# Multicultural Education in a Pluralistic Society

## Twelfth Edition

**Donna M. Gollnick**
*Finance Manager & Past President, National Association for Multicultural Education*

**Philip C. Chinn**
*Professor Emeritus, California State University, Los Angeles*

With
Alison G. Dover, *California State University, Fullerton*
Kevin Roxas, *Western Washington University*
William Toledo, *California State University, Fullerton*

Pearson

**Content Development:** Shannon LeMay-Finn
**Content Management:** Rebecca Fox-Gieg
**Content Production:** Deepali Malhotra
**Product Management:** Drew Bennett
**Product Marketing:** Krista Clark
**Rights and Permissions:** Ritika Akhil

Please contact www.AskPearsonSupport.com with any queries on this content.
Please contact us with concerns about any potential bias at https://www.pearson.com/report-bias.html
You can learn more about Pearson's commitment to accessibility at https://www.pearson.com/us/accessibility.html

Cover Image by: emyerson/E+/Gettyimage, Pixel-Shot/Shutterstock, Photographielove/Shutterstock, Daxiao Productions/Shutterstock. Darrin Henry/Shutterstock, Samuel Borges Photography/Shutterstock, StockImageFactory.com/Shutterstock, Rawpixel.com/Shutterstock, SB Arts Media/Shutterstock, Q88/Shutterstock, Reallord34/Shutterstock, ViDI Studio/Shutterstock

**Library of Congress Cataloging-in-Publication Data**

Names: Gollnick, Donna M., author. | Chinn, Philip C., 1937- author.
Title: Multicultural education in a pluralistic society / Donna M.
   Gollnick, Finance Manager & Past President, National Association for
   Multicultural Education, Philip C. Chinn, Professor Emeritus, California
   State University, Los Angeles.
Description: Twelfth edition. | Hoboken, NJ : Pearson Education, Inc.,
   [2025] | Eleventh edition published in 2021. | Includes bibliographical
   references and index.
Identifiers: LCCN 2024000832 | ISBN 9780138167820 (paperback) |
   ISBN 9780138173739 (epub)
Subjects: LCSH: Multicultural education--United States. | Social
   sciences--Study and teaching (Elementary)--United States. | Cultural
   pluralism--Study and teaching (Elementary)--United States. | Social
   sciences--Study and teaching (Secondary)--United States. | Cultural
   pluralism--Study and teaching (Secondary)--United States.
Classification: LCC LC1099.3 .G65 2025 |
   DDC 370.1170973--dc23/eng/20240125
LC record available at https://lccn.loc.gov/2024000832

5 2024

ISBN 10:     0-13-816782-6
ISBN 13: 978-0-13-816782-0

# About the Authors

**Donna M. Gollnick** is an education author and consultant in multicultural education. She is also the public member of the Early Childhood Higher Education Accreditation Commission of the National Association for the Education of Young Children. Previously, she was the Chief Academic Officer at the TEACH-NOW Graduate School of Education, an online post-baccalaureate program. Dr. Gollnick was Senior Consultant at the Council for Accreditation of Educator Preparation, the Senior Vice President of the National Council for Accreditation of Teacher Education, Director of Professional Development for the American Association of Colleges for Teacher Education (AACTE), and a secondary teacher in South Bend and Carmel, Indiana. Dr. Gollnick is the coauthor of *Introduction to the Foundations of American Education: Becoming Effective Teachers in Challenging Times* (17th edition) and *An Introduction to Teaching: Making a Difference in Student Learning* (4th edition). She is a past president of the National Association for Multicultural Education (NAME). She has been recognized as a distinguished alumna by the College of Consumer and Family Sciences at Purdue University and the Rossier School of Education at the University of Southern California and received an Advocate for Justice Award from the AACTE.

**Philip C. Chinn** is a professor emeritus at California State University, Los Angeles, where he taught multicultural education and special education and served as Special Education Division chair. He served as special assistant to the Executive Director for Minority Affairs at the Council for Exceptional Children, where he coordinated the first national conferences on the Exceptional Bilingual Child and the Exceptional Black Child. Dr. Chinn served as vice president of NAME and coeditor of the NAME journal *Multicultural Perspectives*. NAME named its Multicultural Book Award in his honor. He has coauthored two special education texts. He also served on the California State Advisory Commission for Special Education. Dr. Chinn is a recipient of the President's Award from the National Association for Bilingual Education and the Advocate for Justice Award from AACTE.

# About the Contributors

**Alison G. Dover** is a professor and graduate program advisor for the Department of Secondary Education at California State University, Fullerton. She holds a doctorate in social justice education from the University of Massachusetts, Amherst, and has been a high school teacher and instructional coach in Massachusetts, Rhode Island, Illinois, and California.

Dr. Dover works extensively with local and national students, educators, and school communities to advance social justice, agency, and culturally sustaining pedagogies in K–12 and teacher education. She is coauthor of *Preparing to Teach Social Studies for Social Justice: Becoming a Renegade* (2016; Teachers College Press) and *Radically Inclusive Teaching with Newcomer and Emergent Plurilingual Students: Braving Up* (2022; Teachers College Press) and has published 30 journal articles and book chapters related to literacy, equity-oriented approaches to teacher education, and teaching for social justice. Dr. Dover has won numerous awards for her scholarship, including the 2023 Outstanding Journal of Teacher Education Award from AACTE, the 2023 James N. Britton Book Award from the National Council of Teachers of English/English Language Arts Teacher Educators, and the International Latino Book Award Ambassador Julian Nava Award for the Best Educational Themed Book of 2023.

Currently, Dr. Dover holds leadership roles in the American Educational Research Association (Division K: Teaching and Teacher Education) and the California Alliance of Researchers for Equity in Education and is the principal investigator for a Spencer Foundation Research-Practice Partnership Grant titled Project LEARN: Language, Equity and Action Research with Newcomer Students.

**Kevin Roxas** is the Dean of the Woodring College of Education at Western Washington University. His research examines three interrelated areas of concern: (1) the often inequitable nature of the social contexts of reception in school and communities for immigrant and refugee youth; (2) the dynamic creation of adolescent identity for immigrant and refugee youth in response to systems of oppression and discrimination; and (3) how preservice and in-service teachers and social service providers can and must critically examine and reconceptualize the ways in which they respond to the needs of these students in their classrooms and in local communities.

Dr. Roxas has published more than 25 articles in peer-reviewed journals including *the Harvard Educational Review*, *Educational Studies*, the *Journal of Latinos and Education*, and *Educational Leadership*. In 2019, NAME selected him for the Carl A. Grant Outstanding Research Award, and in 2023, NAME selected him for the Pritchy Smith Multicultural Educator of the Year Award.

**William Toledo** is an Assistant Professor in Secondary Education. He earned his PhD from the University of Michigan in Teaching and Teacher Education. His research focuses on LGBTQ+ issues in education, particularly the experiences of LGBTQ+-identifying in-service and pre-service teachers in K-12 schools. He also researches the collaborative development and implementation of social studies curriculum with practitioners. Dr. Toledo has published peer-reviewed pieces in a variety of avenues, and his first book, *Civics Education in Contentious Times*, was recently released. Prior to joining CSUF, Dr. Toledo was a public-school teacher, and was born and raised in Albuquerque, New Mexico.

# Preface

So much has happened in the years since this book was last published to impact one's perspective on living in and contributing to life in a pluralistic society. The foundations in which people believe have been challenged by the COVID-19 pandemic and growing racial, ethnic, and economic inequality. Beliefs in the dignity of human lives have eroded as innocent people are killed in neighborhoods, mass shootings, and wars around the world. At the same time, a window of opportunity has opened for critical and meaningful change for greater equity and justice as people confront the injustices in protests and lobby for changes at local, state, and national levels.

This book introduces future teachers to the different cultural groups to which they and their students belong, the positive strengths of those cultures, and the importance of building on students' cultures and experiences to engage them actively in their learning and support their hope for their futures. Overcoming current realities such as racism, sexism, discrimination, hate, and inequity in schools and society are discussed throughout the twelfth edition of *Multicultural Education in a Pluralistic Society*. Acknowledging and studying these areas are critical to establishing a more humane and equitable society that honors the dignity of people and ensures educational, social, and economic opportunities for everyone.

Why study multicultural education? The United States is one of the most multicultural nations in the world. The population includes Indigenous peoples—Native Americans, Alaska Natives, Native Hawaiians, and other Pacific Islanders—and others who themselves or their ancestors arrived as immigrants from other countries. Students bring their unique races, ethnicities, socioeconomic statuses, religions, and native languages to the classroom. They differ in gender identity, sexual orientation, age, and physical and mental abilities. Many students have come from different parts of the world and have different experiences based on the communities or place in which they have grown up. As this century evolves, the population will become increasingly more diverse. Children of color already comprise over half of the school-age population, and this percentage will continue to grow.

The culture and society of the United States are dynamic and in a continuous state of change. Understanding the impact of race, ethnicity, class, gender, and other group memberships on students' lives and on your own life will make you a more effective teacher. Education that is multicultural provides a learning environment that values diversity and portrays it as a strength in society. Students are valued and treated with dignity regardless of their membership in different cultural groups. Holding high expectations for students contributes to their educational and vocational potentials. All students should see themselves and their communities reflected in the school curriculum, and they should feel that teachers and other school personnel care for them and are treated equitably and fairly as they attend school. The curriculum must be authentic, truthful, and meaningful to students to engage them in learning.

Adopting and enhancing a curriculum that is multicultural helps students and teachers think critically about institutional racism, classism, sexism, ableism, ageism, and heterosexism as they work for equity and justice in the classroom. As educators promote diversity and equity in schools and their classrooms, they develop instructional strategies and create an equitable and caring learning environment for helping all students learn and realize their own academic and social potentials.

# About the Twelfth Edition

Students in undergraduate, graduate, and in-service courses will find this text helpful in examining social and cultural conditions that impact education. It provides the foundation for understanding diversity and using this knowledge effectively in classrooms and schools to help students learn. Other social services professionals will find it helpful in understanding the complexity of cultural backgrounds and experiences as they work with families and children from diverse groups.

As in previous editions, multicultural education is approached from a broad perspective of the concept. Using culture as the basis for understanding multicultural education, cultural groups are discussed along with the impact of those group memberships on people's perception of themselves and their treatment in society and schools.

The importance of an equitable education for all students is emphasized. Creating a just and equitable learning environment requires educators who not only recognize but also confront racism, classism, sexism, heterosexism, and discrimination based on abilities, language, religion, geography, age, and other factors. Schools can eradicate discrimination in their own policies and practices if educators are committed to confronting and eliminating them. The twelfth edition helps readers develop the habit of self-reflection that will assist them in becoming more effective teachers in classrooms that respect and value the cultures of students and their families and build on their cultures to provide equity for all students.

*Multicultural Education in a Pluralistic Society* explores diversity and equity in society and schools. The first chapter examines the pervasive influence of culture, the importance of understanding one's own as well as students' cultural backgrounds and experiences, the treatment of groups in society and schools, the obstacles of just and equitable classrooms, and the evolution of multicultural education. The next nine chapters examine race and ethnicity, socioeconomic status, gender, sexual orientation, exceptionalities, language, religion, geography (that is, the places in which we live), and youth culture. The final chapter makes recommendations for using culturally responsive, culturally relevant, culturally sustaining, abolitionist, and social justice pedagogies in the implementation of education that is multicultural. The chapters in this edition have been substantially revised and reorganized to reflect current thinking and research in the area. Each chapter opens with a scenario to place the cultural topic in an educational setting.

In our effort to be equitable, we attempt to present different perspectives in the most unbiased manner possible and allow readers to make their own decisions about the issues discussed. However, some issues related to racism, sexism, ableism, equity, the dignity of each person, and so on, are so important to the well-being of society that our positions are clearly stated.

Readers should be aware of several caveats related to the language used in this text. Although we realize that the term *American* is commonly used to refer to the U.S. population, we view *American* as including other North and South Americans as well. Therefore, we have tried to limit the use of this term when referring to the United States. We generally use racial and ethnic identifications such as Alaska Native, Asian American, Black, Latino/a, Native American, Native Hawaiian, Other Pacific Islanders, and White. We generally use *Latino/a* rather than *Hispanic* or *Latinx* to refer to persons with Spanish-speaking heritages who have emigrated from countries as diverse as Mexico, Cuba, Argentina, Puerto Rico, Belize, and Colombia. *First Americans, American Indians,* and *Native Americans* are used interchangeably throughout the book. When data sources and references use other terms such as African Americans to classify populations of people, the terms used in a specific survey or study are used to discuss that data. *White* has been used throughout the text to identify White European Americans. The term *persons of color* refers to groups of Black, Alaska Native, Asian Americans, Latino/a, Native American, Native Hawaiian, and Pacific Islander people and people of two or more races.

# New to This Edition

The twelfth edition of this text offers many new and exciting elements, including new and updated features, content, data, and references.

- **New chapter-opening case studies** (Chapters 5 and 7) address diverse issues and scenarios that teachers face today.
- **New (Chapters 4, 6, and 8) and updated and expanded** (Chapter 7) *Critical Incidents* features highlight important topics covered in the chapter that might challenge teachers in the school environment.
- **New *Explore and Focus Your Cultural Lens* features** (Chapters 8, 10, and substantially revised Chapter 7) present a controversial school issue with multiple perspectives for readers to consider.
- **All chapters reflect recent events and research** that have impacted the topics addressed throughout the book.
- **All tables, figures, and references reflect the latest data and thinking** about the issues explored in the book.

# Key Content Updates by Chapter

The twelfth edition of this text has been substantially updated and expanded to address a number of important contemporary issues in society and schools that are affecting the lives of students, teachers, and parents as they work together to help children and youth learn at high levels. Some of the major changes that you will see in chapters are listed below.

- *Chapter 1* now includes an expanded discussion of racism, antiracism, and critical race theory—issues that have received a great deal of media and state legislative attention over the past few years.
- *Chapter 2* includes more in-depth discussion of the often ignored histories of Native American, Native Hawaiian, Alaska Native, Black, Asian American, and Latino/a Americans. In the section on "Classroom Implications," discussions about acknowledging race and ethnicity in schools have been expanded to interrogate the current climate in a number of states and school districts that limit the curriculum related to the histories and discrimination of people of color. The chapter also includes a greater discussion of ethnic studies, which now are required in some states and prohibited in others.
- *Chapter 3* includes discussions of the impact of the COVID-19 pandemic on students, families, teachers, schools, and the economic conditions in society. An expanded historical context was added to the discussion of the labor movement. The section on classroom implications now includes discussions on the impact of current economic conditions on boys and men, a historical context of the development of public and private schools in the United States, inequitable funding of schools, and digital equity among students.
- *Chapter 4* expands the discussion of gender identity and the gender fluidity that exists in today's society and schools. The new and revised content of the section on classroom implications includes discussion and recommendations for ungendering classroom practices, guiding gender discussions, affirming gender identities, supporting trans and nonbinary students, and Title IX. The chapter also discusses parental rights related to school's recognition of their children's LGBTQ+ (lesbian, gay, bisexual, transgender, queer/questioning) status.

- *Chapter 5* expands the discussion of current cultural, political, and legislative climate for LGBTQ+ people, including an analysis of the impacts of "don't say gay" bills and other state-level policies. The chapter includes new sections on the erasure of LGBTQ+ voices and perspectives in schools, approaches to inclusive curriculum, and curricular backlash. The section on experiences of LGBTQ+ educators, legal considerations, and professional supports for educators has been expanded.

- *Chapter 6* includes a new section that describes the struggles of people with disabilities for respect and equity from a historical perspective that centers the movement on the leadership of people with disabilities. The section on court decisions and legislation has been expanded with the background that led to those decisions and updated with the most recent decision about the meaning of the "best possible education" for students with disabilities. A new table on major milestones in the struggle for civil rights has been added to the chapter. The section on "Disproportionate Placement in Special Education" has been expanded with discussions of the use of IQ tests, disproportionate placements, and the referral process for identifying students with disabilities. The chapter also introduces candidates to inclusive education and the use of the individualized education program and differentiated instruction in those programs.

- *Chapter 7* has been restructured to foreground linguistic diversity as the norm within U.S. schools. The chapter now includes content on named languages, plurilingualism, linguistics, and multilingual learners' linguistic repertoires. The discussions of dialect and varieties of English are now more explicit about bias and linguistic justice with a number of contemporary examples. The section on nonverbal communication has been updated to address high and low context cultures and post-COVID norms regarding proxemics. The focus on English learners has been revised to focus on asset-based approaches to students' linguistic knowledge.

- *Chapter 8* has been substantially reorganized and updated with new sections on White Christian Nationalism, the religiously unaffiliated, antisemitism, Islamophobia, the spiritual way of life for Native Americans, and teaching religion. The descriptions of the major religions in the world have been expanded to place them in a historical context and clarify their similarities and differences.

- *Chapter 9* has been reorganized and revised to focus on the importance and impact of the places in which students live and have lived in the past. A new section has been added to the chapter, "The Intersection of Place with Race and Class," with subsections on environmental justice and segregation. The incorporation of place-based education into the classroom has been added to the section on classroom implications to explore strategies for making the classroom and curriculum more meaningful to students.

- *Chapter 10* has been reorganized and revised to more directly focus on the culture of youth today. New sections in the chapter address the commercialization of youth culture, public and media perceptions of youth, social media in the lives of youth, and the role of youth in using and creating digital technology and media. A new section addresses the well-being of youth that includes discussions about their physical health, mental health, and identity development. New sections on relationships with families and peers and risk-taking have been incorporated into the section on transitioning to adulthood. The section on classroom implications has been expanded to include engaging students in learning and creating safe and supportive school environments for young people.

- *Chapter 11* includes a new section on approaches to multicultural teaching that incorporates expanded discussions of James A. Banks' dimensions of multicultural education, Gloria Ladson-Billings's culturally relevant pedagogy, Geneva Gay's culturally responsive teaching, Django Paris and H. Samy Alim's culturally sustaining pedagogies, and Bettina L. Love's abolitionist teaching. The chapter includes a new section on the importance of making student wellness a priority in schooling. Other new sections address involving families and communities in schools, valuing educator diversity, and applying an equity lens to support education that is multicultural.

# Features

Each chapter includes the following features that illustrate how concepts and events play out in a classroom or school.

## Chapter-Opening Classroom Scenarios

Each chapter opens with a classroom scenario to place the chapter content in an educational setting. Questions at the end of each scenario encourage readers to think about the scenario and reflect on the decisions they would make in relation to the scenario topics.

### Opening Case Study

Guadalupe "Lupe" Gutierrez, a third-grade teacher at Martin Luther King Elementary School, has been asked to see the principal, Erin Wilkerson, after the students leave. Dr. Wilkerson explains that the school is expanding its full inclusion program, in which children receiving special education services, including those with severe disabilities, are fully integrated into general education classrooms. Congruent with school district policy, King Elementary is enhancing its efforts to integrate children receiving special education services into general education settings. Gutierrez's classroom is one of four general education classrooms in which children receiving special education services will be placed in the next few weeks. "What this will involve, Lupe, is two students with severe disabilities. One is a child with Down syndrome who has developmental disabilities; he has severe delays in the acquisition of cognitive, language, motor, and social skills, and he has some severe learning problems. The other child is nonambulatory, with limited speech and severe cerebral palsy.

"You will be assigned a full-time aide with a special education background. In addition, Bill Gregg, the inclusion

specialist, will assist you with instructional plans and strategies. It is important that you prepare your students and the parents so that a smooth transition can be made when these students come into your class in January, just two and a half months from now. I'd like you and Bill to map out a plan of action and give it to me in 2 weeks."

#### Reflect

1. What should the plan of action include?
2. What is the purpose of integrating students with severe disabilities with students without disabilities in the same classroom?
3. In what ways will Ms. Gutierrez have to prepare her current students to effectively integrate her new students?
4. How might the classroom environment and curriculum be affected when a student with severe disabilities is integrated into a general education classroom?

## Critical Incidents in Teaching

This feature presents both real-life and hypothetical situations that occur in schools or classrooms. The feature and discussion questions provide readers with the opportunity to examine their feelings, attitudes, and possible actions or reactions to each scenario.

### Critical Incidents in Teaching

#### Celebrating Ethnic Holidays

Ana Maria Lopez is a teacher in an alternative education class in an urban school. Her college roommate was Chinese American, and she remembers fondly her visit to her roommate's home during the Lunar New Year. During that holiday, the Chinese adults gave all the children, including her, money wrapped in red paper, which was to bring the recipients good luck in the New Year. Ms. Lopez thought it would be a nice gesture to give the students in her class red paper envelopes as an observance of the upcoming Lunar New Year. Since she was unable to give the students money, she wrapped gold-foil-covered chocolate coins in red paper to give to her students.

Unfortunately, on the day of Lunar New Year, a number of students were involved in a sports event at another school. Most of the remaining students were Asian American students. When Ms. Lopez passed out the red envelopes, the students were surprised and touched by her sensitivity to a cherished custom.

When her principal heard what Ms. Lopez had done, he accused her of favoritism to the Asian American students and of deliberately leaving out the other students. When she tried to

convince him otherwise, he responded that she had no right to impose Asian customs on her students. Ms. Lopez responded that this was an important Asian custom of which students should be aware. However, the principal could not be persuaded, saying that this was Asian superstition bordering on a religious observance, and students should not be participating in such activities.

#### Questions for Discussion

1. Were Ms. Lopez's actions inappropriate for a public school classroom? If so, why? If not, why not?
2. When Ms. Lopez learned that a large number of students were absent, what should she have done with the red envelopes? Did her actions create an appearance of favoritism of one ethnic group over other groups? How could she have handled the situation to make it a pleasant experience for all students?
3. Why may the principal have been upset about Ms. Lopez's actions?

## Explore and Focus Your Cultural Lens

### Debate: The Inclusion of Ethnic Studies in the Curriculum

Today, some states are banning the teaching of some ethnic studies courses, as Florida did when the governor declared that a new Advanced Placement course on African American history would not be taught in the state. At the same time, other states are requiring them. Ethnic studies have become a flashpoint in the country's cultural and political wars. What are the rationales for supporting or not supporting ethnic studies in a school or university?

**FOR**

- Ethnic studies content helps make curriculum more relevant to students of color.
- Ethnic studies teach about long-neglected racial and ethnic groups in the United States.
- Ethnic studies allow students from the group being studied and students from other racial and ethnic groups to explore different perspectives on the histories and literature of a group.
- Ethnic studies help students develop empathy toward other groups.
- All students can benefit from learning the culture, history, literature, and experiences of racial and ethnic groups different from their own.

**AGAINST**

- Ethnic studies may constitute a form of "reverse racism."
- Ethnic studies may be divisive and foster resentment among students.
- Ethnic studies may indoctrinate students with anti-American and anti-White ideas.
- Ethnic studies may make students "ethnic radicals."
- Ethnic studies may encourage students whose racial or ethnic group is being studied to see themselves as victims.

### Questions for Discussion

1. Whose racial or ethnic groups and cultures are most represented in the curriculum used by most schools? What racial or ethnic groups are seldom found in the curriculum? What are the reasons for these disparities?
2. How do the personal perspectives and biases of authors impact the content of textbooks and curriculum? What is important about hearing the perspectives of different racial and ethnic groups?
3. How do students learn about the history and experiences of White people?

## Explore and Focus Your Cultural Lens

This feature presents a controversial school issue with *for* and *against* statements for readers to consider. Self-reflective questions as well as end-feature questions guide readers to reflect on their own attitudes and biases toward the topics covered in the features and to critically analyze both sides of the issue, encouraging them to take a side and clearly articulate their reasons for their choice.

## Revisiting the Opening Case Study

When Ms. Lin decided it was time to teach a unit on gender to her seventh-graders, part of her motivation was that the girls were complaining about the boys touching them and the boys were calling each other derogatory names. Her unit raised the students' awareness of stereotypes and gender rules that pigeonhole students into feminine and masculine identities. It also introduced them to sexism. However, much more is needed to help students understand and think critically about gender. The unit did not address the sexual harassment issues about which she was worried. It did not address gender identities beyond masculinity and femininity. She may have been supplementing the curriculum with gender-conscious materials and examples. Ms. Lin is reinforcing the messages from the unit throughout the school year, encouraging respectful interactions with each other regardless of student gender identity, and using transgressions, such as calling each other names, as teachable moments. Teaching about gender is a never-ending project as students mature and question their gender. Teachers can be a catalyst for expanding students' knowledge and improving their behavior toward each other.

### Reflect and Apply

1. How and where in the curriculum of the subject you plan to teach could you insert a unit or information on gender? What topics would you include?
2. How and when could you talk about gender identities with students at the grade level that you plan to teach?
3. How will you handle incidents of sexual harassment in your classroom or in the hallways such as calling other students names or touching each other inappropriately?

## Revisiting the Opening Case Study

This feature brings students back to the chapter-opening case study, now with the knowledge and strategies they have gleaned from the chapter. The feature questions challenge students to apply chapter concepts to the issues presented in the case and charge readers to think about the implications of the issues for their own teaching practice.

# Pearson eTextbook, Learning Management System (LMS)–Compatible Assessment Bank, and Other Instructor Resources

## Pearson eTextbook

The Pearson eTextbook is a simple-to-use, mobile-optimized, personalized reading experience. It allows you to easily highlight, take notes, and review key vocabulary all in one place—even when offline. Seamlessly integrated videos and other rich media will engage you and give you access to the help you need, when you need it. To gain access or to sign in to your Pearson eTextbook, visit: https://www.pearson.com/pearson-etext. Features include:

- **Video Examples** Each chapter includes *Video Examples* that illustrate principles or concepts aligned pedagogically with the chapter.

- **Interactive Glossary** All key terms in the eTextbook are bolded and provide instant access to full glossary definitions, allowing you to quickly build your professional vocabulary as you are reading.

## LMS-Compatible Assessment Bank

With this new edition, all assessment types—quizzes, application exercises, and chapter tests— are included in LMS-compatible banks for the following learning management systems: Blackboard, Canvas, D2L, and Moodle. These packaged files allow maximum flexibility to instructors when it comes to importing, assigning, and reading. Assessment types include:

- **Learning Objective Quizzes** Each chapter learning objective is the focus of a *Learning Objective Quiz* that is available for instructors to assign through their Learning Management System. Learning objectives identify chapter content that is most important for learners and serve as the organizational framework for each chapter. The higher-order, multiple-choice questions in each quiz will measure your understanding of chapter content, guide the expectations for your learning, and inform the accountability and the applications of your new knowledge. Each multiple-choice question includes feedback for the correct answer and for each distractor to help guide students' learning.

- **Application Exercises** Each chapter provides opportunities to apply what you have learned through *Application Exercises*. These exercises are usually short-answer format and can be based on Pearson eTextbook Video Examples, written cases, or scenarios modeled by pedagogical text features. A model response written by experts is provided to help guide learning.

- **Chapter Tests** Suggested test items are provided for each chapter and include questions in multiple-choice and short-answer formats.

## Instructor's Manual

The Instructor's Manual is provided as a Word document and includes resources to assist professors in planning their course.

## PowerPoint® Slides

PowerPoint slides are provided for each chapter and highlight key concepts and summarize the content of the text to make it more meaningful for students.

**Note:** All instructor resources—LMS-compatible assessment bank, instructor's manual, and PowerPoint slides are available for instructor download at www.pearson.com. After searching for your title, be sure you have selected "I'm an educator", then select the "Instructor resources" tab.

# Acknowledgments

The preparation of any text involves the contributions of many individuals. We welcome and greatly appreciate the contributions of our new team members, Alison Dover and Kevin Roxas, who revised Chapter 7. We also thank William Toledo, who assisted Dr. Dover in revising Chapter 7. We appreciate the assistance, patience, encouragement, and guidance of our editors, Rebecca Fox-Gieg and Deepali Malhotra and development editor Shannon LeMay-Finn, who asked critical and probing questions as she guided us through this revision. We appreciate the feedback and recommendations from Dennis Jackson and Michele Clarke on Chapters 2 and 6, respectively. Also, our sincere thanks go out to the project managers at Straive, Prathiba Rajagopal, Shirley Monica, and Sharmila Krishnamurthy, and the copyeditor, Laura Specht Patchkofsky, for this edition.

We also wish to thank the following reviewers, whose recommendations guided improvements in this edition: Katie Crews, Ball State University; Maria Elena Salazar, The University of New Mexico; Renée Martin, The University of Toledo; Roland Pourdavood, Cleveland State University; and Lydiah Nganga, University of Wyoming.

# Brief Contents

# Contents

# Chapter 1
# Foundations of Multicultural Education

 ## Learning Objectives

*As you read this chapter, you should be able to:*

**1.1** Understand and respect the diversity of students and their families in U.S. schools.

**1.2** Describe the role that culture plays in the lives of students and how you can incorporate their cultures in the classroom to support their social and emotional development and their academic learning.

**1.3** Compare different ideologies for incorporating diverse cultural groups in society and how those ideologies impact schooling.

**1.4** Analyze the differences between meritocracy, equality, and social justice and how they are applied in schools.

**1.5** Analyze obstacles to creating just and equitable classrooms and schools and how those obstacles can be overcome.

**1.6** Critique multicultural education and its contributions to just and equitable classrooms.

## Opening Case Study

Sarah Clarke's seventh-graders were enthusiastic about starting school. Several of them were new to the school and new to the United States. They were learning a new language—in a new country, with a new teacher, and with new classmates. The first language of more than one-third of the school's students was a language other than English. Throughout the school district, more than 50 languages were spoken by students who had come from countries around the world.

Ms. Clarke was excited about having such a diverse classroom. She knew that most of the students in her class spoke only English. Because she was bilingual in Spanish and English, she was looking forward to being able to use both languages as she worked with the students whose families had immigrated from

Mexico and Central America. Ms. Clarke had not realized that her class would include a student from Afghanistan whose family had recently arrived from Europe. She had already googled for more information on the languages and cultures of Afghanistan, but she wondered how she would communicate with the family of this student if they did not speak English.

During the orientation for new teachers, Ms. Clarke was reminded that nearly half of the students at the school were eligible for free or reduced-price lunch because their families' incomes were below or just above the poverty level. She was thinking about the teaching strategies that would be most effective for this diverse group of students. Ms. Clarke knew that she would need to differentiate her lessons to ensure that all students were learning and

*(continued)*

1

not falling behind academically. She knew that meeting that goal could be challenging, but she felt lucky to be teaching in a school that valued diversity.

## Reflect

1. What are some reasons Ms. Clarke is excited about having a diverse student population in her classroom?

2. What are some challenges Ms. Clarke is likely to confront in her goal for all students to be at grade level by the end of the year?

3. What do you wish you had learned in your teacher preparation program to help you be a more effective teacher of English learners from diverse countries of origin?

# Student and Family Diversity in U.S. Schools

**Learning Objective 1.1** Understand and respect the diversity of students and their families in U.S. schools.

The student population in U.S. schools is very diverse, with **students of color** now accounting for more than half of the students. Before 2050, the majority of the U.S. population will be people of color, with the largest increases being Latino/a and Asian American residents. Today's media coverage might lead you to believe that the general population does not value the country's diversity. However, a Pew Research Center poll found that 64% of U.S. adults believe that the growing racial and ethnic diversity is neither good nor bad for the country. Nearly one in five believe that the growing diversity is a good thing, with people under age 40 being the most positive (Budiman, 2020).

Racial and ethnic diversity in schools is projected to continue to expand. By 2030, students of color are projected to account for 57% of the elementary and secondary public school population (National Center for Education Statistics, 2021a). However, the race and gender of their teachers match neither the student population nor the general population, as shown in Figure 1.1: 79% of teachers are White and 77% are female (National Center for Education Statistics, 2021d).

The racial and ethnic diversity in public schools in the United States differs greatly from region to region, as shown in Figure 1.2, and from state to state within the region. Students of color account for more than half of the student population in western and southern states. More than 40% of the public school students in western states are Hispanic and 8% are Asian American. Nearly 25% of the public school students in southern states are Black. Schools in midwestern states are the least diverse, with only one in three students being a student of color (National Center for Education Statistics, 2021a). Students of color are the majority in most of the nation's largest school districts, comprising 71% of the student population in cities with a population over 100,000 as compared to 50% in suburban areas, 36% in towns, and 29% in rural areas (Snyder et al., 2019). This racial and ethnic diversity includes the children of recent immigrants from such diverse countries as Afghanistan, Ukraine, and El Salvador, who may speak a language other than English at home, requiring schools to make available programs that help students learn both the subjects being taught and English.

The United States is not only multiethnic; it is also a nation of diverse religious beliefs. Immigrants from around the globe have brought with them religions that are unfamiliar to many U.S. citizens. While small groups of Muslims, Hindus, Buddhists, and Sikhs have been in the country for many decades, they became more visible as the U.S. became involved in conflicts in the Middle East and Central Asia. Even Christians from Russia, Hong Kong, Taiwan, Korea, the Philippines, and Egypt bring their own brands of worship to denominations with strong roots in this country.

Diverse religious beliefs can raise challenges for educators in some communities. The holidays to be celebrated must be considered, along with religious codes related to the **curriculum**, school lunches, interactions of students, and student clothing. Immigrant

**Figure 1.1** Racial and Ethnic Diversity of the U.S. Population in Comparison to Public School Students and Teachers

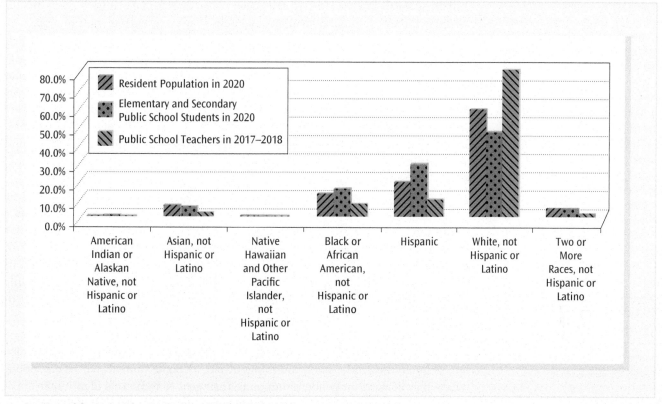

**SOURCES:** National Center for Education Statistics (2021a, 2021d); U.S. Census Bureau (2020).

families generally value education for their children, but they do not always agree with the school's approaches to teaching and learning or accept the public school's **secular** values as being appropriate for their families. Working collaboratively with families and communities is an important step in providing an equitable education to all students.

Another important aspect of diversity that has an impact on schools is the economic level of students' families, especially as the gap in income and wealth among

**Figure 1.2** Percentage of Public Elementary and Secondary School Students by Region and Race and Ethnicity in 2020

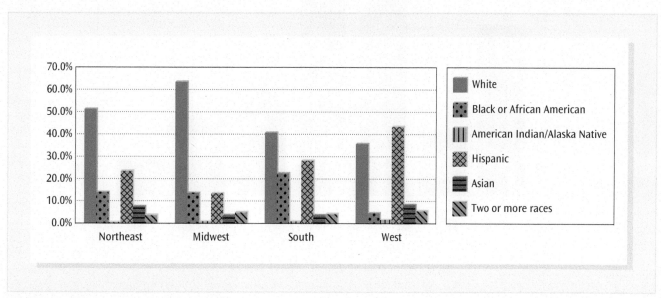

**SOURCE:** National Center for Education Statistics (2021a).

families increases, leading to a smaller middle class and a larger proportion of the population being unable to provide basic needs for their families even when working full time. The Center on Poverty and Social Policy at Columbia University reports that 14.5% of the U.S. population had incomes below the poverty level in August 2022, but 17.2% of U.S. children lived in families with incomes below the official poverty level (Parolin et al., 2022). The percentage of public school students who are eligible for free or reduced-price lunch programs because the incomes of their families are below or near the poverty level increased from 38% in the 2000–2001 school year to 52% in 2019–2020 (National Center for Education Statistics, 2021c). Nearly one in five students attend a **high-poverty school** in which more than 75% of students are eligible for free or reduced-price lunch. Because of historical inequities, students of color are much more likely to attend high-poverty schools, as shown in Figure 1.3 (National Center for Education Statistics, 2021b).

During your teaching career, you are likely to have students with disabilities in your classroom. Depending on the disability, modifications in the curriculum or environment will be needed to provide students with disabilities the opportunity to learn at the same level as other students. The goal is to provide all students the **least-restrictive environment (LRE)** so that they can learn with peers who do not have a recognized disability. The number of children age 3 to 21 with disabilities under the Individuals with Disabilities Education Act increased from 3.7 million in the 1976–1977 school year to 7.2 million, or 17% of the school population, in the 2020–2021 school year (Irwin et al., 2022).

Some of your students will be lesbian, gay, bisexual, transgender, queer/questioning, or otherwise gender-nonconforming (LGBTQ+). Some students will be questioning where they fit along the gender continuum. Their gender and sexual **identity** can impact how they see themselves and how other people view and treat them. Educators and

**Figure 1.3** Percentage of Public School Students Who Attend a High-Poverty School by Race and Ethnicity in Fall 2019

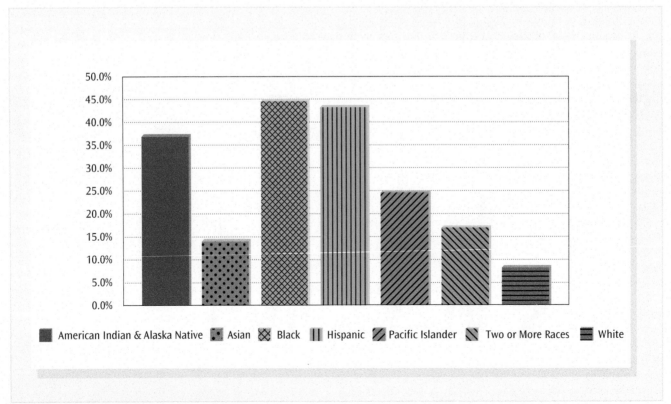

**SOURCE:** National Center for Education Statistics (2021b).

families may be struggling with their acceptance of gender identity beyond male or female, leading to contentious discussions within schools and at school board meetings about gender identity and the use of appropriate pronouns and, sometimes, not respecting or recognizing LGBTQ+ students in the school community. The actions of school districts in recognizing or not recognizing LGBTQ+ students will again be reviewed by the courts, including the Supreme Court, over the coming years.

# The Role of Culture in Students' Lives and the Classroom

**Learning Objective 1.2** Describe the role that culture plays in the lives of students and how you can incorporate their cultures in the classroom to support their social and emotional development and their academic learning.

**Culture** defines who we are. It is the way of life that we experience in our day-to-day living in a particular place at a particular time (Storey, 2018). It influences our knowledge, beliefs, and values. It provides the blueprint that determines the way we think, feel, perceive, and behave. When teachers' cultures are different from their students' cultures, the day may be filled with miscommunications and misunderstandings that lead to children being reprimanded or punished primarily because teachers are not familiar with the cultures and language of their students.

Generally accepted and patterned ways of behavior are necessary for a group of people to live together, and culture imposes order and meaning on our experiences. What appears as the natural and perhaps only way to learn and interact with other people is determined by our culture. It allows us to predict how other people of the same culture will behave in certain situations. Culturally determined norms provide the dos and don'ts of appropriate behavior in our culture. We are generally comfortable with other people who share our culture because we know the meanings of their words and behaviors. In addition, we share the same language, history, religion, traditions, and diet.

Culture has such an impact on us that we may fail to realize that not everyone shares our way of thinking and behaving. This may be, in part, because we have never been in cultural settings different from our own. This lack of knowledge may lead to our responding to differences as personal affronts rather than simply cultural differences. These misunderstandings may appear insignificant to an observer, but they can be important to participants. For example, our culture determines how close we can stand next to another without being rude. Certain hand gestures may be acceptable in one group and offensive in another. Teachers may misinterpret the actions of their students if they do not share the same culture.

Our values are initially determined by our culture. They influence the importance of prestige, status, pride, family loyalty, love of country, religious belief, and honor. Our nonverbal communication patterns also reflect our culture and may be misinterpreted by other group members. Culture also determines our manner of walking, sitting, standing, reclining, gesturing, and dancing.

Language is an important part of our culture and provides a special way of looking at the world and organizing experiences that is often lost in translating words from one language to another. Many different sounds and combinations of sounds are used in the languages of different cultures. People learning a second language may have difficulty verbalizing sounds that are not part of their first language. Also, diverse language patterns found within the same language group can lead to misunderstandings when, for example, one person's joking may be heard by another person as criticism or abuse of **power**.

Being aware and knowledgeable of the diversity of your students is one way to show respect for them and their families. Understanding the community in which the school is

# Critical Incidents in Teaching
## Celebrating Ethnic Holidays

Ana Maria Lopez is a teacher in an alternative education class in an urban school. Her college roommate was Chinese American, and she remembers fondly her visit to her roommate's home during the Lunar New Year. During that holiday, the Chinese adults gave all the children, including her, money wrapped in red paper, which was to bring the recipients good luck in the New Year. Ms. Lopez thought it would be a nice gesture to give the students in her class red paper envelopes as an observance of the upcoming Lunar New Year. Since she was unable to give the students money, she wrapped gold-foil-covered chocolate coins in red paper to give to her students.

Unfortunately, on the day of Lunar New Year, a number of students were involved in a sports event at another school. Most of the remaining students were Asian American students. When Ms. Lopez passed out the red envelopes, the students were surprised and touched by her sensitivity to a cherished custom.

When her principal heard what Ms. Lopez had done, he accused her of favoritism to the Asian American students and of deliberately leaving out the other students. When she tried to convince him otherwise, he responded that she had no right to impose Asian customs on her students. Ms. Lopez responded that this was an important Asian custom of which students should be aware. However, the principal could not be persuaded, saying that this was Asian superstition bordering on a religious observance, and students should not be participating in such activities.

## Questions for Discussion

1. Were Ms. Lopez's actions inappropriate for a public school classroom? If so, why? If not, why not?
2. When Ms. Lopez learned that a large number of students were absent, what should she have done with the red envelopes? Did her actions create an appearance of favoritism of one ethnic group over other groups? How could she have handled the situation to make it a pleasant experience for all students?
3. Why may the principal have been upset about Ms. Lopez's actions?

located will be helpful in developing effective instructional strategies that draw on the cultural background and experiences of students. You should help students affirm their own cultures with an understanding that people across cultures share more similarities than differences. At the same time, you should help students become aware of cultural differences as part of the learning process that will lead to understanding and respecting different cultures, developing empathy for people, and being able to interact effectively with people from cultures and with lived experiences different than your own.

Teachers will find that students have individual differences, even though they may appear to be from the same cultural groups. These differences extend far beyond intellectual and physical abilities. Students bring to the classroom different historical and cultural backgrounds, religious beliefs, and day-to-day experiences that influence the way they behave in school. The cultures of some students will be mirrored in the school culture. The differences between home and school cultures for other students will cause dissonance unless the teacher can accept and respect students' cultures, integrate their cultures into the curriculum, and develop a supportive learning environment. If teachers fail to understand the cultural factors that affect student learning and behavior, it will be difficult to help all students learn.

## Characteristics of Culture

Culture is learned, shared, and dynamic. We learn our culture from the people closest to us—our family, peers, and religious leaders. The ways that we were held, fed, bathed, dressed, and talked to as babies are culturally determined and begin the process of learning our family's culture. Culture affects not only how we dress, what we eat, and how we speak but also what we think, our worldview, and often, our politics. The learning process continues throughout our lives as we interact with members of our own and other cultures.

Shared cultural patterns and customs bind people together as an identifiable group and make it possible for them to live together and function with ease. The shared culture provides us with the context for identifying with a particular group. Although there may be some disagreement about certain aspects of the culture, there is a common acceptance and agreement about most aspects. Actually, most points of agreement are outside our realm of awareness. For example, we may not realize that the way we communicate with each other and the way we raise children are culturally determined. Not until we participate in another culture do we recognize differences among cultural groups.

Our cultures adapt to the environments in which we live and work. While the environment in rural areas is characterized by space and clean air, urban dwellers adapt to smog, crowds, and public transportation.

**SOURCE:** New York City/Alamy Stock Photo

Culture is dynamic, not static. Think about how your ethnic culture has changed from the time that your first family members arrived in the United States or, if your family has been in the United States for a long time, how it differs from the national and ethnic cultures of the countries from which your ancestors came. If you are a First American, think about how your culture has changed as a result of the politics and power that may have led to the relocation of your ancestors and the struggles in which families have been engaged to retain your culture. Think about how female cultures changed as more women entered the workforce and continued to work after they were married and had children. Cultures change as they interact with other cultural groups, adopting characteristics of other cultures when it makes sense for their members. These changes can occur within the same families and across generations. In some Asian groups, especially Chinese families, two or more generations may live under one roof. The grandparents may be slow in adapting to their new U.S. culture; the families may be in the middle of moving into the mainstream U.S. culture, while the children already speak and act like members of the **dominant culture**.

Some cultures undergo constant and rapid change; others are slow to change. Some changes, such as a new word or hairstyle, are relatively minor and have little impact on the culture as a whole. Other changes have a dramatic impact, altering traditional customs and beliefs. For example, cultures change as technology, social and other media, economic growth and decline, and climate change impact their members. Think about the impact on culture that resulted after the Internet and smartphone began to be commonly used around 25 years ago. How has social networking impacted the way we interact? Technology has changed the way we work, communicate, shop, conduct research, and meet each other.

## Cultural Identity

Understanding both the dominant culture and the culture(s) in which we were raised helps us answer the question "Who am I?" Identity is our description of "who we are in relation to ourselves, in relation to others, and in relation to our cultural worlds" (Urriet & Noblit, 2018, p. 26). Our race, ethnicity, class, gender, sexual orientation, native language, disability status, religion, and age comprise our cultural identity. Other sociological labels that may further describe our identity include our political affiliation, our physical characteristics, and our interests, as well as our various roles such as student, parent, and teacher.

Groups in the United States are called **subsocieties** or **subcultures** by sociologists because they exist within the context of a larger society or culture in which political and social institutions are shared. Numerous groups exist in most nations, but the United States is exceptionally rich in the many distinct groups that make up its population. Each of us belongs to multiple subcultures based on our race, ethnicity, religion, gender, sexual orientation, age, class, native language, geographic region, and abilities or exceptional conditions, as shown in Figure 1.4. Our cultural identity is based on traits

**Figure 1.4** Cultural Identity

Our cultural identity is based on our membership in multiple groups that are influenced by the dominant culture, discrimination, and power relations among groups in society.

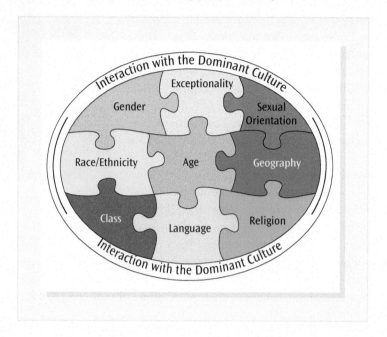

and values learned as part of our membership in these groups. Each of the groups to which we belong has distinguishable cultural patterns shared among the members of the particular group.

We do not simply belong to one cultural group that influences our values, beliefs, knowledge, and behaviors. We belong to many groups that interact with each other, making our cultural identity complex (Lee et al., 2020). Our race, ethnicity, gender, class, religion, and other group memberships impact each other. Sometimes, we may feel that one of these groups has a greater impact on our identity than other groups. Sometimes our membership in one group conflicts with that in another group. Family or friends may think that we are not ethnic or religious enough, for example.

**Intersectionality** was first conceptualized as having an important impact on our identity by Black feminists Kimberlé Crenshaw, Patricia Hills Collins, Audre Lorde, bell hooks, and others who theorized that their gender and class interacted with their race to shape their identity. Researchers, sociologists, and educators now use an intersectional approach to analyze "the relationships of power and **inequality** within a social setting and how these shape individual and group identities" (Tefera et al., 2018, p. viii).

The intersection of the various group memberships within society determines our cultural identity within the power relationships of society and individual groups. Membership in one group can greatly influence the characteristics and values of membership in other groups. For instance, some fundamentalist religions have strictly defined expectations for women and men. Membership in the religious group influences, to a great extent, the way females behave as young girls, teenagers, brides, and wives, regardless of their racial or ethnic group. One's economic level greatly affects the quality of life for families, especially the children and older adults. Having a disability can have a great impact on one's life, especially when society has been unwilling to make accommodations that will provide greater **equity** with people who do not have a disability. Some people with disabilities, such as those who are deaf, are members of distinct cultural groups with their own language and primary interactions with other members of the group.

**Figure 1.5** Changing Cultural Identities

Some cultural group memberships may take on more importance than other groups at different periods of life, as shown here for a woman when she was 24 years old and married without children and again when she was 35, divorced, and a single mother.

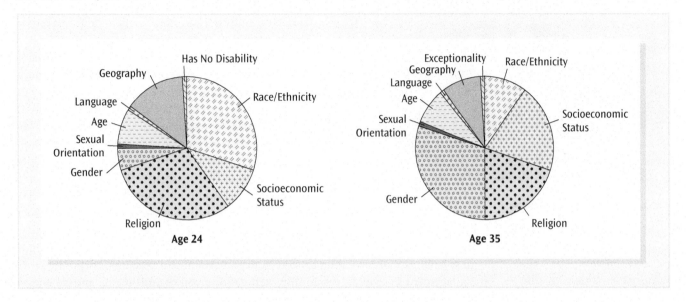

One cultural group may have a greater influence on our identity than other groups. Two people from the same racial and ethnic group may be very different because of their membership in other subcultural groups. This influence may change over time and may be greatly influenced by our life experiences. We can shed aspects of our culture that no longer have meaning, and we can adopt or adapt aspects of other cultures that were not inherent in our upbringing. Identity is not fixed. For example, a 24-year-old, upper-middle-class, Catholic, Polish American woman in Chicago may identify strongly with being Catholic and Polish American when she is married and living in a Polish American community. However, other group memberships may have a greater impact on her identity after she has divorced, moved to an ethnically diverse neighborhood, and become totally responsible for her financial well-being, as portrayed in Figure 1.5. Because she was straight, did not have a disability, and was a native English speaker, her membership in those groups had little to do with how she saw herself. If she later has a disability, membership in that group is likely to take on more importance to her. Think about the group memberships that are most important in your own cultural identity.

Understanding the importance of group memberships to your identity helps answer the question "Who am I?" An understanding of other groups helps answer the question "Who are my students?" Historical and current background on our group memberships and approaches for making a classroom multicultural are explored here.

## The Dominant Culture

Cultures are also influenced by social, economic, and political factors. In the United States, political and social institutions evolved from a western European tradition. Over generations, these political and social institutions have been influenced by other racial and ethnic groups who have used the political and court systems to fight for greater recognition and equity. Nevertheless, the U.S. has a dominant culture "whose values, language, and ways of behaving are imposed on people through economic or political power" (Oxford Reference, 2022). The dominant culture is reflected in most public institutions such as schools, health services, policing, and other

Although Congress is more diverse than in the past, its members do not yet fully represent the racial, ethnic, gender, and religious diversity of the nation's population.

**SOURCE:** AP Photo/Patrick Semansky

Pearson eTextbook
**Video Example 1.1**

In this video, Dr. Olmedo discusses the ways in which teachers can work to bring the culture of students into the classroom.

government agencies. The values, language, and ways of learning and behaving that characterize the dominant culture are included to some degree in our individual cultural identity, but the cultural identity of most White, Christian, middle-class families generally mirrors the dominant culture of the country.

As indicated in the previous section, we all belong to multiple cultures based on our race, ethnicity, gender, class, and other cultural groups. Some groups have more power in society than other groups. For example, the work and voices of men in general have historically been treated as superior to those of women. Men continue to earn greater incomes than women, and they often speak before and over women in meetings. This relationship between culture and power determines who can claim the power and authority to set the rules, norms, and conventions that govern social life (Storey, 2018). In the United States, that power was long ago claimed by affluent, White, Protestant males, but the members of other cultural groups are breaking the glass ceilings that have long existed in the entertainment business, corporate world, management in schools, community and government organizations, and businesses, even though equal representation has not yet been achieved.

It is the dominant culture that many would identify as the national culture of the United States, which has become the norm against which citizens are judged and expected to assimilate. It is the history of the dominant group that is primarily studied in school. It is that group's values, language, and behavior that are rewarded in school, at work, and in society. The dominant group is treated as superior to the subcultures to which much of the population belong. As a result, members of the dominant group receive more benefits and greater rewards from society, such as better jobs and higher-quality education. Members of the dominant group often do not recognize their dominance because their superiority has been internalized; it is the norm they never have to think about (Sensoy & DiAngelo, 2021). They may think of other cultural groups as inferior or defective (Tatum, 2018). They likely do not understand the experiences of **oppressed groups** who seldom experience equity and justice and must constantly focus on survival (McKesson, 2019).

The overpowering value of the dominant culture in the United States is **individualism**, which is characterized by the belief that individuals are in control of their own destiny and advance or regress in society based only on their own efforts (Bellah et al., 2008). This individualism is grounded in a Western worldview that individuals can control both nature and their destiny. Traits that emphasize this core value include industriousness, ambition, competitiveness, self-reliance, independence, and appreciation of the good life. Another core value is **freedom**, which is defined as having the right to self-determination and independence and not having other people or institutions, especially the government, determine your values, ideas, or behaviors. The reaction of many people to the wearing of face masks and mandates for vaccinations during the COVID-19 pandemic is an example of this application of freedom in society.

Within the dominant culture, relations with other people inside and outside the group are often impersonal. Communications may be very direct or confrontational. The nuclear family is the basic kinship unit, but many members of the dominant culture rely more on associations of common interest than on family ties. Values tend to be absolute (e.g., right or wrong, moral or immoral) rather than ranging along a continuum of degrees of right and wrong. Youthfulness is emphasized in advertisements and commercials. Many U.S. citizens, especially if they are middle class, share these traits and values to some degree.

Power differences among groups can lead to conflict. Changing the status quo and sharing power more equally require groups with power to relinquish some of that power. As Frederick Douglass (1857) said, "Power concedes nothing without a demand. It never did and it never will" (para. 7). During the Civil Rights Movement in the 1960s and 1970s, racial and ethnic groups, women, people who were not affluent, and persons with disabilities reignited their long histories of demanding equal rights. They valued and promoted cultural differences and diversity as important characteristics of American democracy. They believed their unique cultural identities should be respected and accepted as equal to the dominant culture, and they should be granted equity with members of the dominant group. The struggle for **equality** across groups continues today.

# Diversity in a Pluralistic Society

**Learning Objective 1.3** Compare different ideologies for incorporating diverse cultural groups into society and how those ideologies impact schooling.

Although many similarities exist across cultural groups, differences exist in the ways people learn, the values they cherish, their worldviews, their behavior, and their interactions with other people. There are many reasonable ways to organize our lives, approach a task, and use our languages and dialects. When we begin to see cultural differences as "us" versus "them," our view of cultures is becoming politicized. By developing an understanding of cultural differences, we can begin to change our simplistic binary approaches of us/them, good/bad, and right/wrong. We begin to realize that a plurality of truths is appropriate and reasonable. We seek out people from different cultural groups for dialogue and understanding rather than speaking about and for them. We begin to move from exercising **privilege** to sharing power.

The theory of **cultural pluralism** portrays a society that allows multiple distinctive groups to function separately and equally without requiring **assimilation** into the dominant culture. Some immigrants have assimilation as their goal; other immigrants try to preserve their native cultures. Refusing or not being permitted to assimilate, some immigrants and racial and ethnic groups maintain their own ethnic communities and enclaves in areas of the nation's cities, such as Chinatown, Harlem, Koreatown, Little Italy, and Little Saigon. The suburbs also include neighborhoods of families from the same racial or ethnic group. Throughout the country are small towns and surrounding farmlands where the population comes from the same racial or ethnic background. Native American nations have their own political, economic, and educational systems. We define ourselves as Black, African American, Hungarian American, Pakistani American, Chinese American, Somali American, Mexican American, or one or more of hundreds of other racial and ethnic identities.

Members of segregated communities may be culturally encapsulated in that most of their primary relationships and many of their secondary relationships are with members of their own racial or ethnic, economic, or religious group. Cross-cultural contacts occur primarily at the secondary level in work settings and political and civic institutions. In segregated communities, families may not have the opportunity to interact with members of other groups, who speak a different language or dialect, eat different foods, or have different values. They may learn to fear or denigrate members of other groups. Many White Americans live in segregated communities in which they interact only with other White people who share the same or a similar culture. Most people of color are forced out of their racial or ethnic encapsulation to try to achieve social and economic mobility. In these cases, they are likely to develop secondary relationships with members of other groups at work, at school, or in interest groups. In this section, we explore ways in which cultural pluralism is suppressed or promoted in society.

## Assimilation

Assimilation occurs when a group's distinctive cultural patterns either become part of the dominant culture or disappear as the group adopts the dominant culture. Two similar processes interact as we learn a new culture: enculturation and socialization. **Enculturation** is the process of acquiring the characteristics of a given culture and becoming competent in its language and ways of behaving and knowing. **Socialization** is the general process of learning the social norms of the culture. Through these processes, we internalize social and cultural rules. We learn what is expected in social roles, such as mother, husband, student, and child, and in occupational roles, such as teacher, banker, or plumber. Most immigrants go through some degree of assimilation as they learn the language and cultural patterns of their new country.

**Structural assimilation** occurs when the dominant group and another cultural group share primary relationships, including membership in social clubs, intermarriage, and equal benefits in society. Although it may require several generations after **immigration**, assimilation has historically worked for most **voluntary immigrants**, particularly if they are White, but has not applied to **involuntary immigrants**, who were forced to emigrate as enslaved people or whose land was forcibly taken by the government. The families of many people of color have been in the country for centuries but have not been allowed to assimilate at the structural level because of long-term **discrimination**.

White European immigrants usually become structurally assimilated within a few generations after arriving in this country. Marriage across groups is fairly common across White ethnic groups and Judeo-Christian groups, and the number of interracial marriages is increasing overall. Three percent of all newlyweds were interracial in 1967, when **miscegenation** laws were repealed in the United States. By 2015, 17% of newlyweds were of a different race than their spouse. Almost one in three Asian American, more than one in four Latino/a, and one in five Black people were marrying outside their racial or ethnic group. White people were less likely to marry outside their group, with only one in 10 choosing to marry a person from a different racial or ethnic group (Pew Research Center, 2017). Young people who are biracial or multiracial are more likely to acknowledge their mixed heritage today than in the past. According to self-reported census data, 5% of the population identifies their race as "two or more races" (U.S. Census Bureau, 2020), with 4.5% of public school students so identified (National Center for Education Statistics, 2021a).

Many immigrants to the United States have become acculturated or have adopted the dominant culture as their own. Although some have tried to maintain the cultures of their native countries, it is often in vain as children go to school and participate in the larger society. Continuous and firsthand contacts with the dominant culture result in changes in the cultural patterns of either or both groups. The rapidity and success of the acculturation process depend on a number of factors, including location and discrimination. If a group is spatially isolated and segregated (whether voluntarily or not) in a rural area, the acculturation process can be very slow.

The degree of acculturation is determined, in part, by individuals or families as they decide how much they want to dress, speak, and behave like members of the dominant culture. In the past, members of many groups had little choice if they wanted to share the American dream of success. Many people have had to give up their native languages and behaviors or hide them. However, acculturation does not guarantee acceptance by members of the dominant group. Most people of color and members of religions that are not Christian have not been permitted to assimilate fully into society even though they may have adopted the values and behaviors of the dominant culture.

Schools historically have promoted assimilation by teaching English and U.S. culture to new immigrants. Before the Civil Rights Movement, students of color would have rarely seen themselves in textbooks or learned the history and culture of their group in classrooms. Even today, in some communities families still do not see their cultures and values represented. When the first set of national history standards was being developed in the early 1990s, the historians involved in the project proposed a multicultural curriculum that celebrated the similarities and differences of the ethnic groups that comprise the United States. Some very influential and powerful individuals and groups accused the project of promoting differences that would undermine national unity and patriotism. When the standards were presented to the U.S. Senate, they were condemned by a vote of 99 to 1 (Symcox, 2002). Multiculturalists, on the other hand, believe that cultural differences should be respected and that cultural diversity contributes to national unity. Even today, whose history and what books are taught in schools are contested at school board meetings and in political elections.

Identifying the degree of students' assimilation into the dominant culture may be helpful in determining appropriate instructional strategies and providing authentic learning activities that relate to the lived experiences of students. One way to know the importance of cultural groups in the lives of students is to listen to them. Familiarity and participation with the community from which students come also help educators know students and their families in ways that contribute to academic success for all students.

## Ethnocentrism

Because culture helps determine the way we think, feel, and act, it becomes the lens through which we judge the world. As such, it can become an unconscious blinder to other ways of thinking, feeling, and acting. Our own culture is automatically treated as innate and the natural and right way to function in the world. We compare other cultures with ours and evaluate them by our cultural standards.

This inability to view other cultures as equally viable alternatives for organizing reality is known as **ethnocentrism**. Although it is appropriate to cherish one's culture, members sometimes become closed to the possibilities of difference. These feelings of superiority over other cultures can become problematic in interacting and working effectively and equitably with students and families of different groups. Our inability to view another culture through its own cultural lens prevents an understanding of the second culture. This inability can make it difficult to function effectively in another culture or with members of another culture. By overcoming one's ethnocentric view of the world, one can begin to respect other cultures and learn to function comfortably in more than one cultural group.

## Cultural Relativism

"Never judge another man until you have walked a mile in his moccasins." This North American Indian proverb suggests the importance of understanding the cultural backgrounds and experiences of other groups rather than judging them by our own cultural standards. The principle of **cultural relativism** is to see a culture as if we are a member of the culture. It is an acknowledgment that another person's way of behaving and thinking is valid. This ability becomes essential in the world today as countries and cultures become more interdependent. To maintain positive relationships with people in a community as well as around the world, we must learn to respect and value other cultures and accept them as equal to our own.

Intercultural misunderstandings among groups occur even when no language barrier exists and when large components of the dominant culture are shared by the people involved. The members of one group are largely ignorant about the culture of another group, giving it little credibility or respect. Our lack of knowledge about people from other cultural groups leads to misunderstandings that are accentuated by differential status based on our group memberships. Cultural relativism suggests that we need to be knowledgeable about our own culture. That must be followed by study about and interaction with other cultural groups. This intercultural process can help us know what it is like to be a member of a second culture and to view the world from another perspective. To function effectively and comfortably within a second culture, that culture must be learned and valued.

## Multiculturalism

Individuals who have competencies and can operate successfully in two or more cultures are bicultural or multicultural and often bilingual or multilingual as well. Having **proficiencies** in multiple cultures allows us to draw on a broad range of abilities in making choices as determined by the particular situation.

Because we participate in more than one cultural group, we have already become proficient in multiple systems for perceiving, evaluating, believing, and acting according to the patterns of the various groups to which we belong. We often act and speak differently when we are in the community in which we were raised than when we are in a professional setting. We may behave differently on a night out with friends than we do at home with family. People with competencies in several cultures develop a fuller appreciation of the range of cultural competencies available to all people.

Many members of oppressed groups are forced to become bicultural, operating in the dominant culture at work or school and in their family's culture at home and in the community. Different behaviors are expected in the two settings. Because most schools reflect the dominant culture, students are forced to adjust to or act like middle-class White students if they are to be accepted and academically successful. In contrast, most middle-class White students find almost total congruence between the cultures of their family, school, and work. Many remain monocultural throughout their lives. They are more likely not to envision the value and possibilities inherent in becoming competent in a different culture.

**Multiculturalism** values the cultural identities of diverse groups as members participate in and interact with the dominant culture. A society that supports multiculturalism promotes diverse group identities. Diversity in the workplace, school, university, or community is valued and affirmatively sought. It allows individuals to choose membership in the cultural and social groups that best fit their identities, without fear of ostracism or isolation from either their original group or their new group.

Educators establish **cultural borders** in the classroom when all activity is grounded in the dominant culture. In our expanding, diverse nation, it is critical that educators be able to participate effectively in more than one culture. As teachers learn to function comfortably in different cultures, they should be able to move away from a single perspective linked to cultural domination. They should be able to cross cultural borders and integrate their students' cultures into the classroom. Understanding the cultural cues of different groups improves their ability to work with all students and makes them more sensitive to the importance of cultural differences in teaching effectively.

# Meritocracy, Equality, and Social Justice in a Democracy and in Schools

**Learning Objective 1.4**  Analyze the differences between meritocracy, equality, and social justice and how they are applied in schools.

The United States is a democracy in which power is vested in ordinary people to influence public policymaking (Page & Gilens, 2020). It is a "system of government with regular, free and fair elections, in which all adult citizens have the right to vote and possess basic civil liberties such as freedom of speech and association" (Levitsky & Ziblatt, 2018, p. 6). U.S. society and government, though not perfect, are promoted as providing steady advancement toward a more prosperous and egalitarian society. However, creating and maintaining a democracy is not an easy task. Former Secretary of State Condoleezza Rice (2017) writes in *Democracy: Stories from the Long Road to Freedom* that "disruption is built into the fabric of democracy" (p. 9) because it is open to "upheaval through elections, legislation, and social action" (p. 9). It involves tensions and contradictions as we debate and negotiate our multiple perspectives about what is best for our communities and the nation.

The principle of equality was codified in the Declaration of Independence when it stated, "We hold these truths to be self-evident, that all men are created equal, that they are endowed by their Creator with certain unalienable Rights, that among these are Life, Liberty and the pursuit of Happiness." Although the declaration did not mention women, a number of amendments to the constitution later clarified that equality referred to women and people of color. Unfortunately, state and federal policies and practices seldom protected these rights for all citizens, particularly for people of color, persons with low incomes, women, persons with disabilities, non-English speakers, and LGBTQ+ people before the Civil Rights Movement of the 1960s and 1970s. Today a number of citizens believe that government leaders are back-pedaling on the ideal of equality and democracy through voter suppression laws passed by a number of states after the 2020 national election and Supreme Court decisions such as *Shelby County v. Holder* that challenged a key pro-

Because of family income and wealth, some students have access to resources and experiences in their schools that are not available to most students from low-income families, as shown in these two classrooms.

vision of the 1965 Voting Rights Act (McGhee, 2021). The country's foundational ideal that people are citizens regardless of their race, ethnicity, or religion is being questioned by some people. Other people such as White supremacists believe that the nation should be governed and controlled by people from the same racial and religious group as the men who wrote the Constitution. To most other people, equality should be reflected in the sharing of power so that no one group would continuously dominate the economic, political, social, and cultural life of the country.

U.S. citizens can both share a common national identity and maintain the cultural identities of their families and communities. Although they do not always agree on ideological and political issues, they share constitutional patriotism (Chua & Rubenfeld, 2018). One strength of a democracy is that citizens bring many perspectives, based on their own histories and experiences, to bear on policy questions and practices. Thus, to disagree is acceptable as long as we are able to communicate with each other openly and without fear of reprisal. Furthermore, most people expect that no single right way will be forced on them. For the most part, they would rather struggle with multiple perspectives and determine what is best for them as individuals within this democratic society than have one perspective forced on them.

At the same time, a democracy expects its citizens to be concerned about more than just their own individual freedoms. In the classic *Democracy and Education*, philosopher and educator John Dewey (1966) suggested that the emphasis should be on what binds people together in cooperative pursuits and results, regardless of our group membership and affiliations. He raised concern about our possible stratification into separate classes and called for "intellectual opportunities [to be] accessible to all on equitable and easy terms" (p. 88). The Internet could help us achieve this goal, although it currently seems to be encouraging divisiveness.

Individualism and equality have long been central themes of political discourse in democratic societies, yet the meaning of equality in society varies according to one's assumptions about humankind and human existence. At least two sets of beliefs govern the ideologies of equality and inequality. The first accepts inequality as inevitable and believes that people's achievements are due totally to their own personal merits. The second set of beliefs supports a much greater degree of equality across groups in society that could be accomplished by not limiting accessibility to quality education, higher-paying jobs, health care, and other benefits of society.

## Meritocracy

Proponents of **meritocracy** accept the theories of sociobiology or functionalism or both, in which inequalities are viewed as natural outcomes of individual differences. They believe that all people have the opportunity to be successful if they are intelligent and talented and work hard enough (Sandel, 2020). They give little credit to conditions such as being born into a wealthy family as a head start to success. Members of families with low incomes, persons of color, and those with disabilities may be seen as inferior and their hardships blamed on their own personal characteristics rather than societal constraints or discrimination.

The belief system that undergirds meritocracy has at least three dimensions that are consistent with dominant cultural values. First, the individual is valued over the group. The individual is believed to have the qualities, ambitions, and talent to achieve at the highest levels in society. Popular stories promote this ideology in their descriptions of the poor immigrant who arrived on U.S. shores with nothing, set up a vegetable stand to eke out a living, and became the millionaire owner of a chain of grocery stores. In reality, **social mobility**, in which individuals and families move up the economic ladder, is less likely to occur today than in the past (Hout, 2019). The second dimension of meritocracy stresses differences through competition. IQ and achievement tests are used throughout schooling to help measure differences. Students and adults are rewarded for outstanding grades, athletic ability, and artistic accomplishment. The third dimension emphasizes internal characteristics—such as motivation, intuition, and character—that have been internalized by the individual. External conditions, such as **racism** and poverty, are to be overcome by the individual; they are not accepted as contributors to an individual's lack of success.

Equal educational opportunity, or equal access to education, applies meritocracy to education. All students are to be provided with equal educational opportunities that allegedly will give them similar chances for success or failure. Proponents of this approach believe it is the responsibility of individuals to use those opportunities to their advantage in obtaining life's resources and benefits. Critics of meritocracy point out that children in families with low incomes do not start with the same chances for success in life as children from affluent families. Even the most capable of these students do not enjoy equal educational opportunities if the schools they attend lack the challenging curriculum and advanced placement courses typically found in middle-class and affluent communities. Thus, competition is unequal from birth. The chances of children from affluent families being educationally and financially successful are much greater than for children from families with low incomes (Stiglitz, 2019). Those with advantages at birth are almost always able to hold onto and extend those advantages throughout their lifetimes.

## Equality

With the persistence of racism, poverty, unemployment, and inequality in major social systems such as education and health, it is difficult to reconcile these realities with the celebrated egalitarianism that characterizes the public rhetoric. In reality, U.S. society is composed of institutions and an economic system that represent the interests of the privileged few rather than the pluralistic majority. Even institutions, laws, and processes that have the appearance of equal access, benefit, and protection are often enforced in highly discriminatory ways. These patterns of inequality are not the product of corrupt individuals as such but rather reflect how resources of economics, political power, and cultural and social dominance are built into the political–economic system.

Even in the optimistic view that some degree of equality can be achieved, inequality is expected. Not all resources can be redistributed so that every individual has an equal amount, nor should all individuals expect equal compensation for the work they do. The underlying belief, however, is that huge disparities of income, wealth, and power are not appropriate. Equality suggests fairness in the distribution of the conditions and goods that affect the well-being of all children and families. It is fostered by policies for full employment, wages that prevent families from living in poverty, and quality child care.

Equality generally implies that "goods and services are distributed evenly, that is, everyone gets the same amounts, irrespective of individual needs or assets" (National Academy of Sciences, Engineering, and Medicine [National Academy], 2019, p. 22). In schools, equality would require that all students have access to the same curriculum, qualified teachers, and resources such as school buildings, laboratories, textbooks, and other resources. Equity, on the other hand, considers need, which means that the distribution of goods and services is unequal across individuals. "For example, the most underserved students may receive more of certain resources, often to compensate or make up for their different starting points" (National Academy, 2019, p. 22). The education results might be more equal achievement by students across groups and similar rates of school dropout, college attendance, and college completion by the members of different cultural groups.

Equity in schools would ensure that students from families with low incomes and those of color would be taught by teachers who are as highly qualified as the teachers of students in affluent families. All students regardless of their cultural identity would attend schools that are conducive to and supportive of learning. They would have access to their own laptops or other mobile devices to use for learning or, at a minimum, access to the Internet in school and at home. Most importantly, students would be engaged in their learning while performing at grade level or above. All schools would be attractive and both physically and environmentally safe with the technology to prepare students for tomorrow's technology jobs.

## Social Justice

**Social justice** is another foundation of democracy that is based on a philosophy that promotes fairness, supports economic and political equality, and respects the basic human rights of all people (Sensoy & DiAngelo, 2017). John Dewey (1966) called for social justice at the beginning of the twentieth century when he said, "What the best and wisest parent wants for his [or her] own child, that must the community want for all of its children" (p. 3). In schools, social justice requires critiquing practices that interfere with equity across groups. It requires the elimination of social and economic inequities that prevent students from learning and participating effectively in schools.

Enormous disparities exist between the very wealthy and the impoverished. The very wealthy have accumulated vast resources, while the poor are unable to obtain the barest essentials for shelter, food, or medical care. Some families lack housing, which leads to a growing number of students who are homeless. Other people lack nutritious meals as well as heat in the winter and air-conditioning in the summer. Every day children from families with low incomes arrive at school having had insufficient sleep because of the physical discomfort of their homes, with inadequate clothing, and with empty stomachs. Tens of thousands suffer from malnutrition and lack of dental care.

When they are sick, many go untreated. Under these conditions, it is difficult to function well in an academic setting.

Bringing about truly meaningful change requires paradigm shifts. Even the middle class may be reluctant to make changes if a change in the status quo diminishes their position. Meaningful change in society requires a universal social consciousness. It requires, to some extent, a willingness of the citizenry to explore the means of redistributing some of the benefits of a democratic society. The end result could be a society in which everyone has a decent place to sleep, no child goes to school hungry, and appropriate health care and a quality education are available to all.

Educators who are committed to social justice are advocates for the education and care of all children. They help their students understand **prejudice**, discrimination, power, racism, and privilege. They value diversity and respect and honor the cultural **funds of knowledge**, history, and lived experiences of their students' families and communities (Moll, 2019). They confront their own biases so that they can deliver an equitable and inclusive education. Social justice educators also engage their students in exploring issues of equity and inequities. They encourage students to study inequities in their lives and communities. Students may become active in supporting the community through food drives, visiting older adults, and fighting for changes to improve the lives of their neighbors. Internationally known researcher and education leader Linda Darling-Hammond (2017) encourages us to "pick ourselves up now and redouble our efforts to demand human rights and educate for social responsibility in order to play our part in bending the arc of history toward justice" (p. 138).

# Obstacles to Just and Equitable Classrooms and Schools

**Learning Objective 1.5** Analyze obstacles to creating just and equitable classrooms and schools and how those obstacles can be overcome.

Unequal power relationships have a great impact on individuals' and groups' abilities to define and achieve their own goals. These differences among and within groups can lead not only to misunderstandings and misperceptions but also to conflict. Cultural differences sometimes result in political alliances that respond to the real or perceived presence of domination and oppression in which policies, practices, traditions, and norms exploit one cultural group to the benefit of another group (Sensoy & DiAngelo, 2017). Over time, oppression becomes normalized in our everyday lives (Bell, 2018), even though it is clearly not just and leads to suffering and the inability of individuals and families to develop their capacities to the fullest (Young, 2018). Feelings of superiority of one's group over another are sometimes reflected in antisemitic symbols and actions, cross burnings, gay bashing, sexual harassment, and **hate crimes**.

Conflicts between groups are usually based on the groups' differential status and value in society. The **alienation** and **marginalization** that many powerless groups experience can accentuate their differences. As long as differences across groups have no status implications in which one group is treated differently from another, conflict among groups is minimal. Unfortunately, cultural borders between groups can separate the home and community from schools. What is valued on one side of the border may be denigrated on the other side. The skills that students have learned in their families and communities may not be accepted at school, and crossing those borders to be successful in school can be easy or difficult. For example, speaking Spanish or a dialect may be valued in the community but not appreciated in a school that expects all students to use English during the school day.

Prejudice, discrimination, racism and other **isms**, privilege, and **hate** stem from a combination of factors related to power relationships. People who are prejudiced have preconceived positive or negative notions about a person or group of people that is based on limited or inaccurate information. Discrimination leads to the denial of privileges and rewards to members of specific groups. Racism is a belief that a racial or ethnic group is superior or inferior to another racial or ethnic group, creating hierarchies of value (Kendi, 2019). Privilege provides advantages and power to groups that have resources and status. Hate is an intense or passionate hostility toward another person or group that can result in discrimination, bullying, and/or violence. In this section, we examine each of these practices and how they affect individuals and society.

## Prejudice

Prejudice can result when people lack an understanding of the history, experiences, values, and perspectives of groups other than their own. Members of a specific group are **stereotyped** when generalizations are applied to the group without consideration of individual differences within the group. We may expect children and their families from a specific culture to behave in a particular manner based on generalizations we have heard or observed without regard to their multiple cultural memberships and their own history and experiences.

Prejudice manifests itself in feelings of anger, fear, hatred, and distrust toward members of a specific group. These attitudes are often translated into fear of walking in a neighborhood, fear of being robbed or hurt by members of a group, distrust of a merchant from the group, anger at any advantages that the other group may be perceived as receiving, and fear that housing prices will be deflated if someone from that group moves next door. Although prejudice may not always directly hurt members of a group, it can be easily translated into behavior that harms members. An ideology based on aversion to a group and perceived superiority undergirds the activities of White supremacists, neo-Nazis, the Ku Klux Klan, skinheads, and other racist groups. A prejudiced teacher may hold high academic expectations for students of one group and low expectations for students of another group. Such prejudice could lead to some students not being encouraged to achieve at high levels and inappropriate placement of students in advanced classes or special education programs.

Children who hold biased attitudes toward other groups may simply be reflecting their families' attitudes, but other implicit messages from peers and the media also impact their thinking about people who are not like them. They may hear older children or adults denigrating a group in jokes or racial and ethnic slurs. They may observe how some individuals do not associate with members of a different group. They may observe how some White teachers associate only with other White teachers in the cafeteria. Unwittingly, these teachers are modeling behaviors for students.

Children are greatly influenced by the media. They watch television and movies. They see pictures in newspapers, magazines, and social media. Hardly a day goes by without students being exposed to stereotyping, misinformation, or exclusion of important and accurate information. Young people are even more likely to be influenced by social media in which they not only communicate with friends but also are exposed to postings that are inaccurate and perpetuate stereotypes about groups of people.

One task for teachers is to reflect on their own biases and ensure that those biases are not influencing their interactions with students and families from cultural groups different from their own. As we learn more about cultures other than our own and interact with more people from different cultures, we should more effectively be able to recognize our own prejudices. We will begin to interpret language and behavior through lenses beyond those of our own cultural group, which should improve our interactions with and understanding of people from other groups as equals.

Because children are cognitively capable of becoming less prejudiced, developing activities that have been shown to reduce prejudice beginning in early childhood programs and through high school is an appropriate goal for teachers. Resources to help you get started with this work are available on the websites of Facing History and Ourselves, Learning for Justice of the Southern Poverty Law Center, and the National Association for Multicultural Education.

## Discrimination

Whereas prejudice is based on attitudes, discrimination focuses on behavior. Discrimination occurs at two levels: individual and institutional. Individual discrimination is influenced by prejudice. Individuals discriminate against members of a group because they have strong prejudicial, or bigoted, feelings about the group. For example, real estate agents, human resources managers, receptionists, and membership chairpersons all work directly with people. Their own personal attitudes about members of a group can influence decisions such as whether a house is sold, a job is offered, a loan is granted, an appointment is made, a meal is served, or membership is granted to an individual. The actions of these individuals can prevent people from gaining the experiences and economic advantages that these decisions offer.

An individual has less control over the other form of discrimination. Institutional discrimination refers to inequalities that have been integrated into the system-wide operation of society through legislation and practices that ensure benefits to some groups and limit them to other groups. Laws that disproportionately limit immigration to people from specific countries are one example. Other examples include practices that lead to a disproportionately large percentage of Black males being incarcerated; single mothers with low incomes being denied adequate prenatal care; and children in low-income neighborhoods suffering disproportionately from asthma as a result of poor environmental conditions. Many examples of discrimination in our public health system were reported during the COVID-19 pandemic as persons of color and those with low incomes often found vaccines and medical treatment not as accessible in their neighborhoods as in more affluent ones. It also became clear that people in these communities had a long history of medical neglect, leading to disproportionate numbers of people with diabetes, asthma, heart disease, and other diseases (Bentley-Edwards et al., 2022).

We have grown up in a society that has a long history of discrimination against people of color, people who earn low wages, women, and people with disabilities. Not all of us realize the extent to which members of some White and affluent groups receive the benefits and privileges of institutions such as schools, health services, transportation systems, and banking systems. Because we think that we have never been discriminated against, we should not assume that other people do not suffer from discrimination.

Some people argue that institutional discrimination no longer exists because today's laws require equal access to the benefits of society. As a result, they believe that individuals from all groups have equal opportunities to be successful. They fight against group rights that lead to what they perceive to be preferential treatment of the members of one group over another group. The government is sometimes accused of going too far toward eliminating discrimination against historically oppressed groups by supporting affirmative action, contracts set aside for specific groups, special education, bilingual education, and legislation that requires comparable resources for men's and women's athletics. However, the goal of these programs is to create equity across groups, not to discriminate against any group, including the dominant group.

The criteria for access to the "good life" are often applied arbitrarily and unfairly. A disproportionately high number of people of color, especially Black households, have had limited opportunities to obtain the economic resources to purchase homes (Joint Center for Housing Studies of Harvard University, 2022). As businesses and industries move from the city to the suburbs, access to employment by those who live in the inner city becomes more limited. A crucial issue is not the equal treatment of those with equal qualifications but equal access to the qualifications and jobs themselves.

The roles of teachers and other professional educators require that they not discriminate against any student because of their group memberships. This consideration must be paramount in assigning students to special education and advanced classes and in administering and interpreting standardized tests. Classroom interactions, classroom resources, extracurricular activities, and counseling practices should be evaluated to ensure that discrimination against students from specific groups is not occurring.

## Racism, Sexism, and Other Isms

Race and racism are topics that are discussed in the news, debated during elections, and fill our social media. They are central to our discussions of police shootings of unarmed Black men, the disproportionately large number of men and women of color who have been incarcerated, attacks on Asian Americans, immigration policies, health disparities, and academic performance. Racism has become a loaded political term that is continually challenged. What is racism? On an individual level, racism is the belief that one race is inherently superior to other races and thereby deserving of opportunities and benefits in society to which other races do not have access. Racism is most dangerous when it becomes systemic or institutionalized, leading to discriminatory policies, legislation, and practices in society that give benefits to one racial group over another. In general, White people and people of color view racism differently. White people are more likely to define racism as prejudice or bias by an individual while people of color are more likely to define it as systemic or institutionalized (Bonilla-Silva, 2022).

Race and racism are an integral part of U.S. history, culture, and life in the twenty-first century. They have been shaped over 600 years by conflict between White domination and resistance by people of color (Omi & Winant, 2015). From the beginning of European settlement in the country that would become the United States, the new settlers forced the native population off their lands and passed policies to eliminate their cultures and languages. When enslaved people from Africa first arrived in Jamestown, Virginia, in 1619, European settlers viewed them not only as inferior to the White population but as property that they owned. For the next 250-plus years, only White people were considered citizens and only White men could vote. People of color did not have access to the rights held by White people.

For the brief period of Reconstruction after the Civil War, not only were Black men able to vote, but they won elections to serve in state legislatures and Congress. However, White Congressmen soon replaced Reconstruction with **Jim Crow laws** that dramatically curtailed freedom for Black people. State and federal laws during that period supported White supremacy and prevented Native American, Black, Hispanic, and Asian people from participating fully in society and taking advantage of the benefits available to most of the White population. The racism that was prevalent during that period prevented most people of color from competing for the same jobs that White people secured, punished them when they became successful (e.g., the Tulsa Massacre in 1919), lynched them, and ensured that they could not easily vote (even though Black men had the right to vote).

Citizens of color did not give up their fight for freedom. Significant numbers of Black people moved out of the South in the first half of the twentieth century and initiated and nurtured their own political organizations in their new locations. After World War II, the Black movement grew and "deepened democracy, not only in terms of racial justice and equality, but in terms of social justice and equality" (Omi & Winant, 2015, p. 161). Nevertheless, this pattern of racism continued until after the Jim Crow laws became unlawful with the 1954 Supreme Court decision, *Brown v. Board of Education*.

Racism did not end in 1954, but the nature of racism began to change. Courts eventually began to enforce the integration of schools, and the Jim Crow regulations that separated White people from Black people and other people of color in the military and at water fountains, bathrooms, swimming pools, dining rooms, and so on gradually disappeared. The 1960s saw the passage of the Civil Rights Act, the Voting Rights Act, and the Fair Housing Act. In the 1940s, the majority of White people supported segregation of and discrimination against Black people. Today, most White people support policies against racial discrimination and prejudice. The brutal tactics of racial domination and the use of degrading terminology of the past have been replaced by what might appear to some people as nonracial practices (Bonilla-Silva, 2022). At the same time, gains in civil rights achieved during the 1960s and early 1970s began to be resisted by Christian Nationalists and other conservative groups. In some cases, civil rights were recast as attacks on White people through reverse discrimination and a redistribution of resources away from White people.

According to Bonilla-Silva (2022), author of *Racism Without Racists*, "systemic racism in America is not about bad people, but about many seemingly good people following racialized norms, rules, ideas, and practices and acting racially, often unaware or in automatic fashion" (p. 32). All residents of the U.S. participate in **systemic racism** because they grew up learning the norms, rules, ideas, and practices of racism as part of everyday life. Most White people are likely to be good and may even be antiracist, but they continue to live in a racist society. Most White people no longer overtly express racist or racially insensitive views about people of color or think that their culture is superior to the cultures of people of color. However, most people of color and White people have different perceptions of how persons of color are treated in society. For example, Black respondents in a Pew Research Center survey were more likely than White respondents to report that racial discrimination, less access to high-paying jobs, and less access to good schools were obstacles to the ability of Black people to get ahead in society (Horowitz et al., 2019). In a national Gallup Poll survey, 45% of Black adults reported unfair treatment due to their race in the past 30 days in dealing with the police, shopping in stores, being on the job, getting health care, and going to restaurants, bars, theaters, or other entertainment places (Brenan, 2020).

According to a recent survey by *U.S. News & World Report* and The Harris Poll, many people believe that systemic racism does not exist in the United States (Johnson, 2022). They argue that they have never discriminated against a person of color and that they cannot be blamed for past events. White people have little or no experience with discrimination and may not believe that members of other racial and ethnic groups are discriminated against. Many people, especially White people, may question the validity of programs or practices that could have real impacts on improving equality for people of color (e.g., affirmative action, untracking of schools, or equitable financial support across schools).

On the individual side of racism, the dominant culture constructs racism as a binary of being either racist or nonracist. However, most people do not want to be labeled as a racist and become defensive when they are (Sensoy & DiAngelo, 2021). Using this binary can become a primary obstacle that prevents people from hearing each other and developing an understanding of racism and its impact on people and society. Internationally known professor of psychology Jennifer L. Eberhardt (2019), who leads conversations about race with police officers, educators, and corporate leaders, has found that "White people don't want to have to worry that something they say will come out wrong and they'll be accused of being racist. And minorities, on the other side of the divide, don't want to have to wonder if they're going to be insulted by some tone-deaf remark" (p. 186). If the goal is to develop an understanding of racism and to take action to eliminate it in classrooms and schools, students, teachers, administrators, and families will need to work together to that end. Most people are somewhat racist based on their own histories and lived experiences. The director of the Center for Antiracist Research at Boston University, Ibram X. Kendi (2019), reminds us that "racial inequity is a problem of bad policy, not bad people" (p. 231).

**Ableism**, **classism**, ethnocentrism, **heterosexism**, **sexism**, and other isms related to individuals or groups of people are also an integral part of U.S. history, culture, and life today, as is discussed in the following chapters. The definitions of other isms used in this text are:

- *Ableism*: The belief that people without disabilities are "normal" and superior to people with physical or mental disabilities that leads to prejudice and/or discrimination against people with disabilities.

- *Classism*: The belief that a person's socioeconomic status determines their value in society and that more affluent people deserve a dominant role in society.

- *Heterosexism*: The belief that the male/female binary and heterosexuality are normal and superior to LGBTQ+ identities, which leads to prejudice and/or discrimination based on LGBTQ+ identity.

- *Sexism*: The belief that men are superior to and more valuable than women, which leads to prejudice and/or discrimination based on sex, typically against girls and women.

Racism, sexism, classism, and other isms continue to contribute to inequality in society. In a survey by the Pew Research Center (2021), 42% of White respondents indicated that "a lot more needs to be done to ensure racial equality" (para. 10) compared to 77% of Black respondents. Over half of Hispanic (59%) and Asian American (56%) respondents agreed that much more needs to be done. Nearly six in 10 Black respondents believed that "most of the nation's laws and major institutions need to be completely rebuilt because they are fundamentally biased" (para. 8) against some racial and ethnic groups. Anybody can become antiracist by working to "undo or resist structures of domination based on racial significations and identities" (Omi & Winant, 2015, p. 129). Until racism and the other isms are removed from society, limited progress will be made toward real equality and equity.

## Privilege

Privilege is a social system that we have inherited. "Privileges are benefits based on social group membership that are available to some people and not others, and sometimes at the expense of others" (Adams & Zúñiga, 2018, p. 46). However, privilege is invisible to most members of the dominant group; they do not have to think about it because they are not affected negatively by their privilege (Sensoy & DiAngelo, 2017).

We all have grown up in a racist, sexist, classist, ableist, and homophobic society. White people generally do not think of themselves as White, financially secure, Christian, English-speaking, or heterosexual. In fact, not all White people are financially secure or Christian or English-speaking or heterosexual. However, they are privileged in society because their race gives them advantages of which they are not always aware. Earlier in this chapter, you learned that everyone is multicultural, being members of multiple groups. Most people are members of both dominant and oppressed groups. Our membership in one group gives us privilege over other groups while we may be oppressed as a result of our membership in another group. For example, a White, heterosexual, working-class, Christian woman has the advantage of privilege as a White, heterosexual Christian but is not privileged as a working-class woman.

Privilege should not necessarily have a negative connotation because one benefits from privilege. However, individuals who are privileged by being born into the dominant group should explore the meaning of privilege and its relationship to the oppression that shapes the lives of people with low incomes, women, people of color, those with disabilities, and people who are LGBTQ+ (Johnson, 2018). Many White people have not had or have not taken the opportunity to explore their own ethnicity and privileged position in society. They often have not studied or interacted with groups to which they do not belong. Therefore, they have not explored where they fall along the continuum of power and inequality in society.

What does privilege look like? How often have you been confronted with the following situations?

- Turning on the television or opening the newspaper and not seeing people of your racial or ethnic group widely represented
- Being asked to speak for all people of your racial, ethnic, or religious group
- Asking to talk to a manager and finding a person of your racial or ethnic group
- Worrying that you have been racially profiled when you are stopped for a traffic violation
- Being followed around by a clerk or security person when you shop (McIntosh, 2020)

To be successful, White people are not required to learn to function effectively in a second culture, as are most members of other groups. The privileged curriculum reinforces this pattern. It is the members of the oppressed groups who must learn the culture and history of White people, often without the opportunity to study in depth their own racial or ethnic group or to validate the importance of their own history and lived experiences. It is as if they do not belong. This feeling can lead to marginalization and alienation from school when students do not see themselves in the curriculum, do not feel a part of the school culture, and are never selected as leaders in the school. Just because people are members of one or more privileged groups, they don't have to consciously support privilege as they interact with people and carry out their responsibilities throughout the day. They can confront the inequities that result from their privilege and work to eliminate them in work and society.

## Explore and Focus Your Cultural Lens

## Debate: Whose Knowledge Should Be Taught?

The curriculum of the first schools in the United States was greatly influenced by the religion of the early European settlers. The *New England Primer*, which was the primary textbook used in the colonies, included the Lord's Prayer, the Ten Commandments, and the books of the Bible. Following the immigration of Irish Catholics in the 1830s and 1840s, families who were Catholic complained that schools reflected a Protestant perspective and ignored a Catholic perspective. These disagreements led to riots in New York City and Philadelphia. Because no agreement about the curriculum was reached, some families chose to establish their own private Catholic schools rather than send their children to the Protestant public schools (Spring, 2018). Although the curriculum gradually became more secular, many schools continued to open school with prayer until the 1960s.

During the Civil Rights Movement of the 1960s and 1970s, the curriculum was again under attack for its almost exclusive reflection of European American history, values, and traditions. College students participated in protests and sit-ins calling for the inclusion of their cultures in the college curriculum. Colleges and some high schools added ethnic studies and women's studies to the curriculum, but they were majors, minors, or electives not required of all students. LGBTQ+ studies programs were not added to college curricula until the 1990s. Advocates for **multicultural education** pushed for the incorporation of the history, literature, music, and art of diverse groups throughout the curriculum and school. To ensure that diverse groups were studied in school, Black History Month (February), Hispanic History Month (September), American Indian History Month (November), Asian/Pacific History Month (May), Women's History Month (March), and Gay and Lesbian Pride Month (June) were initiated. Most major history and language arts textbooks began to reflect more accurate representations of the U.S. population.

Where are we today? The culture wars continue in debates about what should be included in the curriculum. The teaching of **critical race theory (CRT)** and information about LGBTQ+ identity, for example, have been hot-button issues in recent elections. The subject area that is particularly contentious is social studies, but the lessons are important for other subjects as well. What constitutes facts? From whose perspective are those facts interpreted? How do facts inform current debates? How accurate is the history that is being taught in schools? How can we eliminate the privileging of one group's history and culture? These questions are very important because the perspective(s) presented in textbooks become adopted as our shared history. What are the arguments for accurately reflecting the diversity of the nation's population and multiple perspectives in today's curriculum?

## FOR

- All students should see themselves in the books read, the art displayed on school walls, the word problems used in mathematics, and all school activities.

- Most events can be interpreted differently. Exploring multiple perspectives makes the event more transparent and allows students to see how the event impacted on the different groups involved. For example, the westward movement is viewed quite differently from the perspective of Native Americans than the European Americans who made and enforced policy at that time. The union movement is viewed differently by the working class than the owners of businesses.

- The inclusion and exploration of the literature, music, art, history, lived experiences, and contributions of the major cultural groups in the United States and cultural groups in the school community contribute to equity, respect of cultures different than our own, and the elimination of stereotypes and misconceptions about our own and other groups.

- Until racism, sexism, classism, and other isms are confronted and eliminated in schools, the polarization of groups at school and society will remain.

## AGAINST

- The United States has European roots that have served the nation well. The great books of literature and thought from Western culture should serve as the foundation for the U.S. school curriculum.

- The inclusion of important negative milestones in the history of the United States such as the genocide of Native Americans, slavery, and the internment of Japanese Americans is too brutal to be presented to students and makes the United States look bad.

- The culture of White Protestants is being denigrated and lost when other cultures are integrated into the school curriculum.

- Liberal professors and teachers are indoctrinating students with progressive ideas and socialism.

## Questions for Discussion

1. Why do multiculturalists think that the inclusion of the histories and experiences of the multiple cultural, racial, ethnic, and religious groups that comprise the U.S. population should be incorporated in the school curriculum? Do you agree or disagree? Why or why not?

2. Why do some people fight the creation of an inclusive curriculum and the incorporation of multiple perspectives in the curriculum? Do you agree or disagree? Why or why not?

3. Who do you think should be involved in determining the content of the school curriculum? Why?

## Hate Groups

Some groups organize to protect their power by not only preaching hate against other groups but sometimes inciting violence against members of other groups. In 2009 Congress passed a federal law to protect the population against hate crimes. Nevertheless, hate crimes continue, sometimes as mass shootings. For example, six Sikhs were killed at a Sikh Gurdwara in Oak Creek, Wisconsin, in 2012; nine Black people were killed at the Emanuel African Methodist Episcopal Church in Charleston, South Carolina, in 2016; 11 Jewish people were killed at the Tree of Life Synagogue in Pittsburgh in October 2018; 51 Muslims were killed at two mosques in Christchurch, New Zealand, in 2019; 23 Latino/a people were killed at a Walmart store in El Paso, Texas, in 2019; eight women, six of whom were Asian women, were killed near Atlanta, Georgia, in 2021; and 10 Black people were killed at a grocery store in Buffalo, New York, in 2022. On a daily basis, persons of color, girls and women, people who are not Christian, and those who are LGBTQ+ are taunted with verbal barbs, physically harassed, and sometimes killed because of their race, ethnicity, gender, religion, gender identity, or sexual orientation.

Hate groups like the Ku Klux Klan and similar White supremacist groups initially emerged during Reconstruction when they killed thousands of Black people in an attempt to ensure that they would not achieve political and economic equality. With the success of these groups in embedding racism throughout state and federal policies and practices, most of the groups were abandoned by 1890. However, after the release of the film *Birth of a Nation* in 1915, the Klan reemerged with an expanded mission against Jews, Catholics, and immigrants as well as Black people. The Klan's membership also expanded beyond the South with large numbers of members in Indiana, Oregon, and Pennsylvania. Its members included Protestant ministers, sheriffs, and police officers as well as governors and members of Congress, making bigotry even more acceptable. Again, the Klan's membership declined after the 1920s as White people dominated political and social systems (Byman, 2022).

Klan membership increased again after the Supreme Court's 1954 *Brown v. Board of Education* decision, which called for the desegregation of schools. Klan members were concerned not only about the integration of schools and their communities but also the growing Civil Rights Movement. However, membership during this period never achieved more than 18% approval in the South. Nevertheless, violence was prevalent with lynchings, floggings, cross burnings, arson, bombings, and shootings of Black people and Jews. It wasn't until the 1960s that the federal courts began to rule against the actions of the Klan. As "the government, in their eyes, went from an institution that protected white interests to one that opposed it" (Byman, 2022, p. 37), the government became one of the new enemies of the Klan and other White supremacist groups, such as Aryan Nation, by the 1990s.

The Southern Poverty Law Center (SPLC) reported that 733 hate groups and 488 antigovernment groups were actively operating in the United States in 2021, with the majority located east of the Mississippi River (Miller & Rivas, 2022). These groups were defined as *hate groups* because they have official statements or principles, speeches by their leaders, or activities "that attack or malign an entire class of people, typically for their immutable characteristics" (SPLC, 2022, p. 45). They include nativist vigilantes who patrol the border with Mexico, antigovernment patriot groups, neo-Nazis, Klansmen, White nationalists, White supremacists, racist skinheads, and Black separatists.

The federal government defines hate crimes as those "motivated, in whole or part, by the offender's bias(es) against a race, color, religion, national origin, sexual orientation, gender, gender identity, or disability" (Federal Bureau of Investigation [FBI], n.d.). These crimes are often violent, including assault, murder, arson, vandalism, or threats. The U.S. Department of Justice (DOJ; 2022a) reported 8,263 hate crime incidents in 2020 but indicated that the actual number of hate crimes committed each year is nearer to 250,000 (FBI, n.d.). Although hate crimes were reported against all of the groups in Figure 1.6, over three in five of all the crimes were racially based, with 55% of them being against Black people, 17% against White people, 10% against Latino/a people, and 5% against Asian people (DOJ, 2022a). Hate crimes against Asians increased by over 70% during the COVID-19 pandemic (DOJ, 2022b). Of the religiously based hate crimes, 55% were against Jewish people, 9% against Muslims, and 6% against Catholics. Nearly three in five of antidisability incidents were against persons with a mental disability (FBI, n.d.).

An impetus for the overt actions of individuals who commit hate crimes and hate groups is the changing demographics of the nation in which White people will soon be less than half of the population. White nationalists fear the loss of privilege and power, spreading fear that White people will become extinct—their concepts of *White genocide* or *White replacement theory*—and be replaced by people of color, whom they view as inferior to White people (Serwer, 2019). The proposals for a Mexican border wall, a Muslim ban, and a reduction in immigration fuel this *White anxiety* (Frey, 2018). It is not only White nationalists who worry about the increasing diversity in the United States. A Pew Research Center survey showed that people over 65 years old were least likely to support increasing racial and ethnic diversity (Budiman, 2020).

Recruitment efforts by hate groups often target areas of the country that have historical roots of prejudice and discrimination or have experienced economic and racial change, such as factory layoffs or increased diversity in a community. During the recent pandemic, Asian people were blamed for the start and spread of COVID-19. Hate group organizers convince new recruits that members of other groups are taking their jobs and being pandered to by government programs. These hate groups play an active role on

**Figure 1.6** Bias Motivation of Hate Crimes in 2020

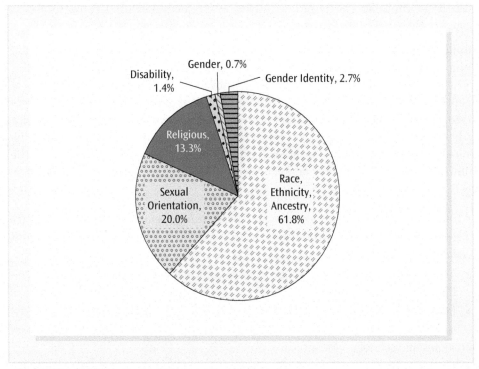

**SOURCE:** U.S. Department of Justice (2022a).

the Internet, frequently using YouTube and other social media platforms like Instagram and TikTok to connect with potential members (Byman, 2022). In addition, a growing number of teenagers are introduced to White supremacy in online multiplayer games like World of Warcraft, Fortnite, Apex Legends, League of Legends, Madden NFL, Overwatch, and Call of Duty (Anti-Defamation League, 2022).

Swastikas and other hate-related graffiti scrawled on the walls of schools, Confederate flags hung at school events, students standing in a "Heil Hitler" salute, a noose hanging on a football goalpost, and homophobic, racist, and sexist slurs, internet posts, and threats are evidence of hate found in some schools. Black, Latino/a, Asian, Native Americans, Jewish, and Muslim students as well as girls, those with disabilities, and LGBTQ+ students are the most likely targets of these incidents in schools. Students say that it is intimidating to report these hateful incidents to school officials, who do not always believe them or do not punish the perpetrators appropriately. As a result, these students feel unsafe in their own schools. School officials should focus on ensuring that potentially targeted students are safe. When a school climate is hostile to students, interventions are necessary. The most common intervention is antibias training for students, teachers, and other school personnel. Schools also introduce multicultural education and sometimes create a diversity committee to improve and monitor the school climate (Vara-Orta, 2018).

As a teacher, you can play a major role in confronting the biases exhibited by students. First, you will need to reflect on your own biases and make sure they do not appear in school. You can take responsibility for learning more about diverse groups in the community, participate in antibias training in person or online, build trust with students and their families, confront hate when it occurs, and work to eliminate it in your classroom and school. *Hate at School* is available for free from the Learning for Justice website as a resource for teachers to combat bigotry and hate in schools. Other resources for fighting hate in schools and society are available online from the Anti-Defamation League.

# Multicultural Education

**Learning Objective 1.6** Critique multicultural education and its contributions to just and equitable classrooms.

Multicultural education respects and values the diversity of students, families, and communities and builds on that diversity to promote academic achievement, equity, and social justice in education. It is "a philosophical concept built on the ideals of freedom, justice, equality, equity, and human dignity as acknowledged in various documents, such as the U.S. Declaration of Independence, constitutions of South Africa and the United States, and the Universal Declaration of Human Rights adopted by the United Nations" (National Association for Multicultural Education, 2022, para. 1). The following beliefs are fundamental to multicultural education:

- Cultural diversity is a strength and value in society.

- Students' life histories, experiences, and perspectives should be integrated throughout the curriculum to help students develop a positive self-concept and the highest levels of academic achievement.

- The school curriculum should incorporate multiple perspectives and support critiques of social inequity.

- Discriminatory practices based on race, socioeconomic status, sex, gender identity, sexual orientation, religion, language, or disability must be eliminated from classrooms and schools.

- In collaboration with families and communities, educators can create an environment that is supportive of academic achievement, multiculturalism, equity, and social justice.

- Teachers are key to students' learning the knowledge, skills, and **dispositions** (i.e., values, attitudes, and commitments) they need to be productive citizens in a democratic society.

Many concepts support multicultural education. The relationships and interactions among individuals and groups are essential to understanding and working effectively with students from groups different from those of their teachers. Educators should understand racism, sexism, prejudice, discrimination, oppression, powerlessness, power, inequality, equality, equity, and stereotyping. Multicultural education includes ethnic studies, global studies, bilingual education, women's studies, human relations, special education, urban education, and rural education. More importantly, it should be integrated throughout the curriculum, interactions with students, and the classroom and school environment. Multicultural education is for all students, including students from the dominant group, who will have the opportunity to learn about the history and experiences of other groups as well as issues of equity and power to which they may otherwise not be exposed. Let's examine how multicultural education has evolved over the past century.

## Evolution of Multicultural Education

Multicultural education is not a new concept. Its roots are in the establishment of the Association for the Study of Negro Life and History in 1915. Through their research and books on the history and culture of Black people, Carter G. Woodson, W. E. B. DuBois, Charles C. Wesley, and other scholars were the pioneers of ethnic studies. Woodson founded the *Journal of Negro History* and the *Negro History Bulletin* to disseminate research and curriculum materials about Black people. These materials were integrated into the curricula of segregated schools and historically Black colleges and universities, allowing Black students to be empowered by the knowledge of their own history (Banks, 2004).

By the 1920s some educators were writing about and training teachers in intercultural education. The intercultural movement during its first two decades had an international emphasis, with antecedents in the pacifist movement. Some textbooks were rewritten with an international point of view. Proponents encouraged teachers to make their disciplines more relevant to the modern world by being more issue oriented. One of the goals was to make the dominant population more tolerant and accepting of first- and second-generation immigrants in order to maintain national unity and social control (Banks, 2021). However, issues of power and inequality in society were ignored. Interculturalists supported the understanding and appreciation of diverse groups but did not promote collective racial and ethnic identities, which were the focus of ethnic studies.

Following the Holocaust and World War II, tensions among groups remained high. Jewish organizations such as the Anti-Defamation League and the American Jewish Committee provided leadership for improving intergroup relations and reducing the antisemitic sentiment that existed at the time. National education organizations and progressive educational leaders promoted intergroup relations in schools to develop tolerance of new immigrants and other groups of color. Like the earlier intercultural movement, many intergroup educators had the goal of assimilating immigrants and people of color into the dominant society (Banks, 2021). Some programs focused on understanding the *folk* cultures of these groups. Other programs were designed to help rid White people of their prejudice and discrimination against other groups. There was disagreement among the supporters of intergroup relations about the degree to which they should promote an understanding of the culture and history of racial and ethnic groups (Banks, 2021).

Although it took a decade after the 1954 ruling of the Supreme Court on *Brown v. Board of Education*, desegregation was being enforced in the nation's schools in the 1960s. At the same time, cultural differences were being described as deficits. Students of color and White people from low-income families were described as **culturally deprived** in that students were perceived as lacking culturally stimulating experiences in their home environment (American Psychological Association, 2022). Their families were

Although the Supreme Court ruled in 1954 that schools should be desegregated, students in many classrooms today are from the same racial, ethnic, or language group.

**SOURCE:** © Michaeljung/Shutterstock

blamed for not providing them with the **cultural capital**—advantages such as skills, norms, language, behaviors, and other social assets—that would help them succeed in schools. Programs like Head Start, **compensatory education**, and special education were established to make up for these shortcomings. Not surprisingly, those classes were filled with students of color, those from families with low incomes, and students with disabilities—the children who had not been privileged in society and whose cultures seldom found their way into textbooks and school curricula.

In the 1970s the term *cultural deficits* was replaced with the label *culturally different* to acknowledge that students of color and immigrant students have cultures, just as European American students do. The Civil Rights Movement brought a renewed interest in ethnic studies, discrimination, and intergroup relations. Racial and ethnic pride emerged from oppressed groups, creating a demand for ethnic studies programs in colleges and universities across the country. Similar programs were sometimes established in secondary schools. However, students and participants in ethnic studies programs were primarily members of the group being studied. Programs focused on students' own racial and ethnic histories and cultures, with the objective of providing them with insights into and instilling pride in their own racial and ethnic backgrounds. Most of these programs were racial or ethnic specific, with only one group studied. Sometimes the objectives included gaining an understanding of the relationship and conflict between racial and ethnic groups, but seldom was a program's scope multiethnic.

Concurrent with the Civil Rights Movement and the growth of ethnic studies, an emphasis on intergroup or human relations again emerged. Often, these programs accompanied ethnic studies content for teachers. The objective was to promote intergroup, and especially interracial, understanding to reduce or eliminate stereotypes and prejudices. This approach emphasized the affective level—teachers' attitudes and feelings about themselves and other people.

With the growth and development of ethnic studies came a realization that those programs alone would not guarantee support for the positive affirmation of diversity and differences in the country. All students needed to learn the history, culture, and contributions of groups other than their own. As a result, ethnic studies expanded into multiethnic studies. Teachers were encouraged to develop curricula that included the contributions of oppressed groups along with those of the dominant group. Social studies textbooks were rewritten to represent more accurately the multiethnic nature of the United States and the world. Students were to be exposed to the perspectives of diverse groups through literature, history, music, and other disciplines integrated throughout the general school program. Curriculum and instructional materials were to reflect multiple perspectives, not just the narrative of the dominant group. In 1973, a professor at the University of Washington, James A. Banks, published *Teaching Ethnic Studies: Concepts and Strategies*, which guided many teachers in their first implementation of multiethnic education. Beginning in the 1970s, national education organizations like the National Council for the Social Studies developed mission statements, guidelines, and resources for multiethnic and multicultural education.

During this period, other groups that had experienced institutional discrimination called their needs to the attention of the public. These groups included women, people with low incomes, those with disabilities, people whose native language was not English, and those who identified as LGBTQ+. Educators responded by expanding multiethnic education to the more encompassing construct of multicultural education. This broader construct focused on the different groups to which individuals belong, with an emphasis on the interaction of race, ethnicity, class, and gender in one's cultural identity. It also called for the elimination of discrimination based on group membership. No longer was it fashionable to fight sexism without simultaneously attacking racism, classism, homophobia, and discrimination against children, older adults, and people with disabilities. Educators who led the movement for multicultural education in the 1970s and 1980s included not only James Banks but also Carl Grant, Geneva Gay, Sonia Nieto, and Carlos Cortés.

The 1990s were characterized by the development of standards for K–12 schools, which led to debates between fundamentalists and multiculturalists, especially around the history standards. The fundamentalists argued that the standards should stress what they believed to be the foundations of democracy: patriotism and historical heroes. The multiculturalists promoted the inclusion of diverse groups and multiple perspectives in the standards. In English language arts, groups disagreed about the literature to which students should be exposed, some arguing for multiple perspectives and others arguing that such literature might promote values they could not support.

These debates continue today. Multicultural education is sometimes criticized as focusing on differences rather than similarities among groups. On the other hand, critical theorists criticize it for not adequately addressing the issues of power and oppression that keep a number of groups from participating equitably in society. Multicultural education as presented in this book does promote **critical thinking** about race and other social categories to ensure that education serves the needs of all groups equitably. At least three schools of thought push multiculturalists to think critically about these issues: **critical pedagogy**, antiracism, and critical race theory.

Critical pedagogy evolved from the theoretical writings of John Dewey, Carter Woodson, Jonathan Kozol, Maxine Greene, Paulo Freire, and others who were concerned with the impact of capitalism and discrimination on students from historically disenfranchised populations (Darder et al., 2017). It focuses on the culture of everyday life and the interaction of class, race, ethnicity, and gender in contemporary power struggles. Its adherents are committed to the development of a school culture that supports students who have been marginalized and oppressed primarily as a result of their race, ethnicity, gender, or class.

**Antiracism** refers to proactively and deliberately working to dismantle racism and promote equity in society and schools. **Antiracist education** is the construct used in Canada and a number of European countries to confront and eliminate racial and ethnic discrimination and racist practices such as **tracking** in which students are placed in classes or groups based on teachers' perceptions of students' academic abilities, **inequitable funding**, and **segregation** in schools. Over the past 5 years, antiracist education has become more well known in the United States, due in part to the scholarly work of Ibram X. Kendi, the author of *How to Be an Antiracist*. Kendi (2019) says that "to be antiracist is to challenge the racist policies that plague racialized ethnic groups across the world" (p. 64) and "to think nothing is behaviorally wrong or right—inferior or superior—with any of the racial groups" (p. 105). Unfortunately, White supremacists have defined antiracism as a code word for anti-White, which has become a mantra for some White families who call for the banishment of any study of race or racism in their schools.

Critical race theory (CRT) was also under attack in the political elections of 2021 and 2022. CRT was introduced in the 1970s by legal scholars Derek Bell, Kimberlé Crenshaw, Richard Delgado, and other legal scholars and activists "to transform the relationship among race, racism and power" (Delgado & Stefancic, 2017, p. 171). CRT declares that racism is a part of everyday life and historically has been embedded in legal systems, legislation, policies, and practices throughout society. The goal is to eliminate racism and the negative impacts it has on the lives of all people. When applied to education, data show that race continues to be a key determinant of inequality in practices such as tracking and disproportionately assigning students of color to schools that are underfunded, have inexperienced and less qualified teachers, and do not include new technologies, laboratories, and enriched curricula (Ladson-Billings, 2021).

Critics of CRT charge that it focuses too much on race and group identity, leading to divisiveness and intolerance among groups as well as discrimination against

White people. Beginning in 2021, legislation passed in a number of states to prevent the teaching of CRT in schools (Sawchuk, 2021). In the state of Florida, legislation in 2022 banned the teaching of concepts or practices that "cause someone to feel guilty or ashamed about the past collective actions of their race or sex" (Craig, 2022). Legislation in Florida and at least 19 other states and school districts are having a chilling effect on teachers who are no longer sure what they can teach about race, ethnicity, class, or gender. Countering such limiting legislation, a recent study by the University of Southern California found that respondents from across the country believed that high school students should be learning about controversial topics in classrooms (Saavedra et al., 2022). Education that is multicultural incorporates the histories and experiences of diverse groups of people. In addition, teachers help students understand discrimination while they ensure that their own words and actions do not discriminate against students and other educators.

Most universities and a number of school districts today offer courses in ethnic studies that provide students the opportunity for in-depth study of a specific racial or ethnic group. These include Black or African American studies, Mexican American studies, American Indian or Native American studies, and Asian American studies. In addition, most public schools have adopted curricula and textbooks that have integrated, to some degree, the history and/or experiences of diverse racial, ethnic and religious groups as well as women, people from different socioeconomic levels, and those with disabilities. The inclusion of people who identify as LGBTQ+ in the curriculum or even acknowledging them remains controversial in many school districts and in a growing number of states. Teaching about race, ethnicity, gender, and sexual orientation is being banned in a number of states in the South and Midwest, and inequities among groups remain.

Today's educators still struggle with the integration of diversity throughout the curriculum and provision of equity in schools. Some classrooms may be desegregated and mainstreamed, and all students may participate in athletic activities, regardless of gender. However, some students are still labeled as at risk, disruptive, lazy, or slow. They are tracked in special classes or groups within the classroom based on their real or perceived abilities. A disproportionate number of students from Black, Latino/a, Native American, and Southeast Asian American groups score below White and Asian American students on national standardized tests. The number of students of color and students from low-income families participating in advanced science and mathematics classes is not proportionate to their representation in schools. They too often are offered little or no encouragement to enroll in the advanced courses that are necessary to be successful in college. These issues are discussed in more detail in the following chapters.

## Multicultural Proficiencies for Teachers

By the time you finish a teacher education program, states and school districts expect you to have proficiencies for helping all students meet state standards. School districts would like to hire qualified teachers who can help students from families with low incomes, students of color, English learners, and students with disabilities meet academic expectations. The expected proficiencies include specific knowledge, skills, and dispositions related to working with diverse student populations and teaching multiculturally. Most state standards for teacher licensure reflect the national standards developed by the Interstate Teacher Assessment and Support Consortium (InTASC).

In working with students from different racial, ethnic, language, and religious groups, the development of dispositions that are supportive of diversity is important. Students quickly become aware of the educators who respect their cultures, believe they can learn, and value differences in the classroom. Examples of the knowledge, skills, and dispositions that the InTASC standards (Council of Chief State School Officers, 2013) expect teachers to develop include the following:

- Teachers understand the role of language and culture in learning and know how to modify instruction to make language comprehensible and instruction relevant, accessible, and challenging.

- Teachers bring multiple perspectives to the discussion of content, including attention to learners' personal, family, and community experiences and cultural norms.

- Teachers believe that all learners can achieve at high levels and persist in helping all learners reach their full potential.

- Teachers value diverse languages and dialects and seek to integrate them into their instructional practice to engage students in learning.

- Teachers communicate verbally and nonverbally in ways that demonstrate respect for and responsiveness to the cultural backgrounds and differing perspectives learners bring to the learning environment.

- Teachers know how to integrate culturally relevant content to build on learners' background knowledge.

- Teachers prepare all learners for the demands of particular assessment formats and make appropriate accommodations in assessments or testing conditions, especially for learners with disabilities and language learning needs.

- Teachers know how to apply a range of developmentally, culturally, and linguistically appropriate instructional strategies to achieve learning goals.

- Teachers reflect on their personal biases and access resources to deepen their own understanding of cultural, racial, ethnic, gender, and learning differences to build stronger relationships and create more relevant learning experiences.

- Teachers respect families' beliefs, norms, and expectations and seek to work collaboratively with learners and families in setting and meeting challenging goals.

## Reflecting on Multicultural Teaching

Teachers who reflect on and analyze their own practices generally improve their teaching practice over time. If you decide to seek national board certification after you have taught for 3 years, you will be required to provide written reflections on videos of your teaching. You are encouraged to begin to develop the habit of reflecting on your practice now and to include in that reflection the multicultural proficiencies listed above. An important part of teaching is to determine what is working and what is not. Are you actually helping students learn the subject and skills you are teaching? Effective teachers are able to change their teaching strategies when students are not learning. They do not leave any student behind. They draw on the experiences and cultures of their students to make the subject matter relevant to them. This critical skill of self-reflection will contribute to teaching effectively.

You can begin to develop skills for reflection while you are preparing to teach. Many teacher education programs require candidates to keep journals and develop portfolios that include reflection papers. Video the lessons that you teach so that you can critique your knowledge of the subject matter, interactions with students, and methods of managing a class. The critique could be expanded to address multicultural proficiencies. You may find it valuable to ask a colleague to periodically observe you while you teach and provide feedback on your multicultural proficiencies. Honest feedback can lead to positive adjustments in your behavior and attitudes.

# Revisiting the Opening Case Study

In the opening scenario of this chapter, Ms. Clarke was excited about the racial, ethnic, socioeconomic, and language diversity in her classroom. She will soon learn that her students have many similarities but also have different experiences based on their gender, religion, physical and mental exceptionalities, age, and the places in which they have lived. Although her school values diversity, she should remain alert to policies and practices that privilege some students over others and work to ensure that all students have opportunities to learn at high levels. In implementing multicultural education, Ms. Clarke will ensure that all of her students see themselves in the curriculum, that their cultures and experiences are respected, that instructional strategies build on their cultural experiences, and that their voices are heard. To expand her knowledge base for working effectively with students and families from diverse backgrounds, she plans to select professional development activities that will fill in the gaps in her knowledge and experiences. For example, Ms. Clarke is committed to learning more about Afghanistan cultures and languages to support the student whose family recently moved to the United States. She is beginning the school year with the dispositions that should support the development of equity and justice in her classroom. The students in her classroom should be well served.

## Reflect and Apply

1. How could you become familiar with the cultures and languages of the students in your classroom?

2. What are some policies and/or practices you have experienced or observed in PreK–12 settings that privilege some students over others?

3. What are the positive dispositions that Ms. Clarke appears to hold regarding the diversity of the students in her classroom? How will these dispositions benefit the students?

# Summary

- Students of color currently account for over half of elementary and secondary school populations, and this proportion is expected to grow to 57% by 2030. They come from diverse racial, ethnic, religious, socioeconomic, language, gender, sexual orientation, and ability groups. Understanding diversity and the cultures of students and knowing how to use that knowledge effectively can enable teachers to deliver instruction to help students learn.

- Culture provides the blueprint that determines the way we think, feel, and behave in society. We are not born with culture but rather learn it from our families and communities. Historically, U.S. political and social institutions have developed from a western European tradition, and they still function under the strong influence of that heritage. At the same time, many aspects of American life have been greatly influenced by the numerous cultural groups that comprise the U.S. population. The dominant culture of the United States is based on its western European roots and the core values of individualism and freedom. Cultural identity is based on the interaction and influence of membership in groups based on race, ethnicity, religion, gender, sexual orientation, age, class, native language, geographic region, and exceptionalities. Membership in one group can greatly affect our participation in another group. Cultural identity is adapted and changed throughout life in response to political, economic, educational, and social experiences that either alter or reinforce our status or position in society.

- Assimilation is the process by which groups adopt and change the dominant culture. Schools have traditionally served as transmitters of the dominant culture to all students, regardless of their unique cultural backgrounds. The theory of cultural pluralism promotes the maintenance of the distinct differences among cultural groups with equal power. Ethnocentrism occurs when individuals believe that their culture is superior to other cultures. Cultural relativism allows us to understand a culture different from our own as though we are members of that culture. Multiculturalism allows groups to maintain their unique cultural identities and choose the degree of their assimilation into the dominant culture.

- Egalitarianism and equality have long been espoused as goals for society, but they are implemented from two perspectives. The emphasis on individualism is supported in a meritocratic system in which everyone is alleged to start out equally, but the most deserving will end up with the most rewards. Equality, in contrast, seeks to ensure that society's benefits and rewards are distributed more equitably among individuals and groups. Equity applies fairness and justice in a way that recognizes and responds to the individual needs of people by providing greater resources to the people who have the greatest need and removing barriers that limit their ability to meet their full potential. The practice of social justice pushes us to explore inequities in society and actively work toward their elimination.

- Prejudice, discrimination, racism, privilege, and hate are major contributors to preventing progress at meeting society's goals for equality and social justice. Almost everyone has some prejudices against persons or groups that are different from their own, but recognizing those prejudices can lead to their elimination. While prejudices are primarily based on positive or negative notions or attitudes about people, discrimination leads to the denial of privileges and rewards to people based on their race, ethnicity, class, gender, or other group membership. Racism is a belief that one cultural group is superior to other groups and results in the systemic or institutionalized discrimination primarily against people of color. Privilege provides advantages and power to the dominant group, which has power, status, and resources based on their group memberships that are not equally available to members of other cultural groups. Hate of people from oppressed groups can lead to violent crimes against members of those groups. Schools are places in which young people can develop the knowledge about diverse cultural groups and the interpersonal skills to collaborate across groups and dramatically reduce these obstacles to equality and social justice.

- Multicultural education is an educational construct that incorporates cultural differences and provides equality, equity, and social justice in schools. For it to become a reality in the formal school setting, the total environment must reflect a commitment to multicultural education. The diverse cultural backgrounds and group memberships of students and families are as important in developing effective instructional strategies as are their physical and mental capabilities. Furthermore, educators must understand the influence of racism, sexism, and classism on the lives of their students and ensure that these are not perpetuated in the classroom.

## Pearson eTextbook Application Videos

The following videos are available in the Pearson eTextbook and can be used to practice observing and applying what you learned in this chapter.

**Pearson eTextbook Application**
### Video Example 1.2
As you engage with this video, consider the process a teacher may go through in order to enhance diversity in the curriculum.

**Pearson eTextbook Application**
### Video Example 1.3
In this video, consider why making cultural assumptions about students is a poor approach to multicultural education.

# Chapter 2
# Race and Ethnicity

## Learning Objectives

*As you read this chapter, you should be able to:*

**2.1** Analyze race and ethnicity as social constructs that affect the lives of all people in the United States.

**2.2** Examine the policies and practices of immigration and its impact on society and education.

**2.3** Describe the Indigenous and immigrant populations of the United States.

**2.4** Explore the struggle for civil rights and its impact on equality.

**2.5** Analyze the impact of racial and ethnic discrimination on communities and students.

**2.6** Develop strategies for affirming race and ethnicity in the curriculum, instruction, and climates in classrooms.

## Opening Case Study

It was a September morning, and a conscious party of resistance, courage, and community uplift was happening on the sidewalk in front of John Muir Elementary School in Seattle. Dozens of Black men were lined up from the street to the school doorway, giving high-fives and praise to all the students who entered as part of a locally organized event called "Black Men Uniting to Change the Narrative." Black drummers pounded defiant rhythms. Students smiled and laughed as they made their way to the entrance. And teachers and families milled about in #BlackLivesMatter T-shirts, developed and worn in solidarity with the movement to make Black Lives Matter (BLM) at John Muir Elementary.

That September morning was the culmination of a combination of purposeful conversations among John Muir administration and staff, activism, and media attention. John Muir Elementary sits in Seattle's Rainier Valley, and its student population reflects the community: 68% of Muir's roughly 400 students qualify for free or reduced-price lunch, 33% are officially designated transition bilingual, 10% are Hispanic, 11% are Asian American, 11% identify as multiracial, and almost 50% are Black—mostly a mix of East African immigrants and families from this historically Black neighborhood.

John Muir Elementary had been actively working on issues of race equity, with special attention to Black students, for months.

The previous year, Muir's staff began a deliberate process of examining privilege and the politics of race. With the support of both the school and the PTA, Ruby Bridges—who as a child famously desegregated the all-White William Frantz Elementary School in New Orleans in 1960—had also visited Muir as part of a longer discussion of racism in education among staff and students. During end-of-summer professional development, with the support of administration and in the aftermath of the police shooting deaths of Alton Sterling and Philando Castile, school staff read and discussed an article on #BlackLivesMatter and renewed their commitment to working for racial justice at Muir.

As part of these efforts, DeShawn Jackson, a Black student support worker, organized the "Black Men Uniting to Change the Narrative" event for that September morning, and in solidarity, school staff decided to wear T-shirts that read "Black Lives Matter/ We Stand Together/John Muir Elementary," designed by the school's art teacher.

A local TV station reported on the teachers wearing BLM T-shirts, and as the story went public, political tensions exploded. Soon the White supremacist *Breitbart News* picked up the story, and the right-wing police support group Blue Lives Matter publicly denounced the effort. Hateful e-mails and phone calls began to flood the John Muir administration and the Seattle School Board, and then someone made a bomb threat against the school. Even though the threat was deemed not very credible by authorities, Seattle Public Schools officially canceled the event at Muir out of extreme caution.

All of this is what made that September morning all the more powerful. The bomb-sniffing dogs found nothing, and school opened that day. The drummers drummed, and the crowd cheered every child coming through the school doors. Everyone was there in celebration, loudly proclaiming that, yes, despite the bomb threat, the community of John Muir Elementary would not be cowed by hate and fear. Black men showed up to change the narrative around education and race. School staff wore their BLM T-shirts and devoted the day's teaching to issues of racial justice, all bravely and proudly celebrating their power. In the process, this single South Seattle elementary school galvanized a growing citywide movement to make Black Lives Matter in Seattle schools.

## Reflect

1. What was the purpose of the BLM event at the John Muir Elementary School in Seattle?
2. Why was it important for the school faculty to involve the PTA and broader community in their event?
3. If you were a teacher at Muir on this day, what would you have taught about racial justice?
4. How would you respond to a parent who accuses you of indoctrinating students with a leftist Marxist perspective as you teach about BLM?

**SOURCE:** Au and Hagopian (2018).

# Race and Ethnicity as Social Constructs That Affect Every Aspect of Our Lives

**Learning Objective 2.1** Analyze race and ethnicity as social constructs that affect the lives of all people in the United States.

**Race** is a concept that was developed by physical anthropologists to describe the physical characteristics of people in the world—a practice that now has been discredited. It is not a stable category for organizing and differentiating people. Instead, it is a socially constructed concept dependent on society's perception that racial differences exist and that these racial differences are important. Although race is a human creation, "it produces real effects on the actors racialized as 'Black' or White'" (Bonilla-Silva, 2022, p. 9). For example, during periods of colonization and enslavement, Indigenous and African people were viewed by most European immigrants as inferior to the White race. Even today, White supremacy is a belief that White people are inherently superior to the races of other people. The classification of groups of people as inferior or superior to other racial and ethnic groups results in inequality and discrimination against people of color.

Race and racism became central factors of human division as early as the fifteenth century in Portugal and have existed in the land that was to become the United States from the beginning of European occupation (Bonilla-Silva, 2022; Kendi, 2016). These racial and ethnic structures impact the life chances of people of color, benefiting members of the dominant White culture (Bonilla-Silva, 2022). They have led to the oppression of people of color and their resistance against that oppression, as reflected in protests against the police killings of unarmed Black men, the unfairness of a justice system that places a disproportionately high number of men of color in U.S. prisons, and the mistreatment of people from Central America, Haiti, and other countries who are seeking asylum at the border with Mexico.

People of northern and western European ancestry have historically been advantaged in the United States. For example, an immigrant had to be a White person to be eligible for **naturalized citizenship** until 1952. Chinese immigrants in the late nineteenth century were charged an additional tax. When immigrants from Ireland and southern and eastern Europe arrived in the nineteenth and early twentieth centuries, they were viewed by some Americans as members of an inferior race. However, European immigrants were eligible for citizenship because they were White; those from other continents were not eligible. Arab American immigrants, for example, needed a court to rule that they were White before they could become citizens.

Madison Grant's *The Passing of the Great Race* in 1916 detailed the U.S. racist ideology. Northern and western Europeans of the **Nordic race** were identified as the political and military geniuses of the world. Protecting the purity of the Nordic race became such a popular and emotional issue that laws were passed to severely limit immigration from any region except northern and western European countries. **Miscegenation** laws in many states prevented the marriage of White people to members of other races until the U.S. Supreme Court declared those laws unconstitutional in 1967. Today, similar ideologies about race/ethnicity are reflected in policies and practices related to immigration, civil rights, criminal justice, economics, and voting. These policies and practices continue to perpetuate inequity across racial and ethnic groups.

## Racial Identity

Parents' races are used to identify a child's race at birth, but the meaning of race is learned from our families and others who share the same **racial identity**. Black adults are more likely than other groups to view their race as central to their identity. Seventy-six percent of Black adults report that their race is extremely or very important to how they think of themselves (Cox & Tamir, 2022). Fifty-six percent of Asian adults see their race as central to their identity (Horowitz et al., 2019), as do over half (54%) of Latino/a adults, but only 23% of White adults view their race as central to their identity (Cohn et al., 2021). White racial identity has risen as it has become clear that the majority of the U.S. population will be people of color before the middle of this century.

Racial **stereotypes** influence the interactions among members of different racial groups. If a group is seen as aggressive and violent, the reaction of the second group may be fear and protective action. The construct of whiteness by many students of color is based on a distrust of White people that has grown out of their own or their communities' lived experiences. Unlike most White people, people of color see the privilege of whiteness and often have suffered the consequences of their lack of privilege and power in society. Their oppression by the policies and practices of the dominant group is often a unifying theme around which they coalesce as a group.

Elementary and secondary students will be at various stages in their development of racial identity. They may be angry, feel guilty, be ethnocentric, or be defensive—behaviors and feelings that may erupt in class. Educators should remember that students of color and those from low-income families face societal constraints, restrictions, and outright discrimination that seldom affect White middle-class students. Such recognition is essential in the development of instructional programs and schools to effectively serve diverse populations who do not yet share equally in the benefits that education offers.

## Ethnic Identity

Are racial groups also ethnic groups? In the United States, many people use the two terms interchangeably. Racial groups include many ethnic groups, and an ethnic group may include members of more than one racial group.

Many definitions have been proposed for the term **ethnic group**. Some writers describe **ethnicity** as a person's national origin, religion, and race. The most basic definition focuses on the native country of people's ancestors. Thus, people identify themselves as German American, Vietnamese American, Polish American, Ethiopian American, or Mexican American. A growing number of citizens identify themselves as having two or more national origins. Other citizens identify themselves simply as American without acknowledging, or maybe not knowing or wanting to identify with, the specific national origins of their ancestors.

Developing a healthy and secure **ethnic identity** helps provide people with a sense of belonging, optimism, and self-esteem, especially for new immigrants. The continued recognition of ethnic identity depends on whether family members view ethnicity as an important part of their identity. When the ethnic group believes that a strong and loyal ethnic identity is necessary to maintain group solidarity, the pressure of other members of the group makes it difficult to withdraw from the group.

A common bond with an ethnic group is developed through family members, friends, and neighbors from whom people learn their culture, language, and ways of living. These are the people invited to marriages, funerals, and family reunions. They are the people with whom one feels the most comfortable. They know the meaning of each other's behavior; they share the same language and nonverbal patterns, traditions, and customs. **Endogamy** (marriage within the same racial, ethnic, cultural, or religious group) along with segregated residential areas and restriction of activities with the dominant group help preserve ethnic cohesiveness across generations. The ethnic group also allows for the maintenance of group cohesiveness by sustaining and enhancing the ethnic identity of its members. It establishes the social networks and communicative patterns that are important for the group's optimization of its position in society. Ethnic communities undergo change as people move, the economic status of members improves or declines, and they experience political and economic struggles.

People do not have to live in the same community with other members of their ethnic group to continue to identify with the group. Many second- and third-generation children have moved from their original ethnic communities, integrating into the suburbs or urban communities—a move that is easier to accomplish if they are White and speak Standard English. Although many Americans are generations removed from an immigrant status, some continue to consciously emphasize their ethnicity as a meaningful basis of their identity. As ethnic group members learn English and adopt the cultural behaviors of the dominant group, their ethnicity becomes less distinct, and they are less apt to be labeled as ethnic by society, especially if they are White. Their ethnicity becomes voluntary, making it possible to choose to identify with their ethnic group or not.

## Identifying People by Race and Ethnicity

Racial and ethnic identification became codified early in U.S. history. People were asked to identify their race on the census in 1790 (Alba, 2020). Most people who emigrated from Europe were classified as White people, especially after they had adopted the Anglo culture. The courts generally classified Latino/a people as White people, but Indigenous populations and Asian American people were generally not considered White people in the courts when families argued that their children should be sent to White schools. However, decisions about the race of families differed from state to state. Black and Native American people were always the "other" and were not allowed to **assimilate** into the Anglo culture even after they had learned the culture and may have desired to assimilate.

Today, the identification of race cannot be legally used to determine where we live, the jobs for which we are qualified, or the public schools to which we can be admitted. It does allow tracking of the participation of groups in schools, colleges, and professional fields to determine the extent of discriminatory outcomes. Federal forms and reports classify the population on the basis of a mixture of racial and **ethnic** or **pan-ethnic** categorizations, as shown in Figure 2.1.

A problem with identifying the U.S. population by such broad pan-ethnic categories is that the categories reveal little about the people in these groups. Whether people are born in the United States or are immigrants may have significance in terms of how they identify themselves. Pan-ethnic classifications impose boundaries that do not always reflect how group members see themselves. Some students rebel against identifying themselves in this way and refuse to select a pan-ethnic identity.

Non-Hispanic White Americans are currently the majority group in the United States, but they belong to many different ethnic groups. The specific ethnic identity of Black Americans is not generally recognized unless they have recently immigrated. The term Latin American includes people from different racial groups and distinct ethnic groups such as Mexican, Puerto Rican, El Salvadorian, Argentinian, and Cuban American.

**Figure 2.1** Racial and Pan-Ethnic Composition of the United States, 2022

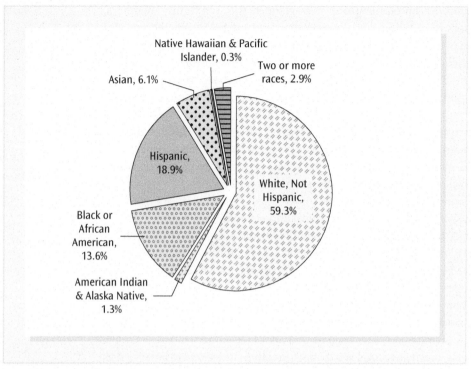

SOURCE: U.S. Census Bureau (2022d).

Black people have become a single pan-ethnic group because of their African history, U.S. history, language, economic life, and culture developed over centuries of living in the United States. They are a cohesive group, in part because of the continuing discrimination they experience in racial profiling by police and others, segregated schools and housing, and treatment as they shop, dine, and work. Not all individuals who appear to be a Black person identify themselves in that way. Some identify as African American or a specific ethnic group—for example, Puerto Rican, Somali, Nigerian, or West Indian. Africans who are recent immigrants may identify themselves ethnically by their nation or tribe of origin, not seeing themselves as members of the long-established Black racial group in the United States.

A growing number of people identify themselves as multiracial. Census data indicate that 3% of the population checked the box for "two or more races" in 2022, but the Pew Research Center estimates that almost 7% of the population could be considered multiracial in 2015 based on the races of their parents or grandparents. People who didn't consider themselves multiracial when their parents or grandparents were of different races generally did so because of the way they were raised or the way they looked. About two in five reported that they identify more with one race than the other (Horowitz & Budiman, 2020).

Many White people see themselves as raceless. They believe they are the norm, against which everyone else is "other." They can allow their ethnicity to disappear because they do not see it as a determinant of their life chances, especially after their family has been in the United States for a few generations. They often deny that their race has had any impact on their ability to achieve, believing that their social and economic conditions are based solely on their own individual achievement. They seldom acknowledge that White oppression of people of color around the world has contributed to the subordinate status of those groups. Many White people are unwilling to acknowledge the **white privilege** that advantages them in social, political, and economic systems. Because "racism privileges [W]hite people does not mean that individual [W]hite people do not struggle or face barriers. It does mean that [they] do not face the particular barriers of racism" (DiAngelo, 2018, p. 14).

**Figure 2.2** Persons Obtaining Lawful Permanent Resident Status by Region and Selected Country of Last Residence, 1950–2019

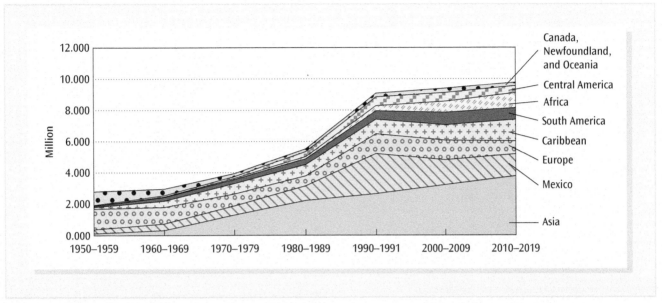

SOURCE: U.S. Department of Homeland Security (2022d).

Biases are largely unconscious. As a result, those people who are White often think they are unbiased and can become very defensive at the suggestion that they are. Even people who champion equality have unconscious biases that they don't always see or admit.

## Factors That Affect Racial and Ethnic Diversity

The proportion of White people in the U.S. population is declining. Currently 59% of the population is non-Hispanic White. By 2045, non-Hispanic White people will be less than half of the population (U.S. Census Bureau, 2018a). Two factors contribute to population growth: births and new immigrants. As shown in Figure 2.2, the majority of new immigrants are coming from Asian countries, Mexico, and the Caribbean.

Birth rate affects population growth. In 1960, the U.S. fertility rate was 3.7 births per woman, but it has steadily declined. In 2020, the rate was 1.6, as compared to 0.8 in South Korea, 1.3 in Japan, 1.5 in Germany, 2.1 in India, 3.6 in Iraq, 4.8 in Afghanistan, and 6.9 in Niger (World Bank, 2022). The replacement rate required to maintain the population is 2.1 children per woman. Therefore, countries with low fertility rates experience a decrease in their populations, while those with high rates are increasing the size of their populations. On average, women from different racial and ethnic groups in the United States have fertility rates below 2.1, with the only exception being Native Hawaiian and other Pacific Islander women (Statista, 2023). Because a greater proportion of women of color are of child-bearing age than White women, racial and ethnic diversity is greater among children. Less than half of children 5 years old and younger were White in 2021, compared to 77% of the population 75 years old and older (Frey, 2022).

Figure 2.3 shows how the diversity of school-age children and youth has changed since 2000 and is projected to change by 2030. Non-Hispanic White students became fewer than half of the student population in 2014, and the majority of the population in many urban schools today are students of color. However, that number is somewhat misleading because many Latino/a people identify their race as White. These demographics will gradually increase the diversity in schools throughout the United States.

**Figure 2.3** The Changing Diversity of the Student Population in Public Elementary and Secondary Schools, 2000–2030

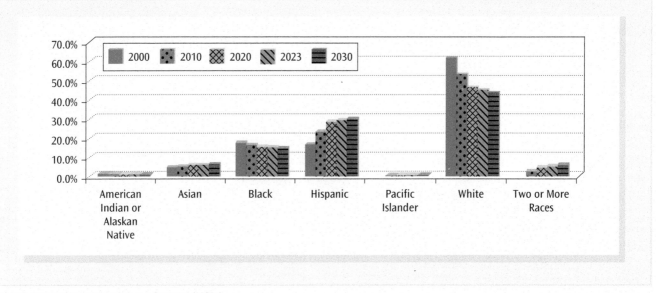

**SOURCE:** National Center for Education Statistics (2022a).

# Critical Incidents in Teaching
## Student Conflict Between Family and Peer Values

Wing Tek Lau is a sixth-grade student in a predominantly White and Black southern community. He and his parents emigrated from Hong Kong 4 years ago. His uncle was an engineer at a local high-tech company and encouraged Wing Tek's father to immigrate to this country and open a Chinese restaurant. It is the only Chinese restaurant in the community, and it was an instant success. Mr. Lau and his family have enjoyed considerable acceptance in both their business and their neighborhood. Wing Tek and his younger sister have also enjoyed academic success at school and appear to be well liked by the other students.

One day when Ms. Baca, Wing Tek's teacher, called him by name, he announced before the class, "My American name is Kevin. Please, everybody, call me Kevin from now on." Ms. Baca and Wing Tek's classmates honored this request, and Wing Tek was "Kevin" from then on.

Three weeks later, Mr. and Mrs. Lau made an appointment to see Ms. Baca. When the teacher made reference to "Kevin," Mrs. Lau said, "Who are you talking about? Who is Kevin? We came here to talk about our son, Wing Tek."

"But I thought his American name was Kevin. That's what he asked us to call him," Ms. Baca replied.

"That child," Mrs. Lau said in disgust, "is a disgrace to our family."

"We have heard his sister call him by that name, but she said it was just a joke," Mr. Lau added. "We came to see you because we are having problems with him at home. Wing Tek refuses to speak Chinese to us. He argues with us about going to his Chinese lessons on Saturday with the other Chinese students in the community. He says he does not want to eat Chinese food anymore. He says that he is an American now and wants pizza, hamburgers, and tacos. What are you people teaching these children in school? Is there no respect for family, no respect for our cultures?"

Ms. Baca, who is Mexican American and was raised in East Los Angeles, began to put things together. Wing Tek, in his attempt to ensure his acceptance by his classmates, had chosen to acculturate to an extreme, to the point of rejecting his family heritage. He wanted to be as "American" as anyone else in the class, perhaps more so. Like Wing Tek, Ms. Baca had acculturated linguistically and in other ways, but she had never given up her Mexican American culture and values. She knew the internal turmoil Wing Tek was experiencing.

### Questions for Discussion

1. Why is Wing Tek rejecting his Chinese name?
2. Why do Mr. and Mrs. Lau say that their son is a disgrace to the family and their traditional family values?
3. What can Ms. Baca do to meet the needs of both Wing Tek's parents and Wing Tek?
4. What can Ms. Baca do to help Wing Tek feel more comfortable with his Chinese heritage in the classroom?

# Becoming a Multicultural Nation: The Role of Immigration

**Learning Objective 2.2**  Examine the policies and practices of immigration and its impact on society and education.

Throughout U.S. history, Congress has restricted the immigration of different national or racial and ethnic groups based on the perceived superiority of the older, established immigrant groups that had colonized the nation. As early as 1729, immigration was discouraged. In that year, Pennsylvania passed a statute that required foreigners in the colony to pay an additional tax. Some leaders, including Benjamin Franklin, worried that Pennsylvania was in danger of becoming a German state. The 1790 Naturalization Act, which allowed only White people to become U.S. citizens, declared that a White immigrant could become a citizen after several years of residency.

In the nineteenth century, native-born citizens again worried that new immigrant groups threatened their majority and superiority status. The resulting movement, known as **nativism**, restricted immigration and protected the interests of native-born citizens. This nativism continued into the twentieth century, when the Dillingham Commission recommended, in 1917, that all immigrants be required to pass a literacy test. The **nativists** successfully lobbied Congress to pass the Johnson-Reed Act in 1924, establishing annual immigration quotas based on 2% of each nation's foreign-born population in the 1890 census, which disproportionately favored immigrants from northern and western European countries.

The Johnson-Reed Act was not abolished until 1965, when a new quota system was established, dramatically increasing the number of immigrants allowed annually from the Eastern Hemisphere and reducing the number from the Western Hemisphere, which resulted in the changes shown in Figure 2.2. The Immigration Reform and Control Act in 1986 provided a pathway to citizenship to unauthorized residents who had arrived in the United States before 1983, and the 1990 Immigration Act increased the quota cap for legal immigration.

Concern about immigration reappeared again in the 1990s in resolutions, referenda, and legislation as a number of states tried to deny education to unauthorized immigrants, restrict communications to the English language, and limit prenatal care and preschool services available to low-income families, who are disproportionately families of color. The 1996 Illegal Immigration Reform and Responsibility Act supported cooperation between local law enforcement and immigration enforcement and established "expedited removal" of noncitizens without proper documentation at the border.

Immigration became a controversial and divisive issue again in the 2016 presidential campaign and continues today. Congress has not passed legislation on immigration since 1996. As the nation continues to become more racially and ethnically diverse, some people again call for more restrictive control of immigration. They worry that the heritage and power of White Americans are being diminished as the population becomes less White. However, the Pew Research Center has found in its surveys that only 24% of U.S. adults say that legal immigration should be decreased while 70% say it should remain at its current level or increase. Two in three respondents believe that immigrants strengthen the country "because of their hard work and talents" (Budiman, 2020, para. 34).

Some of today's immigrants enter the United States lawfully, and others are unauthorized. Legal immigration consists of five different routes, as show in Figure 2.4. The primary path to lawful immigration is the admission of immediate relatives (i.e., spouses, children, and parents), which represented 52% of immigrants in 2021. Other pathways include family members who can be admitted under family-sponsored preferences, refugees and asylees, and diversity immigrants from countries with relatively few immigrants who enter a lottery for 50,000 available openings each year. The fifth route is for people who have come to the United States at the request of employers. They

**Figure 2.4** Persons Obtaining Lawful Permanent Resident Status by Type of Admission, Fiscal Year 2021

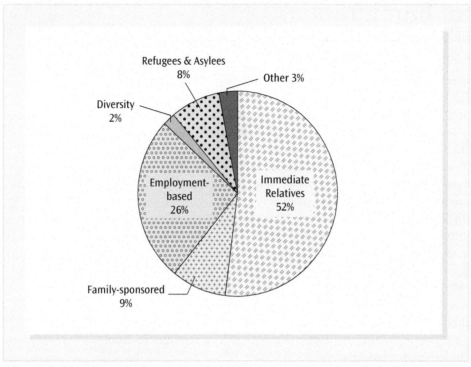

SOURCE: U.S. Department of Homeland Security (2022f).

include workers with "extraordinary ability" in the arts or sciences, professionals with advanced degrees, skilled and unskilled workers, and such special categories as athletes, ministers, and investors (U.S. Department of Homeland Security [DHS], 2022g).

Immigration continues to impact the nation's population today. An average of 1 million people immigrated lawfully to the United States annually from 2002 to 2021. The number of authorized immigrants who entered the U.S. in 2021 was almost 300,000 less than prior to the pandemic, with the largest numbers coming from the countries shown in Figure 2.5. Half of the recent immigrants live in four states: California (18.3%),

**Figure 2.5** Countries from Which Most Immigrants Arrived in the United States, 2021

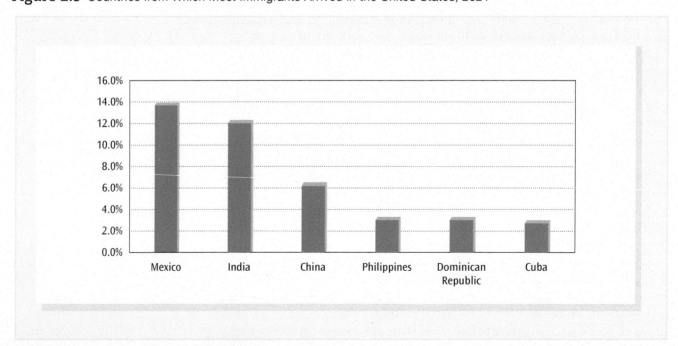

SOURCE: U.S. Department of Homeland Security (2022d).

Florida (11.2%), New York (10.3%), or Texas (10.7%) (DHS, 2022e). The West is home to 34% of the nation's immigrants. Another 34% live in the South, and the fewest (11%) live in the Midwest (Budiman, 2020).

Schools host a multicultural population in which over half of the nation's students are of color. Four percent of U.S. elementary and high school students were born outside the United States, and more than one in four has one or more foreign-born parents (U.S. Census Bureau, 2021b). Only 1.5 million or 5% of the children with one or more foreign-born parents are unauthorized (Abramitzky & Boustan, 2022). This number is lower than might be expected because children of unauthorized mothers who are born in the United States are U.S. citizens.

Protestors at a rally at the University of Michigan support dreamers and the Deferred Action for Childhood Arrivals (DACA) to prevent deportation of students.

**SOURCE:** Susan Montgomery/Alamy Stock Photo

Many citizens value multiculturalism and bilingualism, recalling that their ancestors were immigrants who entered the country with a culture and often a language different from that of the dominant group. Other citizens are anti-immigration, sometimes believing in the superiority of the native-born White population and worrying that the growing cultural and language diversity will destroy the dominant culture. In some states and school districts, these groups of citizens have led the movement to declare English the nation's official language and oppose the use of bilingual signs, bilingual education, and documents written in any language other than English.

## Unauthorized Immigrants

The debate about immigration policy centers primarily on unauthorized immigrants. President George W. Bush proposed immigration reform during his presidency at the beginning of the twenty-first century, but Congress took no action. Many people were hopeful that President Barack Obama would push for immigration reform soon after he was inaugurated in 2009 but were disappointed by his administration's inaction. The Dream Act, intended to allow the children of unauthorized immigrants a conditional pathway to citizenship and allow them to work and attend U.S. colleges, was defeated by Congress in 2011, but President Obama created an executive memorandum, the Deferred Action for Childhood Arrivals (DACA), that temporarily deferred deportation of the "dreamers" and granted them work permits and driver's licenses. The Dream Act of 2023 was introduced by senators Dick Durbin (D-IL) and Lindsey Graham (R-SC) in March 2023. Immigration, especially by unauthorized immigrants, continues to be a major issue in presidential elections.

Not all visitors to the United States are authorized to be there. People from other countries enter the United States as travelers or on student or other special visas. Some of them extend their stay beyond the intended legal limits, never returning to their home country after their visas expire. Many of these people are later reclassified as authorized or documented because they meet the requirements for employment-based visas, they qualify as refugees, or they are sponsored by a family as allowed by law. They may also become lawful immigrants through **amnesty** or similar programs periodically enacted by Congress. The problem is that many more people would like to immigrate to the United States than there are available visas for legal entry (Abramitzky & Boustan, 2022).

The total number of unauthorized immigrants has decreased since 2007, when it was at its peak with 12.2 million people. Of the estimated 11 million unauthorized immigrants living in the United States in 2019, approximately 48% were from Mexico, 19% from Central America, 15% from Asia, 8% from South America, 4% from Europe and

Canada, 3% from the Caribbean, and 3% from Africa (Migration Policy Institute, n.d.). Although the number of unauthorized migrants reaching the U.S./Mexico border was at an all-time high in 2022, the number of unauthorized immigrants living in the United States was estimated to have been 11.35 million in 2022, or 3.5% of the U.S. population (Camarota & Zeigler, 2022).

**Restrictionists** charge that unauthorized immigrants drain the social welfare system as they seek education for their children and medical assistance for their family members. People who are anti-immigration see these unauthorized immigrants as stealing their jobs, causing wages to be deflated, and making it hard for current citizens to make a good living (Watson & Thompson, 2021). State government has the greatest impact on the opportunities available to immigrants, including their ability to find a job, attend college, access government assistance, and encounter Immigration and Customs Enforcement (ICE) agents (Reich, 2021). Some states try to restrict public services, including education, for unauthorized immigrants. Other states are more supportive of immigrant families, passing their own Dream Acts and promoting bilingual education. Some states have passed legislation to provide in-state tuition to children of unauthorized immigrants and increase opportunities for them to attend public colleges and universities in their states.

Unauthorized children have a right to seek a public education under the U.S. Supreme Court decision *Plyler v. Doe* (1982). Educators cannot require students or families to declare their immigration status, provide Social Security numbers, or make inquiries that might expose such status. Teachers should be aware of the local policies related to ICE and its presence in or near schools as it conducts operations for deporting unauthorized immigrants in the neighborhood. The enforcement environments in which many families with unauthorized members live are fear-inducing and lead to stress and hardship for students and their family members, who are constantly worried about deportation (Watson & Thompson, 2021).

## Refugees and Asylees

**Refugees** and **asylees** are recognized by the federal government as being persecuted in their home countries because of race, ethnicity, religion, nationality, or membership in a specific social or political group. During 2021, 11,454 individuals were admitted as refugees and 17,692 as asylees to the United States. These numbers have dropped from highs earlier in this century. The number of refugees in 2021 was 13% of the refugees admitted in 2016, and the number of asylees was 39% of the asylees admitted in 2019 (DHS, 2022a, 2022g).

The number of refugees and asylees from different countries changes over time, as shown in Figure 2.6, based on political conditions in their home countries. People seeking **asylum** in the United States in 2021 came from at least 100 countries, with the largest number from Venezuela, China, El Salvador, Guatemala, Turkey, and Honduras (DHS, 2022b, 2022c).

Although some people worry that refugees will be a burden on society and not fit in, extensive research on immigrants demonstrates that refugees learn English, settle in, and contribute to the economy as soon as they possibly can (Abramitzky & Boustan, 2022).

Nearly half of the refugees are students who may be coping with the stress of the political unrest in their native countries and time spent in refugee camps. They often do not speak English and do not have strong academic backgrounds. They may feel disconnected from their U.S. schools, which contributes to poor academic performance and high dropout rates. Educators should encourage students to share their stories and work with the families of these students to determine their educational goals for their children and provide the necessary support (Cun, 2020).

**Figure 2.6** Home Countries from which Most Refugees Entered the United States, Selected Years 2012–2021

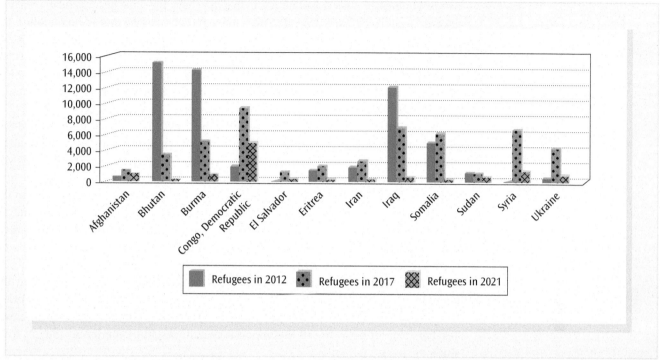

**SOURCE:** U.S. Department of Homeland Security (2022h).

## Education Levels of Immigrants

The education level of immigrants varies greatly, based in great part on their access to education in their home country. The percentage of foreign-born residents with bachelor's degrees is nearly equal to that in the native-born population, 25% and 24%, respectively. Seventeen percent of foreign-born residents have advanced degrees compared with 14% of native-born citizens. At the other end of the scale, 14% of foreign-born citizens do not have a high school degree—over twice as many as in the native-born population (U.S. Census Bureau, 2022c). Studies of immigrants indicate that those with the social and cultural capital of higher education and high literacy, numeracy, and digital skills are more likely to assimilate into the middle class. At the same time, one in five immigrants with bachelor's degrees report that their skills are underutilized as they work in jobs that require no more than a high school diploma or are unemployed (Batalova & Fix, 2022).

# Indigenous and Immigrant Populations in the United States

**Learning Objective 2.3** Describe the Indigenous and immigrant populations of the United States.

**First Americans** comprised 2.1% of the total U.S. population in 2021 (U.S. Census Bureau, 2022b), with 574 federally recognized tribal entities that are **Indigenous** or native to the United States (U.S. Department of the Interior, 2023). Foreign-born individuals who immigrated during their lifetime comprised 13.6% of the population (U.S. Census Bureau, 2021c). Ancestors of the remaining 84% of the population immigrated to the United States from around the world sometime over the past six centuries.

As people from all over the world immigrated to the United States, they brought with them cultural experiences from their native countries. Just because individuals have the same national origins, however, does not mean that they have the same history and experiences as other people who have emigrated from the same country. The time of immigration, the places in which groups settled, the reasons for emigrating, their **socioeconomic status (SES)**, and the degree to which their families have been affected by racism and discrimination affect their immigration experiences and acceptance in the United States. These differences are projected in communities as residents whose families have been in the United States for several generations do not always warmly welcome new immigrants.

Most groups have immigrated to the United States voluntarily to seek freedoms not available in their native countries at the time, to escape dismal economic or political conditions, or to join family members already settled in the United States. However, not all people and groups voluntarily immigrate. The ancestors of most Black people arrived involuntarily on ships transporting enslaved Africans. Mexicans living in the southwestern part of the country became residents when the United States annexed their lands. The reasons for immigration and the way immigrants were treated after they arrive have had a lasting impact on each group's assimilation patterns and access to society's resources.

In this section, we explore the experiences of Indigenous populations in the United States, involuntary immigrants, and voluntary immigrants. Students bring to school the cultures, histories, and languages of their families and communities. Teachers should be aware of the importance cultures and experiences play in their students' lives.

## Indigenous Populations

When Europeans first stepped on land in North America, millions of people were living on that land. First Americans have often been forgotten or neglected in the histories that most people studied in their youth. To set the stage for a discussion of immigration, let's first briefly explore the status of Indigenous peoples on the lands that are now the United States.

**NATIVE AMERICANS**   When Europeans first arrived on the shores of North America, 5 to 15 million Native people in hundreds of tribes populated and controlled the 2.4 billion acres that would become the United States (Treuer, 2021). Excavations have found that the ancestors of the Native people have likely been on these lands for at least 19,000 years (Treuer, 2019). European exploration of Native lands did not begin in earnest until the sixteenth century, when Spanish explorers took over land across the Americas while enslaving Native people and killing them with diseases like smallpox and measles. Soon the Spanish explorers were joined by the French, Dutch, Portuguese, and English, who planned to extract the valuable resources of the land. Toward the beginning of the seventeenth century, colonization began as people from Europe settled on lands that they did not own and created governments that did not recognize the Native inhabitants of the land. The Native people continued to be enslaved. Others were devastated by European diseases that killed as much as 90% of the population of New England tribes between 1616 and 1619 (Treuer, 2019).

Early European settlers were convinced that Native populations needed to be converted to Christianity, learn English, and adopt the culture of the settlers. For the most part, Native people had no interest in adopting the culture of the people who had colonized them. The eastern Cherokee had developed their own governmental structure, were publishing a bilingual newspaper, and announced a capital of the Cherokee nation. Many other tribes in the southeast had "fought for the government, . . . devoted themselves to farming and trade, developed courts and legislative systems—they had proved themselves socially and culturally adaptive" (Treuer, 2019, p. 35). Nevertheless, the new country's leaders saw them "as impediments to the cultivation of the American nation and American character" (Treuer, 2019, p. 32).

When President Andrew Jackson was elected in 1829, he seized the southeastern lands of the Native population, who were fighting in the courts against the privatization and selling of their lands. Congress passed the Indian Removal Act of 1830. Although the Supreme Court ruled that the removal of Native people from their homelands was unlawful, they were removed anyway. Members of the Cherokee, Muscogee, Seminole, Chickasaw, and Choctaw nations were forced from their homes and moved to the Oklahoma Territory. In that forced relocation, as many as one in three of them died on the march, called the Trail of Tears, to the western territory. By 1890, only 250,000 Native people remained in control of 56 million acres, roughly 2% of the land on which they had lived 400 years earlier (Treuer, 2021).

Members of tribes fought the U.S. Army to hold onto their homelands as European colonizers occupied their lands. The Seminole, for example, fought three wars with the U.S. government between 1818 and 1858. At the end of the second and third wars, some members of the Seminole tribe were moved to the Oklahoma Territory, but others refused to surrender. Other tribes west of the Mississippi fought the U.S. Army and colonial settlers who were moving west and settling on land that tribes had inhabited for hundreds or thousands of years. Peace between groups would be reached and then trespassed by one side or the other. Treaties were signed and then ignored. Massacres occurred, killing women and children as well as warriors and soldiers. Native people were arrested, hanged, and executed throughout the nineteenth century, and settlers lost their lives in battles over who belonged on the land that had been the homeland of the Native population. "The last major armed conflict between a Native tribe and the U.S. government ended at Wounded Knee Creek with the massacre of as many as 300 men, women, and children of Spotted Elk's band of Miniconjou" (Treuer, 2021, p. 39).

The U.S. government continued to pass laws to make Native land available to White settlers. The 1887 Dawes Act, for example, split reservations into small acreage plots for Native people, opening the rest of the land to settlement by White people. Native people lost another 90 million acres. The 1889 Indian Appropriations Act replaced tribal landownership with individual ownership of 160 acres. After allotments of land were made to members of tribes, the remainder was given away to homesteaders.

The establishment of national parks also required the removal of Native people from their most revered homelands. Again, people were murdered to remove them

Children from the Cherokee Nation after planting a "victory garden" at a boarding school during World War II.

**SOURCE:** Bettmann Archive/Getty Images

from the land. Yellowstone became the first national park in 1872, eliminating any settlement on the land. The tribes that had lived there for centuries became trespassers on park land. They left the park with the understanding that they would have hunting rights on the park land based on an 1868 treaty. By the end of the century, the government had withdrawn those rights. The establishment of national park after national park was created on the homelands of Native people (Treuer, 2021).

By 1879, children on reservations were being removed from their homes and placed in boarding schools to unlearn the traditional ways and languages of their families. Children were forced to have their hair cut, and they were not allowed to use their native languages. In those schools they were often malnourished, and the school buildings were decrepit and unsafe. They sometimes attended school part of the day and worked the other part of the day to support the school. Reports in the 1920s chronicled the abuse of children, who were schooled many miles and sometimes many states away from their families. Although the goal became less about assimilation, some boarding schools for Native Americans continued to operate into the twenty-first century.

**Sovereignty** is a political and legal concept that refers to the ultimate power to govern and have independence. It is of critical importance to the self-governance of Native American tribes. The U.S. Constitution recognizes Native American tribes as distinct governments within the United States with the power to regulate their internal affairs. Thus, treaties with the federal government are legally binding contracts, which are related to fishing rights, gaming, lands in federal trust, and other rights (Echohawk, 2013). At different periods of time, the federal government has been pro- or antisovereignty for Native American tribes (Hopkins, 2020). Beginning in the 1960s, legislation and practices became more pro-sovereignty. In the 1980s, it expanded beyond the previous treaty rights to include gaming or the right to administer to the civil concerns of the tribe (Treuer, 2019). In 2020, the Supreme Court upheld the sovereignty of the Creek Nation Reservation in Oklahoma when it declined Oklahoma's request to disestablish the reservation. Justice Neil Gorsuch's opinion on behalf of the majority indicated that "once a reservation is created by a treaty, it can be disestablished only by an act of Congress—not a court and certainly not a state" (Chaudhuri, 2020, para. 6).

It was not until the 1960s that Native Americans were granted federal authority to establish and manage their own tribal schools. The Rough Rock Demonstration School, which opened in 1966 in the New Mexico portion of the Navajo Nation, was the first contemporary school that had a locally elected all-Native American governing board and taught the curriculum using a Native American language (McCarty & Roessel, 2015).

The atrocities and near genocide that characterized the treatment of Native Americans have been ignored in most accounts of U.S. history. According to historian Claudio Saunt (2020), "there has been no comparable reckoning with the conquest of the continent, little serious reflection on its centrality to the rise of the United States, and minimal sustained engagement with the people who lost their homelands" (p. xix). Not until 2000 did an official of the Bureau of Indian Affairs apologize for a "legacy of racism and inhumanity that included massacres, forced relocations of tribes and attempts to wipe out Indian languages and cultures" (Kelly, 2000). An official apology, which was buried in a massive defense appropriation bill signed by President Obama in 2019, urged "the President to acknowledge the wrongs of the United States against Indian tribes in the history of the United States in order to bring healing to this land," but no apology has ever been made by a president (Bigpond & Brownback, 2021).

**NATIVE HAWAIIANS**  Native Hawaiian heritage was identified by 620,000 people in the 2020 census; an additional 881,000 people identified themselves as Other Pacific Islanders (U.S. Census Bureau, 2020b). It is believed that the Hawai'i Islands were first settled by explorers from the Marquesas Islands in 300 c.e. and 900 years later by Polynesians from Tahiti (Polynesian Cultural Center, 2023). Over time, they "developed systems of aquaculture (loko i'a), irrigated terraces for planting (lo'i), and other forms of food cultivation situated in a land division system known as an ahupua'a," reinforcing their relationship with the land (Ho-Lastimosa et al., 2019, p. 1). Their experiences of colonization are similar to those of other Indigenous populations around the world as their countries were invaded by Europeans. Spanish explorers had likely set foot on Hawai'i lands earlier, but British explorer Captain James Hook is cited as one of the first Europeans to land on one of the Hawaiian Islands, Kauai, in 1778, followed 42 years later by Christian colonialist settlers, traders, and whalers who brought diseases that devasted the native population.

As White owners of plantations needed more laborers than were available on the island in the mid-1880s, they recruited labor to work on the sugar and rice plantations from China and Japan, and later from Portugal, Korea, Puerto Rico, the Philippine Islands, and Europe. By 1893, U.S. colonists controlled the island's sugar-based economy, and Native Hawaiians were losing both their land and their political power (Lee, 2015). The following year, White sugar planters overthrew Queen Lili'uokalani in an effort to gain control of the island and further their interests. Although Hawaiians organized a counter-revolution to restore the monarchy, they were unsuccessful (U.S. National Park Service, 2019). President Grover Cleveland declared the abdication illegal and called for the monarchy to be restored, but the planters' interests prevailed. A White president of the Republic of Hawai'i was installed, and Hawai'i was annexed by the U.S. government in 1898, becoming a territory in 1900. In 1853, the population of Hawai'i was 97% Native Hawaiians, but it had dropped to 16% by 1923 (History.com Editors, 2022).

Vital to the interests of the United States, Hawai'i became the 50th state in 1959. By then, Hawai'i was the most racially and ethnically diverse U.S. state. In 2020, 37% of the state's population identified their racial or ethnic identity as Asian American, 30% as White American, 25% as two or more races, 11% as Native Hawaiian or Other Pacific Islander, and 2% as Black American (U.S. Census Bureau, 2021a).

Hawai'i is the only state that has designated two official state languages: Hawaiian and English. Over the past few decades, Native Hawaiians have been revitalizing traditional cultural practices to overcome inequities they have faced in self-governance, education, health, and research (Ho-Lastimosa et al., 2019). Like the Native American and Alaska Native peoples, Native Hawaiians strive to reclaim their indigenous voices as they establish Hawaiian language- and culture-based programs (Hawai'i State Department of Education, n.d.).

**ALASKA NATIVES** Thousands of years ago, the ancestors of Alaska Natives settled in the northern part of North America. Indigenous populations in Alaska today include 228 federally recognized tribes that are sovereign governments including the Aleut, Alutiiq, Athabascan, Cup'ik, Eyak, Haida, Iñupiat, St. Lawrence Island Yupik, Tlingit, Tsimshian, Unangax, and Yu'pik people (U.S. Bureau of Indian Affairs, 2023). When Russian explorers first landed in Alaska in 1741, 100,000 Alaska Natives lived there. The Russian empire was able to gain control of the land using their firearms and other weapons, although they met resistance from some tribes. During the early years of Russian occupation, Alaska Natives died from disease, warfare, and enslavement. By the time Russia sold Alaska to the U.S. in 1867, the population had been reduced by half. Alaska Natives claimed that the land was theirs because they were the "original inhabitants and having not lost the land in war or ceded it to any country" (Hensley, 2017, para. 8). In their view, the United States "had bought the right to negotiate with the indigenous populations" (para. 8).

When the United States "bought" Alaska, it was made a military district because its Indigenous inhabitants were considered adversaries (Hensley, 2017). Soon the Alaska Natives came under the management of the U.S. Bureau of Indian Affairs, suffering from the same restrictions that Native Americans experienced, including campaigns "to eradicate their languages, religion, art, music, dance, ceremonies, and lifestyles" (Hensley, 2017, para. 9). Unlike Native Americans, Alaska Natives did not have treaties with the U.S. government to protect their subsistence rights, except for the right to harvest whales and other marine animals.

By the 1890s, gold prospectors and White settlers began to populate Alaska, overtaking the size of the Native population so that Alaska Natives are only 15% of the population today (U.S. Census Bureau, 2021b). It wasn't until 1936 that the Indian Reorganization Act allowed Native people to form their own tribal governments. Nine years later, Alaska outlawed discrimination against Alaska Natives. In 1959, Alaska became the 49th state. The Alaska Federation of Natives filed land claims covering the entire state in 1966. Two years later, oil was discovered in Alaska, and in 1971 the U.S. Congress passed the Alaskan Native Claims Settlement Act to resolve long-standing issues regarding aboriginal land claims in Alaska. The settlement ceded 44 million acres of federal land and $1 billion to Alaska's Native populations that would be managed by Native regional economic development corporations (Hensley, 2017).

Formal schools were first introduced in Alaska by missionaries of the Russian Orthodox Church. By 1888, schools were managed by the Bureau of Education, an agency of the Department of the Interior, whose director was a Presbyterian missionary who viewed Alaska Natives as inferior. Early in the twentieth century, Congress passed the Nelson Act to create two separate school systems: one for Alaska Native students operated under the U.S. Office of Indian Affairs and a second for White and mixed-race students (Jones & Rich, 2019). A 1972 lawsuit ended Alaska's unequal education system that required students in rural areas to attend boarding schools outside their community if they wanted a secondary education. The court decision led to high schools being built in rural areas. In 2022, Alaska passed legislation (Senate Bill 34) to allow the state to reach an agreement with an Alaska Native Tribal entity for the Tribal authority to operate and oversee K–12 schools that "would offer a unique, culturally rich combination of Western and millennia-old tribal educational models" (Alaska Department of Education & Early Development, n.d., para. 1).

**OTHER INDIGENOUS PEOPLE NOW LIVING IN THE UNITED STATES**   Other indigenous people have immigrated to the United States from Central and South America and other areas. For example, half of the population in Guatemala is Indigenous, often from Mayan descent, and speaks one of many Indigenous languages, not Spanish. They are moving from very poor, mostly rural areas of their country. They may be stigmatized and discriminated against as they move through the immigration system (Ramos, 2020). It is not clear how Indigenous people from other countries identify their race/ethnicity on U.S. forms. They may indicate they are Native American or Latino or a specific race. They do not always speak Spanish and there is no checkbox on the forms they complete that aligns with how they see themselves.

## Involuntary Immigrants

Not all people who immigrated to the United States did so by choice. The first **involuntary immigrants** were 20 to 30 enslaved Africans who were aboard the *White Lion* when it landed at Point Comfort (now Fort Monroe in Hampton) in the Colony of Virginia in 1619, a year before the Pilgrims arrived in Cape Cod. Enslaved Africans were forcibly brought to the United States for almost another 200 years. After trading of enslaved people was banned by Congress in 1808, enslaved people were traded domestically. Although 12.5 million Africans were forced onto ships bound for the Americas, only 10.7 million survived the **Middle Passage** from West Africa (Equal Justice Initiative, 2023). The number of Africans who disembarked in the United States was 450,000, a small fraction of the total number of enslaved people who arrived during this period in the Caribbean Islands and North, Central, and South America (Gates, 2014).

Enslaved people were not the only people who entered this country involuntarily. People of color, primarily Mexican Americans, who lived in the current southwestern and western part of the United States became residents of the United States after the

Mexican–American War in 1845–1848 when those territories were annexed by the U.S. government. In this section, the immigration patterns of Black and Latin Americans are introduced.

**BLACK AMERICANS**   Africans were among the early explorers in the 1500s, joining expeditions of Spanish explorers as soldiers, interpreters, or servants; they were sometimes free men and sometimes enslaved by the Spaniards (Library of Congress, n.d.). By the end of the seventeenth century, African men, women, and children were arriving through the forced migration of enslaved people that had expanded to the colonies. They "were not recognized as human beings but were considered property that could be mortgaged, traded, bought, sold, used as collateral, given as a gift, and disposed of violently" (Hannah-Jones et al., 2021). Enslaved people, sometimes joined by **indentured servants**, did not quietly accept their status; they rebelled against their enslavers and the White elite who condoned slavery. For example, in 1739, enslaved Africans near the Stono River near Charleston, South Carolina, raided a local store for weapons and ammunition that they used to raid and burn plantations in the area. Soon after that rebellion, South Carolina legislators passed the Negro Act of 1740 to force enslaved people into "due subjection and obedience" (Alexander & Alexander, 2021). In the Haitian Revolution from 1791 to 1804, enslaved people in Haiti overthrew their French enslavers, which led to laws for even greater control of the Black population in the United States to prevent a similar revolution. According to Leslie and Michelle Alexander (2021), "This notion—that Black people were inherently devious and criminal, and that [W]hite people were required to monitor and police them—ultimately defined the nature of race relations in the United States" (p. 103). By 1793, Congress passed a fugitive slave law that empowered enslavers and local governments to pursue and recapture enslaved people across state lines.

By the Revolutionary War, 50% of the population in the tobacco-growing states of Virginia, Maryland, and North Carolina was comprised of enslaved people. Soon after, rice plantations in Georgia and South Carolina were using enslaved labor (Shah & Adolphe, 2019), followed by the production of cotton, sugarcane, and indigo, which increased dramatically across the South after the War of 1812. By the Civil War, the United States had risen to global prosperity, due in large part to the production of cotton by nearly 4 million enslaved people (Beckert, 2014).

Following the Civil War, the 12-year period of Reconstruction provided some hope for freedom of formerly enslaved people as they were promised land and were elected to local positions, state legislatures, and Congress, but that hope was short-lived. After President Abraham Lincoln was assassinated, his vice president, Andrew Johnson, was responsible for providing the leadership for the inclusion of previously enslaved people into U.S. society. Just before the war ended, Congress created the Bureau of Refugees, Freedmen, and Abandoned Lands, which was known as the Freedmen's Bureau. Among its duties was the leasing of 40-acre parcels of land from abandoned plantations to Black adults who had been enslaved and the establishment of schools for their children across the South. President Johnson, who was an ardent supporter of the Homestead Act to give 160 acres to citizens settling the West, rescinded the order to give land to Black people and reinstated owners of plantations on the land.

President Johnson also pardoned major Confederate leaders, who returned home to lead political revolutions against granting rights to the Black population. Mississippi, for example, passed *Black Codes* that denied Black people land, the ability to hunt and fish, and independent work. Nine more Confederate states soon followed by passing the same or similar codes to control Black people in their states. White Southerners "unleashed a reign of terror and anti-black violence" (Anderson, 2017, p. 18) on the formerly enslaved population. Not only did the president ignore the violence in the South, he declared, "This is . . . a country for White men, and by god, as long as I'm President, it shall be a government for White men" (as cited in Anderson, 2017, p. 18).

The sharecropping system developed for Black farmers to lease land was designed so that they stayed in constant debt to the landowners, almost never earning a profit. The system prevented sharecroppers from leaving the land by having them arrested, assaulted, or murdered when they tried to leave. Black prisoners were sold to plantations, mines, and factories (Rothstein, 2017). In other jobs, neither Black nor White people who were impoverished were paid wages that could raise them out of poverty. Although Congress passed the Civil Rights Act in 1866, state courts were not allowing Black people to sit on juries or provide testimony in court, making it nearly impossible to convict the White people who were committing violent crimes against them. It was during this period that former Confederate officers founded the Ku Klux Klan to defend the Southern way of life. By 1868, the Klan was terrorizing Black men who tried to vote (Glaude, 2017).

Congress tried to change the actions that were preventing Black people from accessing their civil rights by passing the Reconstruction Acts in 1867. At the same time, the House of Representatives voted to impeach President Johnson, but the Senate acquitted him. Congress did pass the Fourteenth Amendment in 1868, granting citizenship to all people born or naturalized in the United States except Native Americans. With the ratification of the Fifteenth Amendment in 1870, Black men were granted the right to vote. However, the laws were ignored or interpreted in ways that continued to deny the vote and civil rights to the Black population until the Voting Rights Act was passed by Congress in 1965, nearly 100 years later. The withdrawal of federal troops from Southern states in 1877 by President Rutherford B. Hayes opened the door for White Southerners to quickly eliminate any gains that Black people had made in Reconstruction, reinvigorating White supremacy ideology and racism (Gates, 2019).

As involuntary immigrants, Africans underwent a process quite different than the Europeans who voluntarily immigrated. Separated from their families and robbed of their freedom, cultures, and languages, enslaved Africans developed a new Black culture based on their experiences in Africa and the United States, which later sometimes included European and/or Native American heritages. Immediately after the Civil War, Black people began establishing their own schools to ensure that the population became literate as quickly as possible.

Early on, the majority of Black people lived in the South, where today they remain the majority population in a number of counties. When industrial jobs in northern, eastern, and western cities began to expand between 1910 and 1920, many Black people migrated to northern and western cities—a pattern that was repeated in the 1940s and 1950s. Another factor that contributed to Black migration north was the racism and political terror that existed across the South at that time. Even today, a racial ideology is implicit in the policies and practices of many of U.S. institutions. It continues to block the full inclusion of Black people into the dominant society. Although the Civil Rights Movement of the 1960s reduced a number of barriers that prevented many Black people from enjoying the advantages of the middle class, the number of Black people, especially children, who live in poverty remains disproportionately high.

The Pew Research Center reports that 8% of the Black population now identifies themselves as biracial, usually with Black and White heritages (Tamir, 2021). However, the increase in the Black population today is due to increasing immigration from Africa. One in 10 Black people in the United States in 2019 was an immigrant, with the majority of them arriving after 2000. Black immigrants are primarily from the Caribbean (46%), particularly from Jamaica and Haiti, and Africa (42%), with the largest number from Nigeria and Ethiopia. A number of immigrants from South and Central America and the Caribbean are Afro-Latino/as. Black immigrants generally settle in large metropolitan areas such as New York City, Miami, Washington DC, Atlanta, Boston, Houston, and Dallas (Tamir, 2022).

**LATINO/A AMERICANS**   Mexican Americans also played a unique role in the formation of the United States. Spain was the first European country to colonize the western and southwestern United States and Mexico. In 1848 the U.S. government annexed the northern sections of the Mexican Territory, including the areas now occupied by Arizona, California, western Colorado, New Mexico, Nevada, Texas, and Utah. The Mexican population living within that territory became an oppressed group in the region where they had previously been the dominant group with power. Although the labor of Mexicans has consistently been sought by U.S. farmers and businesses for more than a century, laborers have been treated with hostility and have been limited to low-paying jobs and subordinate status. Supremacy theories related to race and language have been used against Latino/a people in a way that, even today, prevents many Latino/a people, particularly if they are people of color, from assimilating fully into the dominant culture.

While Mexican American natives were involuntary immigrants when their lands were annexed by the U.S. government, they have been the largest group to voluntarily and lawfully immigrate to the United States in most years since the 1980s. In addition, over half of the unauthorized immigrants at the southern border in 2022 were Mexican (Rosenbloom & Batalova, 2022).

Four in five Latino/a residents were U.S. citizens in 2021 (Krogstad et al., 2022). Figure 2.7 shows the immigrant status by the number of generations people have been in the United States and the countries of origin of the Latino/a population plus the percentage of Afro-Latino/as. At the beginning of the twenty-first century, the Latino/a population became the largest group of color in the United States. Although Latino/a people are usually categorized as people of color, not all are people of color. In 2021, 87% of Latino/a people reported that they were White, 5% were Black, 3% were Native American or Alaska Native, and 3% were bi- or multiracial (U.S. Census Bureau, 2022b).

**Figure 2.7**  Demographics of Latino/a Population in the United States, 2019–2021

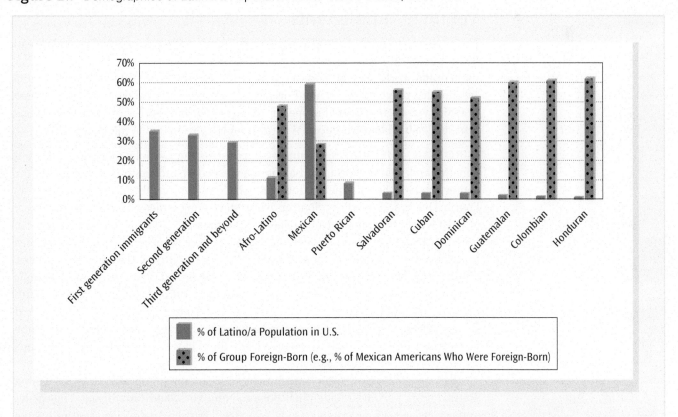

SOURCES: Gonzalez-Barrera (2020, 2022); Krogstad et al. (2022).

Another study found that not all Afro-Latinos, who are primarily from Puerto Rico and the Dominican Republic, identify themselves as Hispanic (Gonzalez-Barrera, 2022).

Latino/a people were 19% of the U.S. population in 2020 and projected to constitute 25% of the U.S. population by 2045 (U.S. Census Bureau, 2018b). In 2021, the Latino/a population was over half of the population in New Mexico and 40% of the population of California and Texas, and the population is growing across most states, with the fastest rates of growth in North and South Dakota (Krogstad et al., 2022). Because the Latino/a population is younger than other racial and ethnic groups, their numbers will continue to grow based more on new births than immigration (Krogstad et al., 2022).

Note that different terms are used to identify the Latino/a population. As it collects data about the population, the U.S. Census uses *Hispanic* or *Latino*, defining the terms as a pan-ethnic group that includes people of "Cuban, Mexican, Puerto Rican, South or Central American, or other Spanish culture or origin regardless of race" (U.S. Census Bureau, 2022a). People completing government forms and surveys determine their identity. If they say they are Hispanic, they are considered Hispanic. About half of the population describe themselves by their family's country of origin while almost 40% describe themselves as Hispanic or Latino/a. Others describe themselves as American, depending primarily on how long they have been in the United States. *Latinx* is another term that has emerged in recent years as a gender-neutral alternative to Latino/a. Latinx is used by some researchers, universities, news and entertainment organizations, corporations, and local governments. Journalist Paola Ramos (2020) felt "Latinx was able to capture what other terms had not in the past—it captured the stories of all these people under one umbrella, spanning so many separate identities" (p. 11). However, only 4% of adults identified themselves as Latinx in 2022 (Newport, 2022). The debate about the use of Latinx has now moved into the political arena, with some governors banning its use in government documents. The authors of this book have chosen to use Latino/a as a gender-neutral term when we refer to Spanish-speaking people with Latin American ancestry.

## Voluntary Immigrants

The ancestors of most of the U.S. population immigrated voluntarily. The majority of these immigrants were Europeans who faced few barriers to entry. People from other parts of the world were periodically banned from entry or faced very limited quota systems that prevented most non-Europeans from immigrating before the law changed in 1965. Even the number of Europeans immigrating from southern and eastern Europe came to a halt when their quotas were also severely restricted in the 1920s.

**EUROPEAN AMERICANS**  Spain began constructing Catholic missions in Central America and then in Florida and along the west coast and southwestern areas of the country and into South America during the sixteenth century. By the late 1500s, English, French, Dutch, and Swedish colonizers were establishing settlements along the east coast of what would become the United States. After the consolidation and development of the United States as an independent nation, successive waves of northern and western Europeans joined the earlier settler colonists. Within 100 years, Germans, Scots, Swedes, Finns, and others left their home countries for the United States to escape economic impoverishment or political repression. These early European settlers brought with them the political institutions that would become the initial framework for the U.S. and state governments. The melding of northern and western European cultures over time formed the dominant Anglo-Saxon or White culture in which other immigrant groups strived or were forced to assimilate.

Between 1820 and 1860, a large number of Irish immigrants arrived in the United States, taking jobs in Philadelphia, Boston, New York, and Providence. The earlier immigrants were Protestants who soon assimilated into the Anglo-Saxon culture, but the Irish immigrants were Catholic and faced greater discrimination than their predecessors.

At the end of the nineteenth century, industries in the nation's cities required more labor than was available. Immigrants from impoverished eastern and southern European countries such as Poland, Hungary, Italy, Russia, and Greece were recruited to accept jobs, primarily in midwestern and eastern cities. The reasons for their immigration were similar to those that had driven many earlier immigrants: devastating economic and political hardship in the homeland and the demand for labor in the United States. Between 1892 and 1954, more than 12 million immigrants were processed through the immigration station on Ellis Island, located between the states of New York and New Jersey.

Many immigrants came to the United States with the hope of enjoying the higher wages and improved living conditions they had heard about, but they found conditions worse than they had expected. Most were forced to live in substandard housing near the business and manufacturing districts where they worked. These urban areas grew into ethnic enclaves in which the immigrants continued to use their native languages and maintain the cultures of their native lands. To support their social and welfare needs, ethnic institutions often were established. Many of the racist policies that were used against Black, Mexican American, and Native American people were applied to these European immigrants. A major difference was that their offspring were allowed to assimilate into the dominant White culture during the second and third generations.

**ASIAN AMERICANS**  The pan-ethnic classification of Asian people includes individuals whose families have been in the United States for generations and those who are first-generation immigrants. Many have little in common other than that their countries of origin are from the same continent. Asian American people have roots in Bangladesh, Bhutan, Borneo, Burma, Cambodia, Chamorro, China, East India, Philippines, Indonesia, Japan, Korea, Laos, Okinawa, Myanmar, Samoa, Sikkim, Singapore, Sri Lanka, Thailand, Vietnam, or one of 27 other Asian countries.

Chinese immigrants began to migrate to the United States early in the nineteenth century. During the Gold Rush in the 1850s, the number of Chinese people, primarily men, arriving in California increased. The industrial opening of the West in the mid-1800s signaled a need for labor that could be met through immigration from Asia. Chinese laborers worked the plantations in Hawai'i and were recruited to provide the labor needed for building railroads along with workers from Japan and the Philippines. They also worked in factories, canneries, fisheries, and fields and worked long hours in laundries and restaurants across the country (Lee, 2015). By 1882, racism and a changing need for labor led to Congress passing the Chinese Exclusion Act, halting all immigration from China. The 1875 Page Act and the 1882 Exclusion Act made it difficult for Chinese women to immigrate to the United States. The 1888 Scott Act prevented Chinese laborers from returning to the United States if they left. By 1910, immigrants from Asia were entering the United States through Angel Island in San Francisco where they were processed and often deported (Lee, 2015).

Between 1910 and 1940, up to 1 million Asian and other immigrants were processed at the Angel Island Immigration Center in San Francisco, where they were exhaustively interrogated for days or even months before they were deported or admitted to the United States.

**SOURCE:** Fotosearch/Stringer/Getty Images

The first group of Japanese immigrants landed in Hawai'i in 1885 to work on the sugar plantations. Because it was hard work, they led work stoppages to protest the physical punishment and poor living conditions on the plantations. Soon they were also going to the continental United States, finding economic security by the early twentieth century (Lee, 2015). But their limited prosperity was not to last. In 1905 in San Francisco, White organizations organized the Japanese-Korean Exclusion League to exclude Japanese and Korean immigrants from the United States, in part to "save the White race." The group also lobbied the school board to segregate Japanese students from White students in San Francisco schools, which resulted in all Japanese and Korean students being sent to the city's "Oriental" School, which Chinese students were already required to attend (Lee, 2015). By 1924, Japanese were barred from entry as part of the Johnson-Reed Act. After Japan bombed Pearl Harbor in Hawai'i in 1941, Japanese American families were arrested and placed in internment camps for most of World War II, many losing their property and belongings in the process. Because of bias against the Chinese and Japanese populations, immigration from Asia was severely limited by Congress until a change in the immigration laws in 1965.

At the end of the Spanish-American War in 1898, the Philippines, Puerto Rico, and Guam became territories of the United States. Filipinos were not willing to give up their sovereignty and fought the U.S. for another 3 years, leading to the loss of over a million lives. As it did with most other groups of color, the U.S. government categorized the Filipinos by using derogatory characteristics and declaring that they could not govern on their own (Lee, 2015). Soon after the end of the war, Filipinos were being recruited to work in Hawai'i; they were also beginning to slowly migrate to the continental United States. With growing and passionate racism against them, Filipinos became victims of violence. Wanting to restrict immigration from the Philippines, Congress granted the country commonwealth status in 1934 and a promise of independence after 10 years. At that point, Filipinos were no longer "nationals" who could travel to the United States. The next year, Congress passed the Filipino Repatriation Act, which would pay all the expenses for a Filipino born in the Philippines and living in the United States to return to the Philippines. Anyone agreeing to return to the Philippines under this plan would never be allowed to return to the United States. Less than 2,200 Filipinos accepted the deal, even though most had become very disillusioned with their treatment in the United States (Lee, 2015).

As with other people of color, the discrimination and violence against Asian Americans still exists in the twenty-first century. After President Donald Trump blamed the Chinese for COVID-19 at the beginning of the pandemic early in 2020, violent attacks against Asian Americans escalated dramatically. Almost seven in 10 of the attacks on Asian Americans between March 2020 and February 2021 were against Asian American women (Ishisaka, 2021). However, violence against Asian Americans began much earlier than the pandemic, as described above. One of the most publicized incidents in the past 50 years was the 1982 murder of Vincent Chin—a Chinese American that was mistakenly identified as Japanese in a Highland Park, Michigan, bar—who was chased and beaten to death with a baseball bat because the perpetrators believed that Japanese workers caused the loss of their jobs in the auto industry. Neither of his attackers served any time in jail (Stop AAPI Hate, 2022a). In 1989, a gunman shot 35 students who were primarily Asian American in a schoolyard in Stockton, California (Au & Yonamine, 2021). More recently, six Asian American women were killed in March 2021 in Atlanta massage parlors. This growing anti-Asian hate has had a major impact on the group's mental health. Over seven in 10 Asian Americans report that discrimination against them is their greatest source of stress and almost half report depression or anxiety (Stop AAPI Hate, 2022b).

Asian Americans today are growing faster than any other group in the United States. They trace almost all of their roots to 19 origin groups across the continent. The national origins of 85% of the Asian American population are China (23%), India (20%), Philippines (18%), Vietnam (10%), South Korea (8%), and Japan (7%) (U.S. Census Bureau, 2023). The newest Asian immigrants are from Myanmar (formerly Burma).

Although some Asian Americans have been in the United States for generations, nearly six in 10 were foreign-born in 2019. Asian Americans are better educated than any other group in the country, with about half of them holding bachelor's degrees. However, 30% of Southeast Asian adults, which includes Cambodian, Vietnamese, and Laotians, have not graduated from high school (Pandey et al., 2022).

# The Struggle for Civil Rights

**Learning Objective 2.4** Explore the struggle for civil rights and its impact on equality.

The fight for **civil rights** by racial and ethnic groups has a long history in the United States. Native Americans fought to maintain their rights, culture, languages, and lands as foreigners appropriated their homelands. Enslaved Africans revolted against their enslavers. Free Black people decried the discrimination and violence they faced in the North. In the early twentieth century, Mexican American miners in Arizona led a strike for better working conditions and pay equal to that of European American miners. Across the Southwest, Mexican Americans established ethnic organizations to fight exploitation and support those who were in dire straits. Chinese and other immigrants used the courts to overturn the 1790 Naturalization Act, which excluded anyone who was not a free White person from citizenship.

*BIPOC* (Black, Indigenous, and People of Color) is an acronym sometimes used to emphasize the long-term harm that Black and Indigenous people and other people of color have experienced as a result of institutional racism and discrimination. These groups and their allies continuously fight against the harsh economic and political realities and injustices imposed on them. These movements for democratic rights and economic justice invariably bolster community solidarity based on race/ethnicity. The fight for civil rights has led over time to the reduction of the overt discrimination and exclusion that has kept many people of color and others who are discriminated against from having access to the basic necessities and benefits of society. The events that initiated these changes in schools and broader society are outlined in this section.

## Antecedents to the Civil Rights Movement

The United States is a nation that espouses the value of equality, but what is meant by equality? Does it mean that everyone has the right to vote without harassment? Does it mean that everyone regardless of race or ethnicity should have access to the jobs for which they are qualified? Does it mean that the median income of workers of color should be equal to the median income of White workers? Does it mean that the children of all families should be able to attend attractive, well-resourced schools with qualified teachers? If the answer to these questions is "yes," the country is not living up to its goal for equality for all people regardless of their race and ethnicity.

In fact, local, state, and federal governments have a long history of passing and implementing policies that made it almost impossible for most people of color to have access to the same opportunities for success and well-being as White people. For example, racial segregation was codified in 1896 when the Supreme Court established the "separate but equal" doctrine in *Plessy v. Ferguson*. The **Jim Crow laws** that followed spread from the South to other regions of the country. Black families were forced out of small towns in which they were living. Sundown laws in numerous communities communicated that Black people were not welcome in their town after sunset. When Woodrow Wilson became president in 1913, Jim Crow laws were applied to the federal government, leading to the separation of federal workers by race. And lynchings continued, with over 4,400 lynchings of Black people documented between 1877 and 1950 (Equal Justice Initiative, n.d.).

By the twentieth century, the Supreme Court had declared that schools for Black children could be closed while a school district continued to provide schools for White children. Courts also approved the use of a poll tax to vote, making it almost impossible for people who were impoverished to vote. These court decisions and government policies continued to limit the civil rights of the population of color until they were outlawed in the 1950s and 1960s. Discrimination had become codified in determining where families could live. In 1910, Baltimore became the first city to adopt zoning rules that prevented Black and White people from living in the same residential area (Rothstein, 2017). Other cities followed suit. The Supreme Court supported these zoning rules with the intent of reserving "middle-class neighborhoods for single-family homes that lower-income families of all races could not afford" (Rothstein, 2017, p. 48).

Zoning decisions contributed to the degradation of Black neighborhoods into slums by zoning those areas to permit industry, even polluting industries, as well as taverns, liquor stores, and nightclubs that could not operate in White neighborhoods. Black people were ineligible for mortgages because the only neighborhoods in which they were allowed to live were viewed by the banks and the Federal Housing Administration as risky loans, a discriminatory practice known as **redlining**. Not only could Black families not get loans for mortgages, their rent was greater for similar housing in White neighborhoods. With no or limited money for upkeep, homes owned by Black families were more likely to deteriorate, reinforcing the poor ratings of their neighborhoods (Rothstein, 2017).

Black citizens continued to be disenfranchised, especially in the South. By 1944, only 5% of eligible Black citizens were registered to vote in the old Confederacy states. By 1960, that rate was less than 2% in Mississippi. More than half of Mississippi's Black population had fewer than 5 years of education compared with 10% of the White population in the state, which led to the use of literacy tests and **understanding clauses** to block Black citizens from voting. The National Association for the Advancement of Colored People (NAACP) worked to eliminate these barriers to voting even though its workers often faced violence from the White population. Poll taxes were outlawed in 1964 with the Twenty-Fourth Amendment of the U.S. Constitution. Other practices such as literacy tests were not outlawed until the 1965 Voting Rights Act. Although *Plessy* was based on a "separate but equal" doctrine, states had failed to provide anything near equal for their Black citizens and other citizens of color.

Native Americans faced similar obstacles to voting; they were not allowed to vote until Congress passed the Indian Citizenship Act in 1924. Because that bill left it up to the states to decide who had the right to vote, full voting rights were not available to all Native Americans until Congress passed the Voting Rights Act in 1965. Obstacles to voting continue today, particularly on reservations where nontraditional mailing addresses and housing insecurity make it difficult to provide proof of residence; access to the Internet is limited; and other barriers such as not accepting tribal IDs for identification and inadequate voting facilities exclude Native voices (Tucker et al., 2020).

## *Brown v. Board of Education*

Schools have long been at the center of the Civil Rights Movement. Before the Civil War, Black children across the South were not allowed to learn to read and write. After the war, they had short school years between harvests in the fall and planting in the spring. Native American students were sometimes barred from attending school by states or school districts into the twentieth century. Later Black and Latino/a and Asian American students were not allowed to attend schools with White children in much of the country as a result of segregated schools in which students of color attended schools without the books and resources to which most White children had access. These circumstances and other Jim Crow laws led to the launch of a campaign in 1935 by the NAACP to overturn *Plessy*. For the next 15 years, the NAACP argued in court case after court case that local school boards were not providing equal schooling as was required in *Plessy*'s "separate but equal" clause.

Four court cases were consolidated for Thurgood Marshall's argument before the Supreme Court in 1952: *Briggs v. Elliott* (1952) in South Carolina, *Davis v. County School Board of Prince Edward County* (1952) in Virginia, *Gebhart v. Belton* (1952) in Delaware, and *Brown v. Board of Education of Topeka* (1951) in Kansas. In 1954, the Supreme Court unanimously declared that "separate but equal" schooling was not equal in its *Brown v. Board of Education* decision. A fifth case, *Bolling v. Sharpe* (1954), settled a year later, declared that the federal government could not segregate schools in the District of Columbia. The Supreme Court returned to the implementation of *Brown v. Board of Education of Topeka* in 1955 when it sent all school integration cases back to the lower courts and asked states to desegregate "with all deliberate speed." Later, courts called for the desegregation of metropolitan areas, requiring students to be bused across city lines to ensure integration.

Many segregated school districts and universities took years to integrate their schools. The resistance by White citizens was not a surprise. Mississippi senator James O. Eastland set the stage when he vowed after the *Brown* decision, "We will protect and maintain White supremacy throughout eternity" (U.S. Congress, 1956). The fierce resistance of many White people required the use of the National Guard to protect Black students who were entering White schools for the first time. Many White families, encouraged by their segregationist state and Congressional legislators, established private schools or moved to the suburbs, where the population was predominantly White, to avoid sending their children to schools with Black children. Some communities, such as Farmville, Virginia, closed their public schools for 5 years rather than desegregate them.

Once schools in the South began to desegregate, the racial composition of schools changed. In 1968, only 22% of the Black students in the United States attended integrated schools with a majority of White students compared with 37% in 1988 (Orfield & Jarvie, 2020). One of the negative outcomes of this movement was the replacement of 30,000 to 50,000 Black educators by White educators who were hired to work in the integrated schools (Walker, 2019). By 1972, schools in the South were more integrated than schools in other parts of the country.

The National Guard protected Black students as Little Rock Cetral High School was desegregated in 1957.
**SOURCE:** Bettman/Getty Images

Other ethnic groups also petitioned the courts to demand an equitable education for their children. In 1914, Mexican American families challenged the Alamosa, Colorado, school district for segregating their children, which was unconstitutional in Colorado. School officials argued that the Mexican American students were White and that race was not the reason for segregation; the reason was language. The judge ruled that "school officials could not prevent English-speaking Mexican American children from attending schools of their choice, particularly schools close to their homes" (Donato & Hanson, 2019, p. 40). Although the Treaty of Guadalupe Hidalgo (1848) classified Mexican Americans as racially White, California schools began to create segregated schools in the 1930s. Preceding the *Brown v. Board of Education* decision, a 9-year-old Mexican American student, Sylvia Mendez, and her brothers were not allowed to attend the all-White Westminster Elementary School District in Orange County, California, because of their Mexican appearance and ancestry. The Mendez family and four other Mexican American families filed a lawsuit in 1945, claiming that school segregation violated the California and U.S. Constitutions. The Ninth Circuit Court of Appeals ruled in *Méndez v. Westminster* (1946) that the segregation of Mexican students in separate schools was unconstitutional.

In *Gong Lum v. Rice* in Mississippi in 1927, a Chinese American girl, Martha Lum, sought the right to attend a White school by arguing that she was a White girl. The court ruled she was not White, giving the school the authority to determine the racial makeup of its students. During the Civil Rights Movement, Chinese American students in San Francisco won the right to have their first language used in instruction in *Lau v. Nichols* (1974). The *Brown* decision also served as the precursor for federal laws that supported educational equity for girls and women in Title IX, passed in 1972, and people with disabilities in Section 504 of the Rehabilitation Act of 1973.

## The Civil Rights Movement

The Civil Rights Movement exploded in the 1950s and 1960s when large numbers of Black Americans challenged their oppressed status. Rosa Parks defied authorities in 1955 when she sat in the Whites-only section at the front of the bus in Montgomery, Alabama, sparking a boycott of the public transportation system for more than a year and leading to its desegregation. Beginning in 1960, students from North Carolina A&T University and other historically Black colleges sat at lunch counters designated for White people only, challenging Jim Crow laws that had forced White people and people of color to use different public accommodations such as water fountains, restrooms, hotels, and restaurants.

Under the leadership of the Reverend Dr. Martin Luther King Jr. and Reverend Ralph Abernathy, the Southern Christian Leadership Conference organized civil rights marches, demonstrations, and sit-ins. They lobbied Presidents John F. Kennedy and Lyndon B. Johnson and members of Congress to enact laws to protect the civil rights of the Black population. At the same time, the Congress of Racial Equality, the Student Nonviolent Coordinating Committee, and the Black Panthers Party organized Black adults and young people to fight the injustices they faced daily.

The March on Washington in 1963, at which Martin Luther King Jr. made his famous "I Have a Dream" speech, inspired Black people and their allies to continue the fight for civil rights. But the violence against them continued. Less than a month after the March on Washington, Addie Mae Collins, Cynthia Wesley, Carole Robertson, and Carol Denise McNair were killed after four known Ku Klux Klansmen and **segregationists** detonated dynamite they had placed under the steps in the basement of the 16th Street Baptist Church in Montgomery, Alabama. Congress finally responded by passing the 1964 Civil Rights Act and the 1965 Voting Rights Act, which banned discrimination in schools, employment, and public accommodations and secured the voting rights of Black people.

Under the leadership of Fannie Lou Hamer, Black Democrats from Mississippi challenged the seating of the all-White delegation at the 1964 Democratic National Convention. Although the Black delegates were not seated, their courage led to the seating of a growing number of ethnically and racially diverse delegates in the years that followed. Facing arrests and beatings, the racially mixed Freedom Riders boarded buses to break the segregation pattern in interstate travel. Black students and adults, sometimes joined by White allies, marched for freedom and established Freedom Schools across the South to teach leadership and social activism.

The call for "Black Power" brought attention to the history and contributions of the Black population to society, from the fact that they had helped build the economy that made the United States a world leader to their intellectual contributions to literature, science, education, and politics. Black studies and other ethnic studies programs were established in colleges and universities. Educators and textbook publishers were pushed to revise books to more accurately reflect the multiethnic history of the United States. Yet societal changes did not necessarily follow. Although legislation guaranteed equality for all racial and ethnic groups, many White people continued to fight against the desegregation of schools and other public facilities.

After a number of large protests during the 1960s, President Lyndon B. Johnson appointed the National Advisory Commission on Civil Disorders (1967), which became known as the Kerner Commission after the name of its chair, the governor of Illinois. The commission warned that "[o]ur nation is moving toward two societies, one black, one white—separate and unequal. . . . Discrimination and segregation threaten the future of every American" (p. 2). The commissioners found that the lack of education had contributed to the unrest in the country.

President Johnson appointed NAACP attorney Thurgood Marshall to the Supreme Court in 1967 as the first Black person appointed to the Supreme Court. Nevertheless, the segregationists in Congress and state legislatures and their allies still had not given up the goal of White supremacy. Johnson's Great Society legislation was seen as "reverse discrimination against hardworking Whites and a government handout that lazy black people choose to take rather than work" (Anderson, 2017, p. 100). Many White people defined racism by the actions of the Ku Klux Klan, ignoring the actions of governments, and working with businesses, realtors, school districts, and powerful people to prevent people of color from having the same opportunities as most White people.

The era of President Richard M. Nixon had a southern strategy that used **dog-whistle** or coded appeals such as *crime, inner city,* and *welfare* as references for Black people. With the appointment of four Supreme Court justices, the president was able to weaken civil rights laws, including the court desegregation orders. Continued frustration with the dominant group's efforts to impede progress on civil rights and equality led Black people and members of other oppressed groups to identify even more strongly with other members of their racial group to fight discrimination and inequality with a unified voice.

## Post-*Brown* Turnaround

Although the Civil Rights Movement provided numerous victories, the 1980s and the policies of President Ronald Reagan further divided Black and White people. The president's budget priorities dramatically cut education, housing, and employment. College enrollment by young Black people plummeted from 34% to 26%. The budget for child nutrition programs was dramatically reduced. Federal workers, who were predominantly Black, were laid off (Anderson, 2017). By the mid-1980s, courts were lifting the federal sanctions that had forced schools to desegregate, stating that the federal requirements were meant to be temporary to overcome **de jure segregation**. Sanctions against segregated schools were eased, allowing school districts to return students to neighborhood schools. Because of **de facto segregation** in communities, students in many neighborhood schools were overwhelmingly of the same race, returning the status of segregation to pre-1970 levels.

The use of race/ethnicity by a university to promote diversity of its student population was considered by the Supreme Court in *Grutter v. Bollinger* (2003). The court endorsed the arguments of the University of Michigan Law School regarding its use of race in its admissions policies to increase integration and meet the need for a diverse workforce. On the same day, the court ruled against the University of Michigan College of Arts and Sciences, which gave bonus points to applicants from specific groups of color. To ensure that race could not be used as a factor in determining admission to a public college or university, the voters of Michigan voted to ban its use—an action that was upheld by the U.S. Supreme Court in *Schuette v. Coalition to Defend Affirmative Action* (2014). Most recently, the Supreme Court ended race-conscious admission programs at colleges and universities across the United States in *Students for Fair Admissions, Inc. v. President and Fellows of Harvard College* (2023) and *Students for Fair Admissions, Inc. v. University of North Carolina* (2023). Chief Justice, John Roberts indicated that "nothing in this opinion should be construed as prohibiting universities from considering an applicant's discussion of how race affected his or her life, be it through discrimination, inspiration, or otherwise" (p. 39). The court also suggested that the nation's military academies may be able to continue with their successful affirmative action programs.

School districts with plans to diversify their student populations have also been sued by families. In 2007 the Supreme Court ruled by a vote of 5 to 4 against programs in Seattle and Louisville that used race in assigning students to schools. The court did not find that either school district could relate its preferred level of diversity in a school to educational benefits. Chief Justice John G. Roberts wrote that "racial balance is not to be achieved for its own sake" (*Parents Involved in Community Schools v. Seattle School District #1*, 2007). These two 2007 Supreme Court rulings have essentially halted the integration of schools. By 2018, only 19% of Black students attended integrated schools with a majority of White students—less than in 1968. Schools and school districts today seek integration with policies that limit their reliance on the race and ethnicity of students in making school assignments. Approaches being used to integrate schools include magnet schools, rezoning of school boundaries, school choice, open enrollments, and transfers across schools (George & Darling-Hammond, 2019). The milestones in the desegregation and resegregation of schools are chronicled in Table 2.1.

The goal of desegregation changed over time from the physical integration of students in a school building to the achievement of equal learning opportunities and outcomes for all students. Civil rights groups are now asking why students of color have unequal access to qualified teachers, advanced mathematics and science classes, and adequately funded schools. Why are Black, Latino/a, Native American, and Alaska Native students disproportionately represented in nonacademic and special education classes, and why do the rates for school suspension and dropping out vary so greatly across racial and ethnic groups? As schools become segregated again, educators have a greater responsibility for ensuring that all students learn regardless of the racial and ethnic composition of the school. Teachers also have the responsibility for helping students understand that the world in which they will work is multiethnic and multiracial, unlike the school they may be attending.

## Racial Equity Today

Even though many more people of color are middle class than before the Civil Rights Movement, the United States is still the two Americas that the Kerner Commission warned the country about in 1967. Affluent White neighborhoods have bounced back since the 2007 recession and the COVID-19 pandemic in 2020–2021, but communities of color, especially Black and Indigenous communities, are still struggling financially.

**Table 2.1** Milestones in Desegregating and Resegregating K–12 Schools

| | |
|---|---|
| 1896 | The Supreme Court authorized segregation in *Plessy v. Ferguson*, finding Louisiana's "separate but equal" law constitutional. |
| 1924 | The California Supreme Court ruled that Alice Piper, a Native American student, could not be denied admission to public school because of race. |
| 1940 | A federal court required equal salaries for Black and White teachers in *Alston v. School Board of City of Norfolk*. |
| 1946 | A federal appeals court struck down segregated schooling for Mexican American and White students in *Méndez v. Westminster School District*. |
| 1954 | In a unanimous opinion, the Supreme Court in *Brown v. Board of Education* overturned *Plessy* and declared that separate schools were "inherently unequal." |
| 1955 | In *Brown II*, the Supreme Court ordered the lower federal courts to require desegregation "with all deliberate speed." |
| 1957 | More than 1,000 paratroopers from the 101st Airborne Division and a federalized Arkansas National Guard protected nine Black students as they integrated Central High School in Little Rock. |
| 1959 | Officials closed public schools in Prince Edward County, Virginia, for 5 years rather than integrate them. |
| 1960 | In New Orleans, federal marshals shielded 6-year-old Ruby Bridges from an angry crowd as she attempted to enroll in school. |
| 1964 | The Civil Rights Act of 1964 was adopted. Title IV of the Act authorized the federal government to file school desegregation cases. Title VI of the Act prohibited discrimination in programs and activities of schools that received federal financial assistance. The Supreme Court ordered Prince Edward Country, Virginia, to reopen its schools on a desegregated basis. |
| 1968 | In *Green v. County School Board of New Kent County*, the Supreme Court ordered states to dismantle segregated school facilities, staff, faculty, extracurricular activities, and transportation—the factors that would gauge a school system's compliance with the mandate of *Brown*. |
| 1970 | In *Cisneros v. Corpus Christi Independent School District*, the federal district court ruled that *Brown* applied to the desegregation of Mexican American students. |
| 1971 | The Supreme Court approved busing, magnet schools, compensatory education, and other tools as appropriate remedies to overcome residential segregation in perpetuating racially segregated schools in *Swann v. Charlotte-Mecklenburg Board of Education*. |
| 1972 | The Supreme Court refused to allow public school systems to avoid desegregation by creating new, mostly or all-White "splinter districts" in *Wright v. Council of the City of Emporia* and *United States v. Scotland Neck City Board of Education*. |
| 1973 | The Supreme Court ruled that education is not a "fundamental right" and that the Constitution did not require equal education expenditures within a state in *San Antonio Independent School District v. Rodriguez*. |
| 1974 | The Supreme Court blocked metropolitan-wide desegregation plans as a means to desegregate urban schools with large populations of students of color in *Milliken v. Bradley*. |
| 1984 | A federal court found that once a school district met the *Green* factors, it could be released from its desegregation plan and returned to local control in *Riddick v. School Board of the City of Norfolk, Virginia*. |
| 1991 | Emphasizing that court orders were not intended "to operate in perpetuity," the Supreme Court made it easier for formerly segregated school systems to fulfill their obligations under desegregation decrees in *Board of Education of Oklahoma City v. Dowell*. |
| 2005 | A federal district court case affirmed the value of racial diversity and race-conscious student assignment plans in K–12 education in *Comfort v. Lynn School Committee*. |
| 2007 | The Supreme Court struck down the use of race in determining the assignment of students to schools in *Parents Involved in Community Schools Inc. v. Seattle School District* and *Meredith v. Jefferson County (Ky.) Board of Education*. |
| 2018 | In *Stout v. Jefferson County Board of Education*, the Circuit Court of Appeals ruled that Gardendale, which is located outside of Birmingham, Alabama, could not withdraw from the Jefferson County schools to create its own school with a "racially discriminatory purpose." |

The unemployment rate for Black people may be near the lowest ever, but it remains almost double the unemployment rate of White people and higher than the rate for other racial and ethnic groups (U.S. Bureau of Labor Statistics, 2023). Home ownership by Black people has dropped from its high of 50% in 2007 to 42% in 2019 compared to 73% of White non-Hispanic people, which has contributed to a widening wealth gap (U.S. Census Bureau, 2020a). In 2019, the median wealth of Black people was 12% of that of White people ($24,100 to $188,200) (Bhutta et al., 2020). The lower wealth level of people of color overall is due to discriminatory governmental policies such as Jim Crow laws, the GI Bill, residential zoning, loan practices, and the denial of housing subsidies that were available to White people. The incomes of Black and Latino/a people in 2021 were 74% the incomes of White people—another contribution to the wealth gap (U.S. Census Bureau, 2021c). In addition, Black people lead the nation in rates of heart disease, type 2 diabetes, obesity, asthma, prison population, and poverty but lag behind the nation in high school and college graduation rates (Hubbard et al., 2022). The people who suffer the most from the generations of government neglect and deepening racial, ethnic and class divisions are the people who live in poverty. They have become profoundly isolated and ignored.

The population is more polarized around issues of race than ever, as evidenced by the rise again of White supremacist and alt-right groups. Some White people believe that discrimination against them is as large a problem as it is for Black people, even though economic and social data show that the White population earns higher incomes, has much more wealth, has lower unemployment, is more likely to finish high school and college, and is more likely to own a home. When White people aren't admitted to their college of choice or selected for an internship or job, they may blame a quota system that they believe required the selection of a person of color. Some White people believe that equality will lead to shutting down all pathways to success for hardworking White people (Serwer, 2017). Some state legislators are limiting access to voting by people of color and people who are impoverished. They are challenging ethnic studies courses, teaching about race, Black studies, and diversity programs. A number of conservative pundits argue that multiculturalism, group identity politics, and immigration are dangerous to the dominant culture of the United States.

Our schools continue to be unequal. Schools in affluent communities are not only better resourced, they attract highly qualified and experienced teachers, offer high-quality courses and advanced course choices, provide broadly supportive environments, and prepare a large number of students for college. On the other hand, implicit bias and stereotypes continue to obstruct the education opportunities for many students of color (Carnevale et al., 2019). "School districts with the most Blacks and Latinos receive about 15% less state and local funding per student than those with the fewest Black and Latinos" (Carnevale et al., 2019, p. 15). Teachers' expectations for academic performance are higher for White and selected Asian American students than for Black and Latino/a students.

# The Impact of Racial and Ethnic Discrimination on Communities and Students

**Learning Objective 2.5** Analyze the impact of racial and ethnic discrimination on communities and students.

Equality among groups is greater today than at any other time in our nation's history, but the egalitarian goals that the United States so proudly espouses to the rest of the world have not yet been achieved. Large numbers of Native American, Black, and Latino/a students are not achieving at a proficient academic level in our schools. Because their educational experiences are generally of a lower quality than those of most White students, a larger proportion of students of color have fewer opportunities for higher education and well-paying jobs. In this section, we explore some of the reasons for these differences.

## Intergroup Relations

Interethnic and interracial conflict is certainly not new in the United States. These conflicts began early during the European colonization of the country. The inequities in income and opportunities for desirable jobs, housing, and education among racial and ethnic groups continue to contribute to poor relations among groups as well as the egregious actions of police and others in the shooting of unarmed Black youth and men or people attending services in churches, synagogues, and other houses of worship. The threats of White nationalism and neo-Nazism have also increased the discord among racial and ethnic groups in both the United States and Europe.

What are the reasons for continued interracial conflict? Discriminatory practices have protected the superior status of the dominant group for centuries. When other racial and ethnic groups try to participate more equitably in the rewards and privileges of society, the dominant group may have to concede some of its advantages. That process can be very difficult. As cultural commentator and film producer Franklin Leonard said, "When you're accustomed to privilege, equality feels like oppression." As long as one racial or ethnic group has an institutional advantage over others, intergroup conflict is likely to occur.

Part of the problem is that most White people have little or no experience with being the victims of discrimination and are less likely to believe that members of other groups are treated unfairly or are discriminated against. While over three in five White respondents to a survey about race in the United States indicate that Black people are treated unfairly by the police and criminal justice system, less than half of the respondents thought Black people were treated unfairly in other settings (Horowitz et al., 2019). In the same survey, respondents indicated situations in which they had been treated unfairly, as shown in Figure 2.8. In all but two situations, a higher percentage of Black adults have had negative experiences than members of other groups. Both Black and Asian American respondents reported that it had become more common for people to express racist views toward them during the COVID-19 pandemic (Ruiz et al., 2020).

Surveys show that people are dissatisfied with the state of race relations in the United States today. A survey by the Pew Research Center in 2019 found that 58% of adults thought race relations in the United States are generally bad. Sixty-five percent of the respondents report that it is now more common for people to express racist or racially insensitive views. Forty-five percent said that not enough progress has been made toward racial equality, and Black adults were skeptical that equality would ever be realized (Horowitz et al., 2019). Since that survey, George Floyd was killed by police in Minneapolis, and people of all races protested police brutality and for racial equity across the United States and the world. How have race relations been affected? By May 2022, 68% of the respondents to a Pew Research Center survey indicated that they worried a great deal or a fair amount about race relations in the United States, with Black Americans having the greatest concern (Saad, 2022). Gallup (Newport, 2020)

**Figure 2.8** Adverse Experiences Due to Race and Ethnicity

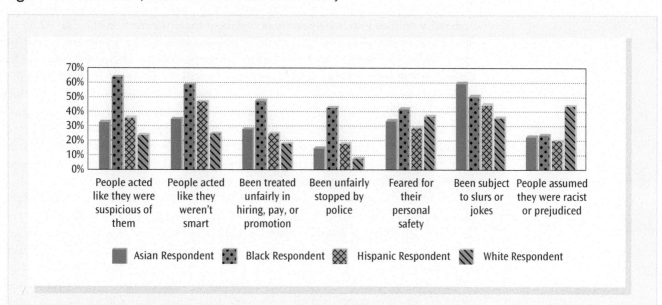

**SOURCE:** Horowitz et al. (2019).

reports that not all trends are negative. The percentage of Americans who say they would vote for an otherwise well-qualified person for president who is Black has risen to 96%, up from 38% in 1958. And the percentage of Americans who approve of marriages between Black and White people moved from 4% in 1958 to 94% in 2021 (McCarthy, 2021). At the same time, more Black men and women who are unarmed continue to be killed. Latino/a, Asian, and Black people are three, five, and eight times, respectively, more likely to worry daily about being threatened or attacked than White people (Noe-Bustamante et al., 2022). Much work needs to be done to overcome White supremacy and the institutional racism in police departments and other institutions in society to ensure equity for all people regardless of their race, ethnicity, economic conditions, gender, and ability.

## School-to-Prison Pipeline

**Pearson eTextbook**
**Video Example 2.1**

Engage with this TED Talk with author Michelle Alexander to learn more about mass incarceration and the threats presented from these types of practices.
https://youtu.be/SQ6H-Mz6h
gw?si=IV7U5ujQs2u5U7k

In the book *The New Jim Crow: Mass Incarceration in the Age of Colorblindness*, Michelle Alexander (2012) makes the case that Black men and other poor people of color are disproportionately arrested and convicted for nonviolent crimes. With a criminal record, they are no longer able to vote or serve on a jury in a number of states after they have served their time. They are legally discriminated against in finding a job, locating housing, and receiving food stamps and other public benefits in ways similar to the restraints of the Jim Crow laws of the twentieth century.

The incarceration rate in the United States is higher than in any other industrialized nation in the world, at over 1.2 million people in 2021. Almost half (47%) of the people serving time in federal prisons in 2021 had been convicted of drug offenses (Carson, 2022). Mass incarceration had become so disproportionate in 2014 that the United Nations' Committee on the Elimination of Racial Discrimination reported that "the United States disproportionately subjects racial and ethnic minorities to harsher sentences," in part because of mandatory drug sentencing policies (American Civil Liberties Union [ACLU] & The Sentencing Project, 2022, p. 3). The high incarceration rates of people of color began to decrease after Congress enacted the First Step Act in 2018 to reduce mandatory sentences for certain drug offenses; 91% of the people whose terms were reduced were Black (ACLU & The Sentencing Project, 2022).

What does imprisonment have to do with schools? The path to prison begins at school for many youth, especially with the **zero-tolerance policies** of a number of schools that can lead to children and youth being handcuffed and arrested at school. Zero-tolerance policies in schools require punishment for any infraction of a rule. Although the initial intent was to ensure safety of the learning environment by removing students for possession of drugs or weapons, students have been suspended and expelled for the possession of cough drops, Tylenol, or paper swords (Whitaker et al., 2019) as well as being late to class, dress code violations, or talking back to teachers (Spencer & Ulluci, 2022). Although punishment for some of these offenses may be appropriate, critics of the zero-tolerance policy would argue that the punishment is far too severe for many of the offenses. When students are expelled from school, they are not only removed from a learning environment but often left on their own and exposed to opportunities for getting in trouble that lands them in the juvenile justice system.

Schools often use out-of-school suspensions to temporarily remove students from schools for infractions against school rules, including minor rules that would not have led to out-of-school suspension in the past. Suspension is one of the leading indicators of students leaving school before graduation, and out-of-school suspension contributes to the risk of students being incarcerated as adults (Losen & Martinez, 2020). Who are the students who are most likely to be suspended? Disproportionately, they are Black students and students with disabilities. Young Black boys too often have been labeled by police and educators as more aggressive and dangerous than other children, leading to harsher punishments at school and inappropriate placement in adult rather than juvenile criminal courts (Nellis, 2023). Nationwide, one in eight Black students received an out-of-school suspension in the 2017–2018 school year, which was 3.5 times that of White students. Native American and Alaska Native students received out-of-school suspensions twice as often as White students. One in 11 students with disabilities was suspended, which was a rate almost twice that of students who were not identified as having a disability. Black and Native American/Alaska Native students and students with disabilities were also more likely to be arrested at school or referred to the police (National Center for Education Statistics, 2022b).

Maintaining a positive climate in the classroom is critical for a safe learning environment that supports all students, regardless of their racial or ethnic background.

**SOURCE:** © stockbroker/123RF

Safe schools do contribute to a positive learning environment for students. Does that require the removal of so many students from an environment in which they should be learning? The Civil Rights Project at the University of California Los Angeles (Losen & Martinez, 2020) and a number of civil rights and education organizations have documented the critical importance of keeping students, especially those who suffer the most from inequality, in school. Promising practices for reducing the risk of violence and disruption in schools do not include the use of zero-tolerance policies. Instead, they include bullying prevention, **threat assessment**, **restorative justice**, and **trauma-sensitive** programs. A growing number of schools are dramatically reducing the number of out-of-school suspensions by figuring out how to keep students in learning environments in schools.

# Classroom Implications: Affirming Race and Ethnicity in Classrooms

**Learning Objective 2.6** Develop strategies for affirming race and ethnicity in the curriculum, instruction, and climates in classrooms.

How educators perceive the race and ethnicity of students can have a significant impact on students' behavior and performance. Because the cultural background and experiences of teachers may be incongruous with the cultural experiences of students, miscommunication and misperceptions can interfere with learning. This incongruity may contribute to student perceptions that their cultures and experiences are not reflected or respected in school. Therefore, it is critical that teachers become aware of the cultures and experiences of the students with whom they work.

Racial discrimination and its harms, both current and historical, affect how children experience their environments and their chances of reaching their full potential (Carnevale et al., 2019). Students of color are more likely than White students to be disciplined for their hairstyles, dress, and music. Children of color, especially Black children, are too often seen as less innocent than other students, older than their actual age, and perceived as more likely to be disruptive in the classroom (Spencer & Ullucci, 2022), which can too easily lead to disproportionate rates of discipline, suspension, and expulsion. As compared to White girls of the same age, Black girls are perceived as needing less protection and nurturing, being more independent, and being more knowledgeable about sex and other adult topics (Epstein et al., 2019). Students of color may be blamed for their "misbehavior" without appropriate investigation, including how educators or other students interact with them. All students, regardless of their racial or ethnic group, should feel safe and cared for at school. When families send their children to school, they should expect that their children will be well, if not better, when they return home. It is critical that teachers "ensure an environment that values students as whole beings, encouraging success within and beyond the scope of their classrooms" (Tintiangco-Cubales et al., 2019, p. 23).

Gloria Ladson-Billings (2021) found that successful teachers of Black students focus on student learning, ensure that students have developed cultural competence in at least two cultures including their own, and promote sociopolitical consciousness. Success does not require a new curriculum or a new behavior performance system or require everyone to wear a uniform. It does require a teacher who believes deeply in students' academic capacity and the teacher's own efficacious abilities. Although Ladson-Billings was writing about Black students in her book, *The Dreamkeepers: Successful Teachers of African American Children* (2022), the principles for being successful apply to all students. Are you up to this challenge as you prepare to enter schools with an increasingly diverse student population? In this section we explore some areas that will be important in developing cultural competence and addressing sociopolitical consciousness.

## Acknowledging Race and Ethnicity in Schools

The social context in which teachers and their students enter school together is one in which their lived experiences "are likely to have been quite different from each other, and in which racial stereotyping is still likely to be an inhibiting factor in cross-group interactions" (Tatum, 2017, p. 9). Teachers may declare that they are **colorblind**, meaning that they do not see a student's race and treat all students equally, regardless of race or ethnicity. The problem is that colorblindness helps maintain White privilege because it does not recognize the existence of race and racial inequality (Bonilla-Silva, 2022). Teachers often do not confront issues of race in schools and classrooms in part because race is not supposed to matter. Teachers' discomfort can become intertwined with their own uncertainties about race and their possible complicity in maintaining racial inequities.

Race and ethnicity matter to many students and their families and have an impact on communications and interactions with teachers and other students. Students of color are reminded of their race almost daily as they face discriminatory practices and attitudes. Rather than pretend that race and ethnicity do not exist, teachers should acknowledge them and be aware of ways they can influence learning. According to Christine Sleeter (2021), "teaching young people about racism is not indoctrination [as some critics suggest], but rather teaching viewpoints and providing factual data related to racism that they otherwise are not likely exposed to. Young people need to make up their own minds about how to think about race, but the better informed they are, the more thoughtfully they will do so" (para. 9). The murder of George Floyd in May 2020, and the Black Lives Matter protests that followed, "fueled a growing discourse about structural racism in American schools, especially over their racially lopsided teaching force, heavy police presence that overdisciplines Black students, and ethnically non-representative curriculum" (Sawchuk, 2021).

As of late June 2023, 23 states had passed laws about teaching racism, antibias training, and/or banning books (PEN America, 2023). In addition, school districts were sometimes passing their own policies restricting what could be taught and the books that could be used (Nathanson, 2023). Teachers should be aware of the state legislation and local district policies related to teaching racism and other controversial issues in their state. A Rand Corporation survey found one in four teachers had revised instructional materials to limit or eliminate references to race or gender and removed books from their classroom libraries (Woo et al., 2023). Although these state bills and district policies may eventually be dismissed in courts as infringements on the right to free speech, educators are forced to implement them or face the loss of their jobs, fines, or lawsuits in some states.

At the same time, some school districts are finding creative ways to teach about racism within the boundaries of the restrictive state laws by ensuring that "all their students have a sense of belonging in schools" and helping "all students realize the ways American racism impacts both [W]hite students and students of color" (Pendharkar, 2021, para. 5). The teaching method used by many English and social studies teachers is discussion about the issues. Using **dialogic pedagogy** recognizes the importance of student voices and interrupts the traditional classroom power dynamic by providing students an equal share in their education. When done well, the discussions help students build confidence (Kay, 2018). (Books such as *Not Light, But Fire: How to Lead Meaningful Race Conversations in the Classroom*, by Matthew R. Kay, can be helpful to teachers in planning discussions.)

Discussing racism and other controversial issues with students requires teachers to carefully plan lessons, think through their own stance and role in guiding the discussions, and be prepared to handle student emotions that may arise during discussions that encourage sharing multiple perspectives. Building a classroom culture of trust and respect and communicating the rationale for the discussion or project to parents and administrators in advance will contribute to limiting the backlash that might otherwise be received from parents or activists (Pace et al., 2022). A strong school administrator who supports teachers who are addressing issues like race and racism contributes greatly to successful implementation.

The pandemic and these politically divisive times contribute to an emotionally fragile state of being for many students of color. For many students, "the fear is real, their anger is palpable, anxiety is high, and sadness is running deep" (Howard, 2020). Once teachers believe that discrimination and racism exist in society and the school, they are more likely to believe students of color when they report incidents of racism or discrimination. Excuses stop being made for the perpetrators. When teachers are able to acknowledge the discrimination that groups of color know from experience, building trust with students and their families should be easier. Teachers cannot start too early. Research indicates that children begin to develop their racial and ethnic identities as early as preschool, including a sense of White superiority (DiAngelo, 2018).

A challenge for teachers is to seriously and intentionally confront these issues on a personal level. Treating students differently on the basis of race or ethnicity can affect students' learning and their spirit. These **implicit racial biases**, which most people have, are reflected in negative attitudes and stereotypes that view students of color as more likely to be threatening, violent, engaged in criminal activities, low in income, and academically inferior. These biases can influence teachers' demeanor and warmth when interacting with students and families of color (Chin et al., 2020) and their expectations for academic achievement.

## Incorporating Race and Ethnicity in the Curriculum

All students should feel like they belong in school. Educators should ensure that they do not reject or neglect students because their racial and ethnic backgrounds are different from the teacher's. One way that these goals can be realized is by accurately and positively reflecting the race and ethnicity of students and their communities in the curriculum, including textbooks and other educational resources. The goal is not just content integration. Educators should be striving for what James A. Banks (2019) calls the *transformation approach*, which "changes the canon, paradigms, and basic assumptions of the curriculum and enables students to view concepts, issues, themes, and problems from different perspectives and points of views" (p. 63). An important part of this approach is teaching students to "think critically and to develop the skills to formulate, document, and justify their conclusions and generalizations" (p. 63).

School curricula in most schools primarily reflect the dominant White culture. All students are being taught about the history and culture of White people, but they are less likely to see the cultures and experiences of students of color as the focus of their learning experiences. The inherent bias of the curriculum prevents candid admissions of racism in society. In fact, it is more likely to support White superiority and provide minimal or no familiarity with the cultures and contributions of Asia, Africa, and South and Central America. When information about and perspectives of other groups are addressed in the classroom, they are often included as a separate unit at some time during the school year or during a specific period such as Black History Month or Hispanic History Month. However, teachers who deliver multicultural education ensure that the cultures, experiences, and perspectives of all students in the classroom are integrated throughout courses, activities, and interactions and issues such as racism, classism, sexism, and discrimination are openly addressed throughout the school year.

The inclusion of the history and experiences of racial and ethnic groups in curriculum and instruction does not require teachers to discuss every ethnic group (that would be an impossible task). It requires that perspectives of racial and ethnic groups as well as the dominant White group be examined in discussions of historical and current events. For example, the perspectives of Mexican and Native American groups as well as the dominant group would be included in presentations on and discussion of White colonizers moving West in the eighteenth and nineteenth centuries. Students listen to the voices of the colonized, enslaved, and oppressed as well as the colonizers and powerful. Students are encouraged to express and justify their own views with impunity.

Multicultural education expects students to read literature by authors from different racial and ethnic backgrounds. It expects that mathematics and science be explored from a Native American as well as a Western perspective. The contributions of different racial and ethnic groups would be reflected in the books that are used by students, in the movies they view, and in the activities in which they participate as they learn and interact with each other. Bulletin boards, textbooks, films, assignments, and school activities should reflect the racial and ethnic diversity of the community and country. However, teachers should not depend entirely on these resources for instructional content about groups. People in the community, including family members, can be very helpful in bringing the community into the school and providing meaningful and authentic cultural resources.

If students do not see themselves in the curricula and in the books they read, they do not feel they are an integral part of school and society. They begin to see themselves as separate, distinct, and inferior to the dominant White group. A multicultural approach requires curricula and instructional practices to intentionally incorporate the histories, experiences, and perspectives of both people of color and White groups. To ensure that all students have opportunities to explore their own or other racial and ethnic groups more in-depth, a growing number of schools include ethnic studies as a required or elective course. Some communities have established public charter or private schools that center the culture of a racial or ethnic group in the design of the curriculum and climate of the school. These two approaches are discussed below.

**ETHNIC STUDIES** In 1968, students at what is now San Francisco State University and the University of California, Berkeley led the movement to demand courses in ethnic studies that would be taught from the lens of the ethnic group rather than a Eurocentric perspective. These protests resulted in the addition of courses and programs at colleges and universities across the country in Black, Asian American, Hispanic, and Native American studies. Some school districts followed suit, offering courses related to specific ethnic and cultural groups.

By 2013, students in California's state universities were protesting budget cuts that were eliminating ethnic studies courses and faculty. A similar pattern was occurring in high schools. In 2010, the governor of Arizona signed a bill banning the teaching of ethnic studies programs that were designed for a particular group or advocated ethnic solidarity, but an Arizona judge found in 2017 that the ban was unconstitutional (Chang, 2022). Taking an opposite approach, the El Rancho School District in California in 2014 adopted a requirement that its students take an ethnic studies course before graduation. Following El Rancho's lead, California now requires all high school students in the state to complete a one-semester course on ethnic studies by the 2029–2030 school year (Fensterwald, 2021). In addition, all students in the California State University system must take an ethnic studies course, beginning with those who graduate in 2024–2025.

By early 2023, at least 11 states required schools to offer ethnic studies, as shown in Figure 2.9. At least nine were requiring the teaching of local Indigenous history and culture. Montana has led the country with visionary language and strategies that have taken decades to implement. When the state passed a new Constitution in 1972, it included language that required all Montanans to learn the histories and cultures of the state's tribes. Because of "broken promises and treaties, genocides and military conquests, land thefts and occupations, forced removals and relocations, and assimilative mission and boarding schools" (Hopkins, 2020, p. 16) over several hundred years, a climate of distrust between Native and non-Native groups existed and had to be confronted to move forward. It was 27 years later when the state passed

**Figure 2.9** State Requirements for the Study of One or More Racial or Ethnic Groups in U.S. Public Schools

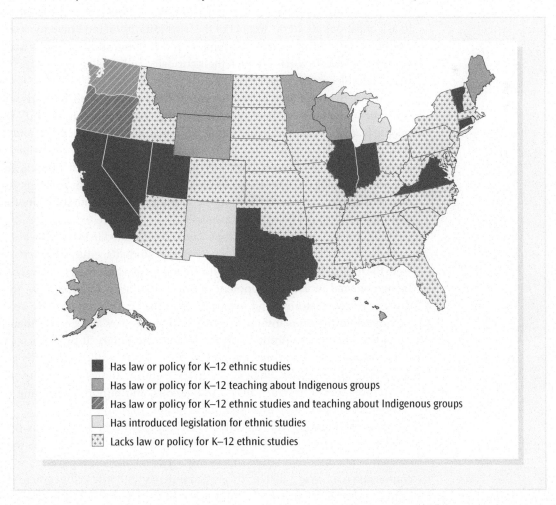

the Indian Education for All legislation, requiring public schools to "include the cultures and histories of Montana's tribal nations in the common school curriculum" and to "work cooperatively with Montana tribes when providing instruction and implementing any educational goals" (Hopkins, 2020, p. 7). Representatives from the state's tribal communities joined public school educators and cultural experts to create Seven Essential Understandings with learning outcomes that all Montana students should know and be able to do. However, there was no state funding to support their implementation until 2005. The inclusion of tribal people in the decision-making process and implementation of this project has been critical to its success and will continue to be essential as the project evolves (Hopkins, 2020).

Ethnic studies courses and programs provide in-depth exposure to the social, economic, and political history of a racial or ethnic group. They are designed to correct the distortions and omissions that prevail in society about racial and ethnic groups. Events that have been neglected in textbooks are addressed, myths are dispelled, and history is viewed from the perspective of the group rather than a dominant White interpretation of history and experiences. It "seeks to humanize the classroom for students of color, who have a history of experiencing dehumanization through silencing of their identities, perspectives, and intellectual abilities" (Sleeter & Zavala, 2020, p. 7). It questions dominant narrative about historical accounts and interpretations and centers the **counternarratives** of the group being studied. Ethnic studies courses and programs also generally include the history, traditions, and beliefs of a group's ancestors before colonization by Europeans. Most students have no experience with this knowledge in classes they have previously taken. For example, most students know little about the history and current conditions of African and Asian countries until they take an ethnic studies course. Ethnic studies includes the analysis of racism, colonialism, and oppression and encourages students to ask questions about the impact of these conditions on their own lives and how they can be eliminated in society. Students in most ethnic studies classes are engaged in complex academic work in which their curiosity and intellectualism are nurtured and respected (Sleeter & Zavala, 2020).

Although ethnic studies is often categorized as part of social studies and history, it is much broader than that. Imagine learning about the thoughts and experiences of people from different racial and ethnic groups through their fictional and nonfictional writings in literature courses; their artistic contributions in art, music, and dance courses and events; and their contributions to, perspectives of, and experiences with science, technology, engineering, and mathematics in those courses. It is a disciplinary or interdisciplinary way of viewing the world from the vantage point of one or more marginalized groups (Sleeter & Zavala, 2020).

Ethnic studies should be developed and implemented in localized ways (Tintiangco-Cubales et al., 2019), involving elders, parents, students, educators, and other experts from the groups in the community who are willing to share their knowledge and stories. Being engaged in the development of ethnic studies courses and the integration of diverse voices, histories, and experiences in the curriculum provide a rich learning experience for teachers if they are willing to be learners and change their teaching to provide greater equity throughout the school community. It provides a gateway into the lives of students and the opportunity to learn about their strengths and interests. According to researcher Ethan Chang (2022), ethnic studies "allows us all to imagine and build a world in which Black, Indigenous, and minoritized young people have greater freedom to thrive now and in the future" (p. 176).

One of the most exciting outcomes of offering ethnic studies is the difference it makes to students not just while they take the course but through the remainder of their schooling. In a study of the impact of a college-preparatory ethnic studies course taken by over 1,400 ninth-grade students with low achievement in the eighth grade in the San Francisco Unified School District over 3 years, researchers found that the students were more likely to stay engaged in high school (as measured by attendance), earn more credits, graduate from high school, and consider postsecondary education. The researchers concluded that ethnic studies provides "the educational potency of pedagogies and content (i.e., anti-racist education) that allow students to experience belongingness and psychological integrity in school" (Bonilla et al., 2021, p. 9). Christine Sleeter also found positive impacts of ethnic studies on students in her review of the research. Except for a few studies, researchers found that ethnic studies programs were positively linked to students' racial or ethnic identity development, sense of empowerment, and academic learning (Sleeter & Zavala, 2020). To achieve these positive outcomes requires (1) a strong, well-developed ethnic studies curriculum that connects the content of the course to students' home and community culture and (2) teachers who effectively use culturally responsive pedagogy in their classrooms.

Ethnic studies is generally offered as separate courses in high schools that students elect from many offerings in the curriculum. Seldom are such courses required for all students. Although the information and experiences offered in these courses are important to members of a specific group, students from other racial and ethnic groups also need to learn about the multicultural nation and world in which they live. If you have limited exposure to the racial and ethnic groups in the community in which you teach, you should consider taking such a course or undertake individual study.

**ETHNOCENTRIC CURRICULUM**  Some ethnic groups have a long history of holding classes in the evenings or on Saturdays to reinforce their cultural values and traditions or to learn the native language of their ancestors. Other racial and ethnic groups have established their own private or charter schools within a public school system with a

## Explore and Focus Your Cultural Lens

### Debate: The Inclusion of Ethnic Studies in the Curriculum

Today, some states are banning the teaching of some ethnic studies courses, as Florida did when the governor declared that a new Advanced Placement course on African American history would not be taught in the state. At the same time, other states are requiring them. Ethnic studies have become a flashpoint in the country's cultural and political wars. What are the rationales for supporting or not supporting ethnic studies in a school or university?

**FOR**

- Ethnic studies content helps make curriculum more relevant to students of color.
- Ethnic studies teach about long-neglected racial and ethnic groups in the United States.
- Ethnic studies allow students from the group being studied and students from other racial and ethnic groups to explore different perspectives on the histories and literature of a group.
- Ethnic studies help students develop empathy toward other groups.
- All students can benefit from learning the culture, history, literature, and experiences of racial and ethnic groups different from their own.

**AGAINST**

- Ethnic studies may constitute a form of "reverse racism."
- Ethnic studies may be divisive and foster resentment among students.
- Ethnic studies may indoctrinate students with anti-American and anti-White ideas.
- Ethnic studies may make students "ethnic radicals."
- Ethnic studies may encourage students whose racial or ethnic group is being studied to see themselves as victims.

### Questions for Discussion

1. Whose racial or ethnic groups and cultures are most represented in the curriculum used by most schools? What racial or ethnic groups are seldom found in the curriculum? What are the reasons for these disparities?
2. How do the personal perspectives and biases of authors impact the content of textbooks and curriculum? What is important about hearing the perspectives of different racial and ethnic groups?
3. How do students learn about the history and experiences of White people?

curriculum centered on the history and values of their ethnic group. For example, some Native American nations have established public tribal schools in which the traditional culture serves as the social and intellectual starting point and Native languages are used and restored. Themes addressed by the educators in these schools include (1) decolonization and Indigenous reclamation, (2) land recognition and relationships with land, and (3) intentional movement toward healing (Pewewardy et al., 2022, p. 201). The Anahuacalmecac International University Preparatory of North America in Los Angeles and the Native American Community Academy in Albuquerque are examples of schools that center Native cultural knowledge to serve Native students in their communities (Sleeter et al., 2019).

Some Black communities support an **African-centered education** to challenge Eurocentrism and tell the truth about Black history. These schools are designed to improve students' self-esteem, academic skills, values, and positive identification with their racial or ethnic group. At the core of this approach is an African perspective of the world and of historical events. One of the goals of these programs is to help students understand the worthiness of their cultures, which have often been ignored, denigrated, and not respected in dominant schools (Asante, 2020). The website for the New Concept School indicates that African-centered education integrates Africa's influences "into all aspects of the curriculum, from science and mathematics to history, literature, and the fine arts. African influences also shape the schools' practices to socialize students to love themselves and other people, to be disciplined and responsible, and to be resilient in the face of adversity" (Institute of Positive Education, n.d., para. 4).

Among the first African-centered schools were those established by the Institute of Positive Education, a nonprofit community service organization in Chicago. The New Concept Development Center was founded in 1974 and still exists today as a preschool. The Betty Shabazz International Charter Schools, named after Dr. Shabazz, who was married to Malcom X, was established in 1998 and now includes two campuses for K–8 students: Betty Shabazz Academy and Barbara A. Sizemore Academy (Lee, 2020). The Nation House was also founded in 1974 in Washington, DC, as an outgrowth of student activism at Howard University; it now supports Watoto School for PreK–4 and Sankofa Institute for fifth and sixth graders. Other African-centered schools in New York City, Detroit, Los Angeles, and other urban areas across the country are immersing Black students in the history, principles, and traditions of African cultures that were intellectual centers of the world prior to colonization.

## Revisiting the Opening Case Study

The activities of the BLM event at John Muir Elementary School did not stop at that single school in Seattle. Because of recent police shootings of unarmed Black men and the institutional racism in Seattle's public schools, the Social Equity Educators (SEE), an organization of union educators, decided they would wear BLM T-shirts to school on October 19, 2016. To raise awareness about police violence against Black women, including queer and transgender women, they added #SayHerName to their T-shirts. In addition, SEE adopted a three-point policy that it would promote to fight institutional racism in schools. The organization would call for the inclusion of ethnic studies in all schools, the replacement

of zero-tolerance discipline with restorative justice practices, and the de-tracking of classes (Au & Hagopian, 2018).

The Seattle teachers' union passed SEE's resolution to publicly support the John Muir teachers and community and to call on all Seattle teachers to participate in the October 19 action. Following the union vote, other organizations in the city endorsed the action, including the Seattle NAACP, Soup for Teachers (a parent group that supported the union in an earlier strike), the executive board of the Seattle Council Parent Teacher Student Association, and 250 professors in the Seattle area. As the support for the Black Lives Matter at Schools action swelled, the school district administrators also officially endorsed the event. On October 19, educators in every Seattle public school were wearing the T-shirts and teaching lessons about institutional racism. In the evening, educators, students, and community members celebrated at a forum and talent showcase. By the end of the day, thousands of Seattle students and parents had been sent a message that their teachers were supportive of Black students and opposed to racism (Au & Hagopian, 2018).

The Black Lives Matter at School Week of Action was still in operation in 2023, defending its ethnic studies programs and supporting reliance on counselors rather than police to foster student safety (Capitol Hill Seattle, 2023). In other parts of the country, students, teachers, and parents have protested to protect their right to learn about race and racism since the teachers and community organized in Seattle. For example, a coalition of teachers and community members protested in Indiana to defeat anti–critical race theory legislation (Rhoden, 2022).

Two students in York County, Pennsylvania, organized a daily protest by students before school began each morning against the school board's banning of hundreds of books and other resources. Soon, students wrote letters to the editor and read excerpts from the banned books on social media. Less than 3 weeks after students began the protest, the school board temporarily lifted the ban (Paz & Cramer, 2021).

## Reflect and Apply

1. What impact do you think your participation in the Black Lives Matter at Schools action would have on your understanding of institutional racism?

2. How would you respond to a question from a reporter who asked you whether teachers were politicizing the classroom by wearing the BLM T-shirt?

3. What action could you take to address institutional racism in your own classroom?

# Summary

- Although no longer useful in describing groups of people, the term *race* continues to be used in this country to classify groups of people as inferior or superior. The popular use of *race* is based on society's perception that racial differences are important—a belief not upheld by scientific study. Nevertheless, government forms request users to identify themselves by race in part to track the extent of discriminatory outcomes. As of 2014, the majority of the student population became students of color. By 2045, less than 50% of the population will be comprised of non-Hispanic White people.

- Ethnicity is a sense of peoplehood based on national origin. Almost from the beginning of European settlement in the United States, the population has been multiethnic, with individuals representing many Native American and European nations, later to be joined by African, Latino/a, and Asian people. The conditions encountered by different ethnic groups, the reasons they came, and their expectations about life here have differed greatly.

- Which and how many people immigrate to the United States and who becomes a citizen has been controlled by Congress from the creation of the country. At different times, Chinese, Japanese, and Filipino immigrants have been excluded and, until 1965, immigration laws strongly favored immigrants from northern and western Europe. Approximately 1 million people per year continue to immigrate legally, including refugees and asylees, to the United States from around the world. Immigration policies, especially for unauthorized immigrants, continues to be a controversial and divisive issue that has become very politicized.

- The United States is composed of three groups of people dependent on the reasons for their original arrival on these lands. The people who were on this land when Europeans first arrived include Native Americans, Alaska Natives, and Native Hawaiians and other Pacific Islanders. Ancestors of most of the population voluntarily immigrated to the United States because of economic impoverishment and political repression in their countries of origin and the demands of a vigorous U.S. economy that required a growing labor force. The third group are involuntary immigrants who arrived here as enslaved Africans or the early Mexican residents of the Southwest.

- People of color have had to fight for their civil rights throughout U.S. history. The efforts of Black people in the 1950s and 1960s led to the removal of Jim Crow laws, the passage of the 1964 Civil Rights Act and 1965 Voting Rights Act, and the expansion of civil rights to women, people with disabilities, and Latino/a, Asian American, and Native American people.

- People of color continue to experience discriminatory treatment and are often relegated to relatively low-status positions in society. Although Americans perceive race relations as better than before the Civil Rights Movement, they are not overly optimistic as the pandemic ends and unarmed Black youth and men continue to be shot by police. With the harsh penalties given by some schools to students who are disruptive or not following school rules, a growing number of students are being pushed out of schools and into the juvenile justice system in a school-to-prison pipeline.

- The school curriculum has historically centered the dominant White culture as the focus of study. However, all students should be able to study the history and contributions of their racial and ethnic groups and see positive portrayals of those groups across the curriculum.

In addition, they should have the opportunity to study and discuss racism and the expectation that they will not be discriminated against while attending school. Since the 1970s, ethnic studies have been added to curricula in a growing number of schools to provide in-depth and accurate study of the history and contemporary conditions of one or more ethnic groups. Some ethnic groups have established schools or programs that center the curriculum on their ethnicity to improve the educational attainment of their children and reclaim their cultural heritages.

## Pearson eTextbook Application Videos

The following videos are available in the Pearson eTextbook and can be used to practice observing and applying what you learned in this chapter.

**Pearson eTextbook Application**
**Video Example 2.2**

In this video, several educators discuss their conversations with students around the concept of diversity. Pay attention to the way the students conceptualize diversity.

**Pearson eTextbook Application**
**Video Example 2.3**

In this video, the experiences of students who are undocumented are discussed including potential fears they may be facing as well as ways to support these students.

**Pearson eTextbook Application**
**Video Example 2.4**

In this video, several students provide first hand insight into the experiences of students who are immigrants. Pay attention to the commonalities in their stories.

# Chapter 3
# Class and Socioeconomic Status

## Learning Objectives

*As you read this chapter, you should be able to:*

**3.1** Describe the measures of socioeconomic status that contribute to a person's economic well-being.

**3.2** Analyze the class differences that exist in the United States.

**3.3** Understand the struggles in which people have been engaged to reduce economic injustice.

**3.4** Probe the intersectionality of class with race and ethnicity, gender, and age and its impact on inequality.

**3.5** Create curriculum, instructional strategies, and classroom environments that open opportunities to students from all socioeconomic groups.

## Opening Case Study

A veteran English teacher, Tyus Loftis taught in a school where most students were from low-income families. Many of the families were working class, and most parents or caretakers had held a steady job until the COVID-19 pandemic. A number of parents held essential jobs in local nursing homes, hospitals, and grocery stores. Many people were laid off or lost their jobs at restaurants and local businesses as they were forced to close. They had found it difficult to find another full-time job, and many of them now worked part time, sometimes holding two jobs with wages that did not match their earlier earnings. Many families had lost their homes, and some were experiencing homelessness, usually sleeping in subsidized hotel rooms, their cars, or the homes of family or friends. They were struggling but not giving up.

By Thanksgiving, Mr. Loftis realized that Christina had not been in his class for several days. He was used to her not being in class periodically, but this was the first time that she had missed an extended period of time. Christina had been turning in her homework on time, for the most part, but she had not been participating as actively in class as she had at the beginning of the semester. Now that he thought about it, she had been exhibiting signs of depression.

Mr. Loftis soon learned that Christina's family had recently moved. They had been staying with neighbors who could no longer share their house with another family of five. They had applied to the city for temporary shelter, but in the meantime, they were living in their car while her parents searched for jobs and a place to stay. Christina, who had been a good student and involved in several school activities, was embarrassed about her family's current economic condition. She was reluctant to go to school where someone might find out that her family was sleeping in their car, especially when it became difficult to shower or wash her clothes. She wanted to help her family and thought she might be able to find a job at a fast-food restaurant nearby.

*(continued)*

Mr. Loftis thought if he could talk to Christina, he might be able to convince her to return to school. School officials could arrange for her to shower at school early in the morning, and she could wash her clothes at school using the equipment there. He worried that if Christina left school now, she might never return, and she had built up an academic record that would make her eligible for a scholarship to college. He recalled attending a professional development session about retaining students who were experiencing homelessness in school but couldn't remember the details. He decided to talk with a school counselor for advice.

## Reflect

1. What steps could Mr. Loftis take to assist Christina during the period in which she and her family are homeless?
2. What are the school's responsibilities for supporting students experiencing homelessness?
3. What safety nets in a community could help support families with financial difficulties?
4. What are some factors that cause families to experience homelessness?

# Socioeconomic Status

**Learning Objective 3.1** Describe the measures of socioeconomic status that contribute to a person's economic well-being.

The economic condition of an individual or group is measured using a criterion called **socioeconomic status (SES)**. It serves as a composite of the economic status of a family or individuals on the basis of their income, occupation, and educational attainment. Related to these three factors are wealth and power, which also help determine an individual's SES but are more difficult to measure. The SES of a family makes a great deal of difference in the experiences of children throughout their formal schooling. It provides advantages or challenges to academic achievement and acceptance in school life.

The five determinants of SES—income, wealth, occupation, educational attainment, and power—are interrelated. Although inequality takes many forms, these factors are probably the most salient for individuals and families because they affect how they live. Families' SES is observable in the size of their homes and the part of town in which they live, the age of the car (if any) that they drive, and the schools their children attend. Many educators place their students at specific SES levels based on observations about their families, the way students dress, the language or dialect they use, and their eligibility for free or reduced-price lunch.

## Income

**Income** is the amount of money a person earns in wages or salaries during a year. One way to look at income distribution is by dividing the population into fifths; the lowest one-fifth has the lowest incomes, and the highest one-fifth has the highest incomes. Figure 3.1 shows the percentage of total income earned by each fifth of the population. The fifth of U.S. families with the highest incomes earned 52% of the total income in 2020, whereas the fifth of the population with the lowest incomes earned just 3% of the total income. The 5% of U.S. families with the highest incomes earned 23% of the total income of all families (Shrider et al., 2021). The wealthiest 1% earned about $2 million annually in 2018 while the approximately 13,000 households in the top 0.01% annually earned about $44.5 million per household (Congressional Budget Office, 2021).

Many people view this income inequality as a natural outcome of the American way. Those people who have contributed at high levels to their professions or jobs are believed to deserve more pay for their efforts. People at the lower end of the continuum either are unemployed or work in unskilled jobs and thus are expected to receive minimal economic rewards. The distance between the two ends of this continuum has grown over the past 40 years. For example, chief executive officers (CEOs) of the 500 U.S. companies in the S&P Dow Jones Indices earned an average income of $18.3 million in 2021, which was 324 times the average earnings of their employees (AFL-CIO, 2022). People earning the federal minimum wage[1] of $7.25 per hour receive $15,080 annually, which is not enough to pay for basic needs such as housing and food and places a

**Figure 3.1** Income in the United States by Fifths of the Population, 2020

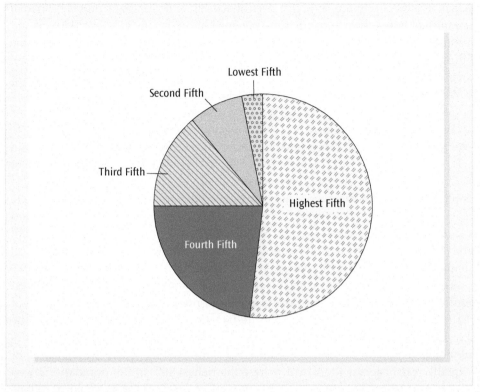

SOURCE: Shrider et al., J. (2021).

family of two or more people below the official U.S. **poverty line**. The Organisation for Economic Co-operation and Development (OECD; 2019) reports that the gap between high and low wage earners is greater in the United States than in almost any other industrialized country in the world.

Between World War II and 1973, the growth of the U.S. economy allowed the incomes of workers at all levels to increase at a faster rate than expenditures. Many middle-class families were able to purchase homes, cars, boats, and luxuries for their homes; money was sometimes also available for savings. During this period, the annual **median income** of all people nearly tripled. The standard of living for most of the population was markedly better in 1973 than in 1940. Beginning in 1973, however, the cost of living (i.e., the cost of housing, utilities, food, and other essentials) began to increase faster than incomes. Except for the wealthy, all families felt the financial pressure. No longer did they have extra income to purchase nonessentials. No longer was one full-time worker in many families enough to maintain a desirable standard of living. The 1990s saw another upswing in the economy that resulted in an annual median family income of $76,784[2] by 2007. Following the 2008 Great Recession, the median income of families dropped to $70,328, rebounding to $84,008 by 2020 (U.S. Census Bureau, 2021d).

## Wealth

Although the difference in income among people and families is great, an examination of income alone does not reveal the vast differences in the way families live. Income reflects the amount of money that people earn for their labors during a year, but the figures do not

[1]Most states and the District of Columbia have adopted a higher minimum wage that ranges from $8.75 to $15.20. Two states (Georgia and Wyoming) have a lower minimum wage of $5.15 (Paycor, 2022).

[2]All the income and wealth numbers throughout this chapter are reported as equivalent to 2020 dollars unless otherwise noted.

include money earned from investments, land, and other holdings. They do not present the **net worth** of a family after they have paid their debts. The **wealth** of a family includes savings accounts, insurance, corporate stock ownership, and property. It provides a partial guarantee of future income and has the potential of producing additional income and wealth. However, for most families, the majority of their wealth comes from the equity value of their homes and the value of household goods. The wealth of the half of the population that is least affluent was only 3.3% of the country's wealth in 2022 (Board of Governors of the Federal Reserve System, 2022a). This figure declined even further during the COVID-19 pandemic as the wealth of billionaires increased dramatically (Chancel et al., 2022).

While income is reported on federal income tax forms, wealth is difficult to determine from these or other standard forms. However, the distribution of wealth is clearly concentrated in a small percentage of the population. The wealthiest 20% of the U.S. population held 80% of the nation's wealth in 2019 (Bhutta et al., 2020). The people in the United States whose net worth grew the most during the pandemic were the wealthiest 1% of the population, who held 32% of the nation's wealth in 2022 (Board of Governors of the Federal Reserve System, 2022b). Figure 3.2 shows how wealth is distributed across fifths of the population. The wealth of the people in the lowest quintile was below zero because they owed more than the value of their assets.

The wealth in the world is held by only a small number of people. The wealthiest families, who represent .05% of the population, hold the largest concentration of wealth since the Great Depression in the late 1920s (Saez & Zucman, 2016). The 10 richest men globally have greater wealth than 40% of the most economically vulnerable people in the world (Oxfam International, 2022). The same pattern of inequality exists across the world, where the richest 10% of the population owns 76% of the wealth (Chancel et al., 2022). The annual revenue of major corporations such as Walmart, Boeing, Facebook, and Exxon exceeds the gross national income of many countries (Smith, 2020).

**Figure 3.2** Distribution of Wealth in the United States by Fifths of Annual Household Income, 2019

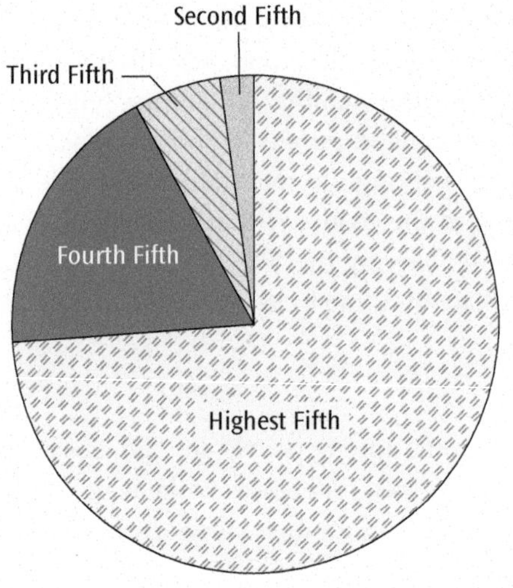

**SOURCE:** Bhutta et al. (2020).

## Occupation

Generally speaking, income is a measure of occupational success—the importance of the occupation to society and of one's skill at the job. In addition to providing an income, an individual's job is an activity that is considered important. Individuals who are unemployed often are stigmatized as noncontributing members of society who cannot take care of themselves. Even individuals with great wealth often hold jobs even though the additional income is unnecessary.

Many jobs that offered a **living wage** in the past are no longer available or are being replaced by automated machinery. This pattern is particularly prevalent in **blue-collar** jobs in manufacturing and production and will impact transportation jobs as vehicles become self-driving. Many **white-collar** jobs for receptionists, clerks, and cashiers are also expected to be replaced by technological advancements over the next decade (Yang, 2018).

What jobs will be available in the future? Figure 3.3 shows the occupations and mean wages for the jobs in which the largest number of people were employed in 2022 including teachers, who comprise the largest number of public employees in

**Figure 3.3** Mean Wages for U.S. Occupations with the Largest Number of Employees Plus Public School Teachers, 2022

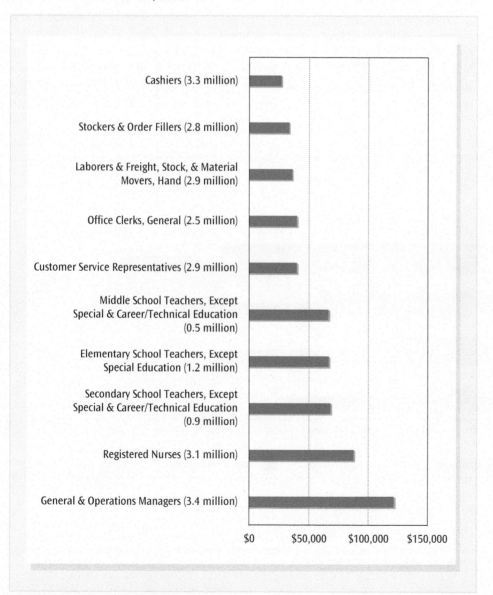

**SOURCE:** U.S. Bureau of Labor Statistics (2022c).

<br>

the United States. Many of the jobs on this list require on-the-job training but no postsecondary preparation. Others require an associate's or bachelor's degree at a minimum. As you can see in Figure 3.3, the difference in income among these jobs varies greatly.

## Education

One of the best predictors of occupational prestige is the amount of education required for a job, with financial compensation generally being greater for occupations that require more years of education. A great discrepancy exists between the incomes of people who have less than a high school education and those who have completed professional training after college. In 2020 the median annual income of a man who was 25 years old or older and worked full time year-round but had not completed high school was $38,763; a man who had attained a bachelor's degree earned $89,847. Most women do not yet earn as much as men, no matter what education level they have. Women who had not finished high school earned a median income of $30,762 compared to $64,723 if they had a bachelor's degree—or 72 to 79 cents for each dollar earned by men with the same education. Earning a professional degree has an even more dramatic impact on income, with a median income of $155,470 for men and $121,311 for women (U.S. Census Bureau, 2021e).

Education is rightfully viewed as a way to enhance one's economic status. However, impressive educational credentials are much more likely to be achieved as a result of family background than other factors. The higher the SES of a student's family, the greater the student's chances of finishing high school and college, as shown in Figure 3.4. The rate of students who enrolled in college soon after high school graduation ranged in 2022 from 48% of those from low-income families to

**Figure 3.4** College Participation and Completion of Bachelor's Degree of Dependent Students* by Family Income, 2020

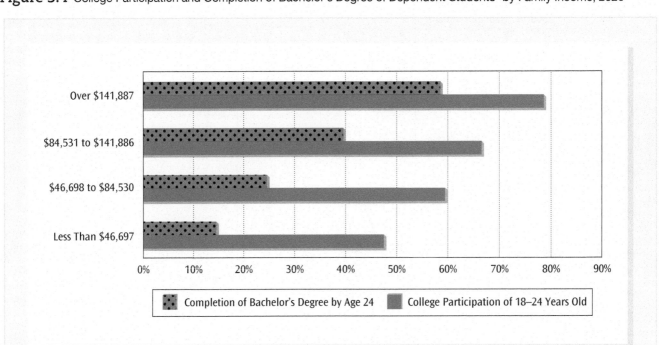

*Dependent students are 18 to 24 years old who are not married and do not earn an income sufficient to be identified as an independent student. The percentage of postsecondary students who are dependent ranges from 50% to 57% annually.

**SOURCE:** Cahalan et al. (2022).

79% of those from high-income families (Cahalan et al., 2022). Another victim of the COVID-19 pandemic was the number of students enrolling in college. In the fall of 2020, the enrollment of students from high-poverty schools declined by 11.4%—four times the rate of decline from low-poverty schools (Whitford, 2021).

The conditions under which students with low incomes live can make it difficult for them to select postsecondary education as an alternative to working. When they do attend college, the colleges they attend are influenced more by the SES of the family than by the academic ability of the student. Many students simply cannot afford to attend private colleges and instead choose community colleges or state colleges and universities. To add to the problems faced by low-income students contemplating college, the cost of tuition has risen continuously over the past decade.

The type of job one holds impacts one's socioeconomic status. Low-wage jobs make it difficult if not impossible to move into the middle class.

**SOURCE:** Jeffrey Isaac Greenberg/Alamy Stock Photo

# Critical Incidents in Teaching

## High Expectations for Educational Attainment

Linda Jackson knew that the ninth grade was the grade at which students were most likely to drop out of school because they weren't engaged, especially in urban schools with large numbers of students from low-income families. Therefore, she organized her ninth-grade class around project-based activities to try to engage students actively in learning and keep them in school.

Ms. Jackson wanted her students to know the importance of a college degree in meeting their future goals. She created activities in which they could explore colleges and potential careers online. During those activities, she realized that most students had never been on a college or university campus even though there were eight of them in the city. Most students were interested in attending college but expressed concern about how their families would pay the tuition. Ms. Jackson proposed that they invite a college admissions officer to talk with them about applying for college and financial aid. Several students asked why they couldn't visit one of the colleges to talk to an admissions officer. Ms. Jackson agreed and received permission from the principal, contacted a local private college that could be reached via the subway, sent permission forms home with students to be signed by one of their parents or guardians, and identified several people who would chaperone the field trip.

It was a beautiful spring day when Ms. Jackson, the ninth-grade students, and the chaperones boarded the subway for their tour of the local college. When they arrived at the admissions office, the admissions officer asked to meet with Ms. Jackson alone. The admissions officer told her that they had never accepted a student from Roosevelt High School and that she should be careful about encouraging her students to go to the college. The admissions officer suggested that she should instead take them to the community college. Nevertheless, the admissions officer would try to answer their questions, but they would have to take a self-guided tour of the campus. Ms. Jackson was devastated by the admission officer's attitude about Roosevelt's students but never let on to them that their chances of attending this college or a similar one would be near impossible. She was going to do everything she could to help them know their potential and plan to attend college, even an elite college if they were qualified to do so.

## Questions for Discussion

1. Why was Ms. Jackson discussing college with ninth-grade students who were primarily from low-income families who would have a difficult time providing financial support for their children to attend college?

2. How important is it for students from low-income families to have a teacher with high expectations for their academic performance? What is Ms. Jackson doing to help students have high expectations for themselves?

3. How would you have responded if you were met by this admissions officer during the field trip? Does Ms. Jackson have unrealistic expectations for her students? Why or why not?

4. How do the policies and practices of colleges and universities contribute to continuing or disbanding inequity in society?

## Power

Individuals and families at upper SES levels exert more power than those at lower levels. These individuals are more likely to sit on state or local policy boards, boards of colleges and universities, and boards of corporations. Groups and individuals with power control resources that influence their lives and the lives of others. They determine who receives benefits and rewards in governmental, occupational, and community affairs. Groups or individuals with little power do not have the means to get what they need or access to the people who could promote their interests. They continually obtain a lower share of society's benefits, in part because they lack access to sources of power.

People with higher incomes are more likely to participate in national and local politics as well as vote in local, state, and national elections. Contributing financially to political candidates pays off for this portion of the population. Voters with low or moderate incomes have little or no influence on policies, while advantaged voters have great influence. This power translates to legislative action that benefits people, families, and corporations that are wealthy. Other segments of the population become disillusioned with a political system in which they reap few if any benefits (Stiglitz, 2019).

However, power is not always limited to the most affluent members of society. Other citizens can generate power as members of collective units that protest for higher minimum wages, racial justice, affordable housing, and environmental justice. Teachers, for example, may strike or protest against insufficient funding for schools or better pay and working conditions (Royce, 2023).

Education is not exempt from the exercise of power. Wealth and affluence can create an uneven playing field for many students, as families with higher incomes use their power to ensure that their children have access to the best teachers, Advanced Placement courses, enrichment programs, and private schools. Families are able to financially contribute to the hiring of teachers for programs such as music and art, which some school districts cannot afford. They do not tolerate the hiring of unqualified or incompetent teachers. In addition, their children participate in extracurricular activities that enhance their college applications. Wealthier families are able to pay for tutors and SAT prep classes and hire consultants to help their children draft their college applications. The steps that some wealthy families will take became transparent in the 2019 scandal in which a number of parents were charged with bribing university coaches and administrators to ensure that their children attended elite universities.

# Class Differences in the United States

**Learning Objective 3.2** Analyze the class differences that exist in the United States.

**Class** is a system of sorting society into groups that share the same or similar SES, giving them different access to economic, political, cultural, and social resources. It determines the schools we attend, the stores in which we shop, the restaurants at which we eat, the community in which we live, and the jobs to which we have access.

Most people remain in the socioeconomic strata into which they were born; the political–economic system helps keep them there. However, some individuals become socially and economically mobile. Stories abound about the athletes, celebrities, and CEOs who have moved from poverty to successful careers and great wealth. In reality, few people have the opportunities to translate their experiences into the high salaries of elite stars of the corporate, entertainment, and sports worlds.

A college education is the most effective path for moving from low-income to a middle-class or higher status, but family background accounts for a large part of the variation in educational and occupational attainment. The opportunity to participate equally in the generation of wealth is usually thwarted before a child is born (Stiglitz, 2019). Children born into a wealthy family are likely to be wealthy as adults. Children born into poverty are significantly more likely to be adults in poverty. Barriers that exist in society often lead to the perpetuation of inequalities from one generation to the next.

Despite the popular myth, most people in the United States are not affluent by U.S. standards. A budget that allows a family of four to meet basic needs was above $55,500 in 2022, compared with the federal government's poverty line of $27,750 for a family of four (U.S. Department of Health and Human Services [DHHS], 2022). In 2020, one in three U.S. families earned less than $55,000 (U.S. Census Bureau, 2021e). Many of these individuals identify themselves as middle class, but they may be unable to obtain the material goods and necessities to live comfortably. In this section we explore the different classes by which people in the United States identify themselves or are identified by others.

## Poverty

**Poverty** is one of the major challenges for societies around the world, but the World Bank, the International Monetary Fund, and UNESCO have identified goals to reduce poverty. In 1990, nearly 2 billion, or 36%, of the world's population lived in **extreme poverty**. Because of global growth and the rising wealth of many developing countries, that number is projected to have decreased to 657 million people living in extreme poverty by 2022, which is 75 million to 95 million people less than expected as a result of the global impact of COVID-19, inflation, and the Ukraine war (The World Bank, 2022).

Poverty has become more entrenched in countries affected by violent conflict and weak institutions. Formal schooling is less likely to be available to households in poverty, especially in rural areas. Countries in Sub-Saharan Africa and South Asia now account for the majority of the population in extreme poverty. At the same time, billions of people live above extreme poverty but continue to live with low incomes that prevent access to their basic housing and food needs as well as access to safe water, sanitation, and core health services, negatively affecting their overall well-being.

Even though the United States is one of the richest countries in the world, 11.4% of its population lived in poverty in 2020 (Shrider et al., 2021). The populations who suffer the most from the lack of a stable income or other economic resources are the unemployed and people experiencing homeless. People in extreme poverty fall into this group, but most others are temporarily at this level, moving in and out of poverty as they work sporadically at low wages. Six million people, or 3.7% of the U.S. civilian workforce, were unemployed in August 2022. Another 4.1 million people were employed part time because full-time jobs were not available or their hours had been reduced (U.S. Bureau of Labor Statistics, 2022b). Because many working-age people have stopped looking for employment, they are not included in these federal unemployment figures; therefore, the actual number of unemployed is higher. However, it is not just the unemployed who may be in poverty. One in 10 of the people who are in poverty actually work full time all year but don't earn enough to pull themselves out of poverty (Bauer, 2019).

Families and people in poverty may find it difficult to stay healthy, clean, punctual, and well-fed—characteristics that contribute to getting and keeping a job (Goldblum & Shaddox, 2021). As a result, they may become socially isolated from the dominant society. They generally are not integrated into or welcome in communities of the more affluent. For example, recommendations to establish low-income housing, shelters for people experiencing homelessness, or halfway houses in middle-class communities are often met with vocal outrage from residents. Many people experiencing homelessness are ostracized and dehumanized as they are blamed for their economic conditions. A number of U.S. cities have enacted laws that criminalize life-sustaining practices such as camping, sleeping, and panhandling (National Law Center on Homeless & Poverty, 2019).

Children suffer the most from persistent poverty. Their families may be criminalized for their poverty as they are charged for failing to provide their children with adequate shelter, food, or clothing. Children, especially Black children, may be permanently separated from their families and placed in foster care (Elliott, 2022).

As a result of no or low incomes, children and families may end up living on the streets of U.S. cities, comprising a large portion of today's population experiencing homelessness, as shown in Figure 3.5. But homelessness is not limited to urban areas. Twenty percent of the people experiencing homelessness in the United States live in rural areas in cars, campers, or tents or with relatives (Henry et al., 2021). Nearly three in five of the people experiencing homelessness are located in five states with large cities (i.e., California, New York, Florida, Texas, and Washington) (National Alliance to End Homelessness, 2021).

Annually, the U.S. Department of Housing and Urban Development (HUD) conducts a count of people experiencing homelessness on one night in January but was unable to count the number of people who were living on the streets, in parks, or in vehicles in 2021 and 2022 because of the pandemic. HUD was able to count people staying in emergency or temporary shelters and transitional housing programs, identifying more than 326,000 people in those facilities in 2021, which is approximately 60% of the people experiencing homelessness (Henry et al., 2022). In January 2020, before COVID-19 was declared a national emergency, over 580,000 people were identified as experiencing homelessness in the United States, which was a 2% increase over the previous year (Henry et al., 2021). However, the number of people who were homeless is significantly undercounted by leaving out people who are staying with friends or family due to economic hardships or who have been hospitalized or

**Figure 3.5** Who Were the People Experiencing Homelessness in the United States in 2020?

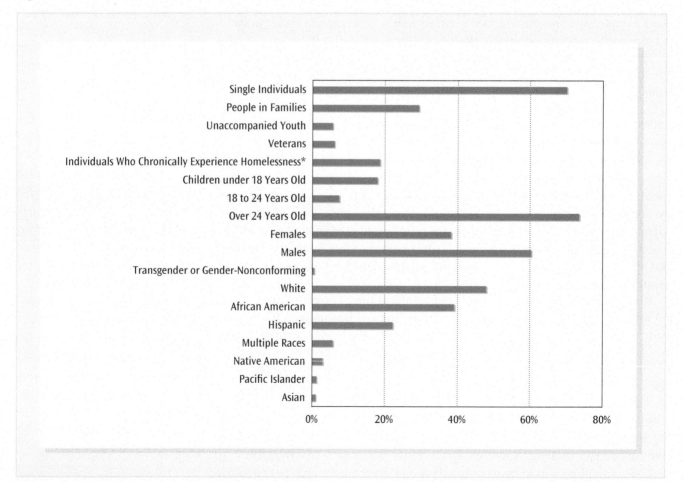

*Individuals in this category include people with a disability who have been continuously homeless for 1 year or more or have experienced at least four episodes of homelessness in the last 3 years adding up to 12 months.

**SOURCE:** Henry et al. (2021).

incarcerated (National Law Center on Homelessness and Poverty, 2017). The National Homelessness Law Center (2022) reports that more than 3.5 million people experience homelessness in the United States at some time during the year.

Based on a national survey conducted by Chapin Hall at the University of Chicago, researchers estimated that one in 10 youth age 18 to 25 and one in 30 youth age 13 to 17 have experienced homelessness at least once (Morton et al., 2017). These youth may sleep in a shelter, but most of them **couch surf** or sleep on the streets or in abandoned buildings or cars. Two of five youth experiencing homelessness identify as LGBTQ+ (lesbian, gay, bisexual, transgender, queer/questioning); 7% are transgender or identify as neither male or female. Black and Latino/a youth are disproportionately overrepresented in the youth population experiencing homelessness (Waguespack & Ryan, 2020). Three in 10 of the youth who are homeless report substance use problems, seven in 10 report mental health issues, one in three have been in foster care, and half have been in juvenile detention (Morton et al., 2017).

The number of households experiencing homelessness has declined by 32% since 2007 when many people lost their jobs because of the Great Recession. Just under 172,000 people in family households were homeless in January 2020, with an average family size of 3.2 people. Sixty percent of the adults experiencing homelessness in families with children were women, and 60% of the people in these families were under age 18 (Henry et al, 2021). Nearly 1.3 million students experiencing homelessness were enrolled in public schools in 2019–2020 (National Center for Homeless Education, 2022).

Why do people experience homelessness? A lack of affordable housing is a primary reason, followed by unemployment, poverty, and low-paying jobs. Even when people find housing, they are often charged unreasonably high rents for housing that is unsafe and lacks working furnaces, refrigerators, or sanitation systems (Elliott, 2022). The federal definition of *affordable housing* is rent equal to 30% of one's income. To spend no more than 30% of one's income on housing, an individual would have to earn $25.82 per hour to afford a modest two-bedroom rental home or $21.25 per hour for a modest one-bedroom rental home in many areas of the country (National Low Income Housing Coalition, 2022). Thus, housing has become unaffordable for low-wage workers. To afford a two-bedroom apartment in most parts of the country, an individual who makes the minimum wage needs one or more additional wage earners in the household. In 2020 at the beginning of the pandemic, 30% of households were paying more than 30% of their incomes for housing, and 14% of households were spending more than half of their income on housing (Joint Center for Housing Studies of Harvard University, 2022), leaving little money to cover expenses such as health care, child care, and basic necessities such as food and diapers.

Domestic violence is another cause of homelessness; women escaping violent relationships do not always have someplace else to go (Goldblum & Shaddox, 2021). Other people experiencing homelessness are without a place to stay because the number of facilities to care for people with mental disorders is limited. Some people who are homeless are dependent on drugs or alcohol, resulting in the loss of their jobs, the inability to keep a job that earns enough to pay for their housing, or estrangement from their families.

An increasing number of adults, families, and children experiencing homelessness are found in communities around the country.

**SOURCE:** © Discha-AS/Shutterstock

People who are unemployed and people experiencing homelessness suffer from economic insecurity as well as social, political, and economic deprivation. When they hold full-time jobs, they are generally of the lowest prestige and at the lowest income levels. The jobs are often eliminated when economic conditions tighten. The work for which they are hired is often dirty work—not only physically dirty but also dangerous, menial, undignified, and degrading. Most people just want a stable job that pays a decent wage (Reeves, 2019).

## The Working Class

The **working class** includes two categories of workers: manual workers and service workers. Just over one in three U.S. workers are engaged primarily in manual work. Workers in service occupations such as the protective services, personal care, and health care support comprise 9% of employed workers. Many of these workers are paid by the hour, work part time, and have no formal control over their schedules, sometimes knowing their schedules less than a week in advance (Reeves, 2019). Many people in these occupations are independent contractors such as long-distance truckers or some construction workers. They are involved in **gig work** such as painting, household cleaning, ride-share driving, and food delivery in which they are generally responsible for their own health insurance, pension protection, and other benefits. Some of these jobs require postsecondary training or an associate's degree; others require no specific skill. Of the employed population, 43% have the working-class jobs shown in Figure 3.6.

The income of the working class varied in 2021 from a median hourly wage of $13.65 in food services to $23.18 for construction and extraction occupations (U.S. Bureau of Labor Statistics, 2021b), which provide different standards of living. Although the income of the working class is equal to and sometimes higher than that of community, social service, and education workers, the working class generally has less job security.

**Figure 3.6** Percent of U.S. Population in Working-Class Jobs, 2021

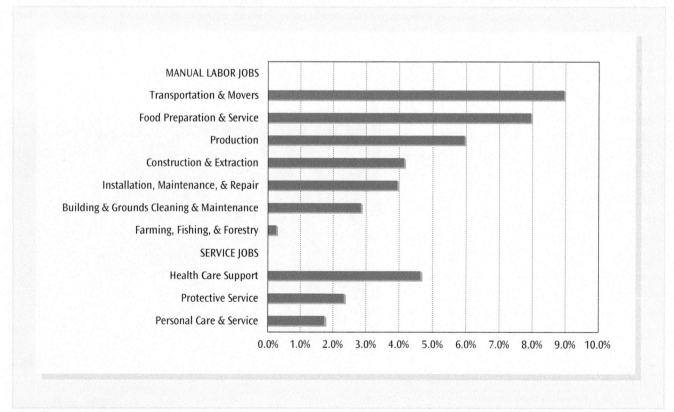

**SOURCE:** U.S. Bureau of Labor Statistics (2021a).

Vacation time is usually less, health insurance is not always available, and working conditions can be more dangerous. Another worrisome factor for working-class people is the projected loss of jobs as a result of artificial intelligence, software, and automation.

People at the low end of the wage scale perform the jobs that most people with more education choose not to do. Although many work one or more jobs at the federal minimum wage of $7.25 per hour, they can't pull themselves out of poverty. People who work but earn low incomes are more likely than other workers to hold part-time jobs, be women, be Black or Latino/a, and lack a high school diploma. Food preparation workers are among the working population who participate in one of the lowest-paid occupations, in which the annual median wage is $27,030 (U.S. Census Bureau, 2022a). Although union workers generally receive higher incomes and enjoy negotiated health care and retirement benefits, many low-income workers either do not join unions or work in states or companies that aggressively discourage union membership.

## The Middle Class

The **middle class** includes members who are blue-collar workers, white-collar workers, professionals, and managers whose annual household income is between 2/3 and 200% of the national median income. It includes families from all racial and ethnic groups and both immigrant and native families. When asked in polls, 52% of the population indicate they are middle class or upper middle class, and 35% identify themselves as working class (Jones, 2022). In fact, 50% of U.S. adults lived in middle-class households[3] with incomes that ranged from $45,014 to $135,042 in 2020, down from 61% in 1971 (Kochhar & Sechopoulos, 2022b). This income range leads to very different lifestyles at the two ends of the continuum. Although some members of the middle class have comfortable incomes, many have virtually no wealth. Many live from paycheck to paycheck, with little cushion against the loss of earning power through catastrophe, recession, layoff, wage cuts, or old age.

Members of the middle class generally adhere to a set of beliefs and values that are inherent in the good life. Many believe in attributes such as thriftiness and dedication to work (Wenger & Zaber, 2021). Depending on where they live, a family at the high end of the middle-class income continuum will find it easier to achieve their financial goals. Even when they are at the lower end, most families are working toward meeting their aspirations for owning a home in a safe neighborhood, saving for retirement, sending their children to college, having decent health care, and being able to take a vacation (Reeves et al., 2018).

The middle class has become more racially and ethnically diverse than in earlier periods of U.S. history. Forty-seven percent of Black and Asian adults were in the middle class in 2021 as compared to 49% of Hispanic adults and 52% of White adults (Kochhar & Sechopoulos, 2022a). Even when they earn the same income, however, Black and Latino/a families are less likely than White families to identify themselves as middle class (Wenger & Zaber, 2021).

The jobs held and incomes earned by people in the middle class vary greatly. The median income of full-time, year-round retail sales workers was $39,650 in 2019; secretaries and administrative assistants in offices earned more, at $40,240, but the middle class also includes elementary and middle school teachers at $53,030, nurses

---

[3]The income for the middle class is based on the Pew Research Center's definition of adults whose annual household income is between 2/3 and 200% of the national median income, which was $67,521 in 2000.

at \$70,380, mechanical engineers at \$92,130, nurse practitioners at \$105,100, software developers at \$112,400, airplane pilots at \$121,700, and lawyers at \$131,700 (U.S. Census Bureau, 2022a). The SES of individuals and households changes over time based on a new job, the loss of a job, an unexpected illness, marriage, divorce, and many other circumstances. Moving into the middle class and maintaining that status often requires two wage earners.

More than 30 years ago, sociologists warned that the middle class was beginning to disappear. At that time, workers were losing their manufacturing jobs, and many of the replacement jobs paid lower wages, making it difficult for workers to maintain their lifestyles. Other workers faced the loss of the better-paying jobs that they held in the past and declining or stagnant salaries. The COVID-19 pandemic contributed to fewer people being in the middle class as many middle- and lower-income families faced serious financial hardships when people lost their jobs. Temporary government programs such as expanded unemployment benefits, Economic Impact Payments (i.e., stimulus checks), and expanded child tax credits provided some assistance to people with lower incomes during this period. Other people were able to work from home, being able to retain their jobs, saving money spent on transportation to and from the job, but adding to their workload as they provided full-time child care and shared computers with their school-age children.

Between 1970 and 2020, the middle-class share of income earned in the United States declined from 62% to 42%, while the incomes of the upper class increased from 29% to 50% (Kochhar & Sechopoulos, 2022b). Limited **intergenerational income mobility** from low-income to middle-income levels contributes to the decline of the middle class. Children of the middle class are less likely to earn more than their parents, as had been the pattern for several decades after World War II (Chetty et al., 2017).

Although children born in the bottom income quintile are still highly likely to earn more than their parents, it has been difficult for them to move into the middle class as adults. At the same time, the children of wealthy families are much less likely to fall out of their class (Krause & Sawhill, 2018). Why is the size of the middle class important? According to Sitaraman (2017), having a large middle class who can live comfortably and accumulate some degree of wealth is critical to a healthy democracy with relative economic equality and limited strife among the classes.

## The Upper Middle Class

Professionals, managers, and administrators are the elite of the middle class. They represent the status that many upwardly mobile families are trying to reach. Their income level allows them to lead lives that are, in many cases, quite different from those of people in the working and middle classes. With much less difficulty than the middle class, they can own a home and a couple of cars, take regular vacations, and accumulate wealth. They can provide amenities for the development of the cultural capital that will contribute to their children's success through life. These advantages include access to books, the latest technology, trips inside and outside the United States, tutors, the best schools and colleges, and access to internships and jobs. Most **upper middle-class** families work toward securing their higher status in a market meritocracy by acquiring college degrees and nurturing networks for their advancement in society—and ensuring that their children do the same (Reeves, 2018).

Although they are at a level far below the median income of the upper class, the upper middle class are the affluent members of the middle class. However, this class is not as diverse as the middle class. White families are 2.5 times and Asian families are 2.9 times more likely than Black and Latino/a families to be members of the upper middle class (Reeves & Joo, 2017).

The professionals and administrators who best fit this category are those who must earn professional or advanced degrees and credentials to practice their professions.

One in three U.S. workers have a professional job. Judges, lawyers, architects, physicians, college professors, teachers, computer programmers, scientists, and social workers are among these professionals. Excluding teachers, nurses, and social services occupations, many professionals earn far more than the $67,521 median income of the U.S. population (Shrider et al., 2021). Upper middle-class families are in the 80 to 95% of the highest income earners in the country, with annual salaries between $174,001 and $319,768 (U.S. Census Bureau, 2022b). Incomes of the upper middle class are pulling away from the middle class, growing at a rate almost double that of the middle class (Congressional Budget Office, 2021). The incomes and opportunities to accumulate wealth are higher for upper middle-class individuals compared with other members of the middle class because they have enough money to invest and earn additional income.

The occupations of the people in this group play a central role in their lives, often determining their friends as well as their business and professional associates. Their jobs allow autonomy and a great amount of self-direction. In the past, they believed in the American dream of success because they had achieved it. However, this dream now appears to be working primarily for college graduates who choose careers in the financial and corporate world. College graduates who choose fields such as reporting, teaching, social work, and other human services professions do not generally earn enough these days to be eligible for many of the opportunities available to the upper middle class.

## The Upper Class

High income and wealth are necessary characteristics for entering the upper class. For this discussion, the **upper class** includes the top 5% of income and wealth earners. Within the upper class, however, are great variations in the wealth of individual families. The upper class includes individuals with top-level, highly paid positions in large financial institutions, entertainment companies, and business corporations as well as people whose wealth allows them to live comfortably on their income without working. The wealthiest 400 people in the United States include individuals with great inherited wealth, who comprise nearly one-third of the group; 69% of the wealthiest individuals created their fortunes rather than inheriting them (Peterson-Withorn, 2022).

The disparity in both income and wealth between members of the upper class and members of other classes is growing. The income that is no longer being earned by the middle class is fueling the increase in the wealth of the upper class. Each year after the Great Recession, the wealth of this class increased while that of the middle class decreased.

The wealthiest families have been able to increase their share of income and wealth consistently over the past 40 years, whereas low-income families have seen limited gains, and the incomes of middle-class families have decreased. For the first time, in 2005, all those on the *Forbes* list of richest people in the United States were billionaires. By 2022, there were 2,668 billionaires in the world, which had decreased by 87 from 2021 as a result of the Russian invasion of Ukraine and a government crackdown on tech companies in China. The United States is home to the largest number of billionaires (28%), followed by China (23%) (Dolan & Peterson-Withorn, 2022).

The power possessed by these people allows them to protect their wealth. The only progressive tax in this country is the federal income tax, in which a greater percentage of the income is taxed as income increases. Loopholes in the tax laws provide benefits to those whose unearned income is based on assets. What does this mean in terms of advantage to the rich? Tax laws in the 1980s were regressive, resulting in a decline in the taxes of higher-income families. The 1990s saw a more progressive structure in which the taxes of higher-income families rose in comparison to the taxes of low-income families. The tax cuts of 2001 reduced taxes for everyone but more so for high-income families than for others.

The most recent tax cuts in 2017 again reduced taxes for the wealthy and corporations that has led to the richest 400 families in the United States paying tax rates that are 1.2 percentage points less than that paid by the half of the U.S. population who earn the lowest incomes (Saez & Zucman, 2019). The debate about taxes continues, with one side arguing that the wealthy should be taxed more and the other side arguing that taxes should be cut for the wealthy because they assert such cuts will stimulate the economy.

Although families with inherited wealth do not represent a completely closed status group, they do have an overrepresentation of Anglo Protestant members who were born in the United States. They tend to intermarry with other members of the upper class. They are well educated, although a college degree is not essential. The educational mark of prestige is attendance at elite private prep schools and prestigious private colleges and universities. Greater assimilation of lifestyles and values has occurred within this class than in any other. Although diversity exists among them, members of the upper class may be the most homogeneous group, and they are likely to remain so as long as their cross-cultural and cross-class interactions are limited.

# Struggles Against Economic Injustice

**Learning Objective 3.3** Understand the struggles in which people have been engaged to reduce economic injustice.

The ability to earn a living wage that will support the basic needs of families and allow them to have a decent standard of living is the major goal for an economically just society. Among the goals of most nations are the elimination of poverty, education of all children and youth, and provision of sanitation and clean water and air. In a democracy, it is also very important that the population maintains confidence in the country's institutions and votes in elections (OECD, 2019). Inequality in income and wealth among families is one factor that contributes to distrust and instability in a society. In 2022, inequality in the United States was almost as great as it was in 1929 before the Great Depression. In this section, we look at how members of the working class have fought to improve wages and standards of living for themselves and their families over time. You should see throughout the next sections of this chapter the reality of one of the principles on which Dr. Martin Luther King, Jr.'s (1958/2010) work was based: "[T]he inseparable twin of racial injustice is economic injustice" (p. 77).

## Setting the Stage for the Labor Movement

From the beginning of the European colonization of the land that became the United States, ownership of land has been a major source of wealth and power. When the Constitution left the details of voting to the states, White men with property were generally the only people who could vote. It wasn't until around 1860 that most White men over 21 years old with or without property could vote, and it wasn't until 1964 when the Voting Rights Act was signed that all citizens could vote regardless of their race, ethnicity, and gender.

During the Colonial period before the American Revolution, the enslavement of workers was at the core of the labor system. Most people who were not enslaved earned a living on their family farm or in a family craft shop. Wage earners were the minority of workers at the beginning of this period, but their numbers steadily increased in coastal cities and towns. They were free laborers, former indentured servants and enslaved people, and Native Americans who had been forced off their lands. According to Murolo and Chitty (2018), they were the "sailors, journeyman artisans, women and girls employed as domestic workers or in cloth and clothing production, and men and boys who plowed fields, hauled freight, and performed other back-breaking jobs" (p. 11). With the exception of people with craft skills, these wage earners were members of the poorest segment of free society.

Laborers were not happy with their economic conditions and rebelled against their enslavers and other authorities before and after the Revolutionary War. Armed revolutions were initiated by enslaved people and sometimes indentured servants and Native Americans in Maryland in the 1650s; in Virginia from the 1660s to 1680s, including Bacon's Rebellion in 1676; in New Mexico in 1680; in Massachusetts in 1690; in French New Orleans in the 1730s; in New York in 1712 and 1741; in South Carolina in 1739; in Spanish New Mexico in 1784, 1793, and 1810; in Florida in 1768; and in other areas of the country (Murolo & Chitty, 2018).

Free workers fought their employers for better working conditions and wages through work stoppages and protests. They also irritated the elites by asserting their rights to dress as they pleased and entertain themselves in venues such as taverns and theaters not deemed appropriate for their class. Although the labor force at this time comprised 90% of the population, the people in the labor force earned little, often lived in squalid conditions, and did not have the right to vote (Murolo & Chitty, 2018).

## The Rise of Unions

Soon after the Revolutionary War, skilled workers began organizing trade societies when their interests clashed with their employers, who were primarily interested in increasing profits as they moved into a merchant-capitalist class. The craftspeople included "carpenters and masons, shipwrights and sailmakers, as well as tanners, weavers, shoemakers, tailors, smiths, coopers (barrel makers), glaziers (glass makers), and printers" (Dubofsky & McCartin, 2017, p. 2). Maximum wages for both the skilled and unskilled workforce were set by law.

During the first half of the nineteenth century, craftspeople began fighting for higher wages, shorter hours, and better working conditions. They fought for **closed shops** in which employers could hire only members of the union or trade society. They introduced **collective bargaining** and called for strikes when their employers would not meet their demands. They also became involved in political action. Although they made some progress in improving their conditions, the courts almost always ruled in favor of the employers. One of the union's successes occurred in 1836 when President Martin Van Buren signed an executive order to establish a 10-hour day for all government projects. Every time a depression occurred, which was almost every 10 years until the 1940s, the unions would collapse, and workers took whatever jobs were available (Dubofsky & McCartin, 2017).

By the middle of the nineteenth century, new industries such as ironworks and textile mills were hiring large numbers of workers. The need for workers continued to increase throughout the century as canals, roads, and railroads were constructed. To meet these labor needs, workers were recruited from northern and western Europe and China, hardening further the division between skilled and unskilled and immigrant and nonimmigrant workers. Most skilled workers were born in the United States, while most unskilled workers were immigrants, Catholics, and women.

After the Civil War, industries such as coal and copper mines, steel mills, and packinghouses drew workers from farms, immigrants, and formerly enslaved people at low wages. Employers treated these workers as commodities and seemed not to care that they were living in abject poverty in packed slums. At the same time, the federal government established 8-hour workdays for all of its employees in 1868. The American Federation of Labor (AFL) was established to unite unions across the country to fight for a living wage. Not to be deterred, employers continued to try to break up the unions, accusing them of restraining trade (Dubofsky & McCartin, 2017).

The last two decades of the nineteenth century were called the Great Upheaval as unions called numerous strikes in their fight for higher wages and better working conditions. The Great Railroad Strikes broke out in 1877 to protest wage cuts. The Haymarket Square Riot in Chicago in 1877 ended with four dead and 50 injured workers plus seven dead and 67 injured police officers during and after a strike at the

Pearson eTextbook
**Video Example 3.1**
In this video, a brief history of labor unions is explored. Pay attention to the ways in which these unions have prioritized the wellbeing of workers.
https://youtu.be/ewu-v36szlE?si=AsFQupFLknNsy2Bg

McCormick Harvester plant and the protest that followed. When negotiations failed in 1892 at the steel mills in Homestead, Pennsylvania, which were owned by Andrew Carnegie, the company's general manager hired Pinkerton guards (an independent police force named after its founder) to break the union. The union members fought back, leading to the surrender of the Pinkerton guards. Six days later, the governor sent in 8,000 state militia members to take control of the steel mill under **martial law**. By the end of the strike, strikebreakers had replaced more than half of the original Homestead working force of nearly 4,000 (Dubofsky & McCartin, 2017).

The workers who built the Pullman sleeping cars for railroads also lived in the Pullman community outside of Chicago, where they rented their houses from the Pullman Company as well as paid utilities and bought supplies at the company store at prices that were higher than in neighboring communities. When Pullman laid off more than 3,000 of its 5,800 employees and cut wages by 25 to 40% for those who still had jobs in 1894, the union called for a strike. The company countered by laying off all workers and closing the plant. The strike soon expanded to all members of the American Railway Union, who refused to handle any Pullman car. The government sent the Fifteenth Infantry to Chicago to safeguard the mail and protect interstate commerce. A judge of the Federal District Court issued a blanket injunction against anyone interfering with the operation of the mail or other railroad transportation. One outcome of the Pullman strike was that the union's leader, Eugene Debs, was sent to jail, making him a hero of the labor movement (Dubofsky & McCartin, 2017).

By the end of the nineteenth century, industrialists were reigning. Cornelius Vanderbilt, Leland Stanford, and Edward Henry Harriman controlled the railroads. Andrew Carnegie was responsible for a quarter of all American steel. J.P. Morgan's banking empire was involved with almost every sector of industry, and John D. Rockefeller's Standard Oil Company produced 90% of the crude oil in the United States. These men and their families used their wealth to control the government at the federal, state, and local levels. In addition, they had great influence over the press, universities, and the church (Sitaraman, 2017).

The period before World War I was influenced by progressive policies. Some states were regulating the work of women and children and enacted protective laws for men in dangerous occupations. By 1910, 35 states had adopted worker compensation laws, and Congress had adopted an 8-hour workday for workers on public contracts and created the Department of Labor. Congress passed the Sixteenth Amendment, which allowed it to levy an income tax. The Clayton Act passed Congress in 1914 to strengthen earlier antitrust legislation; it also declared that humans are not commodities and that the existence of unions could not be forbidden. In the Great Migration, which began in 1916, millions of Black people moved from the rural South to cities in the North and West, providing a large source of workers at low wages for industries in those areas. Unions were flourishing, but only 10% of wage earners belonged to unions, which were still primarily for skilled artisans who were White men (Dubofsky & McCartin, 2017).

This period did not escape union strikes. One of the best known was the 1912 Lawrence Strike, in which 20,000 textile workers in Lawrence, Massachusetts, walked out after the company reduced their wages while they were experiencing long hours and pressure to speed up their work. When strikers tried to send their children to temporary homes in Philadelphia, the police began clubbing them and dragging them to a military truck. The nation was outraged at the treatment of these women and their children. The American Woolen Company soon settled by increasing wages from 5 to 25%, providing overtime pay, and agreeing not to discriminate in rehiring the strikers (Dubofsky & McCartin, 2017).

In his acceptance speech in 1928, President Herbert Hoover proclaimed that "we in America are nearer to the final triumph over poverty than ever before in the history of any land" (Dubofsky & McCartin, 2017, p. 206). Working-class families with steady jobs and good wages for the first time were able to use credit to buy products such as washing machines, refrigerators, vacuum cleaners, radios, and even automobiles and pay for them later.

No longer needing immigrant labor along with **nativist** beliefs about immigrants led to Congress ending mass immigration by excluding immigration from Asia and limiting it from southern and eastern Europe. The dramatic turn of events in 1929 reversed the progress that had been made toward eliminating poverty. When the stock market crashed, millions of investors lost everything, leading to steep declines in industrial outputs and employment. By 1932, 20% of the U.S. labor force had lost their jobs (Isenberg, 2017), and unemployment was over 50% in some cities.

## Improving the Standard of Living for Workers

Under President Franklin D. Roosevelt and the New Deal, labor unions were encouraged, not just tolerated. That did not mean that strikes did not occur. In 1934 alone, 2 million workers were involved in 4,270 strikes (Dubofsky & McCartin, 2017). At the same time, Congress passed legislation for the welfare of the people, including Social Security and unemployment insurance. The right to unionize and bargain collectively was guaranteed in the National Industrial Recovery Act. The Wagner or National Labor Relations Act strengthened bargaining rights and created the National Labor Relations Board to supervise union elections. The Fair Labor Standards Act in 1938 established a minimum wage and a 44-hour work week, to be reduced to 40 hours in 3 years. It also prohibited children under the age of 16 from working in industries whose products entered into interstate commerce. Because of the resistance of Congressmen from southern states, the economic sectors that employed most Black and women workers were not covered under this act. The courts were now ruling in favor of the unions and working people. They exempted unions from being prosecuted under antitrust laws and reversed other policies that prevented them from striking, boycotting, or picketing (Dubofsky & McCartin, 2017).

By 1938, the president of the United Mine Workers, John L. Lewis, was arguing for the inclusion of unskilled workers in the AFL. When the AFL rejected his recommendation, Lewis founded the Congress for Industrial Organizations (CIO) and began organizing workers in the steel, auto, rubber, and radio industries. The CIO promoted interracial solidarity and included immigrants and women, although most of the local unions continued to reject workers who were not White. The exception to this rule was the Brotherhood of Sleeping Car Porters, the nation's first major Black labor union, which decided to remain in the AFL. Its president was A. Philip Randolph, who was also a leader in the Civil Rights Movement and was awarded the Presidential Medal of Freedom by President Lyndon B. Johnson in 1964 (Dubofsky & McCartin, 2017).

World War II overturned the economic woes of the Great Depression (Dubofsky & McCartin, 2017) as White women, Black, and Mexican American workers moved from the secondary to the primary labor market. The end of the war was followed by a postwar boom of 30 years. It was in this period that corporations negotiated contracts with unions that led to the rising standards of living for union workers. Unions won higher wages and expanded fringe benefits, including provisions for holidays and vacations with pay, but they still struggled to organize unskilled workers. One of the major losses for unions during this period was the passage of the Taft-Hartley Act in 1947 with the purpose of prohibiting specific union practices, banning closed shops, and opening the door to **right-to-work** states. Even with this rollback on union practices, 35% of nonagricultural workers had joined a union by 1954.

The dual labor market continued to include (1) White men who earned good wages, held stable jobs, and had union protections and (2) everyone else. Most unions still resisted accepting Black, Mexican American, immigrant, and women workers as members. During this period, public-sector unions began to act like traditional trade unions. They included the American Federation of State, County, and Municipal Employees (AFSCME),

Dolores Huerta was one of the most influential labor organizers and civil rights activists of the twentieth century. After briefly teaching elementary school, she co-founded with Cesar Chavez the United Farm Workers to support the Latino/a farm worker community in California.

**SOURCE:** Kathy Hutchins/Shutterstock

the American Federation of Teachers, and the National Education Association, which was the largest union for teachers and included more women and people of color than other unions. In 1962, César Chávez formed the United Farm Workers Association in California with dedicated organizers Dolores Huerta and Larry Itliong. They organized a boycott of California grapes that resulted in grape growers signing a contract with the farm workers (Dubofsky & McCartin, 2017).

By 1955, the two major industrial unions merged into the AFL-CIO that continues today to organize both skilled and unskilled workers and lobby on their behalf from a national office in Washington, DC. Although automation in many of the industries in which union members worked was beginning to reduce the number of needed workers in the 1960s, the unions had many legislative victories for progressive social legislation under Presidents John F. Kennedy and Lyndon B. Johnson. They were among the most effective lobbyers for Johnson's War on Poverty, which led to passage of Medicare, Medicaid, Head Start, the Elementary and Secondary Education Act, the Economic Opportunity Act that provided Job Corps and work-training assistance, and the Immigration and Nationality Act that removed the quota systems that had governed immigration. The United States had created an affluent society with union members who now had steadily rising wages, fringe benefits, and job security that placed many of them in the middle class. By the end of the 1960s, these factors and economic policies that supported families with low incomes had pulled millions of people above the poverty line (Dubofsky & McCartin, 2017).

## Losing Ground Again

By the 1970s, the expansion of equality came to an end. With the election of Richard Nixon as president, minimal protections for people with low incomes were dramatically reduced. In the 1973 case *San Antonio Independent School District v. Rodriguez*, the U.S. Supreme Court allowed unequal funding of schools in Texas because education was not a fundamental right in the Constitution. Wealth again became increasingly stratified. The welfare system was dividing the country as Nixon supporters complained that "welfare 'breeds weak people'" (Isenberg, 2017, p. 275) who don't want to work. They ignored the fact that many adults in poverty were already working hard at low-paying jobs below the poverty level. Single mothers argued that government assistance was needed to help provide for child care and prevent starvation (Isenberg, 2017). Even with this declining support for union organizing, unions still represented around 25% of the workforce at the end of the 1980s (Krugman, 2021).

Industries began moving to the nonunion South and to other countries with right-to-work laws and cheaper labor, leaving cities and towns in the Great Lakes states with many unemployed workers. Service jobs were growing, and technological innovations substituted capital for human labor. Blue-collar employment was falling, and incomes had become more unequal than they had been for 60 years (Dubofsky & McCartin, 2017). Strikebreaking by employers became more prevalent after President Ronald Reagan crushed the strike of the Professional Air Traffic Controllers Organization and declared that the strikers would never be rehired to their former positions. By the end of the twentieth century, union membership had decreased to 10% of the labor force, and unions were experiencing few successes in organizing workers in nonmanufacturing and technology sectors (Dubofsky & McCartin, 2017).

After 9/11, the economy slowed further, and wages began to lag behind prices. The federal government began to subcontract services to private agencies without unions and waived collective bargaining rights for the new Department of Homeland Security and Transportation Security Administration screeners. When the Great Recession hit in 2007, many workers again lost their jobs or had their wages reduced and, as a result, lost their homes when they no longer could pay their mortgages. The working class and middle class were frustrated with the government. The system was perpetuating the privileges of the wealthy. The bankers whose practices had led to the Great Recession were not prosecuted, and hedge fund managers were paying lower tax rates than their secretaries (Sitaraman, 2017). The people experiencing wage increases were primarily people with higher education or graduate degrees.

During President Barack Obama's term, laws were passed to eliminate gender wage discrimination in employment, provide more jobs through an economic stimulus bill, make health insurance available to a larger proportion of the population with the Affordable Care Act, and raise the minimum wage to $10.10 for all federal contractors. But little other progress was made in improving the economic status of the majority of workers. In 2010, the Supreme Court granted more power to the wealthy and corporations when it gave them the authority to spend unlimited amounts of money on ads and other political tools for an individual running for political office in *Citizens United v. Federal Election Commission*. By 2021, only a little more than 5% of private-sector workers were union members (Gould, 2022). By 2022, 28 states had adopted right-to-work laws (FindLaw, 2022). Nevertheless, workers at Starbucks, McDonalds, Amazon, and other companies were fighting for the right to union representation, losing in some localities and winning in others.

Teacher unions have had similar experiences as the rest of the labor force. After *A Nation at Risk: The Imperative for Educational Reform* was released by President Reagan's National Commission on Excellence in Education in 1983, educational reform movements across the country began to undercut teacher unions and create charter schools. Some hope for the revival of the union movement came with the 2012 strike by the Chicago Teachers Union, which garnered public support and ended in teachers winning major concessions. However, a setback occurred in 2018 in *Janus v. AFSCME* when the U.S. Supreme Court overturned a 1977 decision that had allowed unions to charge fees to nonunion members, which many feared would reduce the number of union members. However, teachers regained their voices in numerous strikes across the country in 2018 as more than 485,000 teachers participated in work stoppages, often in statewide strikes in Arizona, Colorado, Kentucky, North Carolina, Oklahoma, and West Virginia (Van Dam, 2019). Strikes over pay, mental health support, and staffing ratios resumed again in numerous districts as teachers returned to in-person teaching after the COVID-19 pandemic subsided in 2022 (Will, 2022).

Public support for unions is stronger today than in the past 55 years. A recent Gallup Poll found that 71% of the respondents approved of labor unions, although only 16% of the U.S. population live in a household with at least one union member (McCarthy, 2022). Strong unions continue to support the interests of workers, which is of critical importance in a healthy democracy.

# The Intersection of Class with Race and Ethnicity, Gender, and Age

**Learning Objective 3.4** Probe the intersectionality of class with race and ethnicity, gender, and age and its impact on inequality.

Equality is often espoused as an important American value. We have seen ourselves as a classless society in which all individuals have an equal status, regardless of the economic status of their families. However, the United States is not living up to this ideal.

**Figure 3.7** Characteristics of the U.S. Population in Poverty, 2020

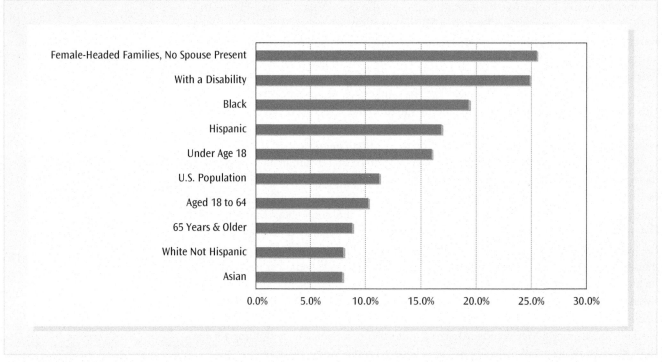

**SOURCE:** Shrider et al. (2021).

The gap between the country's wealthiest residents and all others has grown significantly over the past four decades, making us one of the most unequal industrial countries in the world. Poverty persists in the country, especially for the young, people of color, women, and workers in low-status jobs, as shown in Figure 3.7. People in poverty or with low incomes are a very heterogeneous group. To many, their ethnicity or religion is the most important determinant of the way they live within the economic constraints of poverty. To others, the devastating impact of limited resources is the greatest influence in determining their lifestyles, which are limited severely by the economic constraints they encounter in their daily lives. In this section, we examine the intersection of economic inequalities across social groups in the United States.

## Racial and Ethnic Inequality

The Great Recession that began in 2007 was devastating to almost everyone, but its impact on groups of color and low-income families has been the most difficult to overcome. The wealth that was lost when financial companies foreclosed on their homes can take decades to replace. The recovery of wealth becomes even more difficult for families whose incomes are not equal to others based on their race. In 2020, which includes the first year of the pandemic, Black families earned 60% of the $96,168 median income of White non-Hispanic families; Hispanic families earned 62%, and Asian families earned 114% (U.S. Census Bureau, 2021c). One of the reasons for these income differences is that people of color are more likely to work in low-paying jobs, as shown in Figure 3.8. Black and Latino/a workers are heavily overrepresented in the semi-skilled and unskilled positions. Even though the gap between the incomes of White, Black, and Latino/a families decreases with more education, Black and Latino/a families still do not catch up with the incomes of White families.

During the Great Recession in 2007, many people of color had their wealth dramatically reduced as banks and mortgage lenders foreclosed on their homes, in great part due to the unethical behavior of those lenders who charged high mortgage rates

**Figure 3.8** Workers by Specific Racial and Ethnic Groups and Job Category, 2021

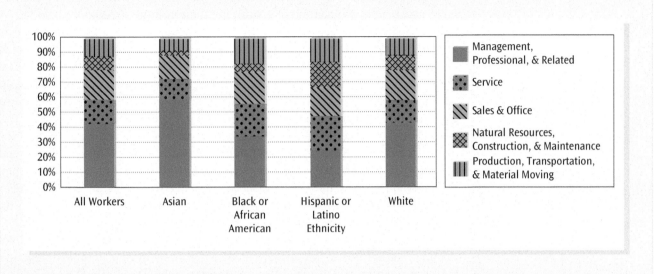

**SOURCE:** U.S. Bureau of Labor Statistics (2022a).

that continued to increase during the recession. Black and Hispanic families lost nearly half of their wealth during this period—almost twice as much as White families lost (McKernan et al., 2014). Differences in the wealth of Black, Hispanic, and White families didn't begin with the Great Recession. Government policies and discriminatory practices by financial institutions have made it much easier for White families to purchase homes for generations, as was discussed in Chapter 2. At times, Black families were prohibited from buying a home or accumulating wealth (Goldblum & Shaddox, 2021).

Many Black and Hispanic families today still face obstacles to homeownership. They are often charged higher mortgage rates, and their homes are undervalued when they are ready to sell them if they live in a specific community (Jan, 2022). These discriminatory policies and practices have led to much lower levels of wealth for families of color. For example, White families had a median net worth of about $188,000 compared to $24,000 for Black families in 2019—almost eight times less than White families (Shiro et al., 2022). Lower levels of wealth make it very difficult to handle the severity of economic shocks such as losing a job, repairing a roof leak, replacing an appliance, caring for a sick child, or weathering a pandemic.

Although more White non-Hispanic people are in poverty (15.9 million) than any other group, the percentage of White people in poverty is less than any group other than Asians. Of the White non-Hispanic population, 8.2% fall below the poverty level, compared with 19.5% of Black people, 17% of Hispanic people, and 8.1% of Asian American people (Shrider et al., 2021).

This inequitable condition is perpetuated by several factors. Students from low-income families are more likely not to graduate from high school, limiting their income potential. High school completion and college attendance are more correlated with the income and education of the parents than with any other factors. Continuing discrimination against groups of color contributes to fewer opportunities to learn at high levels, which results in lower academic achievement, lower educational attainment, and lower-status jobs. Even though the gaps in educational attainment have narrowed among racial and ethnic groups since the 1970s, only 74% of American Indian and Alaska Native students, 80% of Black students, and 82% of Hispanic students graduate from high school within 4 years after entering as first-year students compared to 89% of White students and 93% of Asian and Pacific Islander students (National Center for Education Statistics [NCES], 2022a).

## Gender Inequality

As a group, women earn less and are more likely to suffer from poverty than any other group, with women of color suffering the greatest oppression. The origins of such inequality, however, are different from inequality based on race and ethnicity. Institutional discrimination based on gender began in a patriarchal society in which women's roles were mother and wife. Overt discrimination against women resulted in the use of gender to determine wages, hiring, and promotion of individuals using mechanisms similar to those that promote inequality for members of other oppressed groups. Until recently, this status limited their job opportunities and kept their wages lower than those of men. Although the number of women in most professions except engineering and technology has grown over the past 50 years, they remain overrepresented in jobs such as personal care, food service, health support, and teaching, especially at the early childhood and elementary levels. They are underrepresented in the production and science, technology, engineering, and mathematics (STEM) jobs that generate higher earnings than traditional women's jobs.

Women, especially those who are single heads of household, are more likely than men to fall below the poverty level. Nearly one in four families maintained by women without a spouse earn an income below the official poverty level (U.S. Census Bureau, 2021a). The large number of families in this group is a result of a combination of low-paying jobs, a single wage earner in the family, and an increase in the number of single mothers. Households headed by women without a spouse earn a median income of $43,895, which is only 73% of the median income of men without spouses who head households and 43% of the median income of a married couple (U.S. Census Bureau, 2021f).

Today young men, especially those at the bottom of the economic ladder, also face inequalities that impact their economic status. They are less likely than young women to graduate from high school or attend and graduate from college. Boys and young men are more likely to be placed in special education programs. Young men of color are more likely than White young men to be killed by police and incarcerated for similar crimes. A recent study at the Brookings Institution found that "boys raised in families in the bottom fifth of the income distribution are less likely than girls either to be employed or to move up the income ladder once they become adults" (Reeves & Nzau, 2021, p. 2).

## Age Inequality

Both women and men earn their maximum income between ages 45 and 54. The income of women remains fairly constant throughout much of their working lives, whereas the income for a large percentage of men increases dramatically during their lifetimes. The highest incidence of poverty occurs for young people, as shown in Figure 3.9, with 16.1% of the population under 18 years old in poverty. The youngest children are most likely to live in poverty. Nearly one in six children who are 6 years old and younger live in families who are in poverty. Half of those children live in extreme poverty, which makes them food and housing insecure and lacking essential health care (Children's Defense Fund, 2021). At the other end of the age continuum, the difference in poverty rates is most equal across racial and ethnic groups after they reach age 65 (U.S. Census Bureau, 2021b).

Children's class status depends on their families, leaving children little or no control over their destiny during their early years. Research indicates that families in the United States need an income of about twice as much as the U.S. poverty threshold, which was $18,310 for a family of two with one child and $27,750 for a family of four with two children in 2022 (DHHS, 2022). The National Center for Children in Poverty at Columbia University reports that 38% of all U.S. children lived in low-income families

**Figure 3.9** Persons in Poverty by Age and Race/Ethnicity, 2020

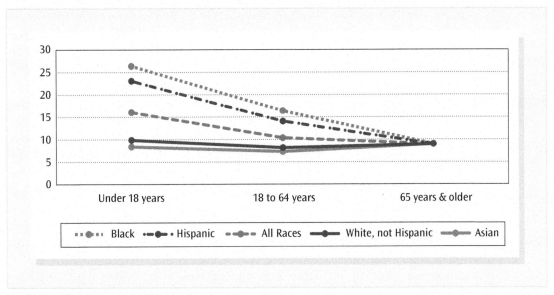

**SOURCE:** U.S. Census Bureau (2021b).

**Figure 3.10** Percentage of U.S. Children Under 18 Years Old Living in Low-Income* Families, 2019

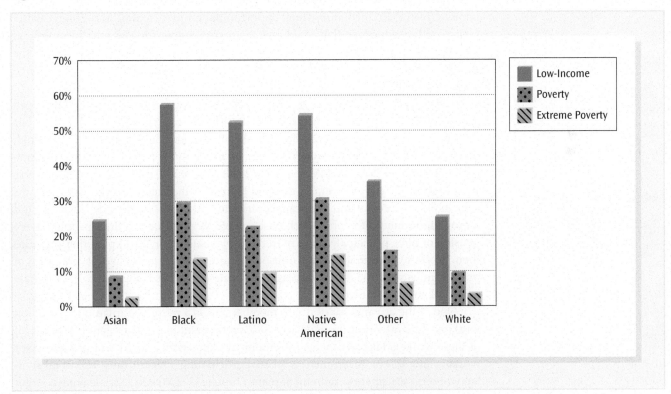

*Low income is defined as family income less than twice the federal poverty level. Poverty is defined as family income below the federal poverty threshold, which was $25,926 in 2019. Extreme poverty is defined as family income below one-half of the federal poverty threshold.

**SOURCE:** Koball et al. (2021).

in 2019, with 17% of all children living below the poverty level and 7% living in extreme poverty. As shown in Figure 3.10, Black and Native American children are over three times as likely to be raised in families that live in extreme poverty, which is 50% of the federal poverty level (Koball et al., 2021).

In schools, poverty is tracked, in part by the number of students eligible for free or reduced-price lunches (FRPL). Children who are eligible for free meals are in families with incomes that are below 130% of the poverty level. If they are in families with incomes between 130 and 185% of the poverty level, they are eligible for a reduced-price meal. Just over half of U.S. students are eligible for FRPL. Although the percentage of low-income families with children is higher in urban areas, low-income families are also found in suburbs, towns, and rural areas. Low-poverty schools are defined as those in which fewer than 25% of the students are eligible for FRPL; in high-poverty schools, more than 75% of the students are eligible. Twenty-four percent of the nation's public school students attended a high-poverty school and 21% attended a low-poverty school in fall 2019. Latino/a and Black students were 5.3 and 5.4 times, respectively, more likely than White students to attend a high-poverty school. Asian and White students were 5.5 and 4.2 times, respectively, more likely to attend low-poverty schools than Black students (NCES, 2021).

What is the impact of poverty on students in schools? Low-poverty schools are twice as likely to have no reported violent incidents. There is greater racial and ethnic diversity among staff in high-poverty schools, with more Black and Latino/a principals and teachers. The real inequality is in the academic area. During the COVID-19 pandemic, student performance on national reading and mathematics assessments declined from previous years. However, the performance of students continued to differ across economic, racial, and ethnic groups. On average, students who are eligible for the National School Lunch Program do not perform as well on the National Assessment of Educational Progress (NAEP) assessments as their peers who live in more affluent families (NAEP, 2022b), limiting their opportunities for participating in the high-quality postsecondary education that could give them greater access to jobs with incomes that could pull them out of poverty. For example, 21% of low-income students read at the proficient or advanced level in fourth grade in 2019 compared to 51% of higher-income students (NAEP, 2022a).

The proportion of the U.S. population that is younger than 18 years old has been gradually decreasing to 22% whereas the proportion who are 65 years and older has steadily increased to 17% in 2020. By 2030, all baby boomers will be at least 65 years old, and by 2034, the number of seniors is projected to outnumber children for the first time and will continue to expand (Vespa et al., 2020). Figure 3.10 indicates that the poverty level is lower for people over 65 years old than any other age. Government programs such as Social Security and Medicare contribute to this drop in the poverty level, and a growing number of people work past age 65. More affluent retired people have a pension or have participated in a retirement plan such as a 401(k) plan that provides them access to additional financial resources after they retire. However, only 68% of private industry workers have access to retirement plans as compared to 92% of state and local government workers.

One of the advantages of union membership is a retirement plan; 91% of union workers in private industry have access to a retirement plan. A problem is that not all of these workers take advantage of retirement plans, with only 51% of private-sector workers and 82% of government workers participating. Overall, only 56% of all civilian workers participate in retirement plans (Topoleski & Myers, 2021), leaving a larger proportion of retirees with limited income as they age unless they have accumulated savings on their own. One-quarter of older people live on a "bare-bones" budget and sometimes have to eliminate or limit medication dosages to pay rent and/or buy food. Half of the older people who live alone are in this same situation, disproportionately affecting women and Black, Hispanic, Asian American, Pacific Islander, and LGBTQ+ older adults (RRF Foundation for Aging, 2021).

# Classroom Implications: Providing Equality and Equity Across Socioeconomic Groups

**Learning Objective 3.5**  Create curriculum, instructional strategies, and classroom environments that open opportunities to students from all socioeconomic groups.

Many social reformers, educators, and families view education as a powerful device for achieving social change and reducing poverty. At a global level, the United Nations Educational, Scientific and Cultural Organization (2022) views education as "a basic human right that works to raise men and women out of poverty, level inequalities and ensure sustainable development" (para. 1). Many people see education as the great equalizer, and countries around the world have created public school systems to serve children across socioeconomic levels. The United States has a history of supporting education, but not always for all children. The Boston Latin School was founded as the first public school in 1635. Although communities in Massachusetts established public schools during the colonial period of the country's history, they were not broadly supported until the 1840s, when they were called common schools that admitted primarily White boys and girls. Private academies were established in the 1700s for the White male children of wealthy families. Although most private schools now admit girls and young women, the expensive private schools of the highest quality remain the choice for the education of the children of wealthy families, contributing to the segregation of the wealthy and the inequities in our educational system.

One of the lofty goals of education is to provide both equality and equity for all students. What is the difference between the two terms? Equality is the belief in social, political, and economic rights for all people. The state of being equal is one in which a group is not viewed or treated as inferior or superior to another and all groups have access to the same rights and benefits of society regardless of their group memberships. The core of equity is fairness and justice that are applied in a way that recognizes and responds to the individual needs of people by eliminating policies, practices, and other actions that discriminate against an individual or group. Providing equity in education is an ongoing process in which educators "identify and overcome intentional and unintentional barriers arising from bias or systemic structures" (National Association of Colleges and Employers, 2022, para 1).

How equitable are today's schools? One of the major determinants of educational equity is the funding of schools. In the United States, schools are financially supported by states (47%), local sources (45%), and federal sources (8%) (NCES, 2022b). Local sources are collected through local school district property taxes, which vary greatly based on the incomes of the families living in the district. Local sources sometimes include donations from families and others, which usually supplement inadequate school budgets. State support could make up the differences that exist between low-income and high-income districts, but not all states choose to use their funds for that purpose. Federal sources support programs for students with specific needs such as those in low-income families, whose first language is not English, and students with disabilities.

What other factors contribute to inequities in educational outcomes based on economic differences? Students from low-income families typically take fewer courses in advanced mathematics, science, and college preparation than their more affluent peers (NCES, 2021), which contributes to later disparities in college enrollment and vocational choices. In many schools with large numbers of low-income students, advanced courses in these subjects may be offered, but the number of them is fewer than in affluent schools, and they may lack the academic rigor of more advantaged schools. Thus, low-income students who are high achievers are stifled in their attempts to move to higher levels in the advanced courses available at their schools. It is no wonder that students from low-income families don't score as high on standardized assessments: They lack the opportunity to take the same high-level courses as their middle-class peers, and they often lack high-quality teachers and resources.

It is not just the course inequities that lead to differences in achievement. Low-income students, particularly Black students, are more likely than other students to be suspended or expelled or not be promoted to the next grade (Carnevale et al., 2019). In addition, students from low-income families attend the most inadequately funded schools that are more likely to be infested with insects, mice, and rats; are dirty and not well maintained; and have large classes, the least experienced teachers, and few extracurricular options (Gorski, 2018).

The opportunity gaps between students based on the SES of their families begin early in a child's life. Students from low-income families do not always have access to nutritious balanced meals, medical and dental care, clean environments, and safe and private housing. They are more likely than their more affluent peers to attend schools in areas polluted by industry and traffic. The exposure to air pollutants can impact children's test scores, suspension rates, and absenteeism (Persico, 2019). They are much more likely than their affluent peers to suffer from trauma as a result of homelessness, be a victim of a crime, or experience deaths in their families or communities. These traumas can affect their ability to engage consistently and effectively with the educational process.

Children from low-income families are also less likely to attend preschool as 3- and 4-year-olds than children whose families are at the highest income levels. Even when children from the lowest-income families have high test scores in kindergarten, they have fallen behind their peers from higher-income families by eighth grade. Researchers at Georgetown University's Center on Education and the Workforce found that "early academic preparation can provide a powerful boost, and children who develop and maintain strong academic skills by high school are much more likely than their peers to achieve the American Dream" (Carnevale et al., 2019, p. 33).

Rather than provide equal educational opportunity for all students regardless of their SES, many schools perpetuate existing social and economic inequities in society. They prove over and over that parents' education and income are the best predictors of the academic performance of children and youth. The challenge is to change that pattern so that there is much greater equity across socioeconomic groups and in sharing the positive outcomes of an education. More than school reform is needed to raise the academic achievement of low-SES students. The social and economic conditions of their families' lives must

Suburban schools are more likely than inner-city schools to have the technology, resources, extracurricular activities, and attractive playground space that make a school welcoming to students.

also be improved through higher wages and social policies that support low-income families and create a more equal society (Royce, 2023).

Many stereotypical notions about people in poverty need to be overcome for teachers to effectively serve students from low-income families. Some people believe that individuals and families live in poverty because of their moral failings or because they simply do not want to work. People with low or no incomes are often treated with condescension, not as equals. These perceptions are based on deficit thinking in which the environment and cultures in which people with low incomes live are blamed for instilling social and educational deficiencies in their members. Students are blamed for their educational failures and lack of academic achievement, with no consideration of the larger historical and sociopolitical contexts and ideologies that produce and perpetuate inequities for historically oppressed populations (Davis & Museus, 2019). In this section, we examine five areas that influence socioeconomic equity in schools: teacher expectations, tracking, curriculum, **digital equity**, and support for students experiencing homelessness.

## Teacher Expectations

Ethnographic studies of schools document how students are classified, segregated, and taught differently, starting in their first days in school. Most teachers can identify the personal characteristics of students that will lead to academic success. They then develop instruction and interactions with their students to ensure that the students will, in fact, behave as the teachers expect—a phenomenon called the **self-fulfilling prophecy** or the **Pygmalion effect**. Kindergarten teachers who divide their class into three reading and mathematics groups based on students' academic skills by the third week of school have limited knowledge about the academic abilities of the students. Too often, the groups are organized according to nonacademic factors. Students in the highest group may be dressed in clean clothes that are relatively new and tidy. They interact well with the teacher and other students, are quite verbal, and use Standard English. Students in the lower two groupings may be dressed in unclean clothing or use a dialect or are English learners. Their families may appear to be less stable than those of students in the highest group.

If the teacher's goal is to spend time with students in the lower group to ensure that they develop the language and reading skills they will need to be successful in the first grade, this grouping strategy may be successful. The development of these skills is critical for future academic success. Students who read at grade level by the end of the third grade are three times as likely to graduate from high school (Hernandez, 2011). The problem is that many teachers do not expect the students who are in the lower academic group at the beginning of the year to perform at grade level by the end of the year. The result is that students in the highest group continue to perform better academically. As the teacher had projected, these students are more successful throughout their schooling than students from lower socioeconomic levels.

When teachers make such judgments about students, they take the first step in preventing students from having an equal opportunity for academic achievement. Rather than ensure that they have access to an egalitarian system, such classification and subsequent treatment of students ensure the maintenance of an inequitable system. This action is not congruent with the democratic belief that all students should be provided equal educational opportunities. All students can learn, including those in the lower-ability group; they can learn at the same level as more affluent students with the assistance and support of effective teachers.

Schools are generally middle-class institutions with a **hidden curriculum** that reinforces the behaviors that middle-class students learn at home, allowing them an advantage as they work with middle-class teachers. When students from low-income families do not behave in the same way because they do not know the middle-class rules, teachers' biases can lead to students from low-income families being thought of as less capable than their more affluent peers. They are also more likely to be harshly disciplined and provided with fewer opportunities for high-quality learning (Calarco, 2018).

Too many teachers blame the students, their families, and their communities for students' failure to learn rather than examine and change their own teaching practices to improve student learning. Effective teachers make a difference. Educators should take on the challenge to provide opportunities for students from low-income families to develop the knowledge and skills that will help them learn at high levels. The strategies that teachers use with advanced students will also actively engage students from low-income and middle-income families in their own learning.

All of us have made a false start or stumbled at some period of our life. When we are economically advantaged, however, we are more likely to know people who can help pick us up and steer us along the academic pathway or toward a new job (Carnevale et al., 2019). Students from economically marginalized families are more likely to fall and stay behind. In an ethnographic study of an elementary and middle school, Jessica McCrory Calarco (2018) found that teachers were providing more support to their middle-class students than to their working-class students, often without realizing it, especially at the elementary level. Students from working-class families had been taught "to take responsibility for their own success in school and to avoid burdening teachers with requests for support" (p. 9). As they had been taught at home, middle-class students were more likely to seek help from their teachers, who generally honored their requests. The teachers also responded to the working-class students when they asked for support, but those students asked less often and, when they requested assistance, they were less likely than their middle-class peers to push for more thorough or helpful responses from the teacher. Calarco argues that "middle-class advantage is, at least in part, a *negotiated advantage*" (p. 9). Middle-class students pressured teachers for assistance, accommodations, and attention in excess of what was fair or required, and teachers responded positively to the requests even when they were inclined to say no. In addition, middle-class families regularly intervened with teachers and administrators to secure advantages for their children.

In helping to overcome the stigma of poverty, educators must consciously review their expectations for students. One in five teenagers from low-income families reports not feeling hopeful for the future; many don't believe they have a chance of earning a middle-class income (Carnevale et al., 2019). Students' feelings of low esteem should not be reinforced by teachers. Seeing students as individuals rather than as members of a specific socioeconomic group may assist educators in overcoming the **classism** that exists in the school and the community. Information about a student's family background can be used to understand the power of environment on a student's expression of self; it should not be used to rationalize stereotypes and label students. Educators should become aware of any prejudices they themselves hold against members of lower socioeconomic groups and work to overcome their biases. Otherwise, discriminatory practices will surface in the classroom in the form of self-fulfilling prophecies that harm students and perpetuate inequities.

## Tracking

Tracking students into different groups or classes based on their intellectual achievement or other factors, which were described in the previous section, is a common educational practice. Teachers divide a class into smaller groups for instructional purposes. These groups could have a heterogeneous makeup, with each group containing students of all genders from different racial and ethnic groups and students who are currently high and low achievers. In these groups, students could help each other. In other cases, teachers may assign students to a group based on their perception of the students' academic achievement, which may be based on students' latest standardized test scores. Teachers may use different instructional strategies in these groups and may have different expectations for learning outcomes.

Supporters of tracking argue that separating students based on their perceived academic achievement allows teachers to better meet the needs of all students. Critics argue that tracking and homogeneous grouping based on achievement is discriminatory and prevents many students from developing their intellectual and social potential.

Tracking is an area in which class matters. High academic achievement appears to be more closely related to race and class than to intellectual potential. Students whose families are already privileged benefit the most from tracking. Students in advanced programs are academically challenged in their courses with enrichment activities that encourage them to develop their intellectual and critical thinking skills. At the other end of the learning spectrum, the learning environment is often uninviting, boring, and not challenging. Rather than prepare students to move to higher-level courses, these courses keep them at the lowest levels of academic achievement.

Student achievement is diminished when students are placed in a class where teacher expectations for students' academic achievement are low. Students in this group have limited access to rigorous courses and to rich and creative experiences that will enhance their opportunities for learning. Critical thinking tasks are reserved for the students for whom teachers have higher academic expectations. Oral recitation and structured written work are common in groups or classes of students for whom academic expectations are low. Students are exposed to knowledge at a slower pace than their peers in other groups, and the knowledge is low in status, causing them to fall further behind in subjects like mathematics and the sciences.

Teachers in classrooms with low academic expectations often spend more time on administration and discipline and less time actually teaching. Student behavior in these tracks is generally more disruptive than in other groups. However, this probably happens, in part, because students and teachers have developed behavioral standards that are more tolerant of inattention and not because of students' individual abilities. To compound the problem, the more experienced and more successful teachers are disproportionately assigned to the groups for which academic expectations are high. Unfortunately, many teachers view students for which they have high expectations positively and other students negatively.

Disproportionately large numbers of students from lower socioeconomic levels are assigned to groups or classes for which academic expectations are low beginning very early in their school careers. Even more tragic is the fact that the number of students from low-income families who are classified as being students with an intellectual disability is disproportionately high. This inequitable classification places students of color in double jeopardy because they also disproportionately come from low-income families.

In many schools with diverse student populations, students are segregated based on race, ethnicity, class, and language into separate tracks within the school. White and Asian students have disproportionately high representation in Advanced Placement and International Baccalaureate programs, while Black and Latino/a students, students from low-income families, and English learners comprise the majority of the students in classrooms where academic expectations are low. For the most part, the courts have agreed with plaintiffs that tracking students into these courses and programs is a discriminatory practice that limits their educational opportunities and their potential for later occupational and economic success. Even when students and families are encouraged to choose courses, a school district may be liable for discriminatory action if families have not been appropriately informed of the prerequisites for advanced courses. Other discriminatory practices that are being reviewed by courts today are the inadequate preparation of students from families with low incomes and students of color to pass standardized tests and the assignment of unqualified teachers to the schools in which these students are concentrated.

## Curriculum for Equality

Although it is essential to ensure that all students learn the subject matter, how these skills are taught can vary depending on the cultures of students and the communities in which students live. The curriculum should build on the lived experiences of students

# Explore and Focus Your Cultural Lens

## Debate: Should Schools Be Detracked?

Data in many schools shows that the children of upper middle-class families are overrepresented in Advanced Placement and other courses for students who are high academic achievers and under-represented in special education and general education courses. School officials are being pushed by the courts to change their practices that segregate students by SES or race. One of the remedies for eliminating these discriminatory practices is **detracking**, or dismantling tracks for students based on ability, as determined by standardized tests or teachers' perceptions. Some teachers and middle-class families resist the move to a single track in which students from different academic groups are mixed, in part because they use tracking to negotiate advantages for their children.

Opinions about these strategies differ. Some people believe that detracking will provide greater equality of opportunity across economic and racial and ethnic groups, while others believe that it will lead to a lower quality of education overall. Do you think schools should be detracked? Why or why not? What do you think the impact of detracking would be on the school and the students from low-income and high-income families in the school community?

### FOR

- Eliminates discrimination against students from low-income families and students of color.
- Integrates students from different socioeconomic, racial, and ethnic groups and ability levels.
- Encourages classroom instruction that is challenging and interesting for students from families with low-incomes and students from families who are affluent.
- Supports a classroom environment in which high-ability students learn while assisting peers who may not be at the same academic level.

- Provides students from families with low incomes greater access to effective teachers, improving their chances for learning at higher levels.

### AGAINST

- Is not fair to high-ability students, who need to be challenged at advanced levels.
- Makes it more difficult for teachers to provide appropriate instruction for all students, whose abilities differ greatly.
- May lead to pressure from upper middle-class families, who may withdraw their children from public schools.
- Waters down the curriculum for high-ability students.
- Prevents high-ability students from participating in advanced courses that will give them the advantage needed to be admitted to elite colleges and universities.

## Questions for Discussion

1. How do schools ensure that the voices of families with low and middle incomes are included in discussions about detracking and the provision of educational equity in schools?

2. How does detracking schools contribute to the provision of equal educational opportunity?

3. What other steps could school officials take to provide students from low-income families greater access to advanced and engaging courses?

4. What are your reasons for supporting or not supporting detracking strategies in schools?

to be both engaging and relevant. Helping students achieve academically in schools that serve students from low-income families requires competent educators who know deeply the subjects they teach and believe that all students can learn. To be an effective teacher in communities characterized by poverty, you should examine your own biases, assumptions, and knowledge gaps that may affect how you work with the children and their families in those communities, especially when their race, ethnicity, religious, or native languages or dialects are different from your own.

Achievement can be improved when teachers help students interact with the academic content through discussion and **authenticity**—relating the content to students' prior experiences and real-world applications. Other teaching strategies that have been found effective for low-income students include **cooperative learning** and participatory, inquiry-driven, problem-solving instruction that is relevant to their lives. They respond favorably to interactive or **dialogic** discussions that allow them to discuss topics in depth and develop critical thinking skills (Gorski, 2018).

Being sensitive to the history and experiences of low-income families and communities helps teachers connect with working-class students and students living in poverty (Calarco, 2018). The curriculum should reflect accurately the class structure and inequities that exist in the United States and the world. The existence of nearly half the population is not validated in the curricula of most schools. Curricula and textbooks usually focus on the values and experiences of a middle-class society. They highlight the heroes of our capitalist and political system, who were primarily White males from economically privileged families. They usually ignore the history and heroes of the labor struggle in this country, in which laborers resisted and endured under great odds to improve their conditions. They generally do not discuss the role of the working class in the development of the nation. The inequities based on the income and wealth of one's family are usually neither described nor discussed. In classrooms, students should learn of the existence of these differences.

If students never see their communities in the activities, films, and books used in class, their motivation and acceptance may be limited. All students should be encouraged to read novels and short stories about people from different socioeconomic levels. When studying historical or current events, they should examine the events from the perspective of the working class and people in poverty as well as from the perspective of the middle class, upper middle class, and the country's leaders.

School is not the only place where students learn about life. Students who live in communities in which high-poverty schools are located often have strengths that are not recognized by many educators. Many students are very **resilient** under conditions that present obstacles to their well-being and academic achievement. Differences in school behavior and learning among students from dissimilar socioeconomic levels are strongly dependent on the knowledge and skills needed to survive appropriately in their community environments. Most low-income students, especially those in urban areas, have learned how to live in a world that is not imaginable to most middle-class students or teachers. Yet the knowledge and skills they bring to school are not always valued. Educators should recognize the value of the community's informal education in supporting each other and their children.

All students, no matter what their SES, should be helped to develop strong and positive self-concepts. Many students do not realize the diversity that exists in this country, let alone understand the reasons for the diversity and the resulting discrimination against some groups. Middle-class children tend to believe that most people live like their families. Educators are expected to expand their students' knowledge of the world, not to hide from them the realities that exist because of class differences. In a classroom in which democracy and equity are important, low-income students should receive priority time from teachers and have access to the necessary resources to help them become academically competitive with middle-class students. Educators should recognize when students from low-income families are struggling and provide assistance and support to ensure they are learning rather than waiting for them to request assistance (Calarco, 2018).

Finally, all students should be encouraged to be critical of what they read, see, and hear in textbooks, through the mass media, and from their families and friends. Although teachers traditionally talk about the democratic vision, they generally are unwilling to model it. Students and teachers who become involved through the curriculum in asking why the inequities in society exist are beginning to think critically about our democracy. To work effectively in high-poverty schools will require you "to be persistent, nonjudgmental, a good listener, open-minded, a problem-solver, a networker, a relationship builder, and someone who is not easily dissuaded by difficult bureaucracies, frustrating situations, or horrific events" (Haberman et al., 2018, p. 12).

## Digital Equity

With the onslaught of the COVID-19 pandemic in 2020, most teachers and students were forced on a moment's notice to teach and learn in a digital environment as schools across the country and world were closed to limit the spread of the virus.

Although the **digital divide** or **digital inequity** across groups of people has existed since the first laptops were introduced in the 1970s, the divide became very pronounced as the pandemic affected everyone's life. Owning a computer allowed many people to work from home and students to attend classes virtually. It allowed people to virtually attend business meetings with colleagues and keep in touch with friends. Almost all adults and many children in the United States have cell phones, although not always smartphones (Pew Research Center, 2021), but attending class, conducting a meeting, reading lengthy documents, and completing forms are somewhat difficult to do on a cell phone.

When schools opened again with online education, educators quickly learned that not all students and not all teachers had access to a computer, which led to many school districts distributing laptops or tablets to students. Soon another problem surfaced. Many students and teachers did not have access to the Internet, requiring them to attend classes in wired parking lots or buildings. Students who lived in homes with one or more computers and access to the internet may have had to share computers with each other and their parents or caretakers if they were working from home, making it impossible for all members of the family to use a limited number of computers at the same time. The result of the digital divide was the inability of some students to attend classes online and the loss of learning as a result. One of the positive outcomes of this period was that both teachers and students became more competent in the use of technology for instruction. Hopefully, teachers can become even more competent at using technology effectively to support learning in both in-person and virtual educational settings.

Before the pandemic, educators had to pay attention to homework assignments to ensure that students without computers or internet access would have the opportunity to complete assignments that required the use of the Internet. When many classrooms became virtual in 2020, access to computers and the Internet became essential to attendance and learning. Without access, many students were not able to progress academically at the same level as before the pandemic closed schools. Tests of the academic progress of 9-year-olds in reading and mathematics found modest drops from previous years of around three points in math and two points for high performers compared to drops of 12 and 10 points in math and reading, respectively, for the lowest performers (NAEP, 2022b). In another study conducted for Congress by the U.S. Government Accounting Office (2022), teachers reported "that more of their students started the 2020–21 school year behind and made less academic progress" (p. iii) during the year, ending the year behind grade level.

Not all students attended school remotely during the pandemic. About half (49%) of 8- to 18-year-olds in the United States reported attending school fully or mostly online and another 38% reported attending school remotely for at least part of the time. Thirteen percent reported attending school in person throughout the pandemic. Sixty-one percent of students from lower-income families attended school remotely fully or mostly online as compared to 44% of higher-income students. Black (58%) and Hispanic (67%) students, who disproportionately live in low-income families, attended school online fully or mostly online, while only 35% of White students did (Rideout & Robb, 2021). Although students in low-income families were more likely than other students to attend school online, they were more likely not to have a computer at home and not have broadband in their homes, as shown in Figure 3.11, making it difficult to attend class regularly and complete assignments.

Families with low incomes suffer the most from not having computers and Internet access because they are used not only for virtual education but to visit medical staff, to schedule vaccinations, and to complete job applications and many other forms that previously were completed and filed with an in-person visit. Many families with low incomes may not be eligible for a credit card that is required to order merchandise online and participate in services such as ridesharing. Three reasons are usually cited for the digital divide: affordability, availability, and adoption (Ali et al., 2021). The families

**Figure 3.11** Student Access to Computers and Broadband at Home

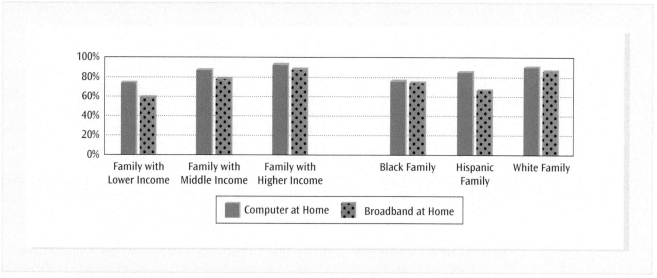

SOURCE: Rideout and Robb (2021).

of up to 60% of the students who do not have computers or are not connected to the Internet simply cannot afford the equipment, installation costs, or monthly fee.

An estimated 25% of the disconnected students live in areas not served by a broadband company or experience intermittent or poor-quality Internet service. The lack of availability of service disproportionately affects Native American students and students who live in rural areas, especially those who live in Alabama, Arkansas, Oklahoma, and Mississippi. This lack of availability is due, in part, to a pattern of "digital redlining" in which Internet companies underinvest in communities that are lower income (Ali et al., 2021). An estimated 40% of disconnected students choose not to access internet services even though they are widely available and affordable for reasons such as the lack of digital skills, language barriers, concerns about sharing personal data, or just a lack of interest (Ali et al., 2021).

Because digital tools are so critical to living and working today, it is very important that all members of society have access to them. All students and adults should have opportunities to expand their digital literacy for both personal and occupational purposes. Every household should have access to a robust Internet connection. Students should be able to attend school virtually or in-person and learn to use technology effectively in either type of school. Teachers should use technology to plan engaging lessons and help *all* students use technology to conduct research and expand their knowledge base. *All* students, not just students from affluent families or who are academically advanced, should be encouraged to use technology for graphing, problem solving, and other higher-order thinking activities to stimulate their creativity and curiosity (Hiefield & Carter, 2021). Federal funds that were available to schools and communities during the pandemic has helped to close the digital divide between groups of people, but they primarily supported short-term projects (Ali et al., 2021). The Infrastructure Investment and Jobs Act passed by Congress in 2022 also includes $65 billion to expand broadband access to underserved areas of the country.

## Support for Students Who Are Experiencing Homelessness

Families and youth may hide their homelessness, in part because of shame. Therefore, knowing which children are experiencing homelessness has been difficult for a number of school districts. One complicating factor is that families often don't know when they will be forced on short notice to leave a shelter, abandoned building, or tent to find new shelter. Around 1.3 million students experiencing homelessness, which is nearly 3% of the student population, were enrolled in public schools in 2019–2020. Even though they may miss school more often than their peers and may be enrolled in several schools during the year, they identify school as the most stable aspect of their lives (Hallett & Skrla, 2017).

Students experiencing homelessness report that it has had a great effect on their education (Ingram et al., 2016). They may find it difficult to access clean clothes, take showers, and arrange transportation to school. Furthermore, they are more likely to be victimized, exploited, and exposed to drugs, alcohol, and sexual activity (Hallett & Skrla, 2017). As a result of the trauma in their lives, they "may have a difficult time fully engaging in the educational process without additional supports" (Hallett & Skrla, 2017, p. 12) or having access to those helping hands available to students from higher-income families. They tend to be invisible in schools, not fully participating in the classroom or in school activities. They often qualify for special education at disproportionately high rates, most often being identified as having emotional/behavior disorders or learning disabilities. Although most of them say that they want to complete high school and attend college, they are not always able to attend school regularly, and completing homework in a shelter or an overcrowded hotel room can be very challenging. Just 64% of students experiencing homelessness graduate from high school within 4 years compared to the national average of 84% of all students and 78% of their low-income peers (Education Leads Home, 2019).

The **McKinney-Vento Homeless Assistance Act**, passed by Congress in 1987, requires public schools to recognize the educational rights of and provide protection for children and youth experiencing homelessness, including students living with relatives or friends because they have lost their housing. The law requires school districts to provide free transportation for these students to remain in the schools they attended before becoming homeless if requested by their families or guardians. A school cannot deny enrollment to students who are homeless because they do not have school records, immunization records, proof of residency, or other documents. The McKinney-Vento Act ensures that students experiencing homelessness have access to schooling and are not denied services such as free meals because of circumstances beyond their control. Schools and school districts cannot segregate students because of their residential instability. The school district's liaison for students experiencing homelessness should serve as an advocate for them, assisting them in accessing available services in the school system and community. This legislation has made a difference. Many more students are being identified and supported today than before 1987.

## Revisiting the Opening Case Study

When Mr. Loftis talked with the school counselor about Christina, he was reminded that the school district has a liaison to work with students experiencing homelessness. The counselor agreed that she would make sure the liaison knew Christina's situation and would confirm that the liaison would work with Christina about returning to school. In some schools, teachers organize clothing drives and food pantries to assist students and their families. In the elementary school in which the daughter of one of this text's authors taught, one of the experienced teachers periodically would leave coats or clothing for a special event on the chairs of her students. Even though this charitable work is likely to be valued by students and families, teachers are not required to use their own money or time for these purposes. Teachers may choose to

volunteer to work with the school's parent–teacher organization or a community or faith-based group on projects such as food pantries or marches to improve the environmental conditions of the community. However, schools should not rely on teachers' voluntary contributions to avoid examining and helping to change the inequities that led to the impoverished and often unsafe conditions in which students live.

Increasing the number of jobs in which families can earn a living wage will be critical to improving not only the well-being of students and their families but the educational opportunities available to students whose families have low incomes, or are working class or middle class. That means that economic conditions will need to improve for the lower half of the income and wealth earners in the country. That is a task that will involve employers and the nation's policymakers, but teachers can contribute to that project as they fight for more equitable funding for the education of all students. It also will require critiquing their own curriculum and classroom practices to ensure they support the academic and social-emotional growth of all students regardless of their families' SES.

## Reflect and Apply

1. In schools that you have attended or observed, how have teachers or other school professionals assisted children or youth who are experiencing homelessness or are impoverished?

2. If you had students experiencing homelessness in your classroom, how could you support them in ways that wouldn't embarrass them?

3. What activities or supports could schools provide to assist families in the community who suffer from poverty or have experienced a devastating event?

4. What is economic injustice, and why is it so prevalent in the United States?

# Summary

- Socioeconomic status (SES) is a composite representing the economic status of a family or of unrelated individuals based on income, wealth, occupation, educational attainment, and power. Where a family falls along this continuum can affect the way its members live, how they think and act, and the way others react to them.

- Class is a system of sorting society into groups that share the same or similar SES with unequal access to economic, political, cultural, and social resources. Individual choice is most limited for those who are in poverty and who can barely meet essential needs. People of color and women who head families are more likely than other groups to earn low wages or be unemployed and experiencing homelessness. The working class and middle class are distinguished by the type of work their members do, but the majority of the population consider themselves middle class. The affluent in society are the upper middle class of professionals and administrators who have many advantages but not the income and wealth of the members of the upper class, who protect their power and privilege.

- People in poverty and with low income historically have been negatively labeled and disparaged in society. The federal government and the courts have sometimes supported initiatives for increasing people's ability to earn a living wage and, at other times, they have favored the wealthy and provided much less support for such policies. Around the Revolutionary War, skilled artisans formed trade societies to negotiate with employers for higher wages, shorter work hours, and better working conditions, calling for strikes when their proposals were ignored. Later those societies became today's labor unions, which lobby Congress for policies favorable to the labor force and negotiate for wages,

fringe benefits, and better working conditions for their members. The teachers' unions surged again in 2018 to fight for increased funding for the improvement of education for children and youth and for their own higher wages and better working conditions, which had been declining since 2007.

- The populations most likely to suffer from income inequality are people of color, children, and single mothers with children. Forty percent of the population are low income or impoverished, struggling to meet their basic needs from week to week. In the United States, almost one in five children under 18 years old lives in poverty, which is among the highest poverty rates in developed countries.

- Disproportionately large numbers of students from lower-SES levels are tracked into low-achievement groups in their early school years. Too often, low-income students are placed in remedial programs because of discriminatory testing and placement. Educators should consciously review their expectations for students and their behavior toward those from different SES levels to ensure they are not discriminating. The curriculum does not serve students well if it reflects only the perspectives of the middle and upper middle class. Students from families with low incomes need to see their own cultural experiences reflected in the curriculum. They also need to have access to the digital equipment and the Internet necessary to complete assignments and attend classes virtually. Without this technology for all students, inequities in learning and preparation for the future are perpetuated in schools. In addition, schools are required to identify and support students experiencing homelessness in ways that will encourage them to continue their education.

## Pearson eTextbook Application Videos

The following videos are available in the Pearson eTextbook and can be used to practice observing and applying what you learned in this chapter.

**Pearson eTextbook Application**
### Video Example 3.2

In this video, an educator discusses her view on student perspectives of social class in the classroom. Focus as she discusses the role teachers may play in helping support students of all social classes.

**Pearson eTextbook Application**
### Video Example 3.3

In this video, Dr. Irma Olmedo discusses the different views of formal schooling as a tool of social mobility.

# Chapter 4
# Gender

## Learning Objectives

*As you read this chapter, you should be able to:*

**4.1** Understand the diverse gender identities of students and adults in today's society.

**4.2** Explain the role of biology and social construction in gender identity.

**4.3** Analyze early and current struggles to gain gender equity and the progress that has been achieved.

**4.4** Describe how sexism and gender discrimination have affected both women and men in their career choices, incomes, and general well-being.

**4.5** Create instructional and classroom management strategies that will promote gender equity in classrooms.

## Opening Case Study

Christy Lin had planned to teach a language arts unit on gender later in the year, but a number of events in her classroom made her decide that it was needed sooner rather than later. Her seventh-grade girls said that boys were touching them without consent, and the boys were harassing each other with the use of derogatory terms about their sexual orientation. Many of the girls were already talking about being married, while most of the boys had an educational or occupational goal.

In class, Ms. Lin asked students to identify the activities in which teenagers participate by their sex. She recorded their responses on posterboard. The responses neatly fit the stereotypes for being masculine and feminine. When she asked who liked football, a number of girls raised their hands as well as almost all of the boys. When she asked who liked to cook, some boys as well as girls raised their hands.

As the class discussed the two lists, they found other crossovers. José offered that his dad cleaned the house, and John said that his dad did most of the cooking. Maria reported that her aunt liked fixing cars and even raced them sometimes on the weekend. Before long, some of the girls were talking about playing soccer with their brothers since they were in the first grade. It seemed more acceptable for girls to identify with the items on the boys' list than

vice versa. When it came to other traditionally "girl" activities such as dressing up or painting one's nails, the boys at first had no examples, and then Carlos remembered that his uncle painted his nails black. Ms. Lin reminded them that a number of rock stars who are men also paint their nails. At the end of this first lesson, they were beginning to see that not everyone followed the **gender rules**, at least not all of the time. But how could this understanding be extended to respect for each other, acceptance of **gender-nonconforming** peers, and actions to overcome gender biases?

Over the next few days, students explored how they learned their gender. They volunteered that they learned it at home and from the Internet, TikTok, and commercials. They began to look at the articles and ads on YouTube and TikTok. When they shared their findings, they quickly saw that men and women were targeted differently. Women were sold ideas about romance, sex, and beauty. Men learned that they should be tough, in charge, and not emotional.

Ms. Lin worried that the students were not yet thinking critically about gender nor connecting their discussion to their own behavior and attitudes. She began to ask them to write about their ideas at the end of each lesson. In those reflections, students would sometimes share an experience or an insight that they were not willing to share in class discussions. Most of the students were expressing more critical thoughts about gender. A few weeks after the completion of the unit, Ms. Lin was quite surprised to hear her students ask candidates running for class representative what they planned to do about sexism in school and in the community.

## Reflect

1. What was Ms. Lin's goal in introducing her seventh-graders to gender? How could the lessons help students broaden their knowledge of the gendered world in which they live?

2. What additional activities would you have included in this unit to help students think more critically about gender?

3. How could Ms. Lin have incorporated information and activities related to gender-nonconforming people into these lessons?

**SOURCE:** Adapted from Espinosa, L. (2016).

# Gender Differences

**Learning Objective 4.1** Understand the diverse gender identities of students and adults in today's society.

During the U.S. Senate's hearings for the appointment of Judge Ketanji Brown Jackson as a Supreme Court justice, Senator Marsha Blackburn asked her to define *woman*. As most judicial nominees respond to questions in hearings, Judge Jackson responded that the question was outside her role on the bench and that she was not a biologist (Weisman, 2022). In this case, the context was political, but the definition of men and women today is debated in the professional literature of **feminists**, philosophers, sociologists, and psychologists.

Before we begin a discussion of gender in today's society, we should be clear about the definition of terms that are used in this chapter. **Sex** is used to identify people as men or women, based on their reproductive and sexual anatomy. **Gender** is the socially and culturally constructed traits and perceptions of being a man, woman, transgender, or nonbinary person. **Gender identity** is people's own sense of self and their gender, which does not always correspond to the traditional ideas of **masculinities** and **femininities**. According to Serano (2018), "There is no such thing as a 'real' gender—there is only the gender we experience ourselves as and the gender we perceive others to be" (p. 430). In this section, we explore gender identities, the role of masculinities and femininities, and the importance of intersectionality in understanding gender differences.

## Gender Identity

Not all cultures limit gender to a binary in which the sex assigned at birth is congruent with one's gender identity and **gender expression**. Some Native Americans recognize the *two-spirits*, persons who have both feminine and masculine traits. They are called *māhū* by Native Hawaiians and *akava'ine* in the Cook Islands. Feminine-acting men-bodied people are identified as *muxe* in Oaxaca, Mexico; *travesty* in Brazil; and *hifra* in Kindia and Bangladesh (Wade & Ferree, 2023). People, especially young people, are expanding the options for gender identity to include **agender**, **bigender**, **cisgender**, **gender fluid**, **genderqueer**, **intergender**, **nonbinary**, and numerous other terms that they think best describe themselves.

Not everyone's biological sex is clear at birth or during puberty. Nearly 2% of the population are **intersex** because they were born with sexual anatomies that do not clearly indicate they are a boy or girl (Ainsworth, 2018). In the past, the sex of intersex people was sometimes determined by a doctor or parent at birth, leading to surgery to ensure that external organs matched the chosen sex. In addition to the surgeries leading to a number of medical problems for the people who underwent them, the resulting

**Pearson eTextbook**
**Video Example 4.1**
This video discusses the importance of supporting transgender students and protecting student health and well-being through caring practices.
https://www.youtube.com/watch?v=AjqHXqH48sU

sex was not always consistent with the gender with which they identified later in life. Intersex people today do not want to feel pressured to hide their real biological sex, and they do not support surgeries on infants. They believe that they should decide their gender when they are old enough to do so (Wade & Ferree, 2023).

Most people are cisgender, taking their gender identity for granted and not questioning it because it corresponds to their sex as it was assigned at birth. Recognition of the appropriate gender identity occurs unconsciously early in life, even for trans and nonbinary people, who in preschool or elementary schools know that something is different about them (Brown et al., 2022). It becomes a basic anchor in people's personality and forms a core part of their self-identity. Children begin selecting toys associated with their gender by the time they start walking. By age 3, most of them identify as either boys or girls and have begun to learn their expected behaviors (Lindsey, 2021). By the time they enter school, children have clear ideas about gender. Most children are taught that there are only two genders (boys and girls), and that the two groups are supposed to behave differently. When they don't follow the rules for their gender behavior, they are often reminded or reprimanded by families, their peers, religious leaders, and sometimes their teachers. Many children strive for conformity with these gender-stereotyped roles, but others are not comfortable in those roles.

However, in reality, gender is fluid, and young people may identify their gender somewhere in between or outside the spectrum of men and women. "The range of potential gender identities mean[s] there are a limitless number of iterations of trans*ness for those who resist, reject, and reimagine their gender apart from the categories of sex and gender assigned at birth" (Catalano et al., 2018, p. 345). When someone's identity, appearance, or behavior falls outside the traditional gender norms, that person may identify as a trans or **transgender** person (American Psychological Association, 2019). A trans woman is a person who was assigned the sex of a boy at birth but who self-identifies and lives as a girl/woman; a trans man is a person who was assigned the sex of a girl at birth but who self-identifies and lives as a boy/man.

In some cases, trans people have surgery and/or use hormones to transform their bodies to match the gender with which they identify—a process sometimes called **gender reassignment** or **gender affirmation**. In the United States, 1.6% of the adult population identified in 2022 as trans or nonbinary, with 5.1% of young adults between

Teenager sends a message about non-binary gender identity.

the ages of 18 and 29 identifying as trans or nonbinary (Brown, 2022); 1.4% of high school students identify as trans students. Of trans adults, there are slightly more trans women (38.5%) than trans men (35.9%); 25.6% of trans adults identify as gender nonconforming (Herman et al., 2022).

Trans students and adults may change their names and pronouns to reflect their gender identity rather than their sex as assigned at birth. Teachers can be supportive of trans students by educating themselves about trans issues, consulting experts, and using names and pronouns appropriate to the students' gender identity. The protocol is to interact with trans students as if they are the sex with which they identify. In other words, teachers would interact with a trans student who identifies as a girl by using pronouns such as *she* and *her* and interacting with the person as they would with other girls in their class. Some students prefer the use of gender-neutral pronouns such as *they/them* or *ze/zir* (Wade & Ferree, 2023). Although some policymakers, including school board members, have adopted policies forbidding educators to use the names or pronouns selected by trans students, over half of U.S. adults say that it is important to use people's new name and pronouns when they've gone through a gender transition (Parker et al., 2022).

Today, people across the world, including families, policymakers, and religious leaders, are grappling with the expansion of the gender binary. Young people are taking the lead as they identify themselves as trans and nonbinary and break the traditional gender rules. Americans do not all agree that people can be anything other than men or women, but views on a broader definition of gender have changed over the past few years and, like the acceptance of people who identify as lesbian, gay, or bisexual and gay marriage over the past 15 years, will probably gain greater acceptance over the next decade. Half of U.S. adults age 18 to 29 already say that people can be a gender that differs from the sex assigned at birth. Adults over 65 years old are most likely to think that the pace of change around issues of gender are progressing too quickly (Parker et al., 2022).

Trans students' rights are among the most controversial topics in education today, including the sports in which trans students can participate and the bathrooms and locker rooms they can use in schools, as discussed in the *Explore and Focus Your Cultural Lens* feature. Educators should be aware of possible harassment and intervene appropriately to protect the legal rights of trans students and ensure their safety in classrooms and the school.

## Explore and Focus Your Cultural Lens

### Debate: How Should Schools Accommodate Transgender Students' Use of Bathrooms?

The U.S. has a century-long history of installing two sets of bathrooms in schools and other public spaces (Schiappa, 2022)—one for girls/women and one for boys/men. What is the appropriate bathroom for transgender students? They generally want to be able to use the bathrooms that are marked for the sex that matches their gender identity.

The administration of President Barack Obama applied Title VII of the Civil Rights Act and Title IX of the Education Amendments of 1972 to protect an employee's and student's right to use bathrooms that correspond to their gender identity. As a result, many school districts or schools adopted a policy that gives trans students the right to use the bathroom that matches their gender

identity. In addition, they may have installed or designated gender-neutral bathrooms in the school similar to the family bathrooms found in airports, sports venues, and public buildings.

The 2016 guidance for Title IX was revoked in February 2017, but President Joe Biden's administration reasserted in 2021 that Title IX includes protection from discrimination based on gender identity. The courts continue to rule in favor of trans students in *G.G. v. Gloucester County School Board* (2016) and *Whitaker v. Kenosha Unified School District* (2017). In May 2018, a federal court in Philadelphia "refused to block a Pennsylvania school district's policy of permitting trans students to use the restrooms or locker rooms consistent with their gender identity" (Walsh, 2018, p. 26).

*(continued)*

At the same time, a federal district judge in Virginia ruled in favor of a trans boy, Gavin Grimm, to use the boy's restroom in his Virginia high school. Nevertheless, some states have introduced legislation to restrict the use of public bathrooms by transgender people by 2023.

Some advocates for transgender rights argue that schools should focus on appropriate behavior in bathrooms rather than policing gender identity. Not only are trans and nonbinary students uncomfortable in school bathrooms, but a number of cisgender students would like different options as well (Myers, 2021). What do you think? How should schools meet the needs of trans students? The arguments used for and against guaranteeing trans students a choice in the bathroom they use include the following:

### FOR

- Trans and nonbinary students should be treated fairly and with dignity in schools, which should include using the bathrooms that reflect their gender identity.
- All people should feel safe using the bathroom. Trans students face significant discrimination and bullying in schools and do not always feel comfortable using bathrooms that do not match their gender identity where they may be outed, bullied, or not allowed to enter.
- Many trans students experience health issues such as kidney stones and bladder infections because they avoid using bathrooms at school and in other public places. Forcing trans students to have restricted use of a specific bathroom could put their health at risk.
- While many trans people experience harassment or assault in gender-restricted bathrooms, there is no evidence that offering gender-neutral bathrooms or allowing trans people to use the bathrooms that match their gender identity puts anyone else at risk (Hasenbush et al., 2019).

### AGAINST

- Schools should continue the long-term practice in the United States of expecting students to use the bathroom that matches the sex they were assigned at birth.
- Nontransgender boys/men may take advantage of gender-neutral bathrooms as an opportunity to stalk, harass, or assault women.
- Schools cannot afford to provide appropriate bathrooms to accommodate the needs of each student's gender identity.
- Cisgender people should not have to change their habits or be uncomfortable in order to accommodate trans people.

## Questions for Discussion

1. Why are trans students fighting for the right to use the bathroom that matches their gender identity?
2. The term *gender* does not appear in either Title IX of the 1972 Education Amendment or Title VII of the Civil Rights Act. Do you think the term *sex*, which does appear in those two laws, should be interpreted to mean gender and include trans people? Why or why not?
3. How would you respond to parents who were concerned about the safety of their daughter under a policy allowing trans students to use bathrooms that match their gender identity?

## The Role of Masculinity and Femininity

Most cultures are **androcentric** in that masculinity is valued over femininity and women are considered inferior to men. Masculinity is often measured by a man's independence, assertiveness, leadership, self-reliance, and emotional stability. Men are expected to demonstrate tough, confident, and self-reliant behaviors as well as be aggressive; they are encouraged to avoid anything feminine. Femininity is stereotypically characterized as emotional, dependent, compliant, empathetic, and nurturing. Men are centered in society as the normal against which others are measured. As a result, men have been bestowed higher status, respect, and power, leading to being identified by some people as the superior sex (Wade & Ferree, 2023).

When these differences are translated into the work environment, women are tracked into the nurturing fields of teaching, health care, and social services. They are often supervised by men with assertive leadership skills and higher incomes. However, progress has been made in changing some of these stereotypes and in the number of women with jobs that were traditionally held by men. Even masculine norms are changing in the United States as men are allowed to be more vulnerable and emotional (Schiappa, 2022).

Few people fall solely at one or the other end of the feminine–masculine continuum. Most people are **androgynous** in that they possess some feminine and masculine characteristics. Generally, women are allowed more flexibility in their gender identification than men. Even young girls receive positive reinforcement for acting like boys by being physically active, participating in sports, and rejecting feminine stereotypical behavior. However, boys and men are susceptible to societal pressures, sometimes going overboard in proving their masculinity. On the other hand, trans women and trans men who are trying to assimilate into the cultures of their chosen gender are not always allowed flexibility; gender norms are applied rigidly to them. In other words, their cisgender peers expect them to reflect traditional expectations for their gender, not supporting their display of masculine or feminine traits or behaviors that no longer match their gender (Schiappa, 2022).

Because of sexism, many cisgender and trans young men are often pressured to engage in hypermasculine behavior, as shown by statistics indicating they are more likely than young women to smoke cigarettes, use steroids, suffer from undiagnosed depression, carry a weapon, commit suicide, and be killed by gunfire or in a car crash (Centers for Disease Control and Prevention [CDC], 2022b, 2023a; Harper et al., 2023; Mayo Clinic, 2022). Boys and men often have to prove their masculinity to peers, fathers, brothers, and coaches. The worst of this behavior is sometimes referred to as **toxic masculinity**, when men or boys hide their emotions and become overly aggressive and even violent. It is one end of a continuum of masculinities that can result when masculinity has been internalized as physical power. However, most men do not display toxic masculinity. As boys become young men, they may feel that they are forced to repudiate the feminine side of their personality and confirm their masculinity. Unfortunately, some of these masculine characteristics also may prevent them from seeking mental health treatment when needed (American Psychological Association, 2018).

As norms change, people are rejecting old, unequal roles. Some people are modifying or rejecting stereotyped masculine behavior. Both men and women are more often able to move to more androgynous behaviors without social repercussions. These changes are resulting in new uncertainties where gender rules are no longer so distinct. As new norms develop, more flexible roles, personalities, and behaviors are evolving for everyone. During this changing period, adolescents are likely to struggle with their gender identity, especially in the middle and high school years, but identifying as trans or nonbinary may be difficult until society becomes more accepting of gender variance.

## Intersectionality

"Beyond sisterhood is still racism," Audre Lorde (1979, para. 22) declared in *An Open Letter to Mary Daly*. She further argued that the "oppression of women knows no ethnic nor racial boundaries. . . . To deal with one without even alluding to the other is to distort our commonality as well as our difference" (para. 21). Lorde and other Black feminists like Kimberlé Crenshaw and Patricia Hill Collins began articulating the essence of intersectionality in the 1970s. The history and experiences of women are different based on their race, ethnicity, class, and religion. Inequities cannot be eliminated by focusing only on gender while ignoring the inequities that result because of people's race, ethnicity, class, or religion.

Race, ethnicity, class, and religion can have a great impact on how people are treated in society. Because of racism, persons of color are more likely than White people to be suspected of wrongdoing as they walk around a store, drive down a street, or walk down the hall of their school. Because of prejudice against some religious groups, a Christian woman may be able to walk through an airport with greater ease than a Muslim woman. Black, Latino, and Native American young men are more likely to be suspended from school, incarcerated, and killed by police than young women and White young men. Young women of color are also more likely than their White peers to be suspended from school and incarcerated.

Religions generally recognize and include gender expectations as part of their doctrines. Regardless of the specific religion, rituals sometimes reflect and reinforce systems of dominance by men. Religion may influence how adherents think about issues of gender identity, sexuality, marriage, reproductive rights, and childrearing. Religious communities have successfully organized politically to influence state and federal policies on family and women's affairs. Religious perspectives on appropriate gender roles sometimes conflict with the school culture in designating the ways students interact with each other in the classroom and hallways. The dress of girls and young women in general and in physical education classes may clash with religious dictates. Educators should be alert to the religious perspectives of the community as they discuss gender issues in classrooms, plan lessons on sexuality, and interact with students in the classroom.

The degree to which gender rules and traditional gender roles are accepted depends, in large part, on the degree to which families maintain the traditional patterns and experiences of their racial, ethnic, and religious groups. Families that adhere to fundamentalist religious and cultural patterns are more likely to encourage adherence to rigid gender rules. New immigrants may find that the gender rules in the United States are not always congruent with those in their native countries and, as a result, may be harassed by their peers. Some students with disabilities may find that they are unable to fulfill their gender role as society expects. Educators should be aware that how they and their students identify and actualize their gender will be influenced by memberships in multiple cultural groups.

# The Role of Biology and Social Construction in Gender Identity

**Learning Objective 4.2** Explain the role of biology and social construction in gender identity.

People generally distinguish men and women by their physical appearance alone. There are differences in hormonal levels of estrogen and testosterone, which control the physical development of the two sexes. Soon after birth, boys and girls have similar hormonal levels, and they are similar in terms of physical development through their early elementary school years. The onset of puberty brings major changes in the hormonal levels of the two sexes. At this time, the proportion of fat to total body weight increases in girls and decreases in boys. The differences in physical structure generally contribute to men's greater strength, greater endurance for heavy labor, greater ease in running and overarm throwing, and less ability to float in water. However, there is significant diversity within the range of "normal" physical characteristics of people of all genders and the extent of sex-related physical differences can also be influenced by environment and culture. They can be altered with nutrition, physical activity, practice, and behavioral expectations.

Researchers have found little evidence that brains are hardwired to make biological males and females behave differently from each other (Lindsey, 2021; Wade, 2016). The claim that structural differences in the brain are associated with gender identity are based on questionable research (Ashwell, 2019). Nevertheless, women and men often segregate themselves at social gatherings. They dress and groom differently. The topics of their conversations often differ. They participate in sex-specific leisure activities and compete in sports that are sex segregated. In classrooms, students are sometimes segregated by sex for school activities. Boys tend to be more rambunctious in their play. Girls and boys often choose different games at recess. For example, girls may jump rope as boys throw balls with each other. These choices generally extend into adulthood as people participate in leisure activities, carry out family responsibilities, and choose occupations.

Are these behaviors and choices due to the sex people were assigned at birth? Or are gender behaviors learned through socialization patterns? Are people born to behave, think, and act differently, or do they learn these differences? How can understanding these differences help teachers support, protect, and provide fair treatment to children and young people as they grow up and progress through school? Let's begin by looking at what is known about the differences between the two sexes.

## Sex Differences Based on Biology

Research on biological differences between the sexes has found few differences after birth. The X and Y chromosomes that determine one's sex represent a very small proportion of the total gene pool; men and women share 99.8% of their genes (Eliot, 2012). The differences in psychological traits (e.g., empathy, ambition, compassion, aggressiveness, and being responsible) and academic abilities between the average sexes are quite small. The differences are much greater within the two sexes than between men and women in general (Ashwell, 2019). The recreational and interpersonal differences between girls and boys are much greater than their cognitive and academic differences (Eliot, 2012). In spite of these research findings, many families and educators believe there are innate differences between boys and girls, which can lead to stereotypes and the development of different expectations for their behavior, academic achievement, and future work.

At one time, it was assumed that men had more intelligence than women due to larger brain size. Today it is known that brain size is related to body size, not to intelligence (Wade, 2016). When Alfred Binet developed the first intelligence test at the beginning of the twentieth century, no differences were found in the general intelligence level between women and men. The only significant difference is related to visual-spatial tasks or mental rotation; men are better at being able to view a three-dimensional figure from different angles in their mind (Ashwell, 2019). However, this skill can be taught, and women can remove the differences through training or playing Tetris or other video games that involve rotating various geometric shapes (Wade & Ferree, 2023).

Different types of classroom activities engage students in the academic areas in which they are not performing proficiently. Boys are in greater need of one-on-one verbal engagement than girls. They need literary immersion as well as opportunities for physical play and hands-on learning (Eliot, 2012). Girls are more likely to need to be engaged in activities to develop their mathematics, science, and spatial skills at higher levels. Expectations for all children and youth need to be high, no matter the subject area. Excuses that students are not performing well because of their gender are no longer acceptable in educational environments in which schools are expected to ensure that all students perform at their grade level or above.

## Socially Constructed Differences

Although biology determines sex for most people at the beginning of life, it does not have to limit their abilities to the gender roles identified for their sex. How children spend their time and what they are taught can help them live the stereotypical role or make it acceptable to break the traditional expectation. Families, teachers, and peers teach the meaning of femininity and masculinity. These gender rules are the guide for how to appear and behave as a girl, boy, woman, or man (Wade & Ferree, 2023). They are primarily determined by our cultures, and they change over time and from context to context, but those rules are being broken by students and adults who identify themselves as nonbinary or other gender nonconforming.

As soon as a baby's sex is known, everything from clothing to furniture to activities is gender driven unless parents intentionally decide they are going to raise their children in a gender-neutral environment. Even when parents are determined not to reinforce the sex stereotypes, society works against them. Gender-specific toys and the actions of girls and boys on the pages of children's books and magazines, on television, and on the Internet as well as in play with their peers reinforce gender expectations. Through this socialization process, children develop social skills and learn their socially and culturally prescribed roles and expectations. Following these gender rules is very easy

Children learn at an early age what types of activities are considered socially acceptable for their gender. Most little girls dress up as princesses, become little ballerinas, or play with dollhouses, but more parents are encouraging their children to engage in non-traditional activities.

**SOURCE:** © fizkes/Shutterstock

for some people, but for others, becoming masculine or feminine under these rules can be brutally painful (Wade & Ferree, 2023).

**THE INFLUENCE OF MEDIA AND ADVERTISING ON GENDER**   Advertising and mass media support **popular cultures** that generally represent masculinity as dominant and femininity as passive. Advertisers shape choices in very gendered ways (Sensoy & DiAngelo, 2017), as Ms. Lin's students were learning at the beginning of this chapter. Even advertisements for shampoo, food, cigarettes, and other products are directed separately to men and women. The media and popular culture perpetuate sexism and androcentrism by showing over and over again the looks and behavior of women and men who play by the gender rules. As children and young people access Facebook, Instagram, Snapchat, TikTok, and other social media, they learn from the ads what is expected for their gender (Sensoy & DiAngelo, 2017).

Children are not immune to the influence of the media and advertising. Cartoon characters, children's movies, and toys reinforce gender rules. The most influential source of gender socialization for young children is television, which projects gender stereotypes 24/7 (Lindsey, 2021). Boys and men in children's cartoons outnumber girl and women characters 10 to 1 (Lindsey, 2021). Programming that deviates from gender stereotypes with smart and adventurous girls in lead roles (e.g., *Dora the Explorer* and *Odd Squad*) is popular, but limited in the number of such shows. Programming with LGBTQ+ (lesbian, gay, bisexual, transgender, queer/questioning) characters has expanded since the 2013 premiere of *Orange Is the New Black* but was down in 2022–2023. Of the 596 LGBTQ+ characters across primetime scripted broadcast and eight streaming services, 32 (5.4%) characters were transgender, including 16 trans women, 11 trans men, and five trans nonbinary characters (GLAAD Media Institute, 2023). The Disney Channel airs the largest number of shows with LGBTQ+ characters as spouses, parents, and classmates as part of Disney's programming for children and families.

Toy stores are filled with aisles of toys that are clearly distinguished by the colors favored by girls (i.e., pink and lavender) and by boys (blue or anything not pink or lavender). Science kits, construction toys, and cars and trucks are for boys while the girl's section is stocked with dolls, Disney princess collections, and beauty kits. Children like board games, but the girl's section has fewer games that stimulate critical thinking or are as cognitively challenging as the games in the boy's section (Hofmann, 2016). The Brookings Institution reports that "Both the scientific and medical communities are united in arguing that children's play provides a critical pathway for the development of important 21st century skills. Toys are platforms for play and can be used to guide children toward some skillsets over others" (Herbst et al., 2021, para. 3). Steering children to toys that are stereotypically for girls or boys limits choices for those children who want to explore beyond gender roles and gain skills that may affect choices they later make. A gender equity approach calls for all toys, books, and activities to be available to all children and that they be encouraged to explore toys and games across gender borders.

**SOCIALIZATION PATTERNS IN SCHOOL**   When a child enters school, educators usually continue the socialization patterns initiated by families that reinforce the stereotyped behaviors associated with gender. The attitudes and values about appropriate gender roles are embedded in the curriculum of schools. Elementary schools with a predominance of women teachers may reinforce maternal roles with an emphasis on obedience. In classrooms, boys and girls may receive different feedback and encouragement for their work. Boys often control classroom conversations and answer questions quickly. Teachers are more likely to praise boys for their intellectual responses. At the same time, boys are more likely to be publicly criticized by teachers when they break a rule (Lindsey, 2021).

Children are also active participants in the socialization process. Playgroups often are determined by the gender of the children, especially in the elementary and middle grades. Even when girls and boys play the same game, they often play it differently, with the boys being more aggressive. However, not all boys and girls follow the socially acceptable ways of their sex. Not all boys participate in large-group activities and are aggressive. Students who do not reflect the stereotypes for their assigned sex may be harassed and/or ostracized by their peers. The forgotten boys whose voices have been silenced and marginalized may follow behavior patterns generally associated with girls, but they risk being labeled as effeminate and can become isolated from other boys. Much the same is true for girls. At the same time, you have probably known a girl who chose to play with the boys rather than the girls. Girls who excel in athletics, even against the boys, usually do not suffer serious consequences.

# Struggles for Gender Equity

**Learning Objective 4.3**  Analyze early and current struggles to gain gender equity and the progress that has been achieved.

Most major changes in society do not occur quietly. Until early in the twentieth century, U.S. and many European societies were **patriarchal**, in which men controlled all institutions, including the family, and had all of the rights. Women were not considered equal to men. In fact, most women were subordinate to men. They were dependent on them for financial well-being as their daughters and their wives. For women on their own, jobs were neither plentiful nor well paid. With some education, women could be hired as teachers if they could convince school authorities that they were moral, upstanding young women. Once they married, they were not always allowed to continue to teach; they became the responsibility of their husbands. Without laws that provided them autonomy from their spouses or fathers, women could not file for divorce, own property, or apply for men's jobs. Their economic dependency on fathers and husbands kept women in a second-class position (Wagner, 2019).

Although patriarchy has been replaced by laws that treat men and women as equal citizens, in some families, in some religions, and in some places, patriarchy still defines relationships between men and women (Wade & Ferree, 2023). Although not all institutions in the United States today are dominated by men and not all men are powerful, boys and men continue to identify with the power that has been culturally bestowed upon them because of their sex, which may give them a sense of entitlement to expect women to meet their needs (Johnson, 2017). In this section, we explore how women and their allies were able to move a patriarchal society to one that is more equitable and how struggles for gender equity have evolved to include trans, nonbinary, and other gender-nonconforming people.

## Gaining the Right to Vote: The First Wave of the Women's Movement

The desire for independence and equal rights has been the backbone of the struggles of women and their allies since the Seneca Falls Convention in July 1848, which was organized by abolitionists Lucretia Mott and Elizabeth Cady Stanton. However, women were working for rights much earlier. For example, the Haudenosaunee (Iroquois) nations had political systems that involved both men and women for over 1,000 years

**Pearson eTextbook**
**Video Example 4.2**
This video discusses the Nineteenth Amendment and the women's suffrage movement.
https://www.youtube.com/watch?v=XcrGQ0npuCw

before Seneca Falls. White women were voting in the colonies before the Constitution made it illegal in 1789, and women and men were petitioning for and winning changes to laws related to property and other issues before Seneca Falls (Wagner, 2019). As the Continental Congress wrote laws for the new country in 1776, Abigail Smith Adams was reminding her husband, who would later become the second U.S. president, to "remember the ladies."

Black women may have initiated the movement for women's rights in 1832 when they organized the first Female Anti-Slavery Society in Salem, Massachusetts. Or it may have started "when the 139 local societies of black and white women . . . held their first national convention in 1837" (Wagner, 2019, p. xxvi). At the Seneca Falls Convention, women organized to fight against their oppression. Their goal was to raise the public's awareness about women's issues, including the right to divorce, own property, speak in public, work, vote, and prevent abuse by husbands. This effort included Frederick Douglass and other abolitionists who were fighting for the human and civil rights of all people. However, not all women supported the women's movement. Many did not view their conditions as oppressive and accepted their roles as wives and mothers as natural (Wagner, 2019).

The Fifteenth Amendment to the U.S. Constitution granted the right to vote to Black men when it was ratified in 1870. However, it did not extend voting rights to women, prompting Stanton and Susan B. Anthony to found the National Women Suffrage Association (NWSA) to fight for a federal amendment to grant women the right to vote. A second organization, the American Woman Suffrage Association (AWSA), was established to seek the right to vote state by state. Twenty years later, the two organizations merged as the National American Woman Suffrage Association (NAWSA) to fight for suffrage (Wagner, 2019), with a membership that was predominantly European American women of the elite class.

Women of color did not feel welcomed in NAWSA or other women's groups. The fight for equal rights was segregated from the struggles of other oppressed groups. White suffragists did not fight to improve the daily lives of women who were working class or who had low incomes (Beck, 2021) and refused to take a stand against Jim Crow laws and other violations of the civil rights of oppressed racial and ethnic groups. Nevertheless, Black women like Sojourner Truth and Ida B. Wells Barnett continued to fight for women's right to vote after the adoption of the Fifteenth Amendment (Wade & Ferree, 2023).

After the merger of the NWSA and AWSA, the strategy for achieving the right to vote adapted AWSA's state-by-state strategy with limited success. Territories in the west were the most supportive of the goal, with Wyoming, Utah, Colorado, and Idaho approving the right of women to vote between 1869 and 1896. Support for women's right to vote picked up again in 1910 as the state of Washington amended its constitution to allow women to vote, followed by California, Oregon, Arizona, Kansas, Nevada, and Montana.

By the beginning of the twentieth century, NAWSA was focusing almost solely on achieving the right to vote over broader women's issues. In the process, leaders of NAWSA "played to the racism and religious conservatism of the [southern] region" (Wagner, 2019, p. 381). They began to affirm White supremacy as they sought the support of women from southern states, arguing that suffrage could not be achieved without them. In addition, they began to call for allowing only educated people to vote, which would limit dramatically voting by people of color who had not been allowed or encouraged to attend school. The leadership of the organization had come under the control of conservative southerners and their religiously conservative sympathizers, who were not allowing Black women to attend their conferences and accepted the segregation of southern affiliates (Wagner, 2019).

By 1913, younger women were joining NAWSA and preparing for their roles by training with militant British suffragettes who introduced them to new tactics

Suffragists became tired of trying to convince legislators to adopt an amendment that would allow women to vote and began protesting in front of the White House in the second decade of the twentieth century.

**SOURCE:** © Everett Historical/Shutterstock

to press for change. Alice Paul and Carrie Chapman Catt were leading the fight for suffrage. The more rebellious of the two, Paul organized and led marches in front of the White House and lobbied Congress, breaking away from NAWSA to found the National Woman's Party in 1916. The protesters were arrested and staged hunger strikes after which they were force-fed in jail. Although some people supported the harassment of these protesters, the general public began to side with the suffragists, and Congress took notice. When Jeannette Rankin, the first woman elected to Congress, reintroduced the amendment for suffrage in January 1918, it passed and was ratified in 1920 by the required 36 states. It had been 50 years since the passage of the Fifteenth Amendment.

However, the Nineteenth Amendment did not guarantee voting rights for all women. Congress did not recognize Native Americans as citizens who had the right to vote until 1924, and then states had the right to deny them their voting rights. Most men and women of color were prevented from voting in some states, especially across the south, until Congress passed the Voting Rights Act in 1965.

By 1920, the activism of women had paid off. They could attend college, enter contracts, hold property in their own name, keep the money they earned, enter professions, and live on their own. Alice Paul introduced the Lucretia Mott Amendment in 1923, which read: "Men and women shall have equal rights throughout the U.S. and every place subject to its jurisdiction." The amendment later was renamed the Alice Paul Amendment and then the Equal Rights Amendment (ERA), which was introduced to Congress every year until it passed in 1972. NAWSA evolved into the National League of Women Voters, which works today to protect and expand voting rights.

## Fighting Sex Discrimination: The Second Wave of the Women's Movement

The push for comprehensive advances in the status of women began again in the 1960s, almost a decade after Black activists had initiated the Civil Rights Movement. One of the catalysts for this new movement was the release of *The Feminine Mystique* by Betty Friedan. Friedan described the unfulfilling lives of college-educated suburban women who were managing households, raising children, and being there for their husbands but saw no hope for their future. Many women around the United States and the world saw themselves in the book.

Attention to women's issues by the government also began to expand in 1963. Congress passed the Equal Pay Act, but it did not prevent discrimination in hiring. President John F. Kennedy created the U.S. Commission on the Status of Women in 1961 to prepare recommendations for overcoming discrimination based on sex. In an attempt to defeat the Civil Rights Bill in Congress, a southern congressman added the words "or sex" to Title VII, declaring that discrimination based on "race, color, national origin, or sex" would be prohibited. Kennedy had thought that the addition of "sex" to Title VII of the legislation would prevent the bill from passing. However, the Civil Rights Bill passed in 1964, extending equal rights to women for the first time. Soon afterward, President Lyndon Johnson signed an executive order that required businesses with federal contracts to hire women and people of color, creating the first affirmative action programs. To enforce Title VII, Congress established the Equal Employment Opportunity Commission (EEOC) to investigate complaints about racial and sexual discrimination.

When the EEOC did not take seriously the thousands of complaints received during its first year, a group of activists decided that a nongovernmental organization was needed to fight for women's civil rights (Wade & Ferree. 2023). The National Organization for Women (NOW) was established in 1966 for that purpose, and Betty Friedan was selected as its first president. By its second annual meeting, members were disagreeing about NOW's stance on the ERA and reproductive freedom, eventually leading some members to establish the more moderate Women's Equity League with a more conservative stance on abortion. At the third annual conference, a group of more radical feminists publicly severed their relationship with NOW. Although Aileen Hernandez followed Betty Friedan as president and Shirley Chisholm was an early member of NOW, its members were predominantly White women (Dicker, 2016).

More women joined women's groups, but tensions grew between women's liberation and leftist political groups. Some groups like the Redstockings picketed legislative hearings. Women began to speak out about their own experiences with abortions and violence. The private worlds of home, marriage, and family and their relationship to the power dynamics of society were being discussed publicly, enacting the words of Carol Hanisch: "the personal is political." During this period, women gained more control of their own bodies. The Supreme Court decriminalized the use of contraceptives by married couples in 1965. Seven years later, the Supreme Court allowed single people to use contraceptives and made abortion legal in *Roe v. Wade*.

Women's groups again pushed for passage of the ERA, which then read, "Equality of rights under the law shall not be denied or abridged by the United States or by any state on account of sex." As noted earlier, it was finally passed by Congress in 1972, but conservative groups concerned about family values lobbied state legislatures to reject the amendment. Although two-thirds of the U.S. population supported the ERA, it was not ratified by the required 38 states by the extended timeline of 1982. By the 1980s, political leaders were no longer disposed to extend full equal rights to women.

There was much for feminists to fight for in the early 1970s. Mothers could not rely on child care centers. Women were earning 52 cents to every dollar earned by a man. Married women were not eligible for a credit card without their husband's approval. Banks and lenders would count half or less of the salary of a wife who was of childbearing age to determine if a couple qualified for a loan. Little support for victims of domestic violence existed. Single women had difficulty renting an apartment. The focus of the second wave movement became the fight for "the same economic, social, and political rights as men" (Williams, 2017, p. 188). Much was accomplished during the second wave to provide greater access to employment and educational opportunities, provide reproductive rights, increase participation in sports, and provide greater sexual freedom. In addition, women were starting to see themselves as political leaders.

Margaret Chase Smith ran for U.S. president for a major political party in 1964, followed by Shirley Chisholm in 1972.

*Sexism in School and Society* by Myra Sadker and Nancy Frazier was released in 1973, making the case that girls were the casualties of sexism in schools, which contributed to the erosion of their future potential, their ideas, and their future careers. Girls were being stereotyped in storybooks, literature, and textbooks used in classrooms. Girls were being guided into gendered roles and expected to follow traditional gender rules. They were counseled into "women's work" and faced discrimination and sexual harassment in schools and on jobs. They were prepared to follow leaders and bosses who were men, rather than being prepared for those roles. The work of researchers and educators during these years led to changes in schools that have improved the academic performance of girls and young women and opened career options to many of them.

## Intersectionality: The Third Wave of the Women's Movement

The third wave of the women's movement started in 1991 in response to the U.S. Senate Judiciary Committee's treatment of law professor Anita Hill, who had charged Clarence Thomas with sexual harassment in his confirmation hearings for appointment to the Supreme Court. The committee of all men stumbled in their treatment of her as a professional and an equal.

Women's groups were also still disconcerted about the backlash against women's progress in the 1980s. NOW's membership had dropped dramatically. Benefiting from the changes that had resulted from the work of previous feminists, young women were not identifying themselves as feminists, signaling that sexism may have been eradicated. In the third wave, feminists developed their identity in a neoliberal global context (Evans, 2015).

The 1990s ushered in a change in the feminist movement toward broader support for the civil rights of all groups, no longer limiting their agenda to the issues and interest of professional working women. The movement began to include more women of color, women with low incomes, lesbians, and trans women with a focus on working together to overcome inequities based on race, ethnicity, gender, socioeconomic level, sexual orientation, and religion.

The third wave also saw the growth of organizations for girls such as Girls Who Code, Black Girls Code, and Girls Educational and Mentoring Service, whose goal was to empower young women who have experienced sexual exploitation. Groups were founded to fight rape culture, sexual harassment, and other issues that address the experiences of girls and women. These groups included End Rape on Campus and Know Your IX, which focused on ending rape. Participants in Right To Be, a global movement to end harassment, protested street harassment and worked to make public spaces safer. Other groups such as the New York Radical Women and Redstockings "called attention to men's domination of women in all phases of a woman's life, including financial disparity, reproduction, sexual violence, and interpersonal relationships" (Lindsey, 2021, p. 192). Some of the milestones of the women's and gender rights movements are listed in Table 4.1.

## Today's Movement for Gender Equity

The fourth wave of the women's movement may have started the day after the inauguration of President Donald J. Trump on January 21, 2017, when more than 3 million people marched in cities and suburbs across the United States and other countries to advocate for legislation and policies for civil rights, including women's rights.

## Table 4.1 Milestones in the Women's Movement, 1920–2022

| | |
|---|---|
| 1920 | The Nineteenth Amendment was ratified, giving most women the right to vote. |
| 1923 | The Equal Rights Amendment is introduced in Congress. |
| 1923 | Congress granted citizenship to all Native Americans born in the United States, but it was 1957 before all states allowed Native Americans to vote. |
| 1963 | President John F. Kennedy's Commission on the Status of Women released its report. |
| | The Equal Pay Act was passed by Congress. |
| | *The Feminine Mystique* by Betty Friedan was published. |
| 1964 | The Civil Rights Act was passed. Title VII of the Act established the Equal Employment Opportunity Act. |
| 1965 | The Supreme Court decriminalizes the use of birth control by married couples in *Griswold v. Connecticut*. |
| 1968 | The EEOC outlawed sex-segregated want ads in newspapers. |
| | Two hundred women protested the Miss America Pageant in Atlantic City. |
| 1971 | The National Women's Political Caucus was established to involve women in politics. |
| 1972 | Congress passed the Equal Rights Amendment (ERA). |
| | Congress passed Title IX of the Higher Education Act to prohibit sex discrimination in schools receiving federal funds. |
| | The Supreme Court allowed single people to use contraceptives. |
| | Gloria Steinem and Patricia Carbine published the first issue of *Ms.* magazine. |
| 1973 | The Supreme Court made abortion legal in the first and second trimesters in *Roe v. Wade*. |
| | The National Black Feminist Organization was formed to provide a space for Black women. |
| 1974 | Congress passed the Women's Educational Equity Act to provide federal money for programs to fight sexism. |
| | The Supreme Court declared that public school teachers who are pregnant could not be dismissed from their jobs. |
| 1975 | U.S. military academies were ordered by Congress to admit women. |
| 1978 | Congress amended Title VII of the Civil Rights Act to require employers to treat pregnancy like any other temporary disability. |
| | Suzanne Kessler and Wendy McKenna question scientific and medical definitions of gender and question the gender binary in *Gender: An Ethnomethodological Approach*. |
| 1979 | Janice Raymond writes *The Transsexual Empire* that claims trans women are appropriating femininity and feminism. |
| 1981 | Sandra Day O'Connor became the first woman Supreme Court Justice. |
| | Women were allowed to enlist in all military branches. |
| 1982 | The ERA was defeated in the state ratification process. |
| 1985 | Emily's List was founded to support pro-choice Democratic women in elections. |
| 1991 | Sandy Stone writes the essay "The Empire Strikes Back: A Posttranssexual Manifesto," critiquing antitrans feminist attitudes and challenging the gender binary. |
| 1999 | Tammy Baldwin (WI) became the first openly gay person to serve in Congress. |
| 2009 | The Lily Ledbetter Fair Pay Restoration Act overturned a Supreme Court decision that prevented women from challenging past pay discrimination. |
| | Sonia Sotomayor became the first woman of color on the Supreme Court. |
| 2016 | Hillary Rodham Clinton became the first woman nominated by a major political party for president of the U.S. |
| 2017 | The day after Donald Trump's inauguration as the president of the U.S., women protested for women's rights in one of the largest marches in U.S. history. |
| | Danica Roem (VA) became the first openly trans state legislator in the U.S. |
| 2018 | Tammy Duckworth became the first senator to give birth while in office. |
| 2020 | Virginia became the 38th state to ratify the ERA, but deadlines set by Congress for ratification had passed. |
| 2021 | Kamala Harris began her term as Vice President of the United States as the first woman to hold that position. |
| | Debra Haaland, a tribal citizen of the Laguna Pueblo, was confirmed as Secretary of the Interior, becoming the first Indigenous American in the U.S. President's Cabinet. |
| | Openly transgender athletes competed in the Olympic Games in Tokyo. |
| 2022 | Supreme Court overturns *Roe v. Wade*, ending a woman's right to an abortion, leaving decisions about abortion up to the states. |
| | Ketanji Brown Jackson became the first Black woman to serve on the Supreme Court. |

An estimated half million women and their allies marched for gender equality and civil rights in Washington, DC, on the day after the 2017 inauguration of President Donalid J. Trump.

**SOURCE:** Jim West/Alamy

The organizers and leaders of this march were Black, Latina, and White Christian, Jewish, and Muslim women. In the year that followed, women worked to save the Affordable Care Act (aka Obamacare); demonstrated at airports to support victims of the Muslim ban; supported the victims of the MeToo explosion; and stepped forward to run for elected local, state, and federal offices in record numbers.

States were being pushed to recognize more gender categories than the binary. By 2023, at least 22 states and the District of Columbia allowed people to identify as neither a man nor a woman on official documents such as driver's licenses, covering just over half of the LGBTQ+ population (Movement Advancement Project, 2023).

The number of women in elected office continued to grow but has not yet reached 50% of elected officials. In the 2018 midterm elections, more women than ever were elected to Congress (Spillar, 2018). Kamala Harris became the first woman to take the oath of office for Vice President in the U.S. in 2021. She was also the first woman of color, the first Black person, and the first South Asian person elected to this national office. In 2023, 25 women (25% of the voting members) were serving in the U.S. Senate, and 125 women (28.7% of the voting members) were serving in the U.S. House of Representatives. Four of the nine Supreme Court justices were women. Thirty-three percent of the women in Congress were women of color (Center for American Women and Politics, 2023), and at least one woman was seeking the nomination for president during the 2023–2024 primaries. At the state level, 12 governors, 22 lieutenant governors, and 32.7% of state legislators were women. Transgender and nonbinary people are also being elected to state and local governmental bodies. In 2023, trans people were elected to state and local governmental bodies in 24 states and the District of Columbia; 14 states had elected nonbinary representatives (LGBTQ+ Victory Institute, 2023).

The business world is also still dominated by men, with only 15% of chief executive officers at *Fortune* 500 companies being women (Buchholz, 2022). Thirty-one percent of the board members of these companies were women in 2022, with only 7% of the board members being women of color (Leech, 2022). Men also continue to dominate the senior professorial ranks and presidencies in higher education. In 2022, only 36% of full professors (American Association of University Women, n.d.) and 39% of university and college presidents were women (Melidona et al., 2023).

The ERA is again in the news. In 2020, Virginia became the 38th state to ratify the ERA that was originally passed by Congress in 1972. Although Article 5 of the Constitution requires 38 states for full ratification, attorney generals from Alabama, Louisiana, and South Dakota claim that their states rescinded their ratifications and sued to block the ERA. The U.S. Department of Justice argued that the three recent state ratifications had been submitted after the deadline, leading to the state attorneys general dropping their lawsuit. In turn, the attorney generals of Nevada, Illinois, and Virginia filed suit for the U.S. Archives to certify the ratification (Baker, 2022). The U.S. House of Representatives voted to ratify the ERA in 2020 and 2021, but the ERA had not passed the U.S. Senate as of 2023.

In addition to these gains, supporters of civil rights are continuing to fight for equality in jobs, pay, schooling, responsibilities in the home, and the nation's laws. They believe that everyone should have a choice about working in the home or outside the home, having children, making choices about their own bodies, and acknowledging gender and sexual orientation. They believe that women should not have to be subordinate to men at home, in the workplace, or in society. They fight to eliminate the physical and mental violence that has resulted from such subordination by providing support groups and shelters for abused women and children as well as by pressuring the judicial system to outlaw and punish people who perpetuate such violence. They question stereotypical gender roles and challenge the socialization of children with traditional gender rules. They fight the culture that values a homogeneous beauty for girls and women. They work to eradicate sexism. They also lobby for policies to help working women live sane and healthy lives, including paid leave for parents of newborn children, reliable and affordable child care, the ability to use a breast pump at work, and flexibility in work schedules. These are changes that would improve the lives of both men and women.

Although progress has been made in the recognition and acceptance of trans and nonbinary people, trans youth and adults are now increasingly under attack. Of the 492 anti-LGBTQ+ bills presented by April 2023 for the last legislation session, 118 (26%) were anti-trans bills on health care, participation in sports, use of public accommodations such as bathrooms and locker rooms, the use of students' pronouns in classrooms, and **education gag orders** (American Civil Liberties Union [ACLU], 2023).

Conservative state legislators are proposing legislation that is based on biological determinism (Schiappa, 2022). These legislators define gender only as binary, which they view as "divinely ordained and assigned to each person according to divine will" (Kolakowski, 2022, para. 3). They do "not accept a person's stated gender identity, and they will not accept the possibility that there are any nonbinary people" (para. 4). As a result of their beliefs, some legislators have introduced legislation that prevents schools from recognizing or supporting any gender identity other than the sex assigned at birth.

The number of banned books in classrooms and school libraries about characters who identify as LGBTQ+ or themes related to LGBTQ+ identities reached the highest level ever in the 2022–2023 school year as a small group of families and conservative organizations labeled the books as "harmful" and "explicit" (Meehan & Friedman, 2023). However, most people do not agree with those bans. A poll by the American Library Association (2022a) found that three in four parents of public school children have a high degree of confidence in school librarians to make appropriate decisions about the books that their children read, and 7 in 10 voters oppose the removal of books from public libraries.

Legislation in at least 10 states declares that "teachers, staff, and classmates aren't required to use students' pronouns or names if they don't align with the student's sex assigned at birth" (Pendharkar, 2023, para. 1). Courts are now considering cases in six states in which teachers are being obliged to tell parents their child might be trans. School districts argue in these cases that students have privacy rights and may be concerned about coming out to their parents, who may be very uncomfortable with their gender identity. In considering all of the proposed anti-trans legislation, ACLU lawyer Chase Strangio concluded that the anti-trans legislation is trying to stop "a trans young person's sense that they can be a part of anything" (Ciesemier & Strangio, 2023, para. 22).

# The Cost of Sexism and Gender Discrimination

**Learning Objective 4.4** Describe how sexism and gender discrimination have affected both women and men in their career choices, incomes, and general well-being.

Sexism is the systemic oppression of girls and women based on the belief that women are inferior to men. Often, it occurs in personal situations of marriage and family life where the husband or father "rules the roost." It also occurs in the workplace when women hold lower-status jobs, work for men, and receive lower wages than men. Society's deep-rooted assumptions about how men and women should think, look, and behave continue to lead to discriminatory and oppressive behavior based on gender alone. In its worst form, sexism is based on **misogyny**, which is contempt for women and the characteristics associated with femininity.

Women are oppressed in countries around the world. For example, girls and women are sewing clothes for U.S. companies at low wages in sweatshops in many developing countries. Their home countries offer limited, if any, rights or protections. The United Nations has found that "when [women's] lives are improved, the benefits reverberate across society" as the lives of their children and other dependents as well as their own improve (UN Women, 2018, p. 73). However, much work remains to achieve gender equity, as shown in the following statistics about the status of women on a global level:

- Around 2.4 billion women of working age do not have equal economic opportunity and 178 countries maintain legal barriers that prevent them from working (The World Bank, 2022).
- Globally, 47% of women are in the labor force compared to 72% of men (International Labour Organization, 2022a).
- One in three women in the world have experienced sexual violence in their lifetime (World Health Organization, 2021).
- Women's work remains undervalued, as shown by a gender pay gap of 20% globally (International Labour Organization, 2022b).
- As many as 90% of adolescent girls in some countries are not in upper secondary school, and as many as 44% of girls and 34% of boys in some countries do not have the opportunity to learn to read or write in a primary school (The World Bank, 2016, 2019).

Many people discriminate on the basis of gender without realizing it. Because people were raised in a sexist society, they think their behavior is natural and acceptable and may not recognize discrimination when it occurs. Women may not be aware of the extent to which they do not participate equally in society, and men may not acknowledge the privilege that their gender bestows on them—signs that the distinct roles have been internalized well during the socialization process.

**Gender discrimination** is not only practiced by individuals; it has been institutionalized in policies, laws, rules, and precedents in society. These institutional arrangements benefit one gender over the other, as described in the following sections that examine gender differences in jobs and income, as well as sexual abuse and harassment, in the United States.

## Jobs

Although more women are entering jobs traditionally held by men, women and men continue to be overrepresented in the traditional occupations for their sex, as shown in Table 4.2. The jobs in which women predominate are accompanied by neither high prestige nor high income. People in professional positions, such as teachers and nurses, do not compete in income or prestige with architects and engineers. Most of the jobs traditionally held by men are regarded as more prestigious than "women's jobs," in large part because men have traditionally been more highly valued in society, with greater access to power and resources, contributing to continuing discrimination against women in ways that devalue the jobs to which they have the greatest access (Schutz, 2022).

Women comprise over 70% of the workers in health care support, office and administrative support, personal care, health care practitioners, and education and libraries, while men are at over 80% of the workers in engineering, construction, extraction, transportation, installation, maintenance, and repair (U.S. Census Bureau, 2023). It has been difficult for women to enter administrative and skilled jobs. These jobs have fewer entry-level positions than less prestigious jobs. The available jobs for many women are often those with short or no promotion ladders, few opportunities for training, low wages, little stability, and poor working conditions. Clerical and sales positions are examples of such jobs, but even professions such as teaching and nursing offer little opportunity for career advancement.

When men enter traditionally women's careers, they typically do not hold the same positions as women, as shown for school positions in Figure 4.1. Many preschool teachers in child care settings other than public schools earn a median salary of $30,210, half the salary of other teachers (U.S. Bureau of Labor Statistics [BLS], 2023b).

**Table 4.2** Examples of the Most Sex-Segregated Occupations in 2021

| Occupations Traditionally Employing Women | Women Working in This Job | Median Annual Earnings | Occupations Traditionally Employing Men | Men Working in This Job | Median Annual Earnings |
| --- | --- | --- | --- | --- | --- |
| Skincare specialists | 98.3% | $32,805 | Brick masons, block masons, and stonemasons | 99.0% | $42,838 |
| Preschool and kindergarten teachers | 97.6% | $34,569 | Roofers | 98.7% | $38,911 |
| Legal secretaries and administrative assistants | 95.9% | $53,487 | Automotive body and related repairer | 98.3% | $45,302 |
| Speech-language pathologists | 94.6% | $70,955 | Crane and tow operators | 98.2% | $64,828 |
| Executive secretary and executive administrative assistants | 94.4% | $63,646 | Carpenters | 98.0% | $42,914 |
| Child care workers | 94.1% | $25,365 | Electricians | 98.0% | $56,709 |
| Other personal appearance workers | 93.5% | $26,868 | Construction laborers | 96.7% | $40,054 |
| Dental assistants | 92.7% | $35,349 | Aircraft mechanics and service technicians | 95.8% | $70,247 |
| Dental hygienists | 92.0% | $62,489 | Telecommunications line installers and repairers | 95.8% | $63,341 |
| Medical assistants | 91.4% | $35,170 | Firefighters | 95.3% | $73,806 |
| Dietitians and nutritionists | 91.1% | $59,469 | Surveying and mapping technicians | 94.0% | $56,467 |
| Medical records specialists | 90.3% | $45,177 | Construction managers | 92.4% | $79,863 |
| Receptionists and information clerks | 89.6% | $32,397 | Industrial truck and tractor operators | 91.4% | $37,329 |
| Hairdressers, hairstylists, and cosmetologists | 89.5% | $31,311 | Electrical and electronics engineers | 90.6% | $106,087 |

SOURCE: U.S. Census Bureau (2023).

**Figure 4.1** Teachers and Principals by Sex, 2020–2021

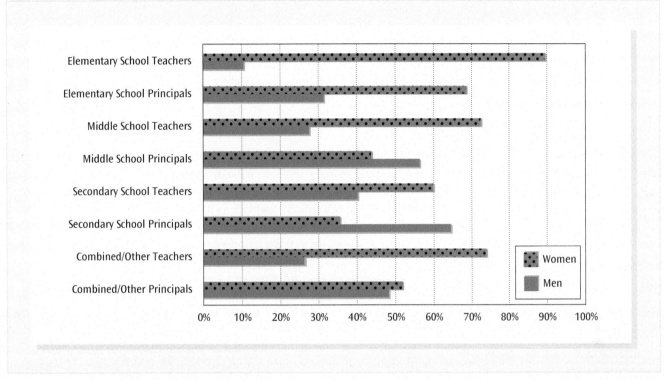

SOURCES: National Center for Education Statistics (2022d, 2022e).

A higher percentage of principals are men in elementary schools than are teachers, and at the middle school level and higher, principals are more likely to be men than women. And, not surprisingly, public school principals earn more than teachers with an average salary of $113,470 as compared to $61,600 for teachers in 2020–2021 (National Center for Education Statistics [NCES], 2022a, 2022c).

The participation gap between men and women in a number of professions has narrowed over the past few generations but has not been eliminated. Women are still underrepresented in mathematics, science, and technology fields. In 1950 only 6.5% of all physicians and surgeons were women; in 2021, 36.7% were women. The percentage of women lawyers has increased from 4% to 38.7%, but only 15.9% of engineers, 17.9% of computer programmers, and 15.9% of clergy are women (U.S. Census Bureau, 2023). The number of women in some professional jobs should continue to rise because women are earning an increasing number of degrees in these fields. For example, women earned 21% of the undergraduate degrees in computer and information science in 2019–2020 (NCES, 2022b). Their participation in these fields is likely to grow as an increasing number of girls learn to code.

Men generally earn more than women because they are working in higher-paying jobs than women, as shown in Table 4.1 and Figure 4.1. In applying intersectionality to jobs and income, it becomes clear that young men who have grown up in families with low incomes are less likely than young women in similar families to finish high school and college, leaving them, for the most part, to lower-paying and less stable jobs with limited or no fringe benefits. Fewer vocational and technical programs are available in high schools than in the past, but research studies indicate that young men in those schools have a higher graduation rate than in traditional schools (Reeves, 2022).

What do these trends suggest to educators? First, schools have prepared a growing number of young women to see themselves as professionals and have helped them obtain the knowledge and skills to pursue those fields. At the same time, a limited number of young men are pursuing jobs that traditionally employ women. In the past, young women were often not encouraged by guidance counselors and other educators to prepare themselves for the higher-paying and more prestigious jobs in engineering and computer science. Even more overwhelmingly, men are not being prepared to work in the health, education, administration, and literacy careers, in which many more people will be needed in the future (Reeves, 2022). What educational strategies could equalize the numbers of men and women pursuing the fields in which the respective groups currently have limited representation?

## Income

**Pearson eTextbook**

**Video Example 4.3**

This video discusses the gender pay gap and the consequences of inequity in pay.

https://www.youtube.com/watch?v=DKrgRBiSnPM

Historically, men in the United States have been expected to be the breadwinner for the family. Until the 1960s, many women were the primary care providers for their children and managers of the household. In more recent years, the higher educational levels of women, the high cost of living, and other factors have contributed to larger percentages of women in the workforce. Only 16.7% of all married women worked outside the home in 1940; by 2022, 56.8% of them were employed, with the rate being above 75% for women between the ages of 25 and 54 (BLS, 2023a).

Women who were working full time and year-round in the United States in 2022 earned 84% of the income earned by men (U.S. Department of Labor, 2023). The wage gap has narrowed over the years—it was 60% in 1980, but it persists. One reason for the reduction in the difference between men and women's earnings is that women are earning more, but the problem is that men are earning less than in the past, which could be the result of the decline in manufacturing jobs as well as the decline of organized labor unions (Stein, 2018). However, the increase in women's earnings is no longer much greater than the increase of men's earnings (Kochhar, 2023). Women are much more likely to report that employers treat women differently. At the same time, women are more likely to interrupt their career to balance family and work (Aragão, 2023). The pay differential may also be related to discrimination in the workplace, as more women (42%) report discrimination than do men (22%) (Parker & Funk, 2017).

An increase in the wages earned by women in the United States and around the world contributes greatly to eliminating poverty and providing their children a better education and nutrition (UN Women, 2018). Figure 4.2 compares the median annual earnings of men and women in the United States over the past 56 years. The salary differential is less for younger women than for older women. Women age 25 to 34 working full time were making 92% of what men were making. However, by age 35, the salaries

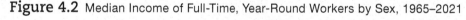

**Figure 4.2** Median Income of Full-Time, Year-Round Workers by Sex, 1965–2021

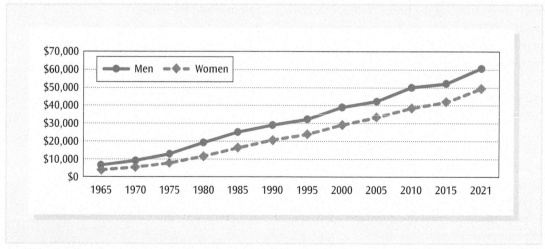

**SOURCE:** U.S. Census Bureau (2023).

for women start to lag behind those of men (Kochhar, 2023). While education typically increases earnings, it is not a deterrent to the gender pay gap. At each level of enhanced academic achievement, the median income for men exceeds that of women. Race and ethnicity are also a factor in women's salaries, with both White and Asian women's salaries exceeding those of Latina and Black women at all levels of education.

Even as income and job equity has improved over the past 50 years, women in the United States are more likely than men to be in poverty or on the verge of poverty. In 2021, 12.6% of all women in the United States earned wages below the official poverty level of $13,788 for one person (U.S. Census Bureau, 2022b). Families with households headed by women with children under age 18 and no spouse present were even more likely to be in poverty; 37% of them were in poverty compared with 18% of men-headed families and 7% of married couples (U.S. Census Bureau, 2022a). Transgender people also have high levels of poverty; 21% were living at the poverty level or below in 2021 (Wilson et al., 2023).

Although more men than women over the age of 25 have earned doctoral degrees and professional degrees in fields such as law and medicine, that pattern is changing (U.S. Census Bureau, 2022a). The percentage of women who are completing postsecondary degrees across all degree levels is now higher than men, as shown in Figure 4.3. Completing a vocational or technical program in high school or a postsecondary degree does give young people a better chance of finding a job that will provide a comfortable and secure life, which is often the primary expectation families have for education.

## Sexual Abuse and Harassment

**Sexual harassment** is a form of sex discrimination that has long existed in the workplace, where workers have been the recipients of unwanted and unwelcome sexual behavior. The perpetuator often is in a position of power over the victim and uses that power to secure favors or to make sexual advances. In other cases, it is a coworker who makes unwanted advances. **Sexual abuse** and harassment have been underreported for years. Both women and men were often not believed when they reported sexual harassment or violence. They were frequently condemned for their accusations at a time when they greatly needed support to overcome the damage of an assault.

In 2006, activist Tarana Burke initiated the "MeToo" movement when she began to speak out about the sexual violence experienced by her and the young women of color with whom she worked. Burke's goal was to help survivors of sexual violence heal. When actress Ashley Judd publicly accused film producer Harvey Weinstein of sexual harassment in October 2017, the world was ready to take notice. A week later, actress

**Figure 4.3** Degrees Awarded by Sex, 2020–2021

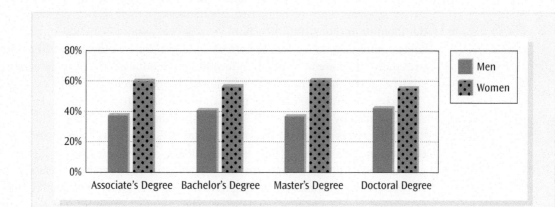

**SOURCE:** U.S. Census Bureau (2021).

Alyssa Milano called for women who had been sexually harassed to reply to her tweet with "#Me Too." She had 30,000 responses by the next morning (Zacharek et al., 2017). Girls, women, and men spanning all races, ethnicities and income levels around the world began sharing their experiences at the hashtag #MeToo, initiating an international dialogue about sexual violence. The movement toppled CEOs, media moguls, entertainers, TV news anchors and analysts, professors, and politicians. While one of the goals of the movement was to hold perpetrators accountable, another goal was to support survivors by connecting them to community resources and support systems. Activists continue to call for the reform of legal systems so that people who report sexual abuse are believed and their cases are investigated while they work to prevent sexual violence by educating communities.

The United Nations Women's report *Turning Promises into Action: Gender Equality in the 2030 Agenda for Sustainable Development* indicated that "eliminating all forms of violence against women and girls . . . [is] critical to ensuring healthy lives and well-being for people of all ages" (UN Women, 2018, p. 73). Much more work is needed to accomplish that goal. Both men and women report receiving unwanted sexual attention:

- Over half of women and almost one in three men in the United States have experienced sexual violence in their lifetime (CDC, 2022a).

- One in four women and one in 26 men in the United States have been raped or a victim of an attempted rape in their lifetime (CDC, 2022a); almost half of the victims were raped by an acquaintance (National Coalition Against Domestic Violence [NCADV], n.d.).

- On some U.S. reservations, Native American women were 10 times more likely to be murdered than other women (NCADV, 2016).

- In 2021, 18 percent of high school girls and 5% of high school boys reported being "forced to do sexual things (e.g., kissing, touching, or being physically forced to have sexual intercourse)" (Clayton et al., 2023, p. 68), with nearly three in five of these incidents occurring on dates.

As in other areas related to gender, sexual harassment also occurs in the halls and classrooms of schools, often while other students watch. Just over half of trans and nonbinary students reported being verbally harassed at school because of their gender identity. One in five of these students were physically harassed (e.g., pushed or shoved), and 8% of them were physically assaulted (e.g., punched, kicked, or injured with a weapon) (Kosciw et al., 2022). Transgender students are at particular risk of harassment and bullying at school, and the results are very serious. Eight-two percent of transgender individuals have considered suicide and 40% have attempted it, with the highest rates among transgender youth (Austin et al., 2020).

In a survey conducted by the U.S. Government Accountability Office (GAO; 2021), 24% of students reported being sexually harassed in their schools because of their gender identity in the 2018–2019 school year. Sexual assault is a widespread problem on college campuses. Forty-five percent of undergraduate women report that it is very or extremely problematic; 20% of undergraduate men and 36% of undergraduate trans students agree. At the undergraduate level, 26% of cisgender women undergraduates, 7% of cisgender men, and 23% of trans and nonbinary students reported nonconsensual sexual contact by force or inability to consent (Canter et al., 2020).

Perpetrators of sexual harassment include teachers, school administrators, janitors, coaches, and bus drivers as well as other students. It is not only boys who harass others; girls are also guilty, although less often. The harassment can be in person or online; it can be verbal (e.g., making insulting remarks or jokes, spreading sexual rumors), visual (e.g., sharing naked pictures, making obscene gestures), or physical (e.g., pinching, fondling, or flashing). At worst, the victim is sexually abused or raped. If actions by other students or adults are unwelcome by victims and make them uncomfortable, scared, or confused, they constitute harassment.

Sexual harassment can be very damaging to its victims, having an impact on their emotions, mental health, and general well-being. They are more likely to suffer from depression, anxiety, interrupted sleep, eating disorders, loss of interest in activities they used to enjoy, physical health complaints, and decreased academic achievement and school participation (GAO, 2021). They may feel powerless and that they can't control their lives. They may feel self-conscious, embarrassed, afraid, and confused. It can also affect their school performance. They may participate less in classrooms and find it difficult to pay attention. They may skip school because they feel unsafe. They are more likely than other students to have been in a physical fight in school and may have been suspended (Patrick & Chaudhry, 2017).

Elementary school and adolescent boys are the primary perpetrators and victims of sexual and **gender harassment**. They harass new students; haze rookies on sports teams; and initiate new members of a fraternity through drinking rites and sexual games that can be dangerous to their health and well-being. These harassers operate on a code that denigrates girls, gay men, lesbians, and anybody else who they feel threatens their privileged gender role. They may do everything possible to prove their masculinity, even if that requires harassing girls and each other. Those boys who do not meet these gender expectations try to avoid settings in which they may be bullied, beaten, or humiliated. While some boys stand up to these pressures, many practice a code of silence where they watch their peers bully others without intervening or reporting incidents to a teacher or parent. Young men between 15 and 19 years old can suffer from the emotional stress that these actions elicit, resulting in a suicide rate that is four times higher than for girls (CDC, 2023b).

Educators and families alike may try to explain away sexual harassment on grounds that it is typical adolescent behavior for boys and place the blame on a few bullies. Young men may be confused by accusations of sexual harassment, in part because the behavior has for too long been viewed as typical for adolescents. Many principals and teachers don't know that harassment is occurring in their schools or ignore it. Most students say they are not comfortable reporting incidents to teachers or other school personnel. They are most likely to tell a friend, but many, especially boys, tell no one. However, sex and gender harassment and discrimination are social justice issues that are included under civil rights laws. Students who have suffered from such harassment are beginning to fight back through the courts. All states have laws governing sexual assault and, with certain type of assaults, such as statutory rape (i.e., sexual intercourse with a minor), the penalties for offenders can be extremely severe, even if the relationships are consensual. When the younger party is under the legal age for consent and the offender over the prescribed age, penalties may result in years of imprisonment and the requirement of registering as a sex offender, sometimes for life.

School officials cannot ignore the sexual harassment and abuse of students, and school districts may be forced to pay damage awards if they do. Educators may be fired if found to be harassing a student, their actions may be reported in the news media, and they will be reported to local police officials. Schools and school districts are legally required to protect students from sexual harassment by Title IX. Any school receiving federal financial assistance must have an antidiscrimination policy and grievance procedures that address sex and gender discrimination, including harassment.

Policies and practices within schools may need to be revised, and discussions should involve the broader community of students and families. Educators can assist in the elimination of harassment, bullying, and other youth violence. They can start by modeling appropriate behavior and avoiding sexual references, innuendoes, and jokes. They should monitor their own behaviors to ensure that they are not using their power as an authority figure to harass students. Educators can also encourage students to form or join school leadership groups that work to educate others about and prevent sexual harassment. Educators can help young men feel empowered enough to resist being bystanders to sexual harassment and other bullying. The positive attributes of masculinity and femininity, such as honor, respect, integrity, ethics, and doing the right thing, should be reinforced in schools. They can help all students be resilient, especially when they do not meet the stereotyped expectations of their gender.

# Classroom Implications: Gender Inclusion

**Learning Objective 4.5** Create instructional and classroom management strategies that will promote gender equity in classrooms.

Gender-conscious and inclusive classrooms and schools support the overall well-being, academic achievement, and social-emotional development of children and youth (Chappell et al., 2018). Teachers who are **gender conscious** recognize how gender affects the lives of students (Kuriloff et al., 2017). As Ms. Lin found in her classroom in the introductory case study, girls and boys receive messages daily about what it means to be a girl and a boy. "These messages influence what they do, how adults and peers interact with them and what paths their lives take. Schools play a particularly large role in shaping students' gender identities, their beliefs about themselves, and the possibilities they picture for their lives" (Kuriloff et al., 2017, p. 5). Schools also contribute to the prevention of bullying, cyberbullying, harassment, and discrimination. They ensure that all students see themselves in the curriculum, in books, on bulletin boards, and in videos.

One of the first steps teachers should take is to evaluate their own biases. Biases related to gender often intersect with biases around race, ethnicity, socioeconomic status, religion, and sexual orientation. Too often when people think of gender, they are thinking of White girls and boys, making students of color invisible. As classrooms become gender equitable, teachers will need to make sure they are consciously including students of color, those who are not Christian, and students from low-income families. Teachers, counselors, teacher aides, coaches, principals, and other school personnel such as custodians and bus drivers all have critical roles in creating educational spaces that affirm gender identities. Let's examine some of the approaches for supporting gender equity in schools.

## Ungendering Classroom Practices

Schools, like most institutions, are gendered. Students are often sorted by their gender as they line up, are assigned a seat, select a partner, or play in a center of an elementary classroom (Mangin, 2022). Statistics on their academic performance and behavior are reported by their sex. They play sports with students of the same sex. They usually dress according to gender rules. And teachers and other educators treat them differently based on their gender. Think about how many times teachers use "boys" and/or "girls" as they manage the classroom, transitioning students from one activity to the next, breaking for lunch or recess, and assigning students to a group or project.

The language used in the classroom is important. The use of inclusive language helps all students feel that they belong and are valued in the classroom. Rather than using binary language (i.e., "boys and girls"), teachers at preschool and elementary levels are beginning to use alternate language such as "scholars," "friends," or "children" (Mangin, 2022).

"Gender identity and gender expression are part of everyone's lives. Restrictive enforcement of the binary can have a negative effect on many people's lives. This doesn't mean that the binary needs to be dismantled; this doesn't mean that everyone ought to be androgynous" (Myers, 2021, p. 58). It does mean that gender should be carefully considered in creating school environments that support students as they learn and clarify their gender. Beginning as early as preschool, students should be free to be themselves and not be forced into following the gender rules based on their sex assigned at birth. Girls should be able to play with trucks and build things with blocks; boys should be able to play with dolls and cook in the play kitchen. In the dramatic play center, children should be able to dress up in clothes of their choice. Even children who identify their gender as binary may feel pressure to be an easily identifiable boy or girl. "Decreasing gendered classroom practices may make students less likely to self-censor or police one another's gender expression, allowing children to develop a sense of self that is not limited by gender restrictions" (Mangin, 2022, p. 331).

**INCLUSIVE CURRICULUM**   Under the current cultural wars in conservative states, some teachers and administrators may be reluctant to include anything related to transgender and nonbinary students in the curriculum. They may be unsure about the content that is appropriate for students of different ages. Many school districts and state departments of education have guidelines for supporting transgender students. At least seven states in 2023 required that the curriculum include LGBTQ+ topics (Meckler, 2022). However, some states ban any attention to LGBTQ+ people or issues in the classroom. You should be familiar with the laws and policies that may impact the content that you teach.

The posters on the walls, the books in the classroom, and the curriculum should reflect the gender, racial, ethnic, religious, and other identities of students in the class. Students should be able to see themselves and others in the resources they use to learn (Myers, 2021). Inclusion of students based on their gender and its intersections with race, ethnicity, class, and religion will be different depending on the subject being taught. Students should be exposed to the contributions of women and trans people as well as men throughout history in their social studies and English classes. Learning about LGBTQ+ historical events and people in the general school curriculum helps trans and nonbinary students see that they are not alone and that role models exist for them as well as cisgender students. History courses that focus primarily on wars and political power focus primarily on men; history courses that focus on the family and the arts more equitably include both sexes. Science courses that discuss the great scientists often neglect to discuss the societal limitations that prevented women from being scientists. Women scientists and writers of the past often used the names of men or were required to turn their work over to men colleagues who either published the work under their names or assumed lead authorship. In biology and health, students could learn about anatomy and reproduction in a way that doesn't assume that all students in the class are cisgender (Myers, 2021). Because teachers control the information and concepts taught to students, it is their responsibility to present a view of the world that includes women, trans people, nonbinary people, and men and their wide ranges of perspectives.

Many outstanding books about gender-nonconforming children help younger children learn that not everyone is like them, and differences are acceptable and valued. Discussions about characters and events in books not only increase students' knowledge but also help combat myths and stereotypes they have about people who are different than them. By middle school, students are ready to explore the images and messages in advertising and media to expand their understanding of gender rules and stereotypes. In high school, they could analyze current events that range from court cases and changing laws to discrimination against women, trans, and nonbinary people as they develop their skills to think critically. All students at all levels of education should be able to see fictional characters and real people with different gender identities in the books they read, the films they watch, and the pictures on the bulletin boards and walls of their classrooms.

Textbooks are generally selected by a school district or state committee. If teachers are fortunate, the books accurately reflect the rich diversity of the United States and encourage students to think critically about the multiple perspectives of the population. Even the best textbooks are not likely to include references to or reflections of all the cultural groups that live in the school's community. Most textbooks do not yet reflect trans or gender-nonconforming identities. Even when teachers are not assigned a textbook with multicultural content, they can supplement it with discussions, debates, research projects, speakers, and other resources to help students understand the history and experiences of their ancestors, families, and communities. Teachers can expose students to multiple perspectives on gender, help them unlearn gender myths, and help them think critically about the stereotypical gender rules under which society operates.

Students are bombarded by subtle influences in schools that reinforce the notion that boys are more important than girls and cisgender students are superior to trans and nonbinary students. This unplanned, unofficial learning—the hidden curriculum—has an impact on how students feel about themselves and others. Sexism and **transmisia** are often projected in the messages that students receive in the illustrations, language, and content of texts, films, and instructional materials.

**INTERACTIONS WITH STUDENTS**   Students value their relationship with teachers (Kuriloff et al., 2017), and educators have control over their own interactions with students. While teachers may not think they respond differently to boys, girls, trans, and binary students, when their interactions are critically examined, they most likely will find that they do, in fact, respond differently based on a student's gender. To overcome the common problem of letting boys respond more often to questions, teachers should focus on making sure other students have an equal voice in the classroom. Also, the type of feedback provided to students should be reviewed for gender bias, including how much time is taken to provide oral feedback and encouragement and the depth of the feedback. To ensure one group of students (e.g., girls/boys/trans/nonbinary students, White girls/boys, Black girls/boys, Hispanic girls/boys, Muslim girls/boys) is not being privileged over another, teachers should ask themselves the following questions and make changes as necessary to ensure all students are being treated fairly:

- To what group do I give more detailed and useful feedback?
- Whom do I call on first to answer questions?
- Who is not participating actively in discussions or group activities?
- Who am I most often disciplining? For what reasons am I disciplining them?
- Who is receiving most of my positive verbal responses in class or my written responses on assignments?
- Who is taking the leadership roles in group and whole-class activities?

One of the goals of gender-conscious education is to eliminate power relationships based on gender in the classroom. Teachers can monitor the tasks and activities in which students participate in the classroom by tracking their responses to the questions above. Boys often receive more attention because of their misbehavior than for their academic performance (Lindsey, 2021). Girls and boys may not always share leadership in classroom activities and discussions. Girls and young women may need to be encouraged to participate actively in math and science whereas boys may need more encouragement in reading and writing activities.

Girls are particularly affected by negative stereotypes such as being perceived as overly emotional and less capable than boys in areas such as science, engineering, mathematics, and technology (Kuriloff et al., 2017). They sometimes internalize these negative stereotypes, leading them to perform worse on tasks than they are capable of—the implementation of the **stereotype threat theory** (Steele, 2011). Teachers can help students overcome stereotype threat by ensuring that they are not reinforcing negative stereotypes as they interact with students and helping students develop self-confidence about their abilities. In a qualitative study of the instructional experiences of girls in single-sex schools, Kuriloff and his colleagues (2017) found that discussions about gender, its role in society, and being a woman in the twenty-first century contributed to girls having a deeper connection to classroom material.

So far, we have focused primarily on teachers' interactions with girls and boys in the classroom, but a classroom may also include one or more trans or gender-nonconforming students. Those students may find that their peers are not very welcoming and may have even ostracized them. Teachers should intentionally make sure that all students are included in all activities, that other students are respectful, and that trans and gender-nonconforming students' voices are heard. "A sense of belonging in school can help counteract other negative environmental influences that could otherwise decrease children's well-being" (Mangin, 2020, p. 99). In addition, teachers could become an **ally** to trans and gender-nonconforming students by being willing to listen and advocate on their behalf. Gender-conscious teachers create and maintain a safe, welcoming, and inclusive space for all students regardless of their gender identity.

## Guiding Gender Discussions

Gender discussions will appear in classrooms whether or not teachers planned for them. A preschooler or primary student may ask why Susie has two mommies, why Eric dresses up like a girl in the drama center, or why Tiana's dad stays home with the children. Older children may harass boys who have feminine characteristics and tease girls who prefer playing with the boys. Young people may begin to question binary identities and rebel against traditional gender roles. They may ask why a woman has never been elected president of the United States. They may ask why state legislators are being so hard on trans people. Are you prepared to help students understand these issues?

**STUDENT VOICES**   One of the goals of gender inclusive education is to create a space in which all students feel free to speak, be heard, and have their experiences accepted as legitimate. Cisgender girls are often silenced as they enter adolescence and are expected to embrace more feminine or binary roles and become less assertive. Girls of color, girls in low-income families, and trans and nonbinary students may feel invisible in the classroom because they do not see themselves in the curriculum, they have been made to feel that they are inferior to their peers, or they have been victims of sexism, transmisia, racism, or classism. Young men are not often encouraged to break out of the expected masculine role, with its own rules of what is required to be a man. They may become depressed and have lower self-esteem as they try to conform to the rules (American Psychological Association, 2018). Teachers should be aware of the students who are silent and not participating in class or group activities and figure out ways to engage them in learning. Students who have been traumatized because of family problems, violence in the community, harassment, or other events that have seriously disrupted their lives may need additional support, but teachers will not know of those needs if they do not reach out to students.

Young men should have opportunities to explore their roles in society and learn to speak for gender equity and the equity of other oppressed groups. Teachers may not find it easy to provide such opportunities. Many students resist discussions of power relations and how they stand to benefit or lose within those relations. However, the value to students and society is worth the discomfort that such discussions may cause students. The classroom may be the only place in which students can confront these issues and be helped to make sense of them.

**LEARNING TOGETHER**   If left alone, many students choose to sit with and participate in group activities with members of the same gender. To ensure that students interact with students of a different gender and with students who are gender nonconforming, teachers may have to assign seats and groups. Small, heterogeneous, cooperative work groups reduce the emphasis on power relationships that characterize competitive activities. These activities can be designed to provide all students, even those who are often marginalized in the classroom, opportunities to participate at a more equitable level.

How can you help students understand, respect, and be supportive of each other regardless of their gender identity? Trans and nonbinary students may feel uncomfortable or awkward in class and may be misidentified by their peers and even bullied. Teachers should create a classroom environment in which "no one is silenced and everyone is recognized and valued" (Editors of Rethinking Schools, 2016, p. 23).

Gender-inclusive education does not require that boys, girls, trans, and nonbinary students be treated the same in all cases. Gender may need to be emphasized at times to ensure equity. Instructional strategies should be varied to engage all students with the subject matter, as discussed earlier. Engaging more boys in the subject matter may require the use of spatial and graphic aids such as manipulatives in mathematics. A wide repertoire of instructional strategies should include some that are more engaging to some students than others. Girls, boys, and gender-nonconforming students will learn to operate in one another's cultural spheres, and the teacher can avoid the disengagement of one group that typically results with the use of instructional strategies that are geared to only one group of students.

## Affirming Gender Identities and Supporting Trans and Nonbinary Students

Where do trans and nonbinary students fit in classrooms that privilege binary gender? When students are divided into groups by their sex assigned at birth, to which group would an intersex or nonbinary student join? Students who are gender-nonconforming begin to feel excluded or mistreated. Students who dress differently than the school gender norm may face negative comments from peers and be isolated in the classroom. Positively acknowledging gender differences contributes to students' feelings of belonging in the classroom. Using the names and pronouns that students choose to identify themselves shows respect for them and may positively support their self-esteem and feelings of empowerment (National Academies of Sciences, Engineering, and Medicine, 2020).

**PARENTAL RIGHTS**   Under the best conditions, educators and parents or families would work together to support students who are questioning their gender identity, but the issue of educators notifying parents about their children identifying themselves as gender-nonconforming is now in the courts. To protect students from possible harm at home and to affirm students' gender identity, some schools have policies that "allow students to socially transition—change their name, pronouns, or gender expression—without parental consent" (Baker, 2023, para. 13).

Regardless of their political affiliation, parents generally believe that they know what is best for their children and that they should be notified about changes to their children's gender identity unless evidence of physical abuse at home exists (Baker, 2023). Not all trans and gender-nonconforming students, civil rights groups, or courts agree. "In each of the lawsuits, the parents allege that school officials followed formal or informal policies, guidelines, or 'gender support' plans that permit students to choose new names or pronouns, or adopt a different gender identity without their parents' consent." (Sawchuk, 2022, para. 3). In some cases, parents accuse teachers and school officials of actively deceiving them or refusing to abide by their wishes (Sawchuk, 2022). At this point, limited legal precedent exists on students' privacy rights and schools, but state legislators may force teachers or school officials to notify parents if their children confide to an educator that they are questioning their gender.

# Critical Incidents in Teaching

## CJ Comes Out

When Mr. Jackson first took attendance in his algebra class at the beginning of the school year, he asked students to introduce themselves and indicate the name and pronouns they would like him to use as he referred to them. Mr. Jackson did not know whether any of his students were trans or nonbinary, but he had previously had students who were, and he wanted to ensure that he honored their names and pronouns. Based on the introductions and names, all students in this class appeared to be cisgender. However, some students might be worried about the reactions they would receive from classmates if they publicly disclosed their trans or nonbinary identity. Other students may be in the process of questioning their gender identity.

A few months into the semester, Cindy asked Mr. Jackson if she could talk to him privately. When they met at the end of the school day, she informed him that she was transgender and preferred to be called CJ and use *he/him/his* pronouns. Although he wanted Mr. Jackson and other teachers and school officials to use his preferred name and pronouns, he didn't want school personnel to contact his parents because they were "not at all okay with his new gender identity." Mr. Jackson agreed to make the name change in his records and to use CJ's preferred name and pronouns in the classroom, but he had many more questions to ensure the transition proceeded smoothly. Had CJ told all of his teachers? Would he be telling his classmates or let them figure it out? Did his family know? Did he feel safe in school? Had this change affected CJ's emotional and mental well-being as reflected in his attendance and schoolwork?

The middle school that CJ attended had a policy that supported trans and nonbinary students, including the use of their preferred names and pronouns. The school's policy recognized that the safety of some students could be endangered if their families did not accept their gender identity and protected students by not informing families of students' requests for name changes and recognition of their gender identity in school. The next day, Mr. Jackson began using CJ to call on him during class. Over the next few days, Mr. Jackson changed documents for grading and attendance to reflect CJ's preferred name and added a note to his packet for substitutes to ensure the requested name rather than the name in official school records would be used in class.

## Questions for Discussion

1. How should Mr. Jackson interact with CJ's family during a parent–teacher conference without referring to the student's name? How should Mr. Jackson respond if the family asks him directly about CJ's gender identity?

2. What resources would you recommend to CJ to assist him with this transition in and outside school? Where would you seek assistance if you were in Mr. Jackson's position?

3. What are the school policies related to gender-nonconforming students in your local school district? What state legislation, if any, addresses gender-nonconforming students and what impact does the legislation have on school policies and practices?

**SUPPORTING TRANS AND NONBINARY STUDENTS** Over 70% of trans students and 50% of nonbinary students feel unsafe in school compared to less than 10% of cisgender students (Kosciw, 2022). With a goal of making schools safe for all students, GLSEN has identified four resources to promote a safer climate and more positive school experiences for LGBTQ+ students: "1) student clubs that address issues for LGBTQ+ students, 2) school personnel who are supportive of LGBTQ+ students, 3) LGBTQ+-inclusive curricular materials, and 4) inclusive, supportive school policies, such as inclusive anti-bullying policies and policies supporting transgender and nonbinary students" (Kosciw, 2022, p 48). Clubs for LGBTQ+ students are generally **gay–straight alliances** or **gender and sexuality alliances (GSAs)** that provide a safe space for them to meet in what may be a hostile school climate. Students in schools with active GSA clubs were less likely to hear derogatory remarks, felt safer, experienced less victimization, and were less likely to miss school for safety reasons. LGBTQ+ students in schools with GSA clubs also reported lower levels of depression and higher levels of self-esteem than in schools without such clubs.

Supportive school personnel and administrators are also an important resource for LGBTQ+ students, especially if the school climate is hostile to them. Most (96%) of the students in the survey could identify at least one school staff member whom they believed was supportive of LGBTQ+ students. School-based mental health professionals and teachers were identified as the most comfortable talking about LGBTQ+ issues, but less than half of them were "very" or "somewhat" comfortable with the discussions (Kosciw, 2022).

As discussed earlier, an inclusive curriculum helps trans and cisgender students recognize that LGBTQ+ people have always been part of the country's history, contributing in many positive ways to the growth of a democratic nation. In the GLSEN survey, only 3 in 10 students had been exposed to LGBTQ+ people, history, or events in the curriculum and nearly half of the time the representations were presented in a negative way (Kosciw, 2022). Students can also learn about LGBTQ+ people and their experiences through other resources available to them at school. Seventeen percent of LGBTQ+ students reported using textbooks that reference information about LGBTQ+ people, and only 43% of the students had access to LGBTQ+-related books in the school library. However, nearly half of the students could access LGBTQ+-related information on school computers. Students who were in a school with an inclusive curriculum experienced the same benefits as having a GSA club and had higher academic outcomes (Kosciw, 2022).

School policies related to the rights and protections of trans and nonbinary students send the message to the school community that they are an important part of the community. Comprehensive policies "take a firm stance against interpersonal microaggressions (e.g., corrective education and/or consequences for staff or students actively refusing to use youths' preferred name and pronouns) and explicitly support gender diversity (e.g., gender-inclusive restrooms, locker rooms, and dress codes)" (Austin et al., 2020, para. 34) The GLSEN survey found that when schools had these policies, trans and nonbinary students were less likely to miss school because of safety concerns and were more likely to feel a part of the school community. With comprehensive policies in place, trans and nonbinary students were twice as likely to report incidents of harassment and assault than if no policy existed, and school staff were twice as likely to respond effectively. Outcomes for trans and nonbinary students were even more positive in that the chances of all types of discrimination were less likely to occur under comprehensive policies that covered the use of their name and pronouns, clothing choices, bathroom and locker use, and participation on a sports team (Kosciw, 2022)

## Title IX

**Title IX** of the Educational Amendments of Public Law 92-318, passed by Congress in 1972, is among the most significant laws regarding gender equity enacted in the United States. The law states:

> No person in the United States shall, on the basis of sex, be excluded from participation in, be denied the benefits of, or be subjected to discrimination under any education program or activity receiving federal financial assistance.

Title IX addresses the differential, stereotypical, and discriminatory treatment of students on the basis of their gender in preschool through higher education. It protects students and employees in virtually all public school systems and postsecondary institutions in the United States, including (1) the admission of students, particularly to postsecondary and vocational education institutions; (2) the treatment of students; and (3) the employment of all personnel.

Title IX makes it illegal to treat students differently or separately on the basis of sex. It requires that all programs, activities, and opportunities offered by a school district be equally available to boys and girls. All courses must be open to all students. For example, boys must be allowed to enroll in family and consumer science classes, and girls must be allowed in technology and agriculture courses. Regarding the counseling of students, Title IX prohibits biased course or career guidance; the use of biased achievement, ability, or interest tests; and the use of college and career materials that are biased in content, language, or illustrations. Schools cannot assist any business or individual in employing students if the request is for a student of a specific gender. There can be no discrimination in the type or amount of financial assistance or eligibility for such assistance. Because only half of teen mothers attain a high school diploma by age 22 (CDC, 2021), the law was also intended to provide access to schooling for pregnant and parenting teenagers.

The most controversial section of Title IX until recently was related to athletic programs. Girls and young women must be able to participate in intramural, club, or interscholastic sports. The sports offered by a school must be coeducational, with two major exceptions: (1) when selection for teams is based on competitive skill and (2) when the activity is a contact sport. In these two situations,

Since the passage of Title IX in 1972, more girls at all ages participate in athletic program in and outside of school, including sports in which they were previously excluded such as lacrosse and wrestling.

separate teams are permitted but are not required. Although the law does not require equal funding for girls' and boys' athletic programs, equal opportunity in athletics must be provided. The courts apply the following three-part test to determine equal opportunity:

1. The percentage of men and women athletes is substantially proportionate to the percentage of women and men in the student population.

2. The school has a history of expanding opportunities for women to participate in sports.

3. A school fully and effectively meets the interest and abilities of women students even if it may not be meeting the proportionate expectation of the first requirement.

When Title IX was passed in 1972, 3.7 million young men (93% of athletes) and 294,015 young women (7%) were participating in high school sports. By 2021–2022, those numbers had increased to 4.4 million (58%) boys and 3.2 million (42%) girls (National Federation of State High School Associations, 2022). At the college level, the number of men and women also increased, as shown in Figure 4.4. Of collegiate women athletes, 68% were White, 11% were Black, 6% were Hispanic/Latina, 2% were Asian, 4% were international, and 8% were other women. The diversity of collegiate head coaches changed only slightly for men's sports since 1996, but the percentage of women coaching women's teams has decreased from over 90% in 1972 to 41% in 2020, as shown in Figure 4.4. Only 16% of women head coaches of collegiate women's teams were coaches of color; 24% of athletic directors were women in 2020, and 93% of them were White (Wilson, 2022).

Sports are healthy and beneficial to all students, but trans and nonbinary youth face challenges as they participate in sports activities (Meyer, 2021). These challenges have the greatest impact on trans women who are perceived by some people as having an athletic advantage over cisgender women. Participating in sports is very important to some students, including trans and nonbinary students, and contributes to their mental health and well-being. School policies for the inclusion of trans and nonbinary athletes contribute to better school attendance, higher grades, and greater feelings of safety (Goldberg & Santos, 2021). A growing number of states and school districts are developing inclusive policies that promote the involvement of trans and nonbinary students in sports, including at the competitive level, while other states and districts are banning their participation in competitive sports.

Athletic associations and the International Olympics Committee (IOC) have been working for a number of years on the fair way to include trans athletes in competitive events. One of the IOC goals has been to move away from the testosterone-based practices of the past, which denigrated and policed trans athletes, especially trans women.

**Figure 4.4** Participation of Men and Women in College Sports

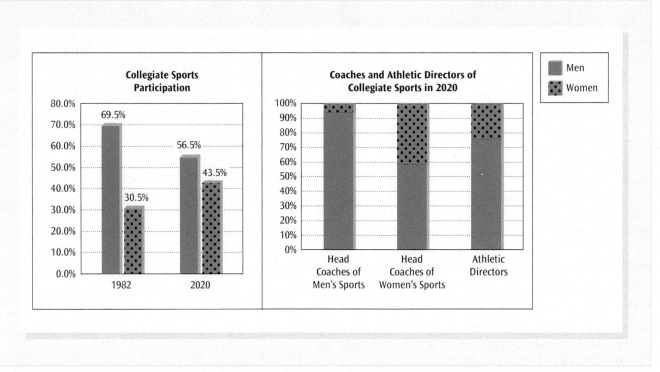

**SOURCE:** Wilson (2022).

The new trans-inclusion framework of the IOC "places the responsibility of establishing guidelines for trans inclusion on each individual sport. It also concludes that sporting bodies should not assume that transgender women have an inherent advantage over cisgender women, nor should transgender women have to reduce their testosterone levels to compete" (De La Cretaz, 2022, para. 8). Other athletic federations are not required to follow the IOC framework, and some have already indicated that they will continue to test testosterone levels.

Current controversial issues related to Title IX are the inclusion of gender and sexual orientation in the law, the rights of accused rapists on college campuses, and the use of bathrooms and locker rooms by trans students. The controversy related to rape is primarily on the rights of the accused for due process, charging that colleges are "exhibiting anti-men bias in disciplinary proceedings" (Kim, 2023, p. 62). On gender, President Joe Biden signed an Executive Order in January 2021 to prohibit discrimination on the basis of gender identity or sexual orientation, which was followed by notification by the Office of Civil Rights of the enforcement of that Order. A federal judge in Tennessee issued a temporary block on the U.S. Department of Education's implementation of its Title IX guidance in the 20 states that were the plaintiffs in *State of Tenn., et al. v. U.S. Department of Education*. These states argued that the department's action "interfered with their ability to enforce laws that prohibit transgender students from using bathrooms and locker rooms or playing on sports teams that align with their gender identity" (Brink, 2022, para. 4)

The law alone has not changed the basic assumptions and attitudes that people hold about appropriate roles, occupations, and behaviors based on gender, but it has equalized the rights, opportunities, and treatment of students within the school setting. More than three in five Americans who have heard of the law believe that it has had a positive impact on gender equality (Igielnik, 2022). Experience has shown that once discriminatory practices are eliminated and discriminatory behavior is altered, even unwillingly, changes in attitudes follow. The Title IX coordinator in a school district should be able to assist teachers with any questions about gender discrimination and equity.

# Revisiting the Opening Case Study

When Ms. Lin decided it was time to teach a unit on gender to her seventh-graders, part of her motivation was that the girls were complaining about the boys touching them and the boys were calling each other derogatory names. Her unit raised the students' awareness of stereotypes and gender rules that pigeonhole students into feminine and masculine identities. It also introduced them to sexism. However, much more is needed to help students understand and think critically about gender. The unit did not address the sexual harassment issues about which she was worried. It did not address gender identities beyond masculinity and femininity. She may have been supplementing the curriculum with gender-conscious materials and examples. Ms. Lin is reinforcing the messages from the unit throughout the school year, encouraging respectful interactions with each other regardless of student gender identity, and using transgressions, such as calling each

other names, as teachable moments. Teaching about gender is a never-ending project as students mature and question their gender. Teachers can be a catalyst for expanding students' knowledge and improving their behavior toward each other.

## Reflect and Apply

1. How and where in the curriculum of the subject you plan to teach could you insert a unit or information on gender? What topics would you include?

2. How and when could you talk about gender identities with students at the grade level that you plan to teach?

3. How will you handle incidents of sexual harassment in your classroom or in the hallways such as calling other students names or touching each other inappropriately?

# Summary

- People develop a gender identity that reflects their deeply held sense of self as a man, woman, transgender, or nonbinary person. Transgender people may identify themselves as trans women or trans men when their gender does not match the sex they were assigned at birth. Other people see themselves as both a man and woman (bigender), neither a man nor woman (agender), genderqueer, gender nonconforming, or another term that describes their nonbinary gender identity. Although some children know when they are fairly young that their sex assigned at birth and gender do not match, many students struggle with their gender identity in middle school and high school.

- Masculinity and femininity are learned through the socialization process, which begins at birth and is reinforced both in the home and at school. People's gender identities interact with their racial, ethnic, class, and religious identities, which influence how people see themselves and how they are treated in society. When addressing gender issues in the classroom, teachers should be aware of the impact of intersectionality on individual students.

- Sex is used to identify people as men or women based on their reproductive and sexual anatomies. Sex as a boy or girl is generally assigned at birth with the exception of intersex children. The two sexes are biologically much alike until puberty, when hormones increase their physical differences. Intellectual differences are small or nonexistent, and those differences can be overcome with education. Families, friends, religious leaders, peers, teachers, television, the Internet, and social media

teach children how to be a boy or a girl. Society has different expectations or gender rules for men and women and socializes children and young people to meet those expectations. Boys are generally raised to be more aggressive, and girls tend to be more supportive and empathetic. Before they begin school, most boys and girls have already learned to select different toys and participate in sex-segregated activities. Girls and women are generally allowed more latitude in adopting masculine characteristics, whereas men are more likely to be bullied or harassed if they exhibit any feminine characteristics.

- The struggles for gender equity came neither easily nor quietly. The first wave of the women's movement began with the Seneca Falls Convention in the mid-1800s as women and their allies began fighting for the right to vote and laws that would give women the right to divorce, own property, speak in public, work, and prevent abuse. The right to vote was granted in 1920. It was not until the 1960s that women's groups again began to work for the civil rights of women. The Equal Pay Act of 1963, the 1964 Civil Rights Bill, and Title IX of the 1972 Education Amendments were major stepping-stones. It was during this second wave that the National Organization for Women (NOW) was founded. The women's movement began to face a backlash in the 1980s as support for women's equality waned. When the women's movement was reignited in the 1990s, feminists tried to appeal to a broader group united in the struggle for equity for all groups, including women of color, low-income women, and lesbians. Today, women continue to fight for equal pay, flexible work schedules, family leave, reproductive rights, and other civil rights issues. The movement made a significant step forward when a large number of women were elected to Congress in the 2018 midterms, but their representation is still less than 30%. The decade beginning in 2021 has been filled with anti-trans legislation at the state level on health care, participation in sports, use of public accommodations such as bathrooms and locker rooms, the use of students' names and pronouns in classrooms, and education gag orders that prevent any acknowledgment of trans and nonbinary people in schools.

- Sexism is the systemic oppression of girls and women based on the belief that men are superior to women, whether in the home or in society. Despite laws prohibiting certain forms of discrimination, many people continue to discriminate on the basis of deeply ingrained discriminatory practices, sometimes without even realizing it. More women than men are taking Advanced Placement classes; more women are completing associate's, bachelor's, and master's degrees than men. However, while more women are seeking degrees in math and technology than in past years, their enrollments are still not on par with their men peers. Women still have not reached income equity with men. Women who work full time year-round earn only 84% of the income earned by men. Over one in three of U.S. single women with children are in poverty or on the verge of poverty. Even though women are more likely than men to earn college degrees at all degree levels, they continue to earn less than men, in part because they are more likely to take time off to raise children or address family issues or are working in jobs with lower

incomes. Sexual abuse and harassment affect all genders, particularly trans and nonbinary people, and continue to be a problem in both schools and the workplace. Sexual harassment and sexual abuse are clear violations of the law and must be reported and stopped. The consequences for the victims are often severe.

- Gender-conscious and inclusive education is designed to treat members of all sexes, trans students, and gender-nonconforming students fairly and equitably in the curriculum, in interactions with teachers, and in instructional activities. To ensure this, textbooks and lessons should reflect the history and experiences of people with diverse gender identities and be devoid of gender bias, each student should be respected, the voices of each student should be heard, and participation and leadership in classroom activities and discussion should be shared among students of different gender identities. Teachers can intentionally monitor their interactions with students to check whether they are encouraging all students to be actively engaged in learning, whether they are asking each student to think more deeply about a topic, whether they are disciplining one group of students (e.g., boys) more often than another, and whether they are providing more detailed and useful feedback to boys, girls, or gender-nonconforming students.

- Title IX, passed into law in 1972, is among the most significant legislation enacted to provide gender equity in schools. It prohibits differential, stereotypical, and discriminatory treatment of students on the basis of their gender. One of the most visible and controversial sections of Title IX involves athletics. When Title IX was passed, girls comprised 7% of high school athletes and less than 30% of collegiate athletes; 50 years later, 42% of high school and 44% of collegiate athletes were women.

## Pearson eTextbook Application Videos

The following videos are available in the Pearson eTextbook and can be used to practice observing and applying what you learned in this chapter.

**Pearson eTextbook Application**
**Video Example 4.4**

In this video, a teacher discusses her study of gender bias in her district's reading materials.

**Pearson eTextbook Application**
**Video Example 4.5**

In this video, two counselors engage in a fictitious conversation. One counselor is uncertain about how to work with a transgender client and the other helps think through the process.

# Chapter 5
# Sexual Orientation

## *Alison G. Dover and William Toledo*

## Learning Objectives

*As you read this chapter, you should be able to:*

**5.1** Define sexual orientation and explain how it is socially constructed in the United States.

**5.2** Explain historical and contemporary civil rights issues impacting LGBTQ+ people in the United States.

**5.3** Analyze the toll that heterosexism has taken on LGBTQ+ youth and educators.

**5.4** Evaluate ways educators can support, affirm, and advocate for LGBTQ+ students within and beyond the classroom.

## Opening Case Study

As an English language arts teacher in a K–8 school, Monica Johnson enjoyed finding books that would interest and engage her seventh-grade students. Her classroom library included a wide array of texts and genres, including fiction and nonfiction, narratives and graphic novels, and contemporary and historical texts. Monica was intentional about selecting texts that reflected her students' diverse interests and identities and believed that while no one book would be right for all students, all students should be able to find a book that spoke to them. As her classroom library grew, students began to come by during lunch and after school to check out books; she even had a few students who weren't in her classes ask if they could borrow something to read.

During Monica's third year as a teacher, she read a news story about book challenges in a neighboring school district. Apparently, some people were concerned that children were being exposed to "inappropriate" content in literature and were demanding an audit of the school library. As Monica looked at the list of books being challenged, she noticed that most of them featured characters of diverse sexual orientations and gender identities and that protesters seemed to be suggesting that reading about LGBTQ+ (lesbian, gay, bisexual, transgender, queer/questioning) people wasn't age-appropriate for elementary and middle school students. But Monica knew that several of her own students had LGBTQ+ family members, and others

identified as LGBTQ+ themselves. She wondered how it would affect students to be told that their families or their own identities were "inappropriate." She also worried about whether she herself was at risk: her classroom library included several of the books being challenged. Monica thought her students and their parents appreciated the breadth and diversity of her library, but she was concerned that the news article might bring negative attention to her classroom. She decided to bring up the issue at the next faculty meeting.

During the faculty meeting, Monica was surprised to learn that some of her colleagues were unaware of parental concerns about library books. It made her question whether the media was sensationalizing the issue of censorship by depicting challenges made by a small number of people as if they were representative of the community. She was also surprised by the diversity of responses among her colleagues: some thought that students shouldn't have access to any books other than those required by the district's curricular frameworks, while others thought that students should have unrestricted access to just about any book in print. Most of Monica's colleagues thought there should be some limits on which books were included in classroom libraries but didn't agree about what those limits should be. When one teacher said that he thought his sixth-graders weren't ready to read books about dating and same-sex relationships, another asked whether that meant they should ban books like *Cinderella* and *Sleeping Beauty*

*(continued)*

for pushing young children toward heterosexuality. It seemed that for every point raised by one teacher, another teacher presented an opposing argument. After 20 minutes of discussion, Monica's principal wrapped up the conversation, suggesting that they form a committee to discuss the matter further.

## Reflect

1. Why is it important for students to have access to books written by and about diverse people, including LGBTQ+ people?

2. Should parents be able to limit or restrict their own child's access to books in public schools and libraries?

Should they be able to limit or restrict the books that other children have access to?

3. What are the implications of suggesting that it is not "age appropriate" to learn about people of diverse genders, sexual orientations, or family structures? How might the concept of "age appropriateness" be used to privilege people with some identities at the expense of others?

4. When did you first read a book featuring an LGBTQ+ character or storyline? Do you think this was the "appropriate" age to first encounter with a book about LGBTQ+ people and communities? Why or why not?

# Understanding Sexual Orientation

**Learning Objective 5.1** Define sexual orientation and explain how it is socially constructed in the United States.

The previous chapter focused on biological and socially constructed aspects of sex and gender, and how educators can promote gender equity and bias-free classrooms for students of all gender identities. People with diverse sexual orientations and gender identities, including people who are **lesbian**, **gay**, **bisexual**, **transgender**, **queer**, or **questioning** (often referred to as members of the **LGBTQ+ community**), are present within every school, community, state, and country. However, despite decades of progress regarding LGBTQ+ civil rights, members of this community continue to face bias and discrimination at the individual and institutional level. Research indicates that LGBTQ+ people are more likely to be targeted by violence than heterosexual and gender-confirming people and that rates of anti-LGBTQ+ violence increase in response to hate speech by politicians and on social media (Center for Countering Digital Hate, 2022). **Homophobic** and **transphobic** attitudes also create hostile climates for LGBTQ+ students and educators, impacting their social-emotional, academic, and professional trajectories. This chapter focuses on the identities and experiences of LGBTQ+ students, communities, and educators; the laws that affect LGBTQ+ people in the United States; and what teachers can do to ensure the health, safety, and academic success of students with diverse sexual orientations and gender identities.

The term **sexual orientation** refers to a person's identity as a romantic and sexual being. Some people—including people who identify as **heterosexual** (or **straight**), lesbian, or gay—are primarily or exclusively attracted to people of only one sex or gender, while other people, including bisexual and **pansexual** people, are attracted to people of multiple sexes or genders. People who describe themselves as **asexual** do not experience romantic or sexual attraction at all, while people who identify as **demisexual** only experience attraction after they form a deep emotional connection with another person.

Many people find that their experience of attraction changes throughout their lifetimes, as sexual orientation for most individuals falls on a continuum; it is rarely stagnant and consistent over time. It is not uncommon for young people to describe themselves as questioning because they are not yet sure of—or ready to label—their sexual orientation. According to the most recent Gallup poll data, 7.1% of all adults in the United States and 21% of adults born between 1997 and 2003 identify as members of the LGBTQ+ community, more than half of whom (56%) self-identify as bisexual (Jones, 2022). While this data may appear to suggest that the size of the LGBTQ+ community is increasing, most researchers think these findings reflect an increased willingness to **come out**, or publicly disclose one's sexual orientation or gender identity, rather than dramatic shifts in people's sexual orientations or behaviors. This may be attributed to victories for LGBTQ+ equality, such as marriage equality and others that are discussed later in this chapter.

All people have a sexual orientation. However, as is the case for members of other dominant religious, cultural, linguistic, and socioeconomic groups, people who are heterosexual may not spend much time thinking about their sexual orientation. As members of the majority group, heterosexual people typically think of their way of experiencing romantic and sexual attraction as "normal," a process referred to as **heteronormativity**—the normalizing of heterosexual relationships and identities while "othering" LGBTQ+ relationships and identities. Most people grow up with heterosexual parents and see positive representations of heterosexuality in literary, religious, social, and media contexts. Many children's fairy tales and movies celebrate heterosexual romance and marriage; heterosexual teachers routinely talk about or display pictures of their partners; classmates tease about heterosexual crushes; and school activities provide opportunities for children to playact heterosexuality through "father–daughter dances," requirements to form "boy–girl" teams in physical education, or the crowning of a prom king and queen. Because of this, children and adolescents may grow up thinking that heterosexuality is the only viable pathway toward a healthy adulthood, especially if they are unaware of or have limited exposure to LGBTQ+ people within their family or their religious or local community.

## The Social Construction of Sexual Identity

The overwhelming majority of people identify as heterosexual and cisgendered. However, LGBTQ+ people have always existed. Artistic representations of same-sex relationships have been found in ancient Greek, Roman, Mesopotamian, Chinese, Japanese, Egyptian, and African art, and same-sex relationships were so common in many ancient cultures that the concept of labeling someone on the basis of their sexual interactions simply did not exist (Mark, 2021). It wasn't until the rise of Christianity, and its emphasis on procreation and the regulation of sexual behavior, that same-sex romantic and sexual behavior was questioned.

The term "homosexual" was first used in the mid-nineteenth century to describe people who are attracted to other members of their sex (Bronski et al., 2013), and it was rapidly adopted by the medical and psychiatric community, who were looking for ways to define a community they did not fully understand. Unlike ancient civilizations, who saw a broad range of romantic and sexual behaviors as acceptable, by the twentieth century, many societies considered homosexuality a psychiatric condition or pathology. In the United States, it wasn't until 1973 that the American Psychiatric Association formally removed homosexuality from its list of mental disorders. Because of this history, the word *homosexual* has a negative connotation in the United States; many LGBTQ+ people find it offensive and prefer to be called gay, lesbian, bisexual, or queer.

Heterosexual people often ask what makes some people lesbian, gay, or bisexual. However, that question is as difficult to answer as what makes some people straight. They simply are. Research suggests that there is a biological component to sexual orientation but that there isn't a simple or single gene that triggers one's sexual orientation. In 2019, researchers at the Broad Institute and Massachusetts General Hospital published a study examining DNA among almost half a million people (Ganna et al., 2019). They found that genetic heritability accounts for between 8 and 25% of an individual's likelihood of having same-sex relationships and that there are hundreds or thousands of genes that contribute to sexual orientation.

Moreover, even when people are genetically predisposed to feel attraction toward people of a particular sex (or of multiple sexes), the way they experience, describe, or act upon feelings of attraction are impacted by an array of environmental factors. People in religiously or socially conservative communities may feel pressure to identify as heterosexual, even if they experience feelings of attraction to people of their own sex, while people in socially liberal communities may be more likely to experiment with or explore relationships with people of multiple genders. Biology alone also cannot account for the ways people's experience of their sexual orientations change throughout their lifespan; it is not uncommon for someone to have relationships with people of a specific gender for most of their lives, and then "suddenly" fall in love with or be attracted to someone of another gender. Although it is a common misconception in some circles, researchers have negated that being lesbian, gay, bisexual, or queer is a "choice."

In fact, most researchers describe sexual orientation as a continuum or social construct, meaning that while people's feelings of romantic or sexual attraction are real, the way society labels people based on their romantic or sexual feelings or behaviors is both arbitrary and artificial. In his famous study of sexual behavior 80 years ago, Alfred Kinsey used a 7-point scale between absolute heterosexuality (a Kinsey 0) and absolute homosexuality (a Kinsey 6) to categorize his interviewees. He found that people's experiences of sexual attraction—as well as their sexual behavior—varied tremendously and that many people exist at neither a 0 nor a 6. Moreover, he found that many people's sexual feelings and behaviors are fluid and change over time. Some people have been attracted to or had sexual relationships with people of the same sex at some time in their lives but are not exclusively gay or lesbian. Others are exclusively attracted to people of one sex or gender, while others are attracted to people of multiple genders, rendering even the labels of "heterosexual," "homosexual," or "bisexual" insufficient descriptors. This fluidity has led many young people to reject labels and are finding new ways to describe their sexual identities.

Our sexual identity is based on sexual attractions, related behaviors, and a connection with others with the same orientation (American Psychological Association, 2019). It is about how people identify themselves. Most researchers agree that sexual orientation is established early in life, even if children are not yet conscious of themselves as sexual beings. As children begin to imagine their future romantic and sexual relationships, they become aware of how their own emerging identities are reflected—or negated—by adults around them.

In the United States, LGBTQ+ is often used as an umbrella term to refer to people of diverse genders and sexual orientations. It emerged as "LGBT" in the 1990s as lesbian, gay, bisexual, and transgender people formed social and political alliances to advocate for their collective civil rights; over time, the *Q* was added to the acronym to include people who identified themselves as queer or questioning. Historically used as a pejorative term for lesbian women and gay men, in the late twentieth century, the word *queer* was reclaimed by some members of the LGBTQ+ community as a term that means "not heterosexual" but does not offer additional detail regarding someone's sexual orientation or gender identity. For some LGBTQ+ people, describing oneself as queer reflects a refusal to assimilate to heterosexual norms (such as traditional gender roles or emphases on marriage and raising a family), while for others it is simply a way of indicating one's membership within the LGBTQ+ community. Sometimes the acronym LGBTQIA+ is used to explicitly include intersex and asexual people; other times, the *A* denotes the inclusion of allies, or heterosexual and cisgender people who are vocal advocates with and on behalf of LGBTQ+ people and communities. However, language is always evolving and, as is the case for other identity groups, it is always best practice to follow peoples' lead regarding the language they use to refer to themselves; it would not be appropriate to call a student who identifies as "queer" a "lesbian" nor to identify a student who refers to themselves as "bisexual" as "gay."

This emphasis on mirroring the language people use to define and describe themselves is especially important for educators. Some children have a strong sense of themselves as gendered, romantic, or sexual beings in early childhood, while others may not think or talk about feelings of romantic or sexual desire until later in adolescence or young adulthood. In either case, it is important to recognize that the feelings children or teens express about their sexual identities and current or future relationships are subject to change over time. LGBTQ+ children who are raised in predominantly heterosexual communities or in schools that do not affirm LGBTQ+ families may struggle with feelings of isolation or disorientation. Research indicates that these feelings of isolation, especially in concert with homophobic bullying in schools and by media figures, have dramatic effects on students' mental and physical health (Kosciw et al., 2022). It is important for educators to be aware of the ways people of diverse sexual orientations and gender identities are discussed—or erased—within their school community and work toward creating affirming and inclusive spaces for all children and families.

Children, including LGBTQ+ youth, move through multiple stages of development as they grow as romantic and sexual beings. For people who are part of socially dominant groups, such as those who are primarily or exclusively heterosexual, this process is often unconscious: They do not think about themselves as exploring their sexual orientation; they think they are simply growing up. For people who don't see their sexual identities reflected or welcomed by others around them, experiences of romantic or sexual attraction can feel confusing and lead them to question the reality of their developing sexual identity. This process may include exploration and experimentation as they determine whether they are LGBTQ+, which could include testing relationships with people of multiple genders, including those to whom they are not necessarily attracted.

As they learn about what "feels right," adolescents may begin to identify themselves with a label or decide that none of the current labels describe them. At some point, many LGBTQ+ people decide to come out or talk about their sexual orientation with others around them; unsurprisingly, this is typically an easier process for students who are in familial, educational, and community environments in which they feel safe and affirmed than for those in environments in which LGBTQ+ people are invisible, silenced, or persecuted.

## Coming Out

Coming out is a complex and important step in the life of an LGBTQ+ individual. Coming out is not a one-time decision and is often one that a person makes based on the context (Human Rights Campaign [HRC], 2019). For example, some individuals may be "out" to their family and close friends, while not disclosing their LGBTQ+ identity in potentially hostile settings. LGBTQ+ people often find that they have to come out again as they change schools, begin a new job, move to a new community, or meet new people. As they move through adolescence, LGBTQ+ and heterosexual students alike are figuring out their sexuality and how to express it appropriately, often receiving mixed messages from their parents, their peers, and the media. Young people, whose understanding of their own gender, sexual, and romantic identities are often in flux, may come out multiple times or as multiple things (first identifying, for example, as "lesbian" and later as "queer," or first as "not straight" and later as "bisexual").

Additionally, coming out requires a great deal of reflection and consideration of safety within varied contexts as individuals make decisions to share their identity with others. Some LGBTQ+ people find that going through coming-out processes strengthens them, making them more empathetic to other oppressed groups, and increases their activism for social justice. LGBTQ+ individuals who are comfortable coming out often feel relief from hiding their identity and feel a sense of freedom in being themselves. **Being out** generally results in positive outcomes for adolescents, including better academic performance, higher self-esteem, and lower anxiety and depression as well as better health and general well-being (HRC, 2018a).

**Pearson eTextbook**
**Video Example 5.1**

In this video, a gay man discusses his coming out process. As he tells his story, consider the complexity of the coming out process for many people.

However, the coming-out process is not easy. Although many youth find affirming environments and acceptance in their households, in some cases, coming out results in the separation of LGBTQ+ individuals from their families due to negative or hostile reactions to their identities, Some political and religious groups continue to portray being gay as a sin or disease that can be eliminated or cured and may advocate a practice called "conversion therapy," which is a widely discredited and abusive form psychiatric intervention intended to change LGBTQ+ people's sexual orientation or gender identity. Antigay activists and parents may push youth and adults into programs designed to make them "normal" by denouncing their LGBTQ+ identity. Organizations such as the American Psychological Association (2019), the American Psychiatric Association (2018), and the American Academy of Child and Adolescent Psychiatry (2018) report that such approaches lack scientific credibility, are clinically unsound, reinforce negative stereotypes about LGBTQ+ people, and are medically and psychiatrically harmful.

Even those young people in supportive families and school communities are aware of anti-LGBTQ+ attitudes in the media and larger community. These attitudes have a negative impact on all LGBTQ+ people. Moreover, although many LGBTQ+ students are happy, well adjusted, and accepted by peers, most students who are or are perceived as such have experienced harassment: Data indicates that almost 80% of LGBTQ+ students have avoided school functions or extracurricular activities because they felt unsafe or uncomfortable (Kosciw et al., 2022). Thus, especially for students who do not have a supportive family or community, the process of becoming aware of their sexual orientation or gender identity may be associated with feelings of depression, isolation, or self-doubt. The messages that they receive from others may indicate that they are abnormal, wrong, or immoral or that their identity is a choice that will not serve them well in the future. They may be afraid of being targeted by peers or religious or political activists. They may not know that multiple sexual orientations have been characterized by psychologists as "normal aspects of human sexuality" (American Psychological Association, 2019, para. 14) or may think that they can or should try to change or hide their sexual orientation.

Students who are not LGBTQ+ themselves but have LGBTQ+ parents or family members may struggle with whether it is safe to talk about their families at school, especially if they only see representations of heterosexual families in the curriculum or at school functions. They may also be afraid of being targeted by homophobic community members or far-right political activists, who are increasingly using school boards as opportunities to enact anti-LGBTQ+ policies and espouse hateful rhetoric (Williams, 2022).

The pressures to be different from who they are contribute to LGBTQ+ students missing school, underperforming academically, and dropping out of school at a higher rate than heterosexual students (Kosciw et al., 2022). Research suggests that the harassment of LGBTQ+ students is increasing in response to media and political targeting of LGBTQ+ communities. In 2023, the Human Rights Campaign declared a "State of Emergency" for LGBTQ+ Americans in response to the dramatic uptick in anti-LGBTQ+ legislation in 2022 and 2023. Many of these bills specifically target LGBTQ+ students, teachers, and school policies (HRC, 2023b), underscoring the tremendous pressures facing these communities.

In response to this hostility, many LGBTQ+ people, and especially those whose families of origin are not accepting of their sexual orientation or gender identity, rely on their close bonds with people they describe as chosen family—supportive friends, peers, teachers, allies, and other members of the LGBTQ+ community—to provide social-emotional support. Schools themselves can play an important role by creating safe places for young people to come out and realize their full human potential. This is part of why **gay–straight alliances** (often called GSAs to reflect their inclusion of all members of the LGBTQ+ and ally communities) are so important for LGBTQ+ young people; they offer a literal lifeline for those experiencing rejection or hostility within or outside of school. GSAs are student-initiated clubs that bring together LGBTQ+ and straight students interested in building an inclusive community. They provide invaluable support to students by offering a supportive environment in which students can build friendships, discuss issues, and meet others with similar interests. When a school has a GSA, LGBTQ+ students report hearing fewer homophobic remarks and that they feel safer at school, they have higher self-esteem and are less likely to be depressed, and they say that school personnel are more likely to intervene when homophobic remarks are made (Kosciw et al., 2022).

In addition to providing a social community, GSAs also offer LGBTQ+ students the opportunity to engage in self-advocacy as they organize events around National Coming Out Day (October 11), the Day of Silence (April 1), and LGBTQ+ Pride Month (June). It is important to know that the federal Equal Access Act of 1984 guarantees that students at public schools have the legal right to form GSAs, and that if a school district allows students to establish other clubs, it must allow the formation of a GSA club. However, some schools require students to have their parents' permission to join any club in the school, which can prevent some LGBTQ+ students from safely joining a GSA (Lugg & Adelman, 2015).

GSAs can be an invaluable source of support to LGBTQ+ students.

**SOURCE:** UPI/Alamy Stock Photo

Every teacher will have students at different points along the gender and sexual identity continuum, in terms of their own identities and experiences but also their beliefs and behaviors. Understanding the influence of students' cultural memberships will be important as teachers try to open up the possibilities for all of them, regardless of their gender and sexual identity. Having teachers who are supportive of LGBTQ+ students and who intervene on their behalf contributes greatly to successful school experiences for these children and youth (Kosciw et al., 2022). In fact, teachers who are supportive of LGBTQ+ students and act as allies may even save the lives of at-risk LGBTQ+ students facing alienation or bullying at school or at home.

# Historical and Contemporary Struggles for LGBTQ+ Equity

**Learning Objective 5.2** Explain historical and contemporary civil rights issues impacting LGBTQ+ people in the United States.

For much of the twenty-first century in the United States, many LGBTQ+ individuals have felt supported in ways that enabled them to come out and live authentic lives as themselves. However, historically, this has not always been the case. Until the early 1980s, many LGBTQ+ people hid their identities, sometimes marrying a person who identified as or was perceived as a member of the "opposite" (or a different) sex, having children, and living as heterosexuals. Up to and continuing into the 2000s, many states had laws that criminalized being gay, allowing gay people to be arrested in their homes as well as public places (American Civil Liberties Union, 2023a). For many years, many laws labeled LGBTQ+ individuals as mentally unsound and considered homosexuality to be a mental disorder (Mora, 2015). This misconception is grounded in anti-LGBTQ+ biases and sometimes results in these individuals being pathologized by some media sources or for political purposes.

The effects of this discrimination and stigma have had dramatic impacts on LGBTQ+ visibility in schools, with some LGBTQ+ people choosing not to, or being forbidden to, teach due to homophobic attitudes among school leaders or community members. While some states, including California, Colorado, Connecticut, Illinois, Nevada, New Jersey, and Oregon, explicitly include LGBTQ+ histories as part of required K–12 curriculum (Movement Advancement Project, 2023d), in others, anti-LGBTQ legislation or school policies continue to create hostile climates for LGBTQ+ educators. In 2022, for example, Florida passed legislation forbidding teachers from discussing sexual orientation (even their own) in the classroom unless expressly required by state standards (Izaguirre & Farrington, 2023), resulting in the erasure of LGBTQ+ people and histories and leading some LGBTQ+ teachers to leave the field rather than hide their identities (Lavietes, 2022).

In the following pages, we trace the history of the LGBTQ+ civil rights movement in the United States, focusing on both the roots and impact of anti-LGBTQ+ discrimination as well as on ways LGBTQ+ people and their allies have organized to ensure that people of all sexual orientations and gender identities have access to basic human, civic, and legal rights.

## The Origins and History of Anti-LGBTQ+ Movements

It is important to note that homophobic and transphobic attitudes are relatively recent phenomena in the history of humanity. LGBTQ+ individuals and same-sex relationships existed and were common in the ancient world and in many different societies. For example, in ancient Greece and Rome, romantic or sexual relationships between two individuals were more often categorized along lines of class and status rather than sex or gender. Similarly, artwork and literature from Mesopotamia indicates that same-sex relationships were as common as opposite-sex ones and that same-sex relationships were treated as equal to those of the opposite sex within their society. Philosophers of the time, such as Aristotle, were not concerned with same-sex relationships, although some did reject the notion of giving up traditionally "masculine" or dominant traits and roles in relationships.

Most scholars point to certain interpretations and translations, and perhaps misinterpretations and mistranslations, of religious texts as the starting point for anti-LGBTQ+ sentiments that continue to this day. The Puritans colonized the Indigenous land that is now the United States and established societal norms that were based on patriarchal and clearly defined gender roles. In the mid-1600s, we saw the beginning of the criminalization of LGBTQ+ communities and relationships when two women, Sarah White Norman and Mary Vincent Hammon, were legally charged with "lewd behavior" in Plymouth, Massachusetts. This legal charge marked the first case in the world in which being a lesbian was criminalized.

**TWENTIETH CENTURY AND BEYOND**   Prior to the 1920s, few LGBTQ+ people in the United States were out. As LGBTQ+ people began being open about their identities and relationships, the United States saw an increase in anti-LGBTQ+ rhetoric and legislative targeting, something that has continued into recent times. Members of the LGBTQ+ community were routinely labeled as "mentally ill" throughout the early twentieth century, and many LGBTQ+ people were subjected to harmful psychiatric treatments such as electroshock therapy. The fight to combat the labeling of LGBTQ+ individuals as mentally ill is a long one and, as noted earlier in the chapter, the American Psychiatric Association finally removed homosexuality from their list of mental illnesses in 1973.

America began to see less conservative representation of relationships and sexuality in the 1950s when the rock 'n' roll era began, with artists such as Elvis Presley, Chuck Berry, and Little Richard. These artists celebrated sensuality and rebellion against society's rules in their lyrics and costuming, but the majority of artists still created exclusively within heteronormative and patriarchal themes. During this time, America also saw legislative efforts banning LGBTQ+ themes from theater and film.

However, literature and music did become sources of expression for the youth who broke the sexual norms, including writers and artists who continued to include queer individuals and content in their art. The Beats were young straight and gay poets and writers who congregated at the bookstores and small galleries in San Francisco during this period. Sexual freedom and the celebration of their gayness were hallmarks of their subculture, contributing to San Francisco becoming a safe and affirming place for gay people and *beatniks* during the 1950s and 1960s.

**INCREASED POLITICAL AND LEGISLATIVE TARGETING**    The post–World War II era in the United States was notable for an increased fear of communism (often referred to as McCarthyism or the "Red Scare" in recognition of the persecution of alleged communists). During this time, LGBTQ+ people were among the many groups targeted as a potential threat to national security, with lawmakers arguing that gay people could be extorted and forced to give up national secrets, a phenomenon historians describe as the "Lavender Scare."

In 1952, Congress passed the Immigration and Nationality Act (McCarran-Walter Act), which banned gay immigrants from entering the country. In 1953, the U.S. Senate called for a purge of gay people from the government, and President Dwight D. Eisenhower signed an executive order to dismiss them from the federal government—a practice that continued into the 1970s. Within a year, the Federal Bureau of Investigation (FBI), under Director J. Edgar Hoover, had identified more than 400 federal employees to be fired. Historians have estimated that tens of thousands of federal and other employees lost their jobs or were dismissed from the military during the next two decades (Faderman, 2015). It wasn't until the year 1995 that discrimination based on sexual orientation was banned in granting security clearances, and the year 1998 that discrimination based on sexual orientation was banned in government employment overall.

In addition to facing employment discrimination, gay men and lesbians were often arrested simply for existing. LGBTQ+ individuals were arrested by the hundreds in bars, parks, and theaters—even at gatherings in their own homes. Throughout the early twentieth century, police routinely raided LGBTQ+ bars and strip-searched people to determine whether they were wearing at least three pieces of clothing associated with the gender they were assigned at birth, leading to many cases of sexual assault, humiliation, and inappropriate arrest (Ryan, 2019). In some states and cities, citizens were encouraged to report their gay neighbors and work colleagues for violating antisodomy laws (laws that criminalized sex between two men), leading to numerous raids on LGBTQ people's homes or workplaces.

Throughout this period, anti-LGBTQ+ activists spread disinformation and propaganda equating LGBTQ+ communities with pedophilia, or engaged in fearmongering, often claiming that these communities were seeking to "recruit children into their ranks." This targeted misinformation was designed to shape public opinion, suggesting that being LGBTQ+ was a choice, that LGBTQ+ people were child or sexual predators, and that being exposed to LGBTQ+ people would somehow change children's own sexual orientations. During this time, calls for justice or equality for these populations were largely ignored by the U.S. government and other legislative bodies.

**ORGANIZING FOR LGBTQ+ RIGHTS**    Like members of other targeted groups, LGBTQ+ people and allies responded to police violence and legislative threats by organizing for their individual and collective civil rights, with especially visible activism in larger cities like San Francisco, Los Angeles, Detroit, Philadelphia, New York, and Washington, D.C. The main goals of those organizing were (1) to change public misconceptions relating mental illness to the LGBTQ+ community, (2) to combat harmful legislation disrupting the lives of LGBTQ+ individuals across the country, and (3) to end the cycle of violent police raids of LGBTQ+ safe spaces and homes across the country.

In recent years, historians have documented the tremendous impact of the many LGBTQ+ activists working toward inclusion nationwide, including people like Harry Hay, who became known as the father of the gay liberation movement and founded one of the first gay rights organizations, the Mattachine Society, in Los Angeles in 1950. The first lesbian civil rights organization, the Daughters of Bilitis, began meeting in 1955 to provide lesbians a place to meet and dance outside the gay bars that were often raided by police. Members Del Martin and Phyllis Lyon, who later were the first lesbian couple married in San Francisco, were leaders of this organization and within the LGBTQ+ civil rights movement throughout their lives (Faderman, 2015).

LGBTQ+ rights organizations were bolstered by the U.S. Supreme Court's 1958 ruling in *One, Inc. v. Olesen*, which provided constitutional protection for LGBTQ+-themed media. With approximately 2,000 subscribers, the Mattachine Society's magazine included articles, editorials, and short stories depicting LGBTQ+ communities. Although the magazine was far from erotic in nature, postmasters in Los Angeles seized and refused to deliver it, arguing that it violated obscenity laws due to its inclusion of LGBTQ+ people and content. In a one-sentence ruling, the U.S. Supreme Court overturned a lower court ruling banning distribution of the magazine. In addition to being the first U.S. Supreme Court case to explicitly address sexual orientation, *One, Inc. v. Olesen* established that material aimed at LGBTQ+ communities was not inherently obscene and that LGBTQ+ organizations and media were protected by the first amendment's free speech clause.

In the decades that followed, LGBTQ+-focused civil rights groups gained momentum and spread nationwide, often led by individual LGBTQ+ people impacted by discrimination. Initially, many LGBTQ+ people focused on building social networks in which they could safely express their identities and protecting themselves and their local community from police violence and employment discrimination. However, as the Civil Rights Movement intensified in the United States, LGBTQ+ people began to increasingly organize at the national level and work in solidarity with other civil rights leaders. The March on Washington on August 28, 1963, rallied a quarter of a million people for human, civil, and economic rights, which led to critical legislation for civil rights being passed by Congress, including the Civil Rights Act of 1964 and the Voting Rights Act of 1965. The LGBTQ+ community noted the success of the movement and continued to organize for LGBTQ+ rights, resulting in increased visibility for these people, communities, and activism.

A key turning point in the fight for equality was the **Stonewall Riots**, also referred to as the **Stonewall Uprising**. New York City's Stonewall Inn was known as a refuge and safe space for racially and socioeconomically diverse members of the LGBTQ+ community, particularly for Black and Latino/a queer and trans people, including **drag queens**. Like other bars frequented by members of the LGBTQ+ community, the Stonewall Inn was regularly raided by police. However, on June 28, 1969, what might have been a routine raid turned into a movement when the patrons of Stonewall refused to leave and resisted the invading police officers' commands. This initial refusal to comply led to a multiple-day demonstration for LGBTQ+ rights, initially led by Black drag queens but supported by a growing coalition of LGBTQ+ people and allies. Over the 4 days that LGBTQ+ community members and allies fought police efforts to forcibly remove them from the Stonewall Inn, their resistance garnered national attention and inspired other demonstrations and demands for LGBTQ+ rights. The Stonewall Uprising was a turning point in the movement for these rights. Although the uprising was violent and disruptive to the community, it also demonstrated the power of the community when people refused to back down from their fight for freedom from oppression and hate.

Ultimately, the Stonewall Uprising is credited as the start to a nationwide LGBTQ+ rights movement. The number of LGBTQ+ groups fighting for rights and equality grew from 50 to more than 800 across the United States. The post-Stonewall era also

**Pearson eTextbook**

**Video Example 5.2**

In this video, gain a deeper understanding of the ways in which the Stonewall Riots sparked a movement.

https://youtu.be/Q9wdMJmuBl A?si=MmEoUdkpExLpjtnS

saw a shift in some LGBTQ+ people's approach to advocacy, as organizations like the Gay Liberation Front led efforts to refuse to comply with unjust laws, reject assimilation, and celebrate the lives and visibility of diverse LGBTQ+ people and communities.

The first Pride Marches for LGBTQ+ rights would take place in New York, Los Angeles, and Chicago on the 1-year anniversary of the Stonewall Uprising, as thousands of LGBTQ+ people and allies celebrated their identities as they marched against discriminatory legislation. In 2019, the New York Police Department finally issued a formal apology for the raid on the Stonewall Inn bar, with Police Commissioner James O'Neill stating that "the actions taken by the NYPD were wrong, plain and simple. The actions and laws were discriminatory and oppressive, and for that I apologize" (Trotta, 2019).

**INCREASING VISIBILITY**  During the second part of the twentieth century, the increasing visibility of LGBTQ+ community members and their allies made it easier for gay men and lesbians to live out lives in which they openly acknowledged their sexual identities, particularly in larger metropolitan hubs and cities. As LGBTQ+ people gained safety and visibility, grassroots organizations grew into nonprofits focused on addressing discrimination in a wide array of legal, educational, political, and policy contexts. In 1973, the National Gay Task Force (later the National Gay and Lesbian Task Force, and now simply the NGLTF) and the Lambda Legal Defense and Education Fund were created, two organizations that proved pivotal to LGBTQ+ movements in terms of fighting LGBTQ+-oppressive legislation. These were followed in 1980 by the Human Rights Campaign political action committee. These organizations assisted with important legislative efforts, including cases related to the AIDS crisis (which disproportionately affected LGBTQ+ communities), legalizing domestic partnerships, and other civil rights issues.

In addition to organizing through advocacy groups, LGBTQ+ people began to seek and win elections in the 1970s. This happened more commonly with individuals who were not "out," such as Allan Spear and Barney Frank winning elections in the early 1970s. After winning, some politicians later came out and fought for LGBTQ+ equality. However, the 1970s also marked the first wave of openly LGBTQ+ individuals winning elections in the United States. Perhaps most famously, gay rights icon Harvey Milk was among the first openly gay citizens to win an election when he was elected to the San Francisco Board of Supervisors in 1977. Although Milk's legacy lives on today, both he and San Francisco's mayor George Moscone were murdered in a hate crime less than 1 year after Milk took office; their killer was a former city supervisor and police officer whose legal defense was that he had eaten too much junk food and was thus not criminally responsible for his actions. Although their killer had confessed to the crime, saying he "saw the city as going kind of downhill" in part due to its tolerance of overt homosexuality, he was ultimately convicted of voluntary manslaughter rather than murder, leading to widespread protests (Lindsey, 1985).

On a national level, the first openly lesbian senator, Tammy Baldwin, was elected to the U.S. Senate in 2012. In 2020, the United States saw Pete Buttigieg, the openly gay mayor of South Bend, Indiana, become a viable candidate for president, winning the most delegates in the first Democratic primary in the state of Iowa. Although Buttigieg did not win the nomination for president, the formal naval officer was appointed to the position of U.S. Secretary of Transportation under President Joe Biden's administration. In 2021, Delaware state senator Sarah McBride became the first openly trans state senator and as of 2023 was running to become the first openly trans member of the U.S. Congress. With these individuals and others, we have seen the number of elected LGBTQ+ legislators continue to increase over the past four decades at the local, state, and national levels.

**BACKLASH IN THE 1970S: ANTI-LGBTQ+ EFFORTS TO HALT PROGRESS**  As is common in civil rights movements, by the 1970s, a backlash had started against the

LGBTQ+ gains achieved over the previous decade. Far-right religious groups, particularly Evangelical Conservative Christians, began to influence politics, calling for a return to what they labeled as "family values." The term denoted that the only acceptable family was a heterosexual nuclear family: a marriage between a biological male and a biological female. The LGBTQ+ community was demonized and blamed for the destruction of the family as they fought for the equal rights of women, lesbians, and gay men and became a scapegoat for sexual liberation and the increasing number of divorces that emerged in the United States during the 1960s. This period marked the beginning of **culture wars** in the United States, in which cultural conflicts between social groups led to efforts to control education, social policy, and laws to force others to ascribe to one's own beliefs about how people should think or behave.

The backlash began in the mid-1970s when Miami's county commissioners proposed an ordinance that prohibited discrimination against people "for their affectional or sexual preference," following the lead of East Lansing (MI), Eugene (OR), St. Paul (MN), and Washington, D.C. The conservative media and far-right churches were outraged. Anita Bryant, a Sunday school teacher who was once fame-adjacent due to her singing and pageant careers, sought to regain relevance and became the face of the anti-LGBTQ+ movement as she traveled around the United States advocating for the repeal of Dade County's equality ordinance. Like other anti-LGBTQ+ activists, Bryant used fearmongering and hateful rhetoric to dehumanize LGBTQ+ people, arguing that the ordinance "would be discriminating against my children's right to grow up in a healthy, decent community" (Bryant, 1977, p. 18). Although a Harris poll found that 62% of registered Dade County voters supported antidiscrimination laws, the ordinance was repealed in a special election in June 1977.

The success of anti-LGBTQ+ activists in Florida led Bryant and her supporters to promote anti-LGBTQ+ efforts nationwide, using hate speech and the phrase "Save Our Children" to pressure other cities to remove LGBTQ+ people from their human rights ordinances. Ultimately, their efforts resulted in anti-LGBTQ+ legislation in cities across the country but also served as a catalyst for a revitalization of the LGBTQ+ civil rights movement. LGBTQ+ people and allies organized protests at Bryant's rallies, spoke out against misinformation at LGBTQ+-focused events and celebrations, and successfully organized against discriminatory policies at the state and local level; the year 1978, for example, saw the defeat of California's Proposition 6, which would have prevented gay people from teaching, and Initiative 13 in Seattle, which would have repealed the city's existing ordinance banning discrimination against gay people in city employment and housing. However, despite these successes, this period emboldened conservative cultural activists, who would continue to use fearmongering, vitriolic rhetoric, and dehumanization to target LGBTQ+ communities for decades to come.

**THE IMPACT OF THE AIDS PANDEMIC** The first cases of what is now called acquired immunodeficiency syndrome (AIDS) were reported by the Centers for Disease Control and Prevention in 1981, when a number of large U.S. cities reported otherwise healthy men were contracting a type of pneumonia that was usually found in cancer patients; the victims in all of the reported cases were gay men. As news of these cases spread across the country, social conservatives suggested the disease was a "punishment" for LGBTQ+ people, especially gay men who were accused of promiscuity, and used fears about contagion to isolate or marginalize LGBTQ+ communities. During this time, many referred to the disease as a "gay cancer" and later "gay-related immune deficiency" or GRID.

In 1984, scientists discovered the virus that was responsible for AIDS (the human immunodeficiency virus, or HIV) and developed a blood test to determine whether an individual was HIV positive. They learned that the virus was spread through the exchange of bodily fluids during sexual activity, needle sharing by drug users, and blood transfusions. However, even though science definitively proved that AIDS was caused by a virus that did not discriminate based on victims' sexual orientation, anti-LGBTQ+ stigma proved pervasive and devastating to HIV research and treatment. Globally, the AIDS pandemic has resulted in more than 40 million deaths worldwide (World Health Organization, 2022); for LGBTQ+ people, the pandemic was notable not only for its early and disproportionate impact on gay men during the late 1970s and early 1980s but also for what it revealed about the impact of anti-LGBTQ+ discrimination on health care policy and treatment.

Because the AIDS pandemic impacted minoritized communities at a higher rate, the U.S. government's level of response and allocation of resources was minimal. For example, between 1981 and 1986, when the U.S. first provided funding to support global AIDS research, 12,000 deaths from the disease were reported (Eaklor, 2008). Even as heterosexual people were increasingly diagnosed with HIV, the general public continued to think of AIDS as a gay disease, resulting in the stigmatization of HIV-positive people and widespread failure to adequately prevent, treat, or fund HIV research. During this period, the LGBTQ+ community mobilized against AIDS and the growing homophobia in society (Eaklor, 2008), with organizations like the AIDS Coalition to Unleash Power (ACT UP) engaging in nationwide campaigns to educate people about the disease, demand research on AIDS prevention and treatment, and raise funds to care for the growing number of people suffering from the disease. The work of these activists led to increasing awareness and funding, as well as broad expansion of sexual health and HIV prevention curriculum in K–12 settings, including medically accurate curriculum regarding the prevention of sexually transmitted infections among LGBTQ+ people, as well as programs to provide condoms and counseling to sexually active teens.

Nevertheless, due largely to the slow governmental response to initial cases of HIV, AIDS evolved into a global pandemic that has killed tens of millions of people and cost hundreds of billions of dollars worldwide. As of 2023, an estimated 39 million people are HIV positive, including 1.2 million people in the United States, and the US currently spends $28 billion per year on domestic HIV/AIDS programs and research (U.S. Department of Health and Human Services [DHHS], 2022). Due to pervasive inequities in health care access and systems, HIV infection continues to disproportionately

Members of ACT UP at the 1989 New York City Pride March.

**SOURCE:** Rita Barros/Getty Images

affect people of color, LGBTQ+ people, and women, particularly women in countries outside the United States (DHHS, 2022).

**ADVANCING EQUITY IN EMPLOYMENT, HOUSING, AND THE LAW**   Throughout the 1980s and 1990s, LGBTQ+ communities made progress in their efforts to fight discrimination, counter antigay legislation, and repeal laws that criminalized gay sexual acts in different states. However, progress wasn't linear: In 1982, Wisconsin was the first state in the country to pass legislation banning discrimination based on sexual orientation, but it would take 9 more years for another state (Massachusetts) to follow suit. The 1980s also saw the passage of the 1984 Federal Equal Access Act, which prohibited public secondary schools from denying students the right to form a GSA if any other types of clubs were permitted on campus.

Over the coming decades, dozens of states would enact laws banning discrimination on the basis of sexual orientation, gender identity, and/or gender expression and, in 2020, the U.S. Supreme Court ruled in *Bostock v. Clayton County* that federal law prohibits discrimination against LGBTQ+ people in employment. While this was a major step forward for LGBTQ+ civil rights, it did not end discrimination against or harassment of LGBTQ+ people in the workplace. Research conducted by the University of California, Los Angeles' School of Law indicated that as 2021, nearly half of LGBTQ+ people have experienced unfair treatment (such as being fired, not hired, or harassed due to their sexual orientation or gender identity) during their lifetimes, with higher rates reported among LGBTQ+ people of color. Researchers also found that 34% of LGBTQ+ people had left a job due to bad treatment by their employer, while more than half of respondents were not out to their current supervisor and 26% of LGBTQ+ respondents are not out to anyone with whom they work (Sears et al., 2021). However, it did give LGBTQ+ individuals the right to legal recourse and an important mechanism with which to ensure their rights. Organizations such as the American Civil Liberties Union took on many such cases pro bono, fighting for LGBTQ+ Americans' rights to employment protections when their rights were threatened or seized.

The Equality Act, which was introduced in both the U.S. House of Representatives and the U.S. Senate on March 13, 2019, would amend existing civil rights laws and laws related to housing, financial credit, jury selection, and employment with the federal government to explicitly include both sexual orientation and gender identity as protected characteristics. This would ensure equal treatment of LGBTQ+ communities across state lines, regardless of previous state, county, or city laws. The Act was passed by the U.S. House of Representatives in February 2021, but despite widespread public support (including a petition started by singer Taylor Swift that collected almost a million signatures), the act was not voted on by the U.S. Senate before the end of the legislative session. This was not only a blow to the LGBTQ+ community but also reflected the way partisanship and culture wars have increasingly hobbled U.S. Congressional processes.

The Equality Act was reintroduced in the 188th Congress on June 21, 2023, and is supported by President Biden. If passed, this act would ensure that LGBTQ+ people's civil rights are protected even if challenged under the guise of religious freedom (as is the case when members of anti-LGBTQ+ religious communities want to deny housing, employment, or business services to LGBTQ+ people due to their personal religious beliefs). As of 2023, the nonpartisan Public Religion Research Institute found that national support for the Equality Act is approximately 70%, and the act has widespread endorsement by business associations including the National Association of Manufacturers, the National Restaurant Association, and the U.S. Chamber of Commerce (HRC, 2023a). However, while some major religious groups—such as many Protestant denominations, the Evangelical Lutheran Church in America, the U.S. Episcopal Church, most U.S. Jewish congregations, and other progressive faith groups— support the Equality Act, others—including the National Association of Evangelicals, the U.S. Conference of Catholic Bishops, the Church of Jesus Christ of Latter-day Saints, and orthodox rabbinical groups—oppose the Equality Act in its current form, arguing that religious people, schools, and institutions should be exempt from requirements to hire, educate, or serve LGBTQ+ people (Gjelten, 2021). Socially conservative and anti-LGBTQ+ political groups continue to lobby against inclusion, and the future landscape of LGBTQ+ rights is currently unknown, particularly as states like Florida and Texas pass extreme anti-LGBTQ+ legislation while other states such as California, Nevada, and New Mexico enshrine LGBTQ+ rights in their state constitutions.

In addition to legislation related to discrimination in employment, housing, and public services, a key legal emphasis of LGBTQ+ activists has been the collection of data regarding and enforcement of laws against hate crimes. These laws, the first of which was passed as part of the Civil Rights Act of 1968, recognize that violent or property crimes that are "motivated in whole or in part by bias on the basis of race, religion, sexual orientation, ethnicity, gender or gender identity" impact not only the individual victim but serve to intimidate an entire community, and thus are prosecuted and penalized differently than crimes against a single individual. As of 2022, 46 states and the District of Columbia have hate-crime laws, all of which cover bias based on race or ethnicity and religion; 34 of these also expressly cover sexual orientation, gender, gender identity, and/or gender expression (Southern Poverty Law Center, 2022).

In 1990, Congress passed, and President George H. W. Bush signed into law, the Hate Crimes Statistics Act, which required the U.S. attorney general to collect data on crimes based on racial, ethnic, religious, or sexual orientation prejudice. This bill was expanded in 2009 with the passage of the Matthew Shepard and James Byrd, Jr. Hate Crimes Prevention Act, which explicitly added gender and gender identity to the federal hate-crime legislation and required the FBI to collect data regarding hate crimes committed by or against people under the age of 18.

**GAINING LEGAL RECOGNITION FOR LGTBQ+ FAMILIES**    LGBTQ+ families have always existed, and the first petition for a same-sex marriage license in the United States was filed in 1970 by Richard Baker and James McConnell in Minnesota. Their application was denied and, while they brought their case to the state Supreme Court, the U.S. Supreme Court refused to hear their appeal, effectively leaving decisions about same-sex marriage in the hands of state courts and legislatures. Over the coming decades, LGBTQ+ couples would unsuccessfully petition for the right to marry in multiple states. In addition to the social stigma associated with governmental refusal to recognize the legitimacy of same-sex partnerships, this meant that LGBTQ+ families did not have access to a broad range of rights afforded to heterosexual families, including access to health insurance, hospital visitation and medical decision-making privileges, the right to file taxes as a couple, and inheritance rights, among many others.

By the late 1980s, some local municipalities, including San Francisco and Washington, D.C., passed ordinances allowing unmarried couples to register as "domestic partners" for the purpose of hospital visitation rights and other benefits; these were intended to provide some measure of protection to LGBTQ+ families but fell short of full legal recognition of same-sex marriages. This began to come in the early 1990s, when three same-sex couples in Hawaii sued for the right to receive marriage licenses in 1991. The couples lost their case, but the Hawaii Supreme Court found that the denial of marriage licenses to these couples was discriminatory. The state legislature responded quickly by defining marriage as taking place only between a man and a woman, a decision that led to another lawsuit. However, rather than wait for the Hawaii case to be resolved, anti-LGBTQ+ members of Congress passed the Defense of Marriage Act in 1996, which specified that only heterosexual couples could be granted federal marriage benefits, even if states passed laws recognizing LGBTQ+ unions.

Over the next several years, state legislatures and courts made multiple decisions regarding the recognition of same-sex marriages and, in 2000, Vermont became the

In 2022, the state of Tamaulipis became the last of Mexico's 32 states to recognize same-sex marriage, rendering it legal nationwide.

**SOURCE:** Gerardo Vieyra/NurPhoto SRL/ Alamy Stock Photo

first state to legalize civil unions (a legal status that afforded same-sex couples the same state rights as people in heterosexual marriages); Massachusetts followed in 2004 when the state Supreme Court formally legalized same-sex marriages. Over the next decade, U.S. marriage regulations looked like patchwork: Same-sex marriage was legal in some states and banned in others. In some states, LGBTQ+ families would win legal recognition in court, only to see those rights rescinded by the legislature or a ballot measure and then reinstated a few years later. In 2008, for example, anti-LGBTQ+ activists successfully lobbied for Proposition 8, which overturned the California Supreme Court's ruling that same-sex couples have a constitutional right to marry; it passed with 52% of the vote, with most Prop 8 supporters identifying as Republican, conservative, weekly attendees of religious service, and over 65 years old (Eagan & Sherrill, 2009). Proposition 8 was overturned by a federal district court judge in 2010 but was appealed. In 2013, the U.S. Supreme Court dismissed the appeal, allowing same-sex marriages to resume in California.

The U.S. Supreme Court finally struck down the Defense of Marriage Act in 2013 in *United States v. Windsor*, which required the federal government to recognize same-sex marriages performed in the states and, in 2015, ruled in *Obergefell v. Hodges* that marriage between same-sex couples was a constitutional right, granting full legal marriage rights to LGBTQ+ couples nationwide. By this time, 37 states and the District of Columbia already allowed same-sex couples to marry, and 780,000 gay and lesbian adults were already legally married (Gates & Newport, 2015). Nevertheless, with this ruling the United States joined more than 20 other countries in providing full legal recognition to LGBTQ+ couples.

Many LGBTQ+ people in the United States considered their fight for relationship recognition over after the Supreme Court's ruling in *Obergefell v. Hodges*. However, the U.S. Supreme Court's 2022 overturning of *Roe vs. Wade* and resultant elimination of abortion rights nationwide raised fears that the current conservative-majority Supreme Court will overturn previous cases, even when precedent, or former rulings, had been established. Thus, in late 2022, President Biden codified protections for same-sex couples by signing the first-of-its-kind bipartisan Respect for Marriage Act, which mandated federal recognition for same-sex marriages and prohibited states from denying the validity of out-of-state marriages based on sex, race, or ethnicity.

However, many LGBTQ+ families continue to face discrimination at the local and state level, especially in states where anti-LGBTQ+ activists or politicians use fearmongering or bigoted religious beliefs as justification for discriminating against LGBTQ+ families. For example, although many LGBTQ+ people have biological children, and same-sex couples can legally adopt children in all 50 states, some anti-LGBTQ+ activists have attempted to restrict discussion of sexual orientation and gender identity in elementary and secondary schools, effectively preventing children from talking about their own families in the classroom. Moreover, while 28 states explicitly prohibit adoption discrimination based on sexual orientation and gender identity, 13 others "permit state-licensed child welfare agencies to refuse to place and provide services to children and families, including LGBTQ people and same-sex couples, if doing so conflicts with their religious beliefs" (Movement Advancement Project, 2023a).

Policies like these carry implicit or explicit messaging that LGBTQ+ people and families are somehow "inappropriate," resulting in the systematic shaming, silencing, and exclusion of LGBTQ+ children, families, and experiences. However, multiple organizations are advocating for LGBTQ+ family rights, including PFLAG (formerly Parents, Families, and Friends of Lesbians and Gays), the Family Equality Council, and the Transgender Law Center, all of which provide legal advocacy and education with and on behalf of LGBTQ+ families and individuals across the United States.

Table 5.1 outlines LGBTQ+ legislative efforts to support and combat LGBTQ+ equality and rights in the United States. The table includes recent history since 2008 into events unfolding today, which are detailed in the following section, "Continuing Challenges for Equity."

## Continuing Challenges for Equity

Although progress is never a straight line, throughout the twentieth and early twenty-first centuries, LGBTQ+ people in the United States have generally seen broader recognition of their social, educational, and civil rights. However, anti-LGBTQ+ propaganda and misinformation began gaining prominence during President Donald Trump's administration and, in the 2020s, the United States saw a dramatic resurgence of anti-LGBTQ+ social and legislative efforts. These include attempts to restrict curriculum about LGBTQ+ history and families; deny trans students and educators

**Table 5.1** Modern Milestones in the Movement for Gay and LGBTQ+ Rights

| | |
|---|---|
| **2009** | Congress passed the Matthew Shepard and James Byrd, Jr. Hate Crimes Prevention Act, expanding federal hate-crime laws to include crimes based on actual or perceived gender, sexual orientation, or gender identity. |
| | Iowa, New Hampshire, Vermont, and the District of Columbia joined Massachusetts in legalizing same-sex marriage. |
| **2010** | A federal district judge in California found Proposition 8, which banned same-sex marriage, unconstitutional. This moment reignited conversations about marriage equality nationwide. |
| | Congress repealed "Don't Ask, Don't Tell," allowing lesbians and gay men to serve openly in the military. This increased visibility of LGBTQ+ people began to change the culture of the military. |
| **2013** | The U.S. Supreme Court decided two landmark cases in favor of LGBTQ+ equality. First, the Supreme Court dismissed the appeal on same-sex marriages in California, allowing them to resume in the state. Second, the Supreme Court outlawed the Defense of Marriage Act in *United States v. Windsor*, requiring the Internal Revenue Service and other government agencies to treat married gay and lesbian couples as heterosexual couples are treated. |
| **2014** | President Barack Obama signed an amended Executive Order that extended protection of federal employees from discrimination based on sexual orientation to include protection based on gender identity, a huge step forward for trans and nonbinary individuals. |
| **2015** | The U.S. Supreme Court ruled in a 5–4 decision that same-sex couples have a constitutional right to marry in *Obergefell v. Hodges*. This was the moment that same-sex marriage became legal across all 50 states. |
| **2017** | A federal District Court overruled Mississippi's ban on adoption by same-sex couples, making adoption by same-sex couples legal in all 50 states. |
| **2019** | The Equality Act, a federal bill that would prohibit discrimination based on sex, sexual orientation, and gender identity in many areas, passed in the House of Representatives. Notable celebrity Taylor Swift began a Change.org petition to pass the bill and collected nearly 1 million signatures. The Republican-held U.S. Senate refused to vote on the bill. |
| **2020** | The U.S. Supreme Court, in *Bostock v. Clayton County*, ruled that all people who work at companies with 15 or more employees are protected against employment discrimination based on sexual orientation or gender identity. |
| **2022** | The Supreme Court overturned *Roe v. Wade*, ending women's right to abortion access in the United States. In his written decision, Justice Clarence Thomas suggested the court also revisit cases related to access to contraception and LGBTQ+ rights. |
| | President Biden signed the Respect for Marriage Act, codifying marriage protections for same-sex couples. This act required states to recognize same-sex marriages across state lines and guarantees federal benefits for all married same-sex couples, even if the court overturns *Obergefell v. Hodges*. |
| | Florida passed the controversial Parental Rights bill (HR 1557), often referred to as the "Don't Say Gay" bill. It prohibited classroom instruction about sexual orientation or gender identity in grades K–3 or in ways that are not "age-appropriate." |
| **2023** | The number of anti-LGBTQ+ bills introduced at the state level skyrockets, indicating a new wave of attacks on the safety and security of LGBTQ+ individuals. In particular, trans individuals were targeted through the introduction of over 500 anti-trans bills between January and August of 2023 (Trans Legislation Tracker, 2023). |
| | Florida expands HR 1557 to prohibit all discussion of sexual orientation or gender identity in grades K–12, except when explicitly required by state standards. Similar bills are adopted by 10 states. |
| | California, Washington, and Oregon were joined by 10 other states in passing "shield laws" protecting trans people who travel across state lines to access gender-affirming health care; these laws also protected health care providers facing state civil or criminal charges for providing such care. The ruling by the U.S. Supreme Court on *303 Creative LLC et al. v. Elenis et al.* opened the door for business entities to legally discriminate against LGBTQ+ communities and other marginalized groups. |

access to restrooms and extracurricular activities such as sports; and the passage of "antidrag" laws similar to those used by police who raided the Stonewall Inn in the 1960s. The political climate and use of hate speech by politicians has emboldened some anti-LGBTQ+ zealots, resulting in a number of small and chaotic demonstrations in communities across the country, such as destroying Pride sections at major retailers and threatening hourly employees (Hernandez, 2023b). Collectively, these have led many historians and activists to worry for the safety of contemporary LGBTQ+ communities (López Restrepo, 2023; Ryan, 2019).

During and after Trump's presidency, the United States witnessed an increase in anti-LGBTQ+ bills introduced in state legislative sessions (see Figure 5.1). In 2020, 77 anti-LGBTQ+ bills were introduced; by 2021, there were 154 bills, doubling the amount in a single year. In 2022, 180 anti-LGBTQ+ bills were introduced, and during the first 6 months of 2023, there were more than 500 anti-LGBTQ+ bills in different state legislative sessions, 70 of which have passed (HRC, 2023b). These legislative efforts target diverse members of the LGBTQ+ community, impacting education, civic rights, public accommodations, health care, sports participation, bathroom access, drag performance, and more. Bills related to education were by far the highest in their number and in their increase, with over 200 bills targeting LGBTQ+ educational efforts. Many of these bills specifically sought to ban the teaching of LGBTQ+ histories in schools, the use of LGBTQ+ curricular resources, and the presence of LGBTQ+-focused school clubs; others require schools to refer to students only by the name and sex they were assigned at birth or to notify the parents if they suspect a student might be trans or gender nonconforming.

**Figure 5.1** Active Anti-LGBTQ Bills Introduced in the United States During the 2023 Legislative Session (updated August 2023)

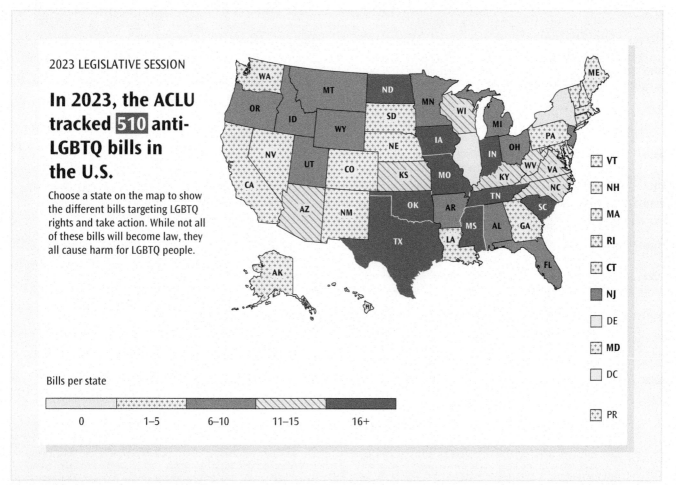

**SOURCE:** American Civil Liberties Union (2023b).

While it is easy to assume the proliferation of anti-LGBTQ+ legislative actions reflect widespread sentiment within the United States, the reality is that many of these bills are advanced by a relatively small number of far-right activists with decades of experience organizing against LGBTQ+ people, such as those responsible for the Save Our Children campaign of the 1970s (HRC, 2023b). For example, an analysis of book challenges in 37 states during the 2021–2022 academic year, for example, found that 60% of book challenges were initiated by just 11 people, many of whom were acting as part of coordinated efforts by far-right activist groups like the Moms for Liberty (Nathanson, 2023). According to 2023 data, the vast majority of Americans support LGBTQ+ equality, including marriage equality and the right of openly trans individuals to serve in the military (Gallup, 2023).

Nevertheless, in recent times, we have seen harmful legislative efforts that privilege so-called "religious freedom" over the safety and lives of LGBTQ+ populations. In May 2023, the state of Florida passed a law stating that health care professionals who held views or religious beliefs that were in conflict with LGBTQ+ acceptance could deny medical care to LGBTQ+ individuals. This ruling could effectively allow doctors, nurses, EMTs, and other medical staff to deny critical care to LGBTQ+ individuals, stating that their religious beliefs prohibited them from providing care. This legislation will likely face legal challenges that will take it to the U.S. Supreme Court in coming years.

How the Supreme Court will rule on cases like these is uncertain, especially given the current far-right conservative majority, and Justice Clarence Thomas's 2022 written opinion recommending that the court consider overturning constitutional rights related to access to contraceptives and LGBTQ+ rights, including the right to have consensual sex and get married, calling them "erroneous decisions" (*Dobbs v. Jackson Women's Health Organization*, 2022). In July 2023, a particularly harsh blow to LGBTQ+ rights occurred with the U.S. Supreme Court ruling in *303 Creative LLC et al. v. Elenis et al*. In the case, a web designer in Colorado fabricated a hypothetical situation in which she might be asked to create LGBTQ+-related wedding materials for digital use (Associated Press, 2023). In a 6–3 decision, the Court ruled that requiring the web designer to create the content would infringe upon her First Amendment right.

The dissenting opinion from the court, written by Judge Sonia Sotomayor, noted that the decision "declares that a particular kind of business, though open to the public, has a constitutional right to refuse to serve members of a protected class" (Sotomayor, dissenting, p. 1). She also noted that with the ruling, "the immediate, symbolic effect of the decision is to mark gays and lesbians for second-class status" (p. 35). In the months following the Supreme Court ruling, anti-LGBTQ+ business owners throughout the United States attempted to use the decision to deny services to LGBTQ+ people, such as the Michigan hair salon that advertised "if a human identifies as anything other than a man/woman, please seek services at a local pet groomer . . . you are not welcome at this salon, period." Although state and national legal experts quickly noted that this type of discrimination is in violation of state law, it illustrates the dangerous potential for the *303 Creative LLC et al. v Elenis et al*. decision to, in the words of HRC Legal Director Sarah Warbelow, "inspire discriminatory behavior and a really disgusting public discourse about LGBTQ people" (Burga, 2023).

# Heterosexism's Toll on LGBTQ+ Students and Adults

**Learning Objective 5.3** Analyze the toll that heterosexism has taken on LGBTQ+ youth and educators.

**Homophobia**, which is the fear of or aversion to LGBTQ+ youth and adults, has historically resulted in laws that prevented LGBTQ+ people from openly acknowledging their sexual orientation or gender identity. While some people clearly hold bigoted beliefs about LGBTQ+ people, it is far more common for people to discriminate against them due to **heterosexism**, or their conscious or unconscious belief that the male/female binary and heterosexuality are normal and superior to other identities. People learn heterosexism when they are exposed to media, religious, political, or familial ideas that portray heterosexuality as a norm or standard, suggest that only two genders exist, or portray the only acceptable sexual or romantic relationships as between a man and a woman.

Heterosexism privileges cisgendered men and women who are heterosexual and categorically excludes the needs, concerns, cultures, and life experiences of LGBTQ+ people (Catalano et al., 2018). It also negatively impacts the self-esteem, academic achievement, school participation, college attendance, and professional trajectories of LGBTQ+ children and adults, who are silenced, shamed, or forced to spend time and energy fighting against prejudice, discrimination, or threats of violence. In this section, we explore the impact heterosexism and homophobia have on young people.

## Erasure of LGBTQ+ Voices and Experiences

Schools have a very important role in promoting a nation's culture and values. Educators accomplish this task through the formal curriculum that they teach and through the hidden curriculum of value-laden rules that guide the daily activities of a classroom and a school. Both the formal and hidden curricula often reinforce the values of the dominant culture; in the United States, this includes the perpetuation of White, middle class, heterosexual, English speaking, able-bodied, and Christian norms and values.

Think of the ways that heterosexuality is supported in the hidden curriculum. The system approves of dating between boys and girls and, as early as elementary school, many schools sponsor "father–daughter" dances or physical education activities that require students to find a partner of the "opposite" gender. A queen and king are often elected for the springtime prom. Preschool children make cards and crafts to celebrate Mother's Day and Father's Day. Cisgender girls and boys routinely hold hands in the hallways or at school events. Teachers distribute permission slips and information cards that ask students to provide the name of their mother and father. Nuclear families with a mother and father are depicted on bulletin boards and discussed in units on the family in primary grades. Heterosexual teachers talk openly about their spouses but rarely display pictures of or reference partners of the same sex. Sports teams are strictly gendered, with dramatic differences in required uniforms for male and female athletes.

For LGBTQ+ students and children in LGBTQ+ families, each of these situations provokes cognitive dissonance: They know that what they see around them does not reflect their own lives, but they may not know how to respond. Should they come out "against" the world around them, or pretend to be someone other than who they are? Next time you enter a school building, view it through the lens of someone with a different sexual orientation or gender identity than your own. Would you feel welcome? Would you be comfortable holding hands with your partner as you walk down the hall, or dancing with them at a school-sponsored dance? Do you see photographs of families that look like yours? Are there faculty and staff members who appear to share your sexual orientation and gender identity? Are you confident that every adult you see would embrace your family and treat you with care and respect?

In addition to shaping the hidden curriculum, heterosexism also impacts every aspect of academic curriculum itself. Reflect back on the history of LGBTQ+ communities included earlier in this chapter. How much of this history was familiar, and how much was new to you? If you are like most people in the United States, it is unlikely that your K–12 education included curriculum related to LGBTQ+ people. In fact, as of 2023, 72% of LGBTQ+ students say they have not had a single lesson about

LGBTQ+ people or histories (Kosciw et al., 2022). This not only prevents LGBTQ+ students from learning about their own community but also denies all children the opportunity to learn about the contributions LGBTQ+ people have made to the arts, sciences, and civic life. This both reflects and perpetuates heterosexism, and children who do not learn about LGBTQ+ people will become teachers who are ill-prepared to teach about LGBTQ+ communities.

**FIGHTING HETEROSEXISM WITH INCLUSIVE CURRICULUM**   In recognition of the importance of representing and affirming the contributions and lived experiences of LGBTQ+ people, a growing number of states across the country have adopted curricular standards that explicitly require teaching LGBTQ+-inclusive curriculum in social sciences, humanities, the arts, and science, technology, engineering, and mathematics (GLSEN, 2024). In addition to providing all students with access to a more inclusive, well-developed curriculum, these standards are grounded in research on school climate and academic performance: When LGBTQ+ students attend schools with an inclusive curriculum, they perform better academically, hear fewer anti-LGBTQ+ comments at school, and experience their classmates as somewhat or very accepting of them (GLSEN, 2024).

LGBTQ+-affirming teachers have always found ways to include LGBTQ+ people in the curriculum, but it wasn't until 2011 that doing so was required by state policy. The passage of the FAIR (Fair, Accurate, Inclusive and Respectful) Education Act in California required history and social studies teachers to explicitly include "a study of the role and contributions of both men and women, Native Americans, African Americans, Mexican Americans, Asian Americans, Pacific Islanders, European Americans, lesbian, gay, bisexual, and transgender Americans, persons with disabilities, and members of other ethnic and cultural groups, to the economic, political, and social development of California and the United States of America, with particular emphasis on portraying the role of these groups in contemporary society" (California Department of Education, 2011). The bill also added explicit prohibitions against textbooks or other instructional materials that "reflect adversely" upon people on the basis of (among other things) sexual orientation.

To help teachers implement the FAIR Act, policymakers provided multiple examples of how teachers might implement the bill in elementary and secondary classrooms, from engaging second-graders in conversations about family diversity in children's books to ninth-grade units about "the legacies of social movements and historic struggles against injustice in California, the Southwest, and the United States as a whole . . . and how different social movements for people of color, women, and lesbian, gay, bisexual and transgender (LGBT) communities have mutually informed each other" (California Department of Education, 2017, p. 312). The framework also includes a comprehensive analysis of LGBTQ+ people's contributions to arts, music, and civil rights movements throughout the twentieth century, providing opportunities for high school students and teachers to explore U.S. history through the lens of complex, diverse, and intersectional perspectives.

In the years following California's implementation of the FAIR Act, six additional states (Colorado, Connecticut, Illinois, Nevada, New Jersey, and Oregon) have adopted similar curricular requirements to explicitly teach about LGBTQ+ people and contributions in history and social studies classrooms (GLSEN, 2024).

In addition to curricular requirements related to LGBTQ+ histories, LGBTQ+ experiences are increasingly visible in young adult literature. Since 2020, publishers have reported record sales of books featuring LGBTQ+ characters and themes: in 2021, almost 5 million LGBTQ+-themed books were sold in the United States, a rate double that of 2020, and sales increased by an additional 39% in the first 6 months of 2022. LGBTQ+-themed young adult fiction drove the increase in sales, selling 1.3 million more copies in 2021 than 2020 (The NPD Group, 2022). Publishers celebrated not only the sheer number of LGBTQ+ books available but also the racial, ethnic, religious, and thematic diversity of the stories being told. The wider availability of this literature makes it easier for teachers to offer book choices that reflect the diversity of students and their families and to address state and federal curricular standards related to analyses of perspective and social context in literature.

Another key advancement has been in the area of health and physical education, where state and national standards increasingly emphasize the importance of comprehensive and LGBTQ+-inclusive curriculum and policy. In 2021, the Society of Health and Physical Educators (SHAPE America) partnered with the GLSEN (formerly the Gay, Lesbian, Straight Education Network) to craft and disseminate model policies and best practices for LGBTQ+ inclusion in physical education (available at *www .shapeamerica.org/standards/guidelines/Transgender/default.aspx*).

In addition to general standards related to health and physical education, an increasing number of states have implemented standards related to *comprehensive sex education*, a curricular approach that does not presuppose heterosexuality when teaching about puberty, relationships, sex, or the prevention of sexually transmitted infections (STIs) but, instead, explicitly affirms and provides guidance regarding STI prevention among people of diverse sexual orientations and gender identities. As of April 2023, California, Colorado, Illinois, Maryland, New Jersey, Oregon, Rhode Island, and Washington have approved sex education standards that explicitly include LGBTQ+ students and communities, while Louisiana, Mississippi, Oklahoma, and Texas have laws forbidding sex educators to speak positively about LGBTQ+ people (GLSEN, 2024). In all U.S. states, parents continue to have the right to review the curriculum prior to instruction and can choose to opt their child in or out of sex education.

**CURRICULAR BACKLASH**  The anti-LGBTQ+ backlash of the early 2020s has led to a series of challenges to LGBTQ+ curricular inclusion. The most notable of these emerged in Florida, where Governor Ron DeSantis adopted a hardline anti-LGBTQ+ stance as part of his far-right presidential campaign platform (Izaguirre, 2023), including a controversial bill (HR 1557) passed under the pretext of protecting "parental rights" in education. This bill, which is often referred to as the "Don't Say Gay" bill, initially prohibited classroom instruction about sexual orientation or gender identity in grades K–3 but was later expanded to include any discussion of sexual orientation or gender identity in grades K–12, except when explicitly required by state standards. Educators who violate HR 1557 are at risk of losing their teaching license or being sued by parents or other community members.

In addition to limiting curricular content, the bill has had a dramatic and chilling effect on LGBTQ+ students, families, and educators, who fear repercussions if they come out, read LGBTQ+-inclusive literature, teach about contemporary civil rights issues, or respond to incidents of harassment or homophobic name calling in the classroom. In announcing the bill, DeSantis (2022) argued that it was necessary to prevent schools from "using classroom instruction to sexualize . . . kids as young as 5 years old." However, the truth is that teaching about LGBTQ+ people is no more sexually explicit than teaching about heterosexual people; policies that restrict instruction about sexual orientation and gender identity are designed to advance cultural and political goals rather than evidence-based research on student learning.

Nevertheless, the introduction of anti-LGBTQ+ school bills and policies has proven an effective political tool and, as of 2023, similar (though less comprehensive) bills have been introduced or passed in 10 states, creating uncertainty for LGBTQ+ students, families, and educators (see Figure 5.2). Curricular tensions have also led to conflict regarding whether students in states with LGBTQ+ curricular bans will be eligible to take Advanced Placement (AP) courses, such as AP Psychology, some of which include required content related to gender and sexual orientation (College Board, 2023).

**Figure 5.2** LGBTQ Curricular Laws

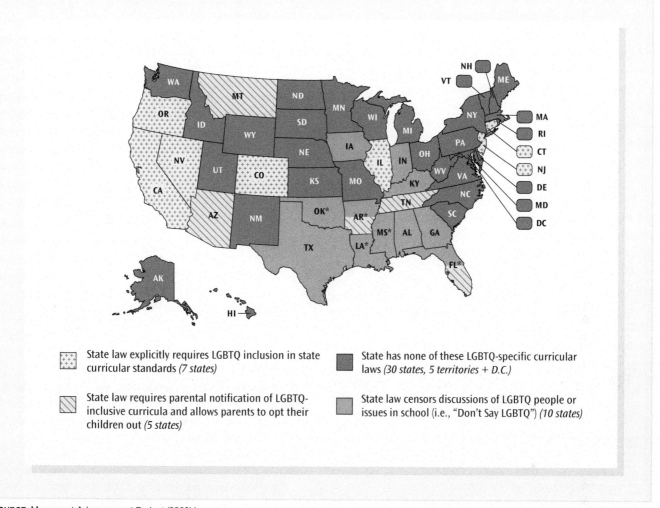

State law explicitly requires LGBTQ inclusion in state curricular standards *(7 states)*

State law requires parental notification of LGBTQ-inclusive curricula and allows parents to opt their children out *(5 states)*

State has none of these LGBTQ-specific curricular laws *(30 states, 5 territories + D.C.)*

State law censors discussions of LGBTQ people or issues in school (i.e., "Don't Say LGBTQ") *(10 states)*

**SOURCE:** Movement Advancement Project (2023b).

In a statement about the impact of the bill, the College Board noted that content related to gender and sexual orientation has been part of AP Psychology courses for 30 years, that any "AP Psychology course taught in Florida will violate either Florida law or college requirements." At the time of publication, it is unclear whether or how this tension will impact students in Florida and similar states.

# Explore and Focus Your Cultural Lens

## Debate: Should Every Educator Address Sexual Orientation and LGBTQ+ Identity in Their Classroom?

State laws vary regarding how elementary and secondary teachers are expected to address sexual orientation and LGBTQ+ identity. In some states, curricular frameworks call for LGBTQ+-affirming lessons about family diversity as early as second grade, include recommended texts by LGBTQ+ authors, and mandate high school units about LGBTQ+ civil rights movements; other states prohibit teachers from mentioning sexual orientation at all. To make matters more complicated, local policies do not always align with state laws: in 2023, for example, anti-LGBTQ+ school board members in Temecula, California, refused to

*(continued)*

adopt the state-approved social studies textbook because the supplementary teacher materials referenced LGBTQ+ lawmaker Harvey Milk; instead, the school board voted to continue using a 2006 textbook that was outdated and noncompliant with state standards. (Ultimately, the district relented after the state threatened a $1.5 million fine but barred teachers from using instructional materials related to Milk.)

Similar tensions are playing out in districts nationwide, with dramatic implications for teachers as well as for their LGBTQ+ students and families. Virtually all teachers will have LGBTQ+ students, families, and colleagues, though only some will be out at school; many teachers will also have students or colleagues who are ignorant of or biased against LGBTQ+ people and communities. As a teacher, you will have to figure out how to navigate these complex political, curricular, and legal landscapes as you create an inclusive and affirming classroom for all students. How you address issues of sexual orientation and LGBTQ+ identity in the classroom will depend, in part, on the context of the community in which you teach and the policies in place in your district. Your approach to LGBTQ+ inclusion will also impact the ways your students learn to see you, to see themselves, and to see each other. How explicit will you be in addressing sexual orientation and LGBTQ+ identity in the classroom? Why? What are your goals for promoting equitable and inclusive classrooms for LGBTQ+ students and families?

**FOR**

- LGBTQ+ people exist, and avoiding discussions about sexual orientation and gender identity is both discriminatory and inaccurate.

- Children and youth of all ages should be taught to be accepting of others, including people of diverse sexual orientations and family structures.

- It is important for LGBTQ+ students and students from LGBTQ+ families to feel a sense of belonging at school, and using inclusive curriculum is part of how teachers can support this.

- All teachers, even those in states that prohibit explicit instruction about sexual orientation or LGBTQ+ identity, have a responsibility to create equitable, inclusive, and affirming environments for all students. It is important

for teachers to be creative in finding ways to use their professional agency to include and advocate for LGBTQ+ students.

**AGAINST**

- Whenever possible, teachers should avoid addressing socially or politically controversial topics.

- Some parents don't want their children to learn about LGBTQ+ people; teachers should respect those parents' preferences, even if they don't agree.

- Due to restrictive curricular policies, there is nothing teachers in some states can do to include or affirm LGBTQ+ students and families.

- Students should learn that bullying against any student is inappropriate; it is not necessary to explicitly talk about sexual orientation or LGBTQ+ identity to prevent bullying.

## Questions for Discussion

1. What did you learn about sexual orientation and LGBTQ+ identity and history during your own K–12 education? How effectively did this prepare you to understand and advocate for the needs of LGBTQ+ students and communities? If you could go back in time, how would you change your own educational experiences in this regard?

2. What are your hopes and fears as you prepare to create equitable, inclusive, and affirming environments for LGBTQ+ students and families? How will you navigate resistance from students or colleagues who express anti-LGBTQ+ biases?

3. What norms, policies, and laws impact the ways teachers address sexual orientation and LGBTQ+ identity in your local community? How do you feel about these?

4. How can teachers navigate state or local policies that require or prohibit classroom discussions about sexual orientation or LGBTQ+ identity? What strategies can they use to include and affirm LGBTQ+ students and families without violating the law? When and how might they challenge or push back on policies that exclude these students and their families?

## School Climate for LGBTQ+ Students

To better understand the experiences of LGBTQ+ students, GLSEN (formerly the Gay, Lesbian, Straight Education Network) conducts a biannual National School Climate Survey examining the experiences of LGBTQ+ students; since 1999, more than 100,000 middle and high school students have participated, offering a comprehensive longitudinal picture of LGBTQ+ students' experiences nationwide. In this section, we summarize data on school climate throughout the United States; however, we encourage you to visit *https://maps.glsen.org/state-research-snapshots/* to learn more about the legislative context and cultural climate of your own state; examine how LGBTQ+ students of different racial, ethnic, ability, and other social identities experience school differently; and analyze changes in student experience overtime.

As of 2023, 22 U.S. states have laws prohibiting bullying on the basis of sexual orientation (Movement Advancement Project, 2023c). Nevertheless, the majority of LGBTQ+ students describe school as a dangerous place. As recently as 2021, 68% of LGBTQ+ students reported feeling unsafe at school because of their actual or perceived sexual orientation, gender identity, or gender expression (Kosciw et al., 2022), while almost 80% have avoided school functions due to a hostile climate and virtually all (97%) have heard antigay slurs used at school. In addition, 76% of LGBTQ+ students have personally experienced verbal harassment or physical assault on the basis of sexual orientation or gender identity, although most (62%) students did not report the incident because they did not think school staff would do anything to stop it (Kosciw et al., 2022).

As indicated in Figure 5.3, verbal abuse in which students were called names or were threatened was the most common form of harassment. It is important to note that anti-LGBTQ+ harassment does not only affect these students; some students who are perceived as LGBTQ+ are also targeted, even if they do not identify as such themselves. Interestingly, GLSEN found that LGBTQ+ students in online-only learning environments were the least likely to report negative school experiences, suggesting that online schooling may offer a layer of protection to some of these students.

In addition to overt harassment, 59% of LGBTQ+ students experienced discriminatory policies or practices at school (see Figure 5.4), including being told they cannot use their chosen name or pronoun (29%); being prohibited from wearing clothes deemed "inappropriate" based on gender (21%); being disciplined for kissing or holding hands (when non-LGBTQ+ students were not disciplined for the same behavior) (25%); being prevented from writing about or doing school projects about LGBTQ+ issues (16%); or being discouraged from playing sports because they identified as LGBTQ+ (11%).

**Figure 5.3** Percentage of LGBTQ+ Students Experiencing School-Based Harassment or Assault on the Basis of Sexual Orientation, Gender Identity, or Gender Expression

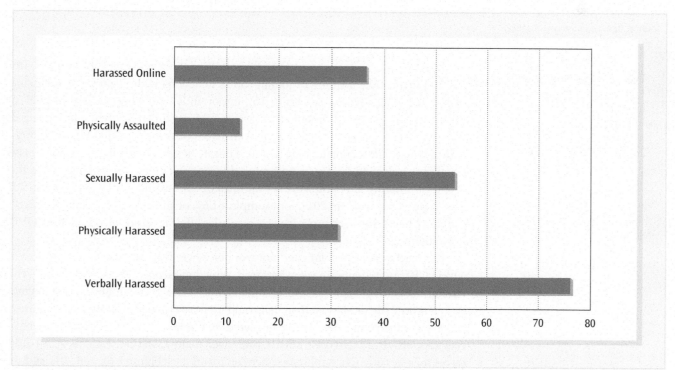

**Figure 5.4** Percentage of LGBTQ+ Students Experiencing Discriminatory Policies or Practices at School

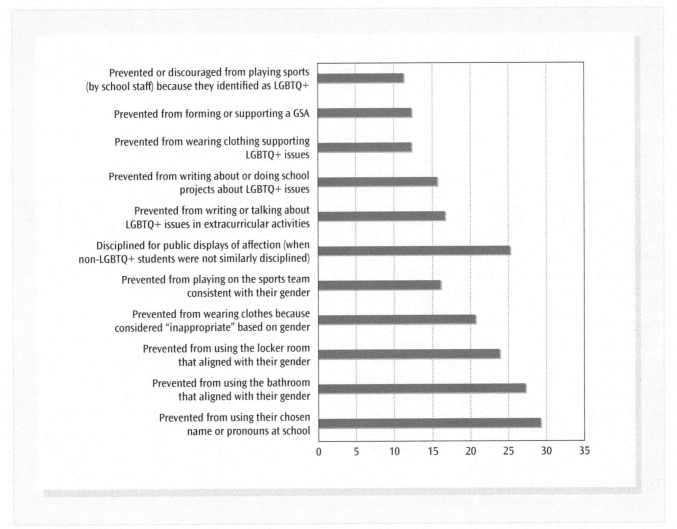

SOURCE: Based on Kosciw et al. (2022).

LGBTQ+ students respond to these conditions in a wide variety of ways, from positive actions like forming or joining GSAs to actions with negative repercussions, such as skipping school (see Figure 5.5). Importantly, while only a third of LGBTQ+ students said that their school had an active GSA or similar student club during the 2020–2021 academic year, those who had an active GSA were less likely to hear homophobic remarks at school; less likely to feel unsafe at school; less likely to have missed school due to feeling unsafe or uncomfortable; and felt greater belonging within their school community. It is noteworthy that rates of GSA availability were lower in 2021 than in previous years (in 2019, for example, 61.6% of students reported having access to a GSA), likely due to changes in extracurricular offerings associated with the COVID-19 pandemic.

It is hard to read this data and not wonder where teachers and administrators are when LGBTQ+ students are being harassed. Why don't school officials intervene? While virtually all LGBTQ+ students (96%) could identify at least one supportive staff member at their school site (and more than half could identify at least six supportive staff members), fewer than a quarter (24%) considered their school administration somewhat or very supportive of LGBTQ+ students. Moreover, many LGBTQ+ students (62%) didn't report their experiences with harassment or assault (see Figure 5.6), and 70% said that

**Figure 5.5** Percentage of LGBTQ+ Students Who Avoided School Events or Facilities Due to Harassment

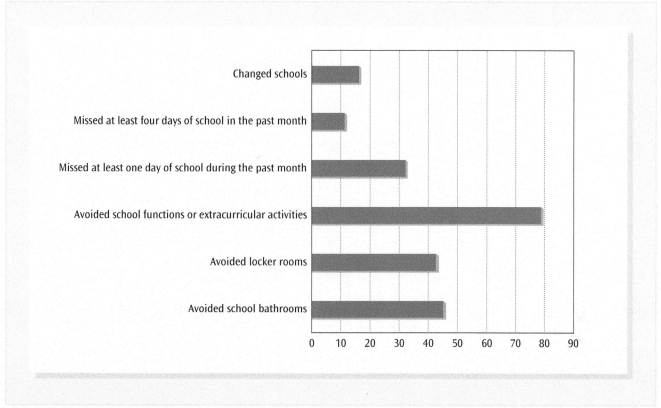

SOURCE: Based on Kosciw et al. (2022).

they didn't believe school staff would do anything even if they reported it. In fact, three in five of the LGBTQ+ students reported that staff members either took no action when a student reported harassment or assault or told them to ignore the incident. One-third of students reported that the staff talked to the perpetrator, and 16% of students were told that they needed to change their own behavior to avoid harassment (e.g., not act "so gay" or dress a certain way).

Hostile climates for LGBTQ+ students affect their academic performance, college aspirations, and psychological well-being. Suicide is the second leading cause of death among young people age 10 to 24 and is more likely to affect LGBTQ+ students than their peers. According to the Trevor Project's 2022 National Survey, which included data from 34,000 LGBTQ+ young people nationwide, 45% of these youth had seriously considered suicide (Trevor Project, 2022). Overall, research indicates that LGBTQ+ young people are three times as likely to think about suicide and four times as likely to attempt suicide as their peers (Johns et al., 2019, 2020).

Due to the compounding effects of homophobia, transphobia, and racism, trans and nonbinary youth and LGBTQ+ youth of color are at increased risk. Data indicates that trans and nonbinary youth are twice as likely to experience depressive symptoms, seriously consider suicide, or attempt suicide as compared to their cisgender LGBTQ+ peers (Price-Feeney et al., 2020), and 12% of LGBTQ+ White youth had attempted suicide, as compared to 21% of Native/Indigenous LGBTQ+ youth, 20% of Middle Eastern/northern African LGBTQ+ youth, 19% of Black LGBTQ+ youth, 17% of multiracial LGBTQ+ youth, 16% of Latino/a LGBTQ+ youth, and 12% of Asian/Pacific Islander LGBTQ+ youth (Trevor Project, 2022). This data underscores the tremendous risks of homophobia and transphobia within and outside of schools.

**Figure 5.6** Why LGBTQ+ Students Don't Report Incidents of Harassment or Assault to School Staff

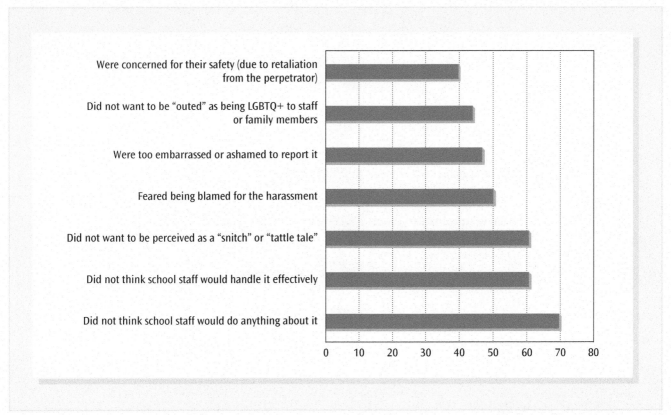

**SOURCE:** Based on Kosciw et al. (2022).

However, resources are available to support LGBTQ+ students. In addition to GSAs, organizations like PFLAG (*www.pflag.org*) and COLAGE (*www.colage.org*) provide support and advocacy to LGBTQ+ children and teens and those with an LGBTQ+ parent. These organizations specialize in helping families navigate the coming-out process and offer support to those whose families are not supportive of their identities.

There are also state and national organizations focused specifically on preventing suicide among LGBTQ+ students. For example, in response to a series of suicides among LGBTQ+ youth at the beginning of the 2010–2011 school year, syndicated columnist and author Dan Savage initiated the "It Gets Better" project in which people were encouraged to send messages of hope to LGBTQ+ youth. Hoping for 100 videos, the project received more than 10,000 within 6 months, including videos from a number of celebrities in which they encourage youth to be strong and to understand that life will be better in the future.

Additional suicide prevention resources are available through organizations like the Trevor Project (*www.thetrevorproject.org*), the Suicide Prevention Resource Center (www.sprc.org), the Family Acceptance Project (*www.lgbtqfamilyacceptance.org*), and the American Medical Association (*www.ama-assn.org/delivering-care/population-care/preventing-suicide-lgbtq-youth*).

Some LGBTQ+ students feel alone in making decisions about acknowledging their sexual orientation or gender identity and facing attacks by others. When school officials and teachers are supportive of LGBTQ+ students, students feel safer in school, miss fewer days of school, and are more likely to attend college (Kosciw et al., 2022). Professional educators have the opportunity and responsibility to provide a safe and inclusive environment at school by eliminating homophobia in the school climate. It is important that teachers and administrators make LGBTQ+ students and families feel welcome in the classroom and confront colleagues and students who exhibit homophobic behaviors. The courts agree. In *Nabozny v. Mary Podlesny, William Davis, Thomas Blauert, et al.* (1996), a Wisconsin court awarded a gay student nearly $1 million in damages for the physical abuse and verbal harassment he endured as school administrators looked the other way. Caring educators can positively affect the lives of LGBTQ+ individuals not only while they are in school but well into adulthood (Sadowski, 2016).

## Experiences of LGBTQ+ Teachers, Staff, and Other Community Members

Adults working in schools—administrators, teachers and student teachers, staff, and other community members—act as role models for students. In the context of LGBTQ+ inclusion, this includes heterosexual and cisgender educators who have the opportunity to model allyship and advocacy as well as educators who are themselves positive representations of what healthy LGBTQ+ adulthood can look like. There is no official data regarding the number of LGBTQ+ educators in the United States; however, given that 7.1% of U.S. adults identify as LGBTQ+ (Jones, 2022), it is reasonable to anticipate that hundreds of thousands of LGBTQ+ teachers, counselors, and school administrators are included among the nation's 3.2 million educators (National Center for Education Statistics, 2023).

While some states have protected LGBTQ+ people from workplace discrimination for decades, beginning with Wisconsin in 1982, it wasn't until 2020 that the U.S. Supreme Court ruled in *Bostock v. Clayton County* that those protections must be extended to all people who work at companies with 15 or more employees. This was a landmark ruling that dramatically improved the living and working conditions for LGBTQ+ people in every state in the country. Figure 5.7 provides examples of some of the kinds of discriminatory actions prohibited by *Bostock*.

However, the presence of legal protections does not always guarantee a supportive workplace, and it is reasonable to expect that LGBTQ+ educators' experiences mirror those of LGBTQ+ adults in other professions: Many are comfortably out at work and feel welcomed and affirmed by their colleagues, whereas others are closeted or impacted by homophobia and transphobia. Additionally, LGBTQ+ educators are unique in that they have to navigate not only official employment policies but also the escalating culture wars playing out in classrooms and school boards across the country. This can create a hostile working environment in which LGBTQ+ educators are asked to enforce policies that harm members of their own community (such as policies forbidding them to acknowledge the existence of LGBTQ+ people, requiring them to use trans students' birth names or pronouns, or mandating they notify parents if students use a chosen name at school).

**Figure 5.7** Examples of Unlawful Discrimination

The school nurse transitions from female to male over the summer. When the fall semester begins, the school principal reassigns the nurse to a position that pays the same amount but doesn't involve contact with students.

An athletic director is interviewing candidates for a football coaching position. She's about to hire someone but realizes the candidate is gay. She worries that some families will be uncomfortable with a gay coach, so she hires someone else.

A female teacher puts a photo of her wife on her desk. The principal tells her she has to remove it, even though many teachers in heterosexual marriages have family photos in their classrooms.

A school bus driver and his husband adopt a baby. The school refuses to grant him paternity leave, even though heterosexual couples who adopt children are granted maternity or paternity leave.

A group of parents complain to the school board after seeing a teacher march in the city's LGBTQ+ pride parade. The school board directs the school principal to transfer any objecting students to another class and warns the teacher that she is on probation because of her disruptive behavior.

A school hires a trans woman who transitioned years before. The school will not allow her to use the women's faculty bathroom but allows her to use a private unisex bathroom.

**SOURCE:** Adapted from National Education Association (2023).

Laws like Florida's "Don't Say Gay" law often feature vague or contradictory language, leaving it up to interpretation whether the laws forbid LGBTQ+ people from discussing their personal life at school. In one section, the bill forbids "classroom discussion about sexual orientation or gender identity"; in another, it focuses specifically on "classroom instruction" about sexual orientation or gender identity. Some LGBTQ+ teachers fear targeting or **doxing**, or the publication of their address and contact information for the purposes of harassment, by anti-LGBTQ+ parents or religious or community groups or worry that normal interactions with students may lead to bigoted accusations of "grooming" or molestation, charges that they are attempting to "recruit" their students into being gay, or scrutiny of their curriculum, pedagogy, and classroom library. In addition, they worry about threats; harassment; vandalism to their cars and homes; and violence by students, parents, colleagues, and other members of the community. Although courts usually protect their jobs, they cannot provide the security and comfort necessary to thrive at work.

In the last two decades of the twentieth century, lawyers argued against the dismissal of LGBTQ+ teachers by drawing on the constitutional protections available to all Americans (McCarthy et al., 2019). The Fourteenth Amendment's Due Process and Equal Protection Clauses provided the primary support for these cases when teachers could prove that their dismissal was based solely on their sexual identity. The landmark case *Lawrence v. Texas* (2003), in which the U.S. Supreme Court found that gay people have a right to privacy in their sexual lives, and California's *Morrison v. Board of Education* (1969) provided the precedents that would generally favor teachers. As a result, the courts began to rule in favor of LGBTQ+ teachers unless a school district could successfully make the argument that a teacher's private sexual behavior had a negative impact on their effectiveness as a teacher (McCarthy et al., 2019).

However, some private schools, especially religious schools, may continue to stipulate in their contracts that teachers will adhere to certain behaviors and cannot be married to a person of the same sex. As recently as 2018, a very popular and successful teacher in Miami was dismissed by a Catholic school after she married another woman (CBS Miami, 2018). Some religious organizations continue to fight against the *Bostock v. Clayton County* decision, seeking exemptions on the basis of religious freedom; however, as of 2023, they have not met legislative success.

More recent court cases are focusing on working conditions related to a teacher's sexual orientation (McCarthy et al., 2019). For example, in 2020, a Maine teacher with a record of "glowing" performance evaluations reported her supervisor for making "degrading and humiliating remarks about her sexuality" (Allen, 2023). The school department did not adequately address the issue, so the teacher filed a complaint with the Maine Human Rights Commission and, after her contract was not renewed, a civil lawsuit alleging discrimination. As of August 2023, her case is still pending. However, legal precedent indicates that schools are responsible for ensuring LGBTQ+ educators are not subjected to a hostile work environment. In *Lovell v. Comsewogue School District* (2002), for example, the court used the Fourteenth Amendment to hold school officials responsible for protecting teachers from harassment by students, parents, and colleagues regardless of the teacher's sexual orientation. What constitutes "sufficient" response, however, is still subject to debate. In *Schroeder v. Hamilton School District* (2002) in Wisconsin, the court ruled in favor of the school district because it had taken minimal action to discipline the students who were harassing a gay teacher.

In addition to their own experiences at work, LGBTQ+ educators are impacted by the lack of legal clarity regarding homophobic or transphobic actions committed by other teachers. For example, when a Virginia teacher was fired in 2021 for refusing to use transgender students' names and pronouns, the Virginia Supreme Court ruled that he had to be reinstated (Associated Press, 2021). In 2023, however, a federal appeals court rejected an appeal from an Indiana teacher who was fired for the same reason (Foody, 2023).

This lack of clarity regarding what happens when educators intentionally misgender transgender students creates a climate that is confusing and hostile for LGBTQ+ students and educators alike. Until federal laws specifically protect LGBTQ+ students, communities, and educators, court decisions are likely to vary across the country.

Moreover, the 2023 passage of anti-LGBTQ+ laws like Florida's HR 1557, as well as other laws banning classroom conversation about sexual orientation and/ or gender identity, have impacted the employment protections not just for LGBTQ+ teachers but for all teachers who include LGBTQ+ content in their classrooms. Some LGBTQ+ educators feel forced to remain closeted or lie about their identity or relationship status and fear coming out would put their job or teaching credential at risk. An increasing number of LGBTQ+ and non-LGBTQ+ teachers have reported censure or termination after reading, showing films, or ordering library materials featuring LGBTQ+ characters or themes. In 2023, for example, Jenna Barbee, a first-year teacher in Florida, was teaching a science unit on ecosystems and environments and decided to show the Disney animated film *Strange World* to demonstrate key concepts from the unit. She had signed permission slips to show films with a PG rating, but one of her student's parents—school board member and member of the anti-LGBTQ+ group Moms for Liberty Shannon Rodriguez—filed a complaint because the film included a gay character (Bowman, 2023). This complaint triggered both a formal investigation by both the county school board and Florida Department of Education (Hernandez, 2023a), national media and activist attention, and an effort to recall the school board member who initiated the complaint. As of August 2023, the county school board has closed its investigation, noting that Barbee had parental permission but did not get explicit administrative approval to show the film; the state's "inappropriate conduct" investigation is ongoing. Regardless, Barbee will not be returning to her classroom. In a media interview, she noted that she decided to resign due to "politics and the fear of not being able to be who you are" (Rosales & Garcia, 2023). Unfortunately, Barbee is not alone in her decision to resign. When testifying during a school board meeting related to the case, the president of the Hernando Classroom Teachers Association noted that the number of resignations of educators had doubled in 2023 (Bowman, 2023).

There are few professions that are as rewarding—or as demanding—as teaching. The demands facing LGBTQ+ teachers can feel especially intense, as they navigate increasingly complex social and political landscapes that include varied national, state, city, and district laws and expectations (Maher & Toledo, 2022; Toledo & Maher, 2021; Verner Chappell et al., 2018). Nevertheless, LGBTQ+ educators make an invaluable contribution to our schools and their students, and there is an ever-growing network of personal and professional supports for LGBTQ+ educators and those working toward educational justice. GLSEN (*www.glsen.org*), for example, offers a tremendous array of free professional resources, advocacy, and support to educators and school administrators seeking to design and implement LGBTQ+-affirming curriculum and policy.

Students and educators attending an Orange County, California school board meeting to show their support for LGBTQ+ students.

**SOURCE:** MediaNews Group/Orange County Register/Getty Images

Similar resources are available from the HRC's Welcoming Schools Program (*www.welcomingschools.org*) and the National Education Association (*www.nea.org/advocating-for-change/racial-social-justice/tools-justice/lgbtq-support-protection*). Additional resources, including legal counsel and advocacy, are often available through local and state teachers' unions, as well as the National LGBTQ Task Force (*www.thetaskforce.org*), GLAD Legal Advocates and Defenders (*www.glad.org*), and the National Center for Transgender Equality (*www.transequality.org*).

# Classroom Implications: Creating Affirming Environments for LGBTQ+ Students

**Learning Objective 5.4** Evaluate ways educators can support, affirm, and advocate for LGBTQ+ students within and beyond the classroom.

The research is clear: LGBTQ+ students who have access to supportive educators and school environments feel safer at school, have fewer absences, perform better academically, are more likely to go to college, have higher self-esteem, and report better psychological well-being (Kosciw, Clark & Menard, 2022). Thus, in addition to the legal imperative to ensure all students have access to health and safe school settings, teachers also have an ethical and professional obligation to do everything in their power to protect and nourish the LGBTQ+ students in their classrooms.

In some school environments, this is easy to do: Many schools across the country have adopted "safe schools" policies affirming LGBTQ+ students and families, while 22 states have explicit laws prohibiting bullying on the basis of sexual orientation (Movement Advancement Project, 2023c). However, classrooms are ideologically diverse spaces, and it is likely that most educators will encounter students and families who are misinformed about or hostile toward LGBTQ+ students and families. Some readers of this book will teach in states where they are explicitly prohibited from teaching about gender and sexual orientation, or where anti-LGBTQ+ activists are pushing for book bans, anti-LGBTQ+ parental notification requirements, or other damaging school policies. In this section, we examine what educators can do to create affirming environments for LGBTQ+ students, families, and colleagues, even in those states with increasingly restrictive legislative or curricular landscapes.

## Advocate for and Create Inclusive Learning Environments

If you are reading this chapter, you have already taken the first step toward being an effective teacher of LGBTQ+ students. You understand what sexual orientation and gender identity are and are aware of the dramatic impact that discriminatory beliefs, behaviors, and policies have on LGBTQ+ students, families, and educators. The next step requires you to learn about the social and political context of your own classroom and develop the skills necessary to teach effectively within that context.

If you have not already done so, now is a good time to research the current laws that impact K–12 students in the state where you live, attend school, or plan to teach. Resources like the GLSEN Navigator (*https://maps.glsen.org*) provide up-to-date information about school climate, antibullying laws, and LGBTQ+-related curricular mandates in each state.

You might also look at the policies and practices in place in your specific school district and school site. For example, does your school district have a policy affirming LGBTQ+ people? Or does it attempt to silence them through prohibitions regarding "controversial content" in the classroom? Is there a GSA at your school site? Does your school library include, or prohibit, resources depicting LGBTQ+ identities, experiences, or histories? Asking questions such as these can help you understand the unique landscape of your school and prepare to create an affirming environment for all your students.

Figure 5.8 outlines additional questions educators might ask as they consider the climate for LGBTQ+ students at their school site. This and additional resources related to creating inclusive schools are freely available within the HRC's Welcoming Schools Toolkit (*www.welcomingschools.org*).

**Figure 5.8** Questions to Ask About School Climate

- Do teachers and administrators use gender-inclusive language at public events and in school communications, rather than language like "Ladies and Gentlemen," "boys and girls," or "Moms and Dads"?

- Do school bulletin boards, newsletters, classroom posters, and community photos include LGBTQ+ people and families? Overall, do they reflect and affirm racial, ethnic, cultural, gender, and other forms of diversity within and beyond the school community?

- Do teachers and school staff avoid gender-based classroom activities, such as lining up children by gender, playing "boys versus girls" games in class, and hosting gender-restrictive school activities (such as "dads and daughters" dances)?

- Are school policies – including dress codes and non-discrimination policies – inclusive and affirming of students and staff with diverse gender expressions? Do students and staff of all races, ethnicities, sexual orientations, and gender expressions feel welcome to dress, wear their hair, and fashion themselves comfortably at school? Do the same dress codes apply to all people, regardless of their gender, gender expression, race, or body type?

- Do curricular materials – including library, classroom, health, and sexual health-related – materials reflect and affirm people of diverse sexual orientations and gender identities?

- Do students, families, faculty, and staff feel comfortable being out at school?

- Do onboarding, training, and professional development offerings reflect the value the school places on LGBTQ+ inclusive education? Do all staff receive training about how to address bullying related to sexual orientation, gender expression, and other aspects of identity?

**SOURCE:** Adapted from the Human Rights Campaign (2023c).

Questions like these can help you assess your own classroom climate. How can you ensure LGBTQ+ students and families know they are welcome in your classroom? Small changes, like telling elementary school children to bring paperwork to the "adults they live with" rather than their "mom and dad," or your use of gender-neutral words like *partner* or *spouse* rather than *boyfriend* or *girlfriend* can signal inclusion. Even in states where teachers are prohibited from explicitly teaching about sexual orientation or gender identity, teachers can always affirm students as individuals and embrace the diversity of students' families and lives.

Laws that attempt to eliminate or silence conversations about LGBTQ+ people and communities are harmful to LGBTQ+ students, families, and the whole school community. They position these students and families as "outlaws" and deny all students the opportunity to learn about history, diversity, and contemporary civic and political issues. Sexual orientation and gender identity should not be taboo subjects in the classroom, and it is important that all teachers are prepared to navigate conversations about LGBTQ+ people and communities whenever they arise.

**EARLY CHILDHOOD AND ELEMENTARY CURRICULUM** Some educators avoid conversations about sexual orientation, gender identity, or family diversity because they think children are "too young" for them. In fact, this was the argument used by anti-LGBTQ+ school board member Shannon Rodriguez, who argued that by showing the PG-rated Disney film *Strange World*, which includes an LGBTQ+ character, a teacher was guilty of "stripping the innocence" of her 10-year-old son (Rosales & Garcia, 2023). The reality, however, is that children begin learning about sexual orientation and gender identity well before they enter the classroom, and all teachers are likely to have children from LGBTQ+ families in their school community. Acknowledging and affirming the existence of the individuals in your classroom is always developmentally appropriate and critically necessary.

Moreover, teaching about sexual orientation and gender identity is ubiquitous in early childhood and elementary classrooms: every time children read a book or see a bulletin board depicting only heterosexual, nuclear families; hear another student tease someone about their favorite color, clothing, or interests; or witness the erasure of LGBTQ+ people, they are implicitly learning that one way of being is considered normal and another is not. Educators often inadvertently reinforce a binary, heterosexist understanding of gender by separating students by gender when building teams or doing classroom activities; referring to students as "boys and girls" rather than "students," "scholars," or "children"; or talking about families as "moms and dads."

It doesn't have to be this way. All educators have the opportunity to promote equity and inclusion by avoiding and interrupting stereotypes. It is easy to use inclusive language, create inclusive classroom displays, and choose literature that reflects diverse people and experiences. Even in states that prohibit teaching about sexual orientation and gender identity, teachers can choose to be inclusive when teaching about families and family relationships. For example, they do not have to limit pictures and discussions to nuclear families with a heterosexual mother and father but can include families with single parents, multigenerational families, and families that double up or live together.

Units on families should reflect the racial and ethnic diversity of the community and larger world, and teachers can emphasize that there are many different types of families—and all can successfully raise healthy, happy children. When doing projects about families, children can be encouraged to draw or write about the "adults they live with" or the "adults who care about them." When talking about relationships in literature or children's lives, teachers can use gender-neutral language like "partner," "spouse," or even "future love," rather than assuming characters, children, or students' family members have or will have a partner of a specific gender. Similarly, LGBTQ+ educators and educators with LGBTQ+ family members can display pictures of their families and extended families in the classroom; even when not explicitly discussed, these images play an important role in showing that all kinds of families are welcome.

Early childhood and elementary educators can also ensure their classroom library depicts a wide range of family structures and emphases on inclusion. Organizations like the National Association for the Education of Young Children (*www.naeyc.org/ article/books-about-families*), the American Library Association (*www.ala.org/advocacy/ literacy/inclusive-booklists*), and the National Education Association (*www.nea .org/professional-excellence/student-engagement/tools-tips/lgbtq-books-schools*) offer booklists to guide educators in selecting inclusive books that are developmentally appropriate for children of various ages and reading levels. There are also books like Todd Parr's *The Family Book* that celebrate diverse families, including large families, small families, and families with two moms, two dads, and moms and dads. Even when not read to the entire class, having an inclusive classroom library can signal to students and families that they are in a safe and supportive place.

In addition to honoring and affirming diverse people and families, early childhood and elementary educators play an invaluable role in establishing climates of respect. Lessons about fairness, valuing differences, inclusion, and respect should be included within any early childhood or elementary classroom and establish a foundation that prepare students for more complex conversations about sexual orientation, gender identity, and the importance of bias-free communities.

**MIDDLE SCHOOL AND SECONDARY CURRICULUM**   As discussed earlier in this chapter, many states have curricular standards that explicitly address the experiences and contributions of LGBTQ+ people in history, science, and literature. Every subject area provides opportunities to include and affirm LGBTQ+ people and perspectives, examine historical and contemporary civil rights movements, or examine current events that impact LGBTQ+ communities. For example, students in a history class might conduct research about Supreme Court cases and examine how they impacted the lives of people from marginalized communities. In math classes, students might analyze data from GLSEN's School Climate Survey, creating charts to depict change over time. In a science class, students can learn about chromosomal variation and how chromosomes impact the sex a person is assigned at birth. Teachers can also provide opportunities for students to learn about diverse scientists, using resources from organizations like the

American Society for Biochemistry and Molecular Biology (*www.asbmb.org/asbmb-today/people/061821/lgbtq-scientists-through-history*) or the American Chemical Society (*https://cen.acs.org/people/lgbtq-scientist-chemist-history/99/web/2021/06*) to identify LGBTQ+ scientists that have shaped the field. In a music or art class, students can study how artists have historically used their medium to critique or respond to pressing social issues, or create original music or artwork based on their own identities, community, or civic passion.

Virtually all state standards for language arts and literature emphasize the importance of reading widely and analyzing differences across diverse perspectives, genres, and literary contexts. Thus, all language arts courses should include books and short stories by authors of, and featuring characters with, diverse races/ethnicities, religious, sexual orientations, genders, and other social identities. Additionally, since analyses of context are important elements of literary critique, teachers can and should talk about the multiple identities of authors and characters in literature, as well as the social, political, and cultural context in which a text was written and is set. Literature with LGBTQ+ characters and themes provide opportunities for LGBTQ+ students to see themselves reflected in the curriculum, and for all students to learn from experiences that are different than their own. This can help students understand the meaning of diversity, the damage of discrimination, and the diversity of LGBTQ+ communities.

The possibilities for curricular inclusion of LGBTQ+ experiences are literally endless and can provide standards-aligned opportunities for students to conduct research about a topic, think critically about issues, and prepare to participate in the civic and political process. Many published resources are available that offer examples of LGBTQ+-inclusive curriculum, including GLSEN, the HRC, and the National Education Association. Early-career teachers may find GLSEN's guide, *Developing LGBTQ-Inclusive Classroom Resources* (*https://www.glsen.org/sites/default/files/2019-11/GLSEN_LGBTQ_Inclusive_Curriculum_Resource_2019_0.pdf*), especially useful. Many LGBTQ+ curricular resources also attend to the intersection of sexual orientation with race, ethnicity, socioeconomic status, gender, and religion (Sadowski, 2016), thus ensuring all students have the opportunity to see themselves within or connect to the curriculum.

Teachers in states or districts with anti-LGBTQ+ curricular mandates, such as those that explicitly ban lessons or books "about" sexual orientation or gender identity, may feel pressure to ignore the existence of their LGBTQ+ students and families or to silence conversations related to LGBTQ+ people and lives. In these cases, teachers may have to find other ways to affirm LGBTQ+ students by, for example, using the inclusive classroom processes described above. They can also build in projects that offer students a choice in selecting texts to read, civil rights issues to explore, art or music to evaluate, or scientists to profile. Teachers can be intentional in ensuring such "choice projects" include options that reflect the diversity of the classroom, community, and field. They can also invite students to analyze the degree to which required curriculum does or does not reflect the diversity of the community in which they live.

Finally, when teaching about LGBTQ+ people and topics, it is important to note that it is never appropriate to position people's basic humanity as the subject of classroom debate. Thus, while it can be useful to study or analyze LGBTQ+ people's experiences with discrimination and advocacy for civil rights, there is no educational value in asking students to debate whether LGBTQ+ people "should" or "shouldn't" be welcomed at school; whether trans students deserve access to health care or safe bathrooms; or whether LGBTQ+ families have legal recognition or civic protection. By framing questions of basic human dignity as something up for debate, such lessons dehumanize LGBTQ+ people and suggest that there is merit or validity in hate-based ideology.

# Critical Incidents in Teaching

## Applying What You've Learned

### Building Allyship: Advocating for LGBTQ+ Students

Teachers serve many roles for some students, and at times are one of the few stable relationships that students may have with adults and mentors. Part of this role often includes advocacy, or ensuring that students are afforded safe, affirming learning environments, free from harassment or bullying. Consider the following case and how you might handle the complexities of the situation:

Eduardo Ramirez, a ninth-grade social studies teacher, just began his first teaching job at Cerrato High School. Eduardo is excited to begin the school year. His administrator has set up individual 10-minute time slots for each student and family to meet their teachers prior to the start of the school year. On his first day of student and family meetings, Eduardo meets Sonia and her parents, Riley and Quinn, who arrive at Eduardo's second-to-last appointment of the day. Sonia expresses her excitement to start the school year and begin her high school experience at Cerrato. However, she also tells Eduardo that she is nervous. Sonia comes out to Eduardo as a member of the LGBTQ+ community and tells him that this will be her first year being out at school. Sonia's parents are very supportive of her identity. They express their love for Sonia, as well as their own nervous feelings. They worry that she will face potential bullying based on her identity, and they want to ensure that her teachers are supportive LGBTQ+ allies. They are also hopeful that Eduardo's social studies curriculum will include, rather than erase, LGBTQ+ people in history. Eduardo assures Sonia's parents of his commitment to her success and safety throughout the year and discusses how Riley and Quinn can be part of his educational team to help Sonia have the best experience possible in his class and at Cerrato.

Sonia and her family go slightly over their time slot talking to Eduardo, but they all leave the conversation feeling hopeful and positive. He welcomes the next student, Brooke, and her family into his classroom for a meeting. The conversation with Brooke's parents, Karen and Carl, gets off to a shaky start. Eduardo notices an agitated tone in their voices and asks if everything is okay. Carl tells Eduardo that he heard the previous conversation with Sonia and her parents and that he does not want his daughter, Brooke, interacting with Sonia or learning about "people like that." He asks that Eduardo separate Sonia and Brooke in the class and asks that they not be placed together for any group or partner work. He also asks Eduardo to keep an eye on the two students outside the classroom when he can to make sure they don't socialize. Brooke does not speak during the meeting, and Eduardo is not sure whether she shares her parents' perspective.

Eduardo doesn't know how to respond and feels overwhelmed and disheartened. After a positive encounter with Sonia and her family, he now feels nervous and anxious about the upcoming school year himself. He knows that it is his professional responsibility to ensure Sonia is not bullied in his classroom and is worried that her physical and mental well-being will be at risk.

## Questions to Discussion

1. How should Eduardo respond to Brooke's parents in this moment? In the future?

2. As the school year begins, what can Eduardo do to create a supportive and affirming environment for Sonia? How, if at all, should he respond to Karen and Carl's requests? How, if at all, should he address this issue with Brooke?

3. Investigate the laws regarding LGBTQ+ students in your own state. Do they offer guidance regarding Eduardo's professional, legal, or curricular responsibilities? If there are laws protecting LGBTQ+ students from bullying, what protections do they provide?

4. How could Eduardo be an effective ally for LGBTQ+ students even if his state does not have laws protecting them or if he teaches in a state that forbids classroom instruction about sexual orientation or gender identity?

5. How can supportive families like Sonia's be a part of creating safe and affirming spaces for LGBTQ+ students in schools?

## Becoming an Effective Advocate for LGBTQ+ Students and Communities

Educators have the opportunity to advocate for LGBTQ+ students, families, and colleagues through their actions within and beyond the classroom. Inside the classroom, teachers can model inclusive and affirming curriculum and pedagogy. They can learn ways to disrupt heterosexist, homophobic, and transphobic speech among their students and colleagues. When homophobic name-calling by students occurs, teachers can follow up with a teachable moment to provide facts and correct myths about LGBTQ+ people. If educators ignore homophobic remarks made by students or other adults, children and youth conclude that something is wrong with LGBTQ+ people and that they can be treated disrespectfully. See Figure 5.9 for simple ways educators can respond when they hear anti-LGBTQ+ comments at school.

**Figure 5.9** Examples of Ways Educators Can Respond to Anti-LGBTQ+ Comments

**Keep It Simple with Quick Responses:**

- "It's not OK at this school to use 'gay' disrespectfully to mean something is bad."

- "You may not have meant to be hurtful, but when you use the word 'gay' to mean something is bad or stupid, it is hurtful." Follow-up with, "Do you know why it is hurtful?"

- "Using the word 'homo' to tease someone is harassment and is unacceptable."

- "Even if you didn't mean to offend people who are gay, it is offensive to call this assignment gay (or queer); if you don't like something, then say you don't like it!"

- "It doesn't matter who said it, I don't want to hear that kind of language again. Is that clear?"

**Don't Ignore It:**

- Harassment does not go away on its own.

- Ignoring mean name-calling and hurtful teasing allows it to continue and possibly get worse.

- Not speaking up teaches the student targeted, as well as anyone within hearing range, that they will not be protected from harassment.

- Almost any response is better than ignoring the situation. You may not know exactly what to say, but you must stop the harassment.

- Interrupting name-calling and harassment isn't always easy. With experience you will become more comfortable in handling it. Practice with colleagues.

- You don't have to be perfect. You can always go back to the student and say or do something else if you feel you did not respond well.

**SOURCE:** Adapted from National Education Association and Human Rights Campaign Foundation (2023).

In addition to ensuring that LGBTQ+ students and families are affirmed within their classrooms, educators can also advocate for policies that protect and nourish LGBTQ+ students in their schools and communities. They can learn about the legislative context within their state, work collaboratively with teachers and school librarians to ensure students have access to inclusive reading materials, or volunteer to be an advisor for their school's GSA. When safe to do so, educators who are LGBTQ+ can choose to come out to students, colleagues, and families, and all educators can be vocal allies to LGBTQ+ students and adults in their community. In so doing, educators have the opportunity to challenge the erasure of LGBTQ+ people and communities, and—by their mere existence—model what an inclusive school community can and should look like.

**SAFE SCHOOL POLICIES**   The overall goal for every school should be to foster a supportive learning environment in which all students can thrive. All states have safe school laws and/or policies to protect students from bullying and harassment. Twenty-two states plus the District of Colombia have passed antibullying laws that specifically include sexual orientation and gender identity, whereas two states (Missouri and South Dakota) have laws that prevent school districts from protecting LGBTQ+ students (Movement Advancement Project, 2023c). To see the status of laws in your state, visit the GLSEN Navigator (*https://maps.glsen.org*).

In addition to district and state policies, many educators participate in **safe zone** or **safe space** programs, where educators "come out" as allies and advocates for LGBTQ+ students. They hang posters, stickers, or flags in their rooms to signal their allyship and assure students that they are welcome. To request a free Safe Space Kit from GLSEN that includes safe space stickers and other material for supporting LGBTQ+ students, visit *https://www.glsen.org*. Similar resources are available from many local teachers' unions and state departments of education.

However, even in schools and states where LGBTQ+ students are protected by laws or policies, schools do not always enforce them as effectively as they should. Some LGBTQ+ students have sued school districts for not protecting them from constant abuse from other students, and courts generally rule in favor of the students. School districts could face litigation if they do not take affirmative steps to prevent harassment and bullying of LGBTQ+ students. For example, the settlement in the *Nobozny v. Podlesny* (1996) case resulted in a $1 million award to a student who had been harassed on the basis of sexual orientation. In another case, after a 13-year-old boy committed suicide because he was bullied at school (*Walsh v. Tehachapi Unified School District*, 2014), the school district was required to reform its policies and conduct school climate surveys and education training sessions. The New Jersey Supreme Court ruled in *L. W. v. Toms River Regional Schools Board of Education* (2007) that school districts were financially liable if the school climate was homophobic. It is important for all educators to be proactive in ensuring their LGBTQ+ students, families, and communities are safe and affirmed at school.

As of 2023, no federal law prevents bullying or harassment of students based on their LGBTQ+ identity. However, bills have been introduced for that purpose. Following the Title IX model, the Student Non-Discrimination Act was reintroduced in 2018 to prevent any federally funded school program or activity from discriminating based on actual or perceived sexual orientation or gender identity. Another bill supported by the GLSEN, the Safe Schools Improvement Act, would amend the Elementary and Secondary Education Act to prohibit bullying and harassment based on race, color, national origin, sex, disability, sexual orientation, gender identity, and religion and was reintroduced in the Senate and House with bipartisan support in 2021. Neither of these bills have yet been passed by Congress, but educators and civil rights leaders around the country continue to advocate for their passage. To learn more about LGBTQ+ civil rights efforts in your state, and how to support local movements toward LGBTQ+ equality, visit GLSEN, the HRC, or your state's LGBTQ+ advocacy organizations.

With every action that they take—or don't take—educators send a powerful message to their LGBTQ+ students, families, and colleagues. By learning about, building relationships with, and advocating for LGBTQ+ students, teachers can ensure their classrooms are spaces in which all students can thrive, grow, and learn.

# Revisiting the Opening Case Study

As Monica listened to her colleagues debate whether the library should include books with LGBTQ+ themes and identities represented and whether students should need parental permission to access them, she struggled with whether or how to respond. She knew how important it was for LGBTQ+ students to see themselves in the curriculum and that restricting access to LGBTQ+-themed literature sent the message that LGBTQ+ people and families were somehow illicit or obscene. Monica also knew of several children with LGBTQ+ family members; while some of these families were out at school, others were not, and all would be hurt if they heard teachers referring to them as "inappropriate" for children. Additionally, she knew the power of inclusive books to build allyship in others and that having access to diverse books was important for all students. She wanted to speak up but wasn't sure how.

Monica decided to do some research to learn about how teachers can advocate for LGBTQ+ students and families. She found that many websites published lists of LGBTQ+-themed children's and young adult literature and that some of these titles had won national awards for literature. Monica also discovered that while her state curriculum standards didn't explicitly require teachers to teach about sexual orientation or gender identity in grades K–8, it did require teachers to teach about "family diversity."

She learned that her school district also had an antidiscrimination policy that prohibited discrimination in curriculum, inclusion, or discipline and discovered resources with tips to prevent bullying and promote inclusion.

Monica gathered book lists from the American Library Association as well as resources about how to create safe and welcoming schools for LGBTQ+ families. She brought them with her to school and shared them with her principal. She also volunteered to be part of the "inclusion committee" he had mentioned. Her principal seemed surprised by Monica's offer, as if he hadn't expected the committee to actually come to fruition, but was glad she was willing to take the lead. They scheduled the first meeting for the following week, and Monica began reaching out to colleagues who had expressed support during her faculty meeting. She wasn't sure what would come next but was excited to be part of a community of teachers poised to make a difference.

## Reflect and Apply

1. Monica realized that she needed professional development and support in order to be a more effective ally to LGBTQ+ students and families. How can you prepare to affirm and advocate for the LGBTQ+ students in your future classrooms?

2. This chapter included many resources and websites related to creating inclusive classroom environments. Which of these did you find most valuable? How might you use this resource in your own classroom?

3. Have you ever encountered an educator or other adult who wanted to restrict conversations about LGBTQ+ identity in school? How did you respond to this person?

In retrospect, is there anything you wish you had done differently?

4. What guidance is provided by your own district and state policies regarding LGBTQ+ students? If they are affirming, what protections do they provide? If they are restrictive, how might teachers promote inclusion without violating the law?

# Summary

- Sexual orientation refers to a person's identity as a romantic and sexual being. All people have a sexual orientation. Sexual orientation exists on a continuum, and the ways people think about and describe their own and others' sexual identities are socially constructed and change over time. Coming out is the process through which people publicly acknowledge their sexual orientation and is an important developmental stage for most LGBTQ+ people. The presence of supportive adults has a dramatic impact on the academic, emotional, and physical health of LGBTQ+ young people at all stages of the developmental continuum.

- LGBTQ+ people have always existed, and discrimination against them was uncommon in ancient societies. In the United States, LGBTQ+ people began to experience discrimination during the Puritan movements of the 1600s, and the struggle for their civil rights continues today. The twentieth century was notable both for persecution of and discrimination against LGBTQ+ people, as well as effective grassroots and legislative advocacy by members of the LGBTQ+ community. The twenty-first century brought major legislative victories for LGBTQ+ communities, including protections against housing and employment discrimination, recognition of LGBTQ+ marriage and families, and safe schools legislation. However, the 2020s saw an increase in anti-LGBTQ+ hate speech and legislative efforts; many of these initiatives have been led by social and religious (typically Christian) conservatives and specifically target LGBTQ+ people in educational settings. These laws seek to ban classroom instruction related to sexual orientation and gender identity; restrict students' ability to use pronouns or names other than those assigned at birth; or prevent students from using facilities that do not align to the sex they were assigned at birth.

- Many LGBTQ+ students feel unsafe in schools due to pervasive experiences of harassment and occasional physical assault. The negative school climate impacts these students' academic and psychological well-being and they are more likely to attempt and commit suicide than their peers. LGBTQ+ educators and allies play an essential role in creating inclusive and affirming educational environments. Additionally, LGBTQ+ educators are protected by antidiscrimination legislation, and school districts are required to protect LGBTQ+ teachers from harassment by students, parents, and colleagues.

- There are many ways educators can advocate for and affirm LGBTQ+ students and families within and beyond the classroom. In some states, educators are required to teach about LGBTQ+ families, communities, and histories as part of the curriculum, whereas other states limit or restrict lessons related to sexual orientation and gender identity. However, all educators can model inclusive pedagogies and create opportunities for LGBTQ+ students to learn and share their identity, family, history, and community. Educators can also be visible as advocates for LGBTQ+ students and families; engage in professional learning related to antibullying, advocacy, and LGBTQ+ inclusion; volunteer for leadership roles within their school site or community at large; and participate in professional and community organizations working to advance LGBTQ+ equity.

# Chapter 6
# Exceptionality

 ## Learning Objectives

*As you read this chapter, you should be able to:*

**6.1** Define people with exceptionalities and be able to affirm their cultural identities.

**6.2** Analyze the struggles people with disabilities have experienced as they fought for respect and equity in society.

**6.3** Summarize court cases and landmark legislation that promoted the educational rights of students with disabilities.

**6.4** Document the impact of ableism and discrimination on the lives of people with exceptionalities.

**6.5** Critique the disproportionate representation of groups in special education classes.

**6.6** Discuss some of the basic needs of exceptional children and identify key instructional strategies for effectively integrating students with exceptionalities in the general education classroom and providing them challenging experiences that improve their academic and functional skills.

## Opening Case Study

Guadalupe "Lupe" Gutierrez, a third-grade teacher at Martin Luther King Elementary School, has been asked to see the principal, Erin Wilkerson, after the students leave. Dr. Wilkerson explains that the school is expanding its full inclusion program, in which children receiving special education services, including those with severe disabilities, are fully integrated into general education classrooms. Congruent with school district policy, King Elementary is enhancing its efforts to integrate children receiving special education services into general education settings. Gutierrez's classroom is one of four general education classrooms in which children receiving special education services will be placed in the next few weeks. "What this will involve, Lupe, is two students with severe disabilities. One is a child with Down syndrome who has developmental disabilities; he has severe delays in the acquisition of cognitive, language, motor, and social skills, and he has some severe learning problems. The other child is nonambulatory, with limited speech and severe cerebral palsy.

"You will be assigned a full-time aide with a special education background. In addition, Bill Gregg, the inclusion specialist, will assist you with instructional plans and strategies. It is important that you prepare your students and the parents so that a smooth transition can be made when these students come into your class in January, just two and a half months from now. I'd like you and Bill to map out a plan of action and give it to me in 2 weeks."

### Reflect

1. What should the plan of action include?

2. What is the purpose of integrating students with severe disabilities with students without disabilities in the same classroom?

3. In what ways will Ms. Gutierrez have to prepare her current students to effectively integrate her new students?

4. How might the classroom environment and curriculum be affected when a student with severe disabilities is integrated into a general education classroom?

# Who Are People with Exceptionalities?

**Learning Objective 6.1** Define people with exceptionalities and be able to affirm their cultural identities.

People with exceptionalities include individuals with disabilities and individuals who are **gifted and talented**.* This fact alone makes the subject of exceptionality complex. The U.S. Census Bureau (2023) reported that there were 42.5 million individuals with disabilities in the United States, or 13% of the U.S. population. Educators continuously come in contact with exceptional children and adults. They may be students in classrooms, professional colleagues, family members, friends and neighbors, and people they meet in their everyday experiences. Teachers and other educators should fairly easily recognize that **accommodations** and **modifications** in the classroom are needed for students with recognizable physical disabilities in which students use a wheelchair, a cane to scan their surroundings, or sign language or speak with a speech impediment. Most other disabilities are not noticeable when first meeting a student with a disability but become noticeable over time.

The school experiences of exceptional children may differ from other children in that they may need accommodations to participate in some aspects of the education process and assistive technology to access the curriculum, communicate with their peers and teachers, and benefit fully from their education. In most cases, they can learn at high levels and be active participants in the classroom even though they may be learning in a different way than their peers. As everyone becomes more familiar with accommodations and modifications in the classroom, the inclusion and acceptance of students with exceptionalities will become the natural and common way to interact and support each other in a classroom. In this section, we explore the identification of students with disabilities and students who are gifted and talented and the role of culture in the lives of exceptional people.

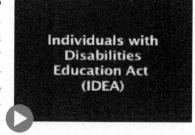

**Pearson eTextbook**

**Video Example 6.1**

This video discusses the landmark legislation, the Individuals with Disabilities Education Act.

## Students with Disabilities

The largest number of children with exceptionalities are children with disabilities, some of whom are also gifted and talented in one or more areas. In the 2020–2021 school year, 7.2 million students age 3 to 21 received special education services under the **Individuals with Disabilities Education Act (IDEA)**, representing 14.5% of all public school students (National Center for Education Statistics [NCES], 2022a). Each of these students brings strengths to the classroom that teachers should intentionally identify. Just because they have a disability does not mean that they cannot learn at high levels and be accomplished and advanced in many ways. Teachers are a critical link in helping students become the person they want to be. "The antidote to ableism in schools is promoting an asset-based approach that affirms worthiness, pride, and the development of disability identity in school" (Forber-Pratt & Minotti, 2023, p. 12).

What is a disability? Generally, it is a physical or mental condition that limits a person's movement, interactions, or activities. For some people, the condition is present at birth. Other conditions, such as autism spectrum disorder and attention-deficit/hyperactivity disorder (ADHD), develop during childhood. Disabilities such as traumatic brain injury or spinal cord injury are the result of injuries. Other conditions related to diabetes, for example, can cause disabilities such as vision loss, nerve damage, or limb loss. Progressive diseases such as muscular dystrophy and multiple sclerosis may affect a person's mobility (Centers for Disease Control and Prevention [CDC], 2020b).

---

*We have used the expression "gifted and talented students" throughout this chapter because the U.S. school system continues to use this term. Note, however, that some people feel the term is no longer appropriate and prefer the use of a term such as "advanced learners."

**DISABILITY IDENTITY** **Disability identity** is a "sense of self that includes one's disability and feelings of connection to, or solidarity with, the disability community" (Dunn & Burcaw, 2013, p. 148). Because disability identities interact with identities based on race, ethnicity, class, gender, religious affiliation, and sexual orientation, they are complex and affected by the strengths, experiences, and social barriers of those groups (Thorius & Waitoller, 2023). Developing a disability identity can be a valuable asset. Bogart and Dunn (2019) report that "research has found that affirming a disability identity is associated with a variety of benefits including higher satisfaction with life, self-esteem, self-efficacy, social support, and lower psychological stress" (p. 657). Embracing a disability identity helps people "recapture their personhood and lay claim to social justice, full citizenship, and participation" (Wehmeyer & Kurth, 2021, p. 19). Thus, affirming students' disability identities in classrooms should be a goal for teachers. In addition, as these students share their own experiences and work together to promote their civil rights, they begin to develop disability pride (Forber-Pratt & Monotti, 2023), which contributes to protecting self-esteem against stigma (Bogart et al., 2018).

**DISABILITIES IN SCHOOLS** Students with specific disabilities in schools are eligible for special education services under the **Individuals with Disabilities Education Improvement Act (P.L. 108-446)** or Section 504 of the Rehabilitation Act of 1973. The disabilities that qualify for services under IDEA include **intellectual disabilities**, hearing impairments (including deafness), speech or language impairments, visual impairments (including blindness), serious emotional disturbance, orthopedic impairments, autism, traumatic brain injury, other health impairments, or specific learning disabilities (U.S. Congress, 2004).[†] Disabilities included under Section 504 are those not included under IDEA. Figure 6.1 shows these categories plus developmental delay, which is included by some states, and the percentage of students being served under IDEA in each category.

For students to be eligible for special education services, they must be declared as having a disability by professionals. Teachers or another professional educator can refer a student for an evaluation if they see signs that a student would benefit from IDEA services; parents must give their consent before an evaluation can be conducted. (Teachers should be careful that they are not referring students who are simply misbehaving or disrupting the classroom.) Families, who know their children better than an educator, can also request an evaluation if they think special education services would be helpful to their children's educational progress. "States, through local school districts, must 'identify, locate, and evaluate every child who may have a disability requiring special education services in both public and private schools'" (Learning Disabilities Association of America, 2023, para. 3) through a process called "Child Find."

Eligibility for special education services is determined by a team that includes students' parents, their general education classroom teacher, a special education teacher, and a specialist such as a school psychologist, speech-language pathologist, or remedial reading teacher. After eligibility has been established, **individualized education program (IEP)** teams write an IEP for students that includes annual goals for their progress and identifies modifications and accommodations to support their learning.

Pearson eTextbook
**Video Example 6.2**
This video discusses the collaborative nature of the IEP process.

## Students Who Are Gifted and Talented

Gifted and talented children "perform—or have the capability to perform—at higher levels compared to other children of the same age, experiences, and environment in one of more domains" (National Association for Gifted Children, 2019, para 2),

---

[†]Note that the federal legislation for IDEA uses the word *impairment* in its categories of disabilities, but its use is no longer generally accepted.

**Figure 6.1** Percentage Distribution of Children Age 3–21 Served Under IDEA, 2021–2022 School Year

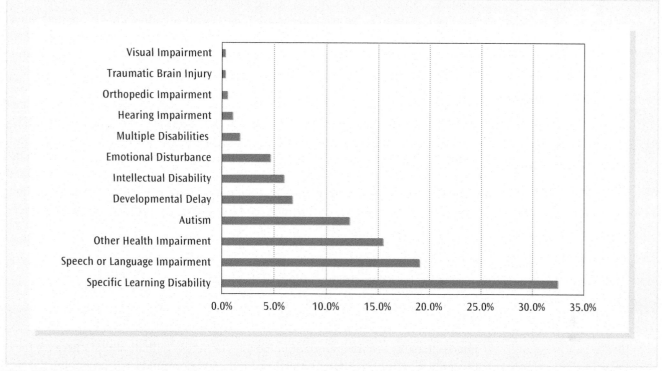

NOTE: "Other Health Impairment" refers to having limited strength, vitality, or alertness due to chronic or acute health problems such as a heart condition, rheumatic fever, sickle cell anemia, leukemia, or diabetes. Deaf and blindness each account for less than 0.4% of the children served under IDEA and are not shown in this figure.

**SOURCE:** National Center for Education Statistics (2022a).

such as intellectual, artistic, creative, physical, or other abilities. Students who were enrolled in enrichment programs represented 6.6% of the public school population in 2017–2018 (NCES, 2022c). In addition, there are students who are considered talented and who could benefit from special educational programming. While the importance of enrichment programs cannot be overstated, it is often overlooked.

While there is permissive legislation for gifted and talented students (i.e., laws that allow gifted and talented programming to take place), there are no federal mandates for the education of this group. A little more than half of the states have a law or rule that requires enrichment programming options for students who are gifted (Rinn et al., 2022). The Javits Gifted and Talented Students Education Act, passed by Congress in 1988, is the only federally funded program specific to gifted and talented students. It does not fund local gifted education programs. Instead, it supports scientifically based research and provides demonstration projects and innovative strategies to enhance the ability of schools to meet the educational needs of these students. The funding for this act is very limited, with only $16.5 million for fiscal year 2023 (National Association for Gifted Children, 2023).

The criteria that are typically used for placement in enrichment programs have been an IQ score of 130 or above or a score above a given percentile on a standardized achievement test. This type of placement criteria favors White children from high socioeconomic backgrounds, which results in the underrepresentation of students of color in these programs (Renzuli & Brandon, 2017). Grissom and Redding (2016) found that Black students, even with high standardized test scores, were much less likely to be assigned to these programs. Renzuli and Brandon (2017) suggest the use of nonverbal tests (e.g., Raven Progressive Matrices) to mitigate the bias of IQ tests. However, nonverbal tests will not by themselves eliminate the disparities in gifted identification and placement. Universal screening might be an option, where every student is screened to support the identification process. Another option is the use of local norms where students' standings are relative to other students in the class rather than their standing nationally when considered in identifying potential gifted candidates.

Black, Latino/a, Native American, Alaska Native, Native Hawaiian, and other Pacific Islander students, English learners, and children from low-income families are all underrepresented in enrichment programs. For example, Black and Latino/a students make up only 28% of students enrolled in enrichment programs while comprising 42% of the population of those schools offering gifted and talented programs. Likewise, English learners make up only 3% of these programs while comprising 11% of the students in school with gifted and talented programming (Renzuli & Brandon, 2017).

Most educators understand the importance of special education for the gifted and talented. Legislators, however, are faced with diminishing fiscal resources, partially related to the mandated funding for children with disabilities. Some may believe that children with disabilities must have special programming to survive, whereas gifted and talented students are more able to fend for themselves. While there is some truth to this belief, failure to provide for the gifted and talented group's educational needs amounts to the waste of a valuable resource. While external funding may not be available to support programs for these students, schools can commit themselves to developing their own programming for these students within their fiscal confines.

## The Intersection of Culture and Exceptionality

Intersectionality is very important in the lives of people with disabilities because they live in families of all different racial and ethnic backgrounds, socioeconomic levels, and gender, religious, and language groups. They are in all age groups and live in small towns, large metropolitan areas, and rural areas across the country. Almost everyone knows people in their family, religious community, or neighborhood who has a disability that may affect the way they live, their mobility, and/or opportunities to participate fully in society. Most families with children and other family members with disabilities have integrated those family members into the family and all of their activities, making appropriate modifications and accommodations as necessary.

People with disabilities "may be the only member of their family or community who shares that identity" (Bogart & Dunn, 2019, p. 652). Not unlike other people, people with disabilities often find comfort and security with each other and, in some instances, they form their own enclaves and social organizational structures. Forming an identity with others who have the same disability could be challenging (Bogart & Dunn, 2019), although it is easier today than in the past with Internet and virtual meetings. Throughout the country, one can find cohesive groups of individuals, such as those who have visual or hearing disabilities and those who have intellectual disabilities. In some instances, they congregate in similar jobs, in the same neighborhoods, and at various social settings and activities.

Near Frankfort Avenue in Louisville, Kentucky, two major institutions provide services for people who are blind or have visual impairments. The American Printing House for the Blind and the Kentucky School for the Blind are adjacent to each other. The American Printing House for the Blind, the leading publisher of materials for individuals who are blind or visually impaired, employs a number of individuals who are blind. The Kentucky School for the Blind is a residential school for students who are blind or visually impaired, and it also employs a small number of people who are blind or visually impaired, including teachers. With the relatively large number of persons who are blind employed by these two institutions, it is understandable that many live in the surrounding residential area.

Settling in this area allows them to live close enough to their work to minimize the potential transportation problems related to their disability. It also provides a sense of emotional security for the many who, in earlier years, attended the Kentucky School for the

Blind and lived on its campus and thus became part of the neighborhood. The neighborhood community can also provide social-emotional security and feelings of acceptance. Individuals who are blind or deaf may be among the most likely to form their own cultural groups as they attend day and residential schools together across the United States. Both have overriding factors that contribute to the tendency for individuals to seek out one another and to form cultural groups. Some people who are blind have limited mobility. Living in cultural enclaves allows them easier access to one another. They share forms of communication—oral language, Braille, and talking books. Social and cultural interests, created partly as a result of their disability, can be shared.

Sign Language is the predominant language used by deaf people in the United States.

**SOURCE:** © Andrii Zastrozhnov/Shutterstock

People with a hearing disability may have communication limitations within the hearing world. Their use of American Sign Language (ASL) provides them with an emotional as well as a functional bond. Religious programs and places of worship for individuals with hearing disabilities have been formed to provide services to assist in total communication and social activities. The first school for students who were deaf, the American School for the Deaf, was established in Connecticut in 1817. Nearly 100 residential and day schools for the Deaf exist across the United States today (American School for the Deaf, n.d.). Gallaudet University was founded in the District of Columbia as a federally funded college for students who were deaf in 1864 and now includes a Model Secondary School for the Deaf and the Kendall Demonstration Elementary School.

People with physical disabilities may or may not become a part of a cultural group related to the disability. Some of them function vocationally and socially as part of the dominant culture. Socialization, however, may depend on the degree of disability and society's acceptance of them. Some individuals with physical disabilities also maintain social contacts with others with similar disabilities. Social clubs for individuals with physical disabilities have been formed to provide experiences commensurate with members' functional abilities as well as a social climate that provides acceptance and security. Athletic leagues for competition in sports, such as wheelchair basketball and tennis, have been formed. Activities such as bocce ball and volleyball enable some athletes with limited mobility to enjoy competition with similar limitations. Many racing events (e.g., the Boston Marathon) now include competition for participants using wheelchairs. The Special Olympics, which were organized in 1968, offers the opportunity for people with intellectual disabilities to compete athletically on a local to international level, while the Warrior and Invictus Games are for wounded service personnel. Paralympic Games for athletes with disabilities began with their first games in Rome in 1960 and now are held in the same cities and venues following the summer and winter games of the Olympics every 2 years.

Many individuals with mild intellectual disabilities live independently or in community-based and community-supported group homes. The group homes provide a family-like atmosphere and house parents provide supervision. Most of the individuals with moderate intellectual disabilities who do not live in institutions tend to live at home. Many individuals with severe and profound intellectual disabilities and some with moderate intellectual disabilities are institutionalized and thus are forced into their own cultural group or enclave, isolated from the rest of society.

The gifted and talented usually do not experience the same type of discrimination and social rejection that many people with disabilities experience. Yet, like individuals with disabilities, they may suffer isolation from the dominant culture and seek others with comparable abilities to gain a feeling of acceptance as well as intellectual or emotional stimulation. The existence of Mensa, an organization whose membership prerequisite is a high score on an intelligence test, attests to the apparent need of some gifted individuals to be with others of similar intellect or talents. Rejection of the gifted and talented may differ from rejection of individuals with disabilities because the roots may stem from a lack of understanding or jealousy rather than from the stigma that may relate to certain disabilities.

# A Brief History of the Struggles of People with Disabilities in Society for Respect and Equity

**Learning Objective 6.2** Analyze the struggles people with disabilities have experienced as they fought for respect and equity in society.

The plight of persons with disabilities, in many respects, closely parallels that of other oppressed groups. The history of the treatment of those with disabilities does not reveal a society eager to meet its responsibilities. Prior to 1800, with a few exceptions, people with disabilities were integrated into their communities. Although they may have been seen as different than other children, they were not considered a major social problem in society (Jarrett, 2020).

In the nineteenth and twentieth centuries, the public was made aware of blindness and deafness by the extraordinary contributions of Louis Braille (1809–1852) and Helen Keller (1880–1968). Louis Braille, who was born in France, lost his sight through an accident before he was 5 years old. He invented the Braille alphabet with a raised dots system that is used by people who are blind; it continues to be used today (Library of Congress, n.d.).

As the result of an illness when she was less than 2 years old, Helen Keller lost both her sight and hearing. With her remarkable teacher, Anne Sullivan (Macy), and education at the Perkins Institution, she learned Braille and, at the Horace Mann School for the Deaf in Boston, she learned to speak and lip-read. Helen later graduated cum laude from Radcliffe College. Her numerous articles, books, and lectures around the world made her a celebrity and provided the public an insight into her life as a person with two disabilities (History.com Editors, 2019).

Other people with disabilities were not recognized or accepted in society to the same degree as most people who were blind and/or deaf during the nineteenth and twentieth centuries. Beginning in the mid-1900s, however, summer camps and rehabilitation centers for children with disabilities whose families could afford them provided nurturing environments where children were accepted for who they were, not what people without disabilities wanted them to be. They were able to develop friendships with people who shared a culture based on their disability (Carmel, 2020b).

Many students with disabilities were not allowed to attend school. Students using wheelchairs often had no way to access a school with steps and classrooms above the first floor. Educators did not know how to provide accommodations for students who were blind or deaf or had a hearing disability, and they did not allow students who tested below a specific level to attend a regular school. Sometimes, especially for students with intellectual disabilities, a school district would assign students to a special school, segregated from their peers without disabilities. When students were allowed to enroll in a school, they were usually segregated in a classroom with other students with disabilities where they were able to cultivate friendships, but they were not always pushed to learn at high levels. When they attended college, neither dorms nor classrooms were accessible, making it difficult to carry out daily functions and attend classes (Carmel, 2020b).

In this section, we examine the treatment of people with disabilities over the past two centuries and the struggles in which people with disabilities have been engaged to gain their civil rights and access to schools, jobs, sports, entertainment, and other societal institutions.

## Institutionalization

During most of the nineteenth century, people with intellectual disabilities were frequently seen as people who needed to be detained and treated under medical supervision in mental asylums or colonies (Jarrett, 2020). Many institutions were deliberately built great distances from population centers so the residents could be segregated and more easily contained. Children with mental illnesses and intellectual disabilities were also institutionalized in schools such as Willowbrook State School on Staten Island in New York City and the Hiwatha Asylum for Insane Indians in Canton, South Dakota. In these schools, students were traumatized with the use of electric shock and other punishments for even minor misbehaviors.

For decades, American society did not have to deal with its conscience with respect to its citizens with severe disabilities. Society simply sent them far away and forgot about them. Most Americans did not know of the sometimes cruel and inhumane treatment that existed in many facilities. One of the successes of the Disability Rights Movement, which started in the 1960s, was the deinstitutionalization of many large, state-funded institutional and hospital wards housing people with psychiatric, intellectual, and/or developmental disabilities. Unfortunately, the number of people with these disabilities grew dramatically in institutional settings like jails as a result (Jaffee, 2023).

Individuals with mild disabilities were generally able to be absorbed into society, sometimes seeming to disappear, sometimes contributing meaningfully to society, often not even being identified as having a disability. As society became more industrialized and educational reforms required school attendance, the academic problems of students with disabilities became increasingly more visible. Special schools and special classes were designated to meet the needs of these children. Thus, society segregated these individuals, often under the guise of acting in their best interests.

## The Eugenics Movement

The word **eugenics** was first introduced in 1883 by Francis Galton, a half-cousin of Charles Darwin, as a policy of social engineering that would increase the number of middle- and upper-class children and limit, or even prevent, the expansion of the "lower classes." Numerous studies at the end of the 1800s blamed intellectual disabilities on families who were impoverished and labeled dysfunctional (Jarrett, 2020).

By the early twentieth century, Alfred Binet of France was determining the intelligence of people with IQ tests that could scientifically identify people with intellectual disabilities, measured by how far from the norm it was (Harry & Klingner, 2022, p. 13). By "norm," Binet was referring to the norm of the White individuals who he was measuring. The eugenics movement in the United States embraced these tests as an appropriate means for sorting the population by their intellectual abilities. Social scientists, psychologists, the medical establishment, and educators ignored the fact that there could be multiple types of intelligence not measured with these tests. They were also not concerned with the cultural biases of the tests that ensured that well-educated middle- and upper-class people would score at higher levels than people with less education and low incomes (Jarrett, 2020).

The supporters of eugenics called for the sterilization of people with intellectual disabilities to "cleanse" society of "undesirable" traits (Forber-Pratt & Minotti, 2023). Again, Black, Latina, and Indigenous women were targeted (Jaffee, 2023). By the 1950s, as many as 30 states allowed the sterilization of individuals with intellectual disabilities, supported by the *Buck v. Bell* (1927) U.S. Supreme Court ruling. Other states prohibited selected people with disabilities from exercising their basic rights of voting, marrying, and applying for a driver's license (Osborne & Russo, 2021). The prospect of marriage prohibitions and eugenic sterilization for persons with intellectual disabilities raised serious social and ethical issues. Those who were responsible for the care and education of individuals with disabilities viewed themselves (not those with disabilities) as having the right to control matters dealing with sexual behavior, marriage, and procreation. In a similar way, educators determined the means of communication for the Deaf, either an oral/aural approach or a manual/total communication approach. Such decisions have profound implications because they determine not only how these individuals will communicate but also, to a great extent, with whom they will be able to communicate.

In addition, during this period, people with disabilities along with people of color were cruelly featured in "freak shows" at circuses, amusement parks, and museums. Scientists used photographic images of people with disabilities to try to convince the scientific community and the public that there were important differences between people with intellectual disabilities and people without disabilities. The most horrific treatment of people with disabilities occurred when the Nazis in Germany determined that they were not worthy of living, killing up to 250,000 people who were sick or disabled (Brown, 2018).

## Disability as a Social Construction

Up until the 1970s, the medical model provided the primary definition of *disability* in western cultures. It defined *disability* as an individual pathology or abnormality that must be treated by a medical specialist with the goal of making the person more able-bodied (Wehmeyer & Kurth, 2021). In the 1970s, psychologists began to view disability as a social construction created by societies that are inaccessible to and biased toward people with disabilities (Bogart & Dunn, 2019, p. 652). It declared that people with disabilities were prevented from full, valued, and inclusive participation in society because of systemic barriers, including **ableism**, racism, and sexism (Waitoller & Thorius, 2016). This social model placed the onus of change on society rather than the individual. It pushed society to reduce social and physical barriers and establish civil rights for people with disabilities.

Most people with disabilities see the disability as one factor of their lives whereas many people without disabilities view the disability as not only a negative factor in the lives of people with disabilities, but the major determinant of their identities. However, the identities of people with disabilities often are much more linked to their race, ethnicity, religion, socioeconomic status, and gender than their disability. In most ways, they live their lives like other members of those groups, making accommodations for their disability as needed. They have many strengths that are not always recognized and affirmed by the professionals and peers with whom they work. They want to make their own decisions about their lives and should be involved in determining their treatment programs based on their own experiences and opinions (Bogart & Dunn, 2019).

## The Fight for Civil Rights

According to The Arc (n.d.), the largest organization of people with intellectual and developmental disabilities, "the history of living with a disability in the United States has largely been one of discrimination, segregation, and exclusion from education, work, housing, and even from routine daily activities" (para. 1). People with disabilities have a long history of being prevented from sharing the same civil rights as their peers without disabilities. For example, as recently as the latter part of the twentieth century, nearly half of the states had miscegenation laws that prohibited marriage between individuals with intellectual disabilities.

Parents of children with disabilities were the early soldiers in the fight for rights to an education. Before the Education for All Handicapped Children Act (Public Law 94-142) was passed by Congress in 1975, many of their children were not allowed to attend schools with students without disabilities. Most school districts or a county or state had special schools for students with intellectual disabilities, those with visual or hearing disabilities, and students with other severe disabilities. If students with disabilities were permitted to attend a regular school, it was likely not to have the appropriate modifications and accommodations needed to support them. Parents had to be advocates for their children, working sometimes with lawyers or other advocates to ensure their children were being appropriately educated. Parents were also major players in the court cases and legislation that led to opening opportunities for their children to receive appropriate services in school and to be educated in the **least-restrictive environment (LRE)** in public schools.

Protesters in New York City demand access to the subway system.

**SOURCE:** Erik McGregor/LightRocket

Following World Wars I and II, veterans who were disabled as they fought in the wars pressured Congress for rehabilitation services and vocational training, but disabilities were still viewed as abnormal conditions that should be medically cured or fixed (Jaffee, 2023). Although individual veterans were receiving services, people with disabilities were prevented from many opportunities to learn and work because they did not have access to public transportation, the telephone, bathrooms, and office buildings (Anti-Defamation League, 2017).

Activists with disabilities demanded changes in the way they were treated, following the blueprint of the struggle for civil rights that Black activists had used in the 1950s and 1960s. They, along with their allies, lobbied Congress and organized protest marches in cities across the country to demand passage of the Rehabilitation Act of 1973 (Section 504) that provided equal opportunity for federal jobs, prohibited discrimination on the basis of physical or intellectual disability, and mandated equal access to public services (Anti-Defamation League, 2017). When the regulations for Section 504 had still not been implemented four years later, sit-ins were organized in cities across the country.

Judy Heumann and Kitty Cone, who both used wheelchairs, led more than 100 people with different types of disabilities, interpreters, and personal care aides in a sit-in at the regional office of the U.S. Health, Education and Welfare Department in San Francisco. They were joined by Brad Lomax and Chuck Johnson of the Black Panthers, who helped provide needed supplies. The mayor of San Francisco, George Moscone, sent mattresses to the demonstrators. The protestors in San Francisco remained in the building for 25 days—one of the longest occupations in history—and the regulations went into effect before they left (Carmel, 2020a).

The sit-ins brought people together across disability groups, contributing to powerful organizing strategies for future action. Judy Heumann, who later served as Assistant Secretary of the Office of Special Education and Rehabilitation Services at the U.S. Department of Education, recognized the importance of this change: "through the sit-ins, we turned ourselves from being oppressed individuals into being empowered people. We demonstrated to the entire nation that disabled people could take control over our own lives and take leadership in the struggle for equality" (quoted in Grim, 2015, para 6). Table 6.1 provides information on other important events in the struggle for civil rights for people with disabilities over the past two centuries.

**Table 6.1** Milestones in the Struggle for the Civil Rights of People with Disabilities

| | |
|---|---|
| 1817 | Thomas H. Gallaudet founded the Connecticut Asylum for the Education and Instruction of Deaf and Dumb Persons in Hartford, Connecticut—the first permanent school for the Deaf in the United States. The institution was later renamed the American School for the Deaf. |
| 1829 | Louis Braille created the raised point alphabet. |
| 1864 | Gallaudet University was founded in Washington, DC, as a federally funded college for the Deaf. |
| 1907 | Indiana enacted the first sterilization law for people with intellectual disabilities and rapists. Similar laws were soon passed by 24 states. |
| 1927 | Compulsory sterilization was ruled illegal. |
| 1935 | The Social Security Act was signed into law, providing assistance to adults with disabilities. |
| 1939–1941 | Up to 250,000 people with intellectual or physical disabilities were killed as a result of Adolf Hitler's order to remove those who were sick and people with disabilities from society. |
| 1947 | The Presidential Committee launched a publicity campaign for businesses to hire people with physical disabilities. |
| | The organization Paralyzed Veterans of America was founded to promote and protect the civil rights of veterans with disabilities. |
| 1950 | The Association for Retarded Citizens (Arc) was founded by the parents of students with intellectual and developmental disabilities. |
| 1954 | The Supreme Court ruled that school segregation had to be abolished in *Brown v. Board of Education*, becoming a foundation for future court action on the education of students with disabilities. |
| 1962 | Ed Roberts and Judy Heumann inspired the Independent Living Movement for people with disabilities. |
| 1965 | Title XIX of the Social Security Act created the federal/state Medicaid program to pay medical costs for specific people with disabilities. |
| 1968 | The Architectural Barriers Act required all buildings designed, constructed, altered, or leased with federal funds to be made accessible to people with disabilities. |
| 1970 | Educator and activist Judy Heumann sued the New York City Board of Education for denying her a teaching license because her wheelchair was a fire hazard—the same reason that she was not allowed to attend kindergarten. |
| 1971 | *PARC v. Commonwealth of Pennsylvania* declared that all children regardless of any physical or intellectual disability should have access to an education. |
| 1973 | Disabled in Action became one of the first advocacy organizations led by people with disabilities. Its motto was "Nothing About Us Without Us." |
| | Congress passed the Rehabilitation Act of 1973, which included Section 504, preventing people with disabilities from being excluded from participation in, being denied any benefits from, and being discriminated against in any program or activity receiving federal financial assistance. |
| 1974 | The last of the so-called "Ugly Laws," which allowed police to arrest and jail people for being "disfigured," was repealed. |
| 1975 | The Education for Handicapped Children Act (P.L. 94-142) was signed, requiring a free, appropriate public education (FAPE) for all children with disabilities in the least-restrictive environment. |
| | The United Nations adopted the Declaration on the Rights of Disabled Persons. |
| 1976 | Actress Linda Bove, who was deaf, was cast as Linda the Librarian on *Sesame Street*. |
| 1977 | Demonstrators with disabilities occupied the regional office of the U.S. Health, Education and Welfare Department in San Francisco, California, and other cities to demand the implementation of Section 504 of the Rehabilitation Act of 1973. |
| 1978 | People using wheelchairs blocked buses in Denver, Colorado, calling for accessible public transportation. |
| 1982 | In *Board of Education of the Hendrick Hudson School District v. Rowley*, the Supreme Court declared that schools were not obligated to provide students with disabilities the best possible education. Schools were required to provide a "basic floor of opportunity." |
| 1988 | Students at Gallaudet University protested the Board of Trustees' appointment of a hearing president, leading to the appointment of the first Deaf president in the history of the institution. |
| 1990 | When passage of the Americans with Disabilities Act (ADA) stalled because public transit companies were lobbying against regulations for transportation accessibility, activists with disabilities tossed aside their wheelchairs, walkers, and crutches to climb the steps of the Capitol, which became known as the "Capitol Crawl Protest." |
| | The ADA, which was signed by President George H. W. Bush, prohibited discrimination of people with disabilities in all areas of public life. |
| 1996 | The Federal Communications Act required computers, telephones, closed captioning, and other telecommunications to be accessible. |
| 1999 | *Olmstead v. L. C. and E. W.* required states to eliminate unnecessary segregation of people with disabilities and to ensure they received services in the most integrated settings. |
| 2001 | Virginia became the first state to formally express its regret for involuntarily sterilizing 8,000 people with disabilities between 1924 and 1979. |
| 2017 | ADAPT activists fought to save the Affordable Care Act and Medicaid by protesting in Senator Mitch McConnell's office and the offices of other elected officials. |
| | In *Endrew F. v. Douglas County School District*, the Supreme Court ruled that the minimal standard in the *Rowley* ruling was not enough. The justices indicated that "all children should have the chance to meet challenging objectives." |
| 2022 | The U.S. Justice Department executed a settlement agreement with the Jefferson County, Kentucky, Board of Elections to ensure people with disabilities have access to polling places during an election. |

**SOURCE:** Temple University (n.d.).

Society has historically sought to dehumanize people with disabilities by ignoring their personal wishes, making critical decisions for them, and treating them as children throughout their lives. When Congress passed IDEA, it indicated that "disability is a natural part of the human experience and in no way diminishes the right of individuals to participate in or contribute to society. Improving educational results for children with disabilities is an essential element of our national policy of ensuring equality of opportunity, full participation, independent living, and economic self-sufficiency for individuals with disabilities." Society has yet to see many people with disabilities as "a natural part of the human experience" who have the right to participate in society as any person without disabilities would. Despite the advances made as a result of the court decisions and federal legislation discussed in the next section, much more work is needed to "make true community integration and recognition of civil rights a reality for ALL, including those with the most significant disabilities" (The Arc, n.d., para 1).

# Court Decisions, Legislation, and the Rights of People with Disabilities

**Learning Objective 6.3** Summarize court cases and landmark legislation that promoted the educational rights of students with disabilities.

Educational rights of people with disabilities were not easily gained. Many educators were reluctant to extend educational rights to children with disabilities and, when they finally did, it was because the children's rights had been won in the courts and the educational community was ordered to provide for these students. In this section, we review the landmark judicial decisions and federal legislation that led to improved civil rights and equity for people with disabilities.

## Early Litigation for Educational Rights

Some of the court decisions and many of the arguments that advanced the rights of Black Americans and other oppressed groups were used by the advocates of children with disabilities. However, in reality, the battles and the rights gained by disability rights advocates came years after similar rights were won by other groups that had been oppressed. Attorneys for children with disabilities and their parents utilized case law to fight their court battles. **Case law** is the published opinions of judges, which interpret statutes, regulations, and constitutional provisions. The U.S. legal system relies on the value of these decisions and the legal precedents they establish.

**SETTING THE STAGE: *BROWN V. BOARD OF EDUCATION***  As with Black students, the initial struggles for children with disabilities involved the right to, or access to, a public education. The Supreme Court decision in *Brown v. Board of Education of Topeka* (1954) discussed in Chapter 2 played a pivotal role in securing educational rights for children with disabilities. Historically, the U.S. Supreme Court had sided with the Louisiana District Court in *Plessy v. Ferguson* in 1896, which upheld the constitutionality of Louisiana's Separate Car Act, providing for separate but equal transportation facilities for Black Americans. The *Plessy* verdict became a part of case law and set a precedent, segregating Black people from White people in transportation, public facilities, schools, restaurants, and so on. This decision "legitimized" the Jim Crow laws that established racially segregated schools, which were supposed to be separate but equal. As history clearly shows, these schools were inherently unequal. This was the setting for the *Brown* case.

The U.S. Constitution mandates that all citizens have the rights to life, liberty, and property. They cannot be denied these rights without due process. *Brown* determined that education was a property right. Although there is no constitutional guarantee of a free public education, in *Brown* the U.S. Supreme Court found that if a state undertakes the provision of free education for its citizenry, the property right of an education is established. The property (education) rights of Linda Brown and the other Black children had been taken without due process, a clear violation of the Fourteenth Amendment to the U.S. Constitution. The *Brown* decision overturned *Plessy* with regard to education (although some of the other rights were not clearly gained until the Civil Rights Act of 1964) and began the integration of all children of color into American schools.

*Brown* did not involve children with disabilities, but the precedent it set in guaranteeing equal educational opportunity for Black children extended to students with disabilities. It would take another 16 years, however, before the concept of equal opportunity would actually be applied to children with disabilities. The Court had essentially ruled that what the Topeka School District had provided Linda Brown and the other Black children was not appropriate. Not only have the courts supported rights of students with disabilities to have a free education, but legislation has also sought to ensure them the right to an appropriate education.

Throughout the history of special education in the United States, children with disabilities have faced a continuous uphill struggle to gain the right to attend public schools. Some special education programs were initiated in the early 1900s, but until the mid-1970s certain children, particularly those with moderate to severe disabilities, were routinely excluded from public education. One of the arguments to deny admission to children with moderate or severe intellectual disabilities was that they could not learn to read, write, or perform arithmetic in the same manner as other students. The argument went that because they were not able to be educated, they did not belong in schools. Parents and supporters of these children countered, arguing that learning self-help skills and other important life skills was indeed learning, and this was education. These children, along with children with severe physical disabilities, could learn, particularly if support services were provided.

***PARC V. COMMONWEALTH OF PENNSYLVANIA*** In 1971, the Pennsylvania chapter of The Arc (PARC) (1971) brought a class action suit against the Commonwealth of Pennsylvania for the failure to provide a publicly supported education to students with intellectual disabilities. The attorneys for the plaintiffs argued that:

- Education cannot be defined as only the provision of academic experiences for children.

- All students with intellectual disabilities are capable of benefiting from programs of education and training.

- Having undertaken a free public education for the children of Pennsylvania, the state could not deny children with intellectual disabilities the same opportunities.

- The earlier the students with intellectual disabilities were provided education, the greater the amount of learning that could be expected.

PARC and the state reached a settlement with a consent decree that was approved by the federal district court. The decree declared that no children who were classified as, or thought to be, intellectually disabled could be excluded from public schools. In other words, all of these children between the ages of 6 and 21 were to be provided a free public education. The court stipulated that it was most desirable to educate children with intellectual disabilities in programs like those provided to their peers without disabilities (Osborne & Russo, 2021; Yell, 2018).

***MILLS V. BOARD OF EDUCATION OF DISTRICT OF COLUMBIA*** Following the *PARC* decision, another class action suit, *Mills v. Board of Education* (1972), was brought before the federal district court for the District of Columbia on behalf of 18,000 out-of-school children with behavior problems, hyperactivity, epilepsy, intellectual disabilities, and physical problems. The court again ruled in favor of the plaintiffs and mandated that the District of Columbia schools provide publicly supported education to all children with disabilities. In addition, the court ordered that:

- The district is to provide due process procedural safeguards.
- Clearly outlined due process procedures must be established for labeling, placement, and exclusion.
- Procedural safeguards include the right to appeal, right to access records, and written notice of all stages of the process. (Osborne & Russo, 2021; Yell, 2018)

While these two high-profile cases were being played out in their respective communities, other states were facing similar challenges. The Arc and other national organizations, such as the Council for Exceptional Children, actively supported disability advocates throughout the country in preparing court briefs and in offering other means of support. Armed with their victories and case law favorable to their cause, parent groups in other states began challenging their legislatures and school districts and winning. More than 46 cases were filed on behalf of children with disabilities in the first 2½ years following the *PARC* and *Mills* decisions (Yell, 2018). Fresh with many court victories, disability advocates in the early 1970s were busy preparing for their next battleground, the Congress of the United States.

## Legislation Related to Individuals with Disabilities

Following critical court victories for children with disabilities in the early 1970s (e.g., *PARC* and *Mills*), Congress began passing key civil rights legislation for individuals with disabilities. Not surprisingly, much of the legislation was patterned after the civil rights legislation for oppressed groups of color. These new laws forever changed the way individuals with disabilities were treated in the United States and served as a model for much of the world. Today it is inconceivable that schools could be inaccessible to students who use wheelchairs, that elevators could have floor buttons not marked with Braille, or that a stadium would be built without ramps. However, as recently as the mid-1970s, restrooms and aisles in restaurants were often too narrow to provide access for individuals who used wheelchairs.

**SECTION 504 OF THE REHABILITATION ACT**   In 1973 Congress enacted **Section 504 of Public Law 93-112** as part of the Vocational Rehabilitation Act. Section 504 was the counterpart to Title VI of the Civil Rights Act of 1964. The language was brief but its implications far-reaching: "No otherwise qualified handicapped individual in the United States . . . shall, solely by reason of his (or her) handicap, be excluded from the participation in, be denied the benefits of, or be subjected to discrimination under any program or activity receiving federal financial assistance" (National Archives, 1982, §15b.1). Instead of trying to fix the person, as was past practice, Section 504 was designed to fix the environment in which people with disabilities live to make it more inclusive and provide them access to opportunities previously not available to them. Although the action applies only to programs and activities that were federally funded, it was the foundation for extending the protections to private institutions and workplaces 13 years later (Carmel, 2020b).

Section 504 prohibited exclusion from programs solely on the basis of an individual's disability. A football coach, marching band director, or university admissions officer cannot deny a student participation solely on the basis of a disability. However, if an intellectual disability inhibits a student's ability to learn football rules and plays, a learning disability prevents a student from learning marching band formations even with accommodations, or a student's test scores are clearly below the university admissions standards and indicative of likely failure, then exclusion may be justified. If denial of participation is unjustified, the school or agency risks the loss of all federal funds, even for programs in the institution that are not involved in the discriminatory practice (Murdick et al., 2014; Yell, 2018).

**INDIVIDUALS WITH DISABILITIES EDUCATION ACT**   In 1975, Public Law 94-142, the **Education for All Handicapped Children Act**, was signed into law. These provisions forever changed the face of American education. Every child age 3 to 21 with a disability became entitled to a free public education that was to be appropriate to each child's needs. The education was to be provided in the LRE, meaning that students were to be educated in a setting as close to a general or regular education class as was feasible. Parents were to have an integral role in their child's education and were to be involved in the development of the education program and to share in other decisions related to their child. When appropriate, the student was also to be involved. Schools were required to follow procedural safeguards to ensure that the rights of the students and parents were observed. Each student was required to have an IEP that was designed to meet the student's unique needs. The identification and evaluation process had to be nondiscriminatory and unbiased, with multifactored methods used to determine eligibility and placement (Murdick et al., 2014; Yell, 2018).

When Congress amended Public Law 94-142 in 1990, it renamed it the Individuals with Disabilities Education Act. Key components of this amendment included the addition of students with autism or traumatic brain injury as a separate class entitled to services. A **transition plan** was an added requirement to be included in every student's IEP by age 14. The transition plan included a needs assessment and individual planning to transition students with a disability successfully into adulthood.

In addition to substituting the term "disability" for "handicap," the new legislation included a far-reaching change in language to emphasize the person first, before the disability. The title of the legislation was changed to "Individuals with Disabilities" rather than "Disabled Individuals." This change resulted in the use of language such as "children with intellectual disabilities," "students with learning disabilities," and "individuals with cerebral palsy." The change occurred because individuals with disabilities are people or individuals first. Their disability is secondary and at times inconsequential to their ability to perform the tasks they undertake (Murdick et al., 2014; Yell, 2018).

The Education for All Handicapped Children Act of 1975 guaranteed a free and appropriate education for all children with disabilities in the least-restrictive environment.

**SOURCE:** © Wavebreakmedia/Shutterstock

In 1948, only 12% of children with disabilities were attending public schools. Just prior to the passage of P.L. 94-142, 79% were attending public schools, increasing to 94% in 2019 (NCES, 2023b). Even after schools began admitting students with disabilities, many of them were not receiving an education appropriate to their needs (Yell, 2018). Many students receiving special education services were isolated in the least desirable locations within the schools. In the first two special education teaching assignments (both prior to P.L. 94-142) experienced by one of the authors of this text, this was very much the case. In the first, all three special education classes were located in the basement of the junior high school, isolated from other students. In the second school, there were two lunch periods to accommodate the large student body. The students receiving special education services were required to eat in the school cafeteria between the two lunch periods, and they were expected to exit the facility before any other students entered. When a new school building was completed next to the old, outdated facility, the students receiving special education services remained in the old facility while the rest of the students moved.

IDEA has been amended twice since 1990 and is now overdue for reauthorization, with no sign that Congress will amend it in the near future (Osborne & Russo, 2021). The most recent amendment, in 2004, renamed the legislation to the **Individuals with Disabilities Education Improvement Act**. IDEA 2004 added new language about academic and functional goals, including the requirement that IEPs must include a statement of measurable annual goals, including academic and functional goals. IDEA 2004 also included a new initiative in the prereferral and identification of children with learning disabilities—a process referred to as **response to intervention (RTI)** that is based on a multi-tiered approach to meeting the needs of children.

Usually associated with learning disabilities, RTI or another multi-tiered system has as its primary aim to provide intervention to students who are not achieving at comparable rates with their peers. RTI includes various levels of support in the general education setting to support students with special challenges. One of the goals is to reduce unnecessary referrals into special education (Lane et al., 2020). Only if students are not responding to research-based quality instruction in general education would they be referred to special education (Hallahan et al., 2019). More recent studies suggest that because of the multi-tiered nature of these programs, they are inherently complicated to implement, and results are still mixed. RTI will require additional long-term research to determine its efficacy in schools (Hallahan et al., 2019).

Under IDEA requirements, emergency or provisional certificates do not qualify an individual to teach special education (Yell, 2018). With the passage of the 2015 Every Child Succeeds Act (ESSA), a special education teacher must have full state certification as a special educator. However, a nationwide survey of schools in 2022 found that 65% of U.S. public schools did not have an adequate number of qualified special education teachers, meaning that a large number of students with disabilities were being taught by teachers with no or limited education or experience in teaching special education. Experts suggest that these shortages may be due to high job demands with inadequate support and resources (Bodenhamer & Taylor, 2023).

When Congress passed Public Law 94-142 in 1975, it mandated services for children with disabilities. It required states and school districts to provide extensive and often expensive services to these children. Congress set a goal in 1978 to fund the mandate at 40% of the cost to educate children with disabilities, but later adjusted federal support to $26 billion, which was far below 40% of the cost, leaving states and school districts to make up the difference. Often the classes for these children are smaller and many require additional staffing with teacher aides, which increases the cost to the schools.

From 2000 to 2016, Congress's appropriations for IDEA increased from nearly $5 billion to $13.3 billion (NCES, 2022e), which is just over half of the federal projection for 2012 (Lieberman, 2023). While this is a significant increase, special education programs have expanded, and Congress's estimate that providing services to students with disabilities would cost 1.5 times the education of a student without disabilities does not match reality. A report from the California Legislative Analyst's Office (Petek, 2019) found that it cost three times as much. This leaves school administrators in a difficult quandary, trying to provide the mandated appropriate services to all children using the underfunded resources of IDEA.

Many parents of children with disabilities are fully aware of the legal rights of their children. They may fight to secure the best possible education for them, regardless of the district's financial ability to provide expensive services (e.g., residential schools, long-distance transportation). In these situations, the cost of providing service may greatly exceed funding from state and federal sources and may be far greater than the average budgeted costs for the typical student. These situations may add to a district's financial distress and may require the use of funds from general education to provide special education services.

**AMERICANS WITH DISABILITIES ACT**  Imagine that you use a wheelchair and have a class on the fourth floor of an older college building with only stairs to reach your destination. Prior to the **Americans with Disabilities Act (ADA)**, a classmate of one of the text's coauthors had to wait at the bottom of the stairs and implore four classmates to carry him and all of his books up and down the four flights of stairs. The individual, books, and wheelchair weighed over 250 pounds. Imagine a teacher who uses a wheelchair discovering on the first day at a new school that the toilet stalls are too narrow to negotiate with a wheelchair. This also happened to a colleague of one of the coauthors. These are only two examples of the hundreds of challenges individuals with disabilities faced in their daily lives prior to laws protecting them.

President George H. W. Bush signed Public Law 101-336, the ADA, into law on January 26, 1990. The ADA was the most significant civil rights legislation in the United States since the Civil Rights Act of 1964. It was designed to end discrimination against individuals with disabilities in private-sector employment, public services, public accommodations, transportation, and telecommunications.

Among the many components of this legislation, the following are a sampling of the efforts to break down barriers for individuals with disabilities (Murdick et al., 2014; Yell, 2018):

- Employers could not discriminate against individuals with disabilities in hiring or promotion if they were otherwise qualified for the job.
- Employers had to provide reasonable accommodations for an individual with a disability, such as attaching an amplifier to the individual's telephone.
- New buses, bus and train stations, and rail systems had to be accessible to persons with disabilities.
- Physical barriers in restaurants, hotels, retail stores, and stadiums had to be removed; if this was not readily achievable, alternative means of offering services must be implemented.
- Companies offering telephone services to the general public had to offer telephone relay services to those using telecommunication devices for the Deaf.

Today, Americans with physical disabilities should expect to be able to travel in public, access buses, and attend events in theaters, arenas, and stadiums, thanks to the ADA.

## Post–P.L. 94-142 Litigation

Even with over 50 years of legislation, amendments, and refinements, many aspects of special education law remain unclear to children, their parents and other advocates, and school district personnel. The laws are extremely precise in some areas and

The Americans with Disabilities Act requires buses and other transportation services to be accessible to persons with disabilities.

**SOURCE:** © John A. Rizzo/Photodisc/Getty Images

deliberately vague in others. In addition, many other variables exacerbate the problem of interpreting and implementing the various laws and regulations.

In addition to inadequate federal funding, staffing is another serious problem facing most states. Even when school districts are committed to full compliance with the laws, the acute national shortage of qualified special education and related services personnel may preclude their ability to comply. Parents are often angry and may feel schools have betrayed the best interests of their children, often successfully addressing their frustrations by taking legal action against schools. In some cases, the schools are at fault for deliberately ignoring IDEA requirements, but their situation is often exacerbated by lack of funding or lack of qualified teachers.

Because P.L. 94-142 did not provide a substantive definition of an "appropriate education," the issue has often been left to the courts. Parents, as might be expected, typically view an appropriate education as the best possible education for their child. In 1982, *Board of Education of the Hendrick Hudson School District v. Rowley* became the first case related to an appropriate education for a student with a disability to reach the U.S. Supreme Court. Amy Rowley was a student who was deaf and was placed in a regular education kindergarten class. Several of the school personnel learned sign language to communicate with Amy. A teletype machine was placed in the school office to facilitate communication with Amy's parents, who were also deaf. Amy was provided with a hearing aid by the school, and a sign language interpreter was assigned to her class. She completed kindergarten successfully and was found to be well adjusted and making better-than-average progress.

Following the kindergarten year, as was required by P.L. 94-142, an IEP was developed for the upcoming school year. The plan specified that Amy was to continue her education in a regular classroom. She was to continue the use of the hearing aid, and she would receive speech and language therapy 3 hours a week. In addition, she was to receive instruction for an hour daily from a tutor who specialized in children with hearing disabilities. The parents disagreed with the IEP, believing that Amy should have a qualified sign language interpreter for all academic classes. The school district, however, concluded that a full-time interpreter was unnecessary and denied the request. As was their right under P.L. 94-142, the parents requested and were granted a due process hearing. The parents prevailed, and the case found its way through the lower courts until it finally reached the U.S. Supreme Court.

The Court, noting the absence in the law of any substantive standard for "appropriate," ruled that Congress's objective was to make a public education available to students with disabilities. The intent was to guarantee access on appropriate terms but not to guarantee a particular level of education. The Court ruled that schools were not obligated to provide the best possible education but a "basic floor of opportunity." It found that a free, appropriate public education (FAPE) standard could be determined only from a multifactorial evaluation on a case-by-case basis. This case essentially ensured the continuation of litigation to resolve disputes about appropriate education (Yell, 2018).

This case was significant in that it was the first case related to P.L. 94-142 to reach the Supreme Court. It set a standard for appropriate education to require more than simple access to education but less than the best possible educational program. The Court also focused attention on the rights of parents and guardians, giving them full participation at every stage of the process. It became part of case law, setting a precedent for similar cases that would follow (Yell, 2018). Consequently, when a school could demonstrate that a student was making satisfactory progress, the district's position tended to prevail.

The courts have had to rule on other provisions of the law. For example, the courts have also ruled in favor of the child when parents have sought nonphysician support services necessary to sustain the student's ability to function in school (e.g., *Irving Independent School District v. Tatro*, 1984). Through the years, a developing body of case law provided parents and other advocates as well as school personnel with a better understanding of how the law should be implemented.

IDEA provided students with disabilities their legal educational rights. However, school districts too often have been found out of compliance, either deliberately or due to the negligence of personnel. Over the past years, numerous court decisions (e.g., *Chandra Smith v. Los Angeles Unified School District*, 1996; *Felix v. Lingle*, 1993) have resulted in massive judgments that cost districts far more in legal fees and staff time than they would have expended if they had initially complied with the law.

One of the most recent cases to reach the Supreme Court revisited the meaning of FAPE for a student with a disability is *Endrew F. v. Douglas County School District* (2017). In this case, the parents of a boy who had been diagnosed as having autism believed that his academic and functional progress had stalled in the fourth grade. When school officials presented his IEP for the fifth grade to the parents, they concluded that it was inadequate for his needs and enrolled him in a private specialized school. When the school district refused to reimburse the parents for the private school tuition, the parents filed a complaint under IDEA with the Colorado Department of Education, who denied the complaint (Wehmeyer & Kurth, 2021).

The Federal District Court and the Tenth Circuit Courts applied *Rowley*, in which the Supreme Court had found a school district was in compliance with P.L. 94-142 if it provided students with disabilities with "some educational benefit." The U.S. Supreme Court disagreed with the lower courts and declared in *Endrew F.* that a minimal standard was not enough. Although the justices indicated that "when it is not reasonable to expect children to progress smoothly through the regular curricula, their IEPs need not aim for grade-level advancement. Insisting that although their goals may be different, all children should have the chance to meet challenging objectives" (Osborne & Russon, 2021, p. 21). Thus, school districts must ensure more than a minimal education benefit for students with disabilities in their classrooms.

More than ever before, children and adults with disabilities are an integral part of the nation's educational system and are finding their rightful place in society. Although the progress in recent years is indeed encouraging, society's attitudes toward individuals with disabilities have not always kept pace with the advancement of legal rights. As long as people are motivated more by fear of litigation than by moral and ethical impulses, educators cannot consider their efforts in this arena a complete success.

# Ableism and Discrimination

**Learning Objective 6.4** Document the impact of ableism and discrimination on the lives of people with exceptionalities.

Even today, the understanding and acceptance of people with disabilities is limited. Because of insensitivity, apathy, or prejudice, some people responsible for implementing and upholding the laws that protect people with disabilities fail to do so. The failure to provide adequate educational and vocational opportunities for individuals with disabilities preclude the possibility of social and economic equality. These social and economic limitations are often translated into rejection by peers who are not disabled and ultimately into social isolation.

When people with disabilities are stereotyped and denigrated because of their disability, they are denied their rightful place in society. Too often, they are denied basic rights and dignity as human beings. In many cases, the disability dominates society's perception of the person's social value and creates an illusion of deviance as well as limits their educational, vocational, and social potential. They may be placed under the perpetual tutelage of those perceived as more knowledgeable and more capable than they. They are often expected to subordinate their own interests and desires to the goals of a program decreed by the professionals who provide services to them. In this section, we explore ableism, the discrimination against people with disabilities in society today, and the results of labeling students.

## Ableism

The general public may be required by law to provide educational and other services to people with disabilities and prohibited by the Americans with Disabilities Act from discriminating against citizens with disabilities. However, no one can require a person to like people with disabilities and to accept them as social equals. Just as racism leads to discrimination and prejudice against other races because of the belief in one's own racial superiority, ableism is stereotyping, prejudice, and discrimination toward people with disabilities because of the perceptions of superiority held by people without disabilities. Ableism contributes to a stigmatized perspective of those with disabilities as flawed individuals. People with disabilities are devalued because they use a wheelchair, use sign language to speak, or use computer-assisted programs to read or compute. They are blamed for being different than a person without disabilities. As a result, ableist policies and practices prevent barriers from being removed and keep people with disabilities from having equal opportunities for education, vocational pursuits, and socialization with friends.

## The Impact of Discrimination

Although the ADA was signed into law over 30 years ago, equality is still elusive for many people with disabilities, especially if they are people of color or in a socioeconomic position that makes it difficult to purchase basic necessities for living. Disabilities are not equitably distributed across groups in society. The CDC (2023b) reported that one in four (27%) adults in the United States has some type of disability, with 12% related to mobility and 13% to cognition. Figure 6.2 shows the percentage of the population with disabilities.

People with disabilities have high rates of co-occurring health conditions and often need more health care than people without disabilities. Those with disabilities can be in good health, but adults with disabilities are more likely to be obese, smoke, have

**Figure 6.2** Diversity of the Adult Population with Disabilities by Age, Sex, and Race/Ethnicity, 2021

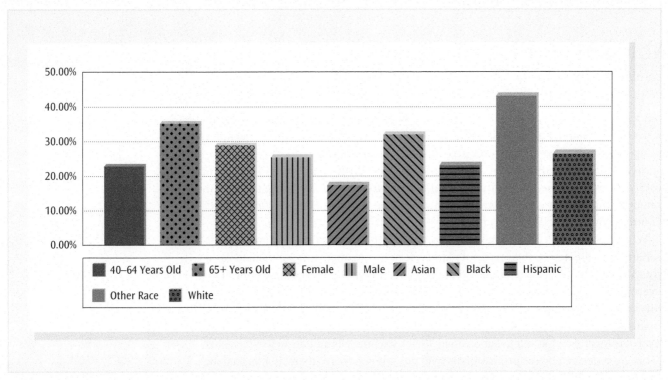

SOURCE: Steinweg (2023).

high blood pressure, be depressed, and be physically inactive (CDC, 2023a). Many people with disabilities face barriers in accessing health care services as often as they are needed. At times, they face the unconscious bias of health professionals, which can affect the way they are treated (Pappas, 2020).

People with disabilities are vastly overrepresented in the incarcerated population. They comprise 13% of the U.S. population but 40% of the state prison population (Wang, 2022). Twenty-four percent of the state prison population have cognitive disabilities, followed by 12% with vision disabilities, 12% with ambulatory disabilities, and 10% with hearing disabilities (Wang, 2022). Another 15% of the state prison population have serious mental conditions such as schizophrenia, bipolar disorder, and major depression (Human Rights Watch, 2015). Prisoners with disabilities and mental illnesses are susceptible to bullying and vulnerable to excessive use of force by both correctional staff and other prisoners (Wang, 2022). Twenty-three percent of people on probation or parole have a disability (Widra & Jones, 2023), and one-third to one-half of people killed by law enforcement had a disability (Perry & Carter-Long, 2016).

In general, people with disabilities are 4 to 10 times more likely to be victimized than people without disabilities, with children with disabilities being more than twice as likely to be victimized as children without disabilities (CDC, 2020a). At the school level, students with disabilities are more likely to be suspended than their classmates without disabilities. Those with disabilities served under IDEA made up 13.2% of the school population in the 2017–2018 school year but represented 20.5% of the students receiving one or more in-school suspensions; 24.5%, one or more out-of-school suspensions; and 23.3%, expulsions (U.S. Department of Education, Office of Civil Rights [OCR], 2021). The disparities increase even further when the data are disaggregated by race. Black students with disabilities are 2.3% of the total school population but receive 6.2% of one or more in-school suspensions and 8.8% of one or more out-of-school suspensions.

The numbers are even higher for school-related arrests and referrals to law enforcement of Black students with disabilities, which are almost four times their share of total school enrollment, starting them down a school-to-prison pipeline as early as elementary school (Hacker et al., 2022). Native American and other Indigenous students also experience exclusionary discipline at rates much higher than their representation in the school population (Fenning & Johnson, 2022). As early as 2002, researchers were finding that Black students were not engaged in infractions that warranted extreme discipline by school officials (Skiba et al., 2011). The evidence showed that Black students were punished more often than other students for subjective reasons such as disrespect and disruption in the classroom whereas White students were punished for more objective offenses such as smoking and vandalism.

Principals' perspectives on discipline were among the strongest predictors of racial and ethnic disparities in school discipline (Skiba et al., 2014). According to Keith Mayes (2022), "the classroom has become a space in which teachers and administrators serve as legal arbiters of student behavior" (p. 274). It is not just Black students with disabilities who are "potential targets of school pushout practices" (Mayes, 2022, p. 265), it is "all [B]lack students who 'act-out' and disrupt" (p. 265) in both special education and general education classrooms. Being Black has become synonymous with being disruptive. Surely there are better ways to integrate students with disabilities in the nation's schools, remove the barriers that prevent them from learning, and support them in ways that provide them the opportunities for learning that they deserve.

Suspensions and expulsions are not the only practices used by schools to try to control and change student behavior. The U.S. Department of Education's Office of Civil Rights reported that over 100,000 students were restrained or placed in seclusion in the 2017–2018 school year. Even though these practices are questionable at any time, they disproportionately affect students with disabilities. Of all students subjected to physical restraint in schools, 80% were students with disabilities, predominantly boys. Seventy-seven percent of those subjected to seclusion were students with disabilities. Again, Black students were more likely to be restrained, especially with the use of a device or equipment to restrict a student's movement; White students were more likely to be secluded in a room or area from which they could not leave (U.S. Department of Education, OCR, 2020).

Suspension from school translates into depriving students from learning opportunities in the classroom while providing them more opportunities for engaging with the juvenile justice system. Being removed from school also increases their chances of not finishing high school or finishing it later than their peers. In the 2019–2020 school year, 71% of students with disabilities graduated with a regular high school diploma within 4 years of the time they started the nineth grade compared to 87% of all students (NCES, 2022d). Ten percent of students with disabilities received an alternative certificate when they finished high school. Students with emotional disturbances were more likely to "drop out" of school and were the most likely to be incarcerated (NCES, 2023c).

With higher rates of not completing high school and disproportionally high rates of being incarcerated, it is not a surprise to learn that people with disabilities are underrepresented in the labor force. The reasons for their low representation are not just because of discriminatory policies and practices that removed them from having an opportunity to work. Persons with disabilities are often viewed as incapable of working because of their disability even when they have college degrees and have demonstrated the resilience to overcome numerous barriers to full participation in society. They are less than twice as likely to be employed as people without disabilities, and almost twice as likely to be employed part time. People with disabilities were more likely to work in service occupations and less likely to work in management, professional, and related occupations than people without disabilities (U.S. Bureau of Labor Statistics, 2023).

## Labeling

Accurately labeling students with their disability may be essential in the development of appropriate instructional strategies and accommodations, but it can lead to overgeneralizations and misconceptions about people with disabilities, neglecting their personhood (Kauffman, 2020). A problem with the IDEA categories and other labels of disabilities is that they often contribute to negative stereotyping of students and limit the recognition of students' full identity primarily to the disability. The categorization and labeling process has its share of critics, who characterize the practice as demeaning and stigmatizing to people with disabilities, with the effects often carried through adulthood, where they may be denied opportunities as a result. Some individuals, including many with learning disabilities and mild intellectual disabilities, were never considered to have disabilities prior to entering school.

Individuals with intellectual disabilities often have problems in intellectual functioning and in determining socially appropriate behaviors for their age group. The school setting, however, intensifies their academic and cognitive deficits. Many, when they return to their homes and communities, do not function as individuals with disabilities. Instead, they participate in activities with their neighborhood peers until they return to school the following day, where they may attend special classes (sometimes segregated) and resume their role in the academic and social structure of the school as students with disabilities. The labels carry connotations and stigmas of being inferior to other people, which may be internalized by students with a disability, similar to a stereotype threat.

Some disabilities are more socially acceptable than others. Visual impairment stimulates public empathy and sometimes sympathy. The public has long given generously to causes for people who are blind, as evidenced by the financially well-endowed Seeing Eye Institute, which is responsible for training guide dogs. People who are blind are the only group with a disability who are permitted to claim an additional personal income tax deduction because of their disability. The general public perceives blindness to be one of the worst afflictions that an individual could have. In contrast, intellectual disabilities and to some extent emotional disturbance are often linked to lower socioeconomic status and people of color. These are among the most stigmatizing disabilities.

Learning disability is one of the more socially acceptable disability conditions. Regardless of the level of general acceptance, middle-class parents more readily accept learning disabilities than intellectual disabilities as the cause of a child's learning deficits. This may also be the case with emotional disabilities or behavioral disorders as compared with ADHD. The former tends to be more stigmatizing, while ADHD may have more social acceptance. Some children have been reclassified from having intellectual disabilities to being learning disabled. It has been said that one person's intellectual disability is another's learning disability and still another's emotional disturbance. The line that distinguishes one of these disabilities from another can be so fine that an individual could be identified as a student with emotional disturbance by one school psychologist and as a student with learning disabilities by another. Harry and Klingner (2022) found in their research that the decision making about placements in special education differed across 12 schools in the same district.

The need for labeling of children with disabilities is being questioned by a growing number of special education professionals because the lines between having a disability and not having a disability are blurred, especially for children with mild disabilities. Are special educators and school psychologists actually able to distinguish between students who are emotionally disturbed and those who are experiencing a temporary behavior problem?

Although the labeling debate persists, even its critics often concede its necessity. Federal funding for special education is predicated on the identification of individuals in specific disabling conditions. These funds, with $13.3 billion appropriated for fiscal year 2022 (NCES, 2022e), are so significant that many special education programs would all but collapse without them, leaving school districts in severe financial distress. Consequently, the labeling process continues, sometimes even into adulthood, where university students may have to be identified with a disability in order to receive the necessary accommodations for their learning needs. Vocational rehabilitation counselors often use labels more indicative of their clients' learning problems than of their work skills. If their work peers become aware of these labels, the result could be stigmatizing and lead to social isolation.

# Disproportionate Representation in Special Education

**Learning Objective 6.5** Critique the disproportionate representation of groups in special education classes.

The overrepresentation of culturally and linguistically diverse students in special education classes has been a controversial issue in education for over 50 years. As schools began to be desegregated in the 1970s after *Brown v. Board of Education* (1954), Black families found their children were becoming victims of intelligence testing that placed them in special education classes, segregated within the schools they had just integrated (Mayes, 2022). As in their earlier history in the United States, Black children again were being labeled as intellectually disabled. Counter to the hereditary explanation for poor performance in schools, psychologists began to blame economic and environmental conditions, including the quality of their education and the conditions in which they attended school.

## The Use of IQ Tests

In 1969, Black professionals founded the Association of Black Psychologists and the Association of Black Social Workers, who questioned the use of intelligence tests that were damaging the self-concept of Black students. Leaders in the field of special education such as Lloyd Dunn (1968) and Jane Mercer (1973) began to highlight the misuse of intelligence tests that led to the disproportionate placement of students of color in special education classrooms. During this period, the educational disability rights movement focused primarily on the rights of middle-class White children, identifying a new category—learning disabled—in which their children who were formerly identified as intellectually disabled could be moved. Black students continued to be labeled as "educable mentally retarded (EMR)" (Mayes, 2022).

Soon it became clear that many schools were tracking students, and Black students were disproportionately assigned to segregated special education classes, learning social adjustment and economic usefulness rather than reading, writing, and mathematics (Mayes, 2022). In 1971, elementary students in the San Francisco Unified School District challenged the California Superintendent of Public Instruction for using IQ tests to place students in EMR classes, arguing in *Larry P. v. Riles* (1979) that the practice was unconstitutional. The court agreed that the tests were culturally biased, favoring White middle-class students. The Ninth Circuit judges agreed that IQ tests misclassified students. The tests were not the only problem. The definition of *mental retardation*, which was the term used for intellectual disabilities at that time, was corrected by the American Association of Mental Deficiency (AAMD) in 1973. Instead of being defined as one standard deviation below the mean general intellectual functioning, it was changed by AAMD to two standard deviations below the mean, which meant that the number of people with intellectual disabilities dropped from 15% to 2% of the population overnight (Mayes, 2022). Helping students who had previously been labelled as intellectually disabled adjust to a general education classroom was a challenge for schools.

As happens in the courts, a similar case resulted in a different decision in Chicago than *Larry P. v. Riles*. In *Parents in Action on Special Education v. Hannon* (1980), Black and Latino/a parents challenged the use of IQ tests for determining the placement of students in EMR classes. However, the court found that Chicago Public Schools did not *purposely* aim to overrepresent their children in those classes. Although the Chicago Public Schools won the court case, they agreed to develop nondiscriminatory placement practice as part of an agreement to settle a desegregation lawsuit with the federal government. Another class action lawsuit was filed by parents in the early 1990s because students with disabilities continued to face restrictive placements. Other lawsuits were filed in Boston and other cities.

## Disproportionate Placements

*Disproportionality* refers to the overrepresentation of groups of students identified and placed in special education in excess of their percentage in the general school population. Typically, it refers to English learners, students from low-income families, and Black, Latino/a, Native American, Alaska Native, and male students. Figure 6.3 shows the distribution of students by sex, race, and ethnicity in special education as compared to overall school enrollment.

English learners became overrepresented in the category of specific learning disability, in part because differentiating between second language acquisition and learning disabilities is difficult, especially when learners are struggling with both their home language and English (Harry & Klingner, 2022). Students living under conditions of poverty experience a variety of issues, including inadequate access to health care, low-performing schools, unsafe neighborhoods, and poor nutrition, which can affect their ability to be academically successful in school (Smith et al., 2018). Other factors such as

**Figure 6.3** Percentage of Students Enrolled in K–12 Schools Compared to Percentage of Students in Special Education

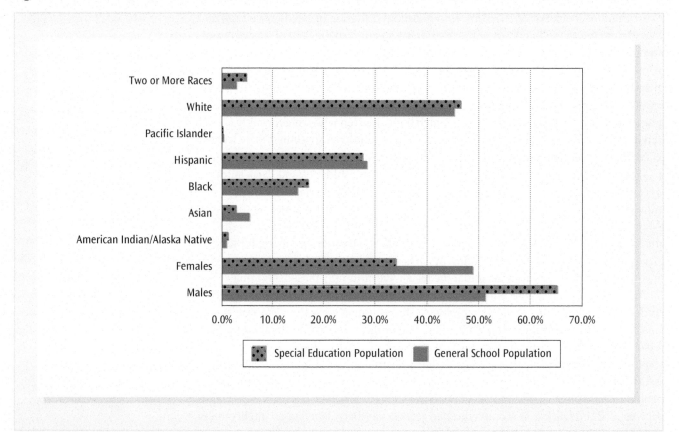

**SOURCES:** National Center for Education Statistics (2022b, 2023a); Statistical Atlas (n.d.).

lead poisoning, contaminated water, and exposure to pollutants can negatively affect the behavior and academic performance of students and the chances of them being overrepresented in special education as a result of external conditions over which they have no control.

While overrepresentation in special education does not necessarily equate with inappropriate placement, it is indicative of problems either within the educational system or in society in general. In some circumstances, it is possible that there are actually more children of color in need of special education than their numbers or percentages in the general school population suggest. Studies suggest that some children of color may in fact be underrepresented in some special education categories (Morgan et al., 2018). While being cognizant of the long history of inappropriate overrepresentation in special education, it is important that educators do not become so consumed with the problem that they fail to place children in need of special education services. If children legitimately qualify for special education services and are in need of such, it would be a disservice to them to withhold such services.

The role of judgment in making referrals for the placement of students in special education contributes to the problem of disproportionality in special education (Harry & Klingner, 2022). Clinicians and educators have limited biological data on which to base their decisions about whether a student has an intellectual disability, specific learning disability, emotional disturbance, and speech and language disabilities. Their judgments may be influenced by implicit or explicit racial, ethnic, or class biases. Making accurate judgments "requires an understanding of the contexts in which children learn, the affective as well as the cognitive processes that influence their learning and the cultural predispositions that prepare children for formal, academic education" (Harry & Klingner, 2022, p. 43).

Although the rates of disproportionality have decreased over time, they remain today. Black students are disproportionately overrepresented in the categories of emotional disturbance and intellectual disabilities, as shown in Figure 6.4. Native American, Alaska Native, and Native Hawaiian students are disproportionately represented in the categories of developmental delay and specific learning disabilities. Latino/a students have the highest representation in the specific learning disabilities, and Asians have the highest representation in the categories of autism and language disability. Overall boys

**Figure 6.4** Percentage Distribution of Children Age 3–21 Served Under IDEA by Sex, Race/Ethnicity, and Disability, 2021–22 School Year

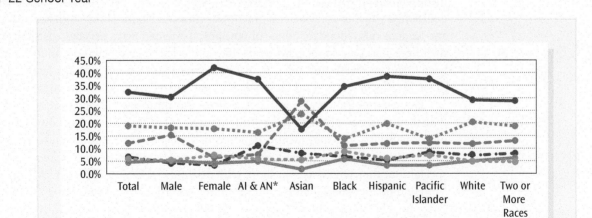

*AI & AN, American Indian and Alaska Native

**SOURCE:** National Center for Education Statistics (2023a).

are overrepresented in most categories with the exceptions of intellectual disabilities and specific learning disabilities.

These placement decisions affect students' lives in many ways for the remainder of their school career and into adulthood. For example, in low-income schools serving predominantly Black students, those in special education are more likely to have inadequately prepared teachers, be taught fragmented instruction that provides limited attention to academics, and face poor management of discipline, which often ends in suspensions and expulsions (Harry & Klingner, 2022). They are generally stuck in these classes and not challenged to move to higher academic levels. Harry and Klingner (2022) found that the reason they are assigned to special education classes is much more than what many educators may blame on family-based deficits. Historical and current beliefs, policies, and practices about race and what is "normal" interact to determine the disability. Some children do benefit from the special education services provided today. However, children who have their humanity devalued as a result of their disability are likely to develop their own self-doubt, which could lead to the internalization of ableism and racism (Boskovich et al., 2019).

## Referrals

How do students become students with disabilities? Teachers are the initiators of referrals in 9 in 10 cases, and more than 3 in 4 of those students will be found eligible after testing. These teachers are most likely to be White, Latino/a, or both; Black teachers refer less often (Harry & Klingner, 2022). There is often incongruity between educators and culturally diverse students with respect to cultural values, acceptable behaviors in school, and educational expectations, which can result in overreferrals of students of color to classes for students with disabilities and underreferrals to classes for gifted and talented students. In underreferrals for placement in classes for gifted students, educators often fail to recognize the strengths of students of color and their potential giftedness and do not make referrals.

Educators generally express confidence in the psychological assessment of students to determine the students who are actually eligible for special education services and make corrections when a teacher made the wrong referral. However, Harry and Klingner (2022) found in their research that decisions about eligibility depended on what the professionals saw as the child's problem without considering possible disconnects in the teaching that was occurring in the classroom. In other words, none of the assessors questioned whether the teacher's practices contributed to the child's difficulties. Harry and Klingner also found that three philosophical orientations of psychologists informed their decisions: the testing instruments they preferred to use, including some that have been found unreliable and subjective; their beliefs about the role cultural and linguistic diversity play in testing; and their beliefs about whether special education is effective.

High-stakes testing also influenced the referral process. Teachers sometimes felt that they were expected to refer students who were demonstrating low academic performance so that they would be identified as special education students before state testing occurred. In other words, "low achievement came to be synonymous with special education eligibility—in short, with disability" (Harry & Klingner, 2022, p. 138).

High-quality special education programs with the goal of preparing students to move to general education as soon as possible would decrease the controversy over placement rates (Harry & Klingner, 2022, p. 207). In reality, students seldom leave special education classes to move to a general education classroom during their elementary years. As with general education classrooms, the quality of instruction in special education varies greatly across classrooms and schools. Until instruction and services in special education programs improve for students with learning and behavioral disabilities, controversies about the benefits of special education programs will continue (Harry & Klingner, 2022).

# Classroom Implications: Teaching Children with Exceptionalities

**Learning Objective 6.6**  Discuss some of the basic needs of exceptional children and identify key instructional strategies for effectively integrating students with exceptionalities in the general education classroom and providing them challenging experiences that improve their academic and functional skills.

The educational implications of working with exceptional individuals are numerous, and entire chapters could be devoted to each type of exceptionality. Educators should remember that exceptional children with disabilities and those who are gifted are more like than unlike nonexceptional children. Their basic needs are the same as all other children's.

Abraham Maslow's theory on **self-actualization** is familiar to most students in education. To be self-actualized, or to meet one's full potential, Maslow (1954) theorized, one's basic needs must be fulfilled. That is, to reach self-actualization, one's physiological needs, safety needs, belongingness or love needs, and esteem needs must first be met. Although some individuals with disabilities may never match the accomplishments of their peers without disabilities, they can become proficient at whatever they are capable of doing. Educators can assist them by helping to ensure that their basic needs are met, allowing them to strive toward self-actualization.

Teachers of children with physical and other health disabilities may find it advantageous to check the student records carefully to determine potential problem situations with students in the classroom. If a child has particular health problems that may surface in the classroom, the child's teachers need to be prepared to determine precisely what to do should the child have, for example, an epileptic seizure. The parents will most likely be able to provide precise instructions, and the school nurse could provide additional recommendations. If the children are old enough to understand, they too can be a valuable source of information. A teacher can ask them what kinds of adaptations, special equipment, or teaching procedures work best for them. Teachers should not be afraid of their own uncertainties. They should feel free to ask students when they prefer to have or not have assistance. Teachers should neither overprotect their students with disabilities nor do more for them than is needed or deserved. Allowing them to assume responsibility for themselves will do much to facilitate their personal growth.

The range and variety of experiences imposed on or withheld from persons with disabilities may result in undue limitations. Too often, parents and teachers assume that a child's visual limitation precludes the ability to approximate the typical everyday experiences of children without such limitations. Children who are blind may not be able to see the animals in a zoo, but they can smell and hear them. They may not be able to enjoy the scenes along a bus route, but they can feel the stop-and-go movements, hear the traffic and people, and smell their fellow travelers. A child who is deaf may not be able to hear the sounds at the symphony or the crowd's roar at a football game. Both events, however, offer the possibility of extraordinary sensory experiences to which the child needs exposure. A child with cerebral palsy needs experiences such as going to restaurants, even if the child has difficulty using eating utensils.

## Meeting the Needs of Children with Exceptionalities

Well-adjusted individuals with a sensory disability usually attain a balance of control with their environment. Individuals who depend completely on other members of the family and on friends may develop an attitude of helplessness and a loss of self-identity. Individuals with disabilities who completely dominate and control their environment with unreasonable demands sometimes fail to make an acceptable adjustment and could become selfish and self-centered.

# Critical Incidents in Teaching
## Integrating Students in an Inclusive Classroom

Andy is a higher-functioning fourth-grader on the autism spectrum. He has very limited oral language, speaking only in syllables, but he has a voice output device in which he types his thoughts and it speaks for him. Andy also uses a laptop in class on which he types with one finger. He is able to participate in all classroom activities and do all of the classwork in this full inclusion classroom. All of Andy's classmates are well aware of his condition and the accommodations that he uses. He has attended school with most of them for 5 years and considers them his friends.

On an October day, Jill appeared in the classroom, having transferred from a school across town. Trying to be friendly, Andy looks up from his desk and says "H-H-H" (for "hi"). She looks at him disdainfully, "What's wrong with you?" Jill sees his equipment and begins complaining to another student, "Why don't we have that? That's not fair."

Julio jumps to Andy's defense, explaining Andy's condition and how he uses the equipment, but Jill continues to complain. Andy fiddles with his laptop and begins typing about his feelings, which would evolve into a creative story. A couple of his classmates asked him if he was okay.

The teacher, who had been talking with students at the front of the room before class began, stops his conversation, moving toward Jill and Julio and asking, "What's wrong?" He wanted to ensure that Jill had a chance to introduce herself and begin her new school on a positive note. At the same time, he needed to ensure that Andy saw himself as a valued member of the class.

### Questions for Discussion

1. How would you approach Jill and make her feel welcome in her new classroom?

2. What would you do to support Andy's self-esteem and ensure that he still feels like a valued member of the class?

3. How would you help Jill understand Andy's strengths and why he uses the technology to communicate with his classmates and teacher?

4. How important is it to help students without exceptionalities understand that those with disabilities are very much like them, but they may speak, hear, write, move, interact, act, and/or learn in different ways than their peers without disabilities?

5. What are the benefits of students with exceptionalities and students without exceptionalities learning together in the same classroom?

It is critical to remember that children who are exceptional are, first and foremost, children. Their exceptionality, though influencing their lives, is secondary to their needs as children. Following are three types of needs for parents and educators to keep in mind for children with disabilities: communication, acceptance, and the freedom to grow. They may also be applicable to some gifted students.

**COMMUNICATION NEEDS** Exceptional children are far more perceptive than many adults give them credit for being. They are sensitive to nonverbal communication and hidden messages that may be concealed in half-truths. They, more than anyone else, need to deal with their exceptionality, whether it is a disability, giftedness, or both. They need to know what their exceptionality is all about so that they can deal with it. They need to know how it will affect their lives in order to adjust appropriately, to make the best of their lives, and to reach their full potential. They need straight, honest communication tempered with sensitivity.

**ACCEPTANCE NEEDS** U.S. society often fails to provide exceptional children with a positive and receptive environment. Even the educational setting can be hostile and lacking in acceptance. A teacher can facilitate the acceptance of a child in a classroom by exhibiting an open and positive attitude. Students tend to reflect the attitude of the teacher. If the teacher is hostile, students will quickly pick up these cues. If the attitude is positive and nurturing, students are likely to respond and provide a receptive environment for their classmates with disabilities.

Kenji, a first-grade student who suffered from a hearing loss, was fitted with a hearing aid. When he came to school wearing the hearing aid, the students in the class immediately began whispering about the "thing" Kenji had in his ear. After observing the class behavior, with the permission of his parents, the teacher privately assisted Kenji in a show-and-tell preparation for the next day. With the teacher's assistance and assurances, Kenji proudly demonstrated his hearing aid to the class, showing them how he could adjust it to allow him to hear even some things they could not. By the end of the demonstration, Kenji was the envy of the class, and all further discussion of the hearing aid was of a positive nature.

**FREEDOM TO GROW** Students with disabilities need acceptance and understanding. Acceptance implies freedom for the exceptional child to grow. At times, it may seem easier to do things for a child than to take the time to teach the child. A number of years ago, one of the coauthors lived and worked at a residential state school for the blind. Recounted next is an actual event that took place at the school.

Having access to blackboards, desks, laptops, and other accommodations in the classroom is important to all students.

**SOURCE:** Bangkok Click Studio/ Shutterstock

Sarah (whose name has been changed) was a 9-year-old girl who was blind and had an orthopedic disability; she studied at the state residential school for the blind. She wore leg braces but had a reasonable amount of mobility with the use of crutches. To save time and effort, fellow students or staff members transported Sarah between the cottage where she lived and the classroom building in a wagon. One day her teacher decided she needed to be more independent in her travel to and from her cottage. To Sarah's dismay, the teacher informed her after school that she would not ride back in the wagon but that he would walk her back. Angered, she denounced him as cruel and hateful. She complained bitterly the full 15 minutes of their walk back to the cottage. After a few days the complaining subsided, and the travel time was reduced. Within a few weeks Sarah was traveling on her own in 5 minutes with newfound independence and self-respect.

Sometimes, it may be tempting for teachers and parents to make extra concessions for an exceptional child. However, these exceptions often hinder the emotional growth of the child and may later cause serious interpersonal problems.

## Inclusion

In the 1960s and 1970s, educators and researchers demonstrated that individuals with intellectual disabilities were capable of higher levels of functioning in their daily living skills and language development than had been previously believed. Bengt Nirje introduced the concept of **normalization**, meaning "making available to all persons with disabilities or other handicaps [disabilities], patterns of life and conditions of everyday living which are as close as possible to or indeed the same as the regular circumstances and ways of life of society" (1985, p. 67).

The principles of normalization as it was introduced were developed with individuals with intellectual disabilities as the primary group. In more recent years, the concept has broadened so that all categories of individuals with disabilities are now included. The term "mainstreaming" has given way to **inclusion**, which is based on a belief that students are more alike than different and that all students, including students with exceptionalities, should be educated together (National Association for the Education of Young Children, 2022). Inclusion should ensure that students who have historically been excluded from and marginalized in school have the same opportunities for learning as students without disabilities (Rufo & Causton, 2022).

Mastropieri and Scruggs (2018) differentiated between inclusion and **full inclusion**, with the latter serving students with exceptionalities entirely within the general classroom. This is an important difference, as students in full inclusion do not receive any of their education in segregated settings. In fall 2021, 67% of students with disabilities spent 80% or more of their time in general education classes; 13% spent less than 40% of their time in general education classes (NCES, 2023b).

The current effort to support full inclusion seeks to provide children with moderate to severe disabilities with similar opportunities to those of students without disabilities. Although resistance to inclusion of students with mild disabilities is far less intense than it once was, it is still felt from some educators. The arguments against integrating children with severe disabilities have often centered on the presumed inability of children without disabilities to accept their peers with disabilities. In reality, some of the reservations may be more a reflection of educators who themselves are unable or unwilling to accept the dignity and worth of individuals with severe disabilities.

The federal special education law, IDEA, does not require inclusion. The law does require the LRE for students with disabilities. Herein lies the basis for considerable controversy in special education. The controversy is often fueled within special education itself, as educators are not in complete agreement regarding what the LRE is. Few special educators would argue against the concept of inclusion. However, disagreement focuses on whether full inclusion is appropriate for every child regardless of the type or the severity of the disability.

To some, and perhaps too many of the advocates of full inclusion, the issue is not the efficacy of general education placement; rather, it is a moral and ethical issue. Advocates for full inclusion find it equally repugnant to prevent children with disabilities from learning in classrooms with their peers without disabilities. Other special educators are concerned that proponents of inclusion have placed too much emphasis on the place in which students with disabilities learn and not enough emphasis on the instruction that is most appropriate for learning, which can be very difficult for teachers in inclusive classrooms to manage. In these cases, they suggest that placement in a special education class may be more appropriate for more students with disabilities (Kaufman, 2020).

In reality, most if not all children with disabilities can be served effectively in a general education classroom if adequate resources and supports are made available. Therein lies a primary problem. An adequate supply of certified or credentialed personnel in special education and related services (e.g., school psychologists) seldom exists in a school district. The courts will not accept an excuse such as "We don't do it because there are inadequate resources." The courts may accept the argument that a particular program or service is not in the best interests of the student, but it must be clearly supported and documented. However, if full inclusion is warranted, the courts will order schools (as they have consistently done) to "find the resources to do it."

In an inclusive classroom it is important that teachers recognize and build on the strengths that students with disabilities bring to the classroom. Instruction is likely to require modifications and accommodations to ensure students have full access to the curriculum and learning experiences. Teachers should plan for students with disabilities to join the class on field trips, in class plays, and on playgrounds as students learn to work together, help each other, and respect each other. Creating an environment that is compassionate and caring for each student will be important in making inclusion work for all students in the classroom (Rufo & Causton, 2022).

Historically, special education in the United States has offered a full continuum of placements for students with disabilities. These services have ranged from the most restrictive placements, such as residential schools and special schools, to the least restrictive settings, such as full inclusion in the general education classroom. Students with the most severe disabilities are more likely to be in segregated schools. Two percent were in separate schools for students with disabilities; 2% had been placed in regular private schools by parents; and 1% were homebound or in hospitals, in separate residential facilities, or in correctional facilities in fall 2021 (NCES, 2023c).

The legal mandates do not eliminate special schools or classes, but they do offer a different philosophical view. Instead of the physical isolation of individuals with disabilities; efforts must be made to enable students with disabilities to assume a more appropriate place in the educational setting. Still, many children with disabilities may not benefit appreciably from an inclusive setting and may be better educated in a special setting. Students who are most likely to be in separate schools are students with emotional disturbance, those with multiple disabilities, and students who are deaf-blind (NCES, 2023c). Black and Native American and Alaska Native students are more likely than others to be placed in segregated special education classrooms (Jaffee, 2023). As attitudes become more attuned to the laws, people with disabilities are beginning to have more options to participate in the decision to be a part of a general classroom or to be segregated into their own classroom or school.

# Explore and Focus Your Cultural Lens

## Debate: How Feasible Is Full Inclusion for All Children with Disabilities?

The Individuals with Disabilities Education Act is a federal law that requires the placement of students with disabilities in the LRE. This means that these students should be placed in or as close to a general education setting as is feasible for them. What is the least restrictive setting for a child with a disability? Is it feasible to place every child with a disability in a general education setting? Are there adequate resources to do this? Do teachers have the skill and the will to make it work? What are your own experiences with individuals with disabilities? Were you ever in a classroom with a student with moderate or even severe disabilities? Was this individual ever disruptive in your class and, if so, how did it make you feel? How feasible is full inclusion of children with disabilities in general classrooms?

### FOR

- Full inclusion for all children with disabilities is a moral and ethical issue. It is immoral to segregate children with disabilities from their peers without disabilities.
- The LRE that is feasible for every child is a general education classroom. Educators have the know-how to deliver quality educational services for every child in an inclusive general education classroom.
- The fact that schools do not have adequate fiscal resources is not the fault of children with disabilities or their families. If schools don't have the resources, then they need to find ways to obtain them.
- Research shows that students with disabilities make academic and social gains in inclusive classrooms, especially at the elementary level. The positive social effects of inclusion for both students with disabilities and those without disabilities include a reduction of fear of each other and a reduction of hostility, prejudice, and discrimination against each other in addition to an increase of tolerance,

acceptance, and understanding of each other (Kart & Kart, 2021).

### AGAINST

- Full inclusion may work for some students with disabilities, but some may be better served in a special education classroom.
- Some students with disabilities lack the maturity, cognitive ability, social skills, or appropriate behaviors to function appropriately in general education.
- Until the federal government makes good on its commitment to fully fund IDEA, adequate resources will not be available to successfully implement full inclusion for all children with disabilities.
- The time it requires general education teachers to work with students with disabilities may detract from the attention required by other students.

## Questions for Discussion

1. What are the advantages for students with disabilities and society to educate those with disabilities and those without disabilities together?

2. The federal government mandates special education for all children and continues to renege on full funding. Parents know the rights of their children and demand the required services even though the schools lack the resources. What should the schools do to meet these demands?

3. What students with disabilities, if any, may be better served in a setting other than the general education classroom? Why?

**THE INDIVIDUALIZED EDUCATION PROGRAM**   Teachers in an inclusion classroom are guided in their work with students with disabilities by the IEP that indicates the modifications and accommodations that should be used in the classroom. The IEP is developed collaboratively by parents or caregivers, teachers, special educators, and other specialists, such as a school psychologist, speech language therapist, or occupational therapist. The purpose of an IEP is to set reasonable learning goals for each child and to clearly state the services that the school district will provide. IEPs also include annual goals for the child, any supplementary aids and services (e.g., a communication device or speech therapy) that will be provided, how much time and for what activity the student will be pulled out of the class, modifications for state-wide assessments, and how families will be informed of their child's progress.

IEPs for students with disabilities indicate accommodations and modifications that will make the curriculum and instructional strategies more accessible to them by removing a barrier. The goal is to provide the same opportunities to learn as are available to their classmates without disabilities. Accommodations do not change the expectations for student performance. In some cases, modifications need to be made to what is being taught such as making an assignment appropriate for students' current academic level, being more advanced for students who are gifted and at a lower grade level when needed to meet a student's needs.

**DIFFERENTIATED INSTRUCTION**   Although students with exceptionalities and without exceptionalities share the same inclusive classroom, they do not always learn or work in the same way, dependent, in part, on their own interests, academic progress, and the nature of their disability if they have one. **Differentiated instruction** is a popular approach for teaching students who have different interests, speak different languages, and are at different levels of learning (Tomlinson, 2022). It requires teachers to plan lessons with multiple options for learning about the academic subject, theme, or skill being taught. A lesson would include different, hopefully engaging activities to meet the needs of each student in the classroom.

Differentiated instruction is a **student-centered approach** that allows students to interact with the content in different ways, submit different types of assignment and projects, and become engaged and responsible for their own learning. Building lessons around students' different learning profiles promotes student learning by taking advantage of their personal preferences, gender, race, ethnicity, culture, and other factors that impact their engagement in learning (Tomlinson, 2022).

Implementing differentiated instruction is likely to be a challenge when teachers first plan for it, but they should not give up; it will become easier with experience and should improve student engagement with the curriculum. Not every lesson will need to be differentiated, but the more that lessons meet students' needs, the better the chances of not leaving any student behind. The chances of succeeding in this effort are improved in nurturing classroom environments in which students know the teacher cares about them, and they are respected and valued as unique individuals (Rufo & Causton, 2022).

After observing students in 12 schools over a 3-year period, Harry and Klingner (2022) reported that the most effective general and special education teachers helped students learn, but they were also empathetic and culturally responsive to them. Effective teachers model anti-ableism as they work with students, making significant and positive differences in student learning and development of each student regardless of their ability classification.

## The Important Role of Families

Teachers and administrators too often blame families for the difficulties their children are experiencing in school and speak disparagingly about those families (Ocasio-Stoutenbery & Harry, 2021). Instead, educators should be emphasizing the strengths of families and drawing on their "funds of knowledge" from their cultures and everyday experiences that contribute to student learning in and outside the classroom (Moll & González, 2004). They are critical partners in the effective education of their children, in part because they know their children, community, and culture well.

As they studied the delivery of special education in schools in Florida, Harry and Klingner (2022) heard educators talk about the families of students eligible for special education services in derogatory terms, usually describing the family as dysfunctional and blaming parents and/or home conditions for students' problems even when the parents attended all of the school meetings. The researchers observed many school-based conferences with 12 families with many challenges and conducted multiple visits to the homes of three families. All of the families were living with the challenges of poverty, personal loss, and limited education. The families who volunteered to be interviewed were, as one mother put it, "doing the best they could." The researchers concluded that the disconnect between educators and families was due to different perceptions of appropriate and important ways of caring and nurturing by educators and families.

The family strengths that the researchers discovered in their interviews had been ignored by school personnel. The researchers found mothers and a grandmother who cared deeply about their children or grandchild and nurtured them by having books in their homes or using the TV for educational activities. The perceptions of school personnel, on the other hand, labeled the families based on negative stereotypes based on race and socioeconomic factors. Tapping into the strengths of these families could have made an important difference in how the families and their children were categorized and treated in school. Because their families lacked the social and cultural capital of other parents, they were less likely to challenge schools' decisions about special education when the recommendations may have not been in the best interest of their children (Harry & Klingner, 2022).

As indicated earlier, families are a required partner in the IEP process and should attend all of the IEP meetings if at all possible. In cases where it is not possible, teachers and administrators should reach out to them through virtual meetings, phone calls, or meetings at times and places at which they are available. Educators have the responsibility for translating special education jargon to parents who are likely to have limited familiarity with the language. Educators also need to actively listen to parents and work collaboratively to set ambitious expectations for their child (Wehmeyer & Kurth, 2021). Building the trust of families by being truthful, listening, communicating effectively, and following through with proposed actions in a timely fashion is critical in maintaining an authentic and effective partnership.

Psychologist Pamela D. Brown (2022) suggests three steps that educators could take to lessen resistance from Black parents. First, *"consider the parent's perspective"* (p. 49). Parents would like teachers to be sensitive to the needs of their children, have high expectations for them, and exhibit dedication to creating a positive and nonbiased academic environment for them. Second, *"be willing to engage with everyone"* (p. 50), especially those families with whom teachers may have the least in common, feel less connected to, and who are less likely to trust them. Teachers should reach out to these families, not wait to be contacted by them. Third, *"know your parents of color and their needs"* (p. 50). Showing genuine interest in the families of students helps communicate caring for both students and their families. "Understanding what parents want enables educators to have more meaningful conversations with the parents of the children they teach about how parents and teachers, together, can help make their children's journeys smoother" (Brown, 2022, p. 50). Building trust with families in these ways will better serve the needs of all students with exceptionalities in both special education and inclusive classrooms.

# Revisiting the Opening Case Study

When Dr. Wilkerson informed Ms. Gutierrez that her classroom was slated for full inclusion with two students with severe disabilities, it should not have come as a shock. The school district had committed itself to implementing full inclusion months earlier, and there had been workshops given in nearly every school on the topic. Lupe Gutierrez had been runner-up for district teacher of the year, and everyone knew she was an outstanding teacher and a likely choice for a full inclusion assignment. However, it still was a surprise to Gutierrez, as she felt unqualified to teach children for whom she had not been prepared to work. How would she be able to work with a child with language and intellectual disabilities? What would she do with a student who uses a wheelchair and has severe speech limitations? Even with an inclusion specialist to work with her, Ms. Gutierrez had many doubts about her ability to deliver a quality education to the new students with disabilities. At the same time, she knew that she could learn how to integrate them into the classroom and engage them in learning. She hoped that a paraprofessional would be assigned to assist her and the students in her classroom in this new challenge.

## Reflect and Apply

1. What experiences have you had with students with severe disabilities? Have any been in any of your classes? What were their disabilities? How did they and their classmates adjust to an inclusive learning situation?

2. If you received Ms. Gutierrez's assignment, what would you expect of the inclusion specialist assigned to you? What if the specialist is not competent in assisting you with the needs of students? Where and how will you access other resources?

3. In what ways is full inclusion in the best interests of society? What are the benefits of full inclusion for everyone involved, including teachers, students without disabilities, those with disabilities, and their families?

# Summary

- There are approximately 10.5 million exceptional students in the United States; just over two-thirds of them are students with disabilities such as intellectual disabilities, learning disabilities, emotional disturbance, and physical and sensory disabilities, and the remaining one-third are students who are gifted and talented. Those with disabilities must be provided special education services under the Individuals with Disabilities Education Act (IDEA) or Section 504 of the Rehabilitation Act of 1973, but programs for students who are gifted and talented are not required by the federal government. Programming options for students who are gifted are required in more than half of the states. In other states, offering programs for students who are gifted is a choice of school districts.

- A disability identity is one's sense of self including the person's disability and identification with others who have a disability. Developing a disability identity contributes to higher satisfaction with life, self-esteem, self-efficacy, social support, and lower psychological stress. People's disability intersects with other identities such as race, ethnicity, gender, sexual orientation, and religion in determining their senses of self. People with disabilities sometimes have strong ties with their disability community, as with the Deaf, who share a language.

- People with disabilities have a long history of trying to gain access to education and other benefits of society. Beginning in the nineteenth century, a few schools for students who were blind and/or deaf were opened, but most other students with disabilities were not allowed to attend school. They stayed at home or were institutionalized. When the eugenics movement grew in popularity at the end of the nineteenth century, the intention was to eliminate people with intellectual disabilities; 30 states had laws for sterilizing those with intellectual disabilities to prevent them from having children and spreading their "deficiency." In the 1970s, psychologists began to change their view of disabilities from a medical model of an individual pathology or abnormality to social construction in which society, not people with disabilities, is responsible for the discrimination against and mistreatment of people with disabilities.

- Parents of children with disabilities had been fighting for years for their children to attend school with students without disabilities rather than being sent to a segregated school with other children with disabilities or being home schooled. The activism of these parents led to Congress passing Public Law 94-142, the Education for Handicapped Children Act, in 1975, requiring free, appropriate public education for all children with disabilities in the least-restrictive environment (LRE). At the same time, people with disabilities were protesting for the implementation of Section 504 of the Rehabilitation as Section 504 of Public Law 93-112, the special education counterpart to the Civil Rights Act of 1964. This law was soon followed in 1975 with Public Law 94-142, the Education for All Handicapped Children Act, which guaranteed a free and appropriate education in the LRE for children with disabilities. The Americans with Disabilities Act in 1990 provided accommodations for individuals in the workplace and accessibility in public places. The 1997 IDEA and subsequent amendments improved and enhanced the provisions of Public Law 94-142.

- Although court decisions, legislation, and state and local policies generally expect that people with disabilities have the opportunities to participate fully in society, they still face discrimination through the ableism of individuals and institutions that do not accept people with disabilities as equal to people without disabilities. People with disabilities generally have more health care needs than other people but often face barriers in receiving that care. They represent 15% of the adult population and 40% of the incarcerated population. At the same time, they are at least four times more likely to be victimized as their peers without disabilities. In schools, they are more likely than their peers without disabilities to be suspended, expelled, and arrested. Eighty percent of students who are restrained in schools are students with disabilities, with Black students with disabilities being restrained at disproportionately high rates. They are also less likely to earn a high school diploma and hold a job as an adult. Labeling of students as having a disability, which is required for them to be eligible for special education services, can lead to overgeneralizations and misconceptions about people with disabilities that extend into adulthood.

- The disproportionate placement of students of color first became evident with the establishment of the National Association of Black Psychologists and the seminal writings of Dunn in 1968 and Mercer in 1973, when they called attention to placement of Black and Latino/a children in classes for those with intellectual disabilities. The Office of Civil Rights has tracked since 1968 the overrepresentation of Black students and in particular Black boys placed in classes for students with intellectual disabilities and severe emotional disturbance. Underrepresentation of Black students and other students of color in classes for the gifted and talented has also been a continuous problem. The reasons for these disproportionate placements are multifaceted, including poverty issues, overreferrals, and biased assessments. Teachers have an important role in the process of referring students to be assessed for eligibility to special education services.

- Maslow indicated that for people to become self-actualized, they must first have their basic needs addressed. While children with disabilities may or may not be able to attain the same level of competency as their peers without disabilities, they too are capable of reaching self-actualization and their full potential if their basic needs are met. Teachers should make themselves particularly aware of the health needs of their students with disabilities and be prepared for any medical emergencies, such as seizures. Student records, parents, a school nurse, and even the student can assist in awareness. Providing for students' needs for communication, acceptance, and the freedom to grow will facilitate not only the students' academic development but their overall life adjustment.

- The inclusion of students with exceptionalities in general education classrooms is based on the belief that students are more alike than different and that all students, including those with exceptionalities, should be educated together. Full inclusion requires that students with exceptionalities receive all of their education within the general education classroom. Sixty-seven percent of the students with disabilities spend at least 80% of their time in a general education classroom, with many of them spending the remainder of their time working with special education teachers or other school specialists. Teachers in inclusive classrooms should recognize and build on the strengths that students bring to the classroom and use differentiated instruction strategies to teach appropriately each student in the classroom. Using the individualized education program for each student with a disability as a guide, teachers should use the recommended accommodations and modifications to ensure that they have full access to the curriculum and learning experiences.

# Pearson eTextbook Application Video

The following video is available in the Pearson eTextbook and can be used to practice observing and applying what you learned in this chapter.

Pearson eTextbook Application
**Video Example 6.4**

In this video, teachers discuss the professional collaborations that take place to include a student with a significant hearing impairment in the general education setting.

# Chapter 7
# Language
## Alison G. Dover and Kevin Roxas

 ## Learning Objectives

*As you read this chapter, you should be able to:*

**7.1** Describe the diversity of languages spoken in U.S. classrooms.

**7.2** Analyze how language and culture impact a student's identity formation.

**7.3** Explain the nature of language and the various components of language development.

**7.4** Describe the various forms of language learners and the characteristics of these learners.

**7.5** Explain the history of language education and policy in the United States.

**7.6** Describe the different programs in place in schools to support multilingual learners.

**7.7** Describe the impact of bias and discrimination against multilingual learners.

**7.8** Evaluate strategies teachers can use to effectively work with multilingual learners.

## Opening Case Study

Angelica Rivera was excited to begin her first year as a ninth-grade science teacher in Chicago, Illinois. She was hired at a school not far from where she grew up and was looking forward to working with a diverse community of students. She anticipated many of her students would speak Spanish (like Angelica's own family), so she spent the summer looking for Latino/a scientists, Spanish language videos, and bilingual posters to hang in her classroom. Angelica also hoped to use her own Spanish skills when talking with students' families or sending letters home. However, a few days before the school year began, she received her class rosters, as well as a partial list of data about her students. She was surprised and a bit intimidated by the linguistic diversity of her students: of the 140 students on her daily roster, 40 were labeled as English learners, and district data indicated her students spoke nine different languages, including Spanish, Mandarin, Cantonese, Polish, Tagalog, Urdu, Arabic, Vietnamese, and Ukrainian. Angelica

had taken classes about working with English learners as part of her credential program, but those classes didn't focus on teaching science, and—despite her fluency in Spanish—she didn't know any of the other languages spoken by her students. Angelica was worried that she wouldn't be able to communicate with many of her students and their families and wondered how any teacher could be successful in a classroom like hers.

### Reflect

1. What is a reasonable expectation for new teachers? Should teachers be expected to learn or provide instructional resources for speakers of multiple languages? Why or why not?

2. Reflect upon your own experiences as a student. What languages were spoken in your elementary, middle, and high school? Did your teachers use multiple languages

when teaching or communicating with linguistically diverse students and families?

3. As a bilingual person, Angelica was looking forward to using her multilingualism to connect with students and families and to support student learning in science. However, she was also aware that she would have students who spoke languages she could neither read nor understand. What linguistic experiences and resources will you bring to your own classroom, and how will they help you be a more effective teacher? What kinds of support will you need in order to teach in a linguistically diverse classroom?

# Linguistic Diversity in the United States

**Learning Objective 7.1** Describe the diversity of languages spoken in U.S. classrooms.

Although the official language of the United States is English, the reality is that virtually everyone will encounter multilingual people throughout their lifetime—and all teachers need the skills to communicate effectively with linguistically diverse students, families, and colleagues. According to 2019 U.S. Census data, almost one in five people (approximately 67.8 million people) in the United States speak a language other than English at home; this represents a rate almost twice that of 1980, when about one in 10 U.S. residents spoke languages other than English (U.S. Census Bureau, 2022).

In some states, such as California, rates of **multilingualism** (the ability to speak more than one language) are far higher: An estimated 40.1% of California's public school students (2.36 million students overall) speak languages other than English at home, with students drawn from 88 distinct language groups (California Department of Education, 2022) (see Figure 7.1). California is not the only state notable for its linguistic diversity: More than 30% of people in Nevada, New Mexico, Texas, Florida, New Jersey, and New York speak languages other than English; this is a marked contrast to states like Mississippi, Montana, New Hampshire, Vermont, West Virginia, and Wyoming, where more than 95% of residents speak English at home (U.S. Census Bureau, 2022).

The linguistic diversity in the United States represents just a minute portion of the linguistic diversity of the broader world, where researchers have documented more than 7,000 unique languages (Ethnologue, 2023). English is the most common language worldwide, spoken by 1.45 billion people, but even so it is only spoken by approximately 19% of the world's population. The next most common language is Mandarin Chinese, spoken by 1.12 billion people; Hindi ranks third, with approximately 602.2 million speakers, followed by Spanish, which is spoken by 548.3 million people (Ethnologue, 2023).

As is the case in the United States, some countries and continents are more linguistically diverse than others. Residents of Europe, for example, speak almost 300 different languages (24 of which are recognized as "official languages" by the European Union), with English spoken by 38% of residents (followed by French [12%] and German [11%]). Asia, home to 4.46 billion people, has speakers of 2,300 languages, including about 1.2 billion Chinese language speakers (including hundreds of varieties of Chinese), 550 million Hindi speakers, and 302 million English speakers (Worldatlas, 2020). Papua New Guinea is the most linguistically diverse country in the world, with more than 800 languages spoken among its population of 9.1 million; its official language is Tok Pisin, with 24 additional languages (including English) used as formal languages of instruction in government-run schools (Ethnologue, 2023).

In the United States, some beginning teachers (like Angelica, from our opening case study) speak multiple languages and are able to use their own multilingualism as an asset in the classroom, whereas others are **monolingual** (meaning that they

Pearson eTextbook
**Video Example 7.1**
This video examines the diversity of languages spoken in classrooms.

**Figure 7.1** Percentage of Public School Students Who Were English Learners, by State, 2019–2020

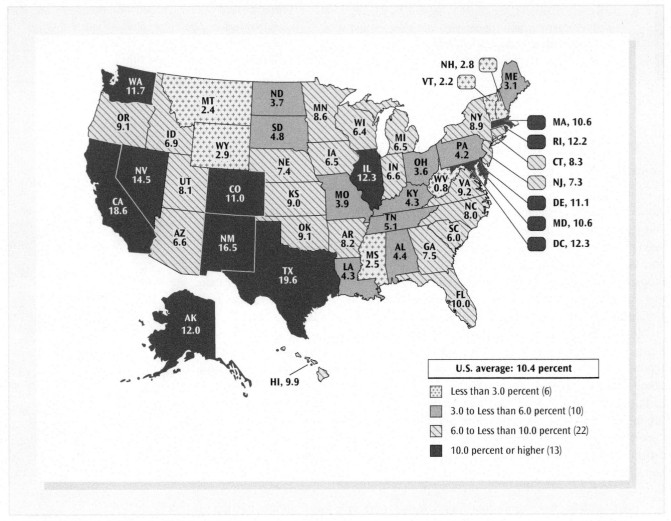

U.S. average: 10.4 percent

- Less than 3.0 percent (6)
- 3.0 to Less than 6.0 percent (10)
- 6.0 to Less than 10.0 percent (22)
- 10.0 percent or higher (13)

**SOURCE:** National Center for Education Statistics (2023).

speak only one language). However, even the most linguistically proficient teachers are unlikely to speak all of the languages reflected in their school community. Therefore, it is important for teachers to develop strategies for engaging linguistically diverse students and families, as well as resources to help students build their skills as effective communicators within and outside the classroom. In this chapter, we explore the nature of language, the relationship between language and culture, approaches to language education in the United States, and ways educators can prepare to teach in linguistically diverse classrooms.

# Language, Culture, and Sense of Identity

**Learning Objective 7.2** Analyze how language and culture impact a student's identity formation.

**Language** is a system of vocal sounds, gestures, and symbols through which people communicate with one another. It is a critical tool in the development of an individual's identity, self-awareness, and intellectual and psychological growth. It can incite anger, elicit love, inspire bravery, and arouse fear. It can also play a key role in providing a group or even a nation a sense of collective identity. Language may also be the means by which one group of people stereotypes another.

For example, in the United States, most schools require students and teachers to communicate in what is called **Standard English**; this refers to the variety (or *dialect*) of English that is commonly used in most governmental, legal, and social institutions in the United States. English-speaking students who do not use the grammar and syntax associated with Standard English are often told that their way of speaking is improper or incorrect and are directed to change their speech to reflect "acceptable" usage. However, there is significant variability in how English is used nationwide; these differences include everything from regional differences in pronunciation or word usage, such as whether people use "soda," "pop," or "coke" to refer to fizzy drinks (Katz & Andrews, 2013), to overarching grammatical rules that change the way people build sentences.

In addition to regional and cultural differences in how people communicate, our approach to communication is also impacted by other languages we speak: Monolingual people typically use only sounds, gestures, and symbols from a single **named language**, such as English or Italian, while multilingual people utilize sounds, gestures, and symbols associated with multiple named languages.

If asked, most people would agree that being multilingual is an asset: It enables people to communicate fluidly with individuals from diverse communities and cultures and is beneficial when traveling or conducting business internationally. Nevertheless, many multilingual people in the United States face bias or discrimination, especially if they speak accented English or are still building their skills in English. Because English is the dominant language in the United States, some people and institutions privilege monolingual English speakers' ways of communicating, rather than valuing the more comprehensive linguistic skills of bilingual and multilingual people; this is a product of systemic **ethnocentrism**, or belief in the superiority of one's own race, ethnicity, or culture. Within the context of the United States, this means that while students from an English-speaking background are required to learn additional languages in school, children who grow up speaking languages other than English are often encouraged or forced to give up their first language in order to gain acceptance as "Americans."

Moreover, because U.S. society has such strong Eurocentric roots, European languages and accents may be given higher status than those from non-European countries; likewise, multilingual people who are perceived as White or of high socioeconomic status (SES) often face less stigmatization than multilingual people who are poor, refugees, or of color. For example, speakers of French and German may be characterized as world travelers who are considered more academic, more sophisticated, and more prestigious in some segments of society, while speakers of Spanish, Korean, or Vietnamese may be labeled as "immigrants" with "limited English." People who hold negative biases against immigrants may characterize multilingual children as low in status or educationally at risk; they may also inappropriately assume parents who don't speak English are uninterested or uninvested in their children's education, rather than examining whether school-based policies alienate or exclude parents who are not fluent in English. Additionally, teachers who are monolingual in English may not know how to build relationships with multilingual learners and families, discourage students from using their home language in the classroom, or assume students who are not fluent in English are not ready for cognitively complex tasks.

It is important to note that no language is inherently better than any other language; all languages have developed to express the needs of their users and, in that sense, all languages are equal. Nevertheless, in most communities around the world, the forms of speech used by dominant racial, ethnic, cultural, and SES groups are privileged. In the United States, people who speak unaccented Standard English tend to be perceived as more educated, wealthier, and higher status than people who speak accented or other forms of English. Thus, as part of their efforts to create classrooms that engage, affirm, and support academic achievement among culturally and linguistically diverse students, teachers need to understand not only the nature of language but also the relationship between language and culture, as well as strategies to minimize linguistic bias within and beyond the classroom.

# The Nature of Language

**Learning Objective 7.3** Explain the nature of language and the various components of language development.

At its most basic level, oral and written language consists of five main components:

- **Phonemic awareness** (the ability to identify the sounds that make up words)
- **Phonics** (the ability to connect written letters or combinations of letters to their sounds)
- **Vocabulary** (the ability to pronounce and understand the meaning of words as they are used in a specific context)
- **Fluency** (the ability to read or understand spoken words accurately and quickly)
- **Comprehension** (the ability to understand and make meaning of oral or written text)

Although there are many theories regarding the development of language, exactly how a language is learned is not completely understood. Research indicates that infants' brains begin to respond to the phonetic units of their native language during the first months of life and that those raised in multilingual households are more able to distinguish between multiple languages in adulthood, suggesting that language learning begins well before children are able to speak themselves (Kuhl, 2010). During early childhood, almost all children learn their first language naturally through constant interactions with and by imitating the people around them; they gradually learn to select almost instinctively the right word, the right response, and the right gesture to fit the situation. As children age, they also acquire the delicate muscle control necessary for pronouncing the words of their native language or for signing naturally if the child is deaf.

As children grow older, it becomes increasingly difficult for them to make their vocal muscles behave in ways necessary to master a new language; they may also struggle to hear nuanced differences in tone or pronunciation in languages with which they are unfamiliar. This sometimes inhibits people from learning new languages and is part of what leads to **accents**, or differences in pronunciation, among people who learn additional languages as adolescents or adults. For example, because some monolingual Japanese speakers have never developed the "l" sound in their speech or language, they may tend to pronounce English words that begin with the letter *l* as if they began with the letter *r*. Thus, the word "light" may be pronounced as if it were "right" and "long" as if it were "wrong."

However, it is important for teachers to realize that speaking with an accent is a normal part of the language acquisition process and that it is more important to support multilingual people in becoming effective communicators rather than emphasizing unaccented speech. Multilingual speakers' accents tend to evolve over time, as they unconsciously mimic the speech patterns of those around them; likewise, people's ears adjust to the accents of those around them, making it easier to understand their speech patterns. It is also common for people to adopt the tonal norms and pronunciation patterns of the people around them, leading to variations in accents in different geographic and cultural communities.

In addition to the physical mechanics of language, by age 5, children have also learned the grammatical syntax used by adults in their community and know that words in different arrangements mean different things. Native speakers of a language unconsciously know and obey the complex rules and customs of their language community, although these skills may vary greatly from what schools may require of them (Adger et al., 2007; American Speech-Language-Hearing Association, 2019).

For multilingual students, knowledge of the lexical and syntactic elements of a first language plays an important role in the process of acquiring and learning a second language. Some concepts acquired through learning their first language (e.g., Spanish) can be transferred to a second language (e.g., English) when a comparable concept in the second language is encountered. However, English speakers should not think of Spanish, French, Chinese, or any other language as consisting of words that, if translated, basically transform into English. There are words and concepts in all of these languages for which there is no English equivalent. There may be no exact English translation to convey the same meaning.

For example, *heung* in the Chinese Cantonese dialect is translated into English as "fragrant." However, *heung* has no exact English translation. The Chinese word has a very distinctive meaning that conveys not only fragrance but a multisensory experience. When Cantonese speakers say that food that they have placed in their mouths is *heung*, it may imply that it tastes, smells, and feels very special. This is just one of thousands of examples: When dictionary-producer Merriam-Webster invited multilingual people to suggest words that could not be translated into English, more than 5,000 people responded in the first 3 days, offering words like صبحيه (an Arabic word that can be written in English script as soubhiyé), which refers to "that quiet time when you're the only one awake in the house and can enjoy a cup of coffee before the day starts," and *apapachar*, a Mexican Spanish word that comes from Nahuatl, translated as "'hug with the soul,' . . . sort of a mix of 'to cuddle,' 'to support' and 'to console': to throw all of your love to someone when they need it the most" (Janse, 2023; Merriam-Webster, 2023).

When we refer to someone as **fluent** in a language, we typically mean that they can read, communicate orally, and write using the conventions of that language in a wide variety of personal, academic, and professional settings. However, language includes far more than simple knowledge of words or sounds; it is deeply and inextricably tied to cultural knowledge and understanding. Additionally, even though we often talk about named languages as separate and distinct entities, the reality is that multilingual people don't store different languages in separate parts of their brains; instead, they have a single, cohesive **linguistic repertoire** (mental collection of linguistic skills, knowledge, and resources) that includes elements from all of the languages they know. Thus, it is natural for multilingual people to think and communicate using words and phrases from multiple named languages simultaneously. It is only when interacting with monolingual people that multilingual learners are expected to limit themselves to the use of words, phrases, and structures from only one language.

In the classroom, this means that multilingual students are constantly integrating sounds and meanings associated with multiple language systems and are making connections between content as it is taught in English and their prior learning in languages other than English. These students often benefit from invitations to think and write about academic content in other languages, so they can utilize their background knowledge and prepare to leverage their multilingualism in future academic, community, and professional settings. Research demonstrates that when children are provided a strong educational foundation in their native language, they gain both knowledge and literacy, and this powerfully supports English language development (Crawford & Krashen, 2007).

## Language and Culture

Although we tend to think about named languages as clearly defined and unchanging, the reality is that language is **dynamic**, meaning that it changes over time. The ways people use language also reflect a complex and ever-changing constellation of cultural, contextual, and historical factors.

For effective communication to take place, it is important that there be enough cultural similarities between the sender and the receiver for the latter to decode the message adequately. Even when one is familiar with a word or phrase, comprehension of the intended meaning may not be possible unless there is some similarity or understanding of the cultural background. For example, in addition to influencing the order of words to form phrases, language influences thinking patterns. A classic example of this is the concept of "time," which is described differently from culture to culture. Some societies view time as something that can be saved, lost, or wasted; punctuality is valued. In other societies, using time "efficiently" is less important than interpersonal connection. In the southern United States, for example, rather than beginning a meeting precisely "on time," people often exchange pleasantries and what they may consider "small talk" prior to substantive or business conversation. Chatting first about Saturday's weather or the spring flowers in bloom may be considered a polite way to lead into the issues that need to be discussed. To do otherwise might be considered rude by some individuals. Others, unaccustomed to southern ways, may consider this behavior a waste of time.

New words and ways of communicating often emerge in response to migrations and cultural and technological shifts; it is also common for different generations of people to use language differently. Psychologist Lev Vygotsky (1962) referred to thought and language as co-creating processes, meaning that language both evolves in response to and sparks changes in the ways we think about ideas and cultural phenomena. For example, people who are raised in monolingual households but live in communities where many languages are spoken may regularly use words or phrases drawn from multiple languages. Similarly, teens often develop language that reflects new ways of interacting on emergent social media platforms; in the early 2020s, the word *rizz* came into popular discourse as a reference to someone (usually male presenting) who is charming or charismatic when creating video content, a characteristic that didn't exist before the widespread use of YouTube and TikTok. Likewise, members of historically marginalized social identity groups may use new forms of language in order to challenge, resist, or draw attention to conditions they find oppressive or colonizing. In recent years, some Spanish speakers have started to use the suffix -*x* or -*e* (as in *Latinx* or *Latine* rather than *Latino/a*) to acknowledge the existence of people who cannot be appropriately characterized using "male" or "female" labels.

Thus, while it can be tempting to think of language as something stable or fixed, it is actually in a constant state of shift, leading many educators to focus on how students are **languaging**, or using language in the classroom, in recognition of the importance of understanding their students' ever-changing linguistic practices rather defining them based on linguistic labels.

When thinking about language, it is also important to recognize that languages do not all have the same conventions of grammar, phonology, or semantic structure and that even within a single named language (such as English), there is wide variability in common usage. The rules of Standard English reflect dominant usage among individuals and institutions that have political, social, and cultural status, enabling them to determine what is socially acceptable and prestigious. However, these rules can change over time. For example, if a noted sportscaster or politician creates a word and uses it repeatedly, and other people begin using it, it may eventually become part of Standard English. In this way, the idea of Standard English is artificial and socially constructed; there is no linguistic reason a standardized variety of English should be considered inherently better than any other variety of English. In fact, some linguists argue that the very concept of "Standard English" is so deeply intertwined with legacies of racism and colonization that educators should stop teaching or expecting students to use it in the classroom (Baker-Bell et al., 2020).

# Varieties of English

Unlike accents, which refer to differences in pronunciation but not in vocabulary or syntax, **dialect** refers to the unique ways language is used by members of a particular region or social group. In the United States, there are multiple regional dialects, such as eastern New England, New York City, western Pennsylvania, Middle Atlantic, Appalachian, southern, central, midland, north central, southwestern, and northwestern. Each of these is notable for a distinct, but shared, set of vocabulary and pronunciation norms that make it different from the normative rules of Standard English.

Dialects differ from one another in a variety of ways, and these differences may be attributed to various factors, including historical speech patterns among native communities, immigrants, and colonizers who settled a region, as well as SES, geography, situational variables, race, and ethnicity. Over time, groups of people who were separated by physical barriers such as mountains or bodies of water developed and maintained their unique linguistic styles. While highways, tunnels, and bridges have all but eliminated these physical separations, dialectical differences have remained relatively stable over time, leading to marked differences in pronunciation and word usage throughout the United States.

Regional dialects are notable for the different words people use to describe things, such as "soda" or "pop," as well as differences in the pronunciations of vowels, whereas consonant differences tend to distinguish social dialects. Regional and social dialects cannot be divorced from one another, however, because an individual's dialect may be a blend of the two. In northern dialects, for example, the *i* in words such as *time*, *pie*, and *side* is pronounced with a long-*i* sound, which is a rapid production of two vowel sounds, one sounding like *ah* and the other like *ee*. The second sound glides off the first so that "time" becomes *taem*, "pie" becomes *pae*, and "side" becomes *saed*. Southern and related dialects may eliminate the gliding *e*, resulting in *tam* for "time," *pa* for "pie," and *sad* for "side" (Adger et al., 2007; Reaser et al., 2017).

Similarly, in what is widely considered the most easily recognized dialect in the world, people from New York often pronounce the *a* in words like "talk" or "caught" as "aw," so "talk" becomes *tawk*, or they drop the closing *r* from words (so "water" becomes *wat-ah*). Other common examples of consonant pronunciation differences are found in the *th* sound and in the consonants *r* and *l*. In words such as "these," "them," and "those," the beginning *th* sound may be replaced with a *d*, resulting in *dese, dem*, and *dose*. In words such as "think," "thank," and "throw," the *th* may be replaced with a *t*, resulting in *tink, tank*, and *trow* (Adger et al., 2007).

In the early 2000s, researchers Burt Vauz and Scott Golder (then at Harvard University) developed a 25-question dialect survey tracking differences in word usage and pronunciation across the United States; they then developed a series of maps illustrating dialectical differences nationwide (Katz & Andrews, 2013). Their survey, which is now hosted by the University of Cambridge, includes questions like "What is your general, informal term for the rubber-soled shoes worn in gym class, for athletic activities, etc.?" and can, in a matter of minutes, predict where in the United States someone was born or lives. Figure 7.2, for example, offers an illustration of which word people use to refer to carbonated beverages. Is the word you use included among the choices at the bottom of the map and, if so, is it matched to the parts of the country where you have lived? To learn more about the survey, take the survey, or view results, visit http://www.tekstlab.uio.no/cambridge_survey/.

As is the case for other aspects of language, people are sometimes privileged or discriminated against based on their dialect. Generally, people who use the dialectical norms most closely associated with Standard English tend to think they speak "correctly" and are perceived as of having higher status. Speakers from regions where people speak quickly may view the long vowel sounds and slower speech common within Southern dialects as indicative of a lack of intelligence, or the substitution of

**Figure 7.2** Responses to "What Do You Call a Carbonated Beverage?"

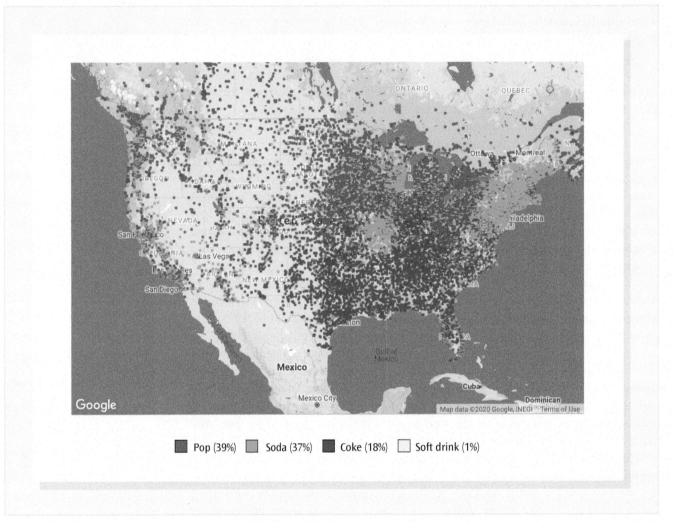

| ■ Pop (39%) | ■ Soda (37%) | ■ Coke (18%) | □ Soft drink (1%) |

**SOURCE:** Cambridge Online Survey of World Englishes, http://www.tekstlab.uio.no/cambridge_survey/.

*d* for *th*, especially when used by people from historically marginalized groups (such as members of poor or working-class, rural, or Black American communities) as indicative of a lack of education. As with all aspects of language, it is important for teachers to recognize that a complex array of social, economic, and cultural factors affect the ways people speak English and that the variety of English spoken by an individual teacher, or even most or all teachers at a given school site, is not necessarily the only socially and academically appropriate variety.

There is some controversy regarding the point at which differences in how people speak should no longer be characterized as differences in dialect but as separate named languages. This controversy is more a product of social, cultural, and political factors rather than linguistic ones. In reality, the distinction between dialect and language is somewhat arbitrary. In common usage within the United States, people tend to focus on the idea of **mutual intelligibility**, or the ability of people to understand one another, as well as whether there are differences in written communication or only oral communication. However, this approach to distinguishing between a dialect and a language is far from perfect. For example, there are many examples of **asymmetric intelligibility**, where speakers of one language are able to understand speakers of another but cannot themselves be understood; speakers of Danish, for example, are better able to understand Swedish than vice versa (Gooskens et al., 2018).

Similarly, definitions that rely on analyses of written language cannot be applied to languages that are exclusively oral or signed (such as American Sign Language). Additionally, historically, speakers of dominant or colonizing languages (such as English and Spanish) have sometimes improperly referred to language spoken by colonized people as dialects. This was due both to colonizers' lack of understanding of linguistic traditions different than their own as well as their sense of cultural, linguistic, and political superiority. Contemporary examples include cases of English speakers referring to African languages as African dialects or the diverse languages spoken by American Indians as Indian dialects. This improper practice is similar to labeling French and German as dialects spoken in the different regions in Europe.

In the United States, one of the most common linguistic varieties is under the umbrella of **African American Language (AAL)** or **Black English** (sometimes called *African American Vernacular English*, or AAVE), which is a fully developed language system that follows different grammatical and syntactic rules than standard English. The grammatical structure of AAL is notable for its use of double negatives ("I don't got no"), habitual be ("they be bothering you"), and perfective tense ("he done did it"), as well as unique vowel sounds and speech patterns (Luu, 2020). However, despite linguists' widespread recognition of AAL as a unique language, linguistic racism has led some teachers and media personalities to condemn it as "slang" or "bad English," even when used by scholars and prominent public figures, such as former president Barack Obama (Hankerson, 2023).

These attitudes reflect biased beliefs in the inherent superiority of White, European speech patterns rather than the legitimacy of AAL as a language. To help educators better understand the linguistic and syntactic rules of AAL, the National Council of Teachers of English has issued a series of statements detailing norms of Black English, as well as the importance of disrupting anti-Black linguistic racism in classrooms (Baker-Bell et al., 2020; Conference on College Composition & Communication, 2021). Speakers of standard English whose students include speakers of AAL may find resources like the University of Oregon's Online Resources for African American Language project (*https://oraal.uoregon.edu*) useful for increasing their understanding of the grammatical structures of AAL, as well as ways to support speakers of AAL in the classroom.

## Code-Switching

Certain situations, both social and professional, may dictate adjustments in the ways people use language. Some individuals have the ability to speak in two or more varieties of English, a skill that is often referred to as **code-switching**. While the term was initially used to refer to the ways speakers of nonstandard forms of English were required to adopt dominant, standardized language practices in order to gain social and academic acceptance, it has evolved to center the ways people strategically alter their language practices in order to communicate effectively in a specific social or cultural context.

Some studies have suggested that students who learn to code-switch achieve better academic or professional results (Owens, 2012), and the English Language Arts Standards used in most states now include criteria related to considerations of audience and purpose when speaking or writing (National Governors Association Center for Best Practices & Council of Chief State School Officers, 2010). However, educators must be careful not to suggest that some varieties of language are more correct or legitimate than others or require students to adopt the dialects of racially and socioeconomically dominant groups in academic settings. Such practices, often cloaked by references to "academic language" or "school talk," can result in psychological harm and a sense of isolation among speakers of racially, culturally, and linguistically marginalized varieties of English; these impacts extend well beyond the classroom and can impact students throughout their professional lives (McCluney et al., 2019). In a TED Talk and spoken word poem viewed more than 5 million times, poet and scholar Jamila Lyiscott

**Pearson eTextbook**

**Video Example 7.2**

In this TED Talk, Jamila Lyiscott sends a powerful message on language, challenging stereotypes, and unpacking linguistic histories. https://www.ted.com/talks/jamila_lyiscott_3_ways_to_speak_english

# Critical Incidents in Teaching

## Whose English?

Julio Plata is the principal of Jackie Robinson Middle School. Named after one of the first Black Americans to play in Major League Baseball, Robinson Middle School served a primarily Black community in Little Rock, Arkansas but, like many schools around the country, had few Black teachers. One afternoon, Principal Plata got a phone call from Ruby Norton, the mother of a sixth-grader at the school, asking for a meeting to discuss her son, Trayson. Since Principal Plata didn't know Trayson, he looked up his record to help prepare for the meeting and found that he had good attendance, was on the honor roll, and was part of the school's track team. He agreed to the meeting and told Ms. Norton he was looking forward to meeting her.

On the day of the meeting, Ms. Norton arrived at the school and told Principal Plata that she wanted to get right to the point: Trayson's science teacher, Ms. Simmons, was racist and didn't understand or respect the culture of Black students. She wanted Trayson moved to another classroom immediately. When Principal Plata asked for more information about Trayson's experience, Ms. Norton replied that Trayson's teacher, who was White, told Trayson that he was smart but "talked Black" and if he didn't fix his grammar, he'd never get into college or get a good job. "That's just plain racist," Ms. Norton said. "I ain't no fool. Trayson, he knows science. He be speaking like his people. This is an attack on Black folk. I want him out of her class."

### Questions for Discussion

1. How should Principal Plata respond to Ms. Norton? To Ms. Simmons?

2. Do you agree with Ms. Norton? Was Ms. Simmons being racist?

3. Should parents be able to pull their children from classrooms when teachers don't understand or respect their cultural or linguistic identity?

4. Should teachers enforce the use of Standard English in the classroom? Why or why not?

5. How did knowing that Trayson was on the honor roll and track team affect your reading of this case? Would your responses have been different had Trayson struggled with attendance, academic achievement, or discipline?

6. What should teachers from linguistically dominant groups do to increase their capacity as effective teachers of culturally and linguistically diverse students?

challenged the ways speakers of nonstandard dialects are referred to as speaking "broken English" and challenges listeners to think of speakers who can move fluidly among multiple varieties of English as "trilingual orators."

## Sign Language

In addition to spoken and written varieties of language, there are languages that do not have a written system, with researchers suggesting that there as many as 2,990 unwritten languages currently used in the world (Eberhard, Simons, & Fennig, 2023). The most widely used of these are visual languages created and used by deaf people. In the United States and Canada, many deaf people communicate using **American Sign Language (ASL)**, a natural language notable for its complex grammar and well-regulated syntax. Children who are deaf are able to pick up the syntax and rhythms of signing as spontaneously as children who hear and pick up their oral languages. Many children, including hearing and deaf children, who are born into deaf families are introduced to ASL from birth. However, those deaf children who have hearing parents may not have the opportunity to learn ASL until they attend a school program for the deaf, where they learn from both their teachers and peers.

With its own vocabulary, syntax, and grammatical rules, ASL does not correspond completely to spoken or written English (Heward et al., 2017; Smith et al., 2018). Thus, ASL, as well as the almost 160 other forms of sign language used around the world, is considered a language in its own right, rather than a variation of spoken English (Eberhard et al., 2023), and a growing number of colleges and universities accept fluency in ASL as meeting a second-language requirement. ASL is different than most spoken languages in that each sign does not represent a single, specific word but, rather, a complete concept; speakers of ASL also use facial expressions, finger spelling, and whole-body movements to convey meaning. Thus, it is impossible to directly translate ASL into English or other oral languages. However, to communicate with the hearing, those who are deaf often also use **signed English**, a system of signing that translates individual English oral or written words into a sign. When one sees an interpreter on television or at a meeting, it is usually signed English that is being used; this means that most interpreters, as well as deaf people who read English, are fluent in at least three languages: ASL, signed English, and English.

## Nonverbal Communication

Although most people think of communication as being **verbal**, or word based, in nature, **nonverbal communication** can be just as important in the total communication process. Because it is so clearly interwoven into the overall fabric of verbal communication, nonverbal communication often appears to be inseparable from it.

Nonverbal communication can serve several functions. It conveys messages through one's attitude, personality, manner, and even dress. It augments verbal communication by reinforcing what one says; for example, a smile or a pat on the back reinforces a positive statement made to a student. It can contradict verbal communication; for example, a frown accompanying a positive statement to a student sends a mixed or contradictory message. Nonverbal communication can replace a verbal message: A finger to the lips or a teacher's hand held in the air, palm facing the students may communicate "Silence" to a class.

It is important to recognize that nonverbal gestures can have significantly different meanings across cultures. For example, a teacher might offer a thumbs-up from across the room as a quick sign of approval. However, a teacher may find an extreme reaction from parents of an immigrant student from Iran or Iraq, where it would be the equivalent of extending a middle finger to the child. The "dog call" or finger curl where a teacher curls the finger to summon a student may be acceptable in the United States but may be highly offensive in some Asian cultures. Likewise, the "OK" sign, with the circle formed by the thumb and index finger, was once commonplace in the United States but has since been co-opted by White Supremacist groups as a reference to the Ku Klux Klan; when used publicly, the symbol is now generally interpreted as a hate symbol (Allyn, 2019; Samovar et al., 2017; Sengupta, 2018).

Just as culture affects the ways people use and interpret language, culture and cultural difference also have profound implications for how individuals interact nonverbally. For example, in **low-context cultures**, including North American, northern European, English, and German cultures, people tend to use direct, linear, and concise oral communication, placing more emphasis on the precise meaning of words and less on how, when, and where communication takes place. By contrast, in **high-context cultures**, which are prevalent through much of Asia, Africa, the Mediterranean, and the Middle East, nonverbal cues, facial expressions, and tone are critically important aspects of communication and oral expressions of disagreement may be experienced as aggressive or confrontational (Hall & Hall, 1990). This can lead to misunderstandings among culturally and linguistically diverse students, educators, and community members, as different people interpret verbal and nonverbal communication differently.

There is often as much or more communicated nonverbally as verbally.

**SOURCE:** Thinkstock/Stockbyte/Gettyimages

Other nonverbal miscommunication may involve the facial expressions or behaviors of the student. Raeburn (2018) suggests that much of our communication is done through eye contact. American teachers typically expect a child to look at them while they are having a conversation. However, some groups consider it disrespectful for a child to look directly into the eyes of a teacher. Consequently, as a sign of respect, a child may look at the floor while either speaking to a teacher or being spoken to. Teachers, however, may view this behavior opposite the manner intended and demand that the child look them in the eyes. While most Western cultures (e.g., U.S., Greek, French, Spanish) tend to value eye contact, many Eastern cultures (e.g., Chinese, Japanese, Vietnamese, Korean) view eye contact as a form of disrespect. In some of these cultures (e.g., Chinese), it may be appropriate for someone in a higher position to make eye contact with someone in a lower position. Some countries are very diverse, so what is expected in some regions and from individuals from those regions may differ from the expectations of those from other regions (Burgoon et al., 2010; Raeburn, 2018), adding to the need for care and sensitivity on the part of educators.

**Proxemics** refers to the ways people move within and use space; it offers a helpful lens through which to think about nonverbal classroom communication. For example, some people feel very comfortable in close proximity to others, while other people may feel crowded or threatened when others enter what they consider their "personal space." It is important to recognize that the concept of personal space varies widely, especially since the COVID-19 pandemic. Some students and families may consider 6 inches an appropriate distance for conversation, while others prefer to maintain a social distance of 3 feet or more.

In the classroom, many teachers use proximity as a means to build relationships with students and unobtrusively redirect student behavior. This might include greeting students with a handshake or high-five as they enter the classroom, walking around the room while lecturing, or standing near the desk of a student who appears to be off task. A light touch on the backs of students can end their talking to their classmates and return them to the lesson at hand. A gentle hug for a tearful second-grader who has lost a pet hamster can ease some of the pain. Neither of these actions requires a single word, yet it can convey much to a student.

However, it is important to be aware that different cultural groups have different expectations when it comes to physical contact with a teacher. Some groups may view a pat on the head of a child as a supportive gesture, whereas others may interpret it as threating or patronizing. Students who have experienced neglect or trauma may cross physical boundaries or avoid physical contact entirely, and students may react to teachers differently depending on their gender expression, racial or ethnic identity, physical size, or age. For this reason, it is important not to make assumptions about how others will interpret physical touch and find ways of interacting that are aligned to the communication norms and policies in your school district.

# The Diversity of Languages Found Within Classrooms

**Learning Objective 7.4** Describe the various forms of language learners and the characteristics of these learners.

In many countries, children are expected to use multiple languages throughout the school day; in Europe, for example, it is common for children to be trilingual prior to graduating secondary school. Officially, the Council of Europe (2023) has adopted a policy of **plurilingual and intercultural education** in recognition of the importance of linguistic and cultural diversity and the value of teaching academic content in multiple languages. As a result, from the time they enter public school, students are not only encouraged to speak and maintain their native language but also to learn additional languages throughout the school day. It is common for academic content (mathematics, science, social studies, and so forth) to be taught in multiple languages, with the goal of preparing students to be effective members of linguistically diverse global communities. By contrast, in the United States, academic instruction is overwhelmingly in English, with many students not taking coursework in other languages prior to high school. This means that despite the linguistic diversity of American students themselves, English is privileged and prioritized in the classroom, limiting opportunities for all learners to develop multilingual fluency.

## Bilingual and Multilingual Learners

Language diversity in the United States has been maintained primarily because of continuing immigration from non-English-speaking countries. In its relatively short history, the United States has probably been host to more linguistically diverse individuals than any other country in the world. As new immigrants enter the country, they bring with them their own cultures, values, and languages and a wealth of knowledge, ways of being, and strengths that can be wonderful assets for their new home communities. As generations of families settle in the United States, schools and teachers often are unsure of how to support children in their home language. In the rush to develop in their English language skills, children and their families can experience great loss in terms of their home languages, cultural ways of being, and connections to their home communities. Teachers then need to develop a clear sense of their work with students learning in a new language and root their work within a framework that builds on the linguistic skills and previous knowledge of the students in their classrooms. Though they might have had limited experience in learning the English language before starting school in the United States, students will have had extensive experience in learning the language they use at home and in their home communities, deep foundational knowledge of subject-matter content in their home language, and other learning experiences in and out of school that they can rely on to learn English as an additional language.

In this regard, it is important for teachers to consider how their students should be considered as **multilingual learners**, or speakers of multiple languages, or as **emergent bilinguals** who are in the process of becoming bilingual rather than "English learners." The description of a student as an English learner is limiting in its approach and perspective because it focuses solely on the child as a learner of English only, while in reality the student is always developing in the language spoken in their home and in their local communities as well as in English. The term *bilingual learner* is also limiting because it implies that learners might only speak one language and are learning a second language. The reality is that some students might know multiple languages before they start learning

English or another language, so the term *multilingual learner* is more appropriate. The term *multilingual learner* highlights a student's existing language abilities and strengths in their home languages, as well as their work in developing fluency in an additional language(s). The term *emergent bilingual* highlights that a student is learning two languages, which are both important, and that the students are emerging and progressing in their development over time.

Many classrooms include multilingual learners.

## Characteristics of Multilingual Learners in U.S. Schools

As explained above, the terms *multilingual learners* and *emergent bilingual* are the most appropriate terms to use when discussing students who are learning English. However, some states continue to track data using the deficit-oriented label **English learner (EL)** or **English language learner (ELL)**. When reporting data, we use the language used by the state or government entity that collected it; however, educators should carefully consider the terms they use when describing multilingual students and how those terms impact students' sense of belonging and value within academic settings.

The arrival of new immigrants annually into the United States results in significant linguistic diversity in our schools and communities. In 2019, the National Center for Education Statistics estimated that 10.4%, or 5.1 million students, were formally designated as ELs, defined as students who do not yet speak enough English to thrive in grade-level academic conversations conducted exclusively in English; by 2025, researchers estimate that one in four public school students will meet this classification (National Education Association, 2020).

Students who are identified as ELs are far from an academically monolithic group: Some enter U.S. classrooms fluent in multiple languages and performing far above grade level when instruction is conducted in those languages; others may struggle with literacy in their native languages or have gaps in their prior schooling. It is important for teachers to get to know the personal, cultural, linguistic, and academic experiences of their students as part of their efforts to promote student engagement and achievement.

It is surprising to many educators that most emergent bilingual students are born in the United States, although many of their parents were born outside the country. Among prekindergarten through the fifth grade, 85% of students who schools identify as ELs are U.S.-born, while 15% are born outside of the United States. Among older students, grades 6 through 12, 62% are U.S.-born, while 38% are born elsewhere (Sanchez, 2017). Figure 7.3 shows the numbers of designated ELs enrolled in U.S. schools between 2000 and 2019. In 2000, there were almost 3.8 million EL students and, by 2019, the number had risen to a little over 5.1 million. Table 7.1 lists the five states with the largest EL enrollments. Percentages shown are those of total school enrollment.

**Figure 7.3** Elementary and Secondary Enrollment of English Learner Students in the United States, 2000–2019

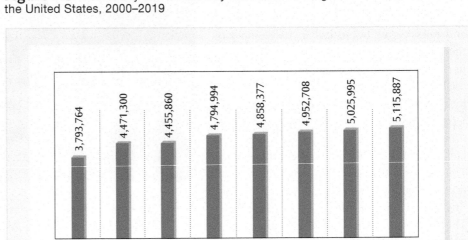

**Table 7.1**  States with the Largest English Learner Enrollments, 2019

| State | Number of EL Students | Percentage of Total Enrollment |
|---|---|---|
| California | 1,148,024 | 18.6% |
| Texas | 1,021.540 | 19.6% |
| Florida | 278,498 | 10.0% |
| New York | 233,627 | 8.9% |
| Illinois | 229,180 | 12.3% |

SOURCE: National Center for Education Statistics (2019).

Spanish is the home language for 75.7% of emergent bilingual students and 7.9% of all K–12 students in the United States; Arabic, Chinese, and Vietnamese each comprise only about 2% of all of the designated ELs enrolled in U.S. public schools (see Table 7.2). However, there are considerable variations among states. For example, in five states, a language other than Spanish was the most common language spoken at home among EL students: The most common home languages in Alaska are Yupik languages (spoken by 17% of EL students); in Minnesota it is Somali (12%); in Vermont, Nepali (11%); in Hawaii, Iloko (9%); and in Montana, German (6%) (National Clearinghouse for English Language Acquisition [NCELA], 2023).

Despite the linguistic diversity of the United States, there are still far too few bilingual teachers and teachers with special training working with emergent bilingual students; only 18 states meet or exceed the number of teachers necessary to effectively serve their English learning population (NCELA, 2021). As of the 2017–2018 school year, some states, such as Hawaii and Kentucky, had fewer than 100 public school teachers who were certified to teach ELs, leading to tremendous shortages in the field (NCELA, 2021). These inequities were exacerbated by the COVID-19 pandemic; during

**Table 7.2**  Top 20 Languages Spoken by English Learners, 2019–2020 Academic Year

| Ranking | Language | Number of Speakers | Percent of Total U.S. EL Students |
|---|---|---|---|
| 1 | Spanish; Castilian | 3,872,159 | 75.69% |
| 2 | Arabic | 124,410 | 2.43% |
| 3 | Chinese | 87,256 | 1.71% |
| 4 | Vietnamese | 57,073 | 1.12% |
| 5 | Portuguese | 32,017 | 0.63% |
| 6 | Haitian; Haitian Creole | 25,404 | 0.50% |
| 7 | Hmong | 19,623 | 0.38% |
| 8 | Cushitic (Other) | 16,829 | 0.33% |
| 9 | Tagalog | 15,787 | 0.31% |
| 10 | Russian | 13,905 | 0.27% |
| 11 | Somali | 12,600 | 0.25% |
| 12 | Urdu | 11,090 | 0.22% |
| 13 | Bengali | 9,291 | 0.18% |
| 14 | Swahili | 8,327 | 0.16% |
| 15 | Navajo; Navaho | 7,235 | 0.14% |
| 16 | Karen Languages | 6,455 | 0.13% |
| 17 | Polish | 6,080 | 0.12% |
| 18 | Marshallese | 5,926 | 0.12% |
| 19 | Yupik Languages | 5,179 | 0.10% |
| 20 | Amharic | 5,133 | 0.10% |

SOURCE: U.S. Office of English Language Acquisition (2023).

the early months of virtual learning, for example, 69% of California parents indicated that their schools hadn't provided any instructional materials in languages other than English, and the Los Angeles Unified School District reported that 40% of designated ELs were logging in to online instruction less than once per week (California Alliance of Researchers for Equity in Education, 2020).

Emergent bilingual students' need for additional academic supports in order to thrive in English-dominant classrooms, as well as the limited availability of teachers with expertise in working with emergent bilingual students, often results in inequitable educational conditions and outcomes. Nationally, students designated as ELs do not perform as well on state tests as do their English-fluent peers; in the most recently released disaggregated data set (from 2017), just 14% of ELs scored "proficient" in fourth-grade mathematics assessments and 6% on eighth-grade mathematics assessments; in reading, 9% of ELs scored proficient in fourth grade and 5% in eighth grade (U.S. Department of Education, 2018). By contrast, 61% of fourth-graders and 68% of eighth-graders nationwide meet proficiency expectations for reading, while 74% of fourth-graders and 60% of eighth-graders met proficiency expectations in mathematics (National Assessment of Educational Progress, 2022).

Moreover, although high school graduation rates for students designated as ELs is increasing, it is still far below that of their English-fluent peers; the most recent national data, from the 2017–2018 academic year, indicates that just 68% of ELs graduate high school in 4 years (as compared to 85% of students overall); in New York, the 4-year graduation rate for ELs is just 31% (NCELA, 2020). Clearly, schools have a lot of work to do to provide a more effective educational experience for emergent bilingual students.

However, this data only tells part of the story. As emergent bilingual students move through the educational system, they are typically retested annually to assess their proficiency level in English. Students who are identified as English-fluent are **reclassified** and are no longer tracked individually. Students who are enrolled in U.S. schools for multiple years but do not qualify for reclassification are sometimes referred to as **long-term English learners (LTELs)**. These students often include those who enter public school at the middle or high school level and may struggle more to learn English than their younger peers.

Emergent bilingual students who enter U.S. schools at older ages, as well as those designated as LTELs, are often impacted by school policies regarding course sequencing and enrollment. They may be required to take courses in basic English rather than electives, lack full access to STEM (science, technology, engineering, mathematics) education, or be denied Advanced Placement or college preparatory classes (Mitchell, 2019). Even when these policies are well intentioned, with the goal of increasing students' fluency in English, they often have a negative impact on students' overall academic trajectory. When programs of study overemphasize basic communication rather than the cognitive demands of more challenging coursework and curriculum, students can become bored, lose opportunities to leverage their bilingualism, and be underprepared for college, the job market, or professions with higher wages and growth potential.

In addition to navigating systemic bias and lack of opportunities at school, many emergent bilingual students in U.S. schools also face complex personal and socioeconomic conditions. Some emergent bilingual students are refugees who have immigrated to flee poverty or violence, and nearly 60% of designated EL students in the United States are from low-income families whose parents have had limited education. Slightly more than 40% of parents of EL students have not completed high school, compared to only 9.3% of the parents of non-EL students (Breiseth, 2015). Some immigrant families were already living in poverty when they left their home countries, and barriers created by racism, lack of documentation, or limited English proficiency limit their economic opportunities upon arrival in the United States. This creates additional burdens for emergent bilingual students as they navigate challenges associated with their overall living conditions, health care, nutrition, books and learning materials, and other important forms of support for optimum cognitive and educational development.

As part of their effort to meet the educational needs of immigrant and emergent bilingual students, educators have taken a wide range of approaches to language education. In the following sections, we explore historical approaches to language education in U.S. public school classrooms, controversies related to bilingual and multilingual education, and strategies that individual educators can employ to engage, affirm, and promote academic achievement among linguistically diverse students.

# History of Language Education in the United States

**Learning Objective 7.5** Explain the history of language education and policy in the United States.

The ways in which learning solely English is privileged and made a priority in the classroom, despite the linguistic diversity of American students themselves, can be seen throughout the history of U.S. language education. As successive waves of families immigrated into the United States, their linguistic diversity and the very existence of their home languages were seen as temporary and transient, rather than as a potential resource for students and their families to draw upon as they learned English as an additional language. Giving up or losing one's home language was deemed in society as a natural process, as one began to develop proficiency in the English language. At times, losing one's home language was seen as a way to prove one's allegiance as a family or as an ethnic group to the United States.

## Overview of Language Policy in the United States

In this section, we present an overview of some of the laws and movements that have impacted the experiences of multilingual people and learners in the United States in order to illustrate the significant role state and national policies play in shaping attitudes and beliefs about language. The examples below trace some of the ways English became the dominant and, at times, exclusive, language of instruction in U.S. schools and how the systematic privileging of English impacted linguistically diverse students in terms of their identity formation, retention of the language spoken in their homes and home communities, and overall educational experience. While these examples are far from exhaustive, they offer insight into the history of language policy in the United States and an opportunity to consider why restrictive language policies endure into the twenty-first century and how they impact contemporary students.

Initially founded in 1824, the Bureau of Indian Affairs (BIA) was developed to oversee the relationship between the U.S. government and the American Indians people and communities who were indigenous to North America. During the nineteenth century, one of the primary functions of the BIA was to assimilate American Indians into mainstream American culture, often by disrupting tribal language or sovereignty. The General Allotment Act (Dawes Act) of 1887 was designed to break down tribal relations through eradicating reservations and tribal lands; as part of this effort, the U.S. government redoubled its efforts to relocate young children away from their families and tribes and send them to boarding schools to be educated. At these reservation schools, students were required to learn, study, and speak in English only, which eventually led to whole generations of people within a tribe not learning its spoken language and a concomitant loss of knowledge about one's own tribe, history, and ways of being.

In addition to attempts to restrict Native American students' use of tribal languages, the 1880s was also a time of backlash against immigrant arrivals in the United States. During this time, anti-immigration laws were introduced in schools, accompanied by a push toward the "Americanization" of all immigrants. The states of Wisconsin and Illinois passed mandates that required English as the sole language of instruction in all public and private schools and, in 1906, the Naturalization Act was passed, requiring all people who were applying for U.S. citizenship to be fluent in English. Effectively, this act required immigrants applying for citizenship to pledge their allegiance to the country as well as to English as a language. Similarly, the Immigration Act in 1917 required immigrants to take literacy tests and barred all immigrants from what was called the "Asiatic zone," a region encompassing much of the continent of Asia.

Over time, these types of laws regulating immigration, as well as expectations that newly arrived children and families from immigrant backgrounds show allegiance to the United States by learning English, became a foundation for educational policies related to citizenship education, the teaching of U.S. history, and expectations regarding English usage in schools. In effect, public schools were seen as one of the primary ways to socialize immigrants into the United States, and this socialization often carried an expectation that students abandon the cultures, languages, and sometimes the names they used in their home countries. Remnants of this belief system are visible in contemporary debates about the daily recital of the Pledge of Allegiance, divergent approaches to teaching about the history of racism and colonization in the United States, and local policies restricting the display of non-U.S. flags in public school classrooms.

## Legislation That Helped Codify Bilingual Education Programs in Schools

With the Civil Rights Movement of the 1960s came a deeper recognition of the implications of this cultural and linguistic erasure. Parents and educators began to advocate for policies that would enable students to develop language skills in both their home languages and in English and to gather data regarding the educational experiences of immigrant and emergent bilingual students. This advocacy resulted in landmark legislation that forced schools to begin to provide equal opportunities for students to learn through the development of new classroom strategies and approaches, including bilingual education.

Bilingual education involves the use of two languages for the purpose of instruction. In 1968, Congress passed the Bilingual Education Act (BEA), which established federal funding through grants for bilingual programs that supported students who were not yet proficient in English at the elementary and secondary school level. The purpose of the BEA—which was reauthorized in 1974, 1978, 1984, 1988, and 1994—was to provide school districts with grants to enact bilingual education as well as other, innovative approaches to supporting bilingual learners in the classroom. The BEA has resulted in a wide array of educational interventions, including dual-language programs, funding for state educational agencies, and professional development for teachers.

Following the BEA, there were a series of court cases that expanded educational offerings for immigrant and multilingual students. In 1974, the U.S. Supreme Court heard a landmark class action suit titled *Lau v. Nichols*. In this case, 1,800 Chinese students claimed that the San Francisco Board of Education failed to provide programs designed to meet the linguistic needs of non-English-speaking children. The failure, they claimed, was in violation of Title VI of the Civil Rights Act of 1964 and the Equal Protection Clause of the Fourteenth Amendment. The plaintiffs argued that if children could not understand the language used for instruction, they were deprived of an education equal to that of other children and were, in essence, doomed to failure. In a unanimous decision, the Supreme Court stated, "Under state-imposed standards, there was no equality of treatment merely by providing students with the same facilities, textbooks,

Parental advocacy has led to important advances in bilingual education policy.

**SOURCE:** Hyoung Chang/Gettyimages

teachers, and curriculum; for students who do not understand English are effectively foreclosed from any meaningful education" (*Lau v. Nichols*, 1974). With this decision, the Court did not mandate bilingual education for non-English-speaking or limited-English-speaking students. However, it did stipulate that special language programs were necessary if schools were to provide an equal educational opportunity for such students. Hence, the *Lau* decision gave considerable impetus to the development of bilingual education as well as English as a Second Language (ESL) programs in public schools in the United States.

Other legislative actions include the 1975 Education for All Handicapped Children Act (amended in 1990 as the Individuals with Disabilities Education Act), which required each state to avoid the use of racially or culturally discriminating testing and evaluation procedures in the placement of children with disabilities. It also required that placement tests be administered in the child's native language and required schools communicate legal matters in languages immigrant and English-learning parents can understand. In 1982, in *Plyer v. Doe*, another landmark court case, the Supreme Court ruled that states could not prevent students from attending schools based on their immigration status. The court ruled that denying a public education to children without documentation violated the Equal Protection Clause, which states that no state "shall deny to any person within its jurisdiction the equal protection of its laws."

Throughout the 1970s, the federal government and the state courts sought to shape the direction of bilingual education programs and mandate appropriate testing procedures for students with limited English proficiency. The *Lau* remedies were developed by the U.S. Office of Education to help schools implement bilingual education programs. However, controversy exists regarding the best or most effective approach to teaching emergent bilingual students in public schools, and especially the relative emphasis educators should place on students' development of biliteracy skills versus their use of English. These tensions were visible in the language of the No Child Left Behind Act of 2002, which renamed the Bilingual Education Act of 1968 as the "English Language Acquisition, Language Enhancement and Academic Achievement Act." As the name of the new act signals, this bill reflected an ideological focus on

English language acquisition, enhancement, and academic achievement as the primary goals of language education in schools.

Although the future level of federal involvement in bilingual education is uncertain and subject to political whimsy, there is little doubt among educators that students thrive when encouraged to develop both in their home language and also in English.

# Programs to Support Multilingual Learners

**Learning Objective 7.6** Describe the different programs in place in schools to support multilingual learners.

There is a wide array of academic programs in schools to support multilingual learners. Each of these programs has different educational goals; some focus on supporting children in building basic English skills as quickly as possible, while others prioritize students' development of biliteracy in English and their home languages. Deciding which approach is best for a given student or school context reflects a complex set of considerations, including the unique characteristics of language learners in a school or community, the types of resources available in a particular school district, and the availability of educators who have specialized training to run these academic programs in the ways that they were designed.

There are also ideological factors that impact multilingual education programs; people who value linguistic diversity are more likely to support programs that result in biliteracy, while those who prioritize assimilation are drawn to programs that emphasize the rapid or exclusive use of English. Research on divergent approaches to bilingual education suggests that no one approach is right for all contexts and that the efficacy of bilingual education depends on its implementation. Historically, some children in bilingual education programs have thrived, whereas others have fared poorly. The national shortage of qualified bilingual educators means that some students are in classrooms with teachers who do not speak their language, have little or no training in multilingual education, or happen to be bilingual but were not trained or certified as bilingual educators.

To better serve emergent bilingual students, most states now require all teachers to take coursework related to teaching ELs and offer specialized credentials—and sometimes financial incentives—for teachers who want to teach in dual-language or bilingual classrooms. This is because decades of research proves that well-developed and well-delivered bilingual education programming delivers positive results (Collier & Thomas, 2004; Fuchs, 2018; Rolstad et al., 2005).

## Dual-Language Immersion Programs

**Dual-language immersion (DLI)**, sometimes referred to as *two-way bilingual immersion*, programs are generally considered the gold standard in bilingual education. In these programs, which co-enroll English-proficient and English-learning students, all academic instruction is conducted in both English and a second language, with the goal of students achieving functional biliteracy in both languages. Students in dual-language programs typically enter the program in kindergarten and continue through elementary school; in recent years dual-language programs have expanded to include opportunities for secondary school students to take advanced coursework in both languages so that they are ready for multilingual college and career pathways.

Interest in and funding for dual-language programs has increased significantly in recent years; during the 2021–2022 academic year, there were more than 3,600 DLI programs across 44 states. Eighty percent of these programs are Spanish, but programs exist for speakers of 27 languages (American Councils for International Education, 2021). While approaches to DLI vary, in most cases, approximately half of students are English proficient and the other half are native speakers of another language; students then take some percentage of their coursework in each language. Many, but not all, DLI teachers are bilingual; however, in some cases DLI programs employ monolingual teachers who teach exclusively in English or the other language of instruction. In some DLI programs, students are expected to use only one language at a time (i.e., with part of the day devoted to each language), whereas in others, students are encouraged to use their full linguistic repertoire throughout the school day (i.e., by moving fluidly among languages within the context of a single academic interaction).

Unlike ESL programs, DLI programs are designed to simultaneously benefit English-dominant students, who become fluent in a second language, and speakers of languages other than English, who develop English fluency. Interest and enthusiasm for dual-language programs reflects not only research on their efficacy but also a desire to preserve students' native languages and the recognition that they provide academic enrichment and competitive advantages to participating students. Some school districts and some states now award a seal of biliteracy to students who achieve proficiency in two or more languages. This recognition can enhance students' college admissions and/or employment opportunities. Other important benefits of becoming bilingual or trilingual are being able to communicate more effectively with people in one's own community, as well as opportunities to navigate multilingual communities within and beyond the United States.

## Transitional Programs

In addition to dual-language programs, which emphasize biliteracy and functional bilingualism, there are approaches that focus on students' use of their native language as a scaffold as they learn new concepts, knowledge, and skills. Students then transition to academic instruction in English, gradually reducing their use of other languages in the classroom. This approach to bilingual education is called a **transitional program** and is the most common approach throughout the United States. Advocates argue that transitional programs provide an affirming and linguistically inclusive space for emergent bilingual students while also prioritizing their development of conversational and academic skills in English. Critics charge that this approach can be considered assimilationist in nature because the focus is on helping multilingual students learn to function effectively in English as soon as possible. Students' native language is used as a tool to help students learn English then is gradually phased out; in this way, bilingual proficiency is framed as less valuable than fluency in English.

Nevertheless, most bilingual educators strongly support the use of bicultural programs even within the transitional framework. By affirming the value of students' home cultures and languages, educators can help students develop or maintain a positive self-image as members of bilingual and bicultural communities.

## English as a Second Language Programs

**English as a Second Language (ESL)** programs are often confused with bilingual education. In the United States, learning English is an integral part of every bilingual program. But teaching English as a second language in and of itself does not constitute a bilingual program. Both bilingual education and ESL programs promote English proficiency for non-native English speakers. However, they are very different in their values and approach to instruction. Bilingual education embraces and leverages students' language and culture as part of the instructional process. Bilingual educators use students' native language as well as English as the medium of instruction.

ESL instruction, however, relies primarily or exclusively on English for teaching and learning. ESL programs are used extensively in the United States as a primary medium to assimilate emergent bilingual children into the linguistic mainstream as quickly as possible. Hence, some educators place less emphasis on the maintenance of home language and culture than on English language acquisition, and they view ESL programs as a viable means for achieving their goals.

Some ESL programs reflect policymakers' ideological goals related to the rapid or exclusive use of English in the classroom, while others emerge from educators' attempts to navigate local constrictions. In some school districts, there may be students from many different language backgrounds but too few speakers of each language to fill an entire class, or insufficient resources to hire teachers who speak each of the languages used by students. In such a situation, ESL may appear to be the most cost-effective approach for delivering services. However, this approach also carries risks. Students in classrooms where only English is emphasized may struggle because they have no main way to access new vocabulary without access to words in their home language. Students who do eventually learn English without continuing to learn and develop in their home language are at risk of losing the ability to converse in their home language with members of their families and communities; they also do not have opportunities to develop biliteracy regarding new academic content (such as the ability to discuss literature, biology, or calculus in their home languages). Some students in ESL pathways experience a sense of disconnection from their home cultures, histories, and communities as they face pressure to primarily develop their skills in English. In effect, rather than becoming functionally bilingual, in the process of gaining one language, students lose another.

# Bias and Discrimination Against Multilingual Learners

**Learning Objective 7.7** Describe the impact of bias and discrimination against multilingual learners.

Linguistic bias affects a wide array of students, including multilingual learners and students who speak diverse varieties of English; as with other forms of bias, students from historically marginalized communities are disproportionately impacted by discriminatory practices. This bias can take many forms, including a deficit-minded approach exhibited by teachers who do not value students' home languages, do not believe that multilingual learners will ever become proficient in English, or equate English proficiency with intelligence.

This bias against multilingual learners on the part of teachers can be rooted in many things, from messages they received in childhood about immigrants or the importance of using Standard English to media representations that portray multilingual people in a negative light. It can also be rooted in negative experiences a teacher might have had in previous interactions with multilingual learners and the attendant negative beliefs the teacher holds in later interactions with members of a newcomer group.

Sometimes teachers are conscious of their beliefs about language learners, while other times unconscious bias shapes their interactions with people who speak differently than they do. Additionally, being multilingual themselves does not preclude a teacher from biased attitudes and behaviors; some multilingual teachers have biases against students who speak languages other than their own or have internalized anti-immigrant attitudes that affect their approach to working with culturally and linguistically diverse students. These beliefs may then lead to a lack of support for bilingual education, a privileging of English over students' home languages, or an overemphasis on grammatical features of Standard English.

As with other forms of bias, teachers' beliefs about language learners invariably shape their work in the classroom. Sometimes teachers are unaware of the impact of their instructional decisions or do not realize that they are not providing emergent bilingual students the same opportunities to learn in class as their peers. They might not call on multilingual learners as often in class; structure classroom discussions in ways that are inaccessible to students who are not yet fluent in English; or fail to provide opportunities for students to leverage their full linguistic repertoires when completing class assignments. Some teachers mete out disciplinary actions for students who speak English as an additional language at a much higher rate than students who are native English speakers. Others use punitive grading systems that block paths toward advanced classes in schools for multilingual learners; track emergent bilingual students into less academically rigorous pathways; or refuse to advocate for multilingual students who are inappropriately placed in remedial classes. It is important for teachers to look carefully at the academic experience and achievement of linguistically diverse students in their school sites and ensure that they are not inadvertently perpetuating oppressive practices.

## Official English (English Only) Controversy

In addition to biased beliefs or actions on the part of individual teachers who are unprepared to be effective teachers of multilingual learners, there are also ideological tensions that have dramatically impacted multilingual students' experiences in public school settings. Among these is the attempted, and sometimes successful, passage of English Only policies at the local and state level. Historically, these movements have emerged not from debate among educators and educational scholars about the best approaches to teaching multilingual learners but from political groups with a history of anti-immigrant sentiment.

One such policy was introduced in 1981 by U.S. senator S. I. Hayakawa, a harsh critic of bilingual education and bilingual voting rights. Hayakawa introduced a constitutional amendment to make English the official language of the United States and prohibit federal and state laws, ordinances, regulations, orders, programs, and policies from requiring the use of other languages. Thus, Hayakawa's efforts were made not only in support of English but also against bilingualism. Had the amendment been adopted, Hayakawa's proposal would have reversed the efforts that began in the 1960s to accommodate linguistic minorities in the United States. The English Language Amendment died without a hearing in the 97th Congress.

In 1983 Hayakawa helped found the organization U.S. English and began lobbying efforts that resulted in a reported 2-million-member organization and an annual budget in the millions of dollars (U.S. English, 2016). This movement, also referred to as the **Official English** or **English Only movement**, supports only the limited use of bilingual education and has mounted an effort to make English the official language of the United States. Some states have adopted laws making English the official language, and three states, including Hawaii, South Dakota, and Alaska, have given official status to non-English languages. To date, English has been adopted in the form of statutes and state constitutional amendments in 32 states (U.S. English, 2016). As recently as March 2023, Ohio senator J. D. Vance introduced a bill seeking to adopt English as the official language within the United States, require all government functions to be conducted in English, and reinstate an English language test for anyone applying for U.S. citizenship (Gans, 2023).

Official English as a proposed legislative policy has become a polarizing issue. For supporters of the English Only movement, English has always been the common language in the United States and a means to become more fully a part of the U.S. society. Supporters of the English Only movement believe that it is a means to resolve conflict in a nation that is diverse in racial, ethnic, linguistic, and religious groups. They also believe that English is an essential tool for social mobility and economic advancement. By contrast, opponents argue that attempts to restrict the use of languages other than English are never only about the language itself but, rather, represent negative bias and discrimination toward the cultures, histories, and home communities of speakers of other languages. They see English Only policies as a form of cultural and linguistic genocide and part of a broader effort to erase the cultures and languages of diverse peoples within the United States.

## Efforts to Dismantle Bilingual Education

One of the outcomes of the English Only movement have been repeated attempts to dismantle bilingual education. Advocates of English Only favor **sheltered English immersion**, or programs where nearly all instruction is in English but there are some curricular and pedagogical supports for language learners, rather than DLI or transitional bilingual education. Most models allow students to be in a sheltered English immersion classroom for a maximum of 2 years; after that, students must be transitioned completely out of bilingual education and into mainstream English usage, irrespective of their level of English proficiency. In essence, these are "sink-or-swim" models, where emergent bilingual students either learn English within a set period of time or fail academically.

English Only advocates met success in 1998, when California voters passed Proposition 227, which required all language-minority students to be educated in sheltered English immersion programs, not normally intended to exceed 1 year. Two years later, in 2000, Arizona voted into law Proposition 203. This law required English-only instruction in the public schools. School districts then began to change the design of their programs for emergent bilingual to English-only instruction. In 2002, Massachusetts voted into law Chapter 386, which mandated sheltered English immersion programs as the method of instruction for emergent bilingual students. This effectively ended transitional bilingual education in the state, and other states across the country began to follow suit.

Research indicates that these efforts were not effective at eliminating gaps between the academic performance of emergent bilingual students and native speakers of English and, in 2016, California voters passed Proposition 58, a statewide referendum that essentially overturned Proposition 227 and returned bilingual education to the state. Similar repeals took place in Massachusetts. Legislative support for bilingual educational programs has both been passed into law by voters in some states and effectively dismantled in other states over time. The impacts of this lack of coherency in programming has resulted in inconsistent programming, curriculum development, and professional development for teachers in bilingual education over time. In effect, ELs and emergent bilingual students have been caught in the crosshairs of warring political movements, as people on both sides of the debate fight for policies that reflect their ideological beliefs about language, culture, and bilingual education.

It is important to note that opponents of the English Only movement readily agree on the importance of learning English. However, they view their adversaries as individuals trying to force conformity by ending essential services in languages other than English. They view the attacks on bilingual education as unjustified because good bilingual education has been shown to be effective. Opponents of bilingual education, they argue, have seen to it that these programs fail by giving inadequate support or resources, by staffing programs with unqualified personnel, by obtaining faulty test results on bilingual education students, by testing all students in English, and by using other means that cast a negative light on bilingual education.

Nevertheless, in spite of their ideological differences, the overwhelming majority of educators are invested in improving academic experiences and outcomes among linguistically diverse students. Their belief systems lead them to different approaches to this critically important work, and sometimes prevent them from learning from perspectives different than their own. Educators and community members must continue to evaluate the most effective approaches in their own local context and then put systems in place that enable culturally and linguistically diverse students to thrive.

# Preparing to Teach in Linguistically Diverse Classrooms

**Learning Objective 7.8** Evaluate strategies teachers can use to effectively work with multilingual learners.

While some teachers will choose to pursue specialized training in multilingual education, virtually all teachers will teach in linguistically diverse classrooms. A first step in preparing to be an effective teacher of culturally and linguistically diverse students is to closely examine one's own beliefs and ideologies about language learning. Instead of looking at linguistically diverse students through a deficit-lens that centers on what students do not know (i.e., English), effective multicultural educators spend time getting to know what students *do* know, learning about their interests and passions, their educational experiences in their home countries, and what subjects they have previously taken in their country of origin. It may, for example, be the case that students have deep and extended experiences in writing in its many forms, but just in another language. Teachers can acknowledge these strengths and experiences as they develop lessons and learning experiences for students in their classes. When teaching about environmental issues, for example, teachers might ask students to interview family members (in any language) about the types of environmental issues that impact people in places they have lived; students can then share what they learned with their peers and identify common themes across diverse regions of the world. In addition to creating an opportunity for students to share their learning with, and learn from, their families, activities like these help all students deepen their understanding of real-world implications of academic content. When teachers remove linguistic barriers, multilingual students can use their cultural knowledge and linguistic assets as resources that benefit themselves and their peers.

There are many small but impactful steps teachers can take to dramatically improve the experience of linguistically diverse students. Teachers can survey students and family members about the languages they speak. They can build multilingual classroom libraries that include resources that are accessible to all students and use free web-based translation services to support oral and written communication with families. Some apps, such as Google Translate, can translate handwritten student work to and from English using the camera function on a smartphone. Teachers can differentiate instruction by providing glossaries and sentence frames for students who need support communicating their ideas in English. Similarly, activities like pre-teaching key vocabulary, modeling reading strategies, and explicitly inviting students to make connections between new concepts and prior learning take very little additional work on the part of teachers but significantly improve students' classroom experiences.

Most teachers begin new instructional units by previewing key vocabulary; teachers can increase accessibility by translating important words and inviting students to explain terms in other languages or varieties of English. Some teachers create—or co-create with students—multilingual "word walls" that provide translations and student-authored definitions of unit vocabulary for students to refer to when in conversation with peers as well as while reading and writing in class. Students can be encouraged to annotate and explain texts using their full linguistic repertoire, to meet in language-alike groups to discuss key concepts, and to write informal summaries about what they are learning.

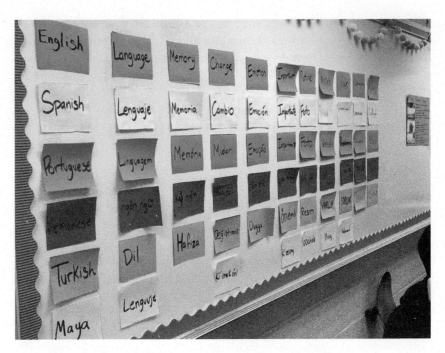

A multilingual word wall created by students and teachers in a Southern California classroom.
**SOURCE:** Alison Dover

Approaches like these reflect a **heteroglossic ideology**, or belief in the value of linguistic diversity and multilingualism. Unlike teachers with a **monoglossic ideology**, who believe that monolingualism is and should be the norm, teachers with a heteroglossic ideology acknowledge the linguistic diversity of the United States and embrace students' linguistic identities. They build in opportunities for students to use their full linguistic repertoire as they reflect on learning in class, ask each other questions and engage in dialogue about what they are learning, and communicate what they know in both small-group and whole-class settings. Activities like these benefit all students, as they are challenged to strategically use and stretch their communicative skills within and beyond the classroom.

All teachers have the capacity to be effective teachers of linguistically diverse students; teachers do not have to be multilingual themselves in order to engage, affirm, and support academic achievement among their students. By adopting an asset-based approach to linguistic diversity and thinking creatively about how to differentiate instruction for their unique students, teachers can prepare all students to succeed within and beyond the classroom.

# Explore and Focus Your Cultural Lens

## Debate: The Use of Standard Academic English in the Classroom

When emergent bilinguals enter a classroom, teachers have many choices to make in terms of curriculum, instruction, and what to focus on for regarding students' English language development. Some teachers may choose to prioritize the development of students' academic language skills in standard academic English. These teachers argue that while emergent bilingual students may use informal English in social settings, they are not prepared for the language demands of academic settings, especially in disciplinary

areas such as U.S. history. Teachers with this perspective focus on teaching students the vocabulary and specialized technical language used in different disciplinary areas. These teachers often require students to communicate exclusively in English and evaluate students' written and oral performance based on their use of English vocabulary and standard grammatical structures.

Other teachers challenge the overemphasis on standard academic English as the primary or privileged mode of instruction in schools. They believe that students, and especially multilingual students and students who speak alternate varieties of English (such as Black English or AAL), should be encouraged to use their full, authentic linguistic repertoire when communicating about academic concepts. These teachers believe that it is more important for students to understand and have mastery of the content rather than communicate using standard academic English, and often create opportunities for students to submit assignments in multiple languages and varieties of English.

As teachers work with students who are learning English as an additional language, they need to consider the ways in which they might be focusing their efforts. Should teachers require students to use standard academic English in the classroom as a way to make sure students can access disciplinary content and communicate effectively in school settings? Or is this approach an example of linguistic bias that penalizes multilingual learners and speakers of nondominant varieties of English?

### FOR

- Teachers need to focus their efforts on teaching multilingual learners in their classrooms standard academic English so that the students will continue to learn content knowledge in specific disciplines (such as social studies).

- If teachers do not focus their work in class on standard academic English, students will be less likely to access disciplinary knowledge (such as social studies topics) and content along with their peers in class. They will then fall further behind their age-group peers in content knowledge, and this will disproportionately impact them as they enter high school and eventually go on to higher education.

- By focusing on standard academic English, teachers will provide students a greater intellectual challenge than focusing efforts on basic interpersonal communication skills.

- Students will rise to this academic challenge and seek to develop in ways that allow them to stay in classes with their age-group peers rather than stay in more remedial content-area classes.

- Allowing students to submit work in languages other than English makes it difficult to assess their work; teachers cannot be expected to evaluate work submitted in languages other than English.

### AGAINST

- Teachers who emphasize the use of standard academic English implicitly suggest that English fluency is more important than multilingualism, thus privileging monolingual speakers of English over multilingual learners.

- Multilingual students may feel silenced or disregarded by teachers who do not value or encourage them to use their full linguistic repertoire; they may also struggle to find ways to communicate their academic knowledge when they are forbidden to use their other languages in the classroom.

- Multilingual students have the potential to be fully biliterate and gain significant economic and professional success. By preventing them from using their full linguistic repertoire when discussing advanced academic concepts, teachers undermine their future success.

- It shouldn't be students' responsibility to translate their work for teachers; instead, it is the responsibility of educators and school systems to use technology and other supports to communicate with and assess work created by multilingual students.

- Creating linguistically affirming classrooms offers opportunities for all students, including monolingual speakers of English, to develop the skills necessary to thrive in a multilingual, global society.

## Questions for Discussion

1. Put yourself in the place of an emergent bilingual student. What types of approaches to teaching English might be most helpful to you?

2. Think back to the teachers you had while in school. In their work with emergent bilingual students and native speakers of English, what approaches did they take in teaching both informal English and academic English in their classrooms?

3. What types of linguistic bias have you seen in schools? How might you work to address those forms of bias in support of emergent bilingual students and other students in schools?

4. How can teachers differentiate instruction in order to engage, support, and assess students who are not fluent in English? What new ideas might you bring to this work based on the new ideas you learned in this chapter?

# Revisiting the Opening Case Study

As Angelica Rivera started the new school year, she was surprised and a bit intimidated by the linguistic diversity of her students. However, as she prepared to meet her classes for the first time, she took a deep breath and reflected on what her credential program taught her about working with emergent bilingual students. Angelica began to apply those concepts as she developed her first few days of lessons. She also reached out to more experienced teachers in her school building, including teachers in her department, teachers who worked with English learners, and paraprofessionals assigned to students in her classroom. Angelica asked them about the strategies that were already in use at the school and that seemed to be successful in their implementation. She learned that experienced teachers at her school met regularly with paraprofessionals in their classes

*(continued)*

to share information about how students were progressing, to learn about students' questions regarding instructional topics, and to make plans for the following class period. She realized that teamwork was essential in meeting the needs of her students and built time for collaboration into her own daily schedule.

Finally, Angelica made efforts from the very first day of classes to create a warm, welcoming, and caring learning environment in her classroom where students were encouraged to grow, make mistakes, and learn together and worked hard to build rapport with each of her students, including those who happened to be emergent bilingual students. She shared her own experiences as a multilingual learner and invited students to teach her about their own languages. As the weeks wore on Angelica began to realize how much more she had to learn as a classroom teacher, but also to appreciate the assets she gained from her previous coursework, through her colleagues in her schools, and the tremendous students she had the privilege of being assigned to work with that first term.

## Reflect and Apply

1. Identify teachers you had while in school who were clearly committed to working with and supporting linguistically diverse students. How did those teachers implicitly and explicitly communicate their commitment to inclusion?

2. What specific teaching strategies did they use in their everyday work? What specific relationship-building strategies did they employ?

3. What are some ways you yourself need to grow and develop during your teacher credential program to prepare yourself to support and connect with linguistically diverse students? What are some previous experiences, strengths, and commitments will you bring personally from your own life and background to this work as a future teacher?

## Summary

- While the United States has historically been Eurocentric educationally and linguistically, it has become increasingly linguistically diverse in recent years. Approximately 20% of U.S. residents speak a language other than English at home, and numerous languages, dialects, and accents are spoken by students in our schools. English is the dominant language in the United States; however, no one language, or variety of language, is inherently better or worse than any other. All languages serve the purpose of meeting the linguistic needs of those who use them and, in that sense, are equal.

- Language is both a means of communication and an expression of individual and group identity. In addition to oral and written communication, people express themselves nonverbally through their attitude, personality, manner, gestures, and proximity. Educators should be cognizant of cultural differences in verbal and nonverbal communication, being aware that typical nonverbal behaviors and gestures in the United States may have very different and even opposite meanings to other cultural groups, even to some who are English speaking.

- Language is a system of both vocal sounds and nonverbal systems by which members of various groups communicate with one another. Monolingual people typically use only sounds, gestures, and symbols from a single named language, while multilingual people utilize sounds, gestures, and symbols associated with multiple named languages. Being multilingual is an asset because it enables people to communicate effectively in culturally and linguistically diverse settings.

- There are currently more than 5.1 million designated English learners (ELs) in U.S. schools, with the vast majority Spanish speaking, followed distantly by those speaking Arabic and Asian or Pacific languages. Students who are designated as ELs are far from an academically monolithic group and enter with different levels of experiences with formal school, opportunities to learn English, and different sociopolitical reasons and contexts for moving to the United States. It is important for teachers to get to know the personal, cultural, linguistic, and academic experiences of their students as part of their efforts to promote student engagement and achievement.

- Federal laws require educators to provide for the linguistic needs of diverse students. There are many different approaches to supporting multilingual learners in schools, including bilingual immersion, transitional, and English as a Second Language programs. Historically, policies regarding language education have been shaped by both political ideologies and educational research as well as the advocacy of parents and community members.

- Linguistic bias affects a wide array of students, including multilingual learners and students who speak diverse varieties of English; as with other forms of bias, students from historically marginalized communities are disproportionately impacted by discriminatory practices. It is important for teachers to look carefully at the academic experience and achievement of linguistically diverse students in their school sites and ensure that they are not inadvertently perpetuating oppressive practices.

- Teachers have multiple and varied ways to support multilingual learners in schools. Effective ways of supporting multilingual learners include taking an expansive and inclusive perspective on the importance of learning multiple languages; having an assets-based orientation toward the languages, cultures, and contributions of multilingual learners; and using curricular and pedagogical supports to support students in communicating their thinking within and beyond the classroom.

## Pearson eTextbook Application Videos

The following videos are available in the Pearson eTextbook and can be used to practice observing and applying what you learned in this chapter.

**Pearson eTextbook Application**

**Video Example 7.3**

In this video, an educator discusses the importance of focusing on academic language. Pay attention to how this focus can enhance the classroom environment.

**Pearson eTextbook Application**

**Video Example 7.4**

In this video, an educator discusses the diversity within her group of students classified as English language learners. Pay attention to these differences.

# Chapter 8
# Religion

 **Learning Objectives**

*As you read this chapter, you should be able to:*

**8.1** Describe the religious diversity of regions of the United States and the U.S. Congress.

**8.2** Characterize the importance of religion and the role of religious freedom in U.S. society.

**8.3** Summarize the major religions in the United States and the changes in religious diversity over the past several decades.

**8.4** Analyze the intersection of religion with gender, LGBTQ+, and racial and ethnic identities.

**8.5** Interpret legal rulings on religion in schools and their implications for school prayer, school vouchers, book banning, and teaching religion.

## Opening Case Study

The teachers and administrators of Daniel Inouye Middle School near San Francisco had put the finishing touches on their plans for the school's honors assembly. They had selected Ramakrishna Patel and Rebecca Rose, who were tied with the highest grades in the eighth grade, to be recognized in a special assembly. Each student was asked to make a 7- to 10-minute speech on the value of education. Because the faculty and Dr. Hovestadt, the principal, wanted the district superintendent to be part of the ceremony, they had agreed to schedule the event at 11:00 a.m. on the fourth Saturday in May, the superintendent's only available time.

Dr. Hovestadt called the Patel and Rose families to inform them of their children's selection as convocation speakers. As expected, both sets of parents were delighted at the news of their son's and daughter's accomplishments and selection. Mr. Rose indicated, however, that Saturday was not possible because it was the Sabbath for their family, who were Orthodox Jews. The Sabbath, a day of religious observance and rest among Jewish people, is from sundown on Friday until sundown on Saturday. Orthodox Jews are a conservative branch of Judaism who strictly observe religious law. Mr. Rose asked that the event

be rescheduled for any other day but the Sabbath so that their daughter could participate. However, Dr. Hovestadt knew no alternative dates were available if the district superintendent was going to be part of the ceremony. "Would you plan the event on a Sunday when you know many of the parents may be attending church?" Mr. Rose asked. "It does not seem right then to schedule it on our Sabbath." Dr. Hovestadt knew the school had to come up with an alternative plan.

### Reflect

1. Why do you think Dr. Hovestadt had not considered that some of the Jewish students in the school would not be able to attend an honors assembly on Saturday?

2. What religious group(s) in most U.S. schools is/are most likely to be privileged in that their religion is reflected in the curriculum, school events, and the dates on which graduations and other special events are scheduled?

3. What would you do to handle the situation that Dr. Hovestadt faces?

# Religious Diversity in the United States

**Learning Objective 8.1** Describe the religious diversity of regions of the United States and the U.S. Congress.

One of the major reasons large numbers of Europeans began to settle in the United States in the seventeenth and eighteenth centuries was to escape religious persecution in their home countries and to practice the religion of their choice. (However, as we discuss later in this chapter, those early settlers paradoxically often forced Native Americans and new immigrants to adopt their Christian religion.) Immigrants during that period were primarily from northern and western Europe and brought with them their families' variations of Protestantism. The Native Americans on whose lands the Europeans were colonizing practiced their own tribal religions. Catholics did not begin to arrive in large numbers until the middle of the nineteenth century, but they quickly felt the domination of Protestants in their daily lives, including their children's schools. Gradually, people from other parts of the world immigrated to the United States, bringing with them new religions or new versions of traditional U.S. religions.

Although freedom of religion was important at the founding of the United States, many people who are not Christian feel that their religions are ignored and/or not respected by many U.S. citizens and institutions. In this section, we examine the degree of religious diversity in different regions of the country and in the U.S. Congress.

## Religious Diversity in U.S. Schools

The religious pluralism of schools is determined, in part, by the school's geographic region. Immigration and migration patterns result in different ethnic and religious groups settling in different parts of the country. The perspectives of the religious community often influence what families expect from the school. If the religious values of the families are incongruent with the objectives of a school, serious challenges for educators are likely. A look at the religious diversity of schools in various sections of the country can provide a sense of the diversity to be found in the nation's schools.

As one visits schools across the United States, distinctive patterns are apparent. In some regions, schools are greatly influenced by religious groups in the community. In these communities, the members of the school board, the appointment of the school administrative leadership, and the curriculum may be shaped by the dominant religious groups. In other regions, religion may have little if any influence on the nature of the schools. Consider these examples:

- A rural high school in the South may be composed primarily of students from Conservative Protestant backgrounds such as Southern Baptist and the Church of Christ. Some students may be members of United Methodist or other less conservative churches. In such a district, local churches serve as the primary social institution for many students. The curriculum and textbooks may be carefully scrutinized by the school board for what it considers objectionable subject matter, such as sex education, evolution, and gender and sexual identity.

- In Ohio, Indiana, Pennsylvania, or Iowa, a visitor may find some students from Amish or Mennonite families. Amish students can be identified by their distinctive attire, and students from Mennonite groups also dress conservatively. Amish students remain in school until they complete eighth grade. In accordance with their beliefs, they then leave school and work on their family farm, which uses neither electricity nor motorized equipment. They often travel in horse-drawn buggies. Most Mennonite students complete high school, and some will attend higher education and face no prohibitions against the use of electricity or motorized vehicles.

Educators will continue to see increasing numbers of students from diverse religious groups in their classrooms, reflecting the growing religious diversity of the United States.

SOURCE: © Ground Picture/Shutterstock

- In Utah and some communities in Idaho, a visitor to the public schools may find that most students are members of the Church of Jesus Christ of Latter-day Saints (LDS), also known as the Mormon church. Although Mormonism is not taught in public schools, church values are reflected in everyday school activities. In many of the predominantly LDS communities, students in secondary schools are given release time from school to attend seminaries, which are adjacent or in close proximity to their public schools. The seminaries provide religious training by instructors employed by the LDS church. Upon completion of high school, many of the LDS young men and a few young women serve for 2 years on church missions.

- In many large metropolitan areas, one encounters a wide range of religious backgrounds. Some students are Presbyterians, Roman Catholic, Baptists, and Jewish, while others are Muslim, Hindu, and Buddhist. A few are atheists, and some are agnostics. **Atheists** believe that there is no God, while **agnostics** argue that the fact that God or gods exist cannot be known. While religion may be important to some students and their families, it does not heavily influence the curriculum or daily life in the schools in this community.

These examples suggest that communities in the United States are religiously very diverse and that the religious makeup of some communities may be influential in the overall culture of the schools. Like other institutions in the United States, most schools have a historical legacy of White Protestant domination. Such influence has determined the holidays, usually Christian holidays such as Christmas and Easter, observed by most public schools. Moreover, the dominant Protestant groups have determined many of the moral teachings that have been integrated into the public schools.

## Religious Diversity in the U.S. Congress

The political leadership in the United States reflects the influence of various religious groups. Nearly all members of Congress indicate a specific religious affiliation; only one identifies as religiously unaffiliated and 20 as "Don't Know/Refused" (Diamant, 2023). Over the past decade, the share of the U.S. population that identifies as Christian has dropped, and people who report no religious affiliation has increased. However, Congress remains overwhelmingly Christian (88%). When the 118th Congress assumed office in January 2023, as in the past, members who were Protestant held the majority of seats with 57%, as shown in Figure 8.1, with the largest percentages being Baptist (12.5%), Methodist (5.8%), Presbyterian (4.7%), Anglican/Episcopalian (4.1%), and Lutheran (4.1%); 20% of the Protestant members did not identify a specific denomination. Other Protestant denominations represented in Congress included Congregationalist, Pentecostal, Restorationist, Adventist, Reformed, Pietist, Nondenominational, Orthodox Christian, and Unitarian Universalist (Diamant, 2023). Catholics are the second largest group (28%) in Congress, followed by Jewish members (6%). Seven members of Congress are Buddhist, Muslim, or Hindu, shown in Figure 8.1 as "non-Christian or Jewish."

While the American electorate has sent significant numbers of Jewish individuals and smaller numbers of Muslims and Buddhists to Congress, religious affiliation continues to be an issue in elections for public office. In 1928, Alfred Smith, a Democratic presidential candidate who was Catholic, lost in a landslide. Many Protestants were fearful that Smith would be strongly influenced by the Vatican. When John F. Kennedy became the Democratic presidential candidate in 1960, some of the same concerns were echoed regarding his Catholic faith. Kennedy was able to overcome these concerns,

**Figure 8.1** Religious Affiliation of Congress Compared to U.S. Population, 2023

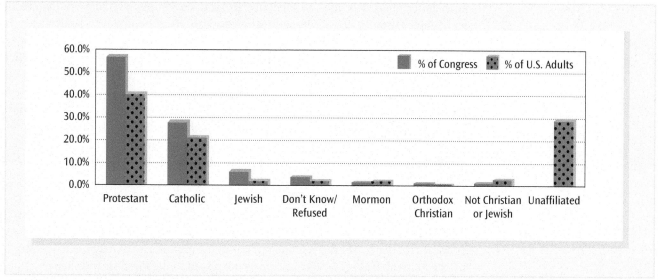

SOURCE: Based on data in Diamant (2023).

and the rest became part of U.S. history. In 2012, Mitt Romney became the Republican Party's presidential candidate, and his affiliation with the Church of Jesus Christ of Latter-day Saints (LDS or Mormon) became an issue among some of the electorate. While Romney lost the election, he won 79% of the Evangelical Christian support, even more than the 73% that Senator John McCain had won in the 2008 election (Ekstrom, 2012). Donald J. Trump won the 2016 presidential election with 77% of Evangelical support and had 84% of their support in the 2020 election when he lost to Joe Biden.

In 2012, Mazie Hirono (HI) was elected as the first Buddhist member of the Senate; a second Buddhist member of Congress in 2023 was Representative Hank Johnson (GA). In 2023, the House also included two Muslim women who had been elected in three consecutive terms: Rashida Tlaib (MI), a Palestinian American, and Ilhan Omar (MN), a Somali refugee who had lived in a camp in Kenya. The third Muslim in the House is André Carson (IN), who was first elected to the House in 2008. The two Hindus who were recently reelected to the House are Ro Khanna (CA) and Raja Krishnamoorthi (IL). The percentage of Buddhist, Muslim, and Hindu representatives in Congress is nearly equal to their representation in the U.S. population. This increasing diversity in Congress reflects the increasing diversity of the country, even though Protestants are still represented at a far higher level than their representation in the U.S. population, as shown in Figure 8.1. Although the United States is not yet free from religious bias, the religious landscape in Congress is slowly changing.

# The Importance of Religion and Religious Freedoms in the United States

**Learning Objective 8.2** Characterize the importance of religion and the role of religious freedom in U.S. society.

For as long as humans have existed, evidence suggests that they have had religious beliefs of some kind, but agreeing on the meaning of religion differs across cultures, academic disciplines, and religious groups themselves (McCutcheon, 2018). Essentially, **religion** involves an inner core of belief in and worship of a superhuman power or powers such as a God or gods who is/are believed to be divine or have control of

Pearson eTextbook
**Video Example 8.1**

In this video, consider the ways in which religious freedom has changed in the history of the United States.

https://www.youtube.com/
watch?v=8goflrYy5T4

human destiny. Some people will say they are **spiritual**, not religious; they focus on their inner faith but generally are not engaged with an institution associated with religion such as churches, mosques, synagogues, or temples. People who identify themselves as religious usually attend worship services with other people who share the same religious beliefs and practices.

Children learn their religion from their families, neighbors, and religious teachers and leaders. The symbols and sacred objects used in worship services "communicate ideological messages concerning the nature of the individual, society, and cosmos" (Bowie, 2018, p. 19). The **rituals** of religious groups are "fundamental to human culture, and can be used to control, subvert, stabilize, enhance, or terrorize individuals and groups" (Bowie, 2018, p. 19). Religion can have a great impact not only on the beliefs and morals of its adherents but also on their attitudes, behaviors, ethics, worldviews, and political views.

Many religions are particularistic, in that members believe that their own religion is uniquely true and legitimate and that all others are invalid. Other religious groups accept the validity of distinct religions that have grown out of different historical and cultural experiences. In this section, we look at the importance of religion in Americans' lives and the role of religious freedom as expressed in the First Amendment.

## Religion in the Lives of the U.S. Population

The United States can be considered a religious country, especially as compared to many countries in Europe. However, there have been changes in what Americans believe or a greater division in their beliefs in the past few decades. Seventy-two percent of Americans said that religion was very or fairly important to them in 2023 (Gallup, 2023), and 81% indicated in 2022 that they believed in God or a universal spirit (Saad & Hrynowski, 2022). A slight majority of Americans (53%) believed that religion can answer most of today's problems, but this number has been on a decline since 2000, when 65% held this belief (Gallup, 2023). In the United States, 20% of adults indicated that they attended a religious service weekly in 2022, while another 10% indicated that their attendance was almost weekly; this number reflects a decline from 2000, when 32% reported weekly attendance (Gallup, 2023). In 2022, 31% indicated that they never attend religious services (Gallup, 2023).

Fifty-nine percent of Americans were satisfied with the influence of organized religion in 2020, whereas 5% wanted more influence and 27% wanted less (Gallup, 2023). In 2022, 75% of Americans felt that religion was losing its influence on American life; only 22% believed that influence was increasing (Gallup, 2023). Conservative Christians have long maintained that the **Bible** is the literal word of God and is inerrant. In 1980, 40% of Americans held this view, while another 45% said that the Bible was inspired by the words of God. By 2022, only 20% believed in the Bible literally, while the percentage of those believing it to be inspired by God was 49% (Gallup, 2023).

## The First Amendment

The First Amendment clearly states that Congress is prohibited from making laws establishing a religion or prohibiting religious worship. This has been consistently interpreted by the courts as affirming the principle of separation of church and state. One of the most valued parts of the U.S. Constitution, this provision is also one of the most controversial. Throughout the country's history, some individuals and groups have sought to interpret this amendment to meet their own needs and interests. For some, religious emphasis is appropriate in the public schools as long as it is congruent with their own religious persuasion. These same individuals, however, may be quick to cite the constitutional safeguards for separation of church and state if other groups attempt to infuse their religious dogmas into school and society. Equity and propriety are often in the eye of the beholder, and one's religious orientation may strongly influence one's perception of what constitutes objectivity, fairness, and legality.

Nationally, adherence to the principle of separation of church and state has been schizophrenic at best. Oaths are typically made on Bibles and often end with the phrase "so help me God." U.S. coins and currency include the words "In God We Trust." The military and Congress have chaplains, and politicians attend congressional prayer breakfasts. The Pledge of Allegiance includes the words "under God." These references have been interpreted by some people to mean that the separation of church and state simply means that there will be no state church.

Complete separation of church and state, as defined by strict constitutionalists, would have a profound effect on social–religious life. It is likely that the American public wants some degree of separation of these two institutions, but it is equally likely that some would be outraged if total separation were imposed. Total separation would mean no direct or indirect aid to religious groups, no tax-free status, no tax deductions for contributions to religious groups, no national Christmas tree, no government-paid chaplains, no religious holidays, no **blue laws**, and so on.

# Major Religions in the United States

**Learning Objective 8.3** Summarize the major religions in the United States and the changes in religious diversity over the past several decades.

The religious diversity of the U.S. adult population in 2022 is shown in Figure 8.2. Until early in the twentieth century, Protestantism was by far the dominant religious force in the country. Protestants are still dominant, but they are no longer the majority of the population, with 42.4% of U.S. residents identifying themselves as Protestant or other Christians, 23.1% as Catholic, 1.5% as Mormon, 1.9% as Jewish, and 0.6% as Muslim (PRRI, 2023). People who did not respond to polling or indicated no religious identity represented 26.8% of the population. Although Judaism has decreased numerically and as a percentage of the U.S. population, it is still routinely listed as one of the five major religious groups in the world along with Christianity, Islam, Hinduism, and Buddhism.

One of the variables contributing to the changing religious landscape of the United States is the demographic characteristics of the newest immigrants granted permanent residency. Over the past two decades, approximately 1 million people immigrated to the United States each year. The geographic origins of these immigrants have been shifting from Europe and the Americas to Asia, Sub-Saharan Africa, the Middle East, and North Africa. These shifts have been accompanied by the religious diversity of the new residents.

While some people may assume that most Asian Americans adhere to Asian-based religions, such as Buddhism, they are often surprised to learn that as many as 34% are reported to be Christian (Chen & Ho, 2023). Some Black Americans have left traditional Black Protestant churches and converted to Islam. Tens of thousands of Latino/as have left the Roman Catholic Church for Pentecostal churches, and some college students from diverse backgrounds have embraced Buddhism.

In the East San Gabriel Valley of Los Angeles County, the Hsi Lai Temple, the largest Buddhist temple in the Western Hemisphere, is located in Hacienda Heights, California. In 2013, a new Islamic center was built in the adjacent community of Rowland Heights. A Korean Southern Baptist church is located just over a mile away in the city of Walnut, and a Sikh temple is also located in Walnut, a mile away. A Hindu temple was completed in 2012 in the nearby community of Chino Hills. These are but a few examples of how America's immigrants have changed not only the ethnic landscape of the country but the religious landscape as well.

**Figure 8.2** Religious Diversity of the Adult U.S. Population, 2022

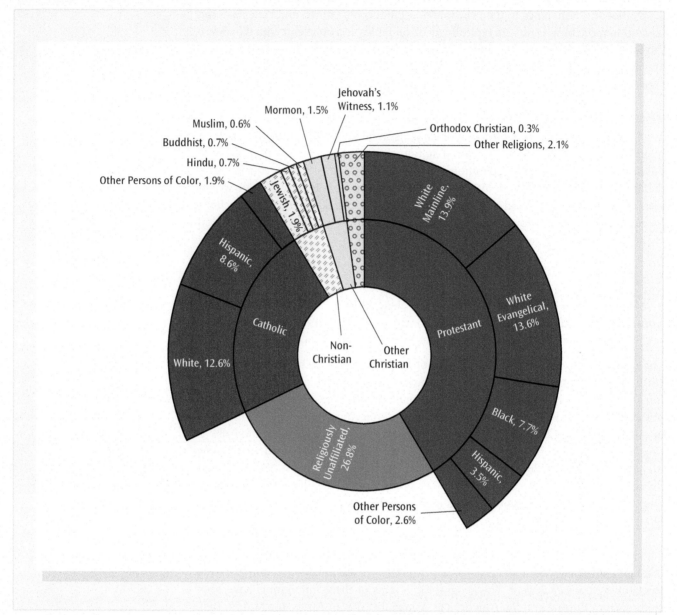

SOURCE: Based on data in PRRI (2023).

Some denominational differences have their origins in ethnic differences. The English established the Anglican (Episcopalian) and Puritan (later Congregational) churches; Germans established some of the Lutheran, Anabaptist, and Evangelical churches; the Dutch, Reformed churches; the Spanish, French, Italians, Poles, and others, Roman Catholic churches; and the Ukrainians, Armenians, Greeks, and others, Eastern Orthodox churches. Over time, many of these ethnic denominations united or expanded their membership to include other ethnic groups (Fisher & Rinehart, 2017).

Although religious pluralism has fostered the rapid accommodation of many American religious movements within society, groups such as Jehovah's Witnesses have maintained their independence. The smaller groups that maintain their distinctiveness have historically been victims of harassment by members of mainline religious groups. Christian Scientists, Jehovah's Witnesses, Children of God, and the Unification Church are groups that have been subjected to such treatment.

The Walnut Gurudwara (Sikh temple) and the First Korean Southern Baptist Church are located within close proximity of each other in the San Gabriel Valley in Southern California.

Conflict among the five major faiths worldwide has also been intense at different periods in history. Antisemitic, anti-Muslim, and anti-Catholic sentiments are still perpetuated in some households and institutions. Although religious pluralism in the past often led to conflict, the hope of the future is that it will lead to a better understanding of and respect for religious differences. In the following sections, we examine in greater detail the five major faiths and a few others that educators may find in some U.S. schools.

## Protestant Branch of Christianity

**Christianity** is the largest religion in the world, with approximately 2.4 billion followers or 30% of the world population (World Population Review, 2023c). The United States is primarily a Christian nation with a strong Protestant influence, but the country has seen slow but steady changes in the past few decades. While 66% of Americans identified themselves as Christians in 2022 (PRRI, 2023), the country is less Christian than it was in 1948, when 91% of Americans were Christians (Newport, 2009). As recently as 1984, 85% identified as Christians (Newport, 2009).

Christianity was founded on the worship of Jesus Christ who was born into Judaism in Bethlehem in Judea, which is now part of the Gaza Strip, the West Bank, and Israel. Most biblical scholars say that he was probably born between 6 and 4 BCE. He began preaching around the age of 30, drawing large crowds and becoming known as a healer. He had an inner group of 12 followers called his "disciples," whom he expected to carry out his mission after his death. Because Jesus claimed to be the messiah and the Son of God, he was tried under Jewish law for blasphemy and convicted to death on the cross by the Roman governor. According to his disciples, he rose from the dead 2 days later. The resurrection of Jesus was the focus of the earliest Christian preaching by his disciples and other followers (France, 2018). The Bible is the sacred text for Christians, with the Old Testament being the Hebrew and Aramaic scriptures of Judaism and the New Testaments about the life and teachings of Jesus.

Although the New Testament envisioned one church, the history of Christianity has been one of fragmentation. For example, the Catholic and Orthodox Churches separated around 1054. In the sixteenth century, Martin Luther led the reformation against the Roman Catholic Church, leading to the creation of **Protestantism**, which over the years split into many distinct Protestant denominations such as the Anglicans, Lutherans, Reformed, Baptists, Methodists, Society of Friends (Quakers), and Pentecostals (Sadgrove, 2018).

Ten percent of the world's population is Protestant, with the largest percentage of them (20%) living in the United States; Nigeria and China have the next largest Protestant populations (World Population Review, 2023e). The Western Europeans who immigrated to the United States in large numbers brought with them various forms of Protestantism. While claiming 42% of the population in 2022 (PRRI, 2023), Protestants in the United States no longer constitute the dominant numerical majority as in previous decades but continue to influence society and institutions. The Pew Research Center revealed some interesting trends. In the 1960s, two out of three Americans identified themselves as Protestants. As recently as 2007, Protestants were still a majority at 51% of the population, but by 2014, they were down to 47% and no longer a majority (Sahgal, 2017).

The first college in the colonies, Harvard College, was founded by the Massachusetts Bay colonial legislature in 1636 to prepare ministers and had general support from the Puritan government. The president of the second college, the College of William and Mary in 1693, was a minister of the Church of England. In 1701, 10 Connecticut clergymen founded Yale, the nation's third-oldest university, to prepare more orthodox ministers. Yale still maintains some religious influence with its prestigious Yale Divinity School. Baylor University (Southern Baptist), Southern Methodist University (United Methodist), Goshen College (Mennonite), and Centre College (Presbyterian) are a few examples of the hundreds of Protestant institutions of higher education in the United States that have educated and influenced the lives of millions of American and international students.

**MAINLINE PROTESTANTS** **Mainline Protestants** stress the right of individuals to determine for themselves what is true in religion. They practice a more liberal theological stance than **Conservative Protestants** or **Evangelical Christians**, believing in the authority of Christian experience and religious life rather than the dogmatic church pronouncements and interpretations of the Bible. They may or may not believe in the virgin birth of Jesus, and they may not share their conservative counterparts' belief in the inerrancy of the Bible. Some may not accept the miracles cited in the Bible as factual. They are likely to support and participate in social justice action, and most churches **ordain** women and members of LGBTQ+ (lesbian, gay, bisexual, transgender,

Parishioners participate in a children's Christmas pageant at an Episcopalian church.

**SOURCE:** Enigma/Alamy Stock Photo

queer/questioning) communities. The United Church of Christ and Episcopal churches are examples, although the degree of liberalism depends on the individual congregation. Methodists and Disciples of Christ represent more moderate denominations within this category. As in most religious groups, Mainline Protestants range across a continuum from conservative to liberal, disagreeing on policies, practices, and social issues within their multiple denominations.

**EVANGELICAL CHRISTIANS** Evangelical Christians have had considerable influence on both U.S. politics and education in recent years. Evangelicals are primarily Conservative Protestants who generally believe that the Bible is inerrant, that the supernatural is distinct from the natural, that salvation is essential, and that Jesus will return in bodily form during the **Second Coming**. They believe they have a personal relationship with God and are much more supportive of individualism than social justice (Winter, 2021). The Southern Baptist Convention is the largest Evangelical Christian denomination in the United States.

**Born-again** Evangelical Christianity is the largest Christian tradition in the United States, at 24% of the population in 2021 (Smith, 2021). They outnumber Christians who no longer go to church (15.5%), Mainline Protestants (12%) (Davis & Graham, 2023), and Catholics (22.8%) (PRRI, 2023). In 2014, 76% of evangelicals were White, 22% were Hispanic, 6% were Black, and 2% were Asian (Masci & Smith, 2018). However, by 2021, Latino/as were the fastest-growing group of evangelicals in the United States (Krogstad et al., 2023; Winter, 2021).

The increased influence of evangelicals has been matched by phenomenal growth in their churches. They have utilized mass communication, including television, to get their message to their faithful. Some churches have become megachurches, with weekly attendance exceeding 10,000 and providing an array of services including job banks, counseling, and even dating services. Life Church in Edmond, Oklahoma, reports an average weekly attendance of 85,000 and annual revenues of over $215 million. The church has 44 campuses and online services (Evangelical Council for Financial Accountability, 2023; Playlister, 2023).

Evangelicals are strong supporters of the antiabortion movement, although younger Evangelicals are more supportive of abortion than older parishioners (Burge, 2022). Opposition to abortion has become a centerpiece of the Catholic–Protestant alliance for conservatives (Jones, 2020). Conservative evangelicals are also fighting against what they view as alarming changes in culture, involving issues such as gender, sexuality, and the family (Whitehead & Perry, 2020). They are concerned about changing sexual standards, the ordination of women, birth control, divorce rates, the decline in family authority, the ban on prayer in schools, and the teaching of evolution. The acceptance of people who identify as LGBTQ+ runs contrary to the values of most evangelicals (Whitehead & Perry, 2020).

Increasing divisions exist between some conservative evangelicals and their moderate counterparts. A number of evangelical and conservative Mainline Christian pastors are leaving the ministry and sometimes the church itself. In some cases, they are leaving of their own accord; in other cases, parishioners are pushing them out because the clerics are not conservative enough in their politics (Wehner, 2021). Moderates, tiring of the divisive politics of religion, may embrace a wider-ranging agenda, with an emphasis on reaching out to those who are experiencing poverty and who are disenfranchised and focusing on other social and human rights issues (Brooks, 2022; Moore, 2023). While evangelical moderates tend to lean more toward the middle both politically and religiously than their **fundamentalist** evangelical counterparts, they are typically far more conservative than most Mainline Protestants.

Burge (2023b) has found in his research that a younger, more diverse group of evangelicals is emerging. They are increasingly Black and Latino/a and may have a greater tolerance of marriage for same-sex couples, abortions, and LGBTQ+ rights. They are also more welcoming and supportive of comprehensive immigration reform.

Evangelical Christians have differing views on education. Some more conservative evangelicals prefer to send their children to private Christian schools, while others prefer to homeschool their children. Some evangelicals support schools instilling a common core of values and morality. They want the schools to focus on basic academics—reading, writing, and mathematics—rather than social concerns such as poverty, human rights violations, racism, gender equity, ethnic studies, diversity, and inclusion (Graham, 2021).

Some evangelicals are among those who reject Charles Darwin's view of evolution. Funk (2019) reported that 38% of Americans surveyed believe that "humans have always existed in their current form." Many Evangelicals are firmly behind the movement to either rid the schools of evolution in the curriculum or establish alternative theories. The most often cited alternative theory is creation science. **Creation science** or **creationism** accepts the creation of all living things in 6 days, literally as presented in the Bible. Opponents of creation science suggest that it is not a science but a theory based on a biblical account. A third theory has been proposed: **intelligent design**. Supporters of intelligent design say that only an intelligent being could have created a natural world that is so complex and so well ordered (Pew Research Center, 2019c). Some scientists and evolutionists suggest that intelligent design is creationism veiled in a relatively new term.

Evangelicals may not be a numerical majority in the United States, but they are an influential force in U.S. society. Their beliefs affect politics, the judicial system, the legal system, and schools. Whether educators agree or disagree with their views and practices, it is important to understand that what evangelicals want for the country is similar to what most other citizens seek. They envision a safer, more moral America that is free of drugs, crime, and violence. However, people from different religious groups disagree on the meaning of morality and religious freedom, particularly around issues of sexuality, gender identity, and equity.

**WHITE CHRISTIAN NATIONALISM** White Christian Nationalism is a cultural framework that blends Christianity with American civic life. It is "a collection of myths, traditions, symbols, narratives, and value systems" (Whitehead & Perry, 2020, p. 10) based on the belief that the United States was founded as a Christian nation. However, the Founders had a wide range of religious views that ranged from atheism through **deism**, and the Constitution was based on a number of influences, not just Christianity (Gorski & Perry, 2022). White Christian Nationalists think that public institutions such as schools should reflect and affirm Christianity as schools did when common schools were first being established in the nineteenth century, and textbooks included Protestant prayers and **catechisms** that taught students Christianity through a set of questions and answers.

In the 1950s and 1960s, members of prominent White churches were employees in state and local governments and members of citizens councils in which the major project was to protect the social and political standing of the White population (Jones, 2020). In his famous Ministers and Marches speech in March 1965, Jerry Falwell said that evangelical ministers were called to be "soul winners," not politicians, as he attacked Martin Luther King, Jr. for leading marches for social justice. Changing direction, Falwell established the Moral Majority in 1970 for the purpose of ensuring that the moral values of Christianity, which he called "pro-family" and "pro-American," advanced conservative social values (Du Mez, 2021). At the same time, the Moral Majority was defending White supremacy in what now is the core of White Christian Nationalism (Jones, 2020).

While American evangelicals had previously avoided political involvement, the Moral Majority embraced the Republican Party (Butler, 2021). To advance their agenda, evangelicals sought to influence the outcomes of local and national elections and shape public policies (Whitehead & Perry, 2020). They have had an impact on state and local elections, the composition of school boards and judicial appointments, as well as the election of conservative U.S. presidents (Whitehead & Perry, 2020). Although the Moral Majority disbanded in 1989, by then, most evangelicals had firmly embraced the Republican party (Haberman, 2018).

Peter Wehner (2021), a senior fellow at the Ethics and Public Policy Center, interviewed dozens of ministers, theologians, academics, and historians regarding the politicization of the Christian faith, concluding that when it is politicized, "churches become repositories not of grace but of grievances, places where tribal identities are reinforced, where fears are nurtured, and where aggression and nastiness are sacralized" (para. 11). Political loyalties sometimes override traditional religious beliefs (Wehner, 2021). According to history professor Kristin Kobes Du Mez (2021), White Christian Nationalists have replaced the Jesus of the Gospels with an idol of rugged masculinity.

The "Christianity" of this framework represents more than religion. Basing their findings on extensive surveys and research, Whitehead and Perry (2020) concluded that Christian Nationalism "includes assumptions of nativism, white supremacy, patriarchy, and heteronormativity" (p. 10). The hundreds of people attending the "Unite the Right" rally in Charlotte, Virginia, in 2017 were White Christian Nationalists who were protesting the proposed removal of the statue of Confederate General Robert E. Lee from a public park. They carried tiki torches and chanted racist and antisemitic slogans on the night before the march and carried White nationalist banners and Nazi flags during the march. The Ku Klux Klan had held a rally in Charlottesville a month earlier (Lord, 2018).

What are the core assumptions held by White Christian Nationalists? First and foremost, they believe that the United States was not only founded as a Christian nation but that it was "divinely chosen and blessed by God" (Burke et al., 2023, p. 287). They believe that a rigidly defined societal hierarchy that preserves God-given freedoms should be overseen by White men to maintain God's dominion. Finally, they believe that "authoritarian and, at times, violent forms of control and governance (rather than deliberative democracy) are needed to maintain proper, God-given order in families, communities, the nation, and the world" (Burke et al., 2023, p. 287). Historically, White Christian Nationalism has been linked to White supremacy and the times when White Protestant Christian beliefs and institutions were clearly dominant and women and people of color were expected to "know their place in society" (Butler, 2021; Jones, 2017). Today, White Christian Nationalists believe that they are the most persecuted group in the United States (Green, 2017). No data support that claim. Their concern is that public institutions are not Christian institutions.

Identification with political conservatism is one of the strongest predictors of Christian Nationalism (Whitehead & Perry, 2020, p. 13), although it does not mean that all political conservatives or evangelicals are Christian Nationalists. Other strong predictors are a literal interpretation of the Bible, especially the Old Testament, the view that society is in destructive decline, and a belief that military action may be necessary to support their views. Whitehead and Perry (2020) argue that there is a difference in the worldviews of people who are religiously committed and who are Christian Nationalists. Surveys show that respondents indicate that religious practice is linked to "caring for the vulnerable, social justice, and even reducing one's consumption patterns for the sake of environmental stewardship" (Whitehead & Perry, 2020, p. 14). Christian Nationalists are less likely than other religious people to "believe that social and economic justice is important to being a good person" (p. 15). To them, fidelity to religion and to the United States are all important. Their tolerance of racial, ethnic, and religious diversity, immigration, the rights of women, and people who identify as LGBTQ+ is limited (Gorski & Perry, 2022).

Only about half of evangelicals embrace Christian Nationalism to some degree; it is also embraced by members of other Christian groups discussed in this chapter (Whitehead & Perry, 2020). Although some people of color connect with a nationalist view of the United States, it is primarily White Christians who support Christian

Nationalism (Burke et al., 2023). However, White Christian Nationalism is less a religion than a political ideology for the purpose of claiming power (Burke et al., 2023; Gorski & Perry, 2022; Stewart, 2019; Whitehead & Perry, 2020). Support of White Christian Nationalism more strongly predicts people's sociopolitical beliefs (e.g., about race, ethnicity, gender, sexual orientation, immigration, and Islam) than political ideology (Whitehead & Perry, 2020). "Religious terms 'Christian' and 'evangelical' are becoming markers of social identity and political views rather than just religious conviction" (Gorski & Perry, 2022, p. 107) and increasingly include secular conspiracy theories such as **QAnon** (Gorski & Perry, 2022). White Christian Nationalism has evolved into "ethno-nationalism," in which being American is based on race (i.e., White), religion (i.e., Christian), and native birth (i.e., born in the United States with parents who are U.S. citizens); it rejects multiculturalism (Gorski & Perry, 2022).

## Catholic Branch of Christianity

The Roman Catholic Church is the largest Christian church in the world, with approximately 1.2 billion adherents, 15% of the world's population in 2023 (World Population Review, 2023c). Twenty-three percent of the U.S. population identified as **Catholic** in 2023 (PRRI, 2023), with over 19,000 congregations (Jones, 2022). The location of Catholics in the United States has changed over time. Seventy-one percent of U.S. Catholics lived in the Northeast 50 years ago, but less than half of them live in the Northeast today. Catholics comprise 30% or more of the population in New York, New Jersey, New Mexico, and Illinois. They comprise the second largest religious group in the United States.

The Catholic Church is headed by the bishop of Rome, referred to as the pope. Central administration of the Church is located in Vatican City, a city-state located on 110 acres in Rome. Within the United States, leadership is provided by the U.S. Conference of Catholic Bishops, which presides over nearly 200 dioceses, which are the geographical areas included in the jurisdiction of a Christian bishop. These bishops are independent in their own dioceses, answering only to Church authority in Rome. In addition, there are 16 active U.S. cardinals (i.e., senior members of the Catholic clergy selected by the pope) in the Catholic Church (U.S. Conference of Catholic Bishops, 2023). Individual dioceses may differ in keeping with the conservative or liberal (progressive)

Pope Francis greets children as he arrives for his weekly general audience in Vatican City.
**SOURCE:** Riccardo De Luca - Update/Shutterstock

views of the presiding bishop. Unlike Protestantism, which includes denominational pluralism, the Catholic faith is a single denomination under the pope, who has authority over all Catholics throughout the world.

The most notable and problematic issue facing the Catholic Church has been the clerical sexual abuse scandals, which have reached worldwide proportions. This misconduct has been widely public in the United States since 2002 when the *Boston Globe* first reported that sexually abusive priests were transferred to new assignments rather than being punished by the Church or reported to law enforcement. By the fall of 2018, 13 states were investigating alleged clerical abuses (Thompson et al., 2018). In Pennsylvania alone, a grand jury report indicated that more than 300 priests had been credibly accused of abusing more than 1,000 children over seven decades, and the accusations continue to grow as 20 additional states conduct investigations today (Graham, 2023). Clergy abuse has also been exposed across Europe, Africa, Australia, Asia, and South America (e.g., National Public Radio, 2018; O'Grady, 2018; Reuters, 2018).

These findings have proven costly to the Catholic Church in credibility and membership losses (Pew Research Center, 2019a). In addition, the U.S. Catholic Church has suffered losses due to religious switching. Like most other religious groups, 32% of U.S. adults who were raised Catholic are now religiously unaffiliated, Protestants, or members of some other religion (Davis & Graham, 2023).

The movement toward conservatism has not been limited to Protestants. In many instances, **Conservative Catholics** have joined forces with Conservative Protestants on such issues as abortion and sexual morality. Some Catholics have abandoned their traditional support of the Democratic Party to support conservative Republican candidates. U.S. Catholics split their votes in the 2020 presidential election. Fifty percent of Catholics voted for Donald J. Trump, while 49% voted for Joe Biden in that election (Nortey, 2021).

Some Catholics have protested the conservative position of their church regarding the limited participation of women in leadership roles; 56% of members support legalized abortion (Fahmy, 2020). Some Catholics ignore the Church's position on certain forms of birth control, whereas others continue to strictly follow Church directives. The diversity of opinion and practice among U.S. Catholics is evidenced by the expressed desire of some to see significant changes in the Catholic Church. For example, 68% of Catholics have used the pill for birth control (Burge, 2023a). Polls by the Pew Research Center have found that the majority of Catholics support the following changes:

- Catholics allowed to use birth control: 76% (Masci & Smith, 2016)
- Priests allowed to marry: 62% (Corichi & Evans, 2019)
- Divorced parishioners allowed to receive communion without annulment: 62% (Masci & Smith, 2016)
- Cohabiting Catholics allowed to receive communion: 61% (Masci & Smith, 2016)
- Women allowed to become priests: 59% (Corichi & Evans, 2019)
- Support of marriage for same-sex couples: 61% (Pew Research Center, 2019b)

Membership in U.S. Catholic churches involves many different racial and ethnic groups. The majority of U.S. Catholics are White (55%), 38% are Hispanic, and 7% are other people of color (PRRI, 2023). Some parishes are predominantly Irish, whereas others are predominantly Italian, Polish, Mexican, Puerto Rican, or other ethnic groups. Although the doctrine and pattern of worship within the Catholic Church are uniform, individual parishes differ to some extent according to the racial or ethnic background and social class of their members. A parish may choose to conduct services in the predominant language group of its parishioners or may have individual masses for different language groups. Cultural events of the ethnic groups may be incorporated into the daily activities of the particular parish (e.g., quinceañera for Latina girls reaching the age of 15).

The Roman Catholic Church in the United States has developed the largest private educational system in the country. Almost 1.7 million students attended 5,920 Catholic schools in the United States in 2022–2023, with 80% of the schools being elementary schools (National Catholic Educational Association, 2023). In many communities, Catholic parochial schools offer quality educational options to both Catholic and non-Catholic students at a lower cost than most other private institutions. With thousands of elementary and secondary schools from Vermont to Hawaii and such internationally recognized universities as Notre Dame, Creighton, and Loyola, Roman Catholic schools and universities have educated millions of Americans and greatly influenced the culture of the country.

## Other Christian Religions

In addition to the major Christian denominations in the United States, there are other Christian religions an educator might encounter in a community. They include Christian religious groups that do not consider themselves either Protestant or Catholic. The largest two of these groups are discussed in this section.

**LATTER-DAY SAINTS**   The **Church of Jesus Christ of Latter-day Saints (LDS or Mormon)** is a rapidly growing Christian group that is neither Catholic nor Protestant. In 1830, Joseph Smith founded the LDS church in western New York State. By his own account, Smith was instructed to translate a history of ancient inhabitants of North America written on tablets of gold, which had been stored in a nearby hillside (Fisher & Rinehart, 2017). The translations were published as the Book of Mormon, which together with the Old and New Testaments of the Bible serve as the scriptural texts for the religion (The Church of Jesus Christ of Latter-Day Saints [LDS], 2023b).

Smith and his followers met opposition from Protestant groups, and they were harassed and violently driven out of various communities. The Mormon practice of polygamy (discontinued in 1890) exacerbated their unacceptability to other groups, and in 1844 Smith and his brother were killed by a mob in Carthage, Illinois. With the death of Smith, Brigham Young became the new leader of the group and led them to Salt Lake City, Utah, now the religious center of the Mormons.

Mormons aggressively proselytize and have a self-reported membership of 6.8 million in the United States and 17 million worldwide (LDS, 2023a). Mormons are the most religious group in the United States, as measured by their belief in the importance of religion in their lives and attendance at religious services (Norman, 2018). Members typically place high value on family and traditional gender roles, preferably where the husband provides and the wife remains at home. They are among the most politically and socially conservative religious groups in the United States. U.S. Mormons have a median age of 47, compared to 56 for White evangelical Protestants and 33 for Muslims (PRRI, 2021). They are racially and ethnically less diverse than the general U.S. population, with 85% of Mormons being non-Hispanic White in 2016 (Sandstrom, 2016).

**EASTERN ORTHODOXY**   The **Orthodox Churches** are other Christian religions that do not fall into the two major groupings of Protestant and Catholic. One reason that Orthodox Churches are lesser known in the United States may be that their members, predominantly from countries such as Syria, Greece, Armenia, Russia, and Ukraine, immigrated during the last century. Ethiopia also has a large population of Orthodox Christians (Diamant, 2017). The Eastern Orthodox Church split with the Roman Catholic Church in 1054 over theological, practical, jurisdictional, cultural, and political differences, particularly related to papal authority (Diamant, 2017). To many outsiders they appear very similar to the pre–**Vatican II** Catholic Church. There are 13 self-governing Orthodox churches worldwide, denoted by their nation of origin (e.g., Ukrainian Orthodox). Each church has its own head bishop as its spiritual leader (Fairchild, 2019).

Worldwide, the Eastern Orthodox churches together had an estimated combined membership of 260 million, or 12% of the world's Christian population in 2010, but its membership was declining at a higher rate than other major Christian religions (Diamant, 2017). Approximately 0.3% of the U.S. population or less than 1 million people were members of Eastern Orthodox churches in 2022 (PRRI, 2023).

## Judaism

**Judaism** is one of the oldest religions known to humanity and provides the historical roots of Catholicism, Protestantism, and Islam. In 2022, the Jewish population was approximately 15.3 million, or 0.19% of the world's population. Israel is home to the largest number of Jews, followed by the United States (The Jewish Agency for Israel, 2022). While the U.S. Jewish population is relatively small, the contributions of Jewish Americans to the fields of medicine, science, academia, business, economics, entertainment, and politics have been notable (Ramsey, 2018).

Ancient Israelites originated with a sense of shared ancestry, myth, ritual, and history sometime before 1000 BCE in historical Israel and Judah in the Middle East where the Egyptian, Babylonian, Assyrian, Hellenistic (Greek), and Roman empires crossed (Ahuvia, 2016). They believed they were descendants of Abraham, his son Isaac, and his grandson Jacob, and they shared the exodus story of God and Moses leading them to liberation from enslavement in ancient Egypt to Mount Sinai and the "Promised Land" where Abraham and his descendants had lived centuries before. Moses is supposed to have disappeared into Mount Sinai for 40 days where God revealed to him the five books of the **Torah** and the Ten Commandments (My Jewish Learning, 2023).

Over the centuries, the Jewish people were conquered and exiled to other countries across the Middle East, Egypt, and later Europe. Periodically their Temple in Jerusalem was destroyed by these outsiders and later rebuilt. Anti-Judaism existed throughout these periods and continued through the medieval period in Europe, when Jews were continually expelled from cities, and into the twenty-first century across the world (Ahuvia, 2016). In the nineteenth century, large numbers of Jews emigrated into the United States from Germany and eastern Europe, and many began moving from Jewish enclaves along the East Coast to other parts of the country. Religious persecution in countries such as Russia, Poland, and Germany led to additional Jewish refugees to the United States in the twentieth century.

People who identified themselves as Jewish by religion were 1.9% of the total U.S. population in 2022 (PRRI, 2023), which rises to 2.4% when Jews who identify as religiously unaffiliated are included (Pew Research Center, 2021). An additional 1.1% of the U.S. population have a Jewish parent or upbringing but identify with a different religion. As a group, Jewish people remain a distinctive, identifiable religious minority. Education, including higher education, has played an important role in the Jewish community by advancing young people from the working class into white-collar and professional positions.

Ninety-two percent of Jewish Americans identify their race as White non-Hispanic, 4% as Hispanic, 1% as Black non-Hispanic, and 3% as non-Hispanic biracial and other people of color. Two in three U.S. Jews identify as Ashkenazi, having descended from Jews who lived in central or eastern Europe (Pew Research Center, 2021). While some Jewish families have maintained their ties to Orthodox (9%) and Conservative (17%) Judaism, the largest number (37%) of American Jews are affiliated with Reform synagogues. Thirty-two percent of Jews do not identify with any specific branch of Judaism; this number includes the 27% who consider themselves culturally or ethnically Jewish but are unaffiliated with the religion (Pew Research Center, 2021).

**DIVERSITY WITHIN JUDAISM**  Jewish identity is a blend of historical, religious, ethnic, and cultural variables. Early Jewish settlers in the United States found it difficult, if not impossible, to practice Judaism in the traditional ways that they had observed in Europe. Jewish religious practices and patterns were modified to meet the needs of the immigrants and in ways that made them characteristically American. In addition to attending a synagogue for traditional religious observances, many Jewish Americans report participating in Jewish cultural activities such as enjoying Jewish foods, visiting historical sites, and reading Jewish literature (Pew Research Center, 2021).

**Reform Jews** represent the more liberal end of the continuum. According to Jewish law, one who is born to a Jewish mother or who converts to Judaism is considered a Jew. Reform Jews also accept children born to non-Jewish mothers as Jews. They are less likely than members of other branches to attend religious services regularly and be religiously observant in traditional ways. They also have high education levels, smaller families, higher rates of intermarriage, and a median age of 53 years (Pew Research Center, 2021).

**Conservative Jews** represent the moderates in Judaism. They are more conservative than the members of Reform congregations and often more liberal than Orthodox Jews. In this instance, "Conservative" indicates the group's attempt to conserve traditional Judaism rather than to reform it. It does not indicate political conservatism. Some Conservative Jews observe **kosher** dietary laws, while others do not. They have the highest median age of 62 years (Pew Research Center, 2021). Both Reform and Conservative Judaism allow women to be ordained as rabbis (i.e., a Jewish religious leader).

**Orthodox Jews** are the most traditionally observant branch of Judaism and tend to hold firm to Jewish law, including rules on diet and dress. They are also more likely to be politically conservative, have larger families, are less likely to intermarry, and have the lowest median age of 35 years (Pew Research Center, 2021).

Although most Jewish people identify with their religion, the Jewish practice of religion is relatively loose regarding synagogue attendance and home religious observance. Nevertheless, the U.S. synagogue is the strongest agency in the Jewish community. Although they may not attend services regularly, a large percentage of Jewish people retain some affiliation with a synagogue. Attendance on High Holidays—Rosh Hashanah and Yom Kippur—is high. The synagogue in the United States serves not only as a place of religious worship but also as a primary base for Jewish identity and cultural survival.

The Torah scroll includes the Five Books of Moses and is the holiest book within Judaism.

**SOURCE:** John Theodor/Shutterstock

The majority of Jewish children attend public K–12 schools. Many of the Reform Jewish temples or synagogues throughout the country operate private preschools and kindergartens. In some of the larger Jewish communities, particularly among the Orthodox groups, *yeshivas*, or private religious schools, provide instruction in both academics and in-depth religious studies. Jewish universities such as Yeshiva University in New York and Brandeis University in Massachusetts have made significant contributions to U.S. higher education.

For decades, American schools have observed the Christian holiday of Christmas. In the past 40 or more years, educators have become increasingly sensitive to the diversity of the students in their schools. December is usually the time of the year when Jewish families observe Chanukah (Hanukkah), an 8-day Jewish holiday commemorating "the victory of a small group of Jewish rebels (led by Judah Maccabee and his brothers, collectively known as 'the Maccabees') over the armies of Syria in 165 BCE and the subsequent liberation and 'rededication' of the Temple in Jerusalem" (Union for Reform Judaism, 2023, para. 1). Many schools, in the spirit of inclusiveness and sensitivity, now refer to the holiday vacation period as the December school recess and December school parties as holiday parties.

**ANTISEMITISM**    Jewish people in the United States and throughout the world have been targets of prejudice and discrimination, sometimes leading to attempted annihilation of the population. During World War II, the Jewish Holocaust resulted in the deaths of approximately 6 million European Jews; approximately two-thirds of all the Jews living in Europe at the time (Smith, 2022). For several years, the world ignored the overwhelming evidence of the Nazi atrocities and did nothing to intervene. Now, in the twenty-first century, neo-Nazis and others falsely claim that the Jewish Holocaust was a myth that never happened.

The people involved in these genocide efforts and their descendants struggle with how to acknowledge them and apologize for the harm done to other people. It took many years after the war for the people of Germany to build museums to describe the Holocaust and honor the people who had been killed. In 1996, German artist Guner Demnig began to illegally place *Stolperstein* or "stumbling stones" among the cobblestones outside the homes of former residents who had been victims of the Nazis between 1933 and 1945. The 10-by-10-centimeter block with a brass plate included the name and the dates of birth, deportation, and death of the former resident. Within 4 years, Germans in most towns and cities were legally allowed to install stumbling stones to memorialize their former neighbors. By 2022, 90,000 stumbling stones filled the streets and sidewalks of 30 European countries (Smith, 2022). After visiting memorials in Germany, Clint Smith (2022) reflected that "no museum can bring back millions of people. It cannot be done, and yet we must try to honor those lives, and to account for this history, as best we can. It is the very act of attempting to remember that becomes the most powerful memorial of all" (p. 41).

**Antisemitism** is rooted in conflicts between Jews and non-Jews that have existed for centuries. In the United States, Jews and Catholics were also targets of the Ku Klux Klan. In the 1960s, some Jewish individuals were forced to flee the South in fear of the Klan (Hopfe et al., 2016). In 2022, there were 3,697 reported antisemitic incidents of harassment, vandalism, and assaults in the United States—the highest number reported since the Anti-Defamation League (2023) began reporting antisemitic incidents in 1979. These incidents occurred in K–12 schools, on college campuses, at Jewish institutions such as synagogues and community centers, and on the streets of America. In 2018 and 2019, 11 worshippers lost their lives at the Tree of Life synagogue in Pittsburgh in October 2018; one woman was killed in an attack at the Chabad of Poway synagogue in Poway, California, in April 2019; three people were killed at a kosher grocery store in Jersey City, New Jersey, in December 2019; and a gunman held hostages for 10 hours at Congregation Beth Israel in Colleyville, Texas, in January 2022.

Three in four Jews report that antisemitism is higher today than in the previous 5 years, with Orthodox Jews being the most likely recipients of antisemitism in part because they are more identifiable by their attire (Pew Research Center, 2021). Over half of Orthodox Jews report seeing anti-Jewish graffiti or vandalism, and over a third of them have been made to feel unwelcome or been called offensive names; 7% of them have been threatened or attacked (Pew Research Center, 2021).

Antisemitism also finds many of its historical roots in the Bible and other religious works. Bach's "Passion of St. John," though musically beautiful and inspiring, has been perceived by some to have antisemitic German lyrics, though others disagree with this contention (Oestreich, 2017). Biblical passages are often used to justify antisemitic behaviors (e.g., Matthew 27:25–26; Romans 3:1).

## Islam

**Islam** is the second-largest religion in the world, with more than 2 billion adherents worldwide or 25% of the world's population in 2023 (World Population Review, 2023d). Worldwide, Islam is the fastest-growing major religion and is expected to nearly equal or surpass the number of Christians by 2050. Americans often mistakenly believe Islam is primarily a Middle Eastern religion. However, Indonesia has the world's largest **Muslim** population. The majority of Muslims live in northern and central Africa, the Middle East, and Southeast Asia. Ninety percent of the population is Muslim in Egypt, Afghanistan, Syria, Pakistan, Turkey, and Iran (World Population Review, 2023d). The PRRI (2023) reported that Muslims were only 0.6% of the U.S. population in 2022. Growth of the Muslim population is reflected in the number of mosques across the country. There were 1,209 mosques in 2000; they had increased to 2,769 in 2020 (Bagby, 2020).

# Critical Incidents in Teaching

## Religious Bigotry in the Classroom

On October 7, 2023, the news media was replete with coverage of the Hamas attack on Israel and the projected retaliation against Hamas in Gaza. Videos and news coverage showed the senseless killing of innocent civilians across Israel. Pundits across cable news were blaming Hamas, Israel, Iran, and/or the United States for policy decisions and practices that led to the disastrous events of that night and the months to come. The attack and subsequent war were the focus of discussions across the world about Muslims, Jews, oppression, protests, and terrorism.

Expressions of antisemitism and Islamophobia were soon to follow. A 6-year-old Palestinian Muslim boy and his mother were stabbed by their landlord because they were Muslim. A swastika appeared on a boys' bathroom wall at a California high school, and it wasn't the first time that a hate crime had occurred at that school (Taketa, 2023). Both schools and synagogues received violent threats (Lapin, 2023). These incidents did not begin in the fall of 2023. Parents in a middle school in Milwaukee were criticizing the school district for not appropriately responding earlier in 2023 to incidents in which swastikas had been drawn on the gym floor, a bathroom stall, and on desks, lockers, and textbooks (Johnson, 2023). Both Jewish and Muslim students were more likely to be harassed and bullied in school because of their religion than other students.

How would you respond if you heard a student or students calling another student a terrorist or pulling the hijab off of another student? How would you respond if a student reported swastika graffiti in a student's notebook or on the bathroom wall?

## Questions for Discussion

1. How should teachers respond to religiously biased incidents they see in their classrooms, the hallways, and other parts of the school?

2. How could these religiously biased incidents lead to discussions about antisemitism and Islamophobia and their impact on classroom peers and the community?

3. What steps should schools take when antisemitic and Islamophobic incidents occur at school or in the community?

4. What could schools do to prevent antisemitic and Islamophobic incidents at school and ensure the safety of all students regardless of their religion, race, ethnicity, socioeconomic status, gender, or sexual orientation?

Islam was born in the city of Mecca in western Saudi Arabia around 610 CE when Muhammad came to believe that he was receiving messages from God to convey to his neighbors and others. These messages were collected over 23 years, becoming the **Qur'an** (or **Koran**), the literal transcript of God's speech that became the sacred scripture of Islam. The messages proclaimed that God was One (Allah) who was merciful and all-powerful and controlled the course of events (Watt, 2018). The persecution of Muhammad's followers in Mecca forced them to move to Medina, where the Islam religion took shape, and he was able to develop enough support to occupy Mecca and expand his base to many tribes across Arabia. Within 12 years of Muhammad's death, Muslims occupied Egypt, Syria, and Iraq and were moving westward into Libya and eastward into the area that is now Iran and later to India. The expansion of their territory continued for a century across North Africa and into Spain and southern France. Military expansion slowed by 750 CE but continued through Muslim traders with camel caravans who spread their religion in Africa and through Central and East Asia to Malaysia, Indonesia, and the Philippines (Watt, 2018).

Muslim worshipers pray at a mosque in New York City during Ramadan.

**SOURCE:** Ron Adar/Shutterstock

As a religious term, "Islam" means "submission to God" (Kerr, 2018). Islam's followers believe in the same God (Allah) as Christians and Jews, although the three religions differ in their beliefs about God (Islam Faith Team, 2023). Muslims are the people who practice Islam. Islam is both a belief system and a way of life for individuals and entire societies that is based on the holy writings of the Qur'an. The Qur'an's basic theme is the relationship between God and His creatures. It provides guidelines for a society that is just, with proper human conduct, and an economic system that is equitable. Muslims believe that Islam began with Adam and continued through the line of prophets including Abraham, Moses, Jesus, and Muhammad. The basic pillars of Islam include:

1. The Shahadah (The Testimony of Faith): Belief in one God (Allah) and in Muhammad as his last messenger. The first words heard by a newborn and the last words spoken at death are "I bear witness that there is no god but God; I bear witness that Muhammad is the Apostle of God." These same words call Muslims to worship around the world.

2. Prayer: Five times daily, facing Mecca and men praying together on Fridays.

3. Almsgiving (Charity): Sharing one's wealth with people who live in poverty.

4. Fasting: No food or water from sunrise to sunset during Ramadan (the ninth month of the Islamic year).

5. The Hajj (Pilgrimage): A visit to Mecca once in one's lifetime if at all possible. (Kerr, 2018)

**DIVERSITY WITHIN ISLAM**   Muslims are generally followers of two major groups. **Sunni Muslims**, who comprise 85% of Islam, believe that the rightful leadership of Islam began with Abu Bakr and that the succession has passed to caliphs, or political leaders. **Shi'a Muslims**, which are also known as **Shi'ites**, are a smaller but highly visible group who comprise the majority population in Iran, Azerbaijan, Bahrain, and Iraq (Sawe, 2018). Shi'a Muslims believe that Muhammad intended the succession of leadership to pass through the bloodline of his cousin and son-in-law, Ali. Shi'a

Muslims have attracted considerable world attention, in part because of their insistence of adherence to Islamic law by their countries' governments (Sergie, 2023).

While the early religious differences between Sunni and Shi'a Muslims continue, they are probably not primary contributing factors to the ongoing violence between the two groups. Politics and the struggle to maintain control of power have been the most likely issues. The hardliners on both sides tend to see this as a struggle for the survival of their sect (Sergie, 2023). For example, after the Shi'a took control of the government in Iraq, they were resistant to sharing the governance of the country with the Sunnis or the Kurds.

While there is often conflict within their own countries, members of the two sects also have been involved in conflicts in other countries. The civil war in Syria has fueled much of the tension and hatred in the Middle East. President Assad's regime has been backed by Shi'a in the region, including Lebanon's Shi'a militant Islamist group Hezbollah, which has sent fighters to the conflict. This action has inflamed the Sunnis throughout the region, leading them to send fighters including the Islamic State of Iraq and Syria, or ISIS, into the conflict (Sergie, 2023).

**A PORTRAIT OF AMERICAN MUSLIMS**   In 2017, the Pew Research Center conducted an extensive survey of 1,000 adult Muslim Americans. Survey respondents included both U.S.-born Muslims and immigrants from 75 countries who spoke and were interviewed in languages including English, Arabic, Farsi, and Urdu. As a group, they were younger and more racially and ethnically diverse than the general U.S. population. Forty-one percent were White, 28% Asian, 20% Black; and 8% Hispanic. Fifty-five percent were Sunni Muslims, while 16% were Shi'a Muslims. Fourteen percent said that they were just Muslims. Two-thirds of the group (65%) indicated that religion was very important to them. Forty-five percent indicated that they observed the ritual prayer (Salalh) five times daily. However, many others indicated that religion was less important to them and that they did not pray regularly (Pew Research Center, 2017).

An overwhelming number of the Muslim respondents (92%) were proud to be Americans. However, they had serious concerns about their place in American society. A majority (75%) believed that Muslims in this country experience discrimination. They felt that being Muslim in the United States was becoming increasingly difficult. Both the U.S. public and American Muslims are concerned about extremism in the name of Islam both at home and abroad. The extremism focuses both unwanted and undeserved attention on innocent Muslims. Furthermore, American Muslims overwhelmingly reject the targeting or killing of innocents for political, social, or religious causes; 76% of the Muslims indicated that targeting innocents can never be justified, while a smaller percentage (59%) of the general public hold those sentiments (Pew Research Center, 2017).

Most Muslim students in the United States attend public schools, but some parents choose private Islamic schools because they offer interactions with other Muslims and support their children in building their Muslim identity (Siddiqui, 2023). Like many immigrant families, Muslim parents may worry that their children will become Americanized and lose their religion and culture (Emerick, 2023). Today, Muslim students attend over 300 elementary and secondary Islamic schools across the country (Islam Icau, 2022). As with other private religious schools, Islamic schools have a mission that extends beyond the curriculum in public schools, allowing them to emphasize aesthetic, spiritual, moral, and ethical dimensions of an individual's behavior based on their religion. In Islamic schools, students can grapple with the reality that Islam is, in the minds of some, associated with terrorism and hate. They are able to discuss terrorist incidents more openly than in a public setting. Research suggests that U.S. Muslim schools may promote more free thinking than public schools can. Students are taught that if they want their religion to be respected, they need to respect other faiths (Gjelten, 2017).

As public schools become more diverse, they become better at recognizing and respecting the diversity of the cultures and religions of their students. Schools with

Muslim students are beginning to recognize the holy month of Ramadan in which many Muslim families fast from sunrise to sunset and engage in self-reflection, study the Qur'an, and spend time with family. Ramadan occurs in the ninth month of the Islamic lunar calendar. Some schools are providing a quiet room (e.g., in the library) for midday prayer and making accommodations such as allowing students to refrain from strenuous physical activity and take tests early in the day. Some school systems recognize Eid al-Fitr—the celebration that marks the end of Ramadan—as a holiday (Chen, 2023).

**BLACK MUSLIMS**   **Black Muslims** in the United States have primarily aligned themselves with the Sunni form of Islam (52%), 2% identify with the **Nation of Islam**, and another 27% do not identify with a particular sect or denomination (Mohamed & Diamant, 2019). American Black Muslims have a unique identity of their own. They tend to be viewed as separate from the rest of Islam. About half of American-born Black Muslims are converts. They account for 20% of the U.S. adult Muslims and are more likely than other Muslims to have been born in the United States (69% to 36%). The Black Muslims who have recently immigrated to the United States are more likely to be from Sub-Saharan African countries like Somalia and Ethiopia, while other Muslims have more likely immigrated from South Asian countries. Compared to Black Christians, they are more likely to live in the Northeast and urban areas (Mohamed & Diamant, 2019).

Elijah Poole (1897–1975), who became known as Elijah Muhammad, led the Nation of Islam into national visibility. In the early 1960s, Malcolm X (1925–1965) became the most well-known spokesperson for the Nation of Islam (Fisher & Rinehart, 2017). Malcolm X and other Black Muslims sought to use the Nation of Islam to engage Black Americans in economic nationalism and to instill in them a sense of pride and achievement. This was accomplished through rejection of Christianity, which was seen as a symbol of White oppression in America.

Wallace Deen Muhammad became the leader of the Nation of Islam after the death of his father, Elijah Muhammad, in 1975. Under his leadership, the Nation of Islam embraced traditional Sunni Islam and changed its name to the American Muslim Mission. During the 1970s and 1980s, W. D. Muhammad, as he was known, dispensed with the racist rhetoric of his sect's past and led his followers toward orthodox Koranic Islam. As a result, the group often supports conservative causes such as the free market. Hard work, personal responsibility, and family values are expected of members (Fisher & Rinehart, 2017).

Louis Farrakhan, the well-known leader of the Black Muslims, led a splinter movement in the 1980s that resumed the use of the original name, Nation of Islam, and the Black separatist position. He continues to receive considerable attention from the press and political leaders because of his sometimes-inflammatory rhetoric as well as his appeal to non-Muslim Black Americans. Members have become role models in many urban areas as they establish businesses. They often serve as visible neighborhood guardians against crime and drug use and have assumed an important role in the rehabilitation of individuals released from prison (Fisher & Rinehart, 2017).

**ISLAMOPHOBIA**   Following the terrorist attacks on the United States on September 11, 2001, innocent American Muslims and people perceived to be Muslims such as Sikhs faced physical assault, emotional abuse, discrimination, and sometimes death in retaliation for the acts of a terrorist group (Pandith, 2021). After the 2017 ban that prevented travel to the United States from seven predominantly Muslim countries, half of the U.S. Muslims interviewed indicated that they had experienced some form of discrimination in the past year (Pew Research Center, 2017). This included being treated with suspicion, singled out at airport security, called offensive names, mistreated by law enforcement, and, in a few instances, threatened or physically attacked. However, half of the respondents indicated that they had received expressions of support because they were Muslim (Pew Research Center, 2017). **Islamophobia**, which is a type of

**xenophobia** against Muslins, continues today. The Federal Bureau of Investigation (2023) reported that 13% of single-bias hate crimes were based on religion. Antisemitic hate crimes (51%) led religious bias attacks followed by those on Sikhs (12%) and Muslims (10%) in 2021.

In a 2020 survey of Muslim U.S. residents by the Othering & Belonging Institute at the University of California Berkeley, researchers found that nearly all (98%) of the respondents believed that Islamophobia exists in the United States (Elsheikh & Sisemore, 2021). Almost three in four thought women were more likely to experience Islamophobia. Two in three of the respondents had experienced it in their lifetimes, with over half of them being treated unfairly by a law enforcement officer. At the same time, 86% of the respondents felt comfortable contacting police for help or protection and almost all of them (97%) felt they were treated fairly by health care professionals. Nevertheless, one in three of the respondents reported having hidden or tried to hide their religious identity, and around 90% of them have censored their "speech or actions out of fear of how people might respond or react to them" (Elsheikh & Sisemore, 2021, p. 6). Black Muslims are more likely than other Muslims to report "a lot of" discrimination against them (Mohamed & Diamant, 2019).

Islamophobia is not unique to the United States; it exists in many countries. The United Nations' Special Rapporteur on freedom of religion and belief, Ahmed Shaheed, reported that Muslims "often feel stigma, shame and a sense that they are 'suspect communities' that are being forced to bear collective responsibility for the actions of a small minority" (United Nations, 2021, para. 5). In 2018 and 2019, an average of 37% of Europeans held unfavorable views of Muslims. In 2017, 30% of Americans held unfavorable views (United Nations, 2021).

The tone of newspaper stories about Muslims in 2020 were more negative than stories about any other group of color, in part because the stories focused on war and extremism (Media Portrayals of Minorities Project, 2021). News media do not adequately emphasize the fact that the vast majority of Muslims are innocent, peace-loving individuals and that Muslims are themselves the primary targets of Islamic extremists (Hayden, 2017). The U.S. National Counterterrorism Center reported that in the prior 5 years, up to 97% of terrorist-related fatalities had been Muslim people (Grant, 2017).

Muslim students also face Islamophobia at school. Long-time educator Sawsan Jaber (2022) reports that negative stereotypes are pervasive in schools, contributing to hostile environments that affect academic performance and feelings of belonging. A study of students age 12 to 18 in California found that 55% of Muslim students felt "unsafe, unwelcome, or uncomfortable" at school (Nittle, 2021). More than one in three students had experienced or observed cyberbullying, which increased in virtual schooling during the pandemic. Muslim girls were primary targets of bullying, especially if they wore **hijabs**. Teachers sometimes were the bullies, calling Muslim students "terrorists" or telling them they did not belong in this country. In a similar study of Muslim students in Massachusetts, 60% reported being "mocked, verbally harassed or physically abused" because of their religion (Nittle, 2021).

Islamophobia is also reflected in textbooks that often include stereotypical information and misconceptions about Islam and Muslims, making students feel like outsiders. Textbooks and discussions do not always differentiate between culture and religion (Jaber, 2020). According to Jaber (2020), "the lack of understanding of students' intersectionality and cultural identities leads to disempowerment, limiting their access to an equitable educational experience in comparison with their white peers" (para. 6).

## Buddhism

**Buddhism**, called Dharma by many of its followers, is the world's fourth largest religion, with over a half billion adherents worldwide or 6.6% of the world's population (World Population Review, 2023a). The largest concentration of Buddhists, approximately

255 million, live in China. Over half of the population is Buddhist in Cambodia, Thailand, Myanmar, Bhutan, Sri Lanka, Laos, and Mongolia. Buddhists account for approximately 0.7% of U.S. residents. Immigration of Asians from countries such as China, Taiwan, Korea, Thailand, Japan, and Tibet brings thousands of additional Buddhists into the United States and continually reshapes the religious demographics of the country.

Buddhism is the only major world religion that is projected to decline both in real numbers and in the percentage of the world's population. While comprising 6.9% of the world population in 2015, Buddhists are projected to increase to 511 million in 2030 and then decrease to 486 million by 2050. These declines are attributable to an aging Buddhist population and comparatively low fertility rates. While it is estimated that a fertility rate of 2.1 children is necessary to maintain the status quo, the fertility rate for Buddhist women is 1.6, compared worldwide with 2.7 for Christians and 3.1 for Muslims (Pew Research Center, 2015, 2017).

Hsi Lai Temple (Buddhist) in Hacienda Heights, California.

**SOURCE:** © Philip Chinn

The history of Buddhism started with the Buddha, Siddhartha Gautama, who lived in North India in the fourth or fifth century BCE. He had been married and had a son but left his family to become a wanderer, seeking the "final truth that would lead to complete freedom from suffering" (Williams, 2018, p. 105). He did not believe in the existence of a God and focused on understanding "the way things really are." His disciples continued to spread his teachings throughout South and East Asia (Williams, 2018).

With Buddhists living in so many regions of the world today, there are invariably different forms of Buddhism practiced (Williams, 2018). "Buddhism is less a set of beliefs than a path, leading from suffering to the cessation of suffering, from ignorance to compassion and wisdom" (Harris, 2018, p. 117). Each school of Buddhism provides a pathway to overcome the meaninglessness of life. Buddha is the solution to life's dilemma (Fisher & Rinehart, 2017). Buddhism teaches that the path to enlightenment is neither through a life of luxury nor through self-deprivation but through the middle way, away from the extremes. Meditation is encouraged to concentrate the mind and see the mind and body clearly (Harris, 2018). Salvation and enlightenment occur when people realize their place of **not-self** in the world. With enlightenment comes the state of **nirvana**, meaning a person's individual desires and suffering go away (Harris, 2018).

Chinese, Japanese, Korean, and Vietnamese individuals are often influenced by Confucian philosophy, which guides daily behaviors in much the same way that a religion does. Thus, some individuals may be Buddhist (or Christian or some other religion) with a strong philosophical overlay of Confucianism. The commitment to academic excellence and respect for parents, elders, and authority are characteristics often found among these groups of Asian students. Many of these cultural traits can be directly or indirectly attributed to the Confucian philosophy deeply instilled in many Chinese, Japanese, Korean, and Vietnamese children from an early age.

## Hinduism

**Hinduism** is the major religion of India and the world's third-largest religion after Christianity and Islam. Approximately 1.2 billion adherents in the world represent 15% of the world's population (World Population Review, 2023b). India is home to more than 9 in 10 of the world's Hindus (Evans, 2022). The number of Hindus in the United States is estimated to be 2.51 million people (World Population Review, 2023b) or 0.7% of the U.S. population (PRRI, 2023). Diwali, the Hindu festival of lights, is the most popular holiday in India and is celebrated in a growing number of U.S. communities, but many Hindus also celebrate Christmas and the Muslim Eid al-Fitr (Evans, 2022).

The seventh-largest Hindu population in the world lives in the United States, where 90% are immigrants and children of immigrants and the remaining 10% are converts. "Hindu concepts, such as karma, veganism, reincarnation, meditation, yoga, and Ayurveda, have become popular in the U.S. mainstream, believed and practiced by millions of non-Hindus" (World Population Review, 2023b, para 8). Hindus in the United States and Europe are the most highly educated religious group in each country (Evans, 2022).

The earliest signs of Hinduism have been traced to the Indus Valley civilization between 2500 and 1500 BCE, making it the world's oldest organized religion. Hinduism does not have a single founder nor a central organization, but it is credited with influencing the development of both Buddhism and Jainism, which believes that all living beings have a soul and teaches that the path to enlightenment is through nonviolence to all living things (Salter, 2018). Like most other religions, Hinduism involves basic beliefs about divinities, life after death, and how followers should conduct their lives. Unlike Judaism, Christianity, and Islam, Hinduism does not limit itself to a single book or writing. Several sacred writings contribute to the basic beliefs of Hinduism. Although Hinduism includes chauvinist and exclusivist forms, "other forms of Hindu belief and practice adopt a more inclusive, universal orientation, emphasizing values such as social justice, peace, and the spiritual transformation of humanity" (Warrier, 2018, p. 77).

Hinduism teaches that the soul never dies. When the body dies, the soul is reincarnated. The soul may be born into an animal or another human being. The law of **karma** states that every action taken by an individual influences how they will be reincarnated. Those who live a good life will be reincarnated into a higher state. Those who do evil will be reincarnated in lower forms, such as a worm. Reincarnation continues until a person reaches spiritual perfection. The soul then enters a new level of existence, referred to as **moksha**, from which it never returns (Fisher & Rinehart, 2017).

## The Spiritual Way of Life for Native Americans

As a result of European colonization and the mission to force Native Americans to convert to Christianity, the faiths of Native Americans were "scorned, forbidden, and almost destroyed" (Newbery, 2018) into the twentieth century. Today Native Americans are engaged in "gathering again in their ceremonial circles, remembering discarded teachings, renewing the traditional ways" (Newbery, 2018, p. 62) as they lay a foundation for recovering harmony with their surroundings. Ancient wisdom and the knowledge of their elders are valued in most Native American communities, and they are reaching back to their earthly ancestral origins to rediscover indigenous spiritual ways of life (Good Feather, 2021).

Native Americans do not have a word for religion. Indigenous spirituality is "a nature-based way of living in alignment with Mother Earth and spiritual laws of the universe" (Good Feather, 2021, p. 1). Every tribe has its own beliefs, but a core philosophy across tribes is the need to live "in harmony with the ways of Mother Earth and in alignment with the natural laws of the universe" (Good Feather, 2021, p. 5). Native Americans believe in a divine energy or creator, which is known by many different names such as the Creator, Great Spirit, God, Jehovah, Allah, Yahweh, and many others. Their story of the Sacred Hoop of Life is about their spiritual relationship with the universe.

Although religious freedom was one of the principal core values on which the United States was founded, it has frequently been denied to Native Americans (Carpenter, 2021). Two of the continuous battles that Native Americans have with the U.S. legal system are over their freedom to practice their own religions and the protection of their sacred lands, waters, and places such as Standing Rock (in South Dakota), Mauna Kea (in Hawaii), and Bears Ears (in Utah) (McNally, 2020). Native Americans continue to fight government decisions that damage their sacred places, sell their sacred land to mining or other companies, and ban their access to places at which they have worshipped and held cultural ceremonies for many generations. On occasion, they have been able to celebrate important legal victories, such as in *McGirt v. Oklahoma* (2020), which prevented the state of Oklahoma from disestablishing the reservation of the Muscogee (Creek) Nation. Nevertheless, Carpenter (2021) concludes that "there remains a shadow of conquest and colonization over the lives of Indigenous Peoples in the United States" (p. 2108).

## The Religiously Unaffiliated

In 1972, only 5% of the U.S. population indicated no religious affiliation. In 1990, 8% did, and by 2022, the religiously unaffiliated had increased to 27% (Newport, 2017; PRRI, 2023). These numbers do not mean that all of the religiously unaffiliated population are not spiritual. A Gallup poll found that 33% of the population say they are spiritual but not religious; only 18% say they are neither spiritual nor religious (Jones, 2023).

Alper (2018) found that questioning religious teachings was the reason most frequently (60%) given for not identifying with a religion. This was followed by disliking the positions taken by religious organizations on social/political issues (49%) and not liking religious organizations (41%). The other reasons given include not believing in God, finding religion irrelevant, and not liking religious leaders. The Pew Research Center (2022) projects that half of the U.S. population will be religiously unaffiliated by 2070.

At a time of increased political and religious discord, some individuals have found themselves weary of religious institutions. Davis and Graham (2023) found that 12% of the **dechurched** evangelicals left religious organizations because of a significant political disagreement with the clergy; another 12% left because of a significant political disagreement with the larger congregation. Some people left churches because they thought right-wing politics were too aligned with the religious organization; others left for the opposite reason (i.e., they thought that the religious organization was not aligned enough with their politics).

# Intersection of Religion with Gender, LGBTQ+, and Racial and Ethnic Identities

**Learning Objective 8.4** Analyze the intersection of religion with gender, LGBTQ+, and racial and ethnic identities.

Religion can significantly influence people's perceptions, attitudes, and values. People who are raised in a specific religion tend to absorb the values of that religious culture and integrate it into their personal value system. Religion can, therefore, shape or at least influence attitudes toward specific issues. We have already seen how religion can influence attitudes about politics. In this section, we explore how religious beliefs intersect with people's perceptions and acceptance of diverse gender, LGBTQ+, and racial and ethnic identities.

## Religion and Gender Identity

In an era of **cultural wars** in the United States, the exclusion or limitations of women in male-dominated religious systems continues to be questioned. In 2017, clergywomen in mainline Protestant churches had grown to 32%, with only two denominations having an equal number of men and women clergy (Campbell-Reed, 2018). However, there are no women priests in the Roman Catholic Church, although 80% of the lay ministers in the Catholic Church are women (Campbell-Reed, 2018). Women cannot attain the priesthood in either the Orthodox Church in America (Orthodox Church in America, 2023) or the Church of Jesus Christ of Latter-day Saints (Riess, 2019).

Few conservative churches or denominations have ordained or are willing to ordain women ministers. For example, Southern Baptist churches had ordained nearly 500 women by 1987, and 18 of them served as pastors. When fundamentalists gained control of the Southern Baptist Convention in the late 1990s, the Convention adopted a revision of its statement of faith to limit the office of pastor to men, arguing that the scriptures indicated that only men could serve in that role. More moderate Baptist churches formed the Cooperative Baptist Fellowship or joined the progressive Alliance of Baptists. Both supported the ordination of women (Shaw, 2021). In 2023, the Southern Baptist Convention expelled from its membership five churches with women pastors, including the largest Southern Baptist church in the United States, Saddleback Church in Lake Forest, California (DeRose, 2023b).

While Lydia, Phoebe, and Priscilla were women mentioned in the New Testament as having prominent roles in the early days of Christianity, other biblical passages are used to justify the limitation of women in religious leadership roles. In supporting the limitations of women's leadership and submission of wives, some draw attention to the fact that Jesus's disciples did not include women. Biblical verses (e.g., I Corinthians 14:34–35) admonish women to submit themselves to their husbands and indicate that the husband is the head of the wife. Some believe that God gave men, through Adam (Genesis 1:26–27), dominion over Eve and, therefore, men dominance over women. However, others argue that such an interpretation is incorrect and that both Adam and Eve (man and woman) were given dominion over every other living thing. There are other biblical examples of women who were leaders or prophets (e.g., Deborah; see Judges 4–5). The participation of women in leadership roles in both Protestantism and Judaism is a function of where the particular denomination falls on the liberal to conservative continuum.

Limitations on the participation of women in religious activities are by no means the sole province of Judeo-Christian groups. Islam and other religions either limit the participation of women or typically place leadership in the hands of men. Islam views women as equal to but different from men (Kharroub, 2015). They worship not alongside the men in their mosques but in separate areas (Al Islam, 2023). They are expected to

A female rabbi leads a service celebrating Rosh Hashanah.

**SOURCE:** Jules Selmes/Pearson Education Ltd

observe all pillars of Islam, including the five daily prayers and fasts during Ramadan. Women in some Muslim countries such as Afghanistan have severe limitations placed on them (e.g., rules against working and attending school and rules regarding dress). In many cases, these limitations may be more a function of the culture of the country or region than they are mandates of Islam. Even the dominant patriarchal interpretations of the Qur'an are "heavily influenced by historic and geopolitical conditions" (Kharroub, 2015, para. 12) and are disputed by feminist Islamic scholars.

Due to the diversity of the backgrounds of adherents as well as the society in which they live, many Islamic women in the United States may function differently than those in other parts of the world. Differences include the extent to which they work outside the home, assume active roles in Islamic centers and community life, and interactions with the non-Muslim community.

In addition to defining the parameters of religious participation of men and women, religion may also be used to prescribe roles of men and women outside the religious context. Such prescriptions may be done either directly or indirectly. In religious groups in which women are given a less prominent status, this may carry over into general family life and other aspects of society as a natural course. In other instances, the pronouncements may be more direct. Religious writings of great importance are continuously interpreted, studied, and analyzed. Consequently, the Bible and other religious writings, such as the Torah and Qur'an, may have a profound influence on many Americans.

It is important for educators to be aware that many of society's attitudes toward gender equality or inequality may be rooted in religious practices. If religious practices dictate that wives are to be subservient to their husbands or if women are prohibited from the highest or even high levels of leadership within a faith, then this practice could carry over into other aspects of everyday life. Regardless of their own beliefs about the role of women in society and family life, educators must not impose limits on the potential for leadership in the classroom, the school, or the future of young women. It is important that all students of all genders at an early age be encouraged and given opportunities to develop leadership skills. Those skills will enable them to pursue their future careers and personal choices and enable them to maximize their full potential.

## Religion and LGBTQ+ Identity

LGBTQ+ issues have become among the most controversial dilemmas facing religious institutions today. Attacks on gay men and lesbians in the religious context are often justified through biblical interpretations or other religious writings. Some argue that the textual interpretation and, in some cases, translation of religious scriptures regarding same-sex relationships are not clear and may be subject to influence by misguided beliefs. Others argue that these documents are clear on the issue of unions for same-sex couples, as in the book of Genesis, where God destroyed Sodom and Gomorrah because of perceived sinful behaviors, including the behaviors of same-sex partners. The debate is serious, as are the consequences. Conservative Christians and conservatives of other religious groups tend to view people who identify as LGBTQ+ as making a choice about their gender or sexual identity, being the result of the way people were raised, or both. They label such an identity as a sin and an abomination. More liberal religious groups contend that being LGBTQ+ is innate and natural and that they are born with a sexual orientation that is not heterosexual or straight (Garretson & Suhay, 2015).

In 2008, California's **Proposition 8**, a voter initiative, repealed a California law allowing marriage between same-sex couples by a 4% margin. It was strongly supported by the Roman Catholic Church, the Church of Jesus Christ of Latter-day Saints (Mormon), and evangelical Christian, Orthodox Jewish, Eastern Orthodox, and other religious groups (Foundation for Apologetic Information and Research, n.d.). The initiative, which passed, received considerable funding from out-of-state church-related groups (Howard University School of Law, 2023). However, all six of the Episcopal diocesan bishops in California, the Board of Rabbis of Southern California, various Jewish groups, the California Council of Churches, and other religious groups voiced their opposition to Prop 8 (Helfand, 2008). In 2013, the U.S. Supreme Court left in place a lower court's decision that Prop 8's ban was unconstitutional (*Hollingsworth v. Perry*, 2013). The Supreme Court's ruling in *Obergefell v. Hodges* (2015) ended the debate when it ruled marriage for same-sex couples to be legal in the United States. By January 2024, 35 countries recognized unions for same-sex couples, primarily in Australia, Europe, New Zealand, and North and South America, but also in Cuba, South Africa, and Taiwan (Human Rights Campaign, 2022).

While the Supreme Court has ruled on marriages for same-sex couples and the majority of the United States public supports it, the issue is not likely to go away. Churches have been forced to reassess their doctrines and positions on the matter. While some churches and denominations have held steadfastly against marriage for same-sex couples and those that identify as LGBTQ+, some welcome LGBTQ+ individuals into their community and have ordained LGBTQ+ ministers and performed marriages for same-sex couples. Views toward these individuals vary considerably among religious groups.

Episcopalians, for example, elevated a gay priest in 2003 and a lesbian priest in 2010 to bishops. These actions strained relations between the parent Anglican Church and the American Episcopal Church and have resulted in a schism in some Episcopal congregations over what some people consider excessively liberal practices. The General Convention of the Episcopal Church "approved in 2018 a resolution granting full churchwide access to same-sex marriage rites" (Millard, 2021, para. 1), and 83% of Episcopalians indicated that "homosexuality should be accepted" (Pew Research Center, 2018). In 2019, the Anglican Church in North America split from the Episcopal Church over theological stances on women's ordination and LGBTQ+ inclusion (Paulsen, 2023). However, members of the LGBTQ+ community and people of color continue not to feel welcomed in some Episcopal churches. These differences among Episcopalians are worldwide, with the clergy in Africa and Asia being much more conservative, not allowing marriages for same-sex couples or the ordination of LGBTQ+ priests and threatening a break with the more progressive Anglican churches (Asadu & Crary, 2022).

For years, Methodists disagreed about the inclusion of LGBTQ+ clergy and members. Nearly half of U.S. Methodists indicated in a 2014 survey that they supported marriage for same-sex couples. Delegates from around the world attending the General Conference of the United Methodist Church in 2019 took a stand by accepting its Traditional Plan, the policy that declared that "homosexuality" was incompatible with Christian teaching. The delegates rejected a plan that would allow individual churches to decide whether to accept LGBTQ+ clergy and perform marriages for same-sex couples (Jackson, 2019). As a result, some U.S. churches are openly not enforcing the new policies in the name of justice, other congregations are leaving the United Methodist Church, and about 20% of the church's membership have left the denomination (DeRose, 2023a).

In addition to the Episcopal Church, Reform and Conservative Jewish congregations, Evangelical Lutherans, the U.S. Presbyterian Church, Quakers, Unitarians, the United Church of Christ, and other progressive congregations sanction marriages for same-sex couples. Other mainline Christian religions such as the Disciples of Christ and the Progressive National Baptist Convention defer to local congregations to determine whether they will bless marriages for same-sex couples or ordain gay clergy (Kilgore, 2022).

The Catholic Church, along with American Baptists, Southern Baptists, the National Baptist Convention, the Assembly of God, Latter-day Saints, Missouri Synod Lutherans, and Orthodox Jews, prohibit marriage for same-sex couples. Same-sex unions in Islam are viewed as lewd and sinful. There are two primary references to gay orientation in the Qur'an (Qur'an 7:80–81 and 26:165). Both address gay behaviors negatively. In South and East Asian Islamic countries, no physical punishment for being gay is considered warranted. However, 62 countries across the world criminalize same-sex relationships by punishments that range from fines and imprisonment to flogging and forced psychiatric treatment (Bandera, 2023). Buddhists and Hindus have no clear position on the matter (Human Rights Campaign, n.d.-a, n.d.-b).

The evangelical community is a major stronghold of antigay sentiment and one of the key political groups in the fight against marriage for same-sex couples. As much of the general public and other religious groups have softened their stance against gay men and lesbians, evangelicals have seemingly been immutable in their stance (Whitehead & Perry, 2020). This, together with immigration and antiabortion issues, has had evangelicals diligently working to place in Congress and the White House conservatives who are sympathetic to their causes. However, a small but significant number of theologians and other conservative Christians have begun to develop moral arguments affirming same-sex relationships within orthodox theology. It is unlikely that the evangelical movement will embrace these unions in the near future, but some are beginning to reach out and welcome LGBTQ+ individuals into their congregations.

These diametrically opposed positions are at the crux of the conversion therapy controversy. Conversion or reparative therapy is based on the assumption that being gay or lesbian is a mental disorder and that individuals can change their sexual orientation. Behavioral, cognitive, psychoanalytic, and other techniques are used in an attempt to change or reduce one's same-sex attraction. Conversion therapy has been aggressively promoted at times by right-wing political and religious groups. The American Academy of Pediatrics, the American Psychiatric Association, and the American Psychological Association, together with other prominent organizations, have taken the position that being gay or lesbian is not a mental disorder and not something that needs to or can be "cured." They assert that conversion therapies lack scientific credibility and can be harmful (American Academy of Child and Adolescent Psychiatry, 2018). Twenty-two states and the District of Columbia have banned conversion therapy for minors (Movement Advancement Project, 2023).

When religion and politics become closely entwined, there is often a concern that legislators will attempt to mandate, through legislation, who may and who may not be allowed to teach, what curriculum is permissible, and what material in textbooks should be censored. Religious views toward LGBTQ+ issues have considerable implications for the educational setting. Educators have a right to their personal views about gender and sexual identity, but they do not have a right to impose their views in the public school setting. They cannot allow students to harass or bully one another, and they cannot allow students to attack other students verbally or otherwise in the classroom or on school grounds. It is the responsibility of every educator, including staff members, to provide a safe and accepting environment for all students.

## Religion and Racial and Ethnic Identity

In the United States, as in many other countries, religion has had a profound impact on racial and ethnic diversity issues. When individuals interpret religious scriptures to justify aberrant behavior, the consequences can be severe. At its 1995 meeting, the Southern Baptist Convention, the country's largest Protestant denomination, in an unprecedented act of contrition, apologized for the role it had played in the justification of slavery and in the maintenance of a culture of racism in the United States. For decades, well into the 1950s, noted ministers and religious leaders from various denominations defended segregation and helped to keep the practice alive. In fact, many Ku Klux Klan groups were led by both evangelical and Mainline Protestant ministers (Butler, 2021; Gorski & Perry, 2022). In this section, we focus on the role of religious groups in oppressing Black people in the United States from 1619 to today and the role of Black churches in the fight for freedom and equality. Religious groups were also complicit in the oppression of other groups of color, especially Native Americans, which was briefly discussed in Chapter 2.

**SLAVERY AND RACISM** The Bible does not condemn slavery, and its practice can be found throughout both the Old and New Testaments. In the New Testament, there is no record of either Jesus or Paul specifically condemning slavery, which was a common practice during that period. Paul returned an enslaved person to his enslaver rather than provide refuge, as was required by Jewish law (Deuteronomy 23:15–16). Therefore, proponents of slavery believed that this institution had a solid biblical foundation. For example, the Catholic king of Spain and his ministers viewed it as their divine right and obligation to enslave and Christianize or slaughter the native peoples of Latin America. Both Cortés and Pizarro operated under papal and governmental authority as they enslaved and killed thousands of people and justified their behavior with biblical texts.

Before the Civil War, both the defenders of slavery and abolitionists who wanted slavery abolished depended on the Bible to uphold their rationale for supporting or not supporting slavery (Jones, 2020). Churches were deeply involved in these debates, resulting in splits in the Methodist, Presbyterian, and Baptist churches (Butler, 2021). Defenders of slavery also claimed that the Bible reinforced the racial supremacy of White people (Jones, 2020). Although abolitionists from both the North and South rejected slavery, they did not always believe in Black equality and, within a few years after the war, Jim Crow laws and segregation again suppressed the freedom of Black people (Jones, 2020).

**ROLE OF BLACK RELIGIOUS GROUPS** In the first century in which enslaved people from Africa lived on the land that would become the United States, they followed primarily traditional West African religions or Islam (Mohamed et al., 2021). Many enslavers would not allow enslaved people to attend church or prayer meetings with them or to be baptized as Christians. When enslaved people did attend religious services, they were likely to hear White clergy emphasizing the importance of obeying their enslavers. To ensure that enslaved people did not interpret Christianity as a path to freedom, at least six colonies passed laws that prevented baptism from leading to freedom from slavery (Mohamed et al., 2021). As a result, "many Christian enslaved people held secret services with distinctive styles of praying, singing and worship" (Mohamed et al., 2021, para. 6). At the same time, some enslaved people began to convert to Christianity in the eighteenth century and attend church with their enslavers, although they would have to sit in the back of the church or in the balcony. When the Black membership of a church in Macon, Georgia, outnumbered the White membership, the White members built a church for Black members next to the original church, which remained under the control of the White congregation (Jones, 2020). As Martin Luther King, Jr. once said, "the most segregated hour of Christian America is eleven o'clock on Sunday morning" (Equal Justice Initiative, 2016, para. 4).

Because enslaved people were prohibited from attending most mainline and evangelical White Christian denominations or their active participation was very limited (Jones, 2020), they established their own denominations. The first Black denomination, the African Methodist Episcopal (AME) Church, was founded in 1816, followed by the African Methodist Episcopal Zion (AME Zion) Church in 1821. Black churches provided leadership opportunities as men became pastors and women

Parishioners attend a Sunday service at a Black Baptist church.

**SOURCE:** Ted Pink/Alamy Stock Photo

organized committees and organizations to support their communities. By 1884, women were allowed to preach in the AME Church. Black churches and religious institutions served their communities in different ways. Some provided food, shelter, insurance cooperatives, libraries, and job training (Mohamed et al., 2021). Other religious organizations, such as the Nation of Islam, provided pride and a self-help philosophy while encouraging education and Black entrepreneurship.

After the Civil War, the AME and AME Zion churches sent missionaries to the South, resulting in a dramatic increase in the number of Black members. Other Black denominations were founded during this period, including the Christian Methodist Episcopal Church (founded in 1870), National Baptist Convention USA (founded in 1880), and National Baptist Convention of America International (founded in 1915). Near the end of the nineteenth century, the Pentecostal church was founded, including the Church of God in Christ (1897), the largest Black Pentecostal denomination. Catholicism also grew among Black Americans during the Great Migration from the South to northern and western cities during the twentieth century (Mohamed et al., 2021). The importance of the Black church to Black people is eloquently expressed by historian Henry Louis Gates, Jr. (2021): "religion enabled them and their descendants to learn, to grow, to develop, to interpret and reinvent the world in which they were trapped; it enabled them to bide their time—ultimately, time for them to fight for their freedom, and for us to continue the fight for ours" (p. xxii).

**CIVIL RIGHTS MOVEMENT AND BLACK CHURCHES**   The Civil Rights Movement in the mid-twentieth century was centered in the South's Black Protestant churches. Many of the civil rights leaders were ministers or church leaders (e.g., Martin Luther King, Jr., Ralph Abernathy, Andrew Young, and Jesse Jackson). In 1957, they formed the Southern Christian Leadership Conference (SCLC), with Martin Luther King, Jr. as its president, to employ nonviolent activities in protests for civil rights across the South. From their pulpits, these religious leaders were able to direct boycotts and organize civil disobedience and nonviolent confrontations such as the 1955 bus boycott in Montgomery, Alabama, where seating for Black bus riders was segregated, as were many everyday activities.

Civil disobedience included sit-ins at segregated public places such as restaurants, where Black individuals refused to leave when asked or ordered to do so. However, not all Black church leaders agreed with the tactics of the SCLC, fearing violence or preferring a more legalistic approach. As a result, King and his supporters established the Progressive National Baptist Convention, which fully supported the "direct-action protests" that other Black denominations did not support (Gates, 2021).

Black churches and their ministers deserve much of the credit for bringing about the civil rights gained in the past 75 years (Gates, 2021). Prevented from voting by suppressive law and practices and alienated and disillusioned by mainstream politics, few Black Americans registered to vote in the past. For example, only 2% of Alabama's eligible Black voters were registered to vote in 1965 (History.com Editors, 2022). After a young Black demonstrator was fatally shot in February 1965 at a peaceful protest in Marion, Alabama, a March for Voting Rights was planned from Selma to Montgomery (54 miles). On March 7, 1965, the 600 protestors were led by activists John Lewis (later to be Congressman John Lewis) and Hosea Williams, who were knocked to the ground and beaten with clubs and whips as protestors were chased, beaten, and sprayed with tear gas by deputies on horseback. The assault, which became known as "Bloody Sunday," was filmed and soon aired on national television, leading to outrage across the county and the passage of the Voting Rights Act in August 1965. But the law alone did not lead to an increase in voting by Black citizens. Clergy in Black churches nationwide advocated church involvement in social and political issues. In recent years, Black churches have been extremely successful in registering millions of voters and played an important role in getting voters to the polls in presidential and midterm elections that resulted in shifts in Congressional seats and the 2008, 2012, and 2020 presidential elections.

# Classroom Implications: Religion in the Classroom

**Learning Objective 8.5** Interpret legal rulings on religion in schools and their implications for school prayer, school vouchers, book banning, and teaching religion.

As part of the curriculum, students should learn that the United States (and indeed the world) is rich in religious diversity. Educators show their respect for religious differences through their interactions with students from different religious backgrounds. Understanding the importance of religion to students and their families is an advantage in developing effective teaching strategies. Instructional activities can build on students' religious experiences to help them learn concepts. This technique helps students recognize that their religious identity is valued in the classroom and encourages them to respect the religious diversity that exists.

Christianity has had a great influence on education from the colonial days in which the students who were attending school were learning religion in private schools to the common schools that were established for White students in the nineteenth century. Catholic families complained in the mid-1800s about the Protestant bible being used in public classrooms. As you will see in the next section, the Supreme Court has considered numerous cases related to the influence of religion on education. One of the most famous of these trials was the Scopes Trial in 1925 in which a high school teacher, John Scopes, was charged with violating Tennessee law by teaching evolution—an issue that is still debated today. Religious groups and leaders continue to be involved in debates about and legislation related to educational issues that undergird cultural wars such as book bans, critical race theory, school prayer, gender diversity, sexual orientation, and parental rights.

Protestants have a long history of involvement in both public and private educational programs. Differences in beliefs among Protestants have resulted in court cases to determine what can or cannot be taught to or asked of students in the public schools. For example, efforts by some fundamentalist Christians to require the teaching of creationism has resulted in litigation. Jehovah's Witnesses have had issues with schools because their children may abstain from saluting the flag, saying a pledge of allegiance, or singing a national anthem because of their belief that these patriotic ceremonies are religious acts reserved for God (Jehovah's Witnesses, 2023). Some Amish have fought in courts to remove their children from public schools after they have completed eighth grade. Other religious groups continue to fight against the 1963 Supreme Court decision that disallowed prayer in school.

Community resistance to cultural pluralism and multicultural education has, at times, been led by families and legislators associated with conservative religious groups. Because cultural pluralism inevitably involves religious diversity, multicultural education is sometimes viewed as an impediment to efforts to maintain the status quo or to return to the religious values of the past. Multicultural education, however, provides a basis for understanding and appreciating diversity and minimizes the problems related to people being different from one another. In this section, we discuss some of the recent court rulings, the status of school prayer in schools, book banning, school vouchers, and teaching religion in schools.

# Legal Rulings on Religion in Schools

School districts and various state legislators who seek to circumvent the principle of separation of church and state continually test the First Amendment. The following are examples of Supreme Court rulings related to education, the First Amendment, and the principle of the separation of church and state:

- *Engel v. Vitale* (1962). The Court ruled that any type of prayer, even that which is nondenominational, is unconstitutional government sponsorship of religion.
- *Abington School District v. Schempp* (1963). The Court found that Bible reading over the school intercom was unconstitutional.
- *Murray v. Curlett* (1963). The Court found that forcing a child to participate in Bible reading and prayer was unconstitutional.
- *Epperson v. Arkansas* (1968). The Court ruled that a state statute banning the teaching of evolution was unconstitutional. A state cannot set a course of study in order to promote a religious point of view.
- *Lemon v. Kurtzman* (1971). The Court ruled that the state could not reimburse private schools (mostly Catholic) for portions of salaries of teachers who used public school textbooks and materials. This case established the "Lemon test" to determine whether government actions violate the Establishment Clause of the First Amendment of the U.S. Constitution. The three-part test requires that government's action must (1) have a secular purpose, (2) neither advance nor prohibit religion, and (3) not result in excessive government involvement with religion.
- *Stone v. Graham* (1980). The Court found that the posting of the Ten Commandments in schools was unconstitutional.
- *Wallace v. Jaffree* (1985). The Court ruled that the state's moment of silence in a public school statute was unconstitutional, as a legislative record revealed that the motivation for the statute was the encouragement of prayer.
- *Edwards v. Aquillard* (1987). The Court found it unconstitutional for the state to require the teaching of creation science in all instances in which evolution is taught. The statute had a clear religious motivation.
- *Lee v. Weisman* (1992). The Court ruled it unconstitutional for a school district to provide any clergy to perform nondenominational prayer at elementary or secondary school graduations. It involves government sponsorship of worship.

Public schools are supposed to be free of religious doctrine and perspective. However, debate about the public school's responsibility in fostering student morality and social responsibility is constant. A major point of disagreement focuses on who should determine the morals that will provide the context of the educational program in a school. Because religious diversity is so great in the United States, that task is nearly impossible. Therefore, most public schools incorporate commonly accepted American values that largely transcend religions.

Although public schools should be secular, they are greatly influenced by the predominant values of the community. Educators must be cognizant of this influence before introducing certain readings and ideas that stray far from what the community is willing to accept within their belief and value structure. Teachers face difficult choices when school administrators give in to parental demands to violate the principles of separation of church and state by infusing school prayer or religious instruction into the curriculum.

There are several controversial issues in schools that challenge the principle of separation of church and state. In many instances, the majority in a given community may support an issue that may already have been ruled as unconstitutional by the courts. Among the controversial issues that are often on the agenda of evangelical

Christians and conservative religious groups are school prayer, school vouchers, the banning of books, and teaching religion in the classroom.

## School Prayer

Despite the 1962 and 1963 Supreme Court decisions regarding school prayer, conservative Christian groups have persisted in their efforts to revive prayer in the schools. What is at issue for the courts is not whether the public favors school prayer but whether it is constitutionally valid. Supreme Court decisions do not prevent teachers or students from praying privately in a school. Teachers or students can offer their own private prayer before the noon meal or pray alone between classes and before and after school. The law forbids public group prayer.

Advocates of school prayer sometimes advance their efforts under the term "voluntary prayer." The interpretation of what constitutes voluntary school prayer has become a main issue in the prayer controversy. Some proponents of school prayer advocate mandated school prayer, with students voluntarily choosing to participate or not participate. The courts had consistently struck down such attempts, indicating that there would be social pressure for students to participate, but the Supreme Court took a different approach in 2022 with *Kennedy v. Bremerton School District*. In this case, high school assistant football coach Joseph Kennedy was placed on paid administration leave for praying midfield after games even after the school district had asked him to stop. He was not rehired the following school year (Brannon, 2022). The Supreme Court declared that the coach's right to pray on the football field with students was protected under the Constitution because it counts as free speech.

Following the *Kennedy* decision, the U.S. Department of Education (2023) released new guidance related to prayer in public schools. It states that "Teachers, school administrators, and other school employees may not encourage or discourage private prayer or other religious activity" (para. 20). It also indicates that the U.S. Constitution allows school employees to engage in private prayer during the workday "where they are not acting in their official capacities and where their prayer does not result in any coercion of students" (para. 21). However, school employees may not "compel, coerce, persuade, or encourage students to join in the employee's prayer or other religious activity, and a school may take reasonable measures to ensure that students are not pressured or encouraged to join in the private prayer of their teachers or coaches" (para. 21). The debates about school prayer and lawsuits to try to overturn other Supreme Court decisions on it are likely to continue.

## Explore and Focus Your Cultural Lens
### Debate: Religious Indoctrination in Schools

In 1647 the first formal American school system was established in Massachusetts to ensure that children would grow up with the ability to read the Bible. Christianity continued to be overtly reflected in textbooks into the twentieth century when court decisions began prohibiting schools from indoctrinating students in a religion (Lupu et al., 2019). Some people today are still very concerned that God and religious sentiment appear to have disappeared from public schools and argue that these exclusions infringe on their First Amendment right for the free exercise of religion.

Conservative Christians, especially those who identify with White Nationalist Christianity, contend that liberal and multiculturalist teachers indoctrinate students in public schools with left-wing ideas about diversity, social justice, and equity

that they perceive being against their religious beliefs. In New York City in 2006, Christian groups argued that schools' promotion of cultural pluralism discriminated against Christianity in the symbols displayed for the holiday season at the end of the year. At the same time, conservatives are accused of trying to impose their fundamentalist values on students in public schools as they have books removed from classrooms and legislate against teaching about topics such as slavery, gender, or LGBTQ+ issues.

Educators are faced with a conflict between the rights of students to engage in religious expression and the rights of other students to be broadly educated in a nonhostile environment without the promotion of religion. Do you agree with the following statement?

Teachers should expose students to multiple ways to think about a subject or about life without promoting a specific religion.

**FOR**

- A strength of considering a content area from multiple perspectives rather than from a specific religious perspective is that it provides students the opportunity to learn reasons for the different perspectives that will help them confirm their own beliefs or change them based on new or different data.

- It is not fair to students from nondominant religious backgrounds to never see nor hear their religious heritage mentioned in class activities or projects, although the heritages, cultures, and contributions of the major U.S. religious groups are continuously addressed because they have been so integrated into the curriculum that they are hardly noticed by anyone other than non-Christians.

- Schools can provide classes that study religions, compare religions, or discuss religions in an objective manner as long as the goal is not to promote a specific religion.

- In most states and school districts, parents can have their children opt out of classes if they do not want their children exposed to specific topics or books, which then allows all other students to fully participate in the study and discussion of those topics.

- Teaching a family's religion and its values should be the responsibility of family members and religious leaders, not public school teachers.

**AGAINST**

- The public school curriculum has become too secular and no longer reflects the moral values that families expect their children to learn.

- Based on the First Amendment and their freedom of speech, teachers should be able teach academic content from the perspective of their religion, especially if they are very committed to it.

- Teachers should not be forced to teach about diversity and social justice when they go against their religious beliefs.

- Teaching students multiple ways to think about a subject or about life may make them think that they have options to live their lives in ways not approved by their families' religions.

- The United States was founded on religious principles that are critical to being an American, and they should be included in the public school curriculum.

## Questions for Discussion

1. In what ways do conservatives and more liberal religious groups perceive the other group is indoctrinating students into particular religious or secular views through the public school curriculum?

2. How do students learn and maintain sound moral values if religious values are not taught in schools?

3. Why do you think it is (or is not) important to separate religion from the content taught in public schools?

# School Vouchers

As with school prayer, **school vouchers** elicit strong emotions and responses from both their supporters and their detractors. Vouchers are intended to partially reimburse parents for monies that would have been used to educate their children in public schools. The first voucher program was created in 1991 in Milwaukee, Wisconsin, to provide families with low incomes access to more high-quality options, public or private, for their children. The funds for vouchers come from tax monies, which vary from state to state and among school districts. Sixteen states plus the District of Columbia offer school vouchers (EdChoice, 2023). The amount families receive varies from state to state and averages from about $2,000 to $5,000, though in some instances it may range as high as $25,000 for students with disabilities (Vevea, 2023). Individual school districts may also provide vouchers. Voucher initiatives are often strongly supported by religious groups that encourage parents to send their children to private religious schools.

Parents and others who support school vouchers point to the failure of the public schools to educate their children adequately. Religious groups may believe that schools face a moral decline as evidenced by school violence, drugs, and teen pregnancies. Some parents believe that school vouchers should be available to pay tuition for religious schools that reflect their religious beliefs, values, and commitments and can integrate religion throughout the curriculum using taxpayer dollars (Chen, 2020). Opponents to voucher initiatives maintain that vouchers will take away needed funds from public schools, exacerbating the fiscal crisis in the public schools and undermining accountability for public funds (National Education Association, 2021).

## Book Banning

Censorship occurs when expressive materials such as books, magazines, films, videos, or works of art are removed or kept from public access, including the removal of materials from textbook adoption lists and materials from school libraries. Censorship may be based on the age and other characteristics of the potential user. Targets for the censors are books and materials that are perceived as disrespectful of authority and religion, destructive to social and cultural values, obscene, pornographic, unpatriotic, or in violation of individual and familial rights of privacy. Just over half (51%) of the book challenges are directed at schools and school libraries, 49% at public libraries, and 1% at college libraries and other public institutions (American Library Association [ALA], 2023).

Books may be banned for a multitude of reasons, including the use of offensive language such as profanity (e.g., *To Kill a Mockingbird*, *The Perks of Being a Wallflower*); the use of racial slurs (*Adventures of Huckleberry Finn*, *Of Mice and Men*); the use of witchcraft (e.g., the *Harry Potter* series); and violence (*The Color Purple*, *Slaughterhouse Five*). Books written by or about people who identify as LGBTQ+ (e.g., *Gender Queer: A Memoir*, *All Boys Aren't Blue*) are also frequently attacked, as are those that are sexually explicit (e.g., *Lawn Boy*, *Out of Darkness*) and those with pictures containing nudity.

The ALA (2023) reported that censors targeted 2,571 unique titles in 2022—the highest number of books since ALA began collecting these data. PEN America—an organization of writers, artists, and journalists who protect free expression—found that 1,557 books had been banned in U.S. public school classrooms and libraries in the 2022–2023 school year. States with the largest number of book bans in school districts were Florida (1,406), Texas (625), Missouri (333), Utah (281), and Pennsylvania (186). Most instances of book bans in schools were young adult books, middle grade books, or picture books for young children (Meehan et al., 2023).

The ALA (2023) reports that book challenges today come primarily from well-organized, conservative political movements to remove books and other material that do not meet their approval. Social media and the Internet are used by a vocal minority of groups and individuals to distribute book lists to local conservative organizations and individual advocates who then present lists of books they want removed from library and classroom shelves to principals, school boards, and state textbook committees (Meehan et al., 2023). A new twist in the censoring of books over the past few years is attacks on school and public librarians who have been subject to "defamatory name-calling, online harassment, social media attacks, and doxing, as well as direct threats to their safety, their employment, and their very liberty" (ALA, 2023, para. 4).

The impact of censorship in the public schools cannot be underestimated. Censorship or attempts at censorship have resulted in the dismissal or resignation of administrators and teachers. Censorship has split communities and has the potential to create as much controversy as did the desegregation of schools. Those who seek censorship feel passionately that the cause they support is just and morally right. Censors believe that they are obligated to continue their fight to rid schools of objectionable materials that in their opinion contaminate the minds of their children and contribute to the moral decay of society.

Opponents of the book bans want their children exposed to multiple perspectives written by and about people from diverse groups. They also believe that censors infringe on academic freedom as they seek to destroy meaningful and inclusive education. Students are also protesting book bans and calling for protection of their freedom to read. According to PEN America, students' "efforts are helping to ensure students have access to a diversity of views and expressions, school libraries serve the educational process by making knowledge and ideas available, and books remain available regardless of the personal or political ideologies of groups and policymakers" (Meehan et al., 2023, para. 59).

The failure to communicate effectively with parents is a contributing source of alienation between educators and parents. Teachers need to communicate the objectives of new curricula and to explain how these programs enrich the educational experience.

Showing families how the curriculum and related readings support rather than conflict with basic family values can prevent potential issues. Teachers are well advised to make certain that they have fully and accurately assessed the climate within the community before introducing new or controversial materials, teaching strategies, or books. Experienced colleagues and supervisors can serve as barometers as to how students, families, and the community will react to various new materials or teaching techniques.

## Teaching Religion

Although religion and public schooling are to remain separate, religion can be taught in schools as a legitimate discipline for objective study. A comparative religions course is part of the curriculum offered in many secondary schools. In this approach, students are not forced to practice a religion as part of their educational program. They can, however, study one or more religions.

In discussing religion in the public school classroom, there are a number of caveats that every teacher should remember:

- Schools are allowed to sponsor the study of religion. However, they may not sponsor a religion.
- Schools may provide instruction on the beliefs of a religion but may not indoctrinate or in any way try to convert students to that religion.
- Schools may teach students what people of various religions believe, but they may not teach students what to believe.

Religious symbols and objects such as the Bible, the Qur'an, Muslim prayer rugs, a cross, a Star of David, and the Ten Commandments may be used for instructional purposes. They may even be placed temporarily on the classroom walls if used specifically for instructional purposes. They may not be used to proselytize nor be displayed beyond the time for instructional purposes. The uses of Christmas trees and Hanukkah menorahs (i.e., candelabra lit each night during Hanukkah) have been determined by the courts to be secular symbols and are permitted to be displayed temporarily. Students and teachers can say "Merry Christmas" to each other. Public school teachers may choose to avoid any possible misunderstandings or conflict by wishing their students "Happy Holidays" rather than "Merry Christmas," especially if there is any question regarding the student's religious preferences.

## Revisiting the Opening Case Study

In the opening scenario for this chapter, Dr. Hovestadt was excited about sharing the good news with the Patel and the Rose families that their children had been selected as the school's honors assembly speakers. In the previous years, the parents of the students selected had always been ecstatic, thanking Dr. Hovestadt and heaping praise on the school and the teachers. He was surprised by Mr. Rose's request that the assembly be rescheduled so as to not conflict with their religious observances. While there were other Jewish children who had attended the school in the past and did so currently, this was the first time that a religious conflict had become an issue. Dr. Hovestadt decided that the honors assembly could be held without the school superintendent. He contacted the Rose and Patel families and the leadership of the parent-teacher organization to determine an appropriate date and time for the event. He also set up a meeting with the school superintendent to discuss how the school system could assist principals and other educators in setting dates for school events that would not conflict with important religious observances of their students' families. Dr. Hovestadt was also thinking that he and other educators may need additional training related to the religious groups in their communities and greater involvement of diverse religious groups in the educational community.

All students in every school should be able to expect that their school will value each student's cultural values, including their religious values and practices. Unexpected conflicts and issues are inevitable when schools serve so many students from so many cultural groups. How the school meets and addresses these challenges is the real determinant of how much a school's administration and staff truly value diversity.

*(continued)*

## Reflect and Apply

1. Why did Dr. Hovestadt contact the leadership of his school's parent-teacher organization as well as the Rose and Patel families before finalizing a new date for the honors ceremony?

2. How can you better inform yourself about the religious diversity of the students and staff in your school?

3. What measures should the school or school district have in place to prevent conflicts that could result because of the lack of attention to the importance of religion in some families' lives?

# Summary

- Immigration and migration patterns have influenced the religious diversity of schools across the United States as people from other countries and other regions of the United States settle in new communities. Historically, the membership of the U.S. Congress was almost all White Christian men. Today, it remains predominantly Christian (88%), with over half of the representatives being Protestant, and the number of members who are not Christian growing to match their representation in the U.S. population. The group least represented in Congress is the population that is not affiliated with a religious organization.

- Religion is an integral part of the American culture and can significantly shape the lives of many students. The vast majority of Americans (72%) indicate that their religion is important to them and that they attend weekly religious services. Many Americans take for granted their religious liberties, since they have enjoyed the freedom of religious choice and worship set forth as a basic right in the country's founding principles. The significance of religion prompted the nation's founders to stipulate by law that there was to be a freedom of religion without government interference and that there would be a separation of church and state. This principle has often been and continues to be challenged by individuals and by religious groups.

- A majority (66%) of the U.S. population identify themselves as Christian, being affiliated with one of the two largest branches, Protestantism or Catholicism, and smaller denominations such as Eastern Orthodoxy or the Church of Jesus Christ of Latter-day Saints (also known as Mormons). The country continues to have considerable religious pluralism within the Christian family, particularly among the conservative and mainline churches. The majority of the earliest European settlers were Protestant, but the religious landscape of the country has been changing with each passing decade. Many immigrants are arriving from areas such

as Asia, the Middle East, and Africa, bringing their religions with them. People who identify as Jewish make up about 2% of the U.S. population while another 2% of the population are Muslim, Buddhist, and Hindu. Many Native Americans are currently trying to revive their native religions that early colonizers, religious leaders, and politicians tried to eliminate over the past 400 years. Although the United States is a religious country compared to some other regions of the world, an increasing number of people (27%) identify as nonaffiliated with a religious organization or religion itself.

- Experiences and values in churches, mosques, synagogues, and temples are transferred into people's everyday lives. Many positive values are transferred into home, work, and school settings. However, care must be taken that restrictive gender practices in religious settings and negative attitudes toward gay men, lesbians, and transgender individuals and toward students of diverse racial and ethnic groups do not become school practices.

- Religious groups, school boards, and parent groups have persisted in attempts to circumvent laws and principles related to the separation of church and state. However, the Supreme Court has historically prohibited open school prayer and the infusion of specific religious perspectives into the curriculum. Nevertheless, these rulings continue to be challenged. Some conservative religious groups advocate for school prayer and school vouchers with the intention of funding private religious education. Some groups and parents have worked diligently to infuse their religious values into school curricula and to control school boards. Educators, like their students, come from different religious backgrounds and may have different values in relation to the importance of religion or what they believe. It is critical that schools provide a safe and accepting environment for every student, every educator, and every staff member regardless of their religion or beliefs.

## Pearson eTextbook Application Videos

The following videos are available in the Pearson eTextbook and can be used to practice observing and applying what you learned in this chapter.

**Pearson eTextbook Application**
**Video Example 8.2**

In this video, two educators discuss the day-to-day activities of a young Muslim student who joined their school community. Pay particular attention to the ways in which this student's cultural norms were not in congruence with the norms of the school.

**Pearson eTextbook Application**
**Video Example 8.3**

In this video, the concept of whether or not evolution or intelligent design should be taught in schools is presented. Pay attention to the approaches from both sides of the debate.

# Chapter 9
# Geography (Place)

## Learning Objectives

*As you read this chapter, you should be able to:*

**9.1** Analyze the role of place in the lives of students and their families.

**9.2** Compare and contrast at least three strengths and challenges across regions of the United States and describe their impact on education.

**9.3** Analyze the benefits of living and attending school in rural, urban, and suburban areas.

**9.4** Explore the impact of globalization on the lives of people and the intersectionality of environmental justice.

**9.5** Analyze how place interacts with race and class to provide inequitable outcomes in society.

**9.6** Create lessons that incorporate students' cultural and geographic backgrounds, are place based, and incorporate global perspectives.

## Opening Case Study

In November, a new student, Imad Amari, appeared at Mark Pulaski's fifth-grade classroom door. Imad, whose family had moved to the United States, was one of the fortunate students able to immigrate from the violence in Syria. He was from a well-educated middle-class family and had enough basic English skills to carry on a conversation. Mr. Pulaski introduced him to the class, assigned him a desk, and began the lesson.

Before a month had passed, Mr. Pulaski noticed that other students had not accepted Imad. In fact, some were making fun of his mannerisms and his accent. Imad's involvement in the class had been minimal up to that point, and Mr. Pulaski was concerned that Imad had been very quiet, not actively participating in the lively discussions that were encouraged. He was performing as well as most other students on the assigned lessons and politely did whatever was asked of him. He ate alone at lunch and did not engage with the other students during recess.

### Reflect

1. What could have Mr. Pulaski done prior to Imad's arrival to enhance the likelihood of his acceptance by his classmates?

2. How does growing up in a different part of the world affect one's experiences in a U.S. school? What cultural capital did Imad have when he came to the United States with his family?

3. How could Mr. Pulaski learn more about Imad's cultural background?

4. If you were Mr. Pulaski, how would you get the students to stop mocking Imad?

# The Importance of Place

**Learning Objective 9.1** Analyze the role of place in the lives of students and their families.

People's identities are closely linked to the place or geographical area in which they grew up and the places they later live. One of the first questions people ask when meeting someone new is "Where are you from?" The answer is then used to determine whether a common background and experiences are shared. Although membership in other groups or subcultures may have a great impact on identity, the place or places in which people have lived provide a cultural context for living.

Because people grew up in the same or a similar geographic area as their neighbors or friends does not mean they experienced the place in the same ways. Some members of a community have lived there much longer than others and have different histories and experiences that sometimes lead to conflict with more recent arrivals. The area takes on a different meaning based on a member's race, ethnicity, religion, age, and language as well as how membership in those groups is viewed by other members of the community. Some people have been the recipients of racism, sexism, or other discriminatory behavior. Other people are privileged because of their race and/or affluence. Almost all adults in one suburban neighborhood may have post-baccalaureate degrees and work as professionals or managers. Farming and related jobs are common in one area, logging and fishing in another, and manufacturing in yet another.

The natural surroundings and climate make a difference in the way people work, relax, and interact. People from Hawaii, Alaska, the mountains of Colorado, and the prairies of Nebraska adapt to their spaces in different ways. People in new environments may find that the "natives" use unfamiliar dialects and phrases and react to events somewhat differently than they are used to. Imad in the opening scenario, for instance, has an accent and mannerisms that are different from those of other students in his new school. Such differences are particularly noticeable when people travel outside the United States, but they also appear to some degree in different parts of the same city and in different regions of the United States.

Different individuals and groups perceive places and events differently. Because their perceptions are different, their responses tend to be different as well. Some will find a given locale the ideal place to live and raise a family; others will feel isolated, crowded, or trapped. Mountains are critical to the well-being of some; others feel the need to be near bodies of water or the desert or greenery. Wide-open spaces in which one can live for a long period of time with little interaction with others provide freedom for some but boredom and confinement for others. Cities can be exciting and stimulating places for some but can be stifling and impersonal to others. Thus, places provide complex multiple identities for the people who live in them. Understanding the place, including the particular part of the city or county, from which students have come helps teachers know the context of their everyday experiences. In this section, we review the meaning of geography and the place of the United States in the world.

## What Is Geography?

You probably studied geography in elementary school as you learned about different parts of the world and memorized state capitals. People may be enticed to learn more about a country when they receive news coverage because of armed conflicts, climate change, and economic turmoil. Major natural disasters in 2023 included floods in Brazil and Pakistan; droughts across central Africa; wildfires in Chile, Greece, and Canada; tropical storms in New Zealand, Madagascar, and Mozambique;

and earthquakes in Turkey and Syria (Atlas Magazine, 2023). Conflicts in Ukraine, Somalia, Syria, and Yemen are covered on the news. During the COVID-19 pandemic, information was readily available about how different countries and cities around the world were handling the situation. Many Americans had never heard of these places and would not have been able to locate them on a map were it not for the news coverage. People who are fortunate enough to travel to other parts of the country and world become familiar with geographic, cultural, and language differences. People who are place-bound and unable to travel far beyond their own neighborhoods may have to learn about these differences in books, from the media, and on the Internet.

The word *geography* comes from the Greek word *geographia*, which means a description of Earth's surface. It is the study of places, cities, countries, mountains, deserts, rural areas, oceans, continents, and communities. Geographers try to determine why places are the way they are. They not only explore the physical features of a place but also examine the economic activities, human settlement patterns, and cultures of the people who live there. The place where one lives is the space or land area that is distinctive and has meaning or symbolism for the people who live there.

**Physical geography** is the study of the physical features of Earth, such as the climate, soils, vegetation, water, and landforms. **Human geography**, on the other hand, is the study of the economic, social, and cultural systems that have evolved in a specific location. It encompasses many of the topics discussed in this text, such as classism, racism, ethnicity, poverty, language, sexual orientation, religion, exceptionalities, and age differences.

Geographers use a number of tools to record and track the physical and human geography of a place. Maps are the most common, as you probably remember from your study of geography. With today's technologies, geographers are able to understand an area in great and intricate detail through the use of computers, global positioning system devices, and satellite images. Teachers use maps to understand the places students live and the importance of place in one's everyday life.

## Our Place in the World

Placing the United States within the world provides a context for understanding where we and others live. First, people are concentrated in certain areas since few choose to live in Earth's coldest or driest areas. Almost 90% of the world population lives in the Northern Hemisphere—the area north of the equator (WorldAtlas, 2023a). Over half of the world's population of nearly 8 billion lives in Asia (World Population Review, 2023a). India, with a population of 1.429 billion, and China, with 1.426 billion, are the two largest countries in the world in terms of population. The United States, the world's third-largest country, had a population estimated to be 340 million in 2023, which was 4.5% of the world's population (World Population Review, 2023d), but the United Nations (2017) projects that Nigeria will overtake the United States by 2050 as the third most populous country.

As discussed in Chapter 2, the United States is culturally diverse, with Indigenous people whose ancestors have lived on the land for thousands of years and other people who have immigrated either by choice or by force from other parts of the world over the past 600 years. It is a resource-rich region that has undergone a great deal of economic development over the past 200 years. Its metropolitan areas are technology rich and oriented to a global economy. The region is very consumer oriented, with many people buying the latest versions of the products its businesses produce. Although it is essentially an affluent area, many of its residents live in poverty.

# Regional Diversity in the United States

**Learning Objective 9.2** Compare and contrast at least three strengths and challenges across regions of the United States and describe their impact on education.

Pearson eTextbook

**Video Example 9.1**

This video discusses the organization Appalshop, which makes art and film devoted to the region of Appalachia. Consider exploring similar groups across the United States.

https://www.youtube.com/watch?v=0S3rWrQmZag

Regional differences become apparent to educators as they move from one area to another to attend college or work. Sometimes local and regional differences are hardly noticeable. At other times, they lead to a number of adjustments in the way one lives, the content that can be taught in the classroom, and the manner in which one interacts with the community. For example, religion plays a more important role in some regions of the country than others, which could influence a teacher's approach to teaching sex education, gender, or evolution.

Not only teachers move around the country and globe, so too do students and their families, especially if the parents are in the military, itinerant agricultural workers, or on a fast track at a multinational corporation. Students such as Imad in the chapter-opening scenario may experience cultural shock, something that should be considered as they settle in a new school. To meet the needs of students, educators should be aware of the influences of geography on the culture of the people who live in the area, especially school-age children.

Regional comparisons are at times difficult to make, with different sources utilizing different regional categories. The federal government tends to use four regions: Northeast, South, Midwest, and West. However, some reporting is broken down into smaller regions (e.g., New England, Appalachia, Southwest, Great Plains). Each region is distinctive, often with different political leanings, racial and ethnic backgrounds and experiences, religious values, and educational priorities.

The U.S. population increased by 7.4% between 2010 and 2020, an increase that was the second smallest decade-long growth rate since 1790, primarily due to two factors: lower immigration levels due to federal restrictions on immigration and fewer births and more deaths due to drug- and pandemic-related deaths (Frey, 2021a). The rate of population growth in the South and West has been two to five times higher than in the Northeast and Midwest since the 1970s. The South's population comprises 38% of the U.S. population compared to 24% in the West, 21% in the Midwest, and 17% in the Northeast (U.S. Census Bureau, 2021b). These regional growth patterns have significant political implications on the balance of power in Congress. State population totals in the 2020 Census determine how many Congressional seats each state will have for the next decade. Beginning with the elections in 2022, Texas had gained two Congressional seats, five states gained one seat, and seven states lost one seat (U.S. Census Bureau, 2021a).

The 2020 Census revealed that the population of color had grown in every region of the United States. The states with the highest percentages of people of color are primarily in the South, followed by the West, while those with the lowest are primarily in the Midwest and Great Plains, as shown in Figure 9.1. Hawaii has the most diverse population and Maine the least diverse population (U.S. Census Bureau, 2021d). Five of the 13 Western states have Latino/a populations of 22% (Colorado) to 47% (New Mexico) of the state population. Florida, New Jersey, New York, and Texas have Latino/a populations that range from 22 to 39% of their populations (U.S. Census Bureau, 2021d).

Immigrants entered the country by boat at Ellis Island on the East Coast from 1892 to 1954, and Angel Island on the West Coast from 1910 to 1940. By the end of the twentieth century, most were entering through airports in New York City, Los Angeles, and Seattle as well as crossing the U.S.–Mexico border. Many of the immigrants over the past 130 years established or moved to ethnic enclaves that were similar to areas they had just left. In these communities, they did not have to assimilate into the dominant culture and could continue to use their native languages. Examples can be found in the metropolitan Los Angeles area, where communities such as Little Saigon, Little Tokyo, Chinatown, and Koreatown have been established.

**Figure 9.1** Percentage of Population of Color by State, 2020

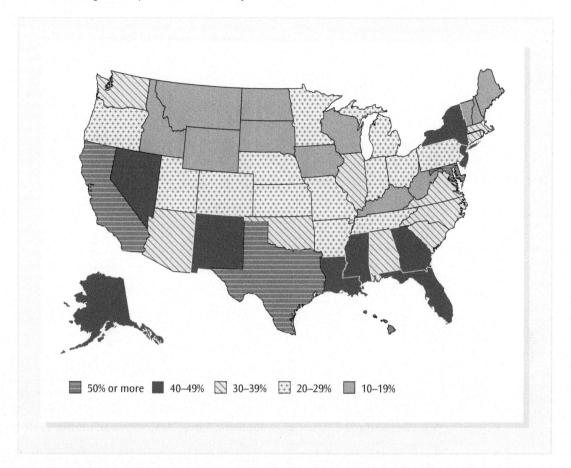

50% or more    40–49%    30–39%    20–29%    10–19%

A larger percentage of more recent immigrants are joining family members who live in **suburbs** or in small towns. Some, especially refugees, have been sponsored by religious groups or community agencies in nonurban areas. Others would like to relocate to the Midwest and South for jobs in the meatpacking and farming industries. Others may want to live in rural areas because they think the values and lifestyle there are closer to their own. And many people who are crossing the southern border are being sent by governors to cities across the country that may not be near the part of the country that the people seeking asylum would like to be located.

The racial, ethnic, and religious diversity of the population varies from one region to another. The interests and perspectives of those who live in various geographic regions often are reflected in their stands on state and federal issues, as shown in national elections. We explore some of these regional educational, religious, and political differences in this section.

## Regional Differences in Education

As one travels across various regions in the United States, significant differences can be found across areas in relation to education. Schools in the western region of the country are considerably more ethnically and racially diverse than other regions, as shown in Figure 9.2. Only 35% of the school population in the West is composed of White students. Latino/a students at 44% are the largest ethnic group. The largest concentration of Asian and Pacific students can be found in the West at 5%. A category of "Two or More Races" in Figure 9.2 includes mixed-race students, who are at 6% in the West. In contrast, the largest concentration of White students is in the Midwest region, with 63%. The largest percentage of Black students can be found in the South, with 22% of the student population (National Center for Education Statistics [NCES], 2022a).

**Figure 9.2** Percentage of Elementary and Secondary School Students by Region and Race, Fall 2021

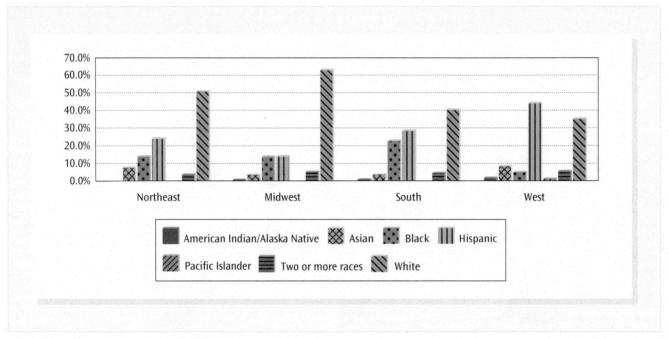

**SOURCE:** National Center for Education Statistics (2022a).

Individuals exploring teaching opportunities will find that the average salaries in some states are considerably higher or lower than in others. Teacher salaries in the 50 states and the District of Columbia average $66,745, as shown in Table 9.1, with starting salaries ranging from $33,568 in Montana to $56,313 in the District of Columbia. Average state teacher salaries range from $47,902 in Mississippi to $91,097 in New York (National Education Association, 2023).

Salaries do not always take into consideration the varying cost of living across the country. In some instances, salaries that may seem reasonable at first glance are far below a living wage in the community. For example, in San Francisco, rent for a one-bedroom apartment would be 47% of a teacher's salary. The same pattern applies to many large

**Table 9.1** States with Highest and Lowest Teacher Salaries, School Year 2021–2022

| Average Starting Salary: $42,844 | | | | | | | | | |
| --- | --- | --- | --- | --- | --- | --- | --- | --- | --- |
| Average U.S. Teacher Salary: $66,745 | | | | | | | | | |
| **Highest** | **Starting Salary Ranking** | **Average Starting Salary** | **Average Salary Ranking** | **Average Salary** | **Lowest** | **Starting Salary Ranking** | **Average Starting Salary** | **Average Salary Ranking** | **Average Salary** |
| District of Columbia | 1 | $56,313 | 4 | $82,523 | Oklahoma | 42 | $38,154 | 37 | $54,804 |
| New Jersey | 2 | $55,143 | 7 | $77,677 | West Virginia | 43 | $38,052 | 50 | $50,315 |
| Washington | 3 | $52,142 | 5 | $81,510 | Kentucky | 44 | $38,010 | 39 | $54,574 |
| California | 4 | $51,600 | 2 | $88,508 | Mississippi | 45 | $38,729 | 51 | $47,902 |
| Alaska | 5 | $50,203 | 9 | $74,715 | North Carolina | 46 | $37,676 | 35 | $54,863 |
| Hawaii | 6 | $50,123 | 12 | $67,000 | Nebraska | 47 | $37,186 | 31 | $57,420 |
| Massachusetts | 7 | $49,503 | 3 | $87,108 | Arkansas | 48 | $37,168 | 47 | $51,668 |
| Maryland | 8 | $49,451 | 10 | $74,006 | Colorado | 49 | $37,124 | 29 | $58,183 |
| New York | 9 | $47,981 | 1 | $91,097 | Missouri | 50 | $34,052 | 46 | $52,481 |
| Pennsylvania | 10 | $47,827 | 11 | $73,072 | Montana | 51 | $33,568 | 44 | $53,628 |

**SOURCE:** National Education Association (2023).

**Table 9.2**  States with Highest Educational Attainment for Individuals 25 Years and Older, 2019

| High School Graduate or Higher | Bachelor's Degree or Higher | Advanced Degree |
|---|---|---|
| U.S. average 88.6% | U.S. average 33.2% | U.S. average 12.8% |
| Wyoming 94.5% | District of Columbia 59.8% | District of Columbia 33.8% |
| Montana 94.2% | Massachusetts 45.0% | Massachusetts 20.3% |
| Alaska 94.0% | Colorado 42.8% | Maryland 19.0% |
| Minnesota 93.5% | New Jersey 41.2% | Connecticut 18.1% |
| New Hampshire 93.5% | Maryland 40.9% | Virginia 17.3% |
| North Dakota 93.4% | Connecticut 40.1% | New York 16.6% |
| Vermont 93.2% | Virginia 39.8% | New Jersey 16.1% |
| Utah 93.1% | Vermont 39.3% | Colorado 16.0% |
| Maine 93.1% | New Hampshire 38.1% | Vermont 15.9% |
| Iowa 92.9% | New York 37.9% | New Hampshire 15.2% |

**SOURCE:** National Center for Education Statistics (2021a).

**metropolitan areas** such as Portland (OR), San Diego, New York City, the District of Columbia, Boston, and Los Angeles as well as Hawaii (Saenz-Armstrong, 2023).

State per capita student expenditures may also be indicative of a state's commitment or ability to support public education. To some extent, the expenditure variations may be a function of the regional cost of living. State expenditures varied considerably, while the reported average per capita student expenditure in the United States was $14,347 in 2021. New York spent a high of $26,571 per student, while Idaho's expenditure was a low of $9,053 (U.S. Census Bureau, 2023b).

Educational attainment varies from state to state. In 2019, 88.6% of the U.S. population age 25 and older held a high school degree. Wyoming led the states with high school graduation rates. The District of Columbia led the nation with the highest percentage of residents with bachelor's degrees and with the highest percentage of advanced degrees, as shown in Table 9.2. California ranked lowest, with 84.1% of its residents age 25 and older with a high school diploma, while West Virginia had the lowest percentage of people (21.5%) with bachelor's degrees (NCES, 2021a). Arkansas and West Virginia had the lowest percentage of people (8.8%) with advanced degrees (Statista, 2023).

## Regional Religious Differences

Religious differences are an important regional difference in the United States as well as other parts of the world. The daily behaviors and values of an individual may have a direct correlation to the individual's religious beliefs. Diet, values, and politics are often functions of one's religion, as discussed in more detail in Chapter 8. Because religious values are often reflected in the platforms of political parties, individuals tend to support either liberal or conservative platforms, parties, and candidates. The Republican Party typically adopts the more conservative platforms and thus has tended to win the support of states and regions where the residents are more likely to be religious conservatives.

Norman (2018) found significant religious differences in various regions of the United States, as shown in Figure 9.3. Based on how important people say religion is to them and how often they attend religious services, 45% of Americans living in the South Central region of the country were considered very religious as were 43% of those living in the Southeast. In contrast, 29% of individuals living in the Pacific region of the country and 26% of those living in New England were reported being very religious (Norman, 2018).

**Figure 9.3** Regional Religiosity in the United States

*South Central*: AR, LA, OK, & TX; *Southeast*: AL, FL, GA, KY, MS, NC, SC, TN, & VA; *North Central*: IA, KS, MN, MO, NE, ND, SD, & WI; *Midwest*: IL, IN, MI, & OH; *Rockies*: AZ, CO, ID, MT, NV, NM, UT, & WY; *Mid-Atlantic*: DE, MD, NJ, NY, PA, & WV; *Pacific*: AK, CA, HI, OR, & WA; *New England*: CT, MA, ME, NH, RI, & VT.

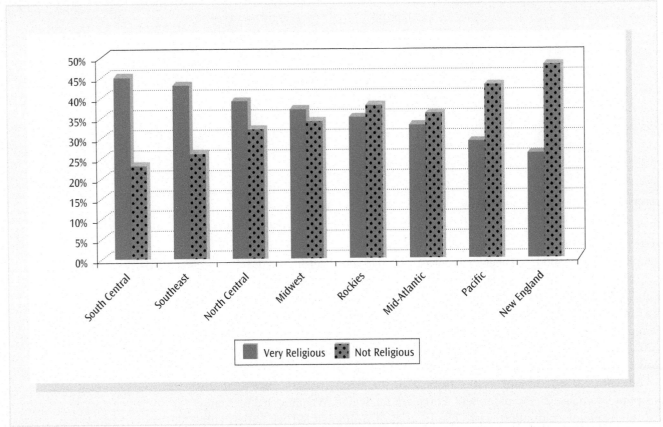

SOURCE: Norman (2018).

Mormons, who are heavily concentrated in Utah and Idaho, are reported to be the most religious group in the United States as determined by "how important people say religion is to them and how often they attend religious services" (Norman, 2018, para. 2). Protestants, the second most religious group, are concentrated in the South, with 77% of Alabama's population identifying as Protestant, and more than 70% of the populations of Mississippi, Arkansas, Tennessee, and South Carolina identifying as Protestant. Muslims are the third most religious group. They are a numerically small group; New Jersey is the state with the largest number of Muslims. Forty percent of Catholics are very religious; they live throughout the country but are more highly concentrated in the Northeast and mid-Atlantic, California, and New Mexico. Eighteen percent of the Jewish population are considered very religious; Jews are most prevalent on the East Coast. Over 30% of the population in Hawaii, Alaska, Washington, Vermont, Oregon, Maine, Colorado, and New Hampshire report that they have no religious affiliation (Gallup, 2019; Norman, 2018).

## Regional Political Differences

During and at the conclusion of every national election, results are posted in the media in the form of color-coded maps of all the states, with red for states won by Republicans and blue for those won by Democrats. The states in the northeastern and far western United States are generally shaded in blue, with the notable exception of Alaska, which is typically Republican. The South, Midwest, and Southwest are primarily Republican and red, as are most of the Mountain West states, such as Idaho, Montana, Utah, and Wyoming.

In 2023, California, Hawaii, Maryland, Massachusetts, and Vermont were the most Democratic-leaning states in the country. Oklahoma, North Dakota, West Virginia, and Wyoming were the most Republican-leaning states (World Population Review, 2023c). In every national election, there are states considered *battleground*, *purple*, or *swing* states, in which neither major political party has such overwhelming public support that election results can be taken for granted. The electorate in one of these states may switch political preferences from one election to another, depending on the major issues at the time of the election (e.g., unemployment, the economy, immigration, war). In 2023, 14 states—Arizona, Colorado, Florida, Georgia, Iowa, Michigan, Minnesota, Nevada, New Hampshire, North Carolina, Ohio, Pennsylvania, Virginia, and Wisconsin—were designated as competitive leading into the 2024 presidential election (World Population Review, 2023c).

There are many other regional differences—too many to include here. However, this sampling of some of the important differences may help you understand how diverse the United States is. Understanding the diversity of one's own country should lead to the realization that many, if not most, other countries are also diverse not only in their racial and ethnic identities but educationally, economically, and in terms of their religious affiliations, political leanings, and other characteristics important in their cultures.

# Rural, Urban, and Suburban Differences

**Learning Objective 9.3** Analyze the benefits of living and attending school in rural, urban, and suburban areas.

Now that we have explored some regional differences in the United States, let's examine differences within each region that also influence people's lives. Life and culture are greatly influenced by the people who share the space and place in which they live. People become very familiar with the place in which they live and know what is expected of them and others. This sense of comfort is a reason many teacher candidates indicate they want to teach in or near the area where they grew up.

Roughly 80% of the U.S. population lived in urban areas in 2020; the other 20% lived in rural areas (U.S. Census Bureau, 2023a). Financial and family constraints tend to keep people from moving to favored areas of choice. Teaching in an isolated rural area a hundred or more miles from a shopping center is very different from teaching in a wealthy suburban area with access to a wide range of cultural and sporting events. Let's examine the characteristics of rural, urban, and suburban areas and the impact the place in which one lives has on education.

## Rural Areas

In 1900, a majority of Americans lived in **rural areas**, but by the early 1900s, large numbers of rural workers were migrating to cities for employment. Today 20% of the U.S. population live in rural areas that are sparsely populated and not urban (U.S. Census, 2023a) and comprise 97% of the country's land (America Counts Staff, 2017). Worldwide, 43% of the population live in rural areas (World Bank, 2023).

Some individuals are born in rural areas and have no option but to live their lives there. Other people choose to live in rural areas because they enjoy the wide-open space; the stars in the sky; and fishing, hunting, and other outdoor activities. Rural areas feature fewer people with whom to contend and the freedom to have more control of one's life.

Many people grew up in rural areas, but others moved from cities to escape the crowding, traffic, crime, pollution, and bureaucracies of city life to recapture a quality of life that some people believe provides a healthier environment for families.

Rural areas are characterized by wide open spaces with farms and small towns.

**SOURCE:** Johnny Adolphson/Shutterstock

The migration of older adults from cities to rural retirement destinations has increased the aging trend in rural areas (Davis et al., 2022). Most people who live in rural areas, especially if they were born there, have a great deal of pride in their place that often includes an emotional attachment to the land and its people (Rose, 2022).

While there may be a tendency to think of rural areas as populated primarily by individuals involved in farming, only a small percentage of Americans farm for a living. Today, there are approximately 2 million farms in the United States (U.S. Department of Agriculture, 2023). While this number is significantly less than the 6.8 million farms at their peak in 1935, today's farms tend to be larger, averaging 446 acres as compared to 155 acres in 1935. While the total amount of land utilized in farming and the amount of labor declined in recent years, total farm output nearly tripled between 1948 and 2019, primarily because of advances in technology, innovations in animal and crop genetics, improvement in chemicals and equipment, and better farm organization (U.S. Department of Agriculture, 2023).

The massive areas of rural land are dotted with small towns, some of which serve as county seats for government purposes. The residents of these towns may work in a nearby city or in local manufacturing establishments. They may provide services to the farming communities as the managers and laborers at grain elevators, where the process of distributing grain to national and world markets begins. Businesses sell supplies needed to raise crops or animals, buy and sell meat products at the stockyards, and produce and deliver gas and oil required for farming. Grocery stores and other retail stores serve farm and small-town residents, although some people must drive many miles to the nearest mall to access larger stores and more options.

**POPULATIONS OF RURAL AREAS**  Over 66.6 million people lived in rural communities across the United States in 2020. The states in which over 50% of the state's population live in rural areas are Vermont (65%), Maine (61%), West Virginia (55%), and Mississippi (53%) (U.S. Census Bureau, 2023c). Over recent decades, the population of rural areas has declined, primarily because the population is aging and younger people are moving to urban areas. A larger proportion of Americans over age 65 live in rural areas (17.5%) compared to metropolitan areas (13.8%). Almost half of this older population lives in the South and one-fourth of them live in the Midwest. In some states, more than half of these older residents live in rural areas, which will require specialized medical and rehabilitation services as well as housing and public transportation options for the aging residents (Smith & Trevelyan, 2019). Fourteen percent of the rural population live below the poverty level (U.S. Census Bureau, 2022d).

The people living and working in rural America are predominantly White but have become more diverse over the past decade. Twenty-four percent of the population in rural counties were people of color in 2020. The degree of racial and ethnic diversity in rural areas depends on the region of the country. Native Americans are the largest population of color in rural areas of eastern Oklahoma, the Four Corners area (Arizona, Colorado, New Mexico, and Utah), and the northern tier of the Great Plains, including southwestern Minnesota, eastern Montana, most of North Dakota and South Dakota, eastern Wyoming, and portions of three Canadian provinces. Black Americans are the largest population of color in rural counties across the South, and Asian Americans are the largest population of color in rural Hawaii and in Kodiak Island Borough and the West Aleutians Census Area in Alaska. The expanding diversity in rural areas is driven by the growth of the Latino/a population, who often work in meatpacking plants, the construction industry, oil and timber industries, their own businesses, or on farms across the country (Rowlands & Love, 2021).

**ECONOMICS IN RURAL AREAS**    Not all is idyllic in rural living. The rural workforce earns less than its urban counterparts, with an annual median income of $53,750. The poverty level is consistently higher in rural America (14.1%) than in suburban areas (9.1%), but about the same as for people who live in large cities (14.3%) (U.S. Census Bureau, 2022d). Regionally, the highest poverty rate is in southern states (Shrider et al., 2021). The highest concentration of persistent poverty is in the Mississippi Delta, Appalachia, Native American lands, and the Black Belt across the South—the counties with predominantly Black populations in Alabama, Arkansas, Georgia, Louisiana, Maryland, North Carolina, South Carolina, Tennessee, and Virginia (Farrigan, 2021). According to the U.S. Department of Agriculture (2022), in 2019, the child poverty rate was 40% or higher in 127 rural counties, primarily on Native American lands and in the South.

The rural economy is sensitive to fluctuations in manufacturing, export rates, and trade wars. Farm production can fluctuate with crop prices, which are controlled by the world economy, and weather. Successful farmers today use technology and business principles, as well as their knowledge about agriculture, to manage a farm. In addition to watching the weather, they monitor the stock market to determine the best time to sell. They must have the resources to store products during times of low prices and adequate finances to sustain them. The nature of the business is making it difficult for small farmers to survive. Global climate change has led to erratic and often unpredictable climatic conditions, which have a severe impact on farming. Drought conditions have brought crop failure, and smaller farms may not have the resources to sustain them in the ways that owners of larger farms and corporate-owned farms can. Today, agricultural and extractive industries such as mining represent only 5% of the employment in rural and **nonmetro areas**, which include cities with populations under 50,000 (Slack & Jensen, 2020).

Multinational corporations have outsourced many of the manufacturing jobs that were once available in rural areas to lower-cost labor markets in other parts of the world. However, processing plants for meat, poultry, and fish continue to be located near the source of the raw product. These are often low-paying, physically demanding, and sometimes dangerous jobs. By 2019, the rural economy "was dominated by four industries: government (3.7 million jobs), manufacturing (2.6 million), retail (2.5 million), and health care and social assistance (2.4 million)" (Davis et al., 2022, p. 10). Jobs in health care and social assistance and hospitality (hotel and restaurant jobs) grew between 2010 and 2020, although the hospitality job market declined during the COVID-19 pandemic. Manufacturing jobs began to increase after 2010 but declined again during the pandemic. The highest growth has been in smaller industries such as real estate and truck leasing. At the same time, new industries began to expand opportunities for some rural communities in professional, scientific, and technical services, educational services, and finance and insurance, requiring postsecondary training (Davis et al., 2022).

To meet the labor demands, immigrants and people of color have been filling these job positions in areas that previously had little racial and ethnic diversity, including health professionals such as doctors and nurses. Over the past 20 years, immigrants accounted for 37% of the overall rural growth (Wang, 2019), contributing to the renewed vitality in a number of communities. As a result, schools began providing services for immigrant children who have significantly changed the diversity of rural schools. At the postsecondary level, the percent of college-educated workers increased over the past decade from 21.5% in 2012 to 23.8% in 2019 (Davis et al., 2022).

Twenty-five percent of rural residents listed drug addiction, particularly opioid addiction, as their leading concern, followed by economic concerns, including the availability of jobs. They indicated that the major problems facing their families were financial problems and health or health care concerns (National Public Radio et al., 2018). The good news is that most rural Americans are optimistic about their lives. "Most say they feel attached to their local community, and they identify the closeness of their local community life in a small town, and being around good people as their community's biggest strengths" (National Public Radio et al., 2018, p. 1).

**RURAL SCHOOLS**   There are advantages and challenges to teaching in a rural area. Schools in rural areas are typically smaller than those in suburban and urban areas, meaning that there are fewer students to manage and a better opportunity to get to know them and their families. The lower enrollment in rural schools usually results in a relatively low student-to-teacher ratio, allowing more individual attention for students. One of the problems in small schools is that teachers often must teach subjects for which they may have little background or experience (e.g., physics, chemistry, biology). Schools often do not have sufficient resources to offer foreign language classes, technology education, music, art, or Advanced Placement courses. However, satellite connections and the internet in some rural areas allow students to take such courses virtually.

The 27,494 rural schools in the United States (NCES, 2022d) served 9.8 million U.S. students in 2021 (NCES, 2021c). They serve critical functions for the community as they help to maintain the social fabric of the community and provide services that reduce the negative effects of poverty. This includes providing health services, continuing education classes, community literacy classes, and well-balanced meals for students. The communities that surround rural schools provide many opportunities for student-centered, hands-on, meaningful, engaging, and place-based experiences in which students can learn science, technology, engineering, and mathematics (STEM) skills. For example, the Teton Science Schools collaborates with Grand Teton National Park to actively involve students in their learning both inside and outside the classroom. To learn more about innovative, place-based learning in rural schools, visit the website of Rural Schools Collaborative.

In spite of the benefits of rural schools, 6,000 have closed since 1998 (Sageman, 2022). Closures are primarily a function of budget issues and low student enrollment. Vermont is one of the rural states that has been faced with the problems of declining student enrollments, rising costs, and tightening budgets. In 2018, the high school in Rochester, Vermont, had only three remaining students. Rathke (2018) describes a junior class student who "moves from one empty classroom to the next, taking mostly online classes or studying alone" (para. 1). The town had already voted to close the combined middle and high schools, leaving the remaining students to face significant changes the following school year. This scenario is repeated in increasing numbers of rural communities.

School closings and consolidation can be a contentious issue in rural communities facing declining enrollments. They affect the civic life of a community as well as its economic vitality, as reflected in higher property values and incomes in areas with schools (Sipple et al., 2019). Moving students to a school located many miles away limits the ability of parents to participate in school activities. Long bus rides to and from the consolidated school may cause hardship for some families. Debates about the value and implications of closing a school can be expected. In Vermont, these debates have expanded to include families' use of school vouchers to pay the tuition for a school of their choice, which has led to the filing of lawsuits (The Associated Press, 2021). The Supreme Court has already ruled that Montana and Maine's educational choice programs must allow families to choose religious schools.

Proponents of consolidation argue that the curriculum can be expanded to include subjects not available in a small school, buildings can be upgraded with educational equipment and technology, and students can be better served when small schools are combined. The advent of online learning has helped save and improve some rural

# Critical Incidents in Teaching

## Moving from the City to a Rural Community

Erica Stevens had just completed her teacher education program at a university in the city where she had lived her entire life. She was determined to leave the city, the traffic, the crime, and the crowds. Erica gladly accepted a high school math teaching position in an isolated rural community nestled at the foothills of a mountain far away from big-city life.

On a Thursday in October, Erica was surprised to find that barely over half the class was present for the first-period class. "Why are so many students absent?" she asked. Julie, seated in the front row, shrugged her shoulders, and no one else responded. She went on with her lesson. When the students came in for her second-period class, again about half the class was missing. "Okay, what's going on?" Erica asked the class. "Why is half the class not here? Come on, I want to know what's going on. Tell me." Finally, Thomas spoke up: "It's no big deal, Ms. Stevens. Deer season starts this weekend, and they have all taken off with their families to get a good site before it starts. Most of them will be back in class on Monday morning, and a few will be gone another day or two." "But they are cutting class," Erica said in frustration. "I have some important lessons planned for today and tomorrow." "Just relax and go with the flow, Ms. Stevens. All the

other teachers do, and we don't do anything very important for the next couple of days."

### Questions for Discussion

1. When moving to a different region of the country, what types of cultural differences might a new teacher anticipate?

2. What biases about the place in which a school is located may affect your interactions with students and their families if you move to a different region of the country?

3. How would you modify your lessons if you were in Erica's situation? Would you do as suggested—relax and "go with the flow—or choose another strategy for working with the students who have gone hunting? Defend your choice.

4. What other cultural events or traditions is Erica likely to experience as she teaches in this rural community?

5. If you were teaching in a rural school, how would you learn more about the community, its history and experiences, and the cultures of students and families?

schools by providing instruction in academic subjects for which they would otherwise be unable to hire teachers. In a Lexington, Mississippi, high school, in the middle of the Mississippi Delta, students in an Advanced Placement physics class can watch a Yale University professor lecture from 1,200 miles away (Mader, 2018). These students are more fortunate than most living in rural areas because they are able to work with high-speed Internet services. Only 72% of people living in rural areas have access to Internet speeds that qualify as broadband, as compared to 79% of those living in suburban areas in 2021, and 24% of rural adults and 9% of suburban adults report that continuous access to high-speed internet remained a major problem (Vogels, 2021).

## Urban Areas

Some people choose to live in **urban areas** because of the excitement and access to amenities such as restaurants, theater, and social opportunities. Large cities offer abundant professional jobs as well as sports complexes, numerous libraries, colleges and universities, recreational activities, restaurants that vary greatly in cuisine and cost, and clubs with entertainment. Other people live in the city because they grew up or accepted a job there. They may choose to remain in the city because they like it or because it adequately meets their needs. Others have no choice because of family or economic obligations or just don't have the opportunity to break loose from the grip of the city. Because of limited incomes, some people who live in the city have never been able to take advantage of the activities that attract other people to the city.

An estimated 27% of the U.S. population live in the cities in a metropolitan area (Bucholtz, 2020). People who live in metropolitan areas, which include both urban and suburban residents, earned over $20,000 more than their rural neighbors, with an annual median income of $73,823. However, people who live in the cities earn only $64,839, compared to $79,599 for people in the suburbs (U.S. Census Bureau, 2022b).

The poverty rate is slightly higher (14.3%) in urban areas than in rural areas (14.1%), but the lowest (9.1%) is in suburban areas (U.S. Census Bureau, 2022d). The pattern of poverty is similar for school-age children, although higher, with 20.9% and 20.8% in urban and nonmetro areas compared to 13.6% and 11.8% in rural and suburban areas (NCES, 2021b).

Geography plays a role in defining the conditions of a city. The upper-middle class and the upper class generally live together in one or more areas of the city; middle-class and low-income families live in other areas of the city. People experiencing homelessness are usually shepherded into specific areas where most others will not see them. Housing in the city is usually more expensive than in other places, as is the cost of living. A small three-bedroom, one-bathroom, 95-year-old house in a modest neighborhood in Berkeley, California, can cost more than $1 million. Low-rent housing is limited and often in disrepair. Most cities do not have enough public housing to meet their needs. The cost of owning a car and paying for parking and insurance in some cities may be exorbitant. Public buses and subway systems serve as major means of transportation.

Some people like the city because they can live their lives free from the prying eyes of neighbors. Some neighbors in the city often don't know each other, let alone details about the families or roots of those who live around them. One is able to live alone within a great mass of humanity. On the other hand, there are communities within cities in which people do know their neighbors and work together on community projects. The city does not allow for a single stereotype that fits all of its residents. Economic conditions, race or ethnicity, and language sometimes divide cities into neighborhoods, such as Little Italy and Chinatown, that clearly distinguish one group from another.

**POPULATION OF A CITY** Urban areas in the South and West grew at the highest rates between 2010 and 2020 (Frey, 2022a). The urban population grew at a higher rate than suburban and rural areas in the past decade, but this pattern changed during the COVID-19 pandemic when people in cities moved to the suburbs, smaller metro cities, and rural areas, causing a negative growth rate in major cities. It is not yet clear whether the move from the cities was because of pandemic health concerns or the ability to work from home (Frey, 2022b).

Over one in four people in the United States live in the 10 largest metropolitan areas, as shown in Table 9.3. People of color were a majority in 20 of the 56 major metropolitan areas in 2020, with the largest increases in the Latino/a and Asian populations (Frey, 2022a). Over two in five of the foreign-born population live in urban areas, half of them living in suburban areas (U.S. Census Bureau, 2022e).

Forty-two metropolitan areas in the United States had more than 1 million residents in 2022. They range in size from the metropolitan New York–Newark–Jersey City area, with 19.6 million, to Fresno, California, with just over 1 million (U.S. Census Bureau, 2022a). Half of the world's population lives in megacities with populations of at least 10 million. New York City is the largest city in the United States, with a population of nearly

**Table 9.3** Ten Largest Metropolitan Areas in the United States, 2022

| Metropolitan Area | Population Estimate | Metropolitan Area | Population Estimate |
|---|---|---|---|
| New York, Newark, Jersey City (NY, NJ, PA) | 19,617,869 | Washington-Arlington-Alexandria (DC, VA, MD, WV) | 6,373,756 |
| Los Angeles, Long Beach, Anaheim (CA) | 12,872,322 | Philadelphia-Camden-Wilmington (PA, NJ, DE, MD) | 6,241,164 |
| Chicago, Naperville, Elgin (IL, IN, WI) | 9,441,957 | Atlanta-Sandy Springs-Alpharetta (GA) | 6,222,106 |
| Dallas, Ft. Worth, Arlington (TX) | 7,943,685 | Miami-Fort Lauderdale-Pompano Beach (FL) | 6,139,340 |
| Houston, The Woodlands, Sugarland (TX) | 7,340,118 | Phoenix-Mesa-Chandler (AZ) | 5,015,678 |

**SOURCE:** U.S. Census Bureau (2022a).

**Figure 9.4** Population of the Largest Cities in the World (in millions) by Ranking

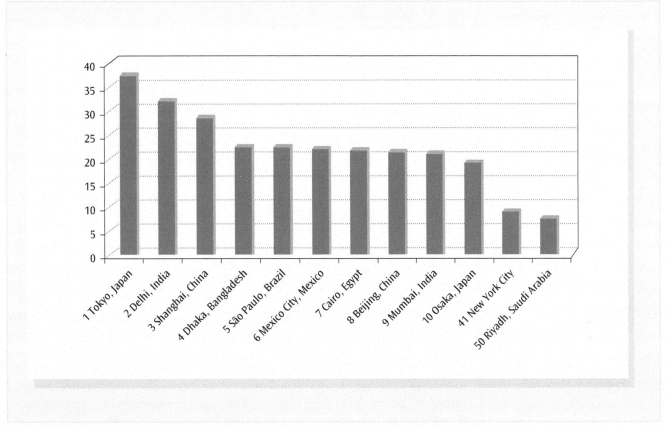

**SOURCE:** WorldAtlas (2023b).

9 million, which grows to almost 20 million when extended into the metropolitan area that includes its suburbs. Figure 9.4 shows how New York City compares in population size to other major cities around the world such as Tokyo, Japan, with 37.3 million, and Mexico City, with 22.1 million (WorldAtlas, 2023b).

**CONTRADICTIONS OF CITIES**   Cities are centers of extremes and contradictions. They are places where people from different cultural backgrounds intermingle. An expensive, elite restaurant may be found on one block and a soup kitchen on the street behind it. Some of the highest salaries in the world are earned in the corporate headquarters housed in or near a city, while large numbers of Black Americans, Puerto Ricans, Mexican Americans, other people of color, and women who work in the city are paid so little that their families live in poverty.

While the city provides creative energy for many, it is oppressive and dangerous for others. Many city residents live in safe and comfortable environments with good schools, parks, and recreational facilities. Others live near waste dumps that have contributed to disproportionately high incidences of asthma and other diseases. The night—and sometimes the daylight—may be interrupted by the sounds of gunshots, ambulances, and police raids in some sections of a city.

For oppressed people in the city, the dominant culture is not serving them effectively. The hope, joy, and freedom associated with living in cities have not been the experience for many. Those who are more advantaged and living comfortably may view the lower-income sections of the city as places of chaos and immorality. Such views are reinforced when they see accounts of violence in the media. City leaders find it difficult to raise the resources necessary to improve city services, ensure adequate housing and food, provide schools of the same quality across the city, and also pay enough to attract and retain highly qualified teachers. Low-income and public housing is seldom built in or near the economically advantaged areas of the city. The aging infrastructure of many cities may be neglected—often tended to only as a response to catastrophic failures.

**URBAN SCHOOLS**   Enrollment in the largest 100 school districts in 2021–2022 ranged from 48,601 in Portland, Oregon, to 956,634 in New York City schools, with its $29,931 per student annual spending being the second highest in the country (NCES, 2022b; U.S. Census Bureau, 2023b). Students at urban schools are more likely to be eligible for free or reduced-price lunches than students at schools in other areas. Thirty-six percent of urban school students attend high-poverty schools in which at least 75% of students are eligible for free or reduced-price lunches, compared to 15% of students in suburban schools, 18% in towns, and 13% in rural areas (NCES, 2023).

Not all schools in a city are equal. Some parents in more affluent school areas are able to raise external funds to help the schools through public school foundations and other means. Parents of children in poverty-area schools may be just as committed to their children's education but lack the fiscal resources and influence of the other parents. They may be actively engaged in their children's education, communicating with teachers and monitoring their children to make certain that they attend school regularly and complete their assignments. However, most low-income parents do not have a great deal of cultural capital. They often do not have incomes that allows them to support school activities (e.g., paying fees for extracurricular activities), and their work situations may inhibit participation in school activities and meetings. Limited English skills on the part of some parents or a lack of education may lead to reluctance to interact with the educational system. One means of enhancing the involvement of immigrant parents is to meet with them in an environment that is perceived as less threatening, such as a community center or a local place of worship.

**Magnet schools** are public schools in which the curriculum emphasizes a particular subject or field, such as performing arts or STEM subjects. Magnet schools usually receive additional funding that provides resources for their students, supplies, teachers, and educational programs (California Department of Education, 2019). Advantaged and well-educated families seek admission to select magnet schools, especially if their neighborhood school does not meet their needs.

A number of school districts allow parents, teachers, community groups, and entrepreneurs to establish **charter schools**. Charter schools are public schools of choice

Suburban communities historically have been composed of single-family homes near a city or town.
**SOURCE:** loft39studio/123RF

that operate free from many of the regulations that apply to traditional public schools. The "charter" includes a performance contract detailing the school's mission, program, goals, students served, methods of assessment, and ways to measure success.

## Suburban Areas

In the 1930s, a relatively small number of Americans lived in the suburbs. Today more than half the U.S. population live in the suburbs and small metropolitan areas. Although suburbs were primarily populated by White families in their early days, today they are more racially and ethnically diverse but still less diverse than major cities. By the beginning of the 21st century, a growing number of Black Americans were leaving cities for the suburbs and more desirable living conditions and schools. They were joined by immigrant groups, especially Latino/a and Asian newcomers. Approximately three in four White people in the United States now live in the suburbs, but over half of Black (54.3%), Latino/a (61.4%), and Asian (63.1%) Americans also live there, with the largest proportion of people of color living in the suburbs closest to a city. By 2020, more than half of the suburban population younger than age 18 were children and youth of color (Frey, 2022c). Diversity in some communities is actively solicited and celebrated. In others, little to nothing is done to encourage it.

Until recently, people who lived in the suburbs were more likely than their urban peers to have a bachelor's degree, but that difference has almost disappeared, with 34% of suburban adults having a degree in 2018 compared to 33% of urban adults. The gaps in other areas such as income have also narrowed over time, with the suburban population being only slightly ahead on many measures. This may be due, in part, to a suburban population that includes more children, 18- to 24-year-olds, and people age 65 and over. Having a larger proportion of the working population may give cities the advantage on the metrics of education, labor market, income, and housing (Fry, 2020).

**DEVELOPMENT OF THE SUBURBS** After World War II, the suburbs offered an opportunity to own a single-family house with a yard in an area that seemed safer than the city and more desirable for raising children. Because many families were unable to afford homes in many U.S. cities in the mid-twentieth century, lower-cost suburban developments became an attractive alternative. Low-interest loans to returning veterans from World War II enhanced the opportunities for many White middle-class families, but they were not made available to most veterans of color. The wage earner—usually the father at that time—commuted to the city daily to work. Most wives stayed at home to care for children and became involved in developing a community.

The early suburbs were a "White racial project" (Omi & Winant, 2015), resulting in racially and economically homogeneous communities. While Black people established their own suburbs in a few places, neither they nor members of other groups of color were encouraged to settle in the suburbs. Racist governmental policies known as **redlining** and discriminatory business practices at the time exacerbated racial and class inequalities and kept suburbia almost exclusively White. At the same time, programs for public housing, urban renewal, and replacement of homes with highways were undermining the stability and vibrancy of Black neighborhoods in the cities. In addition, Black Americans were being denied mortgages to buy homes (Jan, 2018), and Black children were often not allowed to attend school with White students.

Suburbia did not last long as just bedroom communities for people who worked in the city. Soon grocery stores, gas stations, parks, community services, schools, and places of worship were built to support the needs of suburban families. These were followed by malls and a variety of retail stores. In time, more upscale suburban developments were built to meet the needs of affluent families wanting to live there. In some parts of the country, White families were moving from cities to avoid the desegregation of their schools.

Shopping malls were joined by office complexes, high-tech landscaped industrial parks, and an extensive network of highways. Wage earners no longer had to go to the city for work; factories and other businesses existed in their own backyards. Software, electronic, and biotechnology companies found suburban business centers to be ideal for their development and research. They attracted entrepreneurs and professionals, who moved into upscale housing developments near their jobs. These office and research parks began to interact academically and economically with research universities and both public and private groups to develop and use their products. For example, Silicon Valley, south of San Francisco, is the center of much of the U.S. high-tech industry and an example of suburban business and research complexes.

Although racist official housing policies should have been dismantled years ago when Congress passed the Fair Housing Act in 1968, zoning policies and homeowner association building requirements and restrictions still prevented many people of color and people who were not economically advantaged from receiving mortgages or moving into some neighborhoods. By the beginning of the 21st century, banks and mortgage companies were marketing subprime lending to people whose credit records made it difficult for them to buy a home. These loans had low interest rates at the beginning but, after a fixed date, interest rates varied based on marketing conditions. Financial institutions were aggressively marketing to people of color even when they qualified for regular mortgages. As housing prices rose, the Federal Reserve increased interest rates to bring housing prices under control. The increased rates made mortgage payments too high for many people to pay, and the value of their homes fell below the price that they had originally paid. Many people with these loans faced foreclosure. They had become the victims of the Great Recession of 2007 because of inflated housing prices and housing speculation by investors, losing their homes and all the money they had invested in them.

**SUBURBAN SCHOOLS**   The quality of schools is often one of the reasons that families move from cities to suburbs. Wealthy suburbs are more likely to have beautiful schools with the latest technology, qualified teachers, Advanced Placement courses, enrichment programs, and numerous extracurricular activities. However, not all suburban schools are of this high quality. Suburban schools are highly segregated, and "within districts, school attendance zone boundaries play a critical role in either maintaining segregated schools or reshaping those patterns, especially in suburban areas with growing and diversifying student populations" (Asson et al., 2023, p. 12). Schools that predominantly serve students of color, English speakers, and students from low-income families are likely to be the older schools in the region. Not all suburban schools have the resources to adequately support counselors, social workers, and others who can help students deal with the complexity of today's life. Often lacking in facilities, new equipment, and advanced technology, these schools may find the recruitment of teachers challenging.

The problems of urban schools affect many suburban schools as well, including inequitable practices that limit access by students of color to high-status academic offerings, lead to disproportionate disciplinary practices based on race, and are based on deficit-oriented teaching practices, which can limit the ability of students of color to reach their academic potentials (Diamond et al., 2021). Many families in the suburbs indicate that they value the diversity of students in their schools. At the same time, high academic and athletic performance by students of color can be a threat to White status and dominance (Diamond et al., 2021), as reflected in states and schools that are controlling what can be taught about race and history.

White families, especially White upper middle-class families, often are reluctant to give up their privilege of ensuring that their children are enrolled in the most academically challenging classes and are the recipients of other benefits such as awards for their academic and sports accomplishments. Natasha Warikoo (2022) found in her study of a suburban school in an upper middle-class community of White and Asian families that the hard work and high academic achievement of the Asian students led to tensions about appropriate parenting practices. For example, some White families thought that Asian students had an unfair advantage because their parents sent them to a supplementary academic class outside of school.

# The Impact of Globalization on People's Lives

**Learning Objective 9.4** Explore the impact of globalization on the lives of people and the intersectionality of environmental justice.

The realities of the twenty-first century call for people to know not only the places where they live but also the places where others live. The United States is connected to other countries through economic, political, environmental, and cultural systems. All of us live in a global world that is becoming more affected by international conglomerates, armed conflicts, and natural disasters. People think and respond globally for different reasons and in different ways. When major world events occur, responses from the international community are often a function of a number of variables. If countries have a vested political or economic interest in the country affected, the response may be swift and decisive. If nothing is perceived to be in the best interest of a country, then inaction may be the option of choice.

With the Internet and social media, ideas, protests, and misinformation spread across a country and around the world. For example, following the accusations of sexual improprieties by Hollywood mogul Harvey Weinstein, actress Alyssa Milano's #MeToo tweet was influential in encouraging victims of sexual assault to come forward with their experiences. The response went viral and noted celebrities in entertainment, sports, medicine, religion, and other fields were exposed for their predatory behaviors. By 2018, the MeToo movement went global with #*Yoambien* in Spain, with #*BalanceTonPorc* (squeal on your pig) in France, and in other places around the world. The movement was reignited in Spain in the summer of 2023 with #*SeAcabó* (it's over) after star player Jenni Hermoso received an unwanted kiss on the lips from the head of the Spanish football federation at the World Cup trophy ceremony. With a boost from the Internet and other forms of worldwide media, ideas and movements can quickly become global.

Products and the manufacturing of them have moved beyond the countries of their origin. In the case of cars, manufacturers have increased sales by making them in America. Residents of Georgetown, Kentucky, near Lexington, will be quick to let U.S. shoppers know that the Japanese-made Toyota Camry is an American-built car, assembled in Kentucky and nine other plants in the South and Midwest. Honda has produced more than 50 million cars and trucks in the United States since 1979 in its 12 U.S. manufacturing plants in Alabama, Georgia, Indiana, North Carolina, and South Carolina. Mercedes has an assembly plant in Alabama, Nissan in Mississippi and Tennessee, Volkswagen in Tennessee, and BMW in South Carolina. Early in the COVID-19 pandemic, Americans learned that many of the country's medical supplies were manufactured in China (National Academies of Sciences, Engineering, and Medicine, 2022), giving further evidence of **globalization** that affects countries around the world.

The early stages of globalization were initiated when European nations began to colonize the Americas, Africa, and India in the late fifteenth century. Europeans wanted both the raw materials and the labor of these countries, usually taking them by force. The colonizers followed a policy of **manifest destiny**, in which they saw their own cultures as superior to all others and believed they were destined to rule over others. After the United States became independent of England, it became a colonizer itself, making and breaking treaties with Native American tribes and gaining land by annexing it or winning it in wars with Mexico and Spain. In 1898, the United States annexed Hawaii. By the mid-1800s, Europeans had colonized Indonesia, Indochina, and all of Africa except for Ethiopia and Liberia. They controlled the crops that would be produced and limited industrial development. Globalization during this period moved resources primarily in one direction—from the colonized country to Europe or America.

It wasn't until after World War II that many countries gained independence from their colonizers. However, the colonizers quickly centralized their power in 1948 by establishing the General Agreement on Tariffs and Taxes, which later became the World Trade Organization (WTO). With a membership beyond the European colonizers, the goal of the WTO was to reduce barriers of trade so that goods and labor could move more easily across national borders. The International Monetary Fund and World Bank were established to help defend the world's monetary system and make investments through loans in the infrastructure of **developing countries**. Not eager to give up their control of global economic and political issues, the old colonizing countries (Germany, Great Britain, France, and Italy) joined the other economically and politically powerful countries (United States, Canada, Japan, and Russia) to form the Group of Eight (G-8) to oversee the world's future development, which affects the lives of both the richest and poorest people of the world. Russia's membership was suspended by the group in 2014 because of its annexation of Crimea, reconfiguring it as the G-7.

Globalization also affects the ability of the world's population to live without famine, debilitating and deadly diseases, and brutality brought on by poverty, religious beliefs, or war. The United Nations Educational, Scientific and Cultural Organization and other international organizations see the education of children and women as critical to changing their economic status and ability to be self-sufficient. The United National Convention on the Rights of the Child (1989) identified early childhood care and education, especially for the neediest children, as its top goal, and it is collecting data to track the progress of countries in meeting this goal. In this section, we examine the impact of globalization on the movement of people across borders, the economic well-being of populations, and the environment.

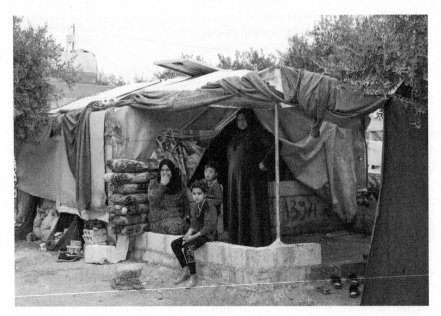

Armed conflicts in many countries have forced families to take refuge in another country, sometimes living in refugee camps for many years before they can return home or become eligible for a visa in another country.

SOURCE: Dogukan Keskinkilic/Anadolu Agency/Getty Images

## Migration Worldwide

**Migration** is a temporary or permanent settling to a new location. Most migration is for short distances in which the migrants remain in the same country. This type of migration is referred to as **interregional migration**, in which moving provides the family with better economic opportunities or sometimes better schools and/or community environments. In the years of the COVID-19 pandemic, for example, migration in the United States was from densely populated, more urbanized areas to smaller cities and rural areas. All regions of the country except the South experienced a loss in population during this period (Frey, 2023). **International migration** is the permanent move from one country to another. Almost 4% of the world's population in 2020 was composed of international migrants who were living in a country other than the one in which they were born (Natarajan et al., 2022).

In much of the world, migration refers to people crossing borders temporarily. The host country views them as temporary guest workers who will eventually return to their homelands. Many immigrants work in countries other than their home country because the higher wages enable them to better provide for their families. In some instances, international migrants send funds, or **remittances**, back to families in the home country. During the pandemic in 2020, worldwide remittances amounted to $722 billion but were expected to rebound to $794 billion in 2022. Funds to India led remittances in 2021 at $89 billion, followed by Mexico ($54 billion) and China ($53 billion). The leading source of remittances that year was the United States at $73 billion (Natarajan et al., 2022).

Historically, migration has been driven by "the clash of powerful nation-states," resulting in "the involuntary and massive displacement of populations" (Suárez-Orozco, 2020, p. 506), People have been forced out of their homelands because of civil war, persecution, uncontrolled crime, or economic depression, and they may be living in refugee camps rather than working in a neighboring or other country. They may later return home once economic and political conditions are stable. However, many migrants never return to their homelands. Dryden-Peterson (2019) found that the average length of exile for people who fled 33 global conflicts was 25 years.

The United Nations reported that 108.4 million individuals were forcibly displaced from their homes due to persecution, conflict, violence, human rights violations, and other events in 2020. Overall, 1 in 74 of the world's population has fled their country of origin, leaving them as refugees, asylum-seekers, or internally displaced or stateless people. In the current decade, over half of all refugees and other people in need of international protection were from three countries: Syria, Ukraine, and Afghanistan (United Nations High Commissioner for Refugees, 2023). Asylum in a new country is difficult to obtain. According to Suárez-Orozco (2020), "only one in ten people seeking asylum will ever make it to a safe high- or middle-income country" (p. 513).

The worldwide trend is interregional migration from rural to urban areas. This trend is particularly salient in less developed countries, where families can no longer sustain themselves in rural areas. They hope to find jobs and greater economic stability in an urban area. The problem is that most cities in developing countries are unable to provide necessary services for a rapidly growing population. Housing, food, water, waste treatment, and jobs are limited or do not exist. As a result, large numbers of migrants are living in villages on city borders without clean water and sanitation. When they can find work, it is often in the informal economy of selling wares on the street, gathering items to sell from garbage dumps, or participating in illegal activities. Death rates are high, and life expectancy is low. Schooling for children in these areas is very limited or nonexistent.

## Economic Ties Across the World

Events in one country can affect other countries around the world. For example, when adjustments are made to the stock market in one country, the stock markets drop or rise in other countries. When rain forests are depleted in Ecuador, the natural production of oxygen for the world is reduced, and the Indigenous groups depending on the rain forests lose their livelihood. During the COVID-19 pandemic, medical supplies, computer chips, and other products produced in other countries were held up in supply chains that took months for delivery, causing dire shortages and closures of companies that needed those supplies. Worldwide, interdependence among countries is so large that almost no country can operate in total isolation from others.

Although economic growth remains strong in countries such as the United States, China, Germany, India, and Japan, many people in the world are struggling to live from day to day. According to the World Bank (2022), nearly half the world population live on less than $6.85 per day. In 1990, 38% of the world's population lived in extreme poverty in which they lived on $2.15 or less per day. By 2019, the poverty rate worldwide had been reduced to 8.6% but increased to 9.3% in 2020 when the world's poorest people suffered the highest loss of income during the COVID-19 pandemic. They also faced the largest setbacks in health and education as lives were lost and children were unable to attend school. The countries in which most of these people live, such as those in Sub-Saharan Africa, have not recovered from the pandemic at the same rates as higher-income countries and have been more affected by natural disasters and conflicts among the world's largest food producers (World Bank, 2022).

Technology has both changed the job market and opened communications across national borders. It provides opportunities to connect people around the world. The use of computers and smartphones around the globe has increased dramatically over the past two decades. The Internet allows individuals to communicate with each other around the world instantaneously. However, the digital revolution is not yet reaching the majority of the world's population, especially people in developing nations.

## The Environment

The environment is also greatly affected by global conditions, changes, and decisions. A volcano, an explosion, a fire, or an oil spill in one country can affect the environment and economy of many other countries, as ash or other pollutants are spread by wind or water around the earth. For example, in 2023, large parts of the United States reached dangerous pollution levels as smoke from wildfires in Canada drifted south.

A number of factors contribute to the degradation of the environment and the world's ecosystem. As the world's population increases, the needs for food, clean water, sanitation, and jobs also increase. Rapid economic growth, which draws on natural resources, is expected to continue in countries such as China and India. Another factor is the increased consumption of natural resources and produced goods by the populations of industrialized countries, with the United States being the major consumer.

Although the destruction of the environment is a global problem, some countries contribute much more to the problem than others. Industrialized nations are the greatest offenders, using more than their equitable proportion of natural resources and adding more than their share of pollutants to the environment. Although the United States accuses China and India of having high rates of pollutants based on their dependence on coal, the United States and other industrialized countries have been polluting the environment through their disproportionately high use of coal and oil for many years.

Although the U.S. population is only 5% of the world population, it consumes more oil than any other nation. It is one of the world's largest consumers of water and creates a significant amount of the world's carbon monoxide emissions. It released the second-highest amount of carbon emissions in the world behind China in 2020, which was 12.6% of the total global emissions. Another measure of a country's carbon footprint is the amount of carbon dioxide emissions per capita, which is 13.68 in the United States, with a ranking of the 13th highest user in the world. Countries with higher $CO_2$ emissions included Australia, Canada, Kazakhstan, Saudi Arabia, and eight much smaller countries in the Middle East, Pacific Islands, Caribbean, and Southeast Asia (World Population Review, 2023b).

One of the tools used to assess how the world's resources are being used is the **ecological footprint**, which determines "how much of the biological capacity of the planet is required by a given human activity or population" (Global Footprint Network, 2023a, para. 1). The Global Footprint Network (2023a) figures an annual **overshoot day** that indicates the day during a year on which the "population's demand on an ecosystem exceeds the capacity of that ecosystem to regenerate the resources it consumes and to absorb its carbon dioxide emissions" (para. 9). In other words, the world is deplenishing its **biocapacity** to support the needs of the world's population. In 2023, that day was August 2 (Global Footprint Network, 2023b). Each year, with the exception of the two years during the COVID-19 pandemic, the time becomes shorter. If you are interested, the internet includes many calculators for individuals to figure their own ecological or climate footprint.

Most scientists believe that the damage to the environment can be halted and steps taken to dramatically improve the environment. Such a change in direction requires a global commitment from multinational corporations, local companies, policymakers, and the public to do things differently. Industrial leaders have traditionally argued against environmental control because of its cost, negatively impacting their competitiveness and profits. However, the tide may be turning. A number of companies are marketing sustainable development, and a growing number of cities are enforcing their own greening policies to support a sustainable environment.

**THE STRUGGLE FOR HEALTHY ENVIRONMENTS**    National and international organizations fight against global warming from fossil fuels, plastic pollution, air pollution, food and water insecurity, and biodiversity loss in the population size of animals and land use such as the conversion of forests into agricultural systems. However, the real battles are at the local level all over the world. These protests are led by Indigenous people, people of color, and other people who are being directly affected by environmental damage that could be controlled with different legislation, policies, and practices at all levels from the local to the global. They are trying to ensure that the places in which they live do not make their family members and neighbors sick with asthma, cancer, depression, heart disease, and many other illnesses. They are trying to protect their children from air pollution and the pollution of water that affects their health and academic outcomes. They "are fighting mines, dump sites, gas flaring, air and water pollution and any number of other environmental travesties. These are not 'greens' or environmentalists, but ordinary people trying to protect their land, water, lives and cultures" (Williams, 2021, p. 142).

Young people are often leading the efforts for environmental justice because their families and communities are being affected today by climate change and other environmental threats. For example, Swedish teenager Greta Thunberg was 15 when she sat outside the Swedish parliament for almost three weeks before an election with a sign that read "Skolstrejk för Klimatet" (School Strike for Climate). She was joined in subsequent days by more and more people, leading to the creation of Fridays for Future, which encouraged students and other activists in other countries to lead their own strikes (Alter et al., 2019). As a teenager, Greta spoke to multiple groups, including the United Nations in 2019, about the current and impending danger of environmental neglect.

Few people fighting for healthy environments and environmental justice have the platform that Greta Thunberg has, but many young people are assuming leadership in their communities to change policies and practices, fix current problems, and seek legal remedies for people who have been harmed from business and governmental decisions that have harmed communities.

## Indigenous People Fight to Save Their Cultures and the Earth

Not all people are excited about the globalization that is opening up the world to the interests of corporations, investors, and politicians. Skeptics do not believe that these groups have the best interests of the people and the environment in mind as they make decisions that primarily consider their profits and their own economic and social well-being. Indigenous people are severely affected by global decisions, but they have had limited or no voice in the decisions that dramatically change their lives.

Indigenous people, who are also known as First people, Aboriginal peoples, or Native peoples, are the descendants of the original inhabitants of a given region of the world. Examples include the Australian Aborigines, Taiwanese Aborigines, Native Hawaiians, Native Americans, Alaska Natives, Maasai in Africa, and Incas in

Indigenous people protest to protect the Earth and save their languages, cultures, religions, artifacts, and traditional knowledge and sciences.

**SOURCE:** NICHOLAS KAMM/AFP/Getty Images

South America. It is estimated that there are more than 476 million Indigenous people living in 90 countries in all geographical regions who represent more than 5,000 cultural groups, constituting 6.2% of the world's population. Many of their languages are endangered, with one Indigenous language dying every 2 weeks (United Nations Development Programme, 2021).

Indigenous people are nearly three times as likely to live in extreme poverty as people who are not Indigenous. They are among the world's most vulnerable people, often lacking social protection and economic resources. Many suffer from malnutrition and have a life expectancy 20 years less than non-Indigenous groups. Child and maternity mortality rates are higher for this group. Because of inadequate health care, they are more susceptible to diseases such as malaria, tuberculosis, HIV, and AIDS (United Nations Development Programme, 2021).

Community values are central in the lives of many Indigenous people. Many in the dominant groups, on the other hand, value individual freedom and the right of individuals to accumulate their own wealth and power. Another core value of many Indigenous people is their reciprocal relationship with nature. As Earth gives them the gifts of water, food, and protection, they must give back to Earth and take care of it. To them, globalization has given the powerful the ability to dominate both people and Earth for the purpose of making money—with no commitment to take care of either. To Indigenous people, these strangers who want to take and even destroy the land on which they have lived for thousands of years have no relationship with their land. The land and its produce have much more meaning to the natives than providing substance for living. Many Indigenous groups practice **subsistence living**, in which they produce enough food for their communities to survive but do not accumulate food or money for private use.

**Collective ownership** is another core value of many Indigenous groups. European settlers in the 1830s tried to convince the Cherokee to divide their lands in the southeastern United States into private plots that would be owned by individual Cherokee. The intent of the European colonizers was to buy the property plot by plot from the owners, thus removing the Cherokee from the land that the new settlers desired. The Cherokee resisted selling their land, which resulted in their being moved forcibly from their homes by federal troops. Indigenous peoples are constantly confronted with others trying to exploit their collective ownership.

Indigenous people view themselves as stewards of the land on which they live. Many Native Americans and Alaska Native communities follow the **Seventh Generation Principle**, which is based on an ancient Haudenosaunee (Iroquois) philosophy about the impact of decisions made today on the world seven generations into the future (Seventh Generation Fund for Indigenous Peoples, n.d.). It emphasizes the importance of being good caretakers of the earth not just for themselves but for the people who come after them. They believe that people's decisions and behaviors must have a positive impact on the land, water, air, animals, and vegetation. In some countries like Australia, Indigenous groups are engaged with the government to provide better management of the lands on which they and other Australians live (Janke et al., 2021).

Many Indigenous groups have suffered from the invasion of their lands by highways and pipelines. They have been relocated to make way for hydroelectric dam projects that flood their lands (e.g., Three Gorges Dam, China) and destroy their livelihoods. Some have been made ill because of contamination from the dumping of oil and chemicals into the water. Others have been plagued with diseases that arrived with the industrial development. When people are removed from their land and subsistence living, they may be forced to enter the competitive economy, in which they have to sell their products to buy the necessities of life. The Indigenous society becomes endangered as family members are forced to find jobs away from their native lands.

Today groups of Indigenous people are fighting in courts and public forums for their rights to sovereignty and self-governance (e.g., Hawaiian sovereignty movement) and collective ownership. Many do not want to assimilate into the dominant society. Indigenous people around the world struggle to protect their languages, cultures, religions, artifacts, and traditional knowledge. Theirs is often a losing battle against the globalization that could destroy their families, languages, and communities.

# The Intersection of Place with Race and Class

**Learning Objective 9.5** Analyze how place interacts with race and class to provide inequitable outcomes in society.

Race and class intersect with place in important ways that prevent the full inclusion of and equity for some groups in society. People become attached to the place in which they live, not always because it is the most desirable place to live but because it is where they have family, friends, and good memories of being together. However, some places exist in better and safer environments than others, and more affluent people generally claim those places for themselves, sometimes restricting the spaces to other people of the same race and socioeconomic status (SES). Even though there are laws against such segregation, the cost of property can serve the same purpose. In this section, we examine societal and governmental policies that discriminate against people of color and people with low incomes to limit their access to healthy environmental spaces and quality schools, the role of environmental justice in changing these disparities, and the limitations of segregation in neighborhoods and schools.

## Environmental Justice

Environmental problems at global and country levels impact the lives of children and their families disproportionately at the local and global level based primarily on their race and class and sometimes their religion. According to some of its early advocates, **environmental justice** is "the right of all people to share equally in the benefits bestowed by a healthy environment" (Adamson et al., 2002, p. 4), not just the people who are wealthy and powerful. It has become a social movement in which activists fight to remove the systemic pollution and other environmental disparities in the communities in which people of color and people with low incomes live, exposing them to disproportionate health disparities. These movements also make it clear that wealth and power often lead to social upheaval and the unequal distribution of society's benefits, including good health. As environmental activist Jeremy Williams (2021) points out, "those who are most responsible for damaging the atmosphere face much lower risks, while the greatest dangers fall on those who are least responsible" (p. 1).

The U.S. Department of Energy (EPA; n.d.) defines environmental justice as "the fair treatment and meaningful involvement of all people, regardless of race, color, national origin, or income, with respect to the development, implementation, and enforcement of environmental laws, regulations, and policies" (para. 1). Furthermore, the EPA indicates that no population group should "bear a disproportionate share of negative environmental consequences resulting from industrial, municipal, and commercial operations" (para. 1). However, previous government policies and business practices such as zoning requirements and other racist practices in housing, lending, and urban planning contributed dramatically to people of color and people with low incomes

**Pearson eTextbook**
**Video Example 9.2**
This video discusses the history of environmental justice.
https://www.youtube.com/watch?v=30xLg2HHg8Q

In oil-producing areas, it is not uncommon to find oil wells and pumpjacks near housing developments.

**SOURCE:** Peter Bennett/Citizen of the Planet/Alamy Stock Photo

being forced to live near industrial plants, major roadways, ports, and other undesirable areas in the past and continuing into today (Gonzalez et al., 2022).

Researchers at the University of California at Berkeley and Columbia University in New York found that people of color and people with low incomes are disproportionately exposed to noise, air, and water pollution, which results in poor health outcomes such as heart disease, impaired lung function, anxiety, depression, preterm birth, and impaired fetal growth (Gonzalez et al., 2022). Black and Latino/a people who were prevented from living in areas with White people as part of the discriminatory practice of redlining in the twentieth century are twice as likely as White people to live in communities today with oil drilling, oil refineries, chemical companies, and other industrial plants (Fears, 2022). These redlined communities expose their residents to smog and fumes from cars, buses, trucks, coal plants, oil refineries, and other industrial sources (Lane et al., 2022).

Some areas of the country are known as "Cancer Alley" because of the concentration of industrial petrochemical plants, which has contributed to people living in that "alley" having disproportionately high rates of cancer. The most notorious Cancer Alley is the 85-mile stretch of land along the Mississippi River from New Orleans to Baton Rouge (Hirsh, 2023). In general, Black Americans are exposed to 38% more polluted air than White Americans, and they are 75% more likely to live close to a chemical plant or other industry where air pollution is toxic, leading to higher risks of cancer, birth defects, and chronic conditions like asthma (Fleischman & Franklin, 2017; Orum et al., 2014).

Farmworkers, who are predominantly Latino/a and other immigrants, also live in these polluted areas. In addition, they are exposed to pesticides while they work as lands close to them are sprayed. Journalist Paola Ramos (2020) wrote that "multiple reports have found that babies with chlorpyrifos[1] in their blood have lower IQs, higher rates of attention deficit hyperactivity disorder (ADHD), and higher risks of developing autism" (p. 28). Farmworkers also worry about the quality of tap water and the possibility of making their children sick and whether their children will have an asthma attack because of pollutants in the air.

---

[1]Chlorpyrifos is a pesticide that has been linked to potential neurological effects in children.

By the time a state-appointed city administrator in Flint, Michigan, switched the source of the city's water from the Detroit Water and Sewage Department to the Flint River in 2014 to save money, 100,000 people lived in the city, half of the 1950s population when the automobile industry was booming. In 2014, the city's Black population was the majority and 45% of the population lived below the poverty line (Natural Resources Defense Council, 2018). Soon after the switch in the water supply, Flint residents began complaining about the taste, smell, and color of the water as well as skin rashes, hair loss, and itchy skin. Mass lead poisoning was the outcome of drinking and using water that had not been properly treated. Seventy percent of the children who were affected were Black children. Even though lead poisoning had been found in the water, little effort was made by the government to fix the problem until Flint residents and state and local groups sued the city and state officials and a judge agreed with them. It took 2 years for the city's water system to be connected to a safe source and 5 years before the lead-corroded pipes were replaced and the water declared safe to drink (Water Defense, 2023). By the 2019–2020 school year, 28% of Flint's children qualified for special education, twice as many as before the water crisis (Green, 2019). Flint was a major crisis that received national news coverage, but the people of Flint are not alone. Over 7,000 water systems across the United States had lead in their drinking water in 2021, affecting 28 million people (Fedinick, 2021).

Jackson, Mississippi, is a city with a different kind of water problem that was also due to government decisions based on structural racism. On August 29, 2022, the largest water treatment plant in Jackson failed, leaving 160,000 people and hospitals, fire stations, and schools without safe drinking water or, in some cases, without any water at all. Jackson's population is majority Black, in part because thousands of White families left the city in the 1970s to avoid their children attending integrated schools. Around 25% of the population live in poverty. The problem in Jackson is the lack of political support at the state level to help maintain the infrastructure of the city. The water treatment plant for Jackson was built in 1914. A new water plant was built near the Ross Barnett Reservoir in 1992, but storms caused water mains to burst, leaving residents without water. At the same time, the city experienced a sanitary sewer overflow. In 2013, a Master Plan indicated $600 million was needed to update and repair the infrastructure; the eroding pipes were 6 inches in diameter and over 100 years old. Storms continued to cause water outages, and in 2019 more than 3 billion gallons of sewage were released into the Pearl River, which flows through the city. In 2020, the governor vetoed a bipartisan bill that would help Jackson fund the water system. Although the state received federal funds in 2021 for pandemic-related expenses, including water, no special session of the state legislature was called to appropriate funds. A 2021 storm left the city's residents without water for a month. When the state legislature met in 2022, it allowed Jackson to apply for funding for water and sewer projects with a one-to-one match, but the legislature required Jackson's funds to be deposited into a state-controlled fund. The day after the water treatment plant failed, President Joe Biden authorized federal funds to cover 75% of all costs related to the emergency, but Jackson cannot access the federal relief because of obstacles set up by the state legislature. As of this writing, the Southern Poverty Law Center (2023) has filed a complaint to the U.S. Department of the Treasury on behalf of the city.

Major natural disasters around the world also hit communities of color and low-income communities disproportionately hard, destroying their homes and lives as those disasters become more violent and more often. "As greenhouse gases pollute the atmosphere from the world's most developed countries, the waters rise or the rains fall in faraway places. Heatwaves claim the weakest. Crops are lost. Places and the memories they hold are erased. Cultural heritage is eroded" (Williams, 2021, p. 83). Most people of color and people living in poverty are facing climate change now, while people with privilege see it as something of the future, marginalizing the reality faced by people of color and those living in poverty. Vulnerable people and countries view climate change as something that is done to them (Williams, 2021). Privileged people and countries, on the other hand, may make decisions that reduce their footprint today, but their past decisions have led to high greenhouse gases that threaten today's environment (Williams, 2021).

**THE IMPACT ON STUDENTS**   The most vulnerable students are exposed daily to toxins, lead, hazardous waste, and other pollutants in their schools and communities that damage not only their bodies but also their ability to learn (Persico, 2019). These children are more likely than children in healthy communities to have asthma, iron-deficiency anemia, cancer, and other illnesses that may make it difficult to attend school or pay attention when they are at school. The World Health Organization (2018) reported that 93% of children worldwide are exposed daily to an unhealthy environment.

The sources of pollution are factories, oil refineries, and power plants, but pollution is also released from cars, buses, planes, trucks, trains, woodburning stoves, wildfires, volcanoes, and wind-blown dust, resulting in eye irritation, lung and throat irritation, breathing problems, and lung cancer (Centers for Disease Control and Prevention, 2022). Researchers Persico and colleagues (2020) examined the relationship of prenatal exposure to **Superfund sites**, which are the most contaminated toxic waste sites in the country, to cognitive and developmental effects on children. They found that "children living within two miles of an uncleaned Superfund site had a 23% increase in cognitive disabilities like learning disabilities, autism, intellectual disabilities, and speech and language impairment. They also had a 42% increase in the likelihood of being suspended from school and a 45% increase in the likelihood of repeating a grade, compared to the average for public school children in Florida" (para. 4).

Persico and Venator (2023) report that 21,800 factories or federal plants in the United States emit harmful classes of pollution. If one of these factories or plants is within one mile of a school, the chances of students scoring lower in school accountability measures such as standardized tests increase. In addition, attending school near a major roadway can also have negative impacts on student achievement and behavior (Heissel et al., 2019). Breathing dirty air, even wildfire smoke and car exhaust, is associated with higher levels of asthma and respiratory diseases. According to Mary Prunicki at Stanford's Sean N. Parker Center for Allergy and Asthma Research, "even brief air pollution exposure can actually change the regulation and expression of children's genes and perhaps alter blood pressure, potentially laying the foundation for increased risk of disease later in life" (Jordan, 2021).

Families are unlikely to choose to live close to polluting sites or in areas with lead in the water, but the costs of houses and rents are generally less expensive in these areas and are the only places that some families can afford. The polluting factories and major highways may have been built after families purchased homes in segregated areas as a result of racist zoning policies that encouraged industrial growth in areas populated by people of color and those with low incomes. As a result of these housing patterns, many children of color and children in families with low incomes disproportionately live and attend schools in places that produce negative cognitive and health outcomes.

## Segregation

**Segregation** is the separation of people based on characteristics such as race, ethnicity, socioeconomic status, gender, and religion. Historically, segregation in the United States was a system for keeping people of different races apart. The Supreme Court decision *Plessy v. Ferguson* (1896) made segregation constitutional, legalizing a Jim Crow system that prohibited people of color, particularly Black Americans, from living in the same neighborhoods, attending the same schools, staying overnight in the same hotel, swimming in the same pool, and sharing the same public facilities with White Americans.

**RESIDENTIAL SEGREGATION**   After Jim Crow laws ended with the passage of the Civil Rights Act in 1964, local governments created zoning restrictions that prevented Black people from purchasing homes in areas in which White people lived. At the same time, banks refused to grant mortgages to most Black people to purchase a home in another part of town, contributing greatly to ensuring that Black people would not be able to begin to create wealth by owning a home. Not until 1968 with the passage of the Fair Housing Act did discrimination in renting and selling homes become illegal. However, the desegregation of neighborhoods and schools is an ongoing project. Many neighborhoods, schools, and businesses still resist sharing the benefits and amenities of their lives with people of color or those of a different religion, SES, or gender.

Just because segregation had been declared unconstitutional did not mean that people, businesses, schools, colleges, and governments would change their practices without a fight. Many Black people who purchased homes in a number of White neighborhoods were driven from their homes by White neighbors. White parents blocked the doors of their schools so that Black children could not enter. Black people and other people of color were turned away from renting apartments in White areas with all kinds of excuses. With the support of powerful people and businesses, White elected officials figured out new ways to prevent widespread desegregation and discourage their communities from becoming more diverse and equitable to all residents (Trounstine, 2018). These decisions have made it difficult to provide a quality, equitable education to students regardless of their race, ethnicity, or SES when some people have access to the most desirable communities and schools while other people have no chance of living in a similarly desirable community with good schools.

Inequality increases on many dimensions with segregation. Professor Jessica Trounstine (2018) has documented that local politics "again and again favored some residents at the great expense of others" (p. 205). The winners have been White property owners, and the losers have been people of color and those with low incomes. Only when these populations have a political voice are segregation and inequality lessened. Trounstine points out that "segregation affects tax rates, wealth acquisition, and educational opportunities, which in turn affects political preferences" (p. 212). Issues related to segregation that are currently debated at local levels include multifamily housing, housing subsidies, and "Yes-in My Backyard" (YIMBY), a campaign that encourages citizens to support higher-density housing units.

Racial segregation persists in the United States today, even though it is more *de facto* **segregation** rather than *de jure* **segregation** as in the past when segregation by race was mandated by local, state, or national laws. Demographers use a **segregation index** to measure "the extent to which two different groups (such as white and Black populations) are unequally distributed across neighborhoods in a single metro area" (Frey, 2022a, p. 15) with a range from zero for complete integration to 100 for complete segregation. The segregation levels range from 36 in Honolulu to 78 in Milwaukee for Black Americans, from 29 in Honolulu to 60 in Los Angeles for Latino/a Americans, and from 25 in Tucson to 58 in Buffalo for Asian Americans.

Frey (2022a) found that the segregation index for Black Americans in the South and West is generally 60 or below, but it is in the 70s in midwestern cities and New York City. Segregation levels are less for Latino/a and Asian American populations. Segregation levels for Latino/a Americans are higher in long-standing immigration areas in the Northeast with large Puerto Rican populations and less in the Southeast and Midwest. Frey concludes that although there have been modest declines in neighborhood segregation, the levels remain "unacceptably high," indicating that "life experiences and access to community resources for nonwhite groups are very different from white residents" (p. 17). White Americans remain the most segregated racial group regardless of the location, even though the U.S. population overall is becoming more diverse. When the size of the White population decreased in a neighborhood, it was usually due to an increase in the Latino/a population. The same pattern was true in predominantly Black neighborhoods; the Latino/a population increased the size of the population (Frey, 2021b).

**SCHOOL SEGREGATION** Until the mid-1900s, schools across the country were segregated by race unless a state or district had restrictions against segregation. The *Mendez v. Westminster* (1946) decision ended the *de jure* segregation of Mexican American children in California schools in 1947, followed by the 1954 *Brown v. Board of Education* decision that ended *de jure* segregation based on the race of students across the United States. However, political resistance to desegregation was intense. Court-ordered desegregation plans aggressively pushed school integration forward after the Supreme Court decision *Green v. County School Board of New Kent County* (1968) (Reardon & Owens, 2014), being more successful in the South than in the cities of the Midwest and Northeast (Anstreicher, 2022). During this period, many White families pulled their children from public schools and enrolled them in private schools that were sometimes established for that purpose. Other White families moved to the suburbs so their children would not attend schools with children of color. By the mid-1970s, the courts began backing away from the enforcement of desegregation efforts and, in 2007, the Supreme Court declared in *Parents Involved in Community Schools Inc. v. Seattle School District* and *Meredith v. Jefferson County (Ky.) Board of Education* that race could not be used to determine the assignment of students to schools.

Today, schools in the United States are more segregated than before these two landmark court cases but not because the government requires segregation. According to a report by the U.S. Government Accountability Office (2022), more than one in three students attended schools where 75% or more students were of a single race or ethnicity in the 2020–2021 school year; almost half of those students were in schools where more than 90% of the student population were of the same race or ethnicity.

As shown in Figure 9.5, White students are the most likely group to be attending schools with other students of the same race or ethnicity. Thirty-one percent of Latino/a students, 23% of Black students, and 19% of American Indian/Alaska Native students attend racially segregated schools. When a school district secedes from an established district, the new district is likely to have higher percentages of White and Asian students than the district they left, taking their higher tax base with them and

**Figure 9.5** Segregation of U.S. School Population by Race or Ethnicity and Socioeconomic Status, Fall 2021

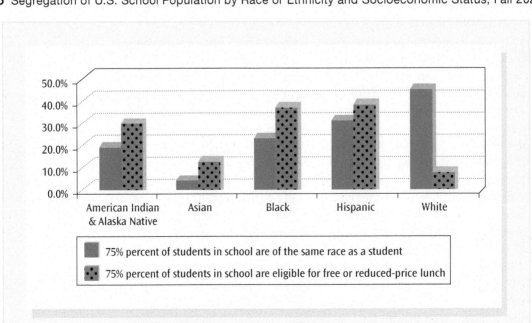

**SOURCES:** National Center for Education Statistics (2022c); U.S. Government Accountability Office (2022).

leaving the original district with fewer resources to support less affluent students (U.S. Government Accountability Office, 2022).

Another problem with segregated schools is that the schools attended by students of color are not only segregated by race but also by SES, as shown in Figure 9.4. A recent study of the impact of segregation on the racial and ethnic achievement gap found attending school with students of the same race or ethnicity had no impact on achievement, but attending school with a concentrated number of students from low-income families has an impact (Reardon et al., 2022). Integrating schools by income level could increase opportunities for higher achievement and also increase racial integration due to the strong relationship of race or ethnicity and SES.

The quality of schools generally plays an important role in the selection of a place to purchase a house by a family with children or planning to have children, and families may resist changes in the diversity of schools that they believe may negatively impact the academic, social, and emotional well-being of their children. If a community is serious about making their schools more racially and economically diverse, they may need to think about the purpose of education. In a study of school attendance boundaries in suburban neighborhoods, the authors (Asson et al., 2023) suggested that "rather than viewing high-quality neighborhood schools as a competitive good to be hoarded for one's own child, we should conceptualize schools as public goods meant to serve all students and society" (p. 16).

The segregation of neighborhoods along with the drawing of school boundaries result in widespread segregation of schools or classes within schools (GAO, 2022). Even when families have the opportunity to choose schools, including public charter schools, the chosen schools are often more segregated than neighborhood schools. When magnet and charter schools that have been designed to serve students from diverse racial, ethnic, and SES groups become successful, more White and middle-class students apply (Hill, 2019). The major problem with segregated schools is that the schools attended by students of color and those from low-income families remain underresourced and have teachers who are less experienced, are absent more often, and do not have the same knowledge and skills as teachers in other schools, resulting in inequalities of educational experiences across groups of students (Reardon et al., 2022)

In a poll conducted for The Century Foundation, over 80% of the respondents indicated that racially and ethnically diverse schools and schools with students from different socioeconomic backgrounds are important (Potter et al., 2021). A Gallup Poll found that just over half of White respondents, 65% of Latino/a respondents, and 66% of Black respondents thought racial segregation was a serious problem (McCarthy, 2019). However, parents' actions are not always aligned with their beliefs that diversity in schools is important, especially when they hear prominent arguments against integration such as it will "come at a cost to students" or might "detract from a child's life chances." The Century Foundation argues that a diverse school "helps reduce racial bias and counter stereotypes, and makes students more likely to seek out integrated settings later in life. Integrated schools encourage relationships and friendships across group lines and prepare students to succeed in an increasingly diverse society and global economy" (Potter et al., 2021, para. 21).

Although most efforts to desegregate schools had stopped by the 1990s, a growing number of school districts are voluntarily integrating their schools. More Black, Latino/a, and Asian American families have moved to the suburbs while more White people are moving into urban areas, which provides more opportunities for integrated schools if planned appropriately. Following the murder of George Floyd in Minneapolis, advocates for school integration are again exploring strategies for increasing the diversity of students in schools because they believe that an integrated education can benefit all students. The Century Foundation identified 185 school districts and charter schools that were considering race, ethnicity, and/or SES in their student assignment or admissions policies (Potter & Burris, 2020).

Drawing on original longitudinal studies going back to the 1960s, economist Rucker C. Johnson (2019) found that integration benefited Black students, leading to higher educational attainment and higher earnings, greater social stability, and lower incarceration rates in adulthood. At the same time, White students lost nothing in the integration process. Johnson's research also found that Black children who attended an integrated school from kindergarten to the 12th grade "had significantly higher educational attainment, including greater college attendance and completion rates, not to mention attendance at more selective colleges" (Johnson, 2019, p. 60). A more recent study found that desegregation of schools in the South resulted in an increase in "high school graduation rates by approximately 15 percentage points, increased employment rates by approximately 10 percentage points, and increased hourly wages by approximately 30%" (Anstreicher et al., 2022), but there were no distinguishable changes for Black students in schools in the North. Other beneficial impacts on Black students in integrated schools were a 25% decrease in poverty in adulthood and an improved adult health status (Johnson, 2019).

The instructional strategies related to intergroup relations, multicultural education, culturally relevant curriculum, and culturally sustaining pedagogy are appropriate approaches to the delivery of curriculum in an integrated school. The cross-racial dialogue and understanding that are built into these approaches are also essential to addressing historical and current racial and ethnic divides, injustices, and structural inequality. Healthy and supportive racial and ethnic communities who live and work together are needed to guarantee the country's future as a democracy (Wells et al., 2016).

# Classroom Implications: Incorporating Place in the Classroom

**Learning Objective 9.6** Create lessons that incorporate students' cultural and geographic backgrounds, are place based, and incorporate global perspectives.

Students and their families may have lived in the community served by a school for all their lives, as with the generations before. But some may have recently moved from another part of the city, another area of the state, or another state or country, as in the chapter's opening scenario. The local protocols for behavior in schools and social settings may be strange to these newcomers. Students may speak a language or dialect for which they are teased or harassed. Teachers should recognize that these differences are not shortcomings on the part of students. Instead, they are an outgrowth of their own histories and experiences outside the local community. Educators may have to become acquainted with other cultures to serve the new students effectively. Meeting with parents and listening to the students' own narratives of their experiences will help in providing a context for effective teaching and learning.

In this section we examine different strategies for incorporating place in instruction and curriculum, including working with migrant and immigrant students, using place-based teaching strategies, and incorporating global perspectives.

## Teaching Migrant and Immigrant Students

The experiences that migrant students bring to the classroom may vary widely. Some will have moved from another region of the United States. Some students in rural areas will be in the school a short time as their parents participate in seasonal agricultural work and then move to another area of the country where they can be employed. Others will be in families who have planned for years to move to the United States or whose parents are beginning graduate school at a nearby university. Some students may be fleeing an armed conflict in their native country and have been admitted to the United States as a refugee; some students may have spent several years in a refugee camp. Some students may have crossed the southern border of the United States with their families who are seeking asylum. Some migrant students have experienced numerous traumatic events during the months or years before they entered the classroom that would be difficult for most teachers to imagine. Migrant students who are undocumented immigrants are likely to be aware of arrests of undocumented immigrants in their community and are fearful that they will return home from school only to find their parents gone, under arrest, and facing deportation.

Where should teachers begin if an immigrant student is assigned to their class? First, they should be welcoming and supportive of the student. Second, they should find out from a school administrator what support the school district offers for migrant students. They should learn whether the district has translators or student advocates who can assist them in working with students and their parents. If students are English learners and the teacher has no background in English as a Second Language or bilingual education, they should consider enrolling in a staff development or local university course. Courses may be available online to provide teachers assistance. Other teachers may be willing to assist teachers in becoming successful at integrating immigrant students into their classrooms and helping them succeed academically.

Immigrant students, especially at the high school level, tend to be overlooked by their teachers and other school officials. Older students in urban areas may be assigned to a special newcomer school or program that is designed to help them learn English and adjust to the U.S. school culture. Most rural schools and many urban and suburban school districts will not have special schools or programs for older immigrant students. Instead, the students will be integrated into current classrooms with or without support to help them adjust to their new settings. Many immigrant students will be English learners who are participating in one of the language programs discussed in Chapter 7.

Migrant parents come from a wide range of backgrounds. Some may be highly educated, while some lack even the most basic educational background. Most believe that education is critical to their children's future success and are supportive of the teacher's efforts to help their children learn. In many cultures, the parents respect the role of teachers and trust them to have the best interests of their children in mind. Teachers should overcome any of the biases they have about immigrants and consider families an ally and partner in the education of their children.

A large number of immigrant students are likely to be living in segregated, low-income communities. As teachers work with immigrant students, they should make it clear that they have high expectations for them and do everything they can to help them meet those expectations. While parents may have hopes that their children will attend college, the children do not always have the appropriate academic preparation for college. They may not have a full understanding of college requirements, admissions procedures, and how they might access financial aid, even if this has been communicated to them in writing or verbally. With the professional staff cutbacks that are occurring in schools, guidance counselors and advisors may be overwhelmed and may not be able to give adequate attention to all students in need. Teachers should be alert to these students and be prepared to assist them in obtaining support.

Teachers should be conscious of the ethnic identification of immigrant students. They may be at very different stages of assimilation, which means they cannot be thought of as a homogeneous group. Some students identify strongly with the dominant group. Others are transcultural or successful in figuring out how to fuse the culture of the dominant society with their native culture. Other students continue to identify with their native cultures and resist or develop opposition to the dominant culture. If teachers understand where students are, they can better understand how to build on students' cultures to help them learn and possibly counter any opposition to academic achievement.

Not all parents feel welcome in schools, in part because most schools reflect the dominant culture and language rather than the culture and language of families. Therefore, school personnel may need to reach out to parents rather than simply wait for them to show up at a meeting. A true collaboration requires that parents and teachers become partners in the teaching process. Teachers need to listen to parents and participate in the community to develop a range of teaching strategies that are congruent with the home cultures of students. Parents can learn to support their children's learning at home but may need concrete suggestions, which they will seek from teachers who they trust and believe care about their children.

Because members of the community may object to the content and activities in the curriculum does not mean that educators cannot teach multiculturally. It does suggest that they know the sentiments of the community before introducing concepts that may be controversial. Only then can educators develop strategies for effectively introducing such concepts. The introduction of controversial issues should be accompanied by the education of parents and by the presentation of multiple perspectives that place value on the community's mores.

## Using Place-Based Teaching Strategies

One of the concerns of many rural residents is that their children will not stay in the community after they finish school, not because they don't want to stay but because they can't afford to raise a family in the area in which they grew up. They worry about the rural economy and wish that more opportunities could be made available. They would like their young people to intentionally choose to stay in their home communities, including young people who are preparing to teach, with the hope that they are interested in improving their communities and sustaining their cultures (Adams & Farnsworth, 2020).

In addition to the place in which people live, place refers to places that have had an important impact on people's lives. These might include a place they have visited in their neighborhood, another state, or another part of the world. They could include a theater, an art gallery, a basketball court, a quiet and calming place in the woods, or a place of cultural significance. Place can promote "agency, equity, and community" and provide "a compelling context for learning" (Vander Ark et al., 2020, pp. 9–10). Vander Ark and colleagues (2020) indicate that "connecting learners to the place where they live can contribute to a sense of identity—a sense of who they are and where they're from. The humblest settings and surroundings have something to teach" (p. 11).

Place-based education promotes study outside the classroom, engaging students in the community and applying academics to real-world settings.
**SOURCE:** Sathachak/iStock/Getty Images Plus

Place-based education relies on the community to actively engage students in their learning of language, arts, mathematics, social studies, science, and other concepts across the curriculum. It is hand-on experiences in the real world that not only promote learning but also active engagement in the community (Center for Place-Based Education, 2023). It expands the place of learning beyond the classroom, encouraging learning at anytime and anywhere.

As teachers think about creating place-based experiences, they should remember that each student is unique, has unbounded potential, and has an innate desire to learn (Vander Ark et al., 2020). In the process of using place-based strategies, teachers become learners along with students. The Teton Science Schools introduced the following six principles of place-based education that have been widely adopted by educators:

1. Communities provide learning experiences for students.

2. Instruction is learner centered.

3. Learning is inquiry-based.

4. Local learning is the foundation for understanding global issues.

5. Students use design thinking to solve problems and confront issues in their local communities, requiring them to think critically and be creative.

6. The curriculum is interdisciplinary to match the real world and is frequently **project based** (City-as-School Toronto, 2021; Getting Smart, n.d.; Vander Ark et al., 2020)

You may be thinking that place-based education is primarily for rural schools where students can conduct projects in nature around their schools or homes. However, it can be implemented in urban and suburban communities as well. In addition to students working on projects related to environmental issues in the local community, place-based strategies include field trips, community service, internships in local businesses and community groups, guest speakers, visits to parks, partnerships with museums, and food gardens. These projects should also contribute to understanding and valuing the local community, the cultural identities of the people who live there, their traditions, and history.

Native peoples have been connecting their cultures and nature to education inside or outside of schools for generations as they had the opportunity to do so. Hopkins (2020) reported that "those classrooms that emphasized place-based interactions, where students learned within tribal communities under the instruction of tribal elders and cultural experts, were characterized by greater empathy toward and knowledge of Indigenous peoples and tribal issues than those classrooms that emphasized more traditional pedagogical approaches" (p. 26).

## Incorporating Global Perspectives

Because the world has become so interdependent and will become even more so in the future, it is important that students develop an understanding of global connections and how they impact their lives. As teachers plan lessons, they should think about how they can integrate worldwide events and actions into the curriculum. A natural disaster such as a tsunami, an earthquake, or a volcanic eruption provides an opportunity to learn about the part of the world in which the disaster occurred, the people affected, and the implications for the United States. Students can learn more about the countries from which immigrant students have come. A lesson on manufacturing could investigate where around the world products are being made and who works in the factories or sweatshops. Students could study child labor laws and how children in some countries are involved in the manufacture of products they buy. A lesson on music could explore the influence of U.S. music around the world and the influence of music from other countries on the United States.

Another strategy for incorporating global issues into the curriculum is to help students think about topics from the perspectives of different groups of people in another country. Their perspectives on an issue could be the same or different from those of students in the classroom. Globalization itself will look quite different from the perspective of a less developed nation than from the perspective of a developed nation. Indigenous people look at the environment in a very different way than oil companies. Presenting different perspectives will help students clarify the issues and understand why different people may think differently about the same issue.

Using the Internet, students can connect to students in classrooms around the world. Some schools connect their students as pen pals to those in other countries. Students in different countries could work together on projects to learn more about each other or on an issue or a project in which both countries are engaged. Students from all kinds of schools participate in exchange programs with families around the world. Teachers sometimes arrange trips for students to visit other countries. The possibilities for interacting with people from other countries will continue to expand as both teachers and students increasingly use technology to work together.

# Explore and Focus Your Cultural Lens

## Debate: How Can Global Perspectives Be Incorporated in the Curriculum?

When a number of teachers at John F. Kennedy High School began to realize the impact that globalization was having on their community, they began to talk to their colleagues about more systematically incorporating global perspectives across the curriculum. Some of the other teachers agreed. They clearly saw that a number of parents had lost their jobs when several factories relocated out of the country. All around them, they could see that they and their students were wearing clothing and buying goods that were made outside the United States. The latest threats to food safety were due to imports from other countries.

Other teachers thought it was unwise to change their curriculum to integrate global issues and perspectives. One teacher expressed concern that such perspectives might politicize the curriculum and was concerned that as it was, students weren't learning enough about the U.S. government and civics.

The principal, however, liked the idea of students developing a greater global awareness. She believed that it might gain community support and provide a unique branding for the school. Would you support the inclusion of global perspectives in the curriculum?

### FOR

- The study of globalization will help students understand how different nations are connected.
- It will help students understand which people benefit from globalization and which ones lose as a result.
- Students will learn to think more critically about the changes that are occurring in the country as a result of globalization.

- Projects in some classes could help students become more involved in their communities by having them organize to fight against inequalities.

### AGAINST

- Social studies courses already cover global issues.
- The approach will provide a distorted view of the problems caused by globalization.
- Including global perspectives in the curriculum will politicize the curriculum.
- The curriculum should concentrate on preparing students for college or jobs.

### Questions for Discussion

1. Why do faculty members disagree about how globalization should be addressed in the curriculum?

2. Why do proponents feel that it is important to help students not only understand globalization but understand the negative impact it is having on many of them who are students, as well as children around the world?

3. Where do you stand on including global perspectives throughout the curriculum? How could global perspectives be integrated into the subject that you will be teaching?

# Revisiting the Opening Case Study

When Imad entered Mark Pulaski's classroom in our opening scenario, his arrival set off a chain of emotions for him, for his new classmates, and for his teacher. For months, the entire country had been bombarded with continuous media coverage of rival politicians squaring off on the country's views of people from the Middle East and allowing refugees into the United States. Middle Eastern and other refugees were desperately trying to escape their war-torn countries.

Mr. Pulaski decided to take three steps with regard to Imad's situation in his class. First, the name-calling related to Imad was unacceptable and must be stopped as soon as he learned of it. Mr. Pulaski had a conference with the two students involved in the name-calling, letting them know why it was wrong and making certain that they understood it would not be tolerated. He also worked at engaging Imad in class activities and discussions and helped the class understand the difficulty of migrating to a new country and adjusting to a new school. Because at this stage Imad was not likely to volunteer his opinions and calling on him would likely cause him discomfort, Mr. Pulaski posed a series of questions to be addressed by changing partners that allowed Imad to work with different classmates and take his turn in reporting responses to the class. This plan enabled different classmates to work with Imad each day and thus learn to interact with him.

Mr. Pulaski also began to introduce current events topics about migration and where and why it is taking place. This discussion provided the class with a geography activity. The class was then able to address the impact on the people having to give up their homes and adjust to new environments. The goal was for the class to gain an appreciation for what Imad and his family had experienced. If and when it is appropriate, Mr. Pulaski plans to help Imad share some of his experiences. It may even be possible for Imad's parents to share with the class why they chose the United States and their hometown to live.

## Reflect and Apply

1. Have you ever been in a situation where you were an outsider who did not really fit in with others? What were your emotions about being in such a situation?

2. As you see and hear the media coverage of migrants trying to escape the violence of their homes and trying to enter our country, what thoughts go through your mind?

3. What is the impact of increasing diversity in the United States?

# Summary

- Where people grow up and live has a profound influence on a person's values as well as their education, vocational opportunities, religion, and political affiliation. People may have no choice in what part of the world—what country, region, or community within a country—they are born and live, but educational opportunities, marriage, or work may take them to other places with different cultures, languages, economic conditions, and religions.

- Populations in different regions of the country not only live with different landscapes (e.g., prairie, mountains, or oceans) and favor different foods, they also share similar values, cultures, educational policies, religiosity, and politics. At the same time, each region is growing more racially and ethnically diverse each year. The diversity of the student population varies across regions, with the largest percentage of Latino/a, Native American, and Asian students in the West and Black students in the South. The Midwest has the least diverse student population. Teachers' salaries and educational policies also differ across regions. The population across the South is more religious than the rest of the country; the least religious populations live in the Northeast and on the Pacific coast. The political differences across regions become clear during national elections when maps show the states in which most of the residents voted for Republicans and Democrats. Specific states can always be counted on to support candidates in one party or the other, but the preferences of people in some states (14 in 2023) change from one election to another.

- Living in urban, suburban, and rural communities provides different opportunities for their residents. Some urban areas tend to become magnets for immigrants seeking housing and work. Large cities offer much to those who are privileged with satisfying jobs and quality housing and are able to enjoy the many offerings of the city, such as restaurants and entertainment. For many, however, the city is a place of misery, featuring unemployment, poor-paying jobs, and substandard housing.

- Education can also be a challenge for some who attend and who teach in underfunded schools lacking adequate materials, supplies, and technology. Some schools in wealthy areas of the city have the advantage of strong parental support, with parents often finding ways to enhance the school facilities and offerings. Suburban schools can also vary considerably; some of them are

American workers in the United States, and American cars contain parts made in countries that many people have only read about. Globalization affects the lives of most people in various ways that many people do not always realize.

- Throughout history, people have been migrating. They move within their own country and migrate or immigrate to other countries, seeking a better life in another place that they hope is free from famine, wars, discrimination, and persecution. Across the world, many people are displaced from their homes because of persecution, conflict, violence, and human rights violations. Some people have the financial resources to travel to a different country or a different part of their home country to study or work, sometimes remaining in that area for all or most of their lives. The United States, the most sought-after immigrant destination in the world, is a country of immigrants. Many of the immigrants to the United States are children, and educators have the responsibility to welcome them and facilitate their adjustment to their new country.

- The environment across the world is influenced by global events such as volcanos, major explosions, wildfires, and oil spills. Climatic conditions are creating havoc for some of the world's residents, forcing them to flee the areas in which they live to avoid drought or rising oceans. Although the U.S. population is only 5% of the world population, it consumes more oil and water and creates more carbon monoxide emissions than most other countries in the world. Indigenous people in the United States and around the world have been fighting to protect the earth's health and protect their lands from highways and pipelines.

- Today, young people are actively engaged in efforts for environmental justice to ensure that all people can live in healthy environments. Data show that people of color and those with low incomes are more likely to be negatively affected by air, water, and noise pollution, in part because they live closer to industrial plants than any other population group. The result is poor health outcomes such as heart disease, impaired lung function, anxiety, depression, preterm birth, and impaired fetal growth.

- Residential areas in the United States remain segregated, with the greatest residential segregation in the South and West. White Americans are more segregated than any other group, even though the population is becoming more diverse overall. Following the Supreme Court decision in *Brown v. Board of Education* in 1954, schools began to focus on desegregating schools, making progress on that goal from the mid-1960s to the mid-1970s when the courts began to pull back from enforcement of that effort. Today, schools are more segregated than before 1954 not because laws require that students from different groups not attend school together but because of residential discrimination and the way school boundaries are drawn.

- As students from other countries arrive in U.S. schools, it is critical that educators are prepared to support them in making their adjustment as seamless as possible. Students may come from a variety of backgrounds. Some come from families that are better educated and financially more comfortable than most students. Others, however, come from families with limited educational backgrounds, limited finances, and limited or no English-speaking skills. While teachers help immigrant students adjust and learn the culture of their new country, there is much that teachers and other students can learn from the rich cultures of immigrant students.

- Place-based education honors the places in which students live and encourages the involvement of students in their neighborhoods. It also expands the place of learning beyond the classroom into the community. Students may be conducting experiments at a local stream, park, garden, or museum. They may be interacting with local people at a farm, fire station, nursing home, or business. They may be investigating the reasons they live in a food desert, why so many people in their community have asthma, or why their school is on the list to be closed. Because of the impact of globalization on communities, teachers are encouraged to also explore the broader world and how decisions made at both the local and global levels can affect students and their communities.

## Pearson eTextbook Application Videos

The following videos are available in the Pearson eTextbook and can be used to practice observing and applying what you learned in this chapter.

**Pearson eTextbook Application**

**Video Example 9.3**

In this video, consider the ways native cultures been changed by the dominance of outside cultures.

**Pearson eTextbook Application**

**Video Example 9.4**

In this video, Dr. Fillmore discusses ways educators can work to create schools that are welcoming spaces for parents and families. Pay particular attention to the roles that educators play in this process.

# Chapter 10
# Youth Culture

## Learning Objectives

*As you read this chapter, you should be able to:*

**10.1** Describe the culture of youth and the characteristics of adolescence.

**10.2** Analyze the impact of digital technologies and social media on the lives of young people.

**10.3** Identify signs of the physical and mental health well-being of youth and discuss identity development during adolescence.

**10.4** Evaluate the challenges young people face as they transition to adulthood, including their relationships with their family members and peers and the positive and negative aspects of risk-taking in their lives.

**10.5** Explain the importance of engaging students in meaningful activities and creating safe and supportive classroom environments.

## Opening Case Study

Bill and Jimmy had grown up in the same neighborhood, attended the same elementary and middle schools, and often played basketball together at a neighborhood park. When they were in middle school, they sometimes hung out, communicated over social media, and considered each other friends. Although they attended the same high school, they became interested in different activities, developed different friendships, and saw each other less often. Bill had shown particular interest in math and science and was even a budding artist. He seldom was in the same class as Jimmy anymore, and they hardly ever interacted socially. Bill also liked most of his classes, and his grades were better for it. Jimmy was still trying to find his place in high school and was unhappy with his social studies teacher, Ms. Mitchell. Jimmy refused to engage in class discussions and activities, but he was worried about passing the upcoming graduation test and the loss of some of his friendships. He was sure Ms. Mitchell didn't care about him and his success. She was just another teacher who was not interested in knowing or helping him.

Jimmy started skipping class but wanted to get back at Ms. Mitchell in some way. One day as he was leaving the school bathroom, Bill was coming in, and Jimmy started complaining about Ms. Mitchell. Bill also was in a class with Ms. Mitchell and thought she was fine, but he felt obliged to listen to Jimmy because they

had been friends. Jimmy had an idea and asked Bill to guard the door so he could tag Ms. Mitchell on the bathroom wall. Knowing that Bill was an artist, Jimmy handed Bill the magic marker and pushed him to add a caricature of Ms. Mitchell to the graffiti. Not wanting to lose his friendship with Jimmy, Bill complied. As Bill was finishing, a school resource officer entered the bathroom. They were caught. Bill's level of stress was skyrocketing. All he could think about was why he did something that he didn't want to do and how he was going to explain his actions to his disappointed parents and teachers, especially Ms. Mitchell.

### Reflect

1. Why are young people susceptible to being pulled into inappropriate activities by their friends or other peers?

2. What are factors that lead to changes in friendships from middle school to high school? Why do young people sometimes feel that they have to stay loyal to previous friends or friends who are misbehaving?

3. What does the research on adolescent development tell us about young people's thinking during their high school years?

**SOURCE:** Adapted from Nakkula & Toshalis, 2021.

# Young People and Youth Culture

**Learning Objective 10.1** Describe the culture of youth and the characteristics of adolescence.

Each person who lives long enough will become a part of every age group. Like other subcultural groups, age influences how people feel, think, perceive, and behave. Although many adolescents behave differently from one another, the ways they think, feel, and behave are at least partly a result of their being adolescents. At the same time, age is not alone in affecting the way a person behaves or functions. Race, socioeconomic status, religion, and gender intersect with age to influence the behavior and attitudes of young people. Classroom behavior and engagement in school is often related to young people's relationships with family members, significant others, and peers as well as the social and economic context in which they live.

American society in general has not always been viewed as particularly supportive or positive in its perceptions of all age groups. In the past, adolescence was often viewed as a time of so-called "storm and stress," which focused on negative views about youth, becoming a form of **ageism** against young people. Adults concentrate on youth's challenges and missteps and "show large-scale resistance to the idea that all youth are capable of thriving and are not inherently problem-prone" (Buchanan et al., 2023). Older people are another group often not viewed in U.S. culture with the respect or reverence that is found in many other cultures. Because most of them are no longer in the workforce, they are often viewed as nonproductive citizens. Ageism is, regretfully, as much a part of our social system as racism, sexism, and discrimination against those with disabilities. Thanks to advances in medical science, people are living longer, which may be positive, but at the same time will require those working to assume a greater tax burden to help support older people through social services.

Students reap benefits if they are able to understand and value the contributions of all age groups to society. By addressing the issues of various age groups in the classroom, educators can help students better understand their family members and other important people in their lives. Knowledge can also eliminate fear of the unknown as students begin to move into different age groups throughout their lives. Just as the school assists students in understanding the problem of racism, teachers can help students understand ageism and dispel the myths related to older people. Field trips to retirement homes or visits to the class by senior citizens may provide useful experiences. As students become aware of the nature and characteristics of each age group, they should be able to develop the perception of each individual, regardless of age, as being an important and integral part of society.

It is important for educators to understand age as it relates to both students and their families. Understanding the particular age group characteristics and needs of students can assist educators in better understanding and managing age-related behavior, such as reactions or responses to peer group pressure. Understanding the nature of families and other important individuals will assist educators in family–teacher relationships and in helping students cope with their interactions with others. For example, when an older grandparent moves into the family setting, this event may affect children and their classroom behavior.

In this section, we examine why youth became a distinctive age group different than childhood. In addition, we explore the definition of youth culture, how adults and the media perceive young people, and how youth have been commercialized.

## Youth as a Distinct Age Group

The concept of youth has not always existed; it developed as countries became more industrialized and controlled by bureaucratic power in the nineteenth century. Legislators and reformers were expressing concerns about the vulnerability of young people as they worked in factories and on farms. Children were just beginning to attend school in larger numbers, but few attended beyond the eighth grade. Modern notions of youth as a distinct age group emerged at the beginning of the twentieth century when psychologist G. Stanley Hall introduced the term *adolescent*. Hall defined it as beginning with puberty and ending in mature adulthood and viewed it as a "volatile period of identity formation" (Osgerby, 2021, p. 6). Over time, sociologists and psychologists "increasingly focused on the social characteristics that were believed to set youth apart as a discrete social group" (Osgerby, 2021, p. 6), with distinct social experiences, values, and behaviors.

Like other identities studied in this book, age is socially constructed in that it is greatly influenced not only by biological and psychological development but by the lived experiences of people as they interact within their social, economic, and political contexts. Development within age cohorts is dependent on relationships of all types. Teachers and other educators are important players in adolescents' development and their interpretations of themselves and the world. Professional educators are active participants in the co-construction of young people as the two groups interact, each influencing the development of the other as young people create themselves though experimentation and theorizing about their possibilities (Nakkula & Toshalis, 2021).

Each age cohort grows up in a particular time period, with events and circumstances such as terrorist attacks, wars, new technology, recessions, and pandemics. These experiences shape the characteristics of the cohort. As the new generation evolves, members of that cohort may themselves contribute to the shaping of that particular generation.

Who are the youth discussed in this chapter? Adolescence is generally defined as the teen years. The primary focus in this chapter is young people between 13 and 17 years old who are generally at the end of middle school or in high school (i.e., grades 8 to 12), but the discussion sometimes includes young adults between the ages of 18 and 24 who may be in college, the military, or their first jobs. The younger cohort includes 21.7 million teenagers in the United States; the older cohort includes 31.3 million young adults. Each cohort includes slightly more young men (51%) than young women (49%) (U.S. Census Bureau, 2023). The percentage of youth in the populations of industrialized countries is much lower than in developing countries. Ninety percent of the world's youth live in Africa, Latin America, and developing countries in Asia (Cooper et al., 2019).

## Youth Culture

Young people are a distinct group with their own unique and evolving identities, languages, music, clothing, values, and ideas. Politically, as a group, they are more liberal than their parents and grandparents. They are more likely than older age groups to identify themselves as gender non-conforming or as part of the LGBTQ+ (lesbian, gay, bisexual, transgender, queer/questioning) community. Regardless of their race and ethnicity, they are more likely than other age groups to support social justice, beginning with the Civil Rights Movement and anti–Vietnam War in the 1960s and more recently the Black Lives Matter movement and women's marches.

Style, music, and fashion are important realms of cultural meaning for many young people, but socioeconomic inequalities and power have a major impact on their cultural experiences (Osgerby, 2021). During adolescence, their identities are fluid and dynamic as they test and experiment with them and interact with friends and family in their socioeconomic contexts (Osgerby, 2021). It is not just their racial and ethnic affiliations that are under consideration but also the clarification of their gender, sexual, and religious identities—struggles that likely will extend into young adulthood and sometimes beyond.

People who grow up in a specific time period share common experiences that lead to distinctive consciousness. Today's young people would have experienced

**Table 10.1** U.S. Population by Generational Cohorts

| Generation | Birth Years |
|---|---|
| Generation Alpha (Polars) | 2011 to 2025 |
| Generation Z (iGen) | 1997 to 2010 |
| Generation Y (Millennials) | 1981 to 1996 |
| Generation X | 1965 to 1980 |
| Baby Boomers | 1946 to 1964 |
| Silent Generation | 1928 to 1945 |
| Greatest Generation | 1901 to 1927 |

the aftermath of the terrorist attacks on 9/11, the Iraq War, Hurricane Katrina, the election of the first Black president, the MeToo movement, the murder of George Floyd, multiple school shootings, the COVID-19 pandemic, the war in Ukraine, the fire that destroyed the historic town of Lahaina on Maui, the 2023 war between Israel and Hamas, and many more landmark events and tragedies. The media, marketers, and even some scholars sometimes refer to these generational cohorts by the names indicated in Table 10.1. These cohorts are purported to have developed a common set of characteristics as a result of sharing a specific historic period of time and having access to technology that affects the way people live and contribute to the changing of cultural "norms" (Twenge, 2023). For example, young adults in Generation Z and Generation Alpha have had Internet all of their lives and smartphones since 2007 when older Gen Zers were starting their teen years.

The following sections include a description of three generations, which encompass the young people addressed in this chapter and most of their parents. These descriptions can be helpful in understanding how societies change over time. However, these generation groups are not scientifically defined, are sometimes stereotypical and oversimplified, focus more on differences than similarities, and may have an upper-class bias. Also, people change over time. Today's youth will not necessarily think or behave the same way in 2050 as they do today (Dimock, 2023).

**MILLENNIALS (GENERATION Y)**  **Millennials** are a large and highly visible generation group within the United States. The majority of demographers and researchers indicate 1981 to 1996 as the birth years for this generational group. The youngest of the millennials are around 30 years old. Many in this group have completed their college education, some have completed graduate school, and they are part of one of the most educated generations to date. The majority entered an increasingly diverse and multigenerational workplace. Few millennials served in the military, and they are less religious than their predecessors (Twenge, 2023).

The older members of this cohort witnessed on TV the Los Angeles riots following the Rodney King incident, and they also have experienced, with their younger cohorts, the wars in Afghanistan and Iraq and the rise and threat of terrorist groups both inside and outside the United States. The recession of 2007 dulled the optimism and high expectations of the millennials, just as it did with the other cohorts. Many millennials are strapped with sizable student loans. Some graduates found the anticipated high-paying jobs elusive and accepted unsatisfying positions for which they believe they were overqualified. However, millennial households today earn more than young adult households did at nearly any time in the previous 50 years, which is due in part to millennial women, who work more—and are paid more—than young women were in earlier years (Twenge, 2023).

This generation is defined by technology, social media, and globalization. Born around the time when the Internet was flourishing and the personal computer came on the scene, they have grown up with technology, and learning to use it came as naturally as learning to walk. Millennials therefore grew up with the ability to access people worldwide through their digital devices. A majority are plugged in 24 hours a day, 7 days a week. They are heavily immersed in the digital world and prefer text messaging, Snapchat, X (formerly Twitter), Facebook, Instagram, and other online technology to telephone calls and time-consuming forms of written communication.

**GENERATION Z (IGEN)**   **Generation Z**, the generational group immediately following the millennials, was born between 1997 and 2010. In 2023, this generation included people between the ages of 13 and 26 years of age. Gen Zers are more racially and ethnically diverse than any previous generation. In addition, they are on track to be one of the best-educated cohorts (Parker & Igielnik, 2020). They are much more likely than previous generations to believe in the existence of more than two genders, and 2.3% of them identified as transgender in 2021 (Twenge, 2023). While Gen Zers are very optimistic about technology use, they are also skeptical about the biases built into logarithms, data breaches of personal information, the monetization of people's intimate personal details to predict and modify their behavior, bot-enabled blackmailing, hacking, fake news, and the disruptions that could be caused by artificial intelligence and genetic engineering (Katz et al., 2021).

Roberta Katz of Stanford University describes a typical Gen Zer as a "self-driver who deeply cares about others, strives for a diverse community, is highly collaborative and social, values flexibility, relevance, authenticity and non-hierarchical leadership, and while dismayed about inherited issues like climate change, has a pragmatic attitude about the work that has to be done to address those issues" (De Witte, 2022, para. 7). Politically, they are more progressive and pro-government than older generations, are more likely to view increasing race and ethnicity as a positive development, and believe climate change is due to human activity. They are less likely to see the United States as superior to other countries (Parker & Igielnik, 2020).

Unlike earlier generations, Gen Zers appear to be in no hurry to grow up. They go out less and, when they do, it is often in the company of family members. In 2015, 18-year-olds were going out less than 14-year-olds did in 2009. This group was less likely to be involved in sexual activity, have babies, or start smoking, drinking, or using drugs than their older counterparts at a comparable age (Twenge, 2023). Many are content to have family members or Uber/Lyft drive them and are in no rush to get their driver's permits or licenses. Compared to previous cohorts, fewer Gen Zers work while still in high school or during the summer. By comparison, those who work choose fewer working hours. Instead, teens devote more time to studying and extracurricular activities. However, some Gen Zers earn money developing apps or adding "product placements" to their blog postings (Katz et al., 2021). Some of them earn significant money as an influencer and endorser of products online.

While most Gen Zers participate in religion to some degree, there are increasing numbers of nonbelievers who do not participate in religion, do not pray, do not believe in God, and never attend religious services. Majorities of millennials and Gen Zers are supportive of racial and ethnic diversity, believing that it is good for U.S. society. One of the most encouraging characteristics of these two generations is their tolerance for differences. Compared to older generations, they tend to oppose racism, sexism, and homophobia and are more likely to support interracial marriage and marriage for same-sex couples (Parker et al., 2019).

**GENERATION ALPHA**   The youth in **Generation Alpha** or **Polars** (according to Twenge) are often the children of millennials. It is the first generational cohort born entirely in the twenty-first century. The oldest Alphas were born in 2011 and afterward, making them 12 years old and younger in 2023; this generation will continue through births in 2025, so the youngest of this generation are not yet born. At its current rate of growth, it will become the largest generational group ever by 2025 (Pate, 2023).

The United States has become even more diverse with the non-Hispanic White population just over 50%, and this generation includes more people who are multiracial than at any other time. At the same time, they are growing up with political polarization and climate change (Twenge, 2023).

Writing for Forbes Media, marketing expert Alpa Pate (2023) reports that "this is a generation that cares *deeply* about the global outlook, education, and equity. Climate change, poverty, refugee crises, digital disinformation, and mental health are some of the issues that Gen Alpha is observing with keen interest" (para. 5). Most Gen Alpha children are using smartphones and tablets. The affluent Gen Alphas are growing up with Siri, Alexa, and other smart voice assistants in their homes and in their family cars. Interacting with artificial intelligence (AI) is becoming more prevalent as ChatGPT has become popular among students. They are destined to be the most technologically advanced generation in the country thus far.

It is possible and highly likely that members of Generation Alpha may see a cure for most if not all cancers in their lifetimes. With the possibility of AI providing advances in medical science including but not limited to diagnosis, the average lifespan of this generation may be extended and the quality of life may be enhanced. The Alphas may also see advances in robots in many different capacities, from education to assisting with health care. Educators in K–12 and higher education need to prepare for the most technologically able and curious generation, the most connected and sophisticated group of students we have ever seen. Teachers and college professors who do not keep up with technology will be doing both their students and themselves a disservice and may be unable to deliver the quality education that students deserve.

## Commercialization of Youth Cultures

As you may have picked up in the discussion of age generations in the previous section, businesses want to know the interests of an existing and new generation so that they can figure out the best way to market their products to young people with money. The origins of the youth market were tied to industrialization and urbanization at the end of the nineteenth century. As a growing number of young people began to attend college at the beginning of the twentieth century, the middle class also began to grow, and college students became an important market for businesses until the Great Depression in the 1930s. The youth market soon rebounded as more young men were employed and had disposable income, fueling the acceptance of young people as a valid consumer group, with independence and influence that flourished during the prosperity of the 1950s and 1960s (Osgerby, 2021).

Young people became even more important consumers in the marketplace as the number of them finishing high school grew from around 30% in the 1920s to 77% in the 1960s, and the percent of graduates attending college increased as well (National Center for Education Statistics [NCES], 2021). Young people began to be called *teenagers* and were seen by businesses as "affluent young consumer[s] who prioritized freedom and fun" (Osgerby, 2021, p. 19). These consumers were children of the middle and upper classes who could spend their money on fashion, grooming, cars, sporting goods, and entertainment. Similar patterns of consumption by young people were occurring in industrialized countries around the world, although in many European countries, working-class youth were more involved (Osgerby, 2021).

The growing teenage market also influenced the movies being produced in the 1950s to attract teenagers and young adults. Beginning in the 1960s, Black youth began to be seen as potential consumers, particularly in entertainment that included the success of Motown Records. In the 1970s, *Soul Train* became the counterpart to *American Bandstand* and some shows for Black audiences began to appear on TV. When shopping malls became popular in the 1980s, they often included multiplex theaters targeted at young people. By the beginning of the twenty-first century, the teen population was again high as the children of baby boomers reached their teens with more money to spend than ever. The sale of video games and digital technology to young people was again rising (Osgerby, 2021). Already, businesses are planning for how and what they will sell to Generation Alpha.

## Public and Media Perceptions of Youth

Youth are sometimes celebrated as society's hope for a prosperous future and at other times vilified as the cause of the country's cultural decline. Fearing young people is not new in the United States, especially since cities became filled with working-class European immigrants in the late nineteenth century. Immigrants were viewed by the elite as immoral and dangerous people. Fears of juvenile delinquency grew and waned throughout the next century and into the twenty-first century.

The times at which the fear is high are often accompanied by major social changes in society and worry about the dangers of the future, creating a **moral panic** for some citizens (Osgerby, 2021). These moral panics were triggered by adults' concern about rock 'n' roll in the 1950s and 1960s, the way youth dressed, their haircuts, and their disrespect of people older than them. Older people found the views of younger people about the Vietnam War and their protests in the streets to be dangerous to the country. As young people adopted hip-hop and rap music and culture in the 1970s, many adults and the media saw a further breakdown in the nation's morality. As feminists and other young women became much more open about their sexuality and sexual expression, other people labeled their ideas and actions as a cultural crisis. Researchers at the Centre for Contemporary Cultural Studies at Birmingham University in England connected these moral panics to shifting political relations in which race and racism were prominent. The concerns about youth in England, the United States, and many other places were not broadly about youth but more specifically youth of color who were viewed as "dangerous and threatening" (Osgerby, 2021).

Older people are more likely than people of other ages to believe that today's youth are declining in areas such as intelligence, work ethic, and delay of gratification. However, research indicates that older people have a *memory bias* in which they exaggerate their possession of positive traits when they were young (Protzko & Schooler, 2022). Such negative views of young people are reinforced by harmful narratives in the media about crime and delinquency of young people and the use of derogatory terms in describing them (Osgerby, 2021).

Concerns about the increase of juvenile delinquency are common and do not always reflect the data, which show that crime rates have declined dramatically from their peak in 1993. Adults think people under the age of 18 commit about half of all violent crimes when they committed only 9% of all serious crimes in 2019 (Puzzanchera et al., 2022). Although the negative perceptions of youth primarily focus on young men, they sometimes also attack young women, accusing them of immorality (Osgerby, 2021).

Young people resist the negative descriptions of them in the media through organizations and the media itself. For example, the Youth in Action network of the American Friends Service Committee organized the "We Are Not At-Risk" campaign in 2018 "to rethink the way they [i.e., media] talk about young people" (Burns, 2020, para. 5). They point out that their "stories of heroes, legacies, and impact are intentionally left out and covered up. Stories of triumph, pride, and resistance are replaced by stories of delinquency and crime to reinforce social and cultural hierarchies" (para. 8). Young people find that an advantage of digital platforms is that they can share their own stories and be more engaged in civic and political action (Center for Information & Research on Civic Learning & Engagement, 2021).

# Connectivity Anywhere, Anytime

**Learning Objective 10.2** Analyze the impact of digital technologies and social media on the lives of young people.

Both adolescents and young adults tend to be connected to the Internet 24/7, relying on digital technology and social media to communicate with their friends and family members.

**SOURCE:** © Rawpixel.com/Shutterstock

Youth today are defined by technology, social media, and globalization. Smartphones and social media are an everyday part of their lives. They interact with friends online, listen to music online, watch videos online, play online video games, and, during the pandemic, attended school online. In 2021, 88% of young people in the United States owned a smartphone, 64% owned a computer, and 36% owned a tablet. A majority are plugged in 24 hours a day, 7 days a week (Rideout et al., 2022). In this section, we explore the role of social media in the lives of young people and their creative contributions to and use of digital technology.

While older educators are often in awe of the computer skills of young students, it is incumbent on educators to provide students with the necessary skills in effective library and research use of the Internet. Without these skills, it is unlikely that they will develop into effective scholars. Although they are familiar with the Internet and know how to utilize search engines such as Google, these young students are not always astute enough to evaluate the quality of sources and to determine whether the information they have found on the Internet is valid. Often seeking the most expedient way to obtain answers or information to complete their reports, they may lack the background to determine whether data should be utilized. Even college students and professors are sometimes led astray by the Internet. There is no close scrutiny to verify the accuracy of materials, which are submitted voluntarily by individuals who are not always qualified to do so. Some students wrongfully assume that anything on the Internet must be correct.

## Social Media in the Lives of Children and Youth

It was just over 20 years ago when LinkedIn, Myspace, Facebook, and Flickr launched, becoming an easy and free way to connect to friends, family, interest groups, businesses, and buyers all over the world. Social media soon became an integral part of the lives of young people, professionals, and people of all ages around the world. At the same time, users' data became the product that social media companies sold. Soon entrepreneurs were promoting themselves or their products and advertising was prevalent on the digital platforms.

In 2021, 13- to 18-year-old youth on average used over 8½ hours of screen time every day, almost 2 hours more than in 2015. Screen time included the time "watching television and online videos, playing video games, using social media, browsing websites, creating content, e-reading, and other digital activities" (Rideout, 2022, p. 3). YouTube was their favorite site in 2022, as shown in Figure 10.1, and the site on which they were most likely to watch online videos regardless of their sex, race and ethnicity, or socioeconomic level. Over 77% of young people watched online videos daily, 62% used social media daily, and 49% watched television daily. The largest amount of time was spent watching TV shows or online videos, followed by online gaming and then social media. Even though they use social media about 1½ hours per day, two-thirds of the teenagers said they enjoy other kinds of media more. Instagram and Snapchat are their favorite social media sites. Boys use screen media more than girls and Black and Latino/a youth use them more than White students (Rideout, 2022).

**Figure 10.1** Most Popular Platforms Used by 13- to 17-Year-Olds, 2022

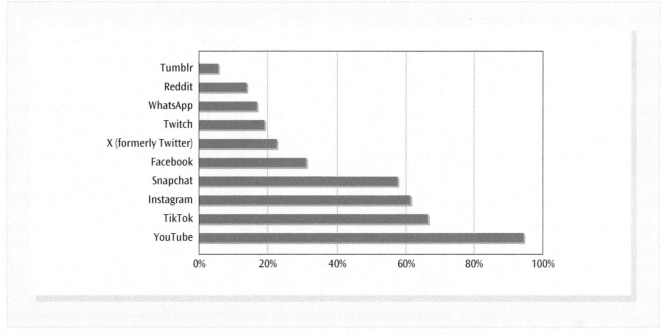

SOURCE: Based on data in Vogels and Gelles-Watnick (2023).

A number of researchers and information technology experts have raised concerns about the negative impacts of social media on the mental health of young people. This concern increased in 2021 when whistleblower Frances Haugen alerted the public that the Instagram app "worsened body image issues for one in three teenage girls, and all teenage users of the app linked it to experiences of anxiety and depression" (Mailman School of Public Health, 2021, para. 1). Watchdog groups have linked Facebook and Instagram to cyberbullying and TikTok to dangerous and antisocial behavior. Critics of social media have accused companies of being addictive by design, spreading misinformation on issues such as vaccine safety and election integrity and contributing to the rise of right-wing extremism.

Claude Mellins at Columbia University stated that social media supports socialization and relationship-building for many young people, but it also serves as "platforms for bullying and exclusion, unrealistic expectations about body image and sources of popularity, normalization of risk-taking behaviors, and can be detrimental to mental health" (Mailman School of Public Health, 2021, para. 4). However, not all researchers support the finding that the use of social media increases the risk for depression; further research is needed (Orben & Przbylski, 2019; Osgerby, 2021). It is not yet clear whether social media leads to poor mental health or whether young people with poor mental health are more likely to use social media.

Young people (32%) are more likely to say social media sites have a positive impact on them; only 9% report that the impact is mostly negative. Others indicate that they have neither a positive nor negative effect. Teenagers report that the most positive effect of social media is to connect and socialize with other people, followed by finding information, learning, and entertainment (Anderson et al., 2022). They feel that "social media helps them feel more accepted (58%), like they have people who can support them through tough times (67%), like they have a place to show their creative side (71%), and more connected to what's going on in their friends' lives (80%)" (U.S. Department of Health and Human Services [DHHS], 2023, para. 4).

Their negative experiences include becoming overwhelmed because of all the drama, feeling like their friends are leaving them out of things, feeling pressure to post content that will receive lots of comments or likes, and making them feel worse about their own life (Vogels & Gelles-Watnick, 2023). Students themselves worry that they spend too much time on social media and other digital technologies. Their families worry about very different possibilities, such as their children being exposed to explicit content on social media, sharing too much personal information about their lives, experiencing anxiety or depression, and spending too much time on social media (Vogels & Gelles-Watnick, 2023).

## Creators and Users of Digital Technology and Media

Young people have been leaders in the development of new technologies. Much of the technology surrounding millennials was developed primarily by companies created by older generations who were young adults when digital devices were developed and marketed for wide use by anyone (e.g., Steve Jobs at Apple and Bill Gates at Microsoft). Much of today's most popular social media was created by millennials who first created their products when they were young adults (e.g., Facebook's Mark Zuckerberg and Instagram's Kevin Systrom). Nothing suggests that this pattern will not continue as digital technology evolves with AI and other new digital products.

Most youth are consumers of the new digital technologies, but young people have also been at the forefront of learning how to use digital technology, sometimes turning it into lucrative businesses. One of the advantages of digital technology is that users can become more than consumers; they can become creators of their own content using the technology to take photographs, produce videos, make beats, create new dances, compose music, or write stories, poetry, or articles. However, only 4% of young people engage with these creative activities on their technology devices on a daily basis; they are more likely to create their written products by hand (Rideout, 2022).

# Explore and Focus Your Cultural Lens

## Using Smartphones in the Classroom

When students first started bringing cell phones to classes, teachers often collected them so that they wouldn't be a distraction and couldn't be used for cheating. Today, almost all middle school and high school students have a cell phone; 88% of them have a smartphone. Teachers now use them to engage students in learning primarily as an enhancement of their teaching. Ehnie (2022) suggests the following six ways to use them for learning:

- Create short videos.
- Use quick-response codes for a scavenger hunt.
- Use an online dictionary and thesaurus for an error-free paper.
- Collaborate and share with Padlet and a social media platform, which may help a shy student participate more often.
- Listen to podcasts and read the news online.
- Use apps to practice using a new language, collect data and feedback, and hundreds of other things.

On their smartphones, students can research anything and at the same time learn how to check the accuracy of what they find and be alert to fake news, which will become more expansive with the application of AI. Students are also able to watch a rocket launch and the swearing-in of a new president and visit almost

any country, zoo, and museum, sometimes taking virtual tours of these attractions. And there are numerous educational games that help make learning fun.

Using technology along with nondigital lessons has been found to have positive outcomes on student learning. It contributes to students having longer attention spans, increased motivation, higher classroom participation and engagement in learning, higher academic performance, and greater digital literacy (Waterford.org, 2020). The use of digital technology also provides the opportunity for students and teachers to learn together, teaching each other how to use the technology effectively as a learning tool. Should smartphones be used in classrooms and how should they be used? Here are common arguments both for and against.

### FOR

- Smartphones should be used for academic purposes only by linking students to apps related to lessons. The focus on academics is more likely to happen if the teacher is walking around the classroom and interacting with students rather than lecturing at the front of the room.
- Smartphones could be used to check on students' knowledge on a unit before the unit starts and as it progresses. There are apps that allow teachers to create

a multiple-choice test in which students' responses are compiled and displayed on a graph. This would help students and teachers know areas for which improvement is needed.

- Smartphones could be used for students to collaborate on projects on which they are doing research, collecting data, and/or preparing a presentation.
- Smartphones provide young people opportunities to conduct online research as well as manage their screen time and balance the time they spend online.

### AGAINST

- Cell phones are a huge distraction to learning by providing students opportunities for watching YouTube, listening to music, playing games, and checking social media instead of participating actively in the class.
- Students will likely use their smartphones to text their friends or update their social media sites.
- Students might use their smartphones to find answers to test questions.
- Students might use their smartphones to bully or harass their classmates during class time.

## Questions for Discussion

1. What additional arguments do you have for and against using smartphones in the classroom?
2. What are the reasons that young people are likely to resist a ban on the use of smartphones in the classrooms?
3. What are some ways that you would like students to use smartphones for learning inside and outside the classroom?
4. How do you project students interacting with you as the teacher to co-construct learning with the use of digital tools?
5. How will you ensure that all students in your class have access to a smartphone? How important will having the smartphone be if students can complete activities with other available digital devices?

# Well-Being of Youth

**Learning Objective 10.3** Identify signs of the physical and mental health well-being of youth and describe identity development during adolescence.

Adolescence is a critical time of physical, cognitive, and social-emotional development. Adolescents' brains are still developing, and they become better at making good judgments as they age. The conditions young people encounter in their families, communities, and society can have positive and negative impacts on their development. According to the National Academies of Sciences, Engineering, and Medicine (NASEM; 2019), children and youth who live in families with low incomes are exposed to high levels of stress and are more likely to develop chronic conditions as they age. They may be living in inadequate and unsafe conditions in homes with high levels of mold, lead, moisture, dust mites, and rodents, which are linked to poor physical and mental health, especially asthma. Poor health affects educational outcomes because, in part, children who are ill miss more days of school.

Young people in low-income neighborhoods have less access to health care, youth-oriented organizations, and learning centers than their more affluent classmates. As indicated in Chapter 9, they are more likely to live in communities where they breathe polluted air, which contributes to the development of asthma and other diseases. Such unhealthy environments deny the residents of those communities the healthy surroundings that would allow them to learn, grow, and thrive at the same levels as more affluent people (NASEM, 2019).

As discussed in Chapter 2, many youth, especially youth of color, are members of groups that have been exposed to historical trauma as a result of slavery, Native American boarding schools, the Jewish Holocaust, the internment of Japanese Americans, lynchings, mass murders, and exposure to other victimization and collective trauma. This historical trauma affects the well-being of generations of people who follow the actual victimization and oppression of their families, friends, and neighbors, impacting the opportunities, risks, and health outcomes of contemporary affected populations (NASEM, 2017).

Being consistently engaged in physical activity is critical to young people's good health and overall well-being.

**SOURCE:** FatCamera/Getty Images

Most students are dependent on their parents or other legal guardians to support their growth, development, self-esteem, and academic progress. However, children face numerous developmental and societal challenges as they mature to adulthood. Other adults—teachers, mentors, coaches, and counselors—are vital in helping children and adolescents make sound choices, as well as recover positively from the inevitable poor decisions they make on the path to adulthood. Caring adults can provide children with different perspectives, self-affirmation, recognition of talents or potential, and links to opportunities. As the Nigerian proverb states, "It takes a village to raise a child." In this section, we examine the roles that physical activity, mental health, and identity development play in the well-being of young people.

## Physical Activity

Physical activity is critical to good health at any point along the age continuum, but it is particularly important in young people's development, providing them a foundation for lifelong health and well-being. Physical activity helps youth improve their bone and heart health and general fitness as well as reduce the risk of depression. Children between the ages of 6 and 17 should participate daily in 60 minutes of moderate-to-vigorous activities such as walking, running, or any other activity that makes their hearts beat faster. They should also be engaged in activities to strengthen their bones and muscles such as jumping rope or playing basketball at least 3 days per week.

Physical activity not only promotes physical development, it also makes people feel better and sleep better as well as reduces the risk of some chronic diseases (DHHS, 2018). A number of young people participate in competitive sports that ensure they meet these requirements if they maintain the activity or related activities throughout the year. Participation in physical activities can be fun as people play with friends and family or provide opportunities to enjoy the outdoors or push themselves to higher levels of performance.

However, most youth are not close to meeting these recommendations. A national survey by the Centers for Disease Control and Prevention (CDC) found that only 32% of high school boys and 16% of girls participated in 60 minutes of exercise on all 7 days before the survey (Michael et al., 2023). Figure 10.2 shows the percentage of high school students who were meeting physical activity guidelines in 2021, including how

**Figure 10.2** Percentage of High School Students Engaged in Physical Activities, 2021

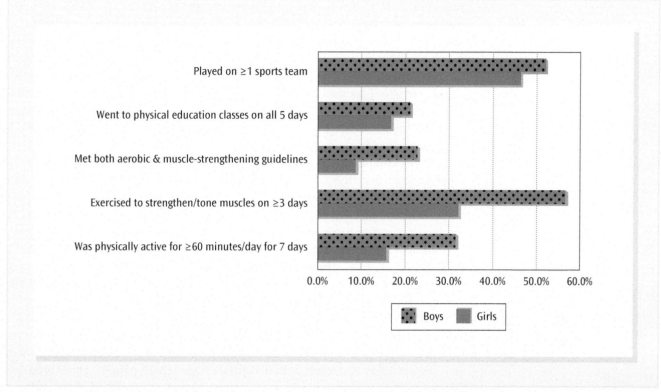

SOURCE: Michael et al. (2023).

many attended physical education classes and played on a sports team. Most young people spend their time outside of school watching TV and online videos, playing video games, and doing homework—all sedentary activities. The amount of exercise that some students get may depend on the neighborhoods in which they live. Families in some neighborhoods may not allow their children to play outside because of poor environmental or other unsafe conditions.

As you would probably expect, students who participate in physical education classes or play on a sports team are more likely to meet the physical activity guidelines. Both physical education classes and sports opportunities contribute to developing social-emotional learning competencies and foster school connectedness (Society of Health and Physical Educators, 2019). Most states require physical education, but they do not always specify the time requirement and allow substitute classes. Just over half of high school students attend a physical education class once a week and only one in four participate in physical education on a daily basis (Merlo et al., 2020). As a teacher, you can promote wellness habits for young people and may even be able to incorporate some guided physical activities in your class.

## Mental Health

Mental health is defined by the World Health Organization (2022) as "a state of well-being that enables a person to cope with the stresses of life, realize their abilities, learn and work well, and contribute to their community" (para. 1). Young people who are mentally healthy are more likely to be ready to learn when they enter school because they do not have to be worried about what is wrong with them. They are also ready to be actively engaged in school activities, make supportive and caring connections to their peers and teachers, use problem-solving skills, behave nonaggressively, and contribute to a positive school culture (youth.gov, n.d.). However, not all young people are mentally healthy.

In a 2021 survey conducted during the COVID-19 pandemic, 44% of high school students felt persistently sad or hopeless and 38% experienced poor mental health (Jones et al., 2022). Almost all youth experience emotional stress at some points in their teenage years as they are faced with new situations, meet new people, worry about their academic work, argue with their families, or make important decisions that could affect their future. However, persistent stress and worry is a sign that something is wrong. The Surgeon General of the United States, Vivek H. Murthy (2022), issued a statement about his concern about the mental health of young people, particularly those that are most marginalized, identifying a broader range of challenges they face such as "the ubiquity of technology platforms, loneliness, economic inequality, and progress on issues such as racial injustice and climate change" (p. 1).

**Adverse childhood experiences** can also negatively affect brain development, leading to mental health disorders. Children and young people whose lives have been marginalized can experience high levels of stress related to food insecurity, housing instability, health care, and many other factors (NASEM, 2019). For example, Black Gen Zers reported that the impact of racism had a significant impact on their mental health as they confronted systemic and institutional racism and experienced multiple **microaggressions** almost daily (Katz et al., 2021). The appearance of mental health conditions during the teenage years is serious, leading to lifelong mental health disorders Thirty-five percent of those disorders appear by age 14 and 63% by age 24 (Solmi et al., 2022).

In 2021, the American Academy of Pediatrics, the American Academy of Child and Adolescent Psychiatry, and the Children's Hospital Association declared a National State of Emergency in Children's Mental Health as a result of the COVID-19 pandemic and "the inequities that result from structural racism" (2022, para. 1). The U.S. Surgeon General issued a similar report. Children and young people had their education disrupted and faced social isolation from their friends. Many also lost a parent or caregiver, faced economic restraints because one or more family members lost a job, and/or were victims of physical or emotional abuse at home. All of this, accompanied by natural disasters, climate change, mass shootings, and political polarization along with the regular challenges of adolescence, felt insurmountable for young people, their families, and their teachers (Abrams, 2023).

Poor mental health can affect youth's lives in many ways, including their ability to achieve successfully in school, make wise decisions, and maintain good health. It can also contribute to the use of drugs and exposure to violence and risky sexual behaviors. However, young people are **resilient**, especially if they feel connected to school and family, and can improve their mental health (CDC, 2023e). Most of the time, mental health distress is episodic, not permanent, and can be treated professionally with the support of family and friends. Educators should focus on the whole child to support mental health wellness, using early intervention strategies such as **response to intervention (RTI)** or **multi-tiered system of supports (MTSS)** to intervene before the situation becomes worse. They can also promote prevention by helping students develop empathy and skills in conflict resolution and problem solving (Lazarus et al., 2021).

Youth's mental health disorders affect more than young people. The disorders also provide challenges for many families and caregivers as they struggle with the best ways to support their children. Some youth have a difficult time in school when behaviors, thoughts, and emotions related to their disorders interfere with their behavior in class, academic performance, and interactions with teachers and classmates. They may have high rates of absenteeism and tardiness and may be diagnosed as needing special education services for emotional trauma.

Youth are likely to have **mental health disorders**, such as anxiety disorders, attention-deficit/hyperactivity disorder, depression, and bipolar disorder, and many others that are less well known. These mental health disorders, plus eating disorders such as bulimia and anorexia, are prevalent among young people. The National Institute of Mental Health (NIMH; 2023b) reports that almost half of adolescents have had a mental health disorder at some time in their lives, affecting girls slightly more than boys and 17- to 18-year-olds more than younger youth. Just over one in four adolescents have had severe impairment or distress from a mental health disorder. More than one in three young adults (18 to 25 years old) in the United States live with a mental health disorder. The NIMH (2023a) suggests that "older children and adolescents may benefit from an evaluation if they:

- Have lost interest in things that they used to enjoy
- Have low energy
- Sleep too much or too little, or seem sleepy throughout the day
- Spend more and more time alone, and avoid social activities with friends or family
- Diet or exercise excessively, or fear gaining weight
- Engage in self-harm behaviors (such as cutting or burning their skin)
- Smoke, drink alcohol, or use drugs
- Engage in risky or destructive behavior alone or with friends
- Have thoughts of suicide
- Have periods of highly elevated energy and activity, and require much less sleep than usual
- Say that they think someone is trying to control their mind or that they hear things that other people cannot hear." (para. 4)

Experts are calling for an increase in the use of mental health assessments and treatment services in schools and the broader community (Abrams, 2023). Strategies for improving mental health care for youth include conducting routine mental health screening as part of regular pediatric care.

**School connectedness** has also been linked to positive mental health by serving as a protective factor for young people who have been traumatized, are stressed, or have been marginalized (Wilkens et al., 2023). "Teachers' relationships with their students are powerful predictors of students' success in school" (Lazarus et al., 2021, p. 4). In addition to teachers, social workers, school counselors, and community organizations can support young people in developing that connectedness by demonstrating that they care about students in ways that make them feel close to people at school. Schools in some communities contribute to the well-being of youth by offering mental health services to students. In one innovative approach, South Carolina schools have telehealth equipment that allows students to access "psychology and social work graduate students and clinicians trained in trauma-focused cognitive behavioral therapy" (Abrams, 2023, para. 32) at no cost to the students.

**SUICIDE**   Poor mental health is a major contributor to people taking their own lives. In 2021, a person died by suicide every 11 minutes, with the highest percentage of deaths among people over 75 years old, followed by adults between 35 and 64 years (CDC, 2023f). However, suicide is the third leading cause of death for high school students, behind unintentional accidents such as car accidents and homicides (CDC, 2023a). Over one in five high school students seriously considered attempting suicide in 2021, 18% had made a suicide plan in the past year, 10% attempted suicide, and 3% attempted suicide that resulted in an injury that had to be treated by a medical professional (CDC, 2023f).

Girls are almost twice as likely as boys to attempt suicide, but boys are four times as likely to die by suicide. American Indian/Alaska Native and Black high school students are more likely to attempt suicide than students in other groups (CDC, 2023f). As indicated in Chapters 4 and 5, over one in five young people who identify as lesbian, gay, bisexual, or queer attempt suicide (CDC, 2023f), and transgender students experience the highest suicide rate, with 40% of polled transgender students having attempted suicide and 82% having considered it (Austin et al., 2022). As a teacher, you may see signs of depression and changed behavior that could lead to suicide attempts. You should report your observations to appropriate school officials to help prevent fatal results.

**ACCESS TO HEALTH CARE** A major barrier to improving the mental health of youth and people of all ages is the lack of access to care by professionals. A part of the problem is the inadequate supply of child psychiatrists, psychologists, licensed clinical social workers, counselors, marriage and family therapists, and advanced practice nurses specializing in mental health care. Both adults and young people often have to wait for months to see a therapist or have access to a bed in a hospital or treatment center. At the end of the pandemic, 70% of schools reported a rise in the number of students seeking mental health services (NCES, 2022).

The director of policy and advocacy at the National Association of School Psychologists reported that the nation's schools have only one-third of the school psychologists needed and only 60% of the needed counselors (St. George, 2023). Only about half of schools say they can effectively provide mental health services to all students who need it (NCES, 2022). The number of professionals in a school should not exceed 250 students per school counselor, 250 per social worker, and 500 per school psychologist (American School Counselor Association, 2023; National Association of School Psychologists, 2023; National Association of Social Workers, 2018).

Youth with mental health problems are particularly underserved. Of youth with major depression, 60% do not receive any mental health treatment from a health professional or receive medication for depression. Less than 30% receive some consistent treatment that amounts to at least seven visits to a specialty outpatient mental health service such as a mental health clinic or private therapist. Not all private insurance plans cover mental health coverage for children. Although mental health treatment for depression is low for all students, less than 10% of Asian, Black, and Hispanic youth have access to treatment from a health professional, as shown in Figure 10.3. The largest percentage of

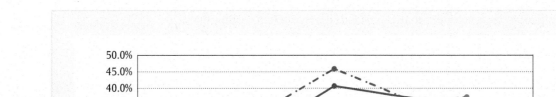

**Figure 10.3** How Were Youth Treated for Depression within a Year by Race and Ethnicity?

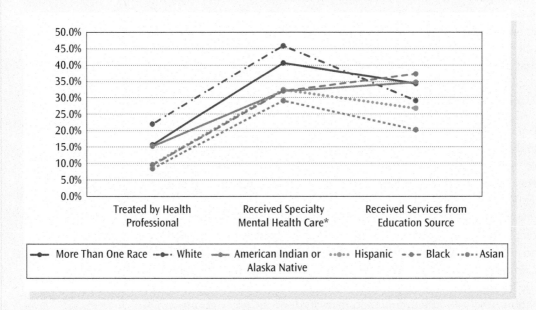

*Specialty mental health care includes staying overnight in a hospital, staying in a residential treatment facility, spending time in a day treatment facility, receiving treatment from a mental health clinic, receiving treatment from a private therapist, or receiving treatment from an in-home therapist.

**SOURCE:** Based on data in Reinert et al. (2021).

young people have received treatment through specialty mental health care such as at a hospital or residential treatment center. They are more likely to receive services at school than from a health professional such as a therapist or psychiatrist (Reinert et al., 2021), in part because their families cannot afford private health care.

## Identity Development

During adolescence, youth are in the process of becoming adults. Their bodies are changing, and they are developing abstract thought. They are learning complex interpersonal skills, negotiating new relationships, reconsidering their values, and thinking about their future. In this process, they are undertaking one of the pivotal tasks for young people: the development of their identities, answering the question of who they are (Nakkula & Toshalis, 2021). The period of adolescence allows young people opportunities to explore their identities, questioning the identities that their families, faith leaders, and society in general have defined for them in the past. They may decide they are happy with their identity and spend little or no time exploring it. In other cases, they discard old identities, construct and test new identities, develop relationships with others who share their identities, and evolve into new identities. They struggle with balancing the desire to be distinct from the people who have been closest to them in the past and the need to maintain meaningful relationships and feel that they belong to a group (Nakkula & Toshalis, 2021).

Most chapters in the book have focused on identities—racial, ethnic, class, gender, sexual orientation, exceptionality, language, religious, and geographic or place. As young people struggle with clarifying their identities, they can be greatly influenced by the expectations of their families, friends, and significant others as well as the perceptions other people have about them. They are also influenced by their experiences with racism, sexism, heterosexism, ableism, and other forms of hatred and discrimination. Their experiences in schools contribute to students' explorations about their identities and the reactions of society to those identities.

As indicated in the chapter on gender, many young people are identifying their gender as nonbinary or nonconforming as well as flexible and fluid, changing as they evolve as a person. They often face resistance, especially from older adults, to their nonbinary identity. A similar pattern is developing for sexual identity, as a growing number of people identify as bisexual. People's class and religious identity can change over time as they move to a different economic level or adopt a different faith or no faith. Over a lifetime, more people have a disability. As people move from one region of the country to another or to a new neighborhood, they may see themselves differently. People generally maintain the racial and ethnic identities of their birth based on the race and ethnicity of their parents, but the meaning of those identities evolves and changes over time. All of these identities develop in complex social contexts that influence how people see themselves. Dominant versions of them are reflected in school curricula, environments, and interactions, but those versions are often challenged and resisted by students and sometimes teachers (Nakkula & Toshalis, 2021).

Everyone in the United States is identified and assessed by their race and ethnicity as forms ask them to declare it, and data on academic achievement, housing, socioeconomic status, access to health insurance, and many other areas are disaggregated by race and ethnicity. Today a growing number of people are identifying as multiracial because their parents are from different racial and ethnic groups. As the racial and ethnic identities of youth evolve, their feelings can be very raw based on their own experiences, engendering feelings of discomfort, guilt, fear, sadness, and anger (Nakkula & Toshalis, 2021). A number of researchers have studied stages of the development of racial and ethnic identities that differ somewhat across groups. Understanding that students are at different places along a continuum of development may be helpful to educators as they try to work effectively with young people. There often is a reason for their anger, resistance, and questioning of their identities.

William E. Cross (1991) was one of the first researchers engaged in this work, developing a model of Black racial identity development. Cross's model includes the following five-stage process that many Black people undergo, which moves from accepting society's view of them to becoming secure in their Black identity:

- *Pre-Encounter:* Black people have adopted many of the beliefs and values of the dominant White culture, believe in meritocracy, and believe that race plays an insignificant role in a person's life.

- *Encounter:* Black people are exposed to the importance of race to one's identity and worldview, forcing them to question their previous stance on assimilation. This stage can lead to confusion, alarm, depression, or anger against White people.

- *Immersion/Emersion:* Black people immerse themselves in the world of Blackness, surrounding themselves with symbols of their racial identity and seeking liberation from Whiteness.

- *Internalization:* Black people become comfortable with their own personal standard of Blackness. Their rage against White people transitions to anger about oppressive and racist systems, and they express more willingness to establish relationships with other oppressed groups and White people who demonstrate race-critical consciousness.

- *Internalization-Commitment:* Black people find ways to translate their personal sense of Blackness as an expression of their sociohistorical experiences and worldviews. (Nakkula & Toshalis, 2021)

Janet Helms (1990) developed a model for White racial identity development and the adoption of an antiracist White identity that requires White people to reject racism and White superiority. The Helms model includes the following six stages:

- *Contact:* White people are oblivious to their racial identity, benefit from racism without necessarily being aware of it, and have limited interactions with people of color.

- *Disintegration:* White people first acknowledge their White identity and may experience guilt, depression, helplessness, and anxiety about the oppression and injustice of racism but do not yet believe that racism is the fault of White people.

- *Reintegration:* White people desire to be accepted by their own racial group, accept the belief of White superiority, believe in meritocracy, and blame people of color for their negative social conditions.

- *Pseudo-Independent:* White people begin to question their definition of Whiteness and justification of racism but continue to interpret cultural and racial differences through White life experiences as the standard.

- *Immersion/Emersion:* White people replace racial myths and stereotypes with accurate information about race in the United States. The desire to change people of color is displaced with the desire to change White people.

- *Autonomy:* White people internalize a multicultural identity that is nonracist, adopts a social justice agenda, and seeks opportunities to interact with people from other racial and ethnic groups. (Nakkula & Toshalis, 2021)

In both of these models and other models related to the development of racial and ethnic identities, people move back and forth across the stages based on their influences and experiences at the time.

As a teacher, you may not like the behaviors of young people when they are at some of these stages as they define themselves in contradiction to others and confront the privilege of White people and the marginalization of people of color.

However, each stage of development may be psychologically healthy and necessary, even if students' actions may seem rude, disrespectful, scornful, or threatening (Nakkula & Toshalis, 2021). Educators should remember that experiences of marginalization and discrimination have a great impact on people's identity and their relationships with other people. The way educators respond to the racist policies and practices in their classrooms and schools can influence students' movements from one stage in their racial and ethnic development to another stage.

Identity construction does not stop at the end of adolescence. It is a dynamic process that continues throughout one's lifetime as one's identity continues to be refined, clarified, and even dramatically changed as the result of an important event or significant experience such as a religious conversion, an unsettling incident, or a powerful joyful event. The development of positive identities is important because they are linked to higher self-esteem, self-confidence, and purpose in life (Nakkula & Toshalis, 2021).

Nakkula and Toshalis (2021) recommend that educators meet students where they are and let them define themselves. Educators should be able to acknowledge how harmful racial and ethnic categorizations have affected the lives of many of their students. Not recognizing the past and current racist practices of schools contributes to the continuation of those practices. Students should not have to abandon parts of their identity while they attend school. Dialogue about the dynamics of race and ethnicity, gender, sexual orientation, and religion should be ongoing with a goal of improving the cultural competence of educators, students, and other school personnel such as cafeteria workers, custodians, and bus drivers (Nakkula & Toshalis, 2021). School spaces that recognize and support the identities of students without judgment promote healthy adolescent development.

# Challenges of Transition to Adulthood

**Learning Objective 10.4** Evaluate the challenges young people face as they transition to adulthood, including their relationships with family members and peers and the positive and negative aspects of risk-taking in their lives.

Adolescence is perhaps one of the most challenging times in the life of students and their families. It is a long transitional period during which they are suspended between childhood and adulthood. During adolescence, emancipation from the primary family unit is a central task. It can be a difficult period for young people, who are attempting to be free from the role of a child but are not fully equipped to assume the responsibilities of adulthood. They are continually challenged to meet their own desires for peer acceptance, their family's expectations, and their own personal interests. Each day they are faced with temptations from easily accessible drugs to other risky behaviors, which can have long-term consequences. In this section, we discuss the important relationships young people have with their family and peers and the positive and negative aspects of risk taking during this critical part of their lives.

Pearson eTextbook
**Video Example 10.1**
In this video, follow along as a son and mother discuss some serious challenges of adulthood transition.

## Relationship with Families

As stated earlier, today's Gen Zers appear to be in less of a rush to loosen their ties with their families. The Gen Zers in one study indicated that their relationship with their families remain strong through their college days (Katz et al., 2021). However, as an adolescent shifts emotional ties from the family to peers, a restructuring may take place in the family–adolescent relationship. The adolescent may view families more objectively. Families may become more concerned about peer influence as they experience increasingly less interaction with their child. In some families, these changes have the potential to turn the period of adolescence into one of dissonance and alienation from parents and other members of the family. One need only observe

Young people's relationships with their parents sometimes become strained or challenging for both teens and their parents during the transition to adulthood.

**SOURCE:** instaphotos/123RF

a few adolescent–family situations, however, to realize that the degree of dissonance and alienation varies greatly.

In their efforts to achieve autonomy and become productive, self-sufficient individuals, some adolescents think they must turn away from the family. In this process of alienation, they can become isolated from their environment and the people with whom they are the most familiar. They may begin to distrust adults and reject the cultural values and expectations of their families (Barclay, 2018). As adolescents assert their rights to assume adult behaviors, they sometimes are unable to assume complementary adult-like responsibilities. Recognizing this shortcoming, families may be reluctant to grant adolescents adult privileges, which further adds to the alienation. Families who have confidence in their children are more likely to promote a feeling of confidence and trust in their children. These children often develop sufficient self-confidence to resist peer pressure when resistance is appropriate.

## The Importance of Peers

Adolescence is a period in which young people are moving away from their close and primary relationships with their families as they spend an increasing amount of time with peers inside and outside of school. Their friends and other peers can have a large influence on their beliefs, attitudes, and behaviors, sometimes replacing the values and behaviors promoted by their families in previous years.

During early school years, friends and peers are usually young people who live in the same neighborhood and attend the same school, often from the same racial and ethnic group. As youth increase in age, they engage with more teenagers from other neighborhoods. Young people tend to select friends who are similar to themselves. They also tend to become more similar to the people with whom they interact over time (Lansford et al., 2021). Thus, families worry about their children being caught up in the "wrong" crowd.

Compared to young people in other countries, youth in the United States have greater freedom to interact with their friends and peers away from the scrutiny of adults. They are allowed greater independence and autonomy outside of adult supervision, which can provide both developmental opportunities and risks for young people. On the positive side, young people have the opportunity to test and refine their social skills, develop friendships with people unknown to their families, and manage conflicts. On the negative side, the peers with whom they interact may be engaging in unhealthy and dangerous behaviors (Lansford et al., 2021).

Peer pressure can be very intense (Nakkula & Toshalis, 2021). Support from friends and other peers can be very positive in young people's academic, social, athletic, and creative growth. On the other hand, friends and peers can push each other to take risks that they might not otherwise take. Those risks may push young people to achieve at higher levels. Sometimes, the risks are related to trying the previously forbidden activities of using illegal substances, having sex, driving too fast or driving after drinking too much, or engaging in violent activities. These can be one-time discretions, but they could also be the beginning of continuing behaviors that could become addictive and lead to dropping out of school, not being able to keep a job, and being arrested for criminal activity.

Belonging is a feeling that young people have when they are accepted by other young people and adults. It often comes with active participation in class, extracurricular activities, clubs, and athletic teams. Some researchers have found that belongingness can affect students' motivation, behavior, and academic performance. In the digital world, peer validation is shown in the number of "likes" received in response to a post (Weinstein & James, 2022), but peer rejection can also have a negative effect on the feelings of youth, resulting in loneliness and lower engagement in school, academic achievement, and self-perception (Pinzone & Reschly, 2021).

## Risk-Taking

Risk-taking is an important part of healthy adolescent development. "It is a way of challenging the limits of one's capacities, the power of authority figures who place limits on one's activities, and the norms of one's peer group, which might be experienced as constraining or dull" (Nakkula & Toshalis, 2021, p. 41). In other words, it is the way young people experiment with different ways of being. Yes, some risk-taking can be unhealthy and dangerous, but for most young people it is a healthy means of exploring the world and how they fit into it. It provides them the opportunity to be creative by doing things that are not typical. What adults consider high-risk behavior is generally not seen as risky to young people (Nakkula & Toshalis, 2021).

**Pearson eTextbook**
**Video Example 10.2**
In this video, a mother and daughter discuss teenage pregnancy and the impacts on well-being.

Positive risks are those in which young people challenge their creativity, their intellect, and their performance in sports and other activities, pushing themselves beyond their comfort zone (Nakkula & Toshalis, 2021). Young people should learn not to be afraid of taking these kinds of risks and that failure is also a learning experience from which they can recover and move forward. Part of the risk-taking for some young people involves creating a world that they see as their own and different from that of adults.

Risk-taking is "common and deeply meaningful" for most young people (Lightfoot, 1997). They ride roller coasters, watch horror movies, play violent video games, and play "extreme" sports as they make meaning of their lives. They create new or novel sounds, fashion, games, and businesses that are usually online; they may become online influencers for their peers. All of these risks can be impulsive or calculated.

How can teachers take advantage of young people's interest in risk-taking? One way is to make their classrooms places where students can experience new, creative, and interesting learning opportunities (Nakkula & Toshalis, 2021). Teachers can also support young people's involvement in positive risk-taking by connecting with students and building together "a value system rooted in care, collaboration, and high achievement of various types" (Nakkula & Toshalis, 2021, p. 56). When teachers are committed to students as persons with dignity, they have a better chance of developing a reciprocal commitment from students and a shared value system (Nakkula & Toshalis, 2021) that supports positive risk-taking. Teachers can also model and teach respect, care, collaboration, and other life skills that can help students be both successful and happy.

On the other hand, risk-taking can also have negative outcomes, as discussed below. Most young people are in good health, but some make decisions about the use of substances that could lead to poor health outcomes. **High-risk behaviors** are activities that make young people vulnerable to physical, social, or psychological harm or negative outcomes. High-risk behaviors include but are not limited to the use of harmful substances such as alcohol or drugs, sexual behaviors leading to unwanted pregnancies or sexually transmitted infections, and violence. These behaviors are often initiated during adolescence, are frequently interrelated, and often extend into adulthood.

SUBSTANCE USE   **Substance use disorder** is the overuse of legal substances or the use of banned or illegal drugs and substances such as opioids. As early as elementary or middle school, some students begin experimenting with alcohol, drugs, and tobacco, and the majority of young people engage in some form of substance use before they finish high school (Hoots et al., 2023). These substances may be linked to desirable adult behavior but can also be a sign of resistance against adult control. Young people may push each other to use substances that are not yet legally available to them as part of their risk-taking experiences. In other cases, they use alcohol and drugs to self-medicate mental health problems such as depression and anxiety. Substance use has been one of the most prominent and publicized challenges faced by families, schools, communities, and law enforcement agencies even though substance use by young people has been declining for over a decade (Hoots et al., 2023).

Figure 10.4 shows the use of alcohol, cigarettes, and drugs by age. Overall, the percentage of young people under 18 years old using these substances is less than most other age groups. In 2022, girls in the 8th, 10th, and 12th grades were more likely to use alcohol and **vaping** than boys, who were more likely to smoke cigarettes (Miech et al., 2023). Even though fewer young people are using these substances, with the exception of vaping, at lower rates than in the past, educators and families should continue to help young people understand the dangers of using these substances and the long-term consequences of addiction.

Alcohol use is a public health problem in society, accounting for more than 140,000 deaths annually in the United States (National Institute on Alcohol Abuse and Alcoholism, 2023). While the vast majority of alcohol-related deaths involve adults,

**Figure 10.4** Use of Alcohol, Cigarettes, and Drugs by Age over the Past Month, 2021

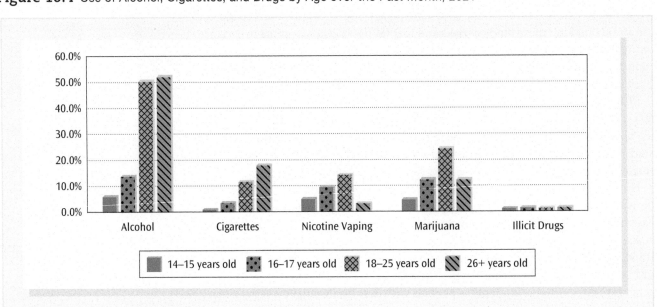

SOURCE: Center for Behavioral Health Statistics and Quality (2022).

more than 3,900 of these deaths were young people under the age of 21 (CDC, 2022b). All alcohol use by adolescents has been declining in recent years, but it is the most popular addictive substance for young people, as shown in Figure 10.4. Among high school students, 23% reported current alcohol consumption in 2021, down from 42% in 2009. Eleven percent reported **binge drinking**, which decreased from 14% in 2019 (Hoots et al., 2023).

Drugs are substances that produce altered states of consciousness. Fifteen percent of high school students report having used an illicit drug at least once, and 14% report misusing prescription drugs (CDC, 2022a), but only 6% were currently misusing opioids in 2021, a decrease from 2019 (Hoots et al., 2023). The adolescents who use drugs often seek relief, escape, or comfort from stress. The social institutions to which the adolescents must relate, including family and particularly the educational system, may be perceived as unresponsive or openly hostile. Their inability to focus on long-range goals, their desire for immediate gratification, and their lack of appreciation for the consequences of their behavior may contribute to some adolescents' misuse of substances.

There are two broad categories of adolescent drug users: experimenters and compulsive users. Experimenters make up the majority of adolescent drug users. Some progress from experimenters to compulsive users. Although most experimenters eventually abandon such use, the possibility of progression to compulsive use is a serious concern of families and authorities. Recreational users fall somewhere between experimenters and compulsive users. For them, alcohol and marijuana are often the drugs of choice. Use is primarily to achieve relaxation and is typically intermittent. For a few, however, the goal is intoxication, and these individuals pose a threat to themselves and others.

In the late 1990s pharmaceutical companies assured medical communities that **opioid** pain relievers were not addictive. At that point, health care providers increased their prescriptions, leading to the beginning of widespread addictions. Between 1999 and 2021, almost 400,000 individuals died from overdoses involving opioids in the United States. In 2021, 80,411 people died from an overdose of these drugs, more than half of them boys and men (National Institute on Drug Abuse, 2023). While the opioid problem may appear to be primarily an adult crisis, children and adolescents have also been severely affected. In 2019, 7% of high school students reported current misuse of opioids (U.S. Department of Justice, 2020). Overdose deaths most often involve the use of fentanyl and other synthetic opioids; more than 150 people die daily from overdoses linked to fentanyl (CDC, 2023c).

The number of children impacted by the opioid crisis far exceeds these numbers. When the adults in the family are involved in addiction, the entire family is at risk. Adult opioid deaths have left thousands of children orphaned or in single-parent homes. The drugs not only take up needed family resources for daily living, but parents under the influence of these drugs often fail to meet their family responsibilities. Schools report chronic absenteeism or tardiness of children whose addicted family members are unable to adequately prepare them daily for school (Superville, 2017).

With budget cuts, many schools no longer have school nurses (Jean, 2022) who might be capable of recognizing students suffering from drug poisonings and taking life-saving actions. There are currently effective medications that can reverse the effects of heroin and other opioid overdoses. One such medication is Naloxone, which is safe and cost-effective and can easily be administered by personnel trained in its use. Some school districts are now taking proactive action by keeping a supply of medications on hand and providing training for teachers and administrators in their use. No agency, group, or individual can wage an effective campaign against substance use alone. Only with a united effort can an effective battle be waged. There are numerous online websites that provide both physical and behavioral warning signs of possible substance use disorder among teens and other individuals.

Cigarette use continues to be a leading preventable cause of death in the United States, accounting for 480,000 related deaths in 2020 (CDC, 2020). Cigarette smoking has declined in recent years, but 12% of adults continue to smoke (CDC, 2023b). Only 2% of high school students were smoking cigarettes in 2022, but 14% of them were using electronic cigarettes or vaping products, which deliver nicotine, cannabis, flavorings, chemical, and other substances (CDC, 2022c). E-cigarettes are popular with young people in part because of the availability of flavors such as mint, fruit, or chocolate (American Lung Association, 2023). High school girls and Native American/Alaska Native, Native Hawaiian or Other Pacific Islanders, and White high schoolers are more likely to use e-cigarettes (Oliver et al., 2023).

Some users of e-cigarettes have been under the false impression that they are a safe alternative to tobacco smoking. While the reviews of these claims are mixed, any relief from the dangers of tar found in tobacco products may be offset by the high levels of addicting nicotine in the vaping products and other additives, metals, and particles, which may include toxins and carcinogens. A number of localities and some states have banned the sale of flavored cigarettes and e-cigarettes with the possible exception of menthol (Campaign for Tobacco-Free Kids, 2023).

**SEXUALITY**   Learning to handle sexual feelings is one of the challenges in the transition to adulthood. The mixed messages about sexuality received from families, peers, religious leaders, movies, and social media can be confusing as young people begin to have sexual feelings during puberty. Young people should know that sexual activity is a basic part of human development and that sexual curiosity is natural as they learn appropriate ways to express and understand their feelings of attraction and sexual orientation. Adolescence is the time that many young people develop romantic and intimate relationships and engage in a range of sexual behaviors. During this period, they date other people and may fall in and out of love several times as they clarify their sexuality, gender identity, and sexual orientation.

Young people who are sexually active are taking a risk of becoming parents much earlier than they had planned or contracting a **sexually transmitted infection (STI)** or **HIV/AIDS**. How engaged in sexual activity are young people? The CDC (2022d) reports that 30% of high school students had ever had sex in 2021, down from 47% in 2011, while 21% were currently sexually active, down from 34% in 2011. Sexual activity was nearly the same for young men and young women and all racial and ethnic groups except for Asians, who were less likely to be sexually active. Unfortunately, a smaller percentage (52%) of high schoolers were using condoms than in 2011; one in three sexually active students used other birth control such as pills, an intrauterine device, or a patch. A contentious issue in some states is the right of young people to contraceptive services without the permission of their parents.

There has been a steady decline in births to teenage mothers over the past 30+ years, but the rates in the United States remain higher than in other industrialized countries (Loudermilk, 2017). The birth rate for 15- to 19-year-old youth in 2020 was 15.4 births for every 1,000 young women, down 75% from its peak of 61.8 births per 1,000 in 1991. Birth rates of teenagers of all racial and ethnic groups have dropped, but they remain higher for youth of color with the exception of Asian youth, and they are higher in states across the South. Five percent of all births in 2020 were to teenage mothers, 76% of those births were to older teenagers who were 18 or 19 years old, and 9 in 10 of the mothers were unmarried (DHHS, n.d.-b). The decrease in birth rates is due primarily to the increased use of contraceptives and reduced sexual activity. Abortion rates among teenagers have also dropped to the lowest level since abortion was legalized in 1973.

Young women who feel more connected to their families and schools are less likely to become pregnant (DHHS, n.d.-b). Adolescents who are pregnant often are not effectively supported by society. They do not always have access to quality prenatal care because of lack of insurance and are not adequately supported and encouraged to finish their education. They may have to depend on public assistance, especially if their family cannot or will not support them during this period. As a result, they are less likely than their nonpregnant classmates to finish high school and enroll in college, and their children are more likely to face educational, behavioral, and health challenges (DHHS, n.d.-a).

Sex education is another controversial program in some communities as families and educators debate what should be taught about sexuality. The fact that almost half of new STIs diagnosed annually are found in young people and young adults (CDC, 2021) is a reason for the dissemination of information on sexuality. Nearly every state has regulations on the inclusion of information and discussions on contraception, sexual orientation, STIs, and nonbinary gender identity, especially transgender identity. Most states require instruction related to healthy relationships and the prevention of sexual violence, but only half of the states mandate the teaching of sex and HIV/AIDS education. Some states require an emphasis on abstinence, and some states allow families the option to remove their children from sex education programs (Guttmacher Institute, 2023). Thus, learning about sexuality differs greatly across school districts and states. Young people may be left to make sense of the mixed messages they receive with limited responsible adult guidance.

**VIOLENCE**   The mental health and well-being of children and youth can be affected negatively by exposure to violence. That violence can be in the form of abuse in their homes or by adults and youth in other settings, including at school and in their neighborhoods. It includes the bullying that some students face from other students or adults in person and online. It includes sexual violence, suicides, the fights and shootings that are disproportionately high in some neighborhoods, and mass shootings in schools. It also includes the killing of Black youth and adults by police. It is inflamed by the hateful language of politicians and on social media. The fact that so many young people are the victims of violence is in itself threatening to many children and youth. This violence also affects the friends and families of those young people who were the direct victims, bystanders who witnessed the violence, and many others who worry incessantly about becoming a victim.

In 2021, firearm deaths of children and teenagers in the United States was 36 times greater than a dozen comparable high-income countries (McGough et al., 2023). The Children's Defense Fund (2023) reported that a child or teenager was killed with a gun every 2 hours and 36 minutes in the United States in 2019. By 2021, there had been an increase of 50% from 2019 in the number of children and teenagers killed by gunfire (Gramlich, 2023). Gun violence has become the leading cause of death of children and teenagers in the United States. In 2021, 2,590 children and teens under the age of 18 were killed by gunfire in homicides (60%), suicides (32%), and accidents (5%), which was higher than any time since the 1990s. Many more children and young people were injured by gunshots, with over 11,000 children and young people being treated in emergency rooms for gunshots in 2020. Members of some groups are more likely to be affected by gunfire than others. For example, boys accounted for 83% of the deaths in 2021 and 12- to 17-year-olds accounted for 86% of the deaths. Black children and teens are six times as likely to die from gunfire in homicides as White and Hispanic children and teens (Children's Defense Fund, 2023).

Before COVID-19 in 2019, the number of high school students who reported carrying a weapon anywhere during the previous 30 days had decreased to 13% from 17% in 2009. Fewer high school students carried weapons (e.g., guns, knives, clubs) to school, with 3.5% carrying a gun in the previous 12 months. Young men, youth who were age 18 or older, and American Indian/Alaska Native, Black, and Hispanic youth were most likely to carry a gun to school (Harper et al., 2023). Harper and his colleagues (2023) report that "gun carrying might be associated with experiences of racism, discrimination, feeling the need to protect oneself because of increased exposure to community violence, mistrust in the criminal justice and other government systems, and poor or inadequate community-level protective factors" (p. 25).

Families and children not only worry about their children being shot on the street or in a drive-by. Children and young people live with the fear of school shootings as they undergo regular drills to prepare for an attack on their school and often face metal detectors, armed security, and even armed teachers in their schools. The first mass shooting at a school was in 1999 at Columbine High School in Colorado. Eight years later, a student at Virginia Tech University killed 33 college students and faculty, followed by the Sandy Hook Elementary School massacre in 2012 in Connecticut, the Marjorie Stoneman Douglas High School shooting in Florida in 2018, the Santa Fe High School shooting in Texas in 2019, and most recently the shootings at Robb Elementary School in Texas in 2022 and The Covenant School in Tennessee in 2023. By Labor Day, 27 school shootings had already occurred in 2023 with 14 deaths and 28 injuries ("School Shootings This Year," 2023).

Following each of these mass shootings, families, communities, and gun control advocates called for legislation to prevent the recurrence of such terrible assaults on young people. Although mass school shootings are horrible and none of them should occur, schools are still one of the safest places for students, with less than 3% of youth homicides occurring in schools or on school property (Cornell & Crowley, 2021). However, they have eroded families' and communities' feelings of safety in their schools.

Youth of color, especially Black youth, receive differential treatment from the juvenile justice system. They are more likely to be arrested, convicted, and incarcerated than White youth for similar offenses. Economically disadvantaged families typically

# Critical Incidents in Teaching
## A Possible Student Threat

James Cawley is one of the 350-plus students in his high school junior class. There is nothing remarkable about him or his closest friend, Kevin Edmunds. They are neither low- nor high-achieving students. They are average students who make average grades, have minimal involvement in school activities, and do not cause any problems for their teachers, classmates, or families.

However, recently, things began to change. Kevin has not been in school for a couple of days, and today, James is the last person remaining in the junior English classroom. James approaches Ms. Carlson's desk and asks her if he can speak to her in private. Jane Carlson has a reputation among the students for being one of the most caring and supportive teachers in the school. She nods affirmatively and motions for James to shut the door. James appears nervous as he tells Ms. Carlson that Kevin is now in his third day out of school and that he appears to be in a very dark place. He is making cryptic remarks about how their classmates hate him, how much he despises the student athletes, and that it is time that they get their just rewards. James knows that Kevin is an excellent marksman, having been brought up in a home where guns are highly valued. His concerns about Kevin's mental state and his access to guns have prompted him to share his concerns with Ms. Carlson. At this point, no specific threats have been made by Kevin.

Reporting these concerns to law enforcement authorities prematurely could cause Kevin's family unnecessary and certainly unwanted attention. It could cause a rift in James's friendship with Kevin if he later learns who reported the concerns to the authorities. Even if the other students never learn of the concerns, Kevin may be branded by the school staff as a potential threat. However, if Ms. Carlson fails to take any action and Kevin has sinister plans, the inaction could be tragic.

### Questions for Discussion

1. At this point, Kevin has done nothing wrong other than miss school for 3 days. What should Ms. Carlson do? Why or why shouldn't she contact Kevin's family to inquire about his well-being before taking any further steps? What should she say if she decides to call?

2. Should Ms. Carlson go immediately with James to the principal to express their concerns? Why or why not?

3. What if James refuses further involvement? How should Ms. Carlson indicate her concerns that Kevin is in "a dark place"?

4. What is the school's responsibility for contacting law enforcement immediately?

have court-appointed attorneys, and the trial and subsequent incarceration often seem like mere formalities. Youth from middle-class and privileged backgrounds may have the benefit of privately retained attorneys who may be able to secure probation, reduced sentences, or even expunged records.

Incarceration severely affects the future of young people, limiting their educational opportunities, employment opportunities, and income. The overrepresentation of juveniles of color in the juvenile justice system is more a result of the inequities of the juvenile justice process than the seriousness or persistence of their offenses. Youth of color and those from economically disadvantaged families are disproportionately incarcerated in large public institutions than in privately operated specialized treatment facilities or group homes where youth from more privileged backgrounds might be sent.

Some schools have implemented **restorative justice** programs to solve or prevent breaches in relationships in the school and broader community. Restorative justice brings together the perpetrator of the crime, the victim, and others who can support and facilitate the process. Often the individual who was harmed negotiates a reparation agreement with the wrongdoer. The goal is to reintegrate the student who has caused the harm back into the community (Cavanagh, 2018).

# Classroom Implications: Affirming and Supporting Young People

**Learning Objective 10.5** Explain the importance of engaging students in meaningful activities and creating safe and supportive classroom environments.

Next to a child's family, a teacher may be in the best position to support a student. Many individuals today can cite the names of teachers who had a profound effect on their development and inspired them to achieve and pursue their academic or vocational careers. Teachers can be a voice of reason, a calming influence in a child's otherwise tumultuous life. As a teacher, you must believe that you can make a difference in the lives of your students.

Adolescents need to feel secure in knowing that their teachers truly care about them, that they believe in them, and that they will communicate forthrightly with them with their best interests at heart. They want to know where their resources are, on whom they can depend for help, and where they can search for information online and elsewhere. They want and need meaningful, not busy, work (Marberry, 2019). As already stated, today's adolescents are well connected to each other through social media. However, many of the connections and contacts are via text messages. Many lack adequate human interaction, and some long for it (Marberry, 2019). Teachers can facilitate appropriate social development for these students and assist them in developing interpersonal relationships with fellow students and other people, not just with smart devices.

Most educators and families have worked diligently to ensure the development of positive self-concepts among youth by structuring successful experiences for them. Some want to see everyone a winner. However, the real world is unlikely to be as protective, suggesting that young people should have the opportunity to learn by working through their problems and be allowed the opportunity to fail at times.

Ware and Rath (2019) suggest that there are four critical elements that enhance classroom success with adolescents: consistency, respect, high expectations, and kindness. Teens need to have a clear understanding of the parameters in which they can function. Knowing their boundaries enables them the freedom to experiment and grow with a sense of security. Teachers and administrators who respect their students will likely have their respect in return. Respect generates realistic expectations, encouraging development to full potential. Kindness evokes kindness in return and a positive learning environment.

In this section, we explore strategies for actively engaging young people in school and creating safe and supportive school and classroom environments that will make them more likely to stay engaged in schooling.

## Engaging Students in Learning

When education is multicultural, student participation and critical analysis are encouraged. Building on students' culture and experiences help them engage in the academic content. Many young people are not interested in attending to their learning if the instruction is not meaningful to them or related to their interests. Today's students are engaged constantly in activities that are interesting and even fun on their cell phones. Keeping them active and engaged in their learning will usually have many positive payoffs, possibly even increasing their standardized test scores. It also increases their connectedness to their school, their teachers, and many of their classmates (Pinzone & Reschly, 2021).

Classroom projects could focus on areas of interest to students and the communities in which they live. As they participate in these activities, they learn to apply and extend to real settings the mathematics, science, language arts, and social studies they have been learning. Teachers and students in these classrooms are developing a vision for a more egalitarian and socially just society. Projects can engage students in collective action to improve their school or communities. These projects include the place-based education projects introduced in Chapter 9. They include social justice projects that investigate conditions in the neighborhood and take action to improve them. They include democratic education in which students have the opportunity to make decisions together about activities in the classroom and school. Through these projects, students become more engaged in actually using their academic, interpersonal, and social skills in making a difference in their lives and the lives of others.

**HIP-HOP FOR LEARNING**   Hip-hop is a culture that has always been a special space for people of color and other marginalized groups. It is also a mindset that legitimizes the rights of students and teachers to their own kind of knowledge, scholarship,

Teaching hip-hop or incorporating it into the curriculum can help make learning more relevant to the experiences of students and engage them more authentically to the content they are studying.

**SOURCE:** victoryt/123RF

communication, brilliance, talent, and professional swag (Jenkins, 2023). It gives teachers and students the freedom to break out of the dominant status quo and curriculum. It encourages teachers to be innovative and resist conformity as they collaborate with students to create classroom environments "where all students work hard, are determined, and have the guts to at least try their hand at being a scholar" (p. 134). The stories that students listen to and create themselves in hip-hop music provide a counter and authentic narrative about themselves and their communities. Jenkins (2023) suggests that educational spaces could also be more "movement-friendly," creating "cultures of welcome, community, release, expression, and participation" (p. 136), maybe even fun while learning.

In an urban classroom, hip-hop could be a tool for meeting educational objectives, especially in humanities and social studies classes. Rap is a "poetic form along with sonnets and the blues, as well as analyzed for vocal rhythm, varying rhyme schemes, and other literary techniques" (Au, 2016, p. 282). The lyrics can be examined for poetic device, imagery, and style, including the complex metaphors and word plays used by many rappers. However, hip-hop is more than its message; it requires innovation and technical skills, which are generally recognized cross-culturally. It draws on the Pentecostal church's call-and-response in which the audience is asked for an "Amen" or other verbal or nonverbal response such as handclapping. The call-and-response approach allows students a safe place to express emotion (Emdin, 2016).

Most urban teens are familiar with rap and are usually open to and enthusiastic about analyzing it. Many of them can write rap as a poetry form in their native language or dialect. Rap is a powerful and important form of cultural communication that can be used effectively in student-centered classrooms. According to James A. Banks (2023), "hip-hop provides a venue for disempowered youth to experience efficacy, protest racism and discrimination, and articulate their cultural identities and affiliations" (p. xi). The music that students are listening to, including country music, can be reviewed and analyzed. The raps that they compose can reflect sociopolitical and other issues that they have researched. They could even highlight their research findings on a specific topic in rap battles among students—a method that would help them develop their writing, research, and oral presentation skills while engaging them in learning academic content (Emdin, 2016).

Hip-hop, like most other artistic and institutional endeavors, has a history of **misogyny**, ableism, and violence, although many artists today have removed those negative components from their work. The field now includes many women artists and some artists who are disabled. Between 2001 and 2004, writer, poet, and community activist Leroy F. Moore Jr. founded Krip-Hop Nation with Rob Da' Noize Temple and Keith Jones with "the mission of advocacy, education, access, music, art, and justice issues that impact Black and Brown disabled communities, but also everyone" (Moore & Jones, 2023, p. 87). These hip-hop artists fight the ableism that has existed in hip-hop and the oppression of Black people with disabilities in society and the hip-hop world. Teachers who incorporate hip-hop in their classroom should remember that it includes artists and fans of all identities.

**RESISTANCE TO LEARNING**  Not all young people are going to appreciate the energy teachers have put into preparing a lesson or creating an innovative and interesting project. In fact, some will actively resist learning for various reasons. Like most things in the educational and health fields, students' resistance to teachers was blamed on the psychological background of the students. Today, psychologists would be more likely to characterize students' resistance as a response to oppressive experiences and relationships (Nakkula & Toshalis, 2021) that operate at both the family and institutional level, including the biases and inequities in schools. Nakkula and Toshalis (2021) have found that the active engagement of students in schools is built on a foundation of trust in their teachers and the school.

Young people sometimes resist their teachers because they feel that they do not care about them and their cultures and that their experiences are not respected nor reflected in their everyday school lives. It can be very difficult to agree to learn from a teacher who appears to know little about you or your community nor shows any respect for either. Capitulating to the desires of such teachers could cause a student a major loss of self-esteem. Thus, students challenge teachers and other educators who demonstrate a deficit orientation about them.

However, teachers are encouraged not to give up on students but to continue to work with them, interacting with them in a way that could become collaborative or co-constructive as teachers listen to them and make appropriate adjustments (Nakkula & Toshalis, 2021). Humor, patience, and trust are helpful attributes in working with resistant students. At the same time, teachers should realize that misunderstandings between teachers and young people are likely to occur. Teachers should not give up on resistant students but, instead, develop the capacity to tolerate those misunderstandings and continue to put forth their best efforts to reach out to students and try again (Nakkula & Toshalis, 2021).

## Creating Safe and Supportive School Environments

Numerous studies have found that marginalized students are stressed and don't think their teachers know or care about them, which can become significant barriers in their school and future success (Lazarus et al., 2021). For years, experts have called for the creation of school environments (or *climates*) to "foster a safe positive, healthy, and inclusive learning environment for all students and staff" (Griffiths et al., 2021, p. 133) to better support the mental health and overall well-being of students. However, teachers and education leaders have not yet been able to create and sustain safe and supportive environments for all students, especially for students of color, those from low-income families, students with disabilities, and those who identify as LGBTQ+ or nonbinary. Too many students still face negative experiences in school, such as verbal assault, harassment, bullying, unfair discipline, bias, and microaggression. However, there are steps that teachers can take to make their classrooms safe and supportive for *all* students.

**CONNECTEDNESS**   Feeling that one belongs in a family, school, or community and among one's peers is not only important to young people but also "is an important protective factor that promotes the health and well-being of students" (CDC, 2023e, para. 1). But **connectedness** is more than just a feeling of belongingness. It is also the caring, valuing, respect, and support that students feel from teachers and other school staff. According to the research reviewed by the CDC (2023e), positive outcomes of connectedness include less involvement of students in risky behaviors such as violence and substance use, more engagement in positive health behaviors, higher grades, better school attendance, higher graduation rates, and less emotional distress and thoughts of suicide.

During the pandemic, 37% of U.S. high school students experienced poor mental health. However, young people who felt close to people at school were more likely to experience good mental health, as shown in Figure 10.5. Although the differences between students who felt close to students and those who did not were less, they were still significant in virtual classrooms, with an advantage for students who felt closer to their classmates (Jones et al., 2022). The researchers who conducted these surveys concluded that schools should promote positive school climates and foster school connectedness among students, families, and school faculty and staff.

**ELIMINATING STEREOTYPES ABOUT YOUNG PEOPLE**   Biases against youth can result in inequitable outcomes for the affected students. According to the National

**Figure 10.5** Status of Young People's Mental Health During the COVID-19 Pandemic

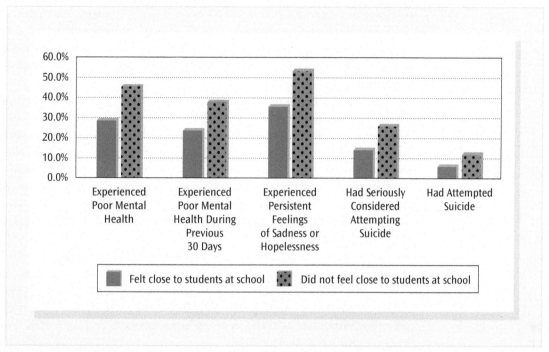

SOURCE: Jones et al. (2022).

Academies of Sciences, Engineering, and Medicine (2019), "adolescents are especially sensitive to the attitudes and behaviors of adult members of the community, on whom they rely for information and encouragement with respect to care-seeking behavior, effort exerted in school, and so on" (p. 131). Students' perceptions about teachers' attitudes and behaviors toward students of color, LGBTQ+ students, and those from economically disadvantaged families influence the teachers they like and from whom they will try to learn (Nakkula & Toshalis, 2021). Experiencing bias and discrimination in the classroom or school can negatively affect the behavioral health of young people, resulting in anger, stress, anxiety, and depression (NASEM, 2019).

Educators do not always hold students to the same expectations and standards based on students' race and ethnicity, class, gender, and sexuality. For example, Black teachers expect more from Black students than White teachers expect from them (Gershenson et al., 2016). The reason for disciplining students differs by race and ethnicity. Students of color are more likely to be disciplined for subjective reasons such as disrespecting the teacher or being perceived as a "threat" while White students are more likely to be disciplined for objective reasons such as smoking or vandalism (Skiba, 2011). In addition, the punishment received by Black students is harsher, even for minimal infractions (Okonofua & Eberhardt, 2015). The latest research and data show that these inequities are beginning to decrease, but the progress is slow (NASEM, 2019).

Research (Buchanan & Hughes, 2009; Qu et al., 2015, 2018) has confirmed that preconceived notions about young people, both positive and negative, can be held by young people themselves, which was described as *stereotype threat* in an earlier chapter. The negative stereotypes about teenagers perpetuated by adults, the media, and even peers can shape young people's understanding of "normal" youth behavior, sometimes leading them to act out the stereotypes about their rebelliousness. When teens transitioning from middle school to high school believed the negative stereotypes about negative risk-taking behaviors, they were more likely to participate in those activities. If impulsive behavior becomes their "norm," developing teenage brains may not exercise cognitive control, making it neurologically more difficult to engage in future self-regulation (Omary, 2022). Negative stereotypes are harmful to young people and sometimes to the people around them. The goal should be for teachers to eliminate those negative stereotypes in all of their interactions with and about teenagers and to provide students with contrasting perceptions about teenage behavior.

Teachers can begin this process by taking a deep look at their own perceptions or stereotypes about their students. The most damaging stereotypes held by many educators are about Black students. Many people view Black children and young people as older than they are—a process called **adultification** that causes harm to students by denying them the protection, nurturing, comfort, or support to which they are entitled (Damour, 2023). Research shows that Black girls are seen as less innocent, more adult-like, and more sexually aware than White girls, and Black boys are perceived as more aggressive and dangerous than White boys. As a result of this racial bias, Black girls and boys are blamed for misbehavior that is seen as intentional and malicious when it is really immature decision making. Another problem is that their complaints about the unfair treatment is often ignored by school personnel (Blake & Epstein, 2017). When teachers react to Black children and adolescents in this way, they are treating them in developmentally inappropriate ways and not providing them the nurturing and comforting responses they need from teachers to promote and support their appropriate academic and social development.

Treating students of color, LGBTQ students, and those with disabilities with the same dignity and respect as White students without disabilities will go a long way to improving the health and wellness of students and the development of safe and supportive schools for *all* students. Teachers can turn the tables on the accusation that they disproportionately pay attention to students who are misbehaving by looking for and publicly commenting on the desirable behaviors of students. In other words, "catch students being good."

**SUPPORTING STUDENTS WITH MENTAL HEALTH DISORDERS**   Just because students seem to feel nervous, sad, bored, angry, frustrated, or worried does not mean that they have depression or anxiety. Almost everyone has these reactions at different times in their lives, and they should only become worrisome if they are persistent and seriously affect students' performance and behavior in and outside the classroom. At the same time, it is important not to downplay the mental health disorders of students or compare them to everyday emotions (Szabo, 2023). In some cases, teachers never know students' mental health disorders and the pain or conditions they must overcome to even make it to school every day.

There appears to be a stigma about seeking help from mental health services that will need to be overcome before large numbers of young people will seek help, especially while they are at school (NASEM, 2019). The question is how educators can help students understand that having a mental health disorder "does not mean that they are broken or that they did something wrong" (Murthy, 2022, p. 5), a somewhat difficult task because of the long-time stigmatization of mental health disorders in the United States. The U.S. Surgeon General emphasizes the importance of safe and supportive climates both in school and in the community and recommends that schools implement culturally responsive and trauma-informed policies and practices to serve students more effectively. Teachers should communicate with families about the best ways to be supportive of their children who are struggling with a mental health disorder and provide them with breaks, rest, love, and support that will help them to have an enriching and enjoyable educational learning experience.

# Revisiting the Opening Case Study

Jimmy was suspended for the incident in the bathroom, and Bill, as a somewhat reluctant accomplice, was required to meet regularly with the school psychologist for at least the next 2 months. The parents of both boys were contacted, and the boys were required to apologize to Ms. Mitchell. Jimmy returned to Ms. Mitchell's class. Even though he had apologized to her, he was still very frustrated with her, and their relationship became more adversarial. After talking with another one of Jimmy's teachers who was not experiencing any problems with him, Ms. Mitchell decided to schedule some time after school to discuss with Jimmy his concerns with the class and plan to listen to him carefully before planning together each of their responsibilities in improving his engagement in the class.

Bill was reluctant to talk about the incident or himself during the first few sessions with the school psychologist as the psychologist tried to help him understand his identities and how they were changing and would continue to change over the next few years. Bill was asked to take notes on when he felt safe and when he felt anxious or uneasy over the next week. This activity led back to a discussion about his behavior in the bathroom and how he relates to different friends who have little in common and don't always share the same social contexts. Bill seemed to be figuring out the complexities and challenges of these relationships himself, but he needed to be able to talk about his challenges with some adults in his life. He also knew what would happen if he tagged a teacher again.

## Reflect and Apply

1. Jimmy and Bill received different punishments for their roles in tagging Ms. Mitchell. Why do you think the differential discipline was appropriate or not appropriate?

2. What strategy is Ms. Mitchell developing to try to overcome the impasse that Jimmy seems to have with her? What steps would you take to improve the relationship between the student and teacher?

3. Bill seems to be struggling with his own identity and his relationship with previous friends. What role does the school have in helping students work though such issues?

# Summary

- Adolescence began to be seen as a distinct period between childhood and adulthood at the beginning of the twentieth century and soon after, capitalists began to treat youth as a potential market, especially if they were affluent and had leisure time. Today's youth face more and significantly different challenges than people in earlier generations and often do not share the same cultural values and attitudes as older cohorts. Understanding today's youth and their challenges enables teachers to better provide for their needs. As a group, members of Generation Z and the Alpha Generation are on track to be the most educated, most technologically proficient, and likely the most liberal-minded cohorts to date.

- Today's youth are defined by technology, social media, and globalization. They are tethered to their smartphones and other electronic devices on a 24/7 basis. Young people between the ages of 13 and 18 years use 8.5 hours of screen time daily, with YouTube being their favorite site in 2022, followed by TikTok, Instagram, and Snapchat. A number of research studies, families, government officials, and media have declared that social media has negative impacts on the mental health of young people. However, not all researchers agree. It is not yet clear whether social media leads to poor mental health or whether young people with poor mental health are more likely to use social media.

- Adolescence is a critical time of physical, cognitive, and social-emotional development. Adolescents' brains are not yet fully developed when then enter their teen years and will continue to develop into young adulthood and beyond. To support the development of their brains and other parts of their body, young people and their families should pay attention to their well-being. Physically, adolescents should be engaged in 60 minutes of moderate-to-vigorous activities every day and in activities to strengthen their bones and muscles at least 3 days a week. Less than one in three boys and less than one in seven girls are meeting this expectation. The mental health of young people has been worsening for a number of years and peaked during the COVID-19 pandemic, with 44% of high school students feeling persistently sad or hopeless and 38% experiencing poor mental health. Unfortunately, less than half of them seek professional support because they are either not interested or do not have access to it. An important part of growing up is developing one's own identity, which may be different from that of families.

- Adolescents face many challenges as they transition to adulthood. Their relationships with family members may remain stable during this period or face some rocky times as young people become closer to friends and peers as they try to become independent of their families. Peer relationships are very important to teenagers as they make efforts to belong to a group. Risk-taking is common during adolescence. Although peer relationships can be very positive and supportive, peers can also influence each other to take risks that could be harmful related to substance use, their emerging sexuality, violence, and other risky behaviors. Data for almost all of these risky behaviors show significant drops since the 1990s, but steps need to be taken to reduce them further. Children and young people live with the fear of school shootings as they undergo regular drills to prepare for an attack on their school and often face metal detectors, armed security, and even armed teachers in their schools.

- Keeping students engaged in school by developing learning experiences that are meaningful to them makes students more satisfied with school. Such activities could integrate hip-hop, place-based activities, project-based

activities, social justice projects, and other interesting projects that enhance and enrich the content being taught. To develop and support positive interactions among teachers and students and establish trust in each other, a safe and supportive school environment must be created in both the classroom and school. This goal requires teachers to eliminate all negative stereotypes against students, including those that denigrate the languages and cultures of students and their families and prevent teachers from providing the care and support that each student needs. It requires teachers to believe that all students can learn at high levels regardless of their race and ethnicity, socioeconomic status, gender, sexual orientation, exceptionality, language, religion, or the place where they live. To support students who are struggling with a mental health disorder, teachers should be able to provide them a break, rest, and other support as needed. Educators who recognize their students' needs and who reach out and demonstrate genuine respect, concern, and kindness may find themselves in a position to help students who may be in distress. Many individuals speak fondly of teachers they remember because of the positive experiences these teachers brought to their lives. Each educator has the potential to be one who makes a difference in a student's life.

## Pearson eTextbook Application Video

The following video is available in the Pearson eTextbook and can be used to practice observing and applying what you learned in this chapter.

**Pearson eTextbook Application**

**Video Example 10.3**

In this video, a counselor has just worked with a teen who has expressed strong feelings of self-harm with the potential for suicide. The counselor is now discussing this event with her principal. Pay attention to the process she describes

# Chapter 11
# Education That Is Multicultural

## Learning Objectives

*As you read this chapter, you should be able to:*

**11.1** Discuss the importance of education that is multicultural.

**11.2** Explain how to place students and their needs at the center of teaching and learning.

**11.3** Analyze classroom climates that promote human rights, antiracism, and equity.

**11.4** Create lesson plans and develop teaching practices that are culturally responsive.

**11.5** Model social justice and equality in the classroom.

**11.6** Expand your knowledge and skills so you can deliver education that is multicultural.

## Opening Case Study

When Janelle Hamilton returned to John F. Kennedy High School where she had taught for 5 years before her daughter was born, she found that her junior English class was stuffed with 40 students as a result of another budget cut. Nevertheless, she was anxious to be engaged again with her Black, Latino/a, Asian American, and White students to develop critical thinking skills as they explored literature about their own and others' lives. Ms. Hamilton had forgotten how difficult it could be to engage high schoolers at the beginning of the year. She was competing with cell phones, side conversations among students, and students who were strolling in and out of the room. Few students were completing the assigned work. Developing productive relationships with students and a classroom community was going to take some serious work.

Ms. Hamilton chose the screenplay *Smoke Signals* by Sherman Alexie, a Spokane/Coeur d'Alene Native American, as the first book the class would tackle because it focused on relationships between children and their families. At first, students weren't engaged with the play. However, when Terrell declared that his father lived with alcoholism, other students began to talk about how the father was

treating his son and why he was drinking. Not all students talked, but it was a positive step forward.

The turning point came when Ms. Hamilton asked students to write a forgiveness poem after reading Lucille Clifton's "Forgiving My Father" and the poems of two students in which one student forgave her mother and the other student forgave his father. Before they wrote their poems, they made a list of the people they wanted to forgive or not forgive. All of the students were writing, and some were sharing their work with a classmate. Near the end of the class, several students read their poems. They cried together as they shared their forgiveness poems written to absent fathers, overcommitted mothers, and themselves. On the following day, they wanted to share more.

Ms. Hamilton was beginning to place the students at the center of the class. The curriculum was becoming their stories, and they were beginning to see themselves as part of a community in which they cared for each other. As they read other books, poems, and short stories that Ms. Hamilton introduced throughout the year, they were encouraged to walk in the shoes of the characters they met, developing empathy for people from cultural groups different from their own. Students shared their reflections on those characters and

*(continued)*

the conditions in which they lived in their dialogue journals. Students interviewed a classmate from a different racial or ethnic group and wrote a profile about their partner to share with the class. They learned the harrowing experiences that some of their immigrant classmates had experienced before coming to the United States. One student learned that her partner's brother had been killed in Iraq before her family fled the country, and an immigrant student learned that his partner's sister had been killed because she was trans. As students learned from each other through these profiles, role playing, writing about different perspectives on historical events, and reflecting on what they were learning, they expanded their knowledge about and empathy toward people whose race, ethnicity, culture, gender identity, [dis]ability status, and/or native language differed from their own.

## Reflect

1. How does Ms. Hamilton's approach to students' sharing their stories and developing a classroom community fit into education that is multicultural?

2. The screenplay *Smoke Signals* includes a number of stereotypes about Native Americans. Why would Ms. Hamilton have chosen a play with such stereotypes?

3. When stereotypes about a group of people surface in students' discussion and writings, how can you help students recognize and critique them?

4. How would you define student-centered teaching versus teacher-centered teaching? What are the advantages and disadvantages to student-centered teaching?

**SOURCE:** Adapted from Christensen (2017).

# Education That Is Multicultural

**Learning Objective 11.1** Discuss the importance of education that is multicultural.

After learning the sociopolitical foundations that provide the framework for multicultural education, you are probably wondering how to put it all together to provide education that is multicultural. There is no recipe for how to respond to students from different cultural groups. For one thing, differences within groups can be as great as differences among groups. In addition, people belong to many groups, depending on their gender and sexual orientation and the racial, ethnic, language, and socioeconomic status (SES) groups into which they were born. The intersections of membership in these groups and where they fit in the power structure of society impact people's cultural identity. Therefore, a recipe would work for some students in a group but not all of them. This chapter is designed to provide suggestions for delivering multicultural education, incorporating the multiple identities of your students into your teaching, and becoming more multicultural yourself.

It is no easy task to incorporate cultural knowledge throughout teaching. In the beginning, teachers must consciously think about multiculturalism as they interact with students and plan lessons and assignments. Multicultural teaching should be approached as an enthusiastic learner with much knowledge to gain from students and community members who have cultural identities different from the teacher. Teachers may need to remind themselves that their way of believing, thinking, and acting evolved from their own culture and experiences, which may vary greatly from those of students in the school in which they teach. Teachers will need to listen to the histories and experiences of students and their families and integrate them into their teaching. Teachers must validate students' lives within the students' in-school and out-of-school realities—a process that is authentic only if teachers value the cultures of their students.

Educators are often at a disadvantage because they do not live, and may have never lived, in the community in which their students live. Too often, the only families with whom teachers interact are those who are able to attend school meetings or who have scheduled conferences with them. In many cases, they have not been in their students' homes or active participants in the community. How do teachers begin to learn the cultures of other people? Using the tools of an anthropologist or ethnographer, they can observe children in classrooms and on playgrounds. They can listen carefully to students and their families as they discuss their life experiences. They can study other cultures. They can learn about the perspectives of others by reading articles and books or watching movies or videos written by LGBTQ+ (lesbian, gay, bisexual, transgender, queer/questioning) and straight individuals from different racial, ethnic, SES, and religious groups. Participation in the religious and ethnic activities in the community can also provide additional perspectives on students' cultures.

Knowledge about students' cultures allows teachers to make the academic content more meaningful to students by relating it to students' own experiences and building on their prior knowledge. It should help teachers make students and their histories the center of the education process in the effort to help them reach their academic, vocational, and social potential. In the process, students can learn to believe in their own abilities and become active participants in their own learning. They should be able to achieve academically without adopting the dominant culture as their own. They should be able to maintain their own cultural identities inside and outside the school.

Teaching multiculturally requires the incorporation of diversity and equity throughout the learning process. If race, ethnicity, class, and gender are not integrated in the curriculum, students do not learn that these are interrelated parts of a whole. For example, if activities are developed to fight sexism but continue to perpetuate racism, multicultural education is not being provided. At the same time, the experiences of women of color and women in poverty should be included when discussing the impact of sexism and other women's issues.

All teaching should be multicultural, and all classrooms should be models of democracy, equity, and social justice. To accomplish this goal, teachers should:

1. Place students at the center of teaching and learning by respecting, valuing, and building on their identities and the histories, cultures, and experiences of their families and communities through culturally responsive teaching.

2. Establish a classroom climate that promotes human rights, antiracism, and equity for all students.

3. Believe that all students can learn.

4. Disrupt the cycle of inequity in schools and eliminate racism, sexism, classism, heterosexism, ableism, and other discriminatory practices in classrooms and schools.

5. Model social justice and equity in the classroom and in interactions with students, families, and the community.

Teachers and other school professionals can make a difference in students' lives. Making teaching and classrooms multicultural is an essential step in empowering both teachers and students. Delivering education that is multicultural requires teachers to ensure an equitable education for all students by removing barriers that prevent many students from being able to access the education that is so critical to their future. At the same time, teachers need to confront their own biases and ensure they are not reflected in their teaching and interactions with students and their families.

Multicultural education is for all students, not just English learners and students of color. White students also belong to racial and ethnic groups and need to understand how their race and ethnicity have been privileged in schools. A strength of multicultural education is that students learn about their similarities and differences as they work together in the classroom and other school activities. Students who are in segregated classrooms or in communities with little religious, language, racial, or ethnic diversity also need to learn about the pluralistic world in which they live and the role they can play in supporting social justice in their communities and beyond. Social justice and equity are integral parts of the commitment to a democratic society.

# Students as the Center of Teaching and Learning

**Learning Objective 11.2**  Explain how to place students and their needs at the center of teaching and learning.

**Pearson eTextbook**
**Video Example 11.1**
Watch as this teacher teaches a lesson that helps students better conceptualize the legal right to self-expression from an inclusive perspective.

Children are the foundation for the future, but they are among the most powerless groups in the country, especially if they are born into a low-income family. Fifteen percent of the nation's children under 18 years old lived in poverty in 2022 (U.S. Census Bureau, 2023). Nearly one in 10 children under age 9 lived in extreme poverty, which is 50% or less of the federal poverty level (Nguyen et al., 2020). In 2021, 13 children died daily from gun violence, with Black children and teens six times as likely to die from gun violence as their White peers (Children's Defense Fund, 2023). These figures suggest a crisis among our children that deserves immediate attention. Nevertheless, most states spend two to three times as much on a person who is imprisoned as they do on a public school student (CNN Money, 2021). Hopefully, educators are major advocates for children, especially for their right to a quality education.

The major purpose of education is to help students learn concepts and skills. However, teaching is much more than knowing the content being taught. Teachers also need to know and understand their students. Who are they? What is important to them? What are their interests? How can students be actively engaged in learning? Teaching should be all about students and moving them to their highest potential academically, socially, physically, and emotionally. Helping them develop their potential in these areas at the same time that they are learning to read and compute at a proficient level is the challenge for teachers. How can teachers ensure that the well-being of students and their learning are the primary goals of their work in schools?

Education that is multicultural requires teachers and other school professionals to possess dispositions that support learning by students from diverse populations. **Dispositions** are the values, beliefs, attitudes, behaviors, commitments, and professional ethics of educators. They influence teaching and interactions with students, families, colleagues, and communities. They affect perspectives on student learning, student motivation, and student development as well as a teacher's own professional growth. They include values such as caring, fairness, honesty, responsibility, and social justice. Multicultural educator Sonia Nieto (2018) indicated that one of the purposes of schools is "to provide all students with an equal and high quality education," which requires that teachers "begin with the belief that all students are capable and worthy of learning to high levels of achievement" (p. 22). It is not just multiculturalists who believe that this disposition is important for all teachers; families also expect as much of their children's teachers.

It is important to teachers who are implementing education that is multicultural that all of their students learn regardless of the obstacles they face because of their disabilities or economic conditions that limit their social capital. These teachers recognize that when some students are not learning, they need to reach out to them and try different pedagogical strategies to help them learn. They do not allow students to sit in their classrooms without being engaged with the content. They do not ignore students who are withdrawn, depressed, or resistant to classroom work. They do everything they can to help students see themselves as learners who value learning. This section explores ways that teachers can implement the belief that all students in their classrooms are valued and can learn at high levels.

## Listening to Students

Seeking, listening to, and incorporating the voices of students, their families, and their communities in the classroom are critically important in providing education that is multicultural. Students should be encouraged to speak from their own experiences and to do more than regurgitate the answers that teachers would like to hear. Teaching that incorporates student voices allows students to make sense of the subject matter within their own lived experiences and realities. Listening to students helps teachers understand students' prior knowledge of the subject matter, including any misinformation or lack of information that may suggest future instructional strategies or interventions. Student voices also provide important information about their cultures.

Most schools today legitimate the voice of the dominant culture—Standard English and the world perspective of the White middle class. Some students, especially those from **marginalized** groups, learn to be silent, which can be a viewed as a source of oppression (Baines et al., 2023). As a result, they end up leaving school without graduating, in part because their voices are not accepted as legitimate in the classroom. Education that is multicultural recognizes the incongruence between the voice of the school and the voices of students. "Valuing voice means providing students with an opportunity to have their thoughts, words, and ideas about the classroom and the world beyond it heard" (Emden, 2016, p. 59) and incorporated in the instructional process. Success in school should not be dependent on the adoption of the voice of the dominant group.

Teachers could use an approach in which instruction occurs as a dialogue between them and students. Rather than depend on a textbook and lecture format, teachers could listen to students and guide them in the learning of the subject matter through dialogue. This approach requires discarding the traditional authoritarian classroom to establish a democratic one in which both teachers and students are active participants and learners.

Too often, teachers ignore students' attempts to engage in dialogue and, as a result, halt their further learning. However, introducing student voices to the instructional process can be difficult, especially when teachers' cultural backgrounds are different from that of students. Teachers may face both anger and silence, which in time can be overcome by the use of dialogue that develops both students' and their own tolerance, patience, and willingness to listen. Although this strategy increases the participation of students in the learning process, teachers will have to become comfortable at handling issues such as racism or sexism that students are likely to raise.

In addition to engaging in dialogue with students, teachers can encourage student voices through written and artistic expression, as Ms. Hamilton did in the chapter-opening scenario. According to Linda Christensen (2017), an experienced English teacher in Seattle and an editor and author for the progressive organization Rethinking Education, students sharing their stories with each other is also important in improving student relationships. "When they hear personal stories, classmates become real instead of cardboard stereotypes. Once they've seen how people can hurt, once they've shared pain and laughter, they can't treat people as objects to be kicked or beaten or called names as easily" (p. 6).

In addition, teachers could ask students to keep journals in which they write their reactions to what is occurring in their lives or in their class, community, or world. These journals would make teachers aware of the learning occurring over time. For journals to be effective, students must feel comfortable writing whatever they want without the threat of reprisal from teachers. The dialogues developed through these approaches can help teachers understand the perspectives brought to the classroom by students from different cultures. The resulting dialogues can help students relate subject matter to their real world and encourage them to take an interest in studying and learning it.

## Holding High Expectations for Students

The belief that each student can learn is essential for the delivery of multicultural education (Howard, 2019). Some teachers have low expectations for the academic achievement of students of color (Gershenson et al., 2021) and students from low-income families based on negative generalizations about their intelligence (Spencer & Ullucci, 2022). In some cases, teachers view high Black intelligence as "something out of the ordinary" (Spencer & Ullucci, 2022, p. 36). When these generalizations are applied to students, grave damage can be done. Students tend to meet the expectations of the teacher, no matter what their actual abilities are. Self-fulfilling prophecies about how well a student will perform in the classroom are often established early in the school year, and both student and teacher unconsciously fulfill those prophecies. However, Spencer and Ullucci (2022) found that the "low performance of Black children . . . is more a symptom of poor teaching than it is representative of Black children's ability" (p. 36). Harry and Klinger (2022) found similar findings for students with disabilities (Milner, 2020).

As children are made to feel "inferior, unimportant, and even dangerous" (Spencer & Ullucci, 2022, p. 36), they become marginalized in the classroom as the negative stereotypes are adopted by other students. To eliminate these beliefs, educators need to rid themselves of deficit views and negative expectations they have for students, stop blaming families and communities for students' "deficiencies," and plan classroom instruction and activities to ensure success for each student, embracing their cultural identities and life experiences.

Heterogeneous grouping can be helpful in improving academic achievement for students from low-income and marginalized groups (Nieto, 2018). Contrary to popular belief, such grouping does not limit the academic achievement of the most academically talented students, especially when the instruction is geared toward challenging all students. The students who experience tracking practices are those who are disproportionately placed in the low-ability groups. Compared with students in other tracks, these students develop more negative feelings about their academic potential and future aspirations. Educational equity demands a different strategy. It requires that all students be academically challenged with stimulating instruction that involves them actively in their own learning.

## Caring

One of the complaints of students is that their teachers don't know them and don't care about them (Nieto, 2018). Students are more willing to work and their performance improves when they feel that teachers care about them. Caring means honoring students and their families. Caring teachers care authentically about students and their families and develop caring relationships with them (Duncan-Andrade, 2022). Caring teachers have overcome their racial and ethnic biases and do not stereotype students. They do not punish students because they do not conform to the dominant culture's expectations. They find them lovable and unproblematic and are able to honor and embrace them without equivocation (Gay, 2018). At the same time, teachers' care extends to having high expectations for their academic success and creating imaginative and authentic strategies to ensure their academic success (Gay, 2023).

Caring teachers authentically care about students, their interests, cultures, and needs as reflected in the way they interact with students and their families.

**SOURCE:** FG Trade/ E+/Gettyimages

Caring teachers are patient, persistent, and supportive of students. They listen to them and validate their cultures. They respond to students' personal lives and the institutional barriers they encounter (Nieto, 2018). Caring requires teachers to adapt to the needs of their students rather than expect them to adapt to the teachers' needs. They empower their students to engage in their own education. Caring teachers don't give up on their students. They understand why students may not feel well on some days or may be having a difficult time outside school. They understand that some children live under chronic stress of which they have little control, but they don't blame the students or their families; instead, teachers try to instill hope, which is possible with a number of caring adults in their lives who can help children heal their wounds (Duncan-Andrade, 2022). Although the spirits of vulnerable and marginalized students may be bruised by their "messy life circumstances," caring teachers and other professional educators can help them heal and "return to a place of wellness" (Wright, 2023, p. 12).

## Prioritizing Student Wellness

According to Jeffrey M. R. Duncan-Andrade (2022), the well-being of children, communities, society, and the planet should be the primary goal of public education. For most families, that means their children leave school being healthier and smarter than when they entered. What would this mean for children and schools? A part of this well-being is the ability to self-actualize, which is the first step in the Blackfoot nation's perspective of wellness and one of the last steps in Maslow's hierarchy of needs (Duncan-Andrade, 2022). Important in this process are three pedagogical domains that build classroom cultures and climates to sustain students' well-being: relationships, relevance, and responsibility that connect to self, family, community, ancestors, and the natural world (Duncan-Andrade, 2022).

Young people are helped most by caring adults who empathize with students by listening, connecting, and understanding them rather than talking, fixing, and solving their problems for them. Empathy requires teachers to be able to see the world as students see it and to be nonjudgmental (Duncan-Andrade, 2022). Students who have been in traumatic events particularly need to be engaged in empathic relationships with adults, including their teachers, other school professionals, and other school personnel such as cafeteria workers, bus drivers, and custodians. Duncan-Andrade (2022) says that students who have been traumatized need schools that are "a place where their relationships with adults give them the medicine of love, time, and patience. They need schools to be a place where they can recharge their armor and feel better protected from a society that has devalued them and taught them that they are undeserving" (p. 77). As teachers work with children and youth, they may need to remind themselves that students experiencing short-term or long-term trauma may be overly aggressive, impulsive, and needy. Their behavior may suggest that an intervention is needed, but punishment is not usually the best choice (Perry & Szalavitz, 2017). They are most likely to need love and safety and to know that adults genuinely care about them (Duncan-Andrade, 2022).

Consider relevance as you think about what to teach children and young people in ways that validate and value them. Making the curriculum and instruction relevant to students usually requires teachers to expand classroom activities and discussion beyond those in the curriculum they have been assigned. It requires ensuring that students see themselves reflected in the curriculum and school activities; relating the curriculum to the community, including how it can be improved; and helping students see their strengths inside and outside of schools (Milner, 2020). More strategies for making education relevant are described in the section of this chapter on approaches to teaching multiculturally.

Responsibility focuses on the purpose of equity. In delivering equity, educators think about how they serve the most marginalized students and those students who have historically been ignored and underserved in the nation's schools and society for generations because of their race, ethnicity, SES, gender, language, sexual orientation, religion, disability, or place in which they live. Those students who are privileged because of their identities are not ignored in this process, but more vulnerable students are no longer neglected. No longer would educators spend their time trying to "fix" students or their families so that they assimilate to White middle-class culture. Instead, educators focus on fixing the injustices that have denigrated vulnerable people and their communities. It requires truth-telling about the history and experiences of communities and the nation that have led to historical levels of inequality and child trauma (Duncan-Andrade, 2022). In many ways, teachers are the first responders in the diagnosis and response to child trauma (Perry & Szalavitz, 2017).

The social and economic conditions in impoverished communities must be considered as educators and health professions work with students to combat the effects of institutionalized racism that has led to real psychological and emotional damage to children and youth (Noguera & Syeed, 2021). To support students and families, some schools make food available through a school food bank, make health care available through community schools, and implement **trauma-informed practices**. Schools could incorporate restorative justice practices to support the healing of wounded students. Some schools have introduced mindfulness and yoga classes to help students cope with stress (Noguera & Syeed, 2021). More support for students could be provided by increasing the number of school counselors, school psychologists, and school social workers to the staff as well as adding mental health professionals. Noguera and Syeed (2021) indicate that these efforts by schools "do not compensate for the effects of structural racism, but they can, to some degree, mitigate them" (p. 288).

The COVID-19 pandemic contributed to an increase in the number of students with mental health illnesses. A psychiatrist and chief medical officer at The Jed Foundation, Laura Erickson-Schroth described the importance of schools in supporting these students: "Young people spend more of their waking hours in school than anywhere else, so we have a responsibility as a society to make school a place where their mental health is supported and where they're learning emotional skills that will help them to develop and thrive as adults" (Stone, 2023, p. 4). To take on this task, mental health professionals recommend that schools focus on "the whole child, in mind, body, and spirit" (Lazarus et al., 2021, p. 2), not just their academic achievements and standardized test scores. The whole-child approach expects that "each student is *safe, healthy, supported, engaged,* and *challenged*" (Jones & Miranda, 2021, p. 63). This strategy suggests that schools should promote and support wellness among all students, a preventive approach with early intervention that may decrease the number of students who are ill and extend wellness into their adulthood.

**Social-emotional learning (SEL),** which could include trauma-informed practice, is one way that many schools have chosen to improve the wellness of students. What is included in SEL differs by school and community. These strategies and programs help students develop skills such as building relationships, empathy, self-awareness, regulation of their feelings, social awareness, handling relationships, and making wise decisions (Sprenger, 2020). Some people worry that focusing on SEL in schools will take time away from learning academic content. Although some schools have a specific course or time of the day or week to focus on SEL, most schools integrate it "by employing evidence-based SEL practices and programs, incorporating SEL into all academic instruction, and fostering a supportive, caring classroom environment where students feel cared for, valued and affirmed in their identity" (Collaborative for Academic, Social, and Emotional Learning, 2023, para. 9). Because students learn more effectively when they are well, attending to their wellness is likely to improve both their academic performance and behavior (Jones et al., 2018). There are times and circumstances in which students need professional help beyond what a teacher can provide (Frey et al., 2019). School counselors, school psychologists, social workers, and mental health professionals can provide that specialized support if they are available to students in a school.

To be effective for the most vulnerable students, SEL should ensure that its application is culturally relevant, acknowledging and accepting that there are cultural differences in the way people communicate, eat, interact, and respond to events (Jones & Miranda, 2021). If educators limit students to the cultural responses of teachers' cultures, many students are not going to be helped by SEL strategies and may end up becoming disengaged and being suspended from school. For example, ignoring the racism that is affecting students' behaviors may convince students that educators do not care enough about them to try to understand them and their experiences. Being community based and confronting racial justice in concrete and practical ways is important in not further damaging students (Noguera & Syeed, 2021).

# Climate for Equity

**Learning Objective 11.3** Analyze classroom climates that promote human rights, antiracism, and equity.

More than 10 years before the Civil Rights Movement reached its zenith in the 1960s and 1970s, the United Nations adopted the Universal Declaration of Human Rights (UDHR), which called on countries around the world to provide human rights and social justice to their populations. It called for the right to an education; social security; equitable wages; an adequate standard of living allowing families to be able to afford housing, food, clothing, and medical care; and participation in the cultural life of the community. The United States and a number of other Western countries supported the civil and political rights that were incorporated into the UDHR but resisted the inclusion of social and economic rights. Nevertheless, the UDHR was adopted by the United Nations General Assembly in 1948.

The UDHR (United Nations, 2015) views education as a basic human right for all people. It also expects schools to teach about human rights, with the goal of eliminating poverty, discrimination, and exploitation—conditions that often have led and continue to lead to conflicts that threaten world peace. After the adoption of the UDHR, the United States made great strides in the human rights area, with the passage of the Voting Rights Act, the Civil Rights Act, and the Equal Pay Act. Congress created Head Start for preschool services and Title I to support the education of children from low-income families. It passed legislation for bilingual education, the Individuals with Disabilities Education Act for students with disabilities, Title IX for gender equity in schools, and technical assistance related to race, ethnicity, and gender equity in schools.

Research finds that people are more creative, more diligent, and harder working when they are around people who are different from them (Gay, 2018). At the same time, students of color, immigrant students, those from low-income families, students whose religion is not Christian, and gender-nonconforming students report that they do not always feel welcome in their schools and communities. They also report that they face or observe harassment in school based on their group membership(s) (Southern Poverty Law Center, 2019). To avoid intergroup strife, students must learn how to relate effectively to people from different cultural backgrounds (Gay, 2018).

Seventy-five years after UDHR was adopted, the U.S. Congress continues to debate the role of the government in enforcing social and economic rights for the population. With government support for public education waning, many multiculturalists are questioning the country's commitment to human rights, especially with respect to the nation's children. Today's issues of racism again are exposed in public policies, police actions, and housing patterns that force students in low-income families into high-poverty schools. The Voting Rights Act passed in 1965 is being undermined by court decision. Conflicts around the world pit one racial, ethnic, or religious group against another, making it clear that the mandate of the UDHR is needed more than ever.

These issues and concerns related to human rights, racism, and inequity carry over to schools. A school's climate sets the tone at a school that is observable and can be felt (Darling-Hammond & Darling-Hammond, 2022). Visitors entering a school can usually feel the tension that exists when cross-cultural communications are unsatisfactory. They can observe whether diversity is a positive and appreciated factor at the school. If only students of color or only boys are waiting to be seen by the assistant principal in charge of discipline, visitors could wonder whether the school is providing effectively for the needs of all of its students. If bulletin boards in classrooms are covered only with the pictures of White people, visitors could question the appreciation of diversity in the school. If the football team is composed primarily of Black students and the chess club of White students, they could wonder about the inclusive nature of extracurricular activities. If school administrators are primarily men and most teachers are women or if the teachers are White and the teacher aides are Latino/a, the visitors could suspect discriminatory practices in the hiring and promotion of staff. These are examples of a school climate that does not reflect a commitment to multicultural education.

A school's climate can make students, teachers, and families feel comfortable or uncomfortable. A positive climate is welcoming to newcomers and families alike regardless of their cultural identities. It is a safe place for students who are feeling the adverse effects of poverty. A positive climate supports students who have been impacted by a traumatic event in their lives rather than denigrating them and damaging their self-esteem. It supports responsive and heathy interactions between students and teachers and maximizes students' ability to learn social-emotional skills along with academic content (Darling-Hammond & Darling-Hammond, 2022). The goals are to create a school climate where students from diverse groups thrive and their cultures are not only valued but sustained (Noguera & Syeed, 2021) and antiracism and equity pervades throughout the school. In this section, we examine some factors that contribute to the positive school climate that is equitable across families and ensures that students are safe and nurtured throughout the school year.

Let's start this discussion with a review of the meaning of equality and equity. *Equality* is the condition of being equal. For example, all students receive the same amount of resources. *Equity*, on the other hand, is that students receive what is fair and just (Duncan-Andrade, 2022). Differentiated instruction is an example in which not all students receive the same instruction because different resources and teaching strategies are required for different students. Gorski and Swalwell (2023) define equity as "*the active process for identifying and eliminating inequity and its underlying oppressions* (such as racism, ableism, and economic injustice). It's also *the active process for intentionally cultivating justice* (including racial justice, disability justice, and economic justice)" (p. 26).

## Thinking About the Hidden Curriculum

In addition to a formal curriculum, schools have a hidden curriculum that consists of the unstated norms, values, and beliefs about the social relations of school and classroom life that are transmitted to students. The hidden curriculum teaches lessons about self-esteem, one's place in society, and the need to submit to authority (Ayers & Ayers, 2014). Although the hidden curriculum is not taught directly or included in the objectives of the formal curriculum, it has a great impact on students and teachers alike. It includes the organizational structures of the classroom and the school as well as the interactions of students and teachers. It is the unwritten, unofficial rules to which students are expected to conform for a successful school experience. The rules are almost always known by the members of the dominant group whose culture is the one most often reflected in schools, but the rules may not be the common pattern for students from other cultures.

The hidden curriculum reflects unequal power. In many ways, this is a dilemma of childhood. By the time students enter kindergarten, they have learned that power is in the hands of adults. The teachers and other school officials require that their rules be followed. In addition to enforcing the rules, teachers may directly or indirectly send the message to students that their home languages or dialects should not be used in the classroom and that behaviors that are common at home and in the community are not respected and not allowed at school. Instead, students should be encouraged to be bicultural, practicing both their home and dominant cultural language and patterns and learning nonacademic skills that are essential in navigating the historically White spaces of schools (Gershenson et al., 2021). Many teachers, especially teachers of color, are able to create their own hidden curriculum to help validate students of color and teach them pride in their identities (Gershenson et al., 2021).

## Eliminating Biased Messages

The hidden curriculum is filled with implicit and sometimes denigrating messages to students who are not members of the dominant groups in a school. In their research, Gershenson and his colleagues found that "implicit biases are pervasive in society" (2021, pp. 49–50) and, knowingly or unknowingly, educators transmit those biased messages to students. Most educators do not consciously or intentionally stereotype students or discriminate against them. They usually try to treat all students fairly and equitably. They have learned their attitudes and behaviors, however, in a society that is ageist, ableist, racist, sexist, and heterosexist. Some biases have been internalized to such a degree that most people do not realize they have them. When educators are able to recognize their unconscious biases in their behaviors and attitudes, positive changes can be made to eliminate them from the classroom.

Students of color are often treated significantly differently than White students. Gloria Ladson-Billings (2001) found that "students of color may become alienated from the schooling process because schooling often asks children to be something or someone other than who they really are. . . . It asks them to dismiss their community and cultural knowledge. It erases things that the students hold dear" (p. xiv). Because many White students share the middle-class culture of the teacher, they also share the cultural cues that foster success in the classroom. For example, students who ask appropriate questions at appropriate times or who smile and seek attention from the teacher at times when the teacher is open to such gestures are likely to receive encouragement and reinforcement from the teacher. When students interrupt class or seek attention from the teacher at a time when the teacher is not open to providing it, they may not receive the reinforcement they are seeking (Milner, 2020).

As a result of the teacher's misreading of cultural cues, racial, ethnic, and class boundaries are established within the classroom (Milner, 2020). This situation is exacerbated when students from the dominant group receive more opportunities to participate in instructional interactions and receive more praise and encouragement from the teacher. Students from families with low SES and students of color generally are provided fewer opportunities to interact with the teacher, and the opportunities may be of a less substantive nature (Gershenson et al., 2021). To address problems that plague some schools, the racial, ethnic, and economic realities of students should be recognized, and teachers should be able to see students as students see themselves (Emdin, 2016).

The ability to recognize and value the cultural differences of students gives teachers of color an advantage at working effectively with students of color (Gershenson et al., 2021). They are not only less biased and have higher expectations for students of color than many White teachers, teachers of color are generally better at teaching them because they understand their students (Gershenson et al., 2021). However, White teachers can successfully teach children of color if they "can develop skills to recognize the ways in which their racist acts can have real consequences for students' mental, emotional, and psychological health" (Milner, 2020, p. 248) and are engaged in disrupting the status quo and racist practices in schools (Gay, 2018).

Unless teachers can critically examine their interactions with students in the classroom, they will not know whether they are treating students inequitably because of cultural differences (Gay, 2018). Once teachers have undertaken self-examination, they can initiate changes to ensure that cultural identity will not be a basis for providing less support to and encouragement of some students. Teachers may need to become more proactive in initiating interactions and in providing encouragement, praise, and reinforcement to students from cultural groups different from their own.

Teachers evaluate students' academic performance through tests and written and oral work and projects, but much more than academic performance is evaluated by teachers. Student misbehavior occurs when classroom rules are not adequately obeyed, which may result in some sort of punishment. Discipline varies with the infraction and student but sometimes is influenced by the gender, race, ethnicity, SES, disability, and the sexual orientation of the student (Lui et al., 2023; U.S. Department of Education, Office of Civil Rights, 2021). Similarly, students who have been assigned low-ability status often receive negative attention from the teacher because they are not following the rules rather than helping them improve their performance on academic tasks (Milner, 2020). Interactions with students should be evaluated to ensure that learning is actually being supported rather than impeding it.

## Developing Positive Student–Teacher Relationships

Although the development and use of culturally responsive materials and curricula are important and necessary steps toward providing multicultural education, alone they are not enough. "The heart of the educational process is the interactions that occur between teachers and students" (Gay, 2018, p. 59). Educators send messages that tell students about their potential and whether they can or cannot learn. Teachers must be "willing to find the good and the worth in students" and be "willing to give students a chance" (Milner, 2020, pp. 221, 222). Teachers can make students feel either very special or incompetent and worthless. Being well grounded in the subject matter, believing that all students can learn, and caring about students as individuals can have a positive impact on students and their learning.

When Gloria Ladson-Billings (2022) observed eight elementary school teachers who were known to help their Black students learn at high levels, she found that the teachers interacted easily with their students and gave them individual attention as needed. When a student was struggling, one teacher sat at the student's desk and asked him to explain the problem to her. The student became the teacher, which required him to explain the process or help the teacher perform the task. Many of the successful teachers expected students to help each other learn by working together to solve problems while the teacher monitored their progress. The classroom was like an extended family

Effective cross-cultural communications between students and teachers promote student learning. When the cultural cues between students and teachers are not understood, communications and learning often are affected adversely.

**SOURCE:** © Rawpixel.com/Shutterstock

that would not let anyone fail. Ladson-Billings (2022) learned from these successful teachers the importance of connecting with their students and developing a community of learners who learned collaboratively and helped each other learn.

Research shows that positive relationships between teachers and students can accelerate learning. In their comprehensive review of the research on effective teaching, Hattie and Zierer (2019) found that "an atmosphere of trust and confidence, of safety, caring, and goodwill, is indispensable for education in general and student achievement in particular" (pp. 95–96). However, the lack of skill in cross-cultural communications between students and teachers can prevent learning in the classroom. For example, the way that teachers talk to students can interfere more with academic engagement than the instructional strategies being used. Too often, more interactions occur between the teacher and some students about undesirable behavior than the development of their academic knowledge and skills (Gay, 2018), which seriously constrains high-level academic achievement. This problem often is a result of misunderstanding the cultural cues of students with cultural identities different from teachers.

Just as cultures differ in the structure of their language, they also differ in the structure of oral discourse. The moves made in the teaching–learning discourse, who is supposed to make them, and the sequence in which they should be made vary from culture to culture. These rules are not absolute laws governing behavior; in fact, students learn them in their interactions within their own cultural groups. But when these patterns differ between the culture of the teacher and the culture of the child, serious misunderstandings can occur as the two participants use different patterns and assign different social meanings to the same actions. When students are not responding appropriately in the classroom, teachers should consider the possibility that their communication cues do not match those of their students and are interfering with learning.

Direct and continuous participation in cultures that are different from teachers can improve their competency in other communication systems and help them be more sensitive to differences in cultures with which they are not familiar. If teachers are aware of these differences, they may be able to redirect their instruction to use the communications that work most effectively with students. Learning more about the interests, dreams, hopes, and aspirations of students can help build positive relationships with students and help teachers build trust, rapport, and connections with them that are likely to improve both their academic outcomes and school experiences (Howard, 2019). How can teachers expand their knowledge about their students? Professor H. Richard Milner IV (2020) at Vanderbilt University suggests the following practices that might help teachers learn more about their students:

- Interview students to learn from and about them rather than depending primarily on the recollections of other teachers and school records. This data collection should provide information about their interests that can later be incorporated into lessons and future interactions with students.

- Make assignments that allow students to share their experiences and interests.

- Plan classroom discussions that allow students to share their perspectives on a topic. In addition to providing additional information about students, these discussions provide space for their voices, opportunities for learning to listen to each other, and the development of speaking skills.

- Attend an extracurricular activity in which a student is involved before or after school. These activities could include sporting events, concerts, theatrical events, or debates.

- Visit places in the community in which students live. These places could include grocery stores, gas stations, libraries, hair salons, community centers, or places of worship. Not only do these visits provide a social context for the community, they send a message that you are supportive of the community.

To provide the greatest assistance to students does not require teachers to apply the same treatment to each student; they should work toward meeting individual needs and differences. With the elimination of bias from the teaching process and the emergence of proactive teaching to meet the needs of individual students, the classroom can become a stimulating place for most, regardless of their cultural identities, abilities, and experiences.

How can classroom interactions and teaching styles be analyzed? Teachers can video themselves teaching a class and then systematically record the interactions as they view or listen to the video later. An outside observer could be asked to record teachers' interactions with students during the school day. An analysis of the data would show how much class time was spent interacting with students and the nature of the interactions. These data would reveal any differences in interactions based on gender, race, ethnicity, or other characteristics of students. Who knows the most about effective teaching? Students themselves can identify teachers who are caring and the teachers who have helped them learn. Teachers could ask students for feedback in a survey or using digital technology. Such an analysis would be a starting point to ensure that teachers are not discriminating against students of different genders or those from different racial, ethnic, or SES groups.

Every effort possible should be made to ensure prejudices are not reflected in teachers' interactions with students. Teachers should continually assess their interactions with students of different genders, those from dominant and marginalized groups, and students with disabilities to determine whether the interactions involve different types of praise, criticism, encouragement, and reinforcement based on the culture of students. Only then can steps be taken to provide equitable treatment.

## Involving Families and Community

Cooperation between teachers and families in "the pursuit of learning, and on an equal footing" (Hattie & Zierer, 2019, p. 39) is correlated with academic achievement. One of the most effective ways to work with families occurs when families and teachers become authentic partners in the education of children and young people (Jones & Miranda, 2021). Building relationships with families is also one of the keys to Black students' success in schools (Toldson, 2019).

Toldson's (2019) research found that families of Black children were less likely than the families of White children to receive regular communications such as newsletters and memos. They were more likely to receive calls from the school to complain about their children's behavior or academic performance. All families are more likely to visit schools when they are satisfied with the academics, quality of teachers, and discipline (Toldson, 2019). Positive relationships between teachers and families contribute to the higher academic performance of students. Those relationships do not require families to attend every teacher–family conference, but they do require regular and transparent communications between teachers and families. Communicating positive achievements of students rather than always misbehavior and poor academic performance would help develop more desirable relationships. Good relationships also require "empathy, unconditional positive regard, compassion, and a mutual interest in educating the whole child" (Toldson, 2019, p. 105).

Many schools are very proud of their international or ethnic festivals, where immigrant families share their native cuisine, traditional dress, music, and dances. Everyone feels good about the diversity in the school during that time. The problem is that the value of diversity expressed during that event does not always extend to the valuing and acceptance of immigrant or racial and ethnic groups in the school culture or curriculum. If the racism, sexism, heterosexism, ableism, or inequality that many students face in and out of school is never discussed, they come to believe that teachers don't really care about them no matter how many events celebrate their diversity. The celebrations become an empty promise for inclusion and equity, and they do nothing to identify and eliminate inequity (Gorski & Swalwell, 2023).

Knowing the community in which students live is an important link in making the classroom relevant to students and their families. It requires knowing what is happening in a community in which teachers may not live. How can teachers know the students' neighborhoods? They can read the local newspaper and watch the local news, but those resources are likely not to capture some of the positive and negative happenings in the neighborhood. Talking to family members, listening to students, and checking in with local businesspeople are likely to provide more information that reflects events and issues that are important to students. Creative teachers are able to make the curriculum relevant to students by having them apply the knowledge and skills they are learning to the community by identifying concerns, collecting and analyzing data, writing their results, and becoming advocates for change (German, 2021).

## Addressing the Opportunity Gap

A disproportionately large number of Black, Latino/a, and Native American students along with English learners, students with disabilities, and those from low-income families are not meeting national standards at the proficiency level (National Assessment of Educational Progress, 2023). These students end up leaving school before high school graduation at higher rates than their middle-class White and Asian American classmates. Too often students' lack of interest or active participation in school is blamed on the poverty in which they live, their upbringing, or their previous teachers. However, teachers are expected to help all students learn, regardless of the discrimination and economic and environmental factors that may make the task challenging.

Why do a disproportionately high number of students of color score lower than White and Asian American students on standardized tests? The reason is that many students of color and those from families with low SES do not have access to the same learning opportunities as most middle- and upper-class students, resulting in an **opportunity gap** (Milner, 2020). For example, studies indicate that:

- Students from low-income households and students of color are more likely to be taught a low-level curriculum with low standards for performance (Darling-Hammond & Darling-Hammond, 2022).

- Fifty percent of Asian American high school students enrolled in a calculus course in 2013, compared to 22% of White, 15% of Latino/a, and 9% of Black students (National Science Board, 2018).

- In high schools with a majority Black population, only 36% of the schools offer calculus compared to 60% of the high schools with majority White populations (Startz, 2019).

- Those in schools that are predominantly students of color or have high poverty levels are more likely to be taught by unqualified and inexperienced teachers who are not certified to teach (Startz, 2019).

Should it be a surprise that many students of color and those from low-SES families do not perform as well as middle-class White students when they have not participated in advanced mathematics and science courses or have not had teachers who majored in the subjects they teach? In urban schools in which students of color are overrepresented, teachers are less likely to be fully licensed than in schools with middle-class White students. Advanced courses in mathematics and science are not always available in the schools attended by a large proportion of students of color. Students must have access to such courses and qualified teachers so that they can study the content on which they will be tested.

These practices have resulted in limited or no progress at reducing the opportunity gap. **Deeper learning** practices have the potential to reverse this trend. When students believe they can succeed, "they engage in mastery learning experiences through which they undertake meaningful questions, conduct inquiries together, present and vet their answers to one another, and continue to revise their findings and products until they have more deeply understood the concepts" (Darling-Hammond & Darling-Hammond, 2022, p. 76). Students who have the opportunity to engage in culturally relevant learning accrue additional benefits as they "critically examine their experiences and cultural histories" (Darling-Hammond & Darling-Hammond, 2022, p. 81).

Teachers should be careful not to label students as intellectually inferior because their standardized test scores are low. These scores can influence a teacher's expectations for students' academic performance. Standardized test scores can help in determining how assimilated into the dominant culture and how affluent a student's family may be, but they provide less evidence about how intelligent a person is. Many other factors can be used to provide information about intelligence—for example, the ability to think and respond appropriately in different situations.

When students do not achieve at the levels expected, some teachers refrain from taking responsibility. They blame the students, their families, or the economic conditions of the community rather than seriously reflecting on why students in their classrooms are not learning and what might be changed to help them learn. A number of research studies report that teacher effectiveness is more important in student achievement than a student's race, ethnicity, poverty status, or parents' education (Gershenson et al., 2017; Sanders & Rivers, 1996).

Students are not always active participants in their academic achievement. They are not always engaged with the schoolwork, and they do not always do their homework. However, effective teachers do not allow students to fail. There are many examples of good teachers who have helped students with low test scores achieve at advanced levels. Your challenge is to become one of the teachers whose students are not allowed to fail.

## Valuing Educator Diversity

Staffing composition and patterns should reflect the cultural diversity of the country. At a minimum, they should reflect the diversity of the geographic area. For example, school administrators should not be predominantly men but should include women and people who identify as nonbinary. The teaching force should include more gender diversity and more people of color than it currently does. Persons of color should not be concentrated in custodial and clerical positions in schools. Students' worldviews and racial and ethnic attitudes are positively expanded when they have the opportunity to see and interact with a diverse group of teachers and administrators who are in positions of esteem and authority in a school (Gershenson et al., 2021). When education is multicultural, faculty, administrators, and other staff see themselves as learners who are enhanced and changed by understanding, affirming, and reflecting cultural diversity.

Having at least some teachers who are from the same racial or ethnic group as students benefits them, especially students of color. "These benefits include increased trust, better communication and relationships, higher expectations, and plain old better teaching, all of which translates to better test scores, fewer absences and suspensions, and higher graduation and college enrollment rates" (Gershenson et al., 2021, p. 2). For example, researchers have found that Black boys who had a Black teacher in grades 3–5 had a 29% increase in interest in pursuing college and 39% less chance of dropping out of school (Gershenson et al., 2017).

The current problem is that the percentage of teachers of color in schools (approximately 20%) is not equal to the percentage of students in schools (over 50%). The ratio of the share of teachers of a specific background to the share of students of the same background in a specific school or geographical area is higher for students and teachers of color in cities than in other geographical areas. Even in cities, the ratio is 0.51 for Black teachers and students compared to 2.41 for White teachers and students. It is lowest (0.27) for Latino/a teachers and students in rural areas (Gershenson et al., 2021). Thus, it is important for teachers to develop cultural competencies that will help them develop the asset-based and caring environments that will support students of color.

## Applying an Equity Lens

When diversity is valued within a school, equity becomes a lens through which all aspects of schooling is viewed. Student government and extracurricular activities include students from diverse cultural groups. In a school where multiculturalism is valued, students from various cultural backgrounds hold leadership positions. Those roles stop being automatically delegated to students from the dominant group in the school.

If the school climate is multicultural, multiculturalism is reflected in every aspect of the educational program. In addition to those areas already mentioned, assembly programs reflect multiculturalism in their content as well as in the choice of speakers. Bulletin boards and displays reflect the diversity of the nation, even if the community is not rich in diversity. Cross-cultural communications among students and between students and teachers are positive. Different languages and dialects used by students are respected. Both girls and boys participate in technology education, family science, calculus, physics, and vocational classes.

In schools that value multicultural education, students from different cultural groups participate in college preparatory classes, Advanced Placement classes, and special education at rates equal to their representation in the schools. Differences in academic achievement levels disappear among students of different genders, White students and students of color, and upper-middle-class and low-income students. Instructional materials are free of biases, omissions, and stereotypes. All students see themselves positively in the books they read and the lessons in which they are engaged. In a positive multicultural climate, they feel that they are an integral part of the school rather than an unwelcome stranger.

In a school climate that promotes human rights, antiracism, and equity, discrimination against students from different cultural groups is not tolerated. Students respect the cultural differences within the school population, and harassment of students disappears. They assist each other in the learning process, helping students who are struggling to understand a concept or a problem. Students are not afraid to let teachers and other students know that they need assistance because they know they won't be labeled academically challenged or lazy. Students and teachers work together to learn and support each other in that process. When respect for cultural differences is reflected in all aspects of students' educational programs, the goals for multicultural education are being attained.

In a multicultural classroom, students from different cultural groups work together on projects such as this one where they are studying natural sources of energy for a joint class project.

**SOURCE:** Yacobchuk/123RF

# Approaches to Multicultural Teaching

**Learning Objective 11.4** Create lesson plans and develop teaching practices that are culturally responsive.

A **multicultural curriculum** supports and celebrates diversity in the broadest sense; it includes the histories, experiences, traditions, and cultures of students in the classroom in accurate and authentic ways. In classrooms with limited diversity, the curriculum introduces students to the major cultural groups in the state and nation. Regardless of the grade level or subject being taught, the curriculum should be multicultural. All students should be able to acknowledge and understand the diversity in the United States and the world. Students in settings with limited diversity may have few opportunities to

**Pearson eTextbook**

**Video Example 11.2**

In this video, Professor Mary Ann Prater discusses the connection between special education and culturally responsive practices.

interact directly with persons from other cultural groups. However, they can learn to value diversity rather than fear it. They should come to know that others have different perspectives on the world and events that are based on different lived experiences.

Although communities are not always rich in racial and ethnic diversity, almost all of them are economically, gender, and religiously diverse as well as diverse in other ways such as (dis)ability and sexual orientation. Educators need to know the cultural groups that exist in the community. Schools on or near Native American reservations include students from the tribes in the area as well as students from other ethnic groups. Urban schools typically include multiethnic populations and students from different SES levels and religions; urban schools have a high proportion of low-income and immigrant students. Rural schools include low-income and middle-class families. Teachers who enter schools attended by students from diverse groups will need to learn about the cultures in the community.

It is important that students see their own identities and experiences reflected in the books and other resources used in classes. In the 1970s, researchers found that children and adults of color were not represented or had very limited representation in textbooks, storybooks, literature, science, and mathematics problems used in the classroom. They are better represented today than in the past, but not at a rate equal to their portion of the U.S. population. Of people of color, Black people are most likely to be found in textbooks. Indigenous people are generally invisible except in a historical context, as are Latino/a and Asian Americans. In 2018, the Cooperative Children's Book Center at the University of Wisconsin–Madison found that Black people were featured in 11% of the children's books published in the United States. About 9% of the featured characters were Asian Americans or Pacific Islanders, about 7% were Latino/a, and 1% were Native American. The inclusion of people of color in school resources is important to promote cultural pride, support self-esteem, improve social-emotional functioning, and improve their engagement in learning as well as to "repair distorted narratives" (Schwartz, 2019, para. 9).

Multicultural teaching should tell it as it is. Diversity existed in North America when Europeans arrived, and it became greater with each passing century. To teach as if only one group is worthy of inclusion in the curriculum is not to tell the truth. Instructional materials and information about different groups are available to students and teachers. It may be more difficult to find resources on groups where the membership is small or somewhat new to the United States, but it is not impossible. Both students and teachers can use the Internet to locate information, including personal narratives, art, music, and family histories. Although teachers cannot possibly address each of the hundreds of ethnic and religious groups in this country, they should attempt to include the groups represented in the school community, regardless of whether all of them are represented in the school.

In western Pennsylvania, a teacher should include information about and examples from the Amish. This approach will signal to other students that the diversity in their community is valued. In schools in the Southwest, the cultures of Mexican Americans and Native Americans should be integrated throughout the curriculum. In other areas of the country, the curriculum should reflect the histories, experiences, and perspectives of Mormons, Muslims, Vietnamese Americans, Lakotas, Jamaican Americans, Black Americans, Chinese Americans, Puerto Ricans, or whatever groups reside in the state or region. If these groups are not included in the textbook, teachers should find other resources, which could provide the opportunity for teachers and students to work collaboratively on projects.

Multicultural education is not about the food, festivals, fun, heroes, or holidays of diverse cultural groups. Celebrating Black history only during February or women's history during March is not multicultural education. It is much more complex and pervasive than setting aside an hour, a unit, or a month to study a specific group. It should become the lens through which the curriculum is presented. The amount of specific content about diverse groups will vary according to the course taught, but awareness and incorporation of the nation's diversity can be reflected in all classroom experiences and courses. No matter how assimilated students in a classroom are, it is the teacher's responsibility to ensure that they understand diversity, know the contributions of members of both dominant and other groups, and hear the voices of individuals and groups who are from cultural backgrounds different from their own. Some states and school districts mandate culturally inclusive curriculum; other states prohibit inclusion of some identity groups and some topics related to issues such as slavery, sexuality, and gender and LGBTQ+ identities.

Multiculturalism is not a compensatory process to make others more like the dominant group. As an educator integrates diversity into the curriculum, the differences across groups must *not* become deficits to be overcome. Teachers who believe that their own culture is superior to students' cultures will have a difficult time building the trust necessary to help all students learn. Trust is built as teachers speak up for students, and students see that teachers are "willing to take risks and challenge the status quo for them" (German, 2021, p. 15).

When teachers begin to teach multiculturally, they may have to allow extra planning time to discover ways to make the curriculum and instruction reflect diversity. With experience, this process will become internalized, allowing teachers to recognize immediately what materials are not multicultural and the need for expanding the standard curriculum to reflect diversity and multiple perspectives. In this section we explore elements of five approaches for delivering multicultural education.

# Critical Incidents in Teaching
## Teaching About Thanksgiving

Michele Johnson was observing a kindergarten class in a school near her campus during the fall semester of her junior year at the same time that she was enrolled in a class on multicultural education. The week before Thanksgiving, the teacher she was observing shared with her the educational resources related to the holiday that she planned to use the following week. When Michele reviewed the materials, she discovered that the kindergartners were to cut out and decorate headbands that they would wear with feathers while sharing a bountiful feast with the newly arrived Pilgrims for Thanksgiving. She was appalled that the teacher was perpetuating stereotypes of First Americans and their relationships with the European settlers.

Michele's multicultural education class had just finished reviewing the historical account of the Pilgrims and other Europeans landing at Plymouth. She learned that she and many of her classmates had received inaccurate information about that event. The stereotypical version of the Wampanoags or other First Americans who lived in that area at the time did not fit the image that the kindergartners were modeling; they looked more like Native Americans who lived on the Plains, much further west of the Northeast coast. If there had been a feast in 1621, the First Americans would have been more likely to have provided the food as they celebrated one of their seasonal thanksgivings as they had for thousands of years. The reality is that many First Americans today consider Thanksgiving a Day of Mourning for the removal from their homelands, enslavement, and the massive number of deaths from diseases introduced by the Europeans who had invaded their country.

The truth is that the Pilgrims did not introduce Thanksgiving. The celebration of Thanksgiving began in 1863 when President Abraham Lincoln declared it a national holiday, and the Pilgrims were not included in the depiction of the holiday until the 1890s. Michael Dorris (2016) of Modoc heritage recommended that the holiday could be "a time for appreciating Native American peoples as they were and as they are, not as either the Pilgrims or their descendant bureaucrats might wish them to be" (p. 105). Michele was worried about the children in the class she was observing already learning stories about First Americans and European settlers that were inaccurate.

### Questions for Discussion
1. Why does Michele think the project to teach about Thanksgiving is not appropriate?
2. What do you know about the first Thanksgiving? Do you think its representation in the classroom that Michele is observing is accurate? Why or why not?
3. How would you tell the truth about Thanksgiving to kindergartners?
4. Should Michele say something to the teacher who might later be evaluating her performance? Why or why not?

**SOURCE:** Stenhouse (2009).

# Dimensions of Multicultural Education

Multicultural education is too often oversimplified by educators who implement it by adding some lessons on people who are not identified as White, Christian, middle class, or cisgender. No effort is made to integrate the histories, contributions, and stories of these groups throughout the curriculum. In some cases, the only attention to diversity in the community is its celebration of ethnic holidays and events. Some educators view the only goal of multicultural education as prejudice reduction and tolerance of each other. To conceptualize multicultural education as a comprehensive approach to changing the curriculum, instruction, and climate of schools, one of the early leaders in the field of multiethnic and multicultural education, James A. Banks, identified five dimensions of multicultural education: content integration, knowledge construction process, equity pedagogy, prejudice reduction, and empowering school culture.

*Content integration* is the inclusion of diverse cultures and groups in the academic subject being taught by teachers (Banks, 2019). It includes key concepts, theories, examples, data, and information that expand the curriculum to address the histories and experiences of more groups than the dominant White group. This integration occurs most easily in social studies, language arts, music, and art. However, teachers of mathematics and the sciences can also ensure that students learn that people of color have contributed to those fields, that the examples they use in class and projects reflect the authentic experiences of diverse groups in their communities and the country, and that the application of mathematics and science can be used to help solve problems in their communities.

The *knowledge construction process* pushes students to think critically about the content in the books they read and resources they access online, in podcasts, and on television. Knowledge is not always accurate, nor value free. It is both subjective and objective (Banks, 2019). Who are the authors of these works and how do their racial, ethnic, gender, SES, religious, and other identities influence what they report as facts? In multicultural education, students explore many resources written by people of diverse identities that provide multiple perspectives on topics that are analyzed and discussed in classrooms.

*Prejudice reduction* focuses on helping students develop positive attitudes about diverse racial and ethnic groups. Most children are aware of racial differences by the age of 4 (Banks, 2019). Therefore, education related to prejudice reduction can begin in preschool. Being able to see people of color, those with disabilities, and girls and women in nontraditional and nonstereotypical roles contribute to prejudice reduction. Cooperative learning and other group activities in which students from different racial and ethnic groups work together support the development of more positive racial attitudes. In today's multicultural education, educators are more aggressively moving toward the elimination of microaggressions against students from marginalized groups and the elimination of racism, sexism, classism, ableism, heterosexism, and other *-isms* in the classroom and school.

Banks's *equity pedagogy* expects teachers to facilitate students' academic achievement by using techniques and teaching methods that incorporate the learning and cultural characteristics of students from diverse groups. Knowing students and their families makes this task easier as teachers draw on students' strengths to engage them in learning.

An *empowering school culture* is seen by Banks (2019) as one that provided all students equal opportunities in school to be successful. It includes assessment activities that are fair to all students and do not favor those from one group over another. It de-tracks students so that they are not sorted in groups or classes by their class, race, ethnicity, gender, or other identity for inequitable instruction. Teachers hold high academic expectations for all students. Such a school culture is expected to lead to a more equitable and fair education for all students.

Banks's five dimensions guided the evolution of multicultural education and new approaches for multicultural teaching over the past few decades, as described in the next section. Based on her research of teachers who were successfully teaching Black students, Gloria Ladson-Billings (2021) first introduced *culturally relevant pedagogy* as an effective pedagogy for students from diverse cultural groups in the 1990s. In 2000, Geneva Gay (2018) introduced *culturally responsive teaching*, and Django Paris and H. Samy Alim introduced *culturally sustaining pedagogies* in 2017. All three approaches are essential components of education that is multicultural and can be used alone or in combination; they build on each other. These pedagogies affirm the cultures of both White students and students of color, view the cultures and experiences of them as strengths, and reflect the students' cultures in the teaching process. They are based on the premise that culture influences the way students learn.

## Culturally Relevant Pedagogy

Ladson-Billings (2021) defines **culturally relevant pedagogy** as "a pedagogy that empowers students intellectually, socially, emotionally, and politically by using cultural referents to impart knowledge, skills, and attitudes" (p. 4). She focuses on three components: student learning, cultural competence, and critical consciousness. Student learning is the academic progress that students make from the time they enter the classroom until they leave at the end of the year. Teachers who practice culturally relevant pedagogy stop asking what is wrong with Black students and other marginalized students. Instead, they change their pedagogy to build on the strengths of students, which contributes to their success in the classroom (Ladson-Billings, 2021).

In culturally relevant pedagogy, cultural competence means that all students become fluent and knowledgeable of at least one culture other than their own. Teachers with Latino/a and White students could use both Spanish and English as they teach. They could integrate the histories, experiences, literature, and stories of the Latino/a students into the curriculum that primarily focuses on the dominant White culture. White students who are in classes with no students of color should also learn other cultures to prepare them to work in a "diverse, globally, interconnected, democratic society" (Ladson-Billings, 2021, p. 5).

Ladson-Billings (2021) defines sociopolitical/critical consciousness as the ability to "apply, analyze, synthesize, and critique [students'] environment and the problems they encounter" (p. 7). Students are pushed to think deeply and learn to problem-solve about issues that are important to them. Issues that appear trivial such as wearing a hat in school or complaining about food on the lunch menu that no one likes may be important to students and can lead to the exploration of more serious issues of discrimination, inequities, how decisions are made, and action that can be taken to make changes.

## Culturally Responsive Teaching

In **culturally responsive teaching**, students' cultural frames of reference become a lens through which the curriculum is delivered, making the content more relevant to students' lives (Gay, 2018). Cultural differences become learning assets as students' race, ethnicity, and cultures are valued, respected, validated, and reflected in the curriculum, instructional strategies, and classroom climate. Culturally responsive teaching helps students maintain their connections with their racial and ethnic groups and communities while contributing to their improving academic achievement (Gay, 2018). Culturally responsive pedagogy opens the curriculum to students of color as it expands the canons of knowledge and ways of knowing beyond that of the dominant culture (Gay, 2018).

Culturally responsive pedagogy empowers ethnically diverse students by making knowledge not only accessible to them but also connected to their lives and experiences outside school (Gay, 2018). A traditional curriculum incorporates the histories, experiences, and perspectives of the White middle class. The problem is that the experiences of other groups are often marginalized or ignored, either not appearing at all or appearing as an afterthought, not as an integrated, important part of society. Culturally responsive teaching incorporates the cultural knowledge, histories, experiences, and perspectives of people of color, people with low SES, and women throughout the curriculum and school environment. It also promotes academic success, validates cultural affiliation, and nurtures personal efficacy for these and other students (Howard, 2019).

Curricula have always been political by privileging the knowledge and experiences of the dominant group. Whose story, whose culture, and whose values should be reflected in the curriculum being taught and the textbooks and readings that are assigned? Why are students of color pushed to assimilate the dominant culture, making its stories their own and ignoring their own stories? How can curricula be changed to value the cultures of all students in the classroom and center their histories and experiences along with those of the dominant culture? "The way that people are written into textbooks, how they are included in stories about history, and constructed as characters in novels and artistic work, influence our understanding of them" (Leonardo & Grubb, 2019, p. 27). Some groups are totally omitted from the official curriculum. Others are portrayed inaccurately or negatively. How students see themselves, their families, and their communities in these resources tells them how the dominant society views them.

Some White teachers are reluctant to make their instruction culturally relevant or responsive because of their lack of understanding of their students' cultures (Howard, 2019). Howard found in his research that it is not the race of teachers that influences their ability to be culturally relevant or responsive. It is their willingness to learn "the complexities of race and culture, develop a healthy sense of their own racial identity and privilege, develop a skill set of instructional practices that tap into cultural knowledge, reject deficit views of students of color, and have an authentic sense of students' ability to be academically successful" (2019, p. 72). Making the classroom culturally responsive provides teachers the opportunity to learn other cultures from their own research, their students, their families, and the community. The work is well worth it as marginalized students begin to see themselves in the curriculum, feel more valued in the classroom, and become more engaged in learning. Strategies that teachers use to teach more multiculturally are discussed in the following sections.

**INTEGRATING CULTURAL DIVERSITY IN ACADEMIC SUBJECTS** Culturally relevant, responsive, and sustaining teaching increases academic achievement because the subject matter is taught within the cultural context and experiences of the students and the communities served. In these approaches, the subject begins to have meaning for students because it relates to their lives and experiences. Today's students are not satisfied with passively listening to a teacher tell them what they need to know. They need to be involved in their learning. They learn from hands-on activities. They like to explore, experiment, and test new ideas. Using technology can help spark their interest.

Teachers must know a subject well to help students learn it. Subject-matter competence alone, however, does not automatically translate into student learning. Without an understanding of students' cultures, teachers are unable to develop

Teachers are a valuable resource in discussions of cultural differences and ensuring that all children see themselves in the curriculum and feel that they are a valued part of the school community.

**SOURCE:** Graham Oliver/Panther Media GmbH/Alamy Stock Photo

instructional strategies related to students' life experiences. They should pay attention to the stories being read in class to ensure that students see themselves in some of the stories while learning about people and families from other cultures in other stories. The projects assigned and classroom activities demonstrate whether some students' cultures are being privileged over others. Teachers may need to substitute word problems used in math and science to better reflect the cultures and experiences of students in the classroom. For example, a problem that focuses on crop production by acre has meaning in a rural setting but little or no meaning to students who have lived in the city all of their lives. A problem asking students to figure out the best route to a location using buses and the subway would present an unfamiliar context for rural students.

**INCORPORATING MULTIPLE PERSPECTIVES**   It is important for students to learn that individuals from other racial, ethnic, religious, SES, and gender groups may have perspectives on issues and events that are different from their own. Movies, books, and music provide different perspectives on local, national, and world issues that expand students' knowledge about the way others live and experience events. Comedians from diverse groups also provide different views of the world from their own and others' experiences. The more teachers listen to others, the more they can expand their own cultural knowledge.

The experiences and histories of one's own group provide a lens for viewing the world. Most members of the dominant group have not had to face the negative, discriminatory experiences that students of color, non-Christians, and trans students have in schools, with the police, in government offices, or in shopping centers. Perspectives vary for good reasons. Understanding the reasons makes it easier to accept that most other perspectives are just as valid as one's own. At the same time, perspectives and behaviors that degrade and harm members of specific groups are unacceptable.

Culturally responsive teaching expects students to examine sensitive issues and topics. It requires them to look at historical and contemporary events from the perspectives of, for example, Black women, Central American and Mexican immigrants, people who are Jewish or Southern Baptists, and other people of color, as well as the perspectives of White men. Reading books, poems, and articles by authors from diverse cultures is helpful because it exposes students to the perspectives of people from other groups. Perspectives on controversial topics can be explored through debates, mock trials, and role playing. These strategies can engage students in topics about which they care and help them develop critical thinking skills.

**ANALYZING EQUITY AND POWER RELATIONSHIPS**   Children ask questions that often make adults uncomfortable. "Why is that man's skin that color?" "Why does Johnny always get to mow the yard while I do the dishes?" "Why does that person talk funny?" "Why does Susie use a wheelchair?" "Why are those women wearing scarves?" These questions are often asked of families when they are with their children in a public place like a shopping center or grocery store, but they are also asked in classrooms. The answers help those who are asking determine appropriate behavior. The answers can clarify or confuse the issues. Children may learn that they shouldn't ask those questions. Adults sometimes answer such questions directly and honestly; at other times, they aren't truthful or forthright in their responses. For teachers, these questions in the classroom and on the playground provide opportunities to discuss issues related to diversity, equity, and social justice. They provide opportunities to denounce name-calling and harassment against other students. They are "teachable moments" that allow the correction of myths or misperceptions students have about people who are different from themselves.

Teachers are sometimes reluctant to answer or address the questions raised above, and the questions and issues become even more complex and controversial as students move from elementary school to middle school to high school. Young people of color begin to ask why so many of them are not learning, why teachers do not care about them, and why they are disciplined more often than other students. Young women struggle with the mixed messages they receive about their expected behavior, sexuality, potential, and self-actualization. Students from low-income families may ask what school is doing for them or wonder how they could possibly afford to attend college. At base, many of these students are questioning the power relationships and inequities that they are experiencing in their lives, although they may not be able to frame their questions and concerns in those terms. Many of them are feeling their powerlessness; others are beginning to rebel against the inequities they are experiencing.

Teachers may feel uncomfortable about addressing these serious but sometimes controversial issues. They may be confused about the issues themselves. They may feel that they don't know enough about the topic to discuss it with students or that talking about the topic would just "rock the boat." Teachers may worry that a discussion of the topic might get them in trouble with families, the principal, their colleagues, or their state legislators. With the focus on preparing students for upcoming standardized testing, teachers may decide they don't have time to address issues such as racism, poverty, homelessness, abuse, sexual identity, disabilities, or religious diversity.

Some educators might think that it is inappropriate to address topics related to social and economic inequities in the classroom, especially with younger children. However, preschool and elementary teachers can address these topics in developmentally appropriate ways, relating topics to the realities of their students' lives (Sapon-Shevin, 2010). Not only can teachers help students understand why something happens, they can also help a student know what to do when another student is called "gay," when a Jewish student questions her participation in Christmas activities, or when a student using a wheelchair can't go on a field trip. Students at any age can learn that they can make a difference and that they can speak up when they see an inequity (Sapon-Shevin, 2010).

Race is an issue that some teachers find difficult to address in the classroom. Yet it affects the work of schools. Most White students are likely to believe that racism is not a factor in their lives; they may even question its existence. Most people of color, on the other hand, feel the pressure of racism all around them. They don't understand how their White peers and teachers could possibly miss it. When racism is included accurately in the curriculum, it confirms students of color's "experience with racism and validates their worldview" (Leonardo & Grubb, 2019, p. 27). Some students react with anger and despair; others are defensive and feel shame or guilt (Tatum, 2017), but they can develop greater clarity about how racism has affected both their lives and the lives of others.

To ignore the impact of racism on society and our everyday world is to negate the experiences of students and families who have experienced its impact. Can teachers afford to ignore it because it is complex, emotional, and hard for some students to understand and handle? As teachers incorporate diversity throughout the curriculum, there should be opportunities to discuss the meaning of race in this country and the debilitating effect that racism (as well as sexism, classism, etc.) has on large numbers of people in this country and the world.

There is value in racial and ethnic groups working together to overcome fears and correct myths and misperceptions. This healing can begin with educators being willing to facilitate the dialogue about race. Discussions of race often challenge teachers' and students' deeply held beliefs about the topic. At the beginning, many White students resist reexamining their worldviews, acknowledging the privilege of Whiteness, and accepting the existence of discrimination. These changes do not occur overnight. They take months, and sometimes years, of study and self-reflection. Some people never accept that racism exists and needs to be eliminated.

Another topic that is difficult to analyze critically is poverty, and especially its causes. Too often, families and individuals are blamed for their own poverty. It is difficult for many, especially those advantaged by the current economic conditions, to acknowledge that not all people have the same opportunities as others. Teachers can help students explore the contributions of the labor class as well as the wealthy and powerful. They can examine various perspectives on eliminating jobs in one area of the country and moving them to cheaper labor markets in another part of the country or world. Students could examine the changing job markets to determine the skills needed for future work. They could research child labor that is used to produce products that are purchased in the United States. They could discuss why companies are seeking labor outside the United States for high-tech jobs as well as low-paying jobs in meat-processing companies and agriculture. They could critique different perspectives on seeking labor outside the country and its impact on U.S. workers and families.

## Culturally Sustaining Pedagogy

Reconsidering the question of the purpose of education in an increasingly pluralistic society such as the United States, Django and H. Samy Alim expanded on Gloria Ladson-Billings's conception of culturally relevant pedagogy. Their **culturally sustaining pedagogies** not only recognized and built on the multiple cultural histories and experiences of students but proposed pedagogies that promote and sustain the cultural pluralism of the community. These pedagogies allow students to be themselves in the classroom, not requiring them to assimilate the White middle-class culture to be academically successful. Culturally sustaining classrooms see the cultures of students as assets to be nourished and further developed rather than deficits that have to be overcome and changed. Children and youth of color continue to learn the dominant culture but also critique the dominant culture as well as "explore, honor, extend, and at times, problematize their [own] cultural practices and investments" (Alim & Paris, 2017, p. 3). To truly sustain a student's culture requires the acceptance of cultural practices that have often been excluded from classrooms and "leverages these as resources both for achieving institutional access and for challenging structural inequality" (Bucholtz et al., 2017, p. 43).

Understanding that young people's interactions with race, ethnicity, language, literacy, and culture are always shifting and dynamic, teachers should incorporate student voices and stories into the curriculum to maximize their engagement in learning. For many urban youth, hip-hop is a form of cultural practice that could be sustained and incorporated into the learning process, but it will also need to be examined for its inclusion, or lack of inclusion, of women, LGBTQ+ youth, and youth who are not Black. Problematic practices such as homophobia and misogyny within cultures should also be explored and critiqued as culturally sustaining pedagogy is implemented (Alim & Paris, 2017).

## Abolitionist Teaching

In her book *We Want to Do More Than Survive: Abolitionist Teaching and the Pursuit of Educational Freedom*, Bettina L. Love (2019) calls for "working in solidarity with communities of color while drawing on the imagination, creativity, refusal, (re) membering, visionary thinking, healing, rebellious spirit, boldness, determination, and subversiveness of abolitionists to eradicate injustice in and outside of schools" (p. 2). Teachers who practice **abolitionist teaching** do not participate in unjust practices such as zero-tolerance and the school-to-prison pipeline. They support restorative practice and ensure that students are safe from violence as they attend school. Abolitionist teachers acknowledge that the United States is "anti-Black, racist, discriminatory, and unjust" (p. 12) and are in solidarity with people of color and people with low SES who are fighting for their dignity and humanity.

According to Love (2019), "abolitionist teaching is not a teaching approach" (p. 89). It is about teachers, students, families, and communities taking action against injustice in schools and society. Teachers can go about this work in many different ways. They may make their classroom safe places to interrogate oppression. They may protest practices that damage students such as gun violence and the use of standardized testing, which can limit students' access to advanced classes and higher education. Some teachers fight to improve the education, housing, health care, or climate for students who have been marginalized in society and in school. They fight for children's dreams not to be crushed by the anti-Blackness and discrimination that prevents them from knowing a just world that recognizes their full humanity, cares about people who have been marginalized in society, thrives as people with diverse identities work together for justice, and makes their dreams possible (Love, 2019).

# Social Justice in the Classroom

**Learning Objective 11.5** Model social justice and equality in the classroom.

Social justice is a philosophy that promotes fairness, supports economic and political equality, and respects the basic human rights of all people. Teaching for social justice requires a disposition of caring and social responsibility for people who have been marginalized in society. But it is much more than a disposition. Teachers who practice social justice confront untruths and stereotypes that contribute to inequality and discrimination against groups. Social justice requires the provision of resources to all students equitably to promote their learning. It means believing in students, having high expectations for them, and providing rigorous and meaningful curriculum and instruction to assist them in developing social and cultural capital to meet their potential. Socially just teachers provide a learning environment that encourages critical thinking and prepares students to be active citizens in a democracy (Nieto, 2018).

Socially just classrooms are democratic, engaging students and teachers in learning together. Establishing a democratic classroom helps overcome the power inequities that exist between students and teachers. Students become active participants in governing classrooms and in critically analyzing school and societal practices related to equity and social justice.

Numerous studies show that interactions and understandings among people from different racial and ethnic groups increase as they work together on **meaningful projects** inside and outside the classroom. In social justice education, meaningful projects address equity, democratic practices, and critical social issues in the community. A classroom can also become a community in which students not only interact with each other for learning purposes but also learn to care and support each other. Teachers can ensure that students from different cultural groups work together in cooperative groups and group work. **Cooperative learning** is a popular strategy for supporting learning communities. It involves grouping students to work together on a project to support and learn from each other. It minimizes competition among students and encourages them to share the work necessary to learn. They can establish opportunities for cross-cultural communication and learning from each other, but teachers should ensure that groups represent the diversity in the classroom.

A socially just curriculum provides students the opportunity to think about issues of injustice and perhaps be able to take action to change them (Milner, 2020). It helps students recognize the biases and discrimination that prevent some students and families from taking advantage of society's benefits. In this environment, students learn to identify discrimination and inequities in the school and the community and become involved in projects working for the elimination of these inequities.

Within the school, students could work toward the elimination of bullying and harassment of LGBTQ+ students, girls, students of color, students who are not Christian, students from low-income families, and students with disabilities. High school students could choose to tutor younger students to improve their chances for academic success. In the community, they could work with community leaders to improve the environment,

# Explore and Focus Your Cultural Lens

## Debate: Teaching About Racism, Classism, Sexism, and Other Social Justice Issues

Social studies teacher Jackson Wright began his teaching career at a school in which one of his students was suspended for "heiling" Hitler at a fall assembly and at which he regularly found swastikas penciled on classroom desks and bathroom walls. Because of these and similar incidents at the school, the administration and teachers had agreed to implement a social justice curriculum, beginning in social studies and English classes. Mr. Wright's first challenge came after he explained to his classes that "Black people can't be racist against White people because they do not hold power over them," which generated a great deal of discussion. During the tutorial period the next day, Jason and several of his friends approached Mr. Wright about what they said was his inaccurate definition of racism. Jason angrily read a definition from an Internet dictionary that confirmed his belief that Black people can also think that their race is superior and thus be racist.

When the class studied discrimination based on gender, students argued that women and girls are no longer discriminated against. By the end of the first semester, Mr. Wright was feeling that he was totally inept at helping his students see the injustices that were manifested in a school in which students of color, those who were not Christian, and LGBTQ+ students felt invisible, underrepresented, and misrepresented. Mr. Wright's students continued to push back on the socially just curriculum and his attempts to build a socially just climate in his classroom. He kept trying to create lesson plans that would honor his students' voices and move them toward empathy with other people's stories. It wasn't until May that Mr. Wright felt that he began to connect with his students as his lessons became more authentic and relevant to them. He stopped shutting down students and began pulling them into meaningful explorations of racism, classism, sexism, and oppression. Do you think that teachers should teach about these and other social justice issues?

### FOR

- One of the goals of education should be to correct the misinformation, inaccuracies, and misperceptions about cultural identities and groups that are circulated daily.
- One of the goals for public schools is to provide equal educational opportunities for all students, which requires

school administrators, educators, and students to eliminate the discrimination that currently exists in schools.

- Helping students understand the issues that prevent equality, equity, and social justice across groups is critical to taking the actions needed to realize a socially just society.
- The teaching of social justice in schools will contribute to students' respect of people from cultures other than their own and the improvement of cross-cultural interactions.

### AGAINST

- Issues of social justice are too sensitive and controversial for teachers to tackle in the classroom.
- Because of the lack of agreement on social justice issues in some communities, families and faith-based organizations, not teachers, should be responsible for teaching about them.
- In today's environment in which immigrants, people of color, LGBTQ+ people, and people who are not Christian are being attacked by some political leaders, schools should not take sides on these political issues.
- Discussions of social justice issues in the classroom will lead to further controversies and disruptions among groups of students.

## Questions for Discussion

1. What are the advantages and disadvantages to studying racism, classism, sexism, and other social justice issues in school?

2. How important do you think it is to teach about social justice in public and private schools? Why is it important or why should it not be taught?

3. What are some of the social justice issues that you could teach about in the subject and at the grade level that you are planning to teach?

**SOURCE:** Adapted from Johnson (2018).

---

establish better services for children, young people, and people over age 65, and create youth centers to promote the physical and intellectual development of young people. In this section, we examine the roles of critical consciousness and democratic classrooms in the delivery of social justice in the classroom.

## Critical Consciousness

As a result of being taught multiculturally, students learn to think critically about what they are learning and experiencing. **Critical consciousness** was first used by Brazilian activist educator Paulo Freire as a tool for "motivating individuals to combat oppression,

As part of social justice education, students often work together on projects in the local community such as packing food for a local food bank.

**SOURCE:** Jose Luis Pelaez Inc/Gettyimages

violence, and dehumanization with their communities" (Seider & Graves, 2020, p. 3). It can lead to challenges of the status quo, encourages questioning of the dominant canon and culture, and considers alternatives to the inequitable structure of society. Students should be supported in questioning the validity of the knowledge presented in textbooks and other resources. They should be encouraged to explore other perspectives. Developing the skills for critical consciousness about issues helps students make sense of the events and conditions that affect their lives.

Most students accept the information written in their textbooks as the absolute truth. However, critical thinkers do not automatically accept the content of textbooks as truth. They understand that authors write from their own perspectives and with their own biases. The presentation is usually from the perspective of the dominant culture rather than from the perspective of persons who have been oppressed because of events and practices supportive of the dominant culture. Teaching for social justice encourages students to question what is written in textbooks or appears in multimedia materials. Students are expected to conduct research that provides other facts and perspectives to balance the content in the textbook. Scholars have found that "marginalized youth, with high levels of critical consciousness are more likely to demonstrate resilience, mental health, self-esteem, academic achievement, high professional aspirations, and civic and political engagement" (Seider & Graves, 2020, p. 3).

Educators can help students examine their own biases and stereotypes related to different cultural groups. These biases often surface during class discussions or incidents outside the classroom. They should not be ignored by the teacher. Instead, they should become teachable moments in which issues are confronted and discussed. Accurate information can begin to displace the myths that some students hold about people from cultural groups different from their own.

## Democratic Classrooms

**Democratic classrooms** are ones in which students practice democracy by being involved in shared decision making about the classroom and understanding their rights and responsibilities in the education process. These classrooms encourage the exchange and exploration of ideas from multiple perspectives. They develop the individual and collective capacity of students to engage in problem solving about not only the structure and workings of the classroom but issues that impact the lives of their families. Teachers in democratic classrooms engage students in the analysis of real-world ideas, problems, and policies, including community issues such as those described earlier in this chapter. The goal is to understand that democracy is not so much an ideal to be pursued as an idealized set of values by which people should live.

A democratic curriculum respects and accepts cultural differences and incorporates multiple perspectives and voices in the materials used and the discussions that ensue. It respects differences in viewpoints and encourages an openness to the world and sensitivity to controversial issues. It does not limit information and study to the areas chosen by members of the dominant group. Harmonious and supportive relationships among students are promoted. Conflict-resolution practices such as restorative justice are used to manage conflicts. In democratic classrooms, students can also have some choice and control of what they study, which increases their engagement, interest, and achievement in the academic content (Epstein, 2019). Students also become aware of political institutions and their responsibility for being involved in the democratic process throughout their lives. Democratic behavior develops over time and includes participating in democratic organizations—a practice that can start early in one's schooling (Applebaum, 2018). The morning meeting or class meeting in a classroom, student government, and extracurricular clubs can provide practice for democratic participation.

Democratic schools reflect democratic structures and processes that provide students with democratic experiences. Students, teachers, families, and community members become active participants in a transparent educational process. Equity undergirds the structure of democratic schools as tracking, biased testing, and other practices that deny access to some students are eliminated. The emphasis on grades, status, test scores, and winning is replaced with an emphasis on cooperation and concern for the common good. Those involved in this democratic project also work toward the elimination of inequities in the broader community as well as in the school.

Establishing a democratic classroom or school is not always an easy undertaking. Sometimes colleagues and families resist it; some people believe that teachers should be authoritarians who exert control over their students rather than sharing power with them and their families. However, the health of a democracy depends on young people understanding democracy and committing to participate in it. Democratic classrooms can contribute to their active participation from an early age.

# Preparing to Deliver Education That Is Multicultural

**Learning Objective 11.6** Expand your knowledge and skills so you can deliver education that is multicultural.

You can undertake a number of actions to prepare to deliver education that is multicultural. First, you should know your own cultural identity and the degree to which you identify with the various groups of which you are a member. Second, you should acknowledge that you have prejudices that may affect the way you interact with students and families. When you recognize these biases, you can develop strategies to overcome or compensate for them in the classroom. In this section, we explore a few actions you can take to be better prepared to work with students and communities who have different cultural histories and experiences from your own.

## Know Yourself and Others

One of the first steps to becoming multicultural is knowing your own cultural identity. Many people, especially if they are White, do not identify themselves as racial, ethnic, or other identities discussed here. They may have not thought deeply about their privilege in society. Students of color may have thought little about their own multiple identities because their race or ethnicity has been the center of their identity. How much do you know about the cultural background of your family?

In addition to knowing yourself, your **cultural competence** could be expanded by learning more about groups other than your own. You can read about other groups, attend ethnic movies or plays, participate in ethnic celebrations, visit different places of faith and ethnic community gatherings, and interact with members of different groups in a variety of settings. If you enjoy reading, you could select authors from different cultures. The perspectives presented may be very different from your own. Books may help you understand that other people's experiences lead them to react to situations differently than you would. It is often an advantage to discuss one's reactions to such new experiences with someone else to clarify and confront your own prejudices or stereotypes.

Teachers should make an effort to interact with people who are culturally different from themselves. Long-term cultural experiences are probably the most effective means of overcoming fear and misconceptions about a group. It must be remembered, however, that there is much diversity within a group. Generalizing about an entire group on the basis of the characteristics of a few persons should be avoided. In direct cross-cultural contacts, people can learn to be open to the traditions and ways of the other culture. Otherwise, their own traditions, habits, and perspectives are likely to be projected as better rather than as just different. If you can learn to understand, empathize with, and participate in a second culture, you will have a valuable experience. If you learn to live multiculturally, you are indeed fortunate.

All people have unconscious racial, ethnic, gender, and other biases that result in preferential treatment of the members of their own racial group (Benson & Fiarman, 2019). Ask yourself if you have the ability to:

1. Confront and name bias, discrimination, and inequity when you see it.

2. React thoughtfully and equitably to bias, discrimination, and inequity when they occur.

3. Study bias, discrimination, and inequity in a sociopolitical context.

4. View all educational work through an equity lens and foster justice in your decisions to support and promote bias-free, discrimination-free schools and communities (Gorski & Swalwell, 2023).

If you are unable to acknowledge the existence of racism and understand the effect it has on your students, it will be difficult to serve communities of color effectively, and it will be nearly impossible to eliminate racism in either schools or society. You are encouraged to take a critical look at your own interactions with peers and students of color. Becoming a multicultural teacher requires deep reflection on one's experiences and perspectives of the students and communities with which you work and the willingness and commitment to change by critiquing your own attitudes and behavior with a social justice lens (Samuels, 2014).

## Reflect on Your Practice

To provide education that is multicultural, professional educators continually reflect on their practice in the classroom. Multicultural educators care that the content of textbooks and district-wide curriculum accurately portray diversity and perspectives beyond the dominant culture. They ask questions about school practices that lead to a disproportionate number of students of color being suspended from school, disproportionate numbers of Asian Americans and upper-middle-class White students in advanced programs, and disproportionate numbers of boys from low-income families and English learners in low-ability classes. They recognize racism, sexism, heterosexism, and ableism and confront students who are not treating others with respect. They correct their own behavior when they learn that their prejudices are showing.

As you begin working with students and other professional educators in schools, continue to observe how you interact with students, families, and colleagues of cultures different from your own. Think about ways you can use the students' cultures to help them learn the subjects and skills you are teaching. By reflecting on what works and does not work in the classroom, you can continuously improve your teaching for all students. Geneva Gay (2018) recommends that the implementation of education that is multicultural will also require courage and tenacity: "The *courage* to stop blaming the victims of school failure" and "the *tenacity* to relentlessly pursue comprehensive and high-level performance for children who currently are underachieving in schools" (p. 53).

# Revisiting the Opening Case Study

Janelle Hamilton's goal was to create student-centered classrooms at John F. Kennedy High School to actively engage students in their learning. She did this, in part, by relating the literature that students were reading to their own histories and experiences and incorporating their stories into her English class, which over time will introduce the role that their membership in racial, ethnic, class, gender, and religious groups plays in their lives. As indicated in this and other chapters, her work can be enhanced by letting students use their home languages and dialects to share their own stories while learning the Standard English that they are likely to need when they seek a job or start college after high school. Throughout the school year, Ms. Hamilton encouraged students to take more responsibility for their own learning as they shared in selecting topics that were important to them. They also informed her of the instructional strategies that were most effective in helping them learn. Ms. Hamilton also co-taught with her students, providing them the opportunity to learn a topic more in-depth as they prepared to teach it and to see her as a co-learner. She continued to believe that all of her students could learn at a high level and monitored their learning through observations of their work and

authentic assessments of their writing, presentations, work together, and support for each other. Ms. Hamilton continued to learn from her students and be an activist in the community to improve the economic conditions for her students' families. She strongly believed that a high-quality education will contribute to the future well-being of her students and was committed to ensuring that they would be provided those educational opportunities in her classroom.

## Reflect and Apply

1. How do you think a student-centered classroom can contribute to the delivery of education that is multicultural?

2. How willing are you to figure out how to share power in the classroom with your students? Why or why not?

3. What steps do you plan to take to expand your knowledge about the cultural history and experiences of students from a racial, ethnic, or religious group that is different from your own?

# Summary

- Education that is multicultural respects the diversity of students and supports equity and social justice with the goal of helping students reach their academic, social, physical, and emotional potentials.

- The voices of students and the community are valued and validated in classrooms that are multicultural. Teachers should make an effort to know all of their students and build on their cultures to engage them actively in their own learning. An important teacher disposition is the belief that all students can learn. These teachers have high expectations for the academic performance of all students, and they care about them. Teachers with this belief do not give up on students. They take on the challenge of finding a way to help a struggling student learn a concept, solve a problem, and develop skills.

- Internationally, education is viewed as a basic human right. A positive school environment makes all students feel comfortable and valued and does not tolerate discrimination against students from different cultural groups. The hidden curriculum can have a negative impact on students who are not members of the dominant cultural group because the expected norms are not part of their cultural experiences. When teachers misread the cultural cues of students, racial, ethnic,

and class borders are created in the classroom. Positive teacher–student relationships can support academic achievement. Oral and nonverbal communication patterns between students and teachers can be analyzed and adjusted to increase the involvement of students in the learning process.

- A multicultural curriculum incorporates the cultures of the community and students in the classroom. Multicultural education starts where people are, builds on the histories and experiences of the community, and incorporates multicultural resources from the local community. Teachers introduce students to the social and historical realities of U.S. society. They help students gain a better understanding of the causes of oppression and inequality, including racism, classism, sexism, ableism, heterosexism, and ageism. In the process, students explore the roots of inequities and oppression and learn how to take action against them. Education that is multicultural can contribute to closing the opportunity gap among students by ensuring that all have access to qualified teachers, advanced curriculum, and culturally relevant, responsive, and sustaining pedagogy.

- By teaching social justice, teachers encourage students to think critically as they consider multiple perspectives and delve into topics and events that explore equity and inequities based on race, ethnicity, SES, gender, sexual orientation, exceptionalities, language, religion, place, and age. Students are encouraged to question the content of textbooks, news reports, movies, and other media as they develop their own knowledge bases and ideas. Teachers foster learning communities among students and establish democratic classrooms in which students are active participants in their own learning and in helping their peers learn.

- One of the first steps in becoming a multicultural educator is the examination and clarification of one's own cultural identity. In addition, teachers should become familiar with the cultures of other groups, especially those in the area in which they will be teaching. Multicultural teaching also requires continuous reflection on one's own teaching practice to determine what is working and what needs to be changed to help all students learn.

# Glossary

**Ableism** The belief that people without disabilities are normal and superior to people with physical or mental disabilities that leads to prejudice and/or discrimination against people with disabilities.

**Abolitionist teaching** Working inside and outside classrooms with communities of color to eliminate injustices that prevent many students from meeting their academic, physical, and social potentials.

**Accent** A distinctive way that an individual pronounces a word or a language.

**Accommodations** Changes in teaching, the classroom, or the school building that remove barriers that prevent students from learning and participating fully in the education process. Accommodations include ramps, texts with large print, audiobooks, more time to take a test, communication devices, and other assistive technologies as indicated in a student's IEP.

**Adultification** The process of treating a child or young person as an adult, denying them the protection, nurturing, comfort, and support that a child or young person is entitled.

**Adverse childhood experiences** Traumatic events experienced by children that can affect their brain development and their response to stress and lead to the development of chronic health problems and mental disorders. These traumatic experiences include exposure to abuse, pollutants, death, violence, and substance use.

**African American Language (AAL)** An umbrella term used to refer to the many varieties of language used in African American communities in the United States.

**African-centered education** Education that is centered on or derived from African history, culture, and values.

**Ageism** Prejudice or discrimination based on age, especially of young and older people.

**Agender** Refers to people who identify themselves as gender neutral, being neither man nor woman or a combination of the two.

**Agnostics** People who argue that we cannot know if a god or gods exist(s); they make no claims of belief nor disbelief in God.

**Alienation** Estrangement or disconnection from oneself or others.

**Ally** Someone who listens to, provides support to, and is an advocate for another individual or group, especially trans students, gender-nonconforming students, and other LGBTQI+ students.

**American Sign Language (ASL)** The predominant sign language of deaf communities in the United States and English-speaking Canada. It is natural language with the same linguistic properties as spoken languages, expressed with hand and facial movements.

**Americans with Disabilities Act (ADA)** 1990 law (Public Law 101-336) designed to end discrimination against individuals with disabilities in private-sector employment, public services, public accommodations, transportation, and telecommunications.

**Amnesty** A pardon for unauthorized immigrants who have been in the United States for a number of years and meet eligibility requirements that allow them to become legal residents and become U.S. citizens.

**Androcentric** A state of being dominated by men or masculine interests.

**Androgynous** The blending of masculine and feminine characteristics or qualities.

**Antiracism** To proactively and deliberately work to dismantle racism and promote equity in society and schools.

**Antiracist education** An education construct that focuses on the confrontation and elimination of racial and ethnic discrimination and racist practices in schools.

**Antisemitism** Hatred, hostility, prejudice, or discrimination against Jewish people.

**Asexual** A term used to describe individuals who do not experience sexual or romantic attraction to others.

**Assimilate** Process by which groups adopt or adapt to the dominant culture.

**Assimilation** Process by which groups adopt and contribute to the dominant culture.

**Asylees** Persons who travel to the United States from another country and request asylum or protection from being persecuted in their native country.

**Asylum** The protection granted people who have left their home countries because of past persecution or a well-founded fear of persecution based on race, ethnicity, religion, nationality, membership in a particular social group, or political opinion. These persons apply for asylum either at a port of entry or at some point after their entry into the United States.

**Asymmetric intelligibility** Speakers of one language are able to understand speakers of another, but cannot themselves be understood; speakers of Danish, for example, are better able to understand Swedish than vice versa.

**Atheists** People who do not believe in the existence of a god or gods.

**Authenticity** Relates the curriculum and activities to real-world applications with meaning in the lives of students.

**Being out** An indication that people have openly acknowledged that they are LGBTQ+ in one or more contexts or settings.

**Bible** The sacred text of the Christian religion that consists of the Old and New Testaments, which Christians believe is the written word of God.

**Bigender** Refers to people who express themselves as both man and woman or any two gender identities.

**Binge drinking** Excessive alcohol consumption in a short period of time.

**Biocapacity** The capacity of ecosystems to produce biological materials such as natural resources and to absorb waste material such as carbon dioxide that have been generated by human activity.

**Bisexual** Sexual attraction to people who identify as either men or women.

**Black English** An umbrella term used to refer to the many varieties of language used in African American communities in the United States.

**Black Muslims** Black people who identify as adherents of the Islam faith, which includes being a member of the Nation of Islam, a small sect of Islam.

**Blue laws** Laws preventing certain activities such as shopping on Sunday.

**Blue-collar** Jobs or workers characterized by manual labor that is often mechanical and routine.

**Born-again**   Christians who have had a conversion experience with a spiritual rebirth into a new life.

**Buddhism**   A major religion or philosophy, sometimes known as Buddha Dharma, that was founded in the fifth century BCE by Siddhartha Gautama in India, the original Buddha. Buddhism is not a religion in the common sense of believing in a Supreme being; it is a search for truth.

**Case law**   Published opinions of judges, which are used to interpret statutes, regulations, and constitutional provisions.

**Catechisms**   A systematic way of providing religious instruction through questions and answers about foundational religious doctrine.

**Catholic**   Person who follows the traditions and beliefs of the Roman Catholic Church, which is a Christian religion that follows the teachings of Jesus Christ.

**Charter schools**   Public schools that are exempt from many of the bureaucratic regulations of traditional public schools.

**Christianity**   A major world religion based on a belief in God and the life and teachings of Jesus of Nazareth as set forth in the Old and New Testaments of the Christian bible.

**Church of Jesus Christ of Latter-day Saints (LDS or Mormon)**   A Christian denomination that was founded by Joseph Smith in 1830 in the United States.

**Cisgender**   Refers to people whose biological sex is consistent with their gender identity.

**Civil rights**   The rights of personal liberty guaranteed by the Thirteenth and Fourteenth Amendments to the U.S. Constitution and by acts of Congress.

**Class**   A form of stratification in which people are sorted into groups that share the same or similar socioeconomic statuses, giving them different access to economic, political, cultural, and social resources.

**Classism**   The belief that a person's socioeconomic status determines their value in society and that more affluent people deserve a dominant role in society.

**Closed shops**   A requirement that a worker be a member of a union to be hired and continue employment.

**Code-switching**   Practice of alternating between two or more languages or language varieties (e.g., dialects) during the course of a single conversation.

**Collective bargaining**   Process in which representatives of a union negotiate wages, benefits, working conditions, and other aspects of a contract with an employer.

**Collective ownership**   Ownership by a group that is for the benefit of all members of the group.

**Colorblind**   A belief that racial group membership should not be taken into account, or even noticed, even though race is an important component of people's culture and identity and how they are treated in society.

**Come (or coming) out**   The act of an LGBTQ+ person acknowledging or disclosing their sexual or gender identity to themselves and others. Sometimes people "come out" at once to everyone in their lives, while at other times people only come out within trusted circles, such as family and/or close friends. It is typically described as a process, as LGBTQ+ people have to decide whether to come out, and how, every time they meet new people or change geographic or professional contexts.

**Compensatory education**   The provision of special services to students who have limited economic or educational advantages.

**Comprehension**   The ability to understand and make meaning of oral or written text.

**Connectedness**   A feeling that one belongs in a family, school, or community and among one's peers.

**Conservative Catholics**   Catholics who rigidly believe in the traditional teachings of the Catholic Church.

**Conservative Jews**   Jewish people, especially in North America, who preserve Jewish tradition and rituals but allow a more flexible interpretation of the law than Orthodox Judaism in its reflection of modern realities.

**Conservative Protestants**   Protestants who believe in the virgin birth of Jesus, the Bible being inerrant, and Jesus as the son of God as essential to salvation.

**Cooperative learning**   Teaching strategy for grouping students to work together on a project or activity to support and learn from each other.

**Couch surf**   Movement from one home to another for sleeping quarters, which often requires sleeping on the couch.

**Counternarratives**   Narratives or stories written or told from the vantage point of people who have been historically marginalized or oppressed by the dominant group.

**Creationism/creation science**   The term advocated by Conservative Protestants who support the teaching of the Biblical account of the beginning of humans on Earth.

**Critical consciousness**   The ability to identify, analyze, and solve real-world problems that have contributed to societal and educational inequities against marginalized people.

**Critical pedagogy**   Study of the impact of capitalism and discrimination on students from marginalized and oppressed groups.

**Critical race theory (CRT)**   An analysis of race and racism that challenges racial oppression, racial inequities, and White privilege in society.

**Critical thinking**   An effort to see an issue clearly and accurately to judge it fairly without a preset bias.

**Cultural borders**   A boundary between groups based on cultural differences that may limit an individual's understanding of persons from a different cultural background.

**Cultural capital**   Endowments such as academic competence, language competence, and wealth that provide an advantage to an individual, family, or group.

**Cultural competence**   The ability to interact and work with people from diverse cultures as a result of understanding and valuing other cultures and having developed cross-cultural skills that facilitate interactions.

**Cultural deficits**   View that the cultures of people of color, those with low incomes, and members of other oppressed groups are deficient in important ways from the cultures of the dominant group.

**Cultural pluralism**   The maintenance of different cultures in society as distinct and equal to the dominant culture in a society.

**Cultural relativism**   The principle that another person's culture can best be understood from the perspective of a member of that culture.

**Cultural wars**   Disagreements between groups about cultural and social beliefs over such issues as culture, equity, identity, race, ethnicity, gender, sexual orientation, abortion, and immigration. These disagreements have become lightning rods in the political arena leading to hundreds of bills in state legislatures about what can be taught in schools, use of bathrooms and locker rooms, and much more.

**Culturally deprived**   View that individuals or groups lack culturally stimulating experiences in their home environment.

**Culturally different**   View that the cultures of groups of people are equal but different because of their histories and experiences.

**Culturally relevant pedagogy**   A pedagogy that empowers students intellectually, socially, emotionally, and politically by building on their cultural background and helping them develop a sociopolitical consciousness.

**Culturally responsive teaching** A pedagogy that affirms the cultures of students, views their cultures and experiences as strengths, and reflects the students' cultures in the teaching process to situate knowledge and skills within their lived experiences.

**Culturally sustaining pedagogies** A pedagogy that values, perpetuates, promotes, and supports the home cultures of students throughout the curriculum, instructional practices, and classroom climate.

**Culture** The socially transmitted values, traditions, and ways of thinking, believing, feeling, and behaving within a group that has a shared history and life experiences.

**Culture wars** Cultural conflicts between different social or political groups that are often based in stark differences in opinion on historically controversial topics.

**Curriculum** A sequence of courses offered by educational institutions.

***De facto* segregation** Separation of people by race that occurs as a result of economic, social, or other circumstances rather than laws or policies that require segregation.

***De jure* segregation** Government-mandated separation of people by race.

**Dechurched** People who used to attend church services at least once a month in the past and now attend less than once a year.

**Deeper learning** Challenging academic content and learning experiences that help students develop the skills to find, analyze, and apply knowledge in new and emerging contexts and situations.

**Deism** Belief in the existence of a supreme being or creator who does not intervene in the universe. The term was part of an intellectual movement in the seventeen and eighteenth centuries.

**Demisexual** A term used to describe individuals who only experience sexual attraction once they have formed deep emotional connections with another person.

**Democratic classrooms** Learning environments that promote values such as inclusion, voice, and representation and in which students are empowered to share decision making with classmates and the teacher.

**Detracking** Eliminating classes and programs that segregate students based on academic ability as determined by standardized tests or teachers' perceptions.

**Developing countries** Countries that have lower per capita income, greater poverty, and much less capital development than the nations that wield global economic power such as the United States, Japan, and most European countries.

**Dialect** A particular form of a language that is unique to a specific social group or region of the country.

**Dialogic** Communication in the form of conversation or dialogue between two or more people.

**Dialogic pedagogy** A teaching strategy in which teachers and pupils critically interrogate the topic of study, express and listen to multiple voices and points of view, and create respectful and equitable classroom relations.

**Differentiated instruction** Teaching in different ways to meet the needs of students based on their learning needs, learning preferences, interests, cultural backgrounds, and readiness of each student.

**Digital divide** The gap between people who do not have access to computers or the Internet and those who do have access.

**Digital equity** Condition that allows all individuals and communities to have access to technology needed for full participation in education and society.

**Digital inequity** See *digital divide.*

**Disability identity** A positive sense of self that includes one's disability and feelings of connection to the disability community.

**Discrimination** The arbitrary denial of the privileges and rewards of society to individuals or members of specific groups.

**Dispositions** Values, attitudes, and commitments that guide the work of teachers and other school professionals.

**Dog-whistle** The use of coded or suggestive language using terms or phrases that have a secondary meaning intended to be understood by a particular group of people for the purpose of gaining political support. Dog whistles are often used to hide feelings of racism or hatred against people of color or people with low incomes.

**Dominant culture** The culture whose values and behaviors have been adopted by most institutions in society, including schools. In the United States, it is the middle-class, White, English-speaking, heterosexual Christian culture with its historical roots in Europe. *Dominant culture* and *dominant group* are used interchangeably.

**Doxing** The publication of addresses and contact information of individuals for the purposes of harassment; most often occurs on social media websites.

**Drag queens** Performance artists who adopt or use exaggerated personalities and performative femininity for the purposes of on-stage entertainment. Historically, many drag queens also identified as gay men; however, people of any sexual orientation and gender can be drag queens. During the 1960s and onward, they were often the most visible members of the LGBTQ+ community.

**Dual-language immersion (DLI)** Educational programs that co-enroll English-proficient and English-learning students in which all academic instruction is conducted in both English and a second language. The goal of DLI programs is for students to achieve functional biliteracy in both languages.

**Dynamic** Something that changes over time; not fixed or static.

**Ecological footprint** The measure of Earth's resources required to maintain one's lifestyle.

**Education for All Handicapped Children Act** Passed into law in 1975, also known as Public Law 94-142, provides a free, appropriate public education for all children with disabilities in the least-restrictive environment.

**Education gag orders** Legislation, policies, or practices that restrict teaching and training in K–12 schools, higher education, and other institutions on race, ethnicity, racism, gender, sexuality, and other issues that some people consider "divisive."

**Emergent bilinguals** People who are in the process of becoming bilingual; often used to refer to students who are fluent in a language other than English and in the process of learning English.

**Enculturation** Process of acquiring the characteristics of a given culture and becoming competent in its language and ways of behaving and learning.

**Endogamy** Marriage within the same racial, ethnic, cultural, or religious group.

**English as a Second Language (ESL)** Programs that focus on the teaching of English, with the goal of rapidly assimilating English learners into mainstream, English-dominant classrooms. Instruction in these programs is typically conducted exclusively in English.

**English language learner (ELL) or English learner (EL)** Students who have limited or no English skills and are in the process of learning English. Although this label is still used by some states and federal agencies, it is increasingly being replaced by the term "emergent bilingual" to avoid portraying students through a deficit lens.

**English Only movement**   A political movement seeking to limit bilingual education and make English the official language of the United States.

**Environmental justice**   A social and scientific movement that calls for all people and communities to have the right to equal environmental protection under the law and the right to live, work, and play in communities that are safe, healthy, and free of life-threatening conditions.

**Equality**   The belief in social, political, and economic rights for all people. The state of being equal is one in which a cultural group is not viewed or treated as inferior or superior to another and all groups have access to the same rights and benefits of society regardless of their group memberships.

**Equity**   Fairness and justice that are applied in a way that recognizes and responds to the individual needs of people, providing greater resources to the people who have the greatest need and removing barriers that limit their ability to meet their full potential.

**Ethnic**   Belonging to a group whose members share a common culture based on the national origin of one's ancestors.

**Ethnic group**   A community or population of people who share a common culture based on the national origin of their ancestors.

**Ethnic identity**   People's sense of belonging to a group based on the national origin of their ancestors.

**Ethnicity**   Group membership based on the national origin of one's ancestors.

**Ethnocentrism**   The belief that one's racial, ethnic, or cultural group is superior to all other groups and deserves dominance in society.

**Eugenics**   The belief in and study of improving human qualities through genetics and breeding of desirable hereditary traits. Early supporters of eugenics believed that social problems such as mental illness, criminal tendencies, and poverty could be eliminated, leading to the involuntary sterilization of people with disabilities and others in the twentieth century.

**Evangelical Christians**   Conservative Christians who fall under a broad umbrella. Some are considered more moderate within the group and focus on social action agendas in addition to their religious agenda. Another group tends to be more conservative and focuses on issues such as an antiabortion, anti-immigrant, and antigay agenda. Evangelicals generally agree on three areas: (1) one must have a "born-again" conversion experience, (2) one must encourage others to believe in Jesus Christ as the son of God, and (3) the Bible is the actual word of God.

**Extreme poverty**   Family income below one-half of the federal poverty threshold in the United States, which makes it difficult for people to meet basic needs of subsistence. In developing nations, the poverty level is much lower than in the United States based on the country's economy, resulting in people not having enough money to meet their basic needs.

**Femininities**   Attributes, behaviors, and roles generally associated with women and girls within a given society. Multiple types of femininity exist in U.S. society.

**Feminists**   Persons who actively support the rights of women.

**First Americans**   Indigenous people who have populated the land now known as the United States for thousands of years; also identified in this book as Native Americans or American Indians.

**Fluency**   The ability to read or understand spoken words accurately and quickly

**Fluent**   The ability to read, communicate orally, and write using the conventions of that language in a wide variety of personal, academic, and professional settings.

**Freedom**   Not being unduly hampered or constrained by other people or institutions in our choices or actions.

**Full inclusion**   Serving students with disabilities entirely within the general classroom. This is an important difference from inclusion, as students in full inclusion do not receive any of their education in segregated settings.

**Fundamentalist**   Conservative Christians who advocate the teaching of creation as presented in the Bible as opposed to the theory of evolution. There are many different groups of fundamentalist Christians. Each has its own unique set of differences that sets it apart from other groups.

**Funds of knowledge**   The knowledge and skills that people develop within their culture and lived experiences in their families and communities.

**Gay**   A term most often used for men who are romantically or sexually attracted to other men. The term is sometimes used to refer to both gay men and lesbians.

**Gay–straight alliances (GSAs)**   School-based groups that bring together members of LGBTQ+ and ally communities with the goal of promoting LGBTQ+ rights, inclusion, and equality.

**Gender**   The socially and culturally constructed traits and perceptions of being a man or a woman or transgender or nonbinary person.

**Gender affirmation**   A range of actions and possibilities for living, surviving, and thriving in one's authentic gender that could involve social, psychological, and medical interventions.

**Gender and sexuality alliances (GSAs)**   Student-initiated clubs of LGBTQ+ and straight students that provide a safe place for students to discuss issues related to sexual orientation and gender diversity and support others with similar interests.

**Gender conscious**   Affirmation that gender is a crucial identity that affects students' lives but should not limit their participation in the classroom and society.

**Gender discrimination**   Action in which an individual or group of people is denied opportunities, privileges, or benefits based on their sex or their gender identity.

**Gender expression**   People's presentation of themselves to others by the way they communicate characteristics such as their attire, voice, hairstyle, body characteristics, and general behavior.

**Gender fluid**   Refers to people who do not identify themselves as a man, a woman, or any other fixed gender.

**Gender harassment**   Unwanted and unwelcome sexual behavior against people who are gender nonconforming that includes verbal, visual, or physical abuse that interferes with the victim's life.

**Gender identity**   People's deeply held sense of self and their view of themselves as a man or a woman or transgender or nonbinary person.

**Gender reassignment**   The process by which people change their physical characteristics through surgery and/or hormone treatment.

**Gender rules**   The social stereotypical expectations for how men and women should speak, dress, groom, and behave in a society.

**Gender-nonconforming**   Gender expression that is not within the socially constructed gender binary of men/women.

**Genderqueer**   Refers to people who do not identify themselves as part of the men/women binary or identify themselves as neither.

**Generation Alpha**   The demographic cohort born between 2010 and 2025/2029.

**Generation Z**   The demographic cohort born between 1996 and 2010, sometimes referred to as *iGen*.

**Gifted and talented**   Students with very high intelligence or unusual gifts and talents in academics, the arts, and other specialty fields that require special educational programming to reach their full potential.

**Gig work**   Work that individuals do as independent contractors or freelancers for a company or individual that has hired them to complete a specific project.

**Globalization**   System that connects countries economically, politically, environmentally, and culturally through a global economy supported by free trade, international corporations, and worldwide labor markets.

**Hate**   An intense or passionate hostility toward another person or group that can result in discrimination, bullying, and/or violence.

**Hate crimes**   Acts of physical, digital, verbal, or other violence that are motivated by an offender's bias(es) against a victim's race, ethnicity, religion, sexual orientation, gender, gender identity, or disability.

**Heteroglossic ideology**   Belief in the value of linguistic diversity and multilingualism.

**Heteronormativity**   The assumption that heterosexuality is normal or the "default" and that any other sexual identity is abnormal. In schools, this often leads to the exclusion or erasure of LGBTQ+ communities.

**Heterosexism**   Discrimination or prejudice against non-heterosexual people based on the assumption that heterosexuality is normal and superior to LGBTQ+ identity.

**Heterosexual**   A term used by men who are exclusively attracted to women and women who are exclusively attracted to men.

**Hidden curriculum**   Unwritten and informal rules that guide the behaviors and attitudes expected of students in school.

**High-context cultures**   A term used to describe cultures in which nonverbal cues, facial expressions, and tone are as or more important than the specific words used in communication.

**High-poverty schools**   Schools in which at least 75% of the students in a school are eligible for free or reduced-price lunch.

**High-risk behaviors**   Acts that make young people more vulnerable to physical, social, or psychological harm or negative outcomes.

**Hijabs**   A covering for the hair and neck that sometimes covers the face and is worn by some Muslim women.

**Hinduism**   A major religion and culture that originated in India before 1500 BCE. It includes multiple perspectives of religious truths and affirms tolerance as a religious virtue.

**HIV/AIDS**   Human immunodeficiency virus and acquired immunodeficiency syndrome. The virus HIV attacks cells that help fight infection and is spread through bodily fluids shared during unprotected sex or the use of infected needles. AIDS is the resulting disease if HIV is not treated, which leads to a badly damaged immune system.

**Homophobia**   Irrational beliefs, attitudes, behaviors, and systems that hurt or deny the existence of LGBTQ+ people.

**Homophobic**   An adjective to describe individuals, groups, or policies that exhibit irrational beliefs, attitudes, and behaviors that hurt or deny the existence of LGBTQ+ people.

**Human geography**   Study of the economic, social, and cultural systems that have evolved in a specific location.

**Identity**   Definitions of ourselves in relation to ourselves, others, and our cultural worlds. Our identity includes our membership in social groups such as race, ethnicity, class, and gender.

**Immigration**   Process for entering a country in which one was not born for the purpose of becoming a permanent resident.

**Implicit racial biases**   Negative attitudes and stereotypes about people of color that are held unconsciously by people.

**Inclusion**   The placement of students receiving special education services in general education settings; see also *full inclusion*.

**Income**   Amount of money earned in wages or salaries.

**Indentured servants**   People who are contracted with their employers to work without pay for a specific period of time as they serve as an apprentice to learn a trade or work to pay the employer the cost for traveling to the U.S.

**Indigenous**   Population that is native to a country or region. In the United States, Native Americans, Hawaiians, and Alaska Natives are Indigenous populations.

**Individualism**   Primary feature of the dominant culture in the United States that stresses the rights, freedom, and importance of the individual over groups.

**Individualized education program (IEP)**   A written program required for all children with disabilities under IDEA. It includes statements concerning the student's present performance, annual goals, short-term objectives, specific educational services needed, relevant dates, participation in regular education, and evaluation procedures. Parents should participate in the development of the IEP and sign the document.

**Individuals with Disabilities Education Act (IDEA)**   Public Law 101-476, which emphasizes the individual over the disability, forever changing how those with disabilities are referred to in the literature (e.g., "students with mental disabilities" took the place of "mentally retarded students").

**Individuals with Disabilities Education Improvement Act (P.L. 108-446)**   Passed in 2004 and sometimes referred to as IDEA 2004, this law added new language about "academic and functional goals." IEPs are required to include "a statement of measurable annual goals," including academic and functional goals.

**Inequality**   Uneven distribution of resources such as income, wealth, educational achievement, educational credentials, and power among people and groups of people.

**Inequitable funding**   Disparities in the financial support for schools that results in higher per-pupil support for students who live in affluent communities compared to those who live in low-income communities. Students who are most affected by underresourced schools are those from low-income families, students experiencing homelessness, those in foster care, students of color, and those with disabilities.

**Intellectual disabilities**   Impaired intellectual functioning with limited adaptive behavior; also referred to as "cognitive disabilities."

**Intelligent design**   A theory that only an intelligent being could have created a natural world so complex and well ordered as ours. Some if not most supporters of evolution theory view this as a new term for creationism or creation science.

**Intergender**   A nonbinary identity that results from contradictory biological evidence about being men or women; it is a term that is sometimes used by intersex individuals.

**Intergenerational income mobility**   The relationship of the income and social status of parents to the income and social status their children will achieve as adults. In other words, will children earn the same, more, or less income and social status than their parents when the children become adults?

**International migration**   Moving from one country to another.

**Interregional migration**   Migration for short distances in which the individuals remain in the same country.

**Intersectionality**   The interaction of race, ethnicity, class, gender, and sexual orientation in determining one's identity and the resulting privileges and/or forms of oppression based on that interaction.

**Intersex**   A person who is born with reproductive or sexual anatomy that is not typical for men or women.

**Involuntary immigrants**   Immigrants who were forced to immigrate through enslavement or being in a region or country when it was acquired through war or annexation.

**Islam**   A major world religion based on a belief in Allah as revealed through the teachings of the prophet Muhammad as set forth in the sacred text of the Qur'an.

**Islamophobia**   The fear, hatred, or distrust of Muslims that often leads to discrimination and hostility.

**Isms**   An oppressive and discriminatory attitude or belief about a specific group that is expressed as racism, sexism, heterosexism, classism, and so on.

**Jim Crow laws**   State and local laws that legalized racial segregation, including the sharing of public accommodations by persons of color and White people.

**Judaism**   The religion developed among ancient Hebrews that is characterized by a belief in one transcendent God who revealed himself to Abraham, Moses, and the Hebrew prophets and is practiced in accordance with Scriptures and rabbinic traditions.

**Karma**   A sum of an individual's action that leads to cause and effect. According to Hindu philosophy, every action (*karma*) such as thoughts, words, and choices has a reaction or outcome. The positive or negative outcome of one's actions may be experienced immediately, later in life, or in the afterlife.

**Kosher**   Usually refers to food prepared in accordance to Jewish dietary laws.

**Language**   A system of vocal sounds, gestures, and symbols through which people communicate with one another

**Languaging**   The process of actively using language in a given context or situation.

**Least-restrictive environment (LRE)**   The educational setting closest to a regular school or general education setting in which the child with a disability can be educated. For many children, this may mean a general education classroom. Others may require a less inclusive setting to best meet their needs.

**Lesbian**   A term most often used to describe women who are romantically or sexually attracted to other women.

**LGBTQ+ community**   Lesbian, gay, bisexual, transgender, queer/questioning, and other gender-nonconforming people.

**Linguistic repertoire**   Mental collection of linguistic skills, knowledge, and resources.

**Living wage**   A wage that is high enough to meet basic needs such as food, housing, clothing, and transportation to support a decent standard of living in the community in which one lives.

**Long-term English learners (LTELs)**   English learners who enroll for the first time in middle or high school and take longer than the usual time to complete their graduation requirements.

**Low-context cultures**   A term used to describe cultures that prioritize direct, linear communication and place more emphasis on the precise meaning of words than on the context, nonverbal cues, facial expressions, and tone that accompany them.

**Magnet schools**   Schools in which the curriculum emphasizes a particular subject or field, such as performing arts or mathematics and science. Generally, students from anywhere in a school district can apply to attend these schools.

**Mainline Protestants**   People who view Christianity in ways meaningful in a world of science and continual change. They stress the right of the individual to determine what is true in religion. They may or may not believe in the virgin birth of Jesus and may or may not believe the Bible to be inerrant. It includes United Methodists, Evangelical Lutherans, Presbyterians, Episcopalians, American Baptists, United Church of Christ, and the Christian Church.

**Manifest destiny**   Policy in which a nation or culture believes itself superior to all others and believes that it is destined to rule over other nations and cultures.

**Marginalization**   Relegation to an insignificant or unimportant position in society.

**Marginalized**   People who have not been allowed to enjoy the benefits of society because of discriminatory policies and practices that limit or make it difficult to access those benefits due to their race, ethnicity, socioeconomic status, gender, or other identities.

**Martial law**   Temporary control *by the military over civilian* rule of a city, state, or other area that may occur *in an emergency such as natural disaster or rebellion.*

**Masculinities**   Attributes, behaviors, and roles generally associated with men and boys within a given society. Multiple types of masculinity exist in U.S. society.

**McKinney-Vento Homeless Assistance Act**   The federal legislation that outlines the education rights and protections for children and youth experiencing homelessness.

**Meaningful projects**   Student projects that address equity, democratic, and social justice issues in the students' communities.

**Median income**   The income at which an equal number of persons, families, or households earn more than this income and less than this income.

**Mental health disorders**   Clinically significant behavioral or psychological disturbances in a person's cognition, emotional regulation, or behavior. Common mental disorders are depression, anxiety, bipolar disorder, and eating disorders.

**Meritocracy**   A system based on the belief that an individual's achievements are based on their own personal merits and hard work and that the people who achieve at the highest levels deserve the greatest social and financial rewards.

**Metropolitan areas**   An urban core area of at least 5,000 people that includes the adjacent counties with which the core area has a high degree of social and economic integration as measured through commuting ties.

**Microaggressions**   Everyday comments or actions that are subtle, intentional and unintentional, negative or insensitive putdowns of a member of a marginalized group.

**Middle class**   Group whose members are blue-collar workers, white-collar workers, professionals, and managers whose annual household income is between 2/3 and 200% of the national median income.

**Middle Passage**   The forced journey by ship in which enslaved Africans were moved from West Africa to the New World during the transatlantic trade period.

**Migration**   Temporary or permanent settling of people to a new location.

**Millennials**   Another name for the demographic cohort born between 1980 and 1995, sometimes referred to as *Generation Y* or the *Me generation.*

**Miscegenation**   Marriage between persons of different races.

**Misogyny**   Hatred of, contempt for, or deep-rooted prejudice against women.

**Modifications**   Adjustments to instruction and assessments for students with disabilities, English learners, and students who are performing above or below grade level to support their learning; they include different types of assignments, tests, and resources to meet the needs of students based on their exceptionalities.

**Moksha**   The Hinduist liberation from the cycle of life, death, and rebirth after the soul has been enlightened following death.

**Monoglossic ideology**   Belief that monolingualism is and should be the norm.

**Monolingual**   Able to communicate in one language only.

**Moral panic**  Widespread feeling of fear, based on false or exaggerated perceptions, that a group of people are dangerous and pose a threat to the values and well-being of a community or society.

**Multi-tiered system of supports (MTSS)**  Framework used by many schools to identify struggling students and provide intervention strategies to support them.

**Multicultural curriculum**  Academic content that has integrated knowledge and skills related to the histories and experiences of students, their families, and communities, including the sociopolitical study of race, ethnicity, class, gender, and other student identities and their intersections, for the purposes of inclusion and making the content meaningful to students.

**Multicultural education**  An educational construct built on the ideals of freedom, social justice, equality, equity, and human dignity. It incorporates the history and experiences of diverse cultural groups throughout the curriculum and supports the elimination of discriminatory practices based on race, ethnicity, socioeconomic status, sex, gender identity, sexual orientation, religion, language, and disability from classrooms and schools.

**Multiculturalism**  The presence of multiple cultural groups who maintain their unique cultural identities while participating equally in the dominant culture.

**Multilingual learners**  People who speak and use multiple named languages.

**Multilingualism**  The ability to speak more than one language.

**Muslim**  A person who believes and follows Islam.

**Mutual intelligibility**  The ability of people to understand one another.

**Named language**  A socially and politically constructed set of linguistic features that are commonly considered part of a single, official language (such as English or Farsi). The term is used to emphasize that boundaries between languages are socially and politically defined, not innate or lexical in nature.

**Nation of Islam**  A religious and political organization founded by Wallace Fard Muhammad in 1930 in Detroit, Michigan, that combined elements of traditional Islam with Black nationalist ideas and promoted racial unity and self-help.

**Nativism**  Policy favoring assimilated ethnic groups in a country over new immigrants.

**Nativist**  Related to beliefs of the superiority of the native-born population of a country over immigrants, leading to policies that protect and favor the native-born population.

**Naturalized citizenship**  Immigrants age 18 and over who have become U.S. citizens.

**Net worth**  Amount of money remaining if all owned property was converted to cash and all debts were paid.

**Nirvana**  State of existence in Buddhism beyond space, time, and definition after the conditions of samsara (i.e., the cycle of birth, death, and rebirth) and dukkha (suffering) have been extinguished.

**Nonbinary**  Refers to people who do not identify as men, women, or a mix of genders; instead, they identify as not having a gender.

**Nonmetro areas**  Cities with populations between 5,000 and 50,000 that are not part of larger labor market or metropolitan areas.

**Nonverbal communication**  Interpersonal interactions that do not rely on words; may include gestures, tone, expressions, or proximity.

**Nordic race**  Germanic people of northern Europe who are White with a tall stature, long head, light skin and hair, and blue eyes.

**Normalization**  Making available to all persons with disabilities patterns of life and conditions of everyday living that are as close as possible to—or, indeed, the same as—the regular circumstances and ways of life of society.

**Not-self**  A Buddhist concept in which a person is not attached to the permanence of any phenomenon, including self, which is always changing.

**Official English**  A position supported by U.S. English, a citizens' action group that is seeking to have English declared the official language of the United States by Congress. Individuals who support this movement believe that all public documents, records, legislation, and regulations as well as hearings, official ceremonies, and public meetings should be conducted solely in English.

**Opioid**  A class of drugs that includes the illegal drug heroin, synthetic opioids such as fentanyl, and pain relievers available legally by prescription such as oxycodone (OxyContin), hydrocodone (Vicodin), codeine, and morphine.

**Opportunity gap**  Circumstances that make it difficult for many students of color and those from low-income families to achieve academically and socially at the same levels as other students. These circumstances include factors such as impoverishment, lack of funds to participate in enhancement educational and sports programs, and attendance at poorly funded and low-quality schools.

**Oppressed groups**  Groups that have limited or no power in society, are subordinate to another group, or have been marginalized or silenced.

**Ordain**  Officially recognize a person a priest, minister, or other member of the clergy in a religious ceremony.

**Orthodox Churches**  Christian groups in Eastern Europe, the Balkan States, and Russia that were established after the Great Schism when Orthodox Churches separated from the Roman Catholic Church during the first century CE.

**Orthodox Jews**  Jewish people who practice a form of Judaism based on the strict observance of Jewish laws and customs.

**Overshoot day**  The date on which humanity's demand for ecological resources and services in a given year exceeds Earth's biocapacity or the resources that can be regenerated during that year.

**Pan-ethnic**  Grouping of people in or from countries within a continent together as a single entity such as Asian, African, European, or North American people or grouping people based on their language or culture such as Hispanics or Latino/as.

**Pansexual**  A term to describe people who are romantically or sexually attracted to people of multiple genders.

**Patriarchal**  Social organization in which the father controls the family and the wife and children are legally dependent on him. It also refers to men having a disproportionately large share of power in society.

**Phonemic awareness**  The ability to identify the sounds that make up words.

**Phonics**  The ability to connect written letters or combinations of letters to their sounds.

**Physical geography**  Study of the physical features of the earth such as the climate, soils, vegetation, water, and landforms.

**Plurilingual and intercultural education**  An educational approach that focuses on the holistic nature of language, especially in contexts where many people are multilingual or draw on elements of multiple languages/varieties when communicating.

**Polars**  Another term for the demographic cohort born between 2010 and 2025/2029, also known as *Generation Alpha*.

**Popular cultures**  Set of ideas, objects, and entertainment that is broadly shared by many people.

**Poverty**  The state of not having enough money and other resources to meet the basic necessities of life, such as food, clothing, health care, and clean, safe, and appropriate housing.

**Poverty line**   The amount of money that the federal government sets as the threshold for determining whether a person has enough money to cover basic needs. The amount is based on the number of people in a household and is used to determine whether a person is eligible for specific government services such as the Supplemental Nutrition Assistance Program (SNAP; formerly known as the Food Stamp Program) and free or reduced-price lunch at school.

**Power**   The control, authority, or influence over others, especially members of oppressed groups.

**Prejudice**   Preconceived positive or negative notions about a person or group of people that is based on limited or inaccurate information.

**Privilege**   Advantages and power over others in society as a result of one's socioeconomic status, race, ethnicity, native language, gender, or other group memberships.

**Proficiencies**   Specific knowledge, skills, or dispositions that students or teachers acquire.

**Project based**   A teaching approach in which students learn by actively engaging in real-world and personally meaningful projects to build their knowledge, creative capacity, and problem-solving skills.

**Proposition 8**   A California ballot initiative passed in 2008 that eliminated the rights of same-sex couples to marry. The initiative was later found unconstitutional and repealed.

**Protestantism**   One of the major branches of Christianity that began in northern Europe in the early sixteenth century by theologian Martin Luther and other Christians who opposed the medieval doctrines and practices of the Roman Catholic Church.

**Proxemics**   The ways people move within and use space, offering a helpful lens through which to think about nonverbal classroom communication.

**Pygmalion effect**   See *self-fulfilling prophecy*.

**QAnon**   A conspiracy theory and political movement that emerged in 2017, declaring that the world is controlled by the "Deep State," a secret cabal of Satan-worshiping liberal elites who traffic, sexually abuse, and cannibalize young children.

**Queer**   A term used by LGBTQ+ communities and individuals to describe their identities; a broad umbrella term that includes individuals from the varied and diverse sexual orientations and gender identities within the LGBTQ+ community.

**Questioning**   Curious, uncertain about, or not ready to label one's sexual orientation.

**Qur'an (or Koran)**   The sacred text of Islam that Muslims believe was revealed by God to the Prophet Muhammad by the Angel Gabriel.

**Race**   A social construct for arbitrarily categorizing people based on the color of their skin and ancestry.

**Racial identity**   People's sense of belonging to a group based on the race(s) of their parents.

**Racism**   The belief that one race is inherently superior to other races and thereby deserving of opportunities and benefits in society to which other races do not have access.

**Reclassified**   A student who has been formally moved from the designation of "English learner" to "English proficient."

**Redlining**   A discriminatory practice of denying or limiting financial services to people in specific geographic areas inhabited by low-income and people of color without regard to the residents' qualifications or creditworthiness.

**Reform Jews**   Jewish people who practice a form of Judaism that is also known as Liberal or Progressive Judaism in which members adapt the Bible and laws of the oral Torah to contemporary moral ideals, emphasizing themes such as social justice.

**Refugees**   Persons and their relatives outside the United States who are recognized by the U.S. government as being persecuted or subject to persecution in their home country because of race, ethnicity, religion, nationality, or membership in a specific social or political group.

**Religion**   An inner core of belief in and worship of a superhuman power or powers such as a God or gods who is/are believed to be divine or have control of human destiny.

**Remittances**   Funds sent back to the home country or families by international migrants.

**Resilient**   Being able to withstand or adapt well after adversity, trauma, or other significant sources of stress.

**Response to intervention (RTI)**   A multi-tiered pre-referral method involving increasingly intensive interventions. Usually associated with learning disabilities, it has the primary aim of providing intervention to students who are not achieving at comparable rates with their peers.

**Restorative justice**   A cooperative approach that involves educators, parents, and students who have been punished or suspended to repair the harm that was done and restore students' relationships in the school with a focus on the student taking responsibility for actions and the adults providing support for the student in the process.

**Restrictionists**   People, political groups, think tanks, or other groups that support reducing legal immigration and getting tough on unauthorized immigration.

**Right-to-work**   Laws that prohibit workers in a state from being forced to join a union or pay union fees.

**Rituals**   Repetitive and patterned behavior that is prescribed by or tied to religious traditions, beliefs, or customs.

**Rural areas**   Parts of the country that are open countryside that may include rural towns of fewer than 5,000 people.

**Safe zones/safe spaces**   Spaces or programs where educators "come out" as allies and advocates for LGBTQ+ students, typically in schools or other educational contexts.

**School connectedness**   Students' feeling that teachers and other adults in their school care not only about their learning but also about them as individuals.

**School vouchers**   Government-funded redemptions toward tuition or fees at a school other than the public school that a student could attend at no cost.

**Second Coming**   The belief that Jesus Christ will return to Earth to judge humanity at the end of the world.

**Section 504 of Public Law 93-112**   Part of the Rehabilitation Act of 1973 designed as a counterpart law for individuals with disabilities to the Civil Rights Act of 1964. It requires reasonable accommodations for those with disabilities and prohibits the denial of participation in any program receiving federal funds solely on the basis of one's disability.

**Secular**   Attitudes or activities, including the educational curriculum, that have no connection to religious or spiritual matters.

**Segregation**   The act or process of separating people in different residential areas, schools, jobs, clubs, and other social settings based on their race, ethnicity, SES, gender, or other identities.

**Segregation index**   A scale of 0 to 100 that measures the degree of which two different groups (such as White and Black populations) are unequally distributed across neighborhoods.

**Segregationists**   People who advocate for policies and practices that enforce the belief that people from different races should not live in the same neighborhoods, attend the same schools, or have the same access to the benefits of society.

**Self-actualization** The fulfillment of one's talents or potential.

**Self-fulfilling prophecy** A prediction of a student's academic achievement that becomes true as the student progresses through the education process. These projections are sometimes based on socioeconomic, social, and cultural factors that lead to placement in an academic track that may or may not match a student's actual academic potential.

**Seventh Generation Principle** A core value of some Indigenous peoples that emphasizes the importance of being good caretakers of earth not just for themselves, but for the people who come seven generations after them.

**Sex** Identification as man, woman, or intersex, which is assigned at birth based on people's reproductive organs and structures.

**Sexism** The belief that men are superior to and more valuable than women, which leads to prejudice and/or discrimination based on sex, typically against girls and women.

**Sexual abuse** Unwelcome sexual activity that occurs without consent. It results in emotional and/or physical damage to the victim of the abuse.

**Sexual harassment** Unwanted and unwelcome sexual behavior against women or men that includes verbal, visual, or physical abuse that interferes with the victim's life.

**Sexual orientation** A term used to describe one's identity as a romantic and sexual being.

**Sexually transmitted infection (STI)** Infections that are passed from one person to another person through unprotected sexual contact.

**Sheltered English immersion** An approach to English language instruction in which nearly all instruction is in English but where temporary curricular and pedagogical supports are provided to language learners. These programs typically emphasize academic vocabulary in English and are designed to rapidly transition students to English-only content learning.

**Shi'a Muslims (Shi'ites)** Adherents to Islam who believe that Muhammad intended the succession of leadership to pass through the bloodline of his cousin and son-in-law, Ali.

**Signed English** A system that translates an English oral or written word into a nonverbal sign. Signed English is distinct from other signed languages, such as American Sign Language, which have unique vocabulary, syntax, and grammatical rules.

**Social justice** A philosophical concept that promotes fairness, supports economic and political equality, and respects the basic human rights of all people.

**Social mobility** The movement of people, families, or households from one social economic level to another. For example, an individual moves from low-income to middle-class status.

**Social-emotional learning (SEL)** The process through which children and young people develop self-awareness and healthy identities, manage their emotions, acquire interpersonal skills that support relationships, show empathy, and make responsible and caring decisions.

**Socialization** Process of learning the social norms and expectations of a culture and society.

**Socioeconomic status (SES)** Composite of the economic status of families or persons on the basis of occupation, educational attainment, income, wealth, and power.

**Sovereignty** The authority of an entity to govern itself. Tribal sovereignty refers to the right of Native Americans, Alaska Natives, and Native Hawaiians to govern themselves.

**Spiritual** Related to the human spirit or soul as opposed to material or physical things.

**Standard English** The English spoken by a particular group of individuals in a community. This group is typically professional, educated, and privileged, with a high degree of influence and prestige in the community.

**Stereotype threat theory** A situation in which people from a marginalized group are apprehensive about conforming to negative stereotypes about the performance of their group to the degree that their actual performance is negatively affected.

**Stereotyped** Application of generalizations, many of which are inaccurate and negative, about a group without consideration of individual differences within the group.

**Stereotypes** Exaggerated and usually biased generalizations and views of a group of people.

**Stonewall Riots (Stonewall Uprising)** A turning point in the movement for LGBTQ+ rights when, in 1969, the LGBTQ+ community and allies fought police efforts to forcibly remove them from the Stonewall Inn. The movement garnered national attention and inspired other demonstrations and demands for LGBTQ+ rights and equality.

**Straight** A slang or casual term for heterosexual.

**Structural assimilation** The acceptance of individuals and groups by the dominant group to the point that they share primary relationships, intermarry, and have equality with the dominant group.

**Student-centered approach** A teaching strategy that focuses on creating connections with the needs, abilities, interests, and learning preferences of students to make learning more meaningful to them and involve them more directly in decision-making regarding their learning.

**Students of color** Children and youth who are Black or African American, Alaska Native, Asian American, Latinx, Native American or Pacific Islander.

**Subcultures** Groups within a society that are connected to cultural group memberships based on gender, sexual orientation, race, ethnicity, socioeconomic status, religion, exceptionalities, language, age, and other identities.

**Subsistence living** Minimal resources such as food, water, and shelter for an individual to survive.

**Subsocieties** Groups within a society such as punks, gangs, skinheads, or hippies that have developed their own values, attitudes, and behaviors that are different from the norm and are often not acceptable to the dominant cultural group.

**Substance use disorder** The use of banned or illegal drugs and substances or the overuse of legal substances.

**Suburbs** Communities that surround a city and are home to many of the city's workers.

**Sunni Muslims** Adherents to Islam who comprise 85% of the religious group and believe that the rightful leadership of the Muslims began with Abu Bakr and that the succession has passed to caliphs, or political leaders.

**Superfund sites** The most contaminated toxic waste sites in the country that have been identified by the U.S. Environmental Protection Agency for cleanup. These sites are due to hazardous waste being dumped, left out in the open, or otherwise improperly managed. They include manufacturing facilities, processing plants, landfills, and mining sites.

**Systemic racism** Discriminatory policies, legislation, and practices in society that give benefits to one racial group over another group that is typically a group of color.

**Threat assessment**   An approach to preventing violent crime in schools by identifying a potential threat, investigating it, and providing appropriate intervention such as mental health counseling to address the issues that are causing a student to consider violence.

**Title IX**   Legislation passed by Congress in 1972 as part of the Educational Amendments of Public Law 92-318 to provide girls and women equal access to all aspects of education, including the curriculum and athletics.

**Torah**   The sacred text of Judaism that Jews believe was revealed to Moses and recorded in the first five books of Hebrew scriptures (the Pentateuch).

**Toxic masculinity**   A form of masculinity in which strength, violence, and aggression are highly valued while being emotional is considered a weakness.

**Tracking**   Assignment of students to a specific class or program (e.g., gifted program) based on how teachers perceive students' academic abilities, educational potential, or vocational interests.

**Transgender**   Refers to people whose gender identity is different from the sex they were assigned at birth.

**Transition plan**   A needs assessment and planning tool for the transition from student into adulthood. Transition plans became a requirement for all children with disabilities by age 14 in IDEA 1990.

**Transitional program**   Educational programs that focus on students' use of their native language as a scaffold as they learn new concepts, knowledge, and skills. Students then transition to academic instruction in English, gradually reducing their use of other languages in the classroom.

**Transmisia**   Irrational beliefs, attitudes, behaviors, and systems that hurt or deny the existence of trans and nonbinary people.

**Transphobic**   Irrational beliefs, attitudes, behaviors, and systems that hurt or deny the existence of trans, gender-fluid, and/or gender nonbinary people.

**Trauma-informed practices**   Teaching strategies and programs that apply an understanding of the impact of traumatic events on a student's learning and social-emotional behavior to provide safe and supportive educational environments for all.

**Trauma-sensitive**   Programs that apply their understanding of the impact of traumatic events on a student's learning and social and emotional behavior to provide safe and supportive educational environments for all students.

**Understanding clauses**   A voting restriction that required a potential voter to explain a part of a state constitution to be eligible to vote.

**Upper class**   Group whose members are wealthy and earn the highest 5% of incomes in the country.

**Upper middle-class**   Group whose members are the affluent middle class people or families who are highly educated professionals, managers, and administrators. They are in the 80 to 95% of the highest income earners in the country.

**Urban areas**   Geographic areas that encompass at least 5,000 people or at least 2,000 housing units.

**Vaping**   The use of a device that heats liquid into an aerosol or vapor that is then inhaled into the lungs.

**Vatican II**   The Second Ecumenical Council of the Vatican in 1962, which addressed the relations between the Catholic Church and the modern world.

**Verbal**   Relating to or consisting of words.

**Vocabulary**   The ability to pronounce and understand the meaning of words as they are used in a specific context.

**Voluntary immigrants**   People who choose to leave their native country to live in another country.

**Wealth**   Accumulated money and property such as stocks, homes, and cars that can be turned into money.

**White Christian Nationalism**   A political ideology that is based on the belief that the United States was founded as a White Christian nation, its laws and institutions were based on Protestant Christianity, and it has been divinely chosen and blessed by God.

**White privilege**   Economic and social advantages that White people hold on the basis of their race that give them greater access to power and resources than people of color have in an inequitable and unjust society.

**White-collar**   Jobs or workers characterized by nonmanual labor in offices, retail stores, and sales.

**Working class**   The socioeconomic group that is comprised of people who are employed in industrial work that is manual or service work.

**Xenophobia**   The fear, hatred, or distrust of strangers or foreigners or things perceived strange or foreign.

**Zero-tolerance policies**   School policies that require punishment, such as suspension or expulsion, for the infraction of a rule.

# References

## Chapter 1

Adams, M., & Zúñiga, X. (2018). Core concepts for social justice education. In M. Adams, W. J. Blumenfeld, D. C. J. Catalano, K. S. DeJong, H. W. Hackman, L. E. Hopkins, . . . X. Zúñiga (Eds.), *Readings for diversity and social justice* (4th ed., pp. 41–49). Routledge.

American Psychological Association. (2022). *APA dictionary of psychology.* https://dictionary.apa.org/cultural-deprivation

Anti-Defamation League. (2022). *Hate is no game: Harassment and positive social experiences in online games 2021.*

Banks, C. A. M. (2021). Responding to diversity in the 21st century: Lessons from the intergroup education movement. In J. A. Banks & C. A. M. Banks (Eds.), *Transforming multicultural education policy and practice: Expanding educational opportunity* (pp. 753–781). Teachers College Press.

Banks, J. A. (2004). Multicultural education: Historical development, dimensions, and practice. In J. A. Banks (Ed.), *Handbook of research on multicultural education* (2nd ed., pp. 21–41). Jossey-Bass.

Bell, L. A. (2018). Theoretical foundations for social justice education. In M. Adams, W. J. Blumenfeld, D. C. J. Catalano, K. S. DeJong, H. W. Hackman, L. E. Hopkins, . . . X. Zúñiga (Eds.), *Readings for diversity and social justice* (4th ed., pp. 34–41). Routledge.

Bellah, R. N., Madsen, R., Sullivan, W. M., Swidler, A., & Tipton, S. M. (2008). *Habits of the heart: Individualism and commitment in American life.* University of California Press.

Bentley-Edwards, K. L., Scott, M. J., & Robbins, P. A. (2022). How systemic racism and preexisting conditions contributed to Covid-19 disparities for Black Americans. In G. L. Wright, L. Hubbard, & W. A. Darity Jr. (Eds.), *The pandemic divide: How Covid increased inequality in American,* pp. 29–45. Duke University Press.

Bonilla-Silva, E. (2022). *Racism without racists: Color-blind racism and the persistence of racial inequality in America* (6th ed.). Rowman & Littlefield.

Brenan, M. (2020, August 19). *New highs say Black people treated less fairly in daily life.* Gallup. https://news.gallup.com/poll/317564/new-highs-say-black-people-treated-less-fairly-daily-life.aspx

Budiman, A. (2020, October 1). *Americans are more positive about the long-term rise in U.S. racial and ethnic diversity than in 2016.* Pew Research Center. https://www.pewresearch.org/fact-tank/2020/10/01/americans-are-more-positive-about-the-long-term-rise-in-u-s-racial-and-ethnic-diversity-than-in-2016/

Byman, D. (2022). *Spreading hate: The global rise of white supremacist terrorism.* Oxford University Press.

Chua, A., & Rubenfeld, J. (2018, October). The threat of tribalism. *The Atlantic, 322*(3), 78–81.

Council of Chief State School Officers. (2013, April). *Interstate Teacher Assessment and Support Consortium (InTASC) model core teaching standards and learning progressions for teachers 1.0: A resource for ongoing teacher development.* https://ccsso.org/sites/default/files/2017–12/2013_INTASC_Learning_Progressions_for_Teachers.pdf

Craig, T. (2022, March 10). Florida legislature passes bill that limits how schools and workplaces teach about race and identity. *Washington Post.* https://www.washingtonpost.com/nation/2022/03/10/florida-legislature-passes-anti-woke-bill/

Darder, A., Baltodano, M. P., & Torres, R. D. (2017). Foundations of critical pedagogy. In A. Darder, R. D. Torres, & M. P. Baltodano, *The critical pedagogy reader* (pp. 1–23). Routledge.

Darling-Hammond, L. (2017). Teaching for social justice: Resources, relationships, and anti-racist practice. *Multicultural Perspectives, 19*(3), 133–138.

Delgado, R., & Stefancic, J. (2017). *Critical race theory.* New York University Press.

Dewey, J. (1966). *Democracy and education: An introduction to the philosophy of education.* Free Press. (Original work published 1916)

Douglass, F. (1857, August 3). *Emancipation in the West Indies.* https://blackpast.org/1857-frederick-douglass-if-there-no-struggle-there-no-progress

Eberhardt, J. L. (2019). *Biased: Uncovering the hidden prejudice that shapes what we see, think, and do.* Viking.

Federal Bureau of Investigation. (n.d.). *Crime data explorer.* https://cde.ucr.cjis.gov

Frey, W. H. (2018, August 3). *Charlottesville, demographic change, and misplaced White anxiety.* https://www.brookings.edu/blog/the-avenue/2018/08/03/charlottesville-demographic-change-and-misplaced-white-anxiety/

Horowitz, J. M., Brown, A., & Cox, K. (2019, April 9). *Race in America 2019.* Pew Research Center. https://www.pewresearch.org/social-trends/2019/04/09/race-in-america-2019/

Hout, M. (2019). Social mobility. *Pathways: A Magazine on Poverty, Inequality, and Social Policy* [Special Issue], pp. 29–32. Retrieved from https://inequality.stanford.edu/publications/pathway/state-union-2019

Irwin, V., De La Rosa, J., Wang, K., Hein, S., Zhang, J., Burr, R., . . . Parker, S. (2022). *Report on the Condition of Education 2022* (NCES 2022-144). National Center for Education Statistics, U.S. Department of Education. https://nces.ed.gov/pubsearch/pubsinfo.asp?pubid=2022144

Johnson, A. G. (2018). *Privilege, power, and difference.* McGraw Hill.

Johnson, S. R. (2022, November 16). U.S. News-Harris Poll survey: As America aims for equity, many believe systemic racism doesn't exist. https://www.usnews.com/news/health-news/articles/2022-11-16/poll-many-americans-dont-believe-systemic-racism-exists

Joint Center for Housing Studies of Harvard University. (2022). *The state of the nation's housing: 2022.* https://www.jchs.harvard.edu/state-nations-housing-2022

Kendi, I. X. (2019). *How to be an antiracist.* Oneworld.

Ladson-Billings, G. (2021). *Critical race theory in education: A scholar's journey.* Teachers College Press.

Lee, C. D., Nasir, N. S., Pea, R., & de Royston, M. M. (2020). Introduction. Reconceptualizing learning: A critical task for knowledge-building and teaching. In N. S. Nasir, C. D. Lee, R. Pea, & M. M. de Royston (Eds.), *Handbook of the cultural foundations of learning* (pp. xvii–xxxv). Routledge.

Levitsky, S., & Ziblatt, D. (2018). *How democracies die*. Broadway Books.

McGhee, H. (2021). *The sum of us: What racism costs everyone and how we can prosper together*. One World.

McIntosh, P. (2020). White privilege: Unpacking the invisible knapsack. In M. L. Andersen & P. H. Collins (Eds.), *Race, class, and gender* (10th ed., pp. 67–71). Cengage.

McKesson, D. (2019). *On the other side of freedom: Race and justice in a divided America*. Oneworld.

Miller, C., & Rivas, C. (2022). The year in hate and extremism 2021. In Southern Poverty Law Center, *The year in hate & extremism 2021* (pp. 2–17). Southern Poverty Law Center.

Moll, L. C. (2019). Elaborating funds of knowledge: Community-oriented practices in international contexts. *Literacy Research: Theory, Method, and Practice, 68*, 130–138.

National Academy of Sciences, Engineering, and Medicine. (2019). *Monitoring educational equity*. National Academies Press.

National Association for Multicultural Education. (2022). *Definitions of multicultural education*. https://www.nameorg.org/definitions_of_multicultural_e.php

National Center for Education Statistics. (2021a, September). *Enrollment and percentage distribution of enrollment in public elementary and secondary schools, by race/ethnicity and region: Selected years, fall 1995 through fall 2030 (Table 203.50)*. U.S. Department of Education. https://nces.ed.gov/programs/digest/d21/tables/dt21_203.50.asp

National Center for Education Statistics. (2021b). *Number and percentage distribution of public school students, by percentage of students in school who are eligible for free or reduced-price lunch, school level, locale, and student race/ethnicity: Fall 2019 (Table 216.60)*. https://nces.ed.gov/programs/digest/d21/tables/dt21_216.60.asp

National Center for Education Statistics. (2021c, November). *Number and percentage of public school students eligible for free or reduced-price lunch, by state: Selected years, 2000–01 through 2019–20 (Table 204.10)*. https://nces.ed.gov/programs/digest/d21/tables/dt21_204.10.asp

National Center for Education Statistics. (2021d, January). *Number and percentage distribution of teachers in public and private elementary and secondary schools, by selected teacher characteristics: Selected years, 1987–88 through 2017–18 (Table 209.10)*. U.S. Department of Education. https://nces.ed.gov/programs/digest/d20/tables/dt20_209.10.asp

Omi, M., & Winant, H. (2015). *Racial formation in the United States* (3rd ed.). Routledge.

Oxford Reference. (2022). *Overview: Dominant culture*. https://www.oxfordreference.com/view/10.1093/oi/authority.20110803095725838

Page, B. I., & Gilens, M. (2020). *Democracy in America?: What has gone wrong and what we can do about it*. University of Chicago Press.

Parolin, Z., Collyer, S., & Curran, M. A. (2022). Monthly poverty in 2022 remains elevated in February. *Poverty and Social Policy Brief, 6*(4). povertycenter.columbia.edu/publication/monthly-poverty-february-2022

Pew Research Center. (2017, May 18). *Intermarriage in the U.S. 50 years after* Loving v. Virginia. http://www.pewsocialtrends.org/2017/05/18/1-trends-and-patterns-in-intermarriage/

Pew Research Center. (2021, August 12). *Deep divisions in Americans' view of nation's racial history – and how to address it*. https://www.pewresearch.org/politics/2021/08/12/deep-divisions-in-americans-views-of-nations-racial-history-and-how-to-address-it/

Rice, C. (2017). *Democracy: Stories from the long road to freedom*. Twelve.

Saavedra, A., Levinson, M., & Polikoff, M. (2022, October 20). *Survey: Americans broadly support teaching about (most) controversial topics in the classroom*. https://www.brookings.edu/blog/brown-center-chalkboard/2022/10/20/americans-broadly-support-teaching-about-most-controversial-topics-in-the-classroom/

Sandel, M. J. (2020). *The tyranny of merit: Can we find the common good?* Picador, Farrar, Straus & Giroux.

Sawchuk, S. (2021, May 18). What is critical race theory, and why is it under attack? *Education Week*. https://www.edweek.org/leadership/what-is-critical-race-theory-and-why-is-it-under-attack/2021/05

Sensoy, Ö., & DiAngelo, R. (2017). *Is everyone really equal?: An introduction to key concepts in social justice education* (2nd ed.). Teachers College Press.

Sensoy, Ö., & DiAngelo, R. (2021). Understanding the structural nature of oppression through racism. In J. A. Banks (Ed.), *Transforming multicultural education policy and practice: Expanding educational opportunity* (pp. 55–79). Teachers College Press.

Serwer, A. (2019, April). White nationalism's deep American roots. *The Atlantic, 323*(3), 84–94.

Snyder, T. D., de Brey, C., & Dillow, S. A. (2019). *Digest of Education Statistics 2017* (NCES 2018-070). National Center for Education Statistics, U.S. Department of Education. https://nces.ed.gov/pubs2018/2018070.pdf

Southern Poverty Law Center. (2022). *The year in hate & extremism: 2021*. Author.

Spring, J. (2018). *The American school: From the puritans to the Trump era*. Routledge.

Storey, J. (2018). *Cultural theory and popular culture: An introduction* (8th ed.). Routledge.

Symcox, L. (2002). *Whose history?: The struggle for national standards in American classrooms*. Teachers College Press.

Stiglitz, J. E. (2019). *People, power, and profits: Progressive capitalism for an age of discontent*. Norton.

Tatum, B. D. (2018). The complexity of identity: "Who am I?" In M. Adams W. J. Blumenfeld, D. C. J. Catalano, K. S. DeJong, H. W. Hackman, L. E. Hopkins, . . . X. Zúñiga (Eds.), *Readings for diversity and social justice* (4th ed.) (pp. 7–9). Routledge.

Tefera, A. A., Powers, J. M., & Fischman, G. E. (2018). Intersectionality in education: A conceptual aspiration and research imperative. *Review of Research in Education, 42*, vii–xvii.

Urriet, L., Jr., & Noblit, G. W. (2018). *Cultural constructions of identity*. Oxford University Press.

U.S. Census Bureau. (2020). *Decennial census (Table P2)*. https://data.census.gov/cedsci/table?q=hispanic&g=0100000US&y=2020&tid=DECENNIALPL2020.P2

U.S. Department of Justice. (2022a). *Hate crime statistics*. https://www.justice.gov/hatecrimes/hate-crime-statistics

U.S. Department of Justice. (2022b, May 20). *Raising awareness of hate crimes and hate incidents during the COVID-19 pandemic*. https://www.justice.gov/hatecrimes/resource/raising-awareness-hate-crimes-and-hate-incidents-during-covid-19-pandemic

Vara-Orta, F. (2018, August 22). Hate in schools. *Education Week, 38*(1), 1, 16–19.

Young, I. M. (2018). Five faces of oppression. In M. Adams, . . . X. Zúñiga (Eds.), *Readings for diversity and social justice* (4th ed., pp. 49–59). Routledge.

## Chapter 2

Abramitzky, R., & Boustan, L. (2022). *Streets of gold: America's untold story of immigrant success*. PublicAffairs.

Alaska Department of Education & Early Development. (n.d.). *Ste-Tribal education compacting*. https://education.alaska.gov/compacting

Alba, R. (2020). *The great demographic illusion: Majority, minority, and the expanding American mainstream*. Princeton University Press.

Alexander, L., & Alexander, M. (2021). Fear. In N. Hannah-Jones, C. Roper, I. Silverman, & J. Silverstein (Eds.), *The 1619 project* (pp. 97–122). One World.

Alexander, M. (2012). *The new Jim Crow: Mass incarceration in the age of colorblindness* (rev. ed.). The New Press.

*Alston v. School Board of City of Norfolk*, 112 F.2d 992 (4th Cir. 1940).

American Civil Liberties Union (ACLU) & The Sentencing Project. (2022, July 14). *Racial disparities in sentencing in the United States*. https://www.sentencingproject.org/policy-brief/shadow-report-to-the-united-nations-on-racial-disparities-in-sentencing-in-the-united-states/

Anderson, C. (2017). *White rage: The unspoken truth of our racial divide*. Bloomsbury.

Asante, M. K. (2020). From critical pedagogy to revolutionary pedagogy: Toward transformative practice. In K. G. Shockley & K. Lomotey (Eds.), *African-centered education: Theory and practice* (pp. 65–83). Myers Education Press.

Au, W., & Hagopian, J. (2018). How one elementary school sparked a citywide movement to make black students' lives matter. In D. Watson, J. Hagopian, & W. Au (Eds.), *Teaching for black lives* (pp. 22–31). Rethinking Schools.

Au, W., & Yonamine, M. (2021, March 23). *Dear educators, it is time to fight for Asian American*. Rethinking Schools. https://rethinkingschools.org/2021/03/23/dear-educators-it-is-time-to-fight-for-asian-america/

Banks, J. A. (2019). *An introduction to multicultural education* (6th ed). Pearson.

Batalova, J., & Fix, M. (2022, December). *The skills and economic outcomes of immigrant and U.S.-born college graduates*. Migration Policy Institute.

Beckert, S. (2014, December 12). Empire of cotton. *The Atlantic*. https://www.theatlantic.com/business/archive/2014/12/empire-of-cotton/383660/

Bhutta, N., Bricker, J., Chang, A. C., Dettling, L. J., Goodman, S., Hsu, J. W., . . . Windle, R. A. (2020, September). Changes in U.S. family finances from 2016 to 2019: Evidence from the survey of consumer finances. *Federal Reserve Bulletin, 106*(5).

Bigpond, N., & Brownback, S. (2021, July 6). For Native peoples, an apology never spoken is no apology at all. *Washington Post*. https://www.washingtonpost.com/opinions/2021/07/06/native-peoples-an-apology-never-spoken-is-no-apology-all/

*Board of Education of Oklahoma City v. Dowell*, 498 U.S. 237 (1991).

*Bolling v. Sharpe*, 347 U.S. 497 (1954).

Bonilla, S., Dee, T. S., & Penner, E. K. (2021, September 7). Ethnic studies increases longer-run academic engagement and attainment. *Proceedings of the National Academy of Science, 118*(37).

Bonilla-Silva, E. (2022). *Racism without racists: Color-blind racism and the persistence of racial inequality in America* (5th ed.). Rowman & Littlefield.

*Briggs v. Elliott*, 342 U.S. 350 (1952).

*Brown v. Board of Education of Topeka*, 98 F.Supp. 797 (1951).

*Brown v. Board of Education of Topeka*, 347 U.S. 483 (1954).

*Brown v. Board of Education*, 349 U.S. 294, at 300 (1955).

Budiman, A. (2020, August 20). *Key findings about U.S. immigrants*. Pew Research Center. https://www.pewresearch.org/fact-tank/2020/08/20/key-findings-about-u-s-immigrants/

Camarota, S. A., & Zeigler, K. (2022, March 29). *Estimating the illegal immigrant population using the current population survey*. Center for Immigration Studies. https://cis.org/Report/Estimating-Illegal-Immigrant-Population-Using-Current-Population-Survey

Capitol Hill Seattle Blog. (2023, January 31). *Seattle Black Lives Matter at school 'week of action' included School Board protest over ethnic studies, cops on campuses*. https://www.capitolhillseattle.com/2023/01/seattle-black-lives-matter-at-school-week-of-action-includes-school-board-protest-over-ethnic-studies-cops-on-campuses/

Carnevale, A. P., Fasules, M. L., Quinn, M. C., & Campbell, K. P. (2019). *Born to win, schooled to lose: Why equally talented students don't get equal chances to be all they can be*. Georgetown University, Center on Education and the Workforce. https://1gyhoq479ufd3yna29x7ubjn-wpengine.netdna-ssl.com/wp-content/uploads/FR-Born_to_win-schooled_to_lose.pdf

Carson, E. A. (2022, December). *Prisoners in 2021-Statistical tables*. Bureau of Justice Statistics. https://bjs.ojp.gov/library/publications/prisoners-2021-statistical-tables

Chang, E. (2022, Summer). Curricular countermovements: How White parents mounted a popular challenge to ethnic studies. *Harvard Educational Review, 92*(2), 157–181.

Chaudhuri, J. O. (2020, July 145). Our Muscogee people suffered for generations in the hope of a better tomorrow. It's finally here. *Washington Post*. https://www.washingtonpost.com/opinions/our-muscogee-people-suffered-for-generations-in-the-hope-of-a-better-tomorrow-its-finally-here/2020/07/14/3caf0638-c60a-11ea-8ffe-372be8d82298_story.html

Chin, M. J., Quinn, D. M., Dhaliwal, T. K., & Lovison, V. S. (2020, November). Bias in the Air: A nationwide exploration of teachers' implicit racial attitudes, aggregate bias, and student outcomes. *Educational Researcher, 49*(8), 566–578.

*Cisneros v. Corpus Christi*, 324 F.Supp. 599 (1970).

*Civil Rights Act of 1964*, Pub.L. 88–352, 78 Stat. 241 (1964).

Cohn, D., Brown, A., & Lopez, M. H. (2021, May 14). *Black and Hispanic Americans see their origins as central to tho they are, less so for white adults*. Pew Research Center. https://www.pewresearch.org/social-trends/2021/05/14/black-and-hispanic-americans-see-their-origins-as-central-to-who-they-are-less-so-for-white-adults/

*Comfort v. Lynn School Committee*, 418 F.3d 1 (2005).

Cox, K., & Tamir, C. (2022, April). *Race is central to identity for Black Americans and affects how they connect with each other: Many learn about ancestors, U.S. Black history from family*. Pew Research Center. https://www.pewresearch.org/race-ethnicity/2022/04/14/race-is-central-to-identity-for-black-americans-and-affects-how-they-connect-with-each-other/

Cun, A. (2020, October-December) Learning about the stories of children with refugee backgrounds through the lens of positioning theory. *Multicultural Perspectives, 22*(4), 178–189.

*Davis v. County School Board of Prince Edward County*, 103 F.Supp. 337 (1952).

DiAngelo, R. (2018). *White fragility: Why it's so hard for white people to talk about racism*. Beacon Press.

Donato, R., & Hanson, J. (2019, February). Mexican-American resistance to school segregation. *Phi Delta Kappan*, *100*(5), 39–42.

Echohawk, J. E. (2013). Understanding tribal sovereignty: The Native American rights fund. *Expedition Magazine*, *55*(3). https://www.penn.museum/sites/expedition/understanding-tribal-sovereignty-the-native-american-rights-fund/

Equal Justice Initiative. (n.d.). *The National Memorial for Peace and Justice*. https://museumandmemorial.eji.org/memorial

Equal Justice Initiative. (2023). *The transatlantic slave trade*. https://eji.org/reports/transatlantic-slave-trade-overview/

Epstein, R., Blake, J. J., & González. (2019). *Girlhood interrupted: The erasure of Black girls' childhood*. Georgetown Law Center on Poverty and Inequality. https://papers.ssrn.com/sol3/papers.cfm?abstract_id=3000695

Fensterwald, J. (2021, October 8). California becomes first state to require ethnic studies in high school. *EdSource*. https://edsource.org/2021/california-becomes-first-state-to-require-ethnic-studies-in-high-school/662219

Frey, W. H. (2022, August 1). *White and youth population losses contributed most to nation's growth slowdown, new census data reveals*. Brookings Institution. https://www.brookings.edu/research/white-and-youth-population-losses-contributed-most-to-the-nations-growth-slowdown-new-census-data-reveals/

Gates Jr., H. L. (2014, January 6). *How many slaves landed in the U.S.?* The Root. https://www.theroot.com/how-many-slaves-landed-in-the-us-1790873989

Gates Jr. H. L. (2019). *Stony the road: Reconstruction, White supremacy, and the rise of Jim Crow*. Penquin Press.

*Gebhart v. Belton*, 91 A.2d 137 (1952).

George, J., & Darling-Hammond, L. (2019). *The federal role and school integration: Brown's promise and present challenges*. Learning Policy Institute. https://learningpolicyinstitute.org/sites/default/files/product-files/Federal_Role_School_Integration_REPORT.pdf

Glaude, E. S., Jr. (2017). *Democracy in black: How race still enslaves the American soul*. Broadway Books.

*Gong Lum v. Rice*, 275 U.S. 78 (1927).

Gonzalez-Barrera, A. (2020, September 24). *The ways Hispanics describe their identity vary across immigrant generations*. Pew Research Center. https://www.pewresearch.org/fact-tank/2020/09/24/the-ways-hispanics-describe-their-identity-vary-across-immigrant-generations/

Gonzalez-Barrera, A. (2022, May 2). *About 6 million U.S. adults identify as Afro-Latino*. Pew Research Center. https://www.pewresearch.org/fact-tank/2022/05/02/about-6-million-u-s-adults-identify-as-afro-latino/

*Green v. County School Board of New Kent County*, 391 U.S. 430 (1968).

*Grutter v. Bollinger*, 123 S.Ct. 2325 (2003).

Hannah-Jones, N., Roper, C., Silverman, I., & Silverstein, J. (Eds.). (2021). *The 1619 Project*. One World.

Hawai'i State Department of Education. (n.d.). *History of Hawaiian education*. https://www.hawaiipublicschools.org/TeachingAndLearning/StudentLearning/HawaiianEducation/Pages/History-of-the-Hawaiian-Education-program.aspx

Hensley, W. L. I. (2017, March 29). There are two versions of the story of how the U.S. purchased Alaska from Russia. *Smithsonian Magazine*. https://www.smithsonianmag.com/history/why-russia-gave-alaska-americas-gateway-arctic-180962714/

History.com Editors. (2022). *Hawaii*. https://www.history.com/topics/us-states/hawaii

Ho-Lastimosa, I., Chung-Do, J. J., Hwang, P. W., Radovich, T., Rogerson, Il, Ho, K., . . . Spencer, M. S. (2019). Integrating Native Hawaiian tradition with the modern technology of aquaponics. *Global Health Promotion*, *26*(3), 87–92.

Hopkins, J. P. (2020). *Indian education for all: Decolonizing indigenous education in public schools*. Teachers College Press.

Horowitz, J. M., Brown, A., & Cox, K. (2019, April). *Race in America 2019*. https://www.pewsocialtrends.org/2019/04/09/race-in-america-2019/

Horowitz, J. M., & Budiman, A. (2020, August 18). *Key findings about multiracial identity in the U.S. as Harris becomes vice presidential nominee*. Pew Research Center. https://www.pewresearch.org/fact-tank/2020/08/18/key-findings-about-multiracial-identity-in-the-u-s-as-harris-becomes-vice-presidential-nominee/

Howard, T. C. (2020, June 3). How to root out anti-Black racism from your school. *Education Week*. https://www.edweek.org/leadership/opinion-how-to-root-out-anti-black-racism-from-your-school/2020/06

Hubbard, L. Wright, G. L., & Darity, W. A., Jr. (2022). Introduction. Six feet and miles apart: Structural racism in the United States and racially disparate outcomes during the COVID-19 pandemic. In G. L. Wright, L. Hubbard, & W. A. Darity Jr., *The pandemic: How COVID increased inequality in America* (pp. 1–26). Duke University Press.

Institute of Positive Education. (n.d.). *About the Institute of Positive Education*. https://www.ipeclc.org/about-us

Ishisaka, N. (2021, March 22). The hidden stories that give rise to violence against Asian American women. *Seattle Times*. https://www.seattletimes.com/seattle-news/the-hidden-stories-that-give-rise-to-violence-against-asian-american-women/

Jones, S., & Rich, E. (2019, July 19). Alaska: A brief history of the state and its schools. *Education Week*. https://www.edweek.org/leadership/alaska-a-brief-history-of-the-state-and-its-schools/2019/07

Kay, M. R. (2018). *Not light, but fire: How to lead meaningful race conversations in the classroom*. Stenhouse.

Kelly, M. (2000, September 9). Indian affairs leaders apologizes. Agency says it's at fault for massacres, relocations. *The Oklahoman*. https://www.oklahoman.com/story/news/2000/09/09/indian-affairs-leader-apologizes-agency-says-its-at-fault-for-massacres-relocations/62182008007/

Kendi, I. X. (2016). *Stamped from the beginning: The definitive history of racist ideas in America*. Nation Books.

Krogstad, J. M., Passel, J. S., & Noe-Bustamante, L. (2022, September 23). *Key facts about U.S. Latinos for national Hispanic heritage month*. Pew Research Center. https://www.pewresearch.org/fact-tank/2022/09/23/key-facts-about-u-s-latinos-for-national-hispanic-heritage-month/

Ladson-Billings, G. (2021). *Culturally relevant pedagogy: Asking a different question*. Teachers College Press.

Ladson-Billings, G. (2022). *The dreamkeepers: Successful teachers of African American children*. Jossey-Bass.

*Lau v. Nichols*, 414 U.S. 563 (1974).

Lee, E. (2015). *The making of Asian America: A History*. Simon & Schuster.

Lee, C. (2020). How shall we sing our sacred song in a strange land—Revisited. In K. G. Shockley & K. Lomotey, *African-centered education: Theory and practice* (pp. 147–167). Myers Education Press.

Library of Congress. (n.d.). *Beginnings: Exploration and colonization*. https://www.loc.gov/classroom-materials/immigration/african/beginnings/

Losen, D. J., & Martinez, P. (2020). *Lost opportunities: How disparate school discipline continues to drive differences in the opportunity to learn*. Learning Policy Institute & Center for Civil Rights Remedies at the Civil Rights Project, UCLA.

McCarthy, J. (2021, September 10). *U.S. approval of interracial marriage at new high of 94%*. Gallup. https://news.gallup.com/poll/354638/approval-interracial-marriage-new-high.aspx

McCarty, T. L., & Roessel, C. M. (2015). Tsé Ch'izhí Diné Bi'ólta'—Rough Rock, The People's School: Reflections on a half-century of Navajo community-controlled education. In E. Rodriguez (Ed.), *Pedagogies and curriculums to (re)imagine public education: Transnational tales of hope and resistance* (pp. 49–63). Springer.

*Méndez v. Westminster, School District of Orange County, et al.*, 64 F.Supp. 544 (S.D. Cal. 1946).

*Meredith v. Jefferson County (Ky.) Board of Education*, 551 U.S. 701 (2007).

Migration Policy Institute. (n.d.) *Unauthorized immigrant populations by country and region, top states and counties of residence, 2019*. https://www.migrationpolicy.org/programs/data-hub/charts/unauthorized-immigrant-populations-country-and-region-top-state-and-county

*Milliken v. Bradley*, 418 U.S. 717 (1974).

Nathanson, H. (2023). Teachers say parents, laws are affecting how they address race and gender. *Washington Post*, p. B2.

National Advisory Commission on Civil Disorders. *(1967, June 27). The report of the National Advisory Commission on Civil Disorders*. https://www.ojp.gov/ncjrs/virtual-library/abstracts/national-advisory-commission-civil-disorders-report

National Center for Education Statistics. (2022a, July). Enrollment and percentage distribution of enrollment in public elementary and secondary schools, by race/ethnicity and region: Selected years, fall 1995 through fall 2030 (Table 203.50). *Digest of Education Statistics*. https://nces.ed.gov/programs/digest/d22/tables/dt22_203.50.asp?current=yes

National Center for Education Statistics. (2022b, March). Percentage of students receiving selected disciplinary actions in public elementary and secondary schools, by type of disciplinary action, disability status, sex, and race/ethnicity: 2017–18 (Table 233.28). *Digest of Education Statistics*. https://nces.ed.gov/programs/digest/d21/tables/dt21_233.28.asp

Nellis, A. (2023, January). *Mass incarceration trends*. The Sentencing Project. https://www.sentencingproject.org/reports/mass-incarceration-trends/

Newport, G. (2020, June 17). *American attitudes and race*. Gallup. https://news.gallup.com/opinion/polling-matters/312590/american-attitudes-race.aspx

Newport, F. (2022, January 7). *Controversy over the term "Latinx": Public opinion context*. Gallup. https://news.gallup.com/opinion/polling-matters/388532/controversy-term-latinx-public-opinion-context.aspx

Noe-Bustamante, L., Ruiz, N. G., Lopez, M. H., & Edwards, K. (2022, May 9). *About a third of Asian Americans say they have changed their daily routine due to concerns over threats, attacks*. Pew Research Center. https://www.pewresearch.org/fact-tank/2022/05/09/about-a-third-of-asian-americans-say-they-have-changed-their-daily-routine-due-to-concerns-over-threats-attacks/

Orfield, G., & Jarvie, D. (2020, December). *Black segregation matters: School resegregation and Black educational opportunity*. Civil Right Project, University of California Los Angeles.

Pace, J. L., Soto-Shed, E., & Washington, E. Y. (2022, January 31). *Teaching controversial issues when democracy is under attack*. Brookings Institution. https://www.brookings.edu/blog/brown-center-chalkboard/2022/01/31/teaching-controversial-issues-when-democracy-is-under-attack/

Pandey, E., Schrag, J., & Oide, T. (2022, May 15). *Redefining Asian America*. One Sandbox. https://onesandbox.com/industry-news/redefining-asian-america/

*Parents Involved in Community Schools v. Seattle School District #1*, 551 U.S. 701 (2007).

Paz, I.G., & Cramer, M. (2021, October 2). How students fought a book ban and won, for now. *New York Times*. https://www.nytimes.com/2021/10/02/us/york-pennsylvania-school-books.html

PEN America. (2023). *PEN America index of educational gag orders*. https://docs.google.com/spreadsheets/d/1Tj5WQVBmB6SQg-zP_M8uZsQQGH09TxmBY73v23zpyr0/edit#gid=1505554870

Pendharkar, E. (2021, June 30). Four things schools won't be able to do under 'critical race theory' laws. *Education Week*. https://www.edweek.org/policy-politics/four-things-schools-wont-be-able-to-do-under-critical-race-theory-laws/2021/06

Pewewardy, C., Lees, A., & Minthorn, R. Z. (Eds.) (2022). *Unsettling settler-colonial education: The transformational indigenous praxis model*. Teachers College Press.

*Plessy v. Ferguson*, 163 U.S. 537 (1896).

*Plyler v. Doe*, 457 U.S. 202 (1982).

Polynesian Cultural Center. (2023). *Culture of Hawaii*. https://polynesia.com/culture-of-hawaii/

Ramos, P. (2020). *Finding Latinx: In search of the voices redefining Latino identity*. Vintage.

Reich, G. M. (2021). *The politics of immigration across the United States: Every state a border state?* Routledge.

Rhoden, G. (2022, April 3). *How a diverse coalition in a red state shut down anti-CRT legislation*. CNN. https://www.cnn.com/2022/04/03/us/indiana-anti-crt-legislation-shut-down-why/index.html

*Riddick v. School Board of the City of Norfolk, Virginia*, 627 F.Supp. 814 (E.D. Va. 1984).

Rosenbloom, R., & Batalova, J. (2022, October 13). *Mexican immigrants in the United States*. Migration Policy Institute. https://www.migrationpolicy.org/article/mexican-immigrants-united-states#unauthorized

Rothstein, R. (2017). *The color of law: A forgotten history of how our government segregated America*. Liveright.

Ruiz, N. G., Horowitz, J., & Tamir, C. (2020, July). *Many Black and Asian Americans say they have experienced discrimination amid the COVID-19 outbreak*. Pew Research Center. https://www.pewresearch.org/social-trends/2020/07/01/many-black-and-asian-americans-say-they-have-experienced-discrimination-amid-the-covid-19-outbreak/

Saad, L. (2022, May 19). *Concern about race relations persists after Floyd's death*. Gallup. https://news.gallup.com/poll/392705/concern-race-relations-persists-floyd-death.aspx

*San Antonio Independent School District v. Rodriguez*, 411 U.S. 1 (1973).

Saunt, C. (2020). *Unworthy republic: The dispossession of Native Americans and the road to Indian territory*. Norton.

Sawchuk, S. (2021, April 21). 4 ways George Floyd's murder has changed how we talk about race and education.

*Education Week*. https://www.edweek.org/leadership/4-ways-george-floyds-murder-has-changed-how-we-talk-about-race-and-education/2021/04?utm_source=nl&utm_medium=eml&utm_campaign=eu&M=59942005&U=1128420&UUID=912fe95ed97529ec8c9325853559066c

*Schuette v. Coalition to Defend Affirmative Action*, 572 U.S. 291 (2014).

Serwer, A. (2017, November 20). *The nationalist's delusion.* Retrieved from https://www.theatlantic.com/politics/archive/2017/11/the-nationalists-delusion/546356/

Shah, K., & Adolphe, J. (2019, August 16). 400 years since slavery: A timeline of American history. *The Guardian.* https://www.theguardian.com/news/2019/aug/15/400-years-since-slavery-timeline

Sleeter, C. (2021, May 15). *Critical race theory.* https://www.christinesleeter.org/critical-race-theory

Sleeter, C., Acuff, J. B., Bentley, C. Foster, S. G. Morrison, P, & Stenhouse, V. (2019). Multicultural education or ethnic studies? In R. T. Cuauhtin, M. Zavala, C. Sleeter, & W. Au (Eds.), *Rethinking ethnic studies* (pp. 12–16). Rethinking Schools.

Sleeter, C. E., & Zavala, M. (2020). *Transformative ethnic studies in schools: Curriculum, pedagogy, and research.* Teachers College Press.

Spencer, J. A., & Ullucci, K. (2022). *Anti-Blackness at school: Creating affirming educational spaces for African American students.* Teachers College Press.

Statista. (2023). *Total fertility rate in the United States in 2020, by ethnicity of mother (births per 1,000 women).* https://www.statista.com/statistics/226292/us-fertility-rates-by-race-and-ethnicity/

Stop AAPI Hate. (2022a, October). *The blame game: How political rhetoric inflames Anti-Asian scapegoating.* https://stopaapihate.org/anti-asian-scapegoating/

Stop AAPI Hate. (2022b, July 20). *Two years and thousands of voices: National report (Through March 31, 2022).* https://stopaapihate.org/year-2-report/

*Stout v. Jefferson County Board of Education*, 448 F.2d 403, 404 (5th Cir., 2018).

*Swann v. Charlotte-Mecklenburg Board of Education*, 402 U.S. 1 (1971).

Tamir, C. (2021, March 25). *The growing diversity of Black America.* Pew Research Center. https://www.pewresearch.org/social-trends/2021/03/25/the-growing-diversity-of-black-america/

Tamir, C. (2022, January 27). *Key findings about Black immigrants in the U.S.* Pew Research Center. https://www.pewresearch.org/fact-tank/2022/01/27/key-findings-about-black-immigrants-in-the-u-s/

Tatum, B. D. (2017). *Why are all the black kids sitting together in the cafeteria? And other conversations about race* (rev. and updated ed.). Basic Books.

Tintiangco-Cubales, A., Kohli, R., Sacramento, J., Henning, N., Agarwal-Rangnath, R., & Sleeter, C. (2019). What is ethnic studies pedagogy? In R. T. Cuauhin, M. Zavala, C. Sleeter, & W. Au (Eds.), *Rethinking ethnic studies* (pp. 20–25). Rethinking Schools.

Treuer, D. (2019). *The heartbeat of Wounded Knee: Native America from 1890 to the Present.* Riverhead Books.

Treuer, D. (2021, May). Return the national parks to the tribes: The jewels of America's landscape should belong to America's original peoples. *The Atlantic*, 327(4), 31–45.

Tucker, J. T., De León, J., & McCool, D. (2020). *Obstacles at every turn: Barriers to polical participation faced by Native American voters.* Native American Rights Fund.

*United States v. Scotland Neck City Board of Education*, 407 U.S. 484 (1972).

U.S. Bureau of Indian Affairs. (2023). *Alaska region.* https://www.bia.gov/regional-office/alaska-region

U.S. Bureau of Labor Statistics. (2023, January 6). *Unemployment rates by age, sex, race, and Hispanic or Latino ethnicity (E-16).* https://www.bls.gov/web/empsit/cpsee_e16.htm

U.S. Census Bureau. (2018a, September). *Projected race and Hispanic origin: Projections for the United States: 2017–2060 (Table 4).* https://www.census.gov/data/tables/2017/demo/popproj2017-summary-tables.html

U.S. Census Bureau. (2018b, September). *Race by Hispanic Origin: Projections for the United States: 2017–2060 (Table 5).* https://www.census.gov/data/tables/2017/demo/popproj/2017-summary-tables.html

U.S. Census Bureau. (2020a, July 28). *Homeownership rates show that Black Americans are currently the least likely group to own homes.* USA Facts. https://usafacts.org/articles/homeownership-rates-by-race/

U.S. Census Bureau. (2020b). *Native Hawaiian and other Pacific Islander alone or in any combination by selected groups (BO2019).* https://data.census.gov/table?q=b02019&tid=ACSDT5Y2020.B02019

U.S. Census Bureau. (2021a, August 12). Race and ethnicity in the United States: 2010 census and 2020 census. https://www.census.gov/library/visualizations/interactive/race-and-ethnicity-in-the-united-state-2010-and-2020-census.html

U.S. Census Bureau. (2021b). *Selected characteristics of the native and foreign-born populations.* https://data.census.gov/table?q=S0501:+SELECTED+CHARACTERISTICS+OF+THE+NATIVE+AND+FOREIGN-BORN+POPULATIONS&g=0100000US&tid=ACSST1Y2021.S0501

U.S. Census Bureau. (2021c). *Selected characteristics of people 15 years and over, by total money income, work experience, race, Hispanic origin, and sex (PINC-01).* https://www.census.gov/data/tables/time-series/demo/income-poverty/cps-pinc/pinc-01.html

U.S. Census Bureau. (2022a, April 15). *About the Hispanic population and its origin.* https://www.census.gov/topics/population/hispanic-origin/about.html

U.S. Census Bureau. (2022b, June). *Annual estimates of the resident population by sex, race, and Hispanic origin for the United States: April 1, 2020 to July 1, 2021 (NC-EST2021-SR11H).* https://www.census.gov/data/datasets/time-series/demo/popest/2020s-national-detail.html

U.S. Census Bureau. (2022c, October). *Educational attainment of the population 25 years and over by sex, nativity, and U.S. citizenship status: 2021 (Table 1.5).* https://www.census.gov/data/tables/2021/demo/foreign-born/cps-2021.html

U.S. Census Bureau. (2022d). *QuickFacts: Population estimates.* https://www.census.gov/quickfacts/fact/table/US/RHI325221#RHI325221

U.S. Census Bureau. (2023, March 3). *Asian-American and Pacific Islander heritage month: May 2023.* https://www.census.gov/newsroom/facts-for-features/2023/asian-american-pacific-islander.html

U.S. Congress, House of Representatives. (1956). *Communist political subversion. Hearings before the Committee on Un-American Activities.* https://archive.org/stream/communistpolitic02unit/communistpolitic02unit_djvu.txt

U.S. Department of Homeland Security, Office of Immigration Statistics. (2022a). Individuals granted asylum affirmatively or defensively: Fiscal years 1990 to 2021 (Table 19). *Yearbook of Immigration Statistics: 2021*. https://www.dhs.gov/immigration-statistics/yearbook/2021

U.S. Department of Homeland Security, Office of Immigration Statistics. (2022b). Individuals granted asylum affirmatively by region and country of nationality: Fiscal years 2012 to 2021 (Table 17). *Yearbook of Immigration Statistics: 2021*. https://www.dhs.gov/immigration-statistics/yearbook/2021

U.S. Department of Homeland Security, Office of Immigration Statistics. (2022c). Individuals granted asylum defensively by region and country of nationality: Fiscal years 2012 to 2021 (Table 16). *Yearbook of Immigration Statistics: 2021*. https://www.dhs.gov/immigration-statistics/yearbook/2021

U.S. Department of Homeland Security, Office of Immigration Statistics. (2022d). Persons obtaining lawful permanent resident status by region and selected country of last residence: Fiscal years 1820 to 2021 (Table 2). *Yearbook of Immigration Statistics: 2021*. https://www.dhs.gov/immigration-statistics/yearbook/2021

U.S. Department of Homeland Security, Office of Immigration Statistics. (2022e). Persons obtaining lawful permanent resident status by state or territory of residence: Fiscal years 2012 to 2021 (Table 4). *Yearbook of Immigration Statistics: 2021*. https://www.dhs.gov/immigration-statistics/yearbook/2021

U.S. Department of Homeland Security, Office of Immigration Statistics. (2022f). Persons obtaining lawful permanent resident status by type and detailed class of admission: Fiscal year 2021 (Table 7). *Yearbook of Immigration Statistics: 2021*. https://www.dhs.gov/immigration-statistics/yearbook/2021

U.S. Department of Homeland Security, Office of Immigration Statistics. (2022g). Refugee arrivals: Fiscal years 1980 to 2021 (Table 13). *Yearbook of Immigration Statistics: 2021*. https://www.dhs.gov/immigration-statistics/yearbook/2021

U.S. Department of Homeland Security, Office of Immigration Statistics. (2022h). Refugee arrivals by region and country of nationality: Fiscal years 2012 to 2021 (Table 14). *Yearbook of Immigration Statistics: 2021*. https://www.dhs.gov/immigration-statistics/yearbook/2021

U.S. Department of the Interior, Bureau of Indian Affairs. (2023, January). *Tribal leaders directory*. https://www.bia.gov/service/tribal-leaders-directory

U.S. National Park Service. (2019). *Did you know: Queen Liliuokalani*. https://www.nps.gov/articles/did-you-know-queen-liliuokalani.htm

Walker, V. S. (2019, April). What black educators built. *Educational Leadership, 76*(7), 12–18.

Watson, T., & Thompson, K. (2021). *The border within: The economics of immigration in an age of fear*. University of Chicago Press.

Whitaker, A., Torres-Guillén, S., Morton, M., Jordan, H., Coyle, S., Mann, A., & Sun, W. (2019). *Cops and no counselors: How the lack of school mental health staff is harming students*. American Civil Liberties Union. https://www.aclu.org/sites/default/files/field_document/030419-acluschooldisciplinereport.pdf

Woo, A., Lee, S. Tuma, A. P., Kaufman, J. H., Lawrence, R. A., & Reed, N. (2023). *Walking on Eggshells—Teachers' responses to classroom limitations on race- or gender-related topics: Findings from the 2022 American instructional resources survey*. Rand Corporation & American Educator Panels.

The World Bank. (2022). *Fertility rate, total (births per woman) – United States*. https://data.worldbank.org/indicator/SP.DYN.TFRT.IN?locations=US

*Wright v. Council of the City of Emporia*, 407 U.S. 451 (1972).

## Chapter 3

AFL-CIO. (2022). *Executive paywatch*. https://aflcio.org/paywatch

Ali, T., Chandra, S., Cherukumilli, S., Fazlullah, A., Galicia, E., Hill, H., . . . Wu, M. (2021). *Looking back, looking forward: What it will take to permanently close the K–12 digital divide*. https://docslib.org/doc/10046343/looking-back-looking-forward-what-it-will-take-to-permanently-close-the-k-12-digital-divide

Bauer, L. (2019, January 3). *Who was poor in the United States in 2017?* Brookings Institution. https://www.brookings.edu/blog/up-front/2019/01/03/who-was-poor-in-the-united-states-in-2017/

Bhutta, N, Bricker, J., Chang, A. C., Dettling, L. J., Goodman, S., Hsu, J. W., . . . Windle, R. A. (2020, September). Changes in U.S. family finances from 2016 to 2019: Evidence from the survey of consumer finances. *Federal Reserve Bulletin, 106*(5). https://www.federalreserve.gov/publications/files/scf17.pdf

Board of Governors of the Federal Reserve System. (2022a, September 7). *Share of total net worth held by the bottom 50% (1st to 50th wealth percentiles)* [WFRBSB50215]. https://fred.stlouisfed.org/series/WFRBSB50215

Board of Governors of the Federal Reserve System. (2022b, September 7). *Share of total net worth held by the top 1% (99th to 100th wealth percentiles)* [WFRBST01134]. https://fred.stlouisfed.org/series/WFRBST01134

Cahalan, M. W., Addison, M., Brunt, N., Patel, P. R., Vaughan III, T., Genao, A., & Perna, L. W (2022). *Indicators of higher education equity in the United States: Historical trend report*. Pell Institute for the Study of Opportunity in Higher Education, Council for Opportunity in Education, and Alliance for Higher Education and Democracy of the University of Pennsylvania.

Calarco, J. M. (2018). *Negotiating opportunities: How the middle class secures advantages in school*. Oxford University Press.

Carnevale, A., Fasules, M. L., Quinn, M. C., & Campbell, K. P. (2019). *Born to win, schooled to lose: Why equally talented students don't get equal chances to be all they can be*. https://cew.georgetown.edu/cew-reports/schooled2lose/#_ga=2.266877451.445204153.1665349038-2081340544.1665349037

Chancel, L., Piketty, T., Saez, E., & Zucman, G. (2022). *Inequality report: 2022*. World Inequality Lab. https://wir2022.wid.world/

Chetty, R., Grusky, D., Hell, M., Hendren, N., Manduca, R., & Narang, J. (2017). *The fading American dream: Trends in absolute income mobility since 1940* (Working Paper No. 22910). National Bureau of Economic Research. https://www.nber.org/papers/w22910.pdf

Children's Defense Fund. (2021). *The state of America's children: 2021*. https://www.childrensdefense.org/wp-content/uploads/2021/04/The-State-of-Americas-Children-2021.pdf

*Citizens United v. Federal Election Commission*, 558 U.S. 310 (2010).

Congressional Budget Office. (2021, August). *The distribution of household income, 2018*. https://www.cbo.gov/publication/57404

Davis, L. P., & Museus, S. D. (2019). What is deficit thinking?: An analysis of conceptualizations of deficit thinking and implications for scholarly research. *Currents: Connecting Diversity to Practice and Society, 1*(1). https://quod.lib.umich.edu/cgi/p/pod/dod-idx/what-is-deficit-thinking-an-analysis-of-conceptualizations.pdf?c=currents;idno=17387731.0001.110;format=pdf

Dolan, K. A., & Peterson-Withorn, C. (2022). Forbes world's billionaires list: The riches in 2022. *Forbes.* https://www.forbes.com/billionaires/

Dubofsky, M., & McCartin, J. A. (2017). *Labor in America: A history* (9th ed.). Wiley Blackwell.

Education Leads Home. (2019, February 15). *Education Leads Home releases homeless student state snapshots.* https://www.schoolhouseconnection.org/education-leads-home-releases-homeless-student-state-snapshots/

Elliott, A. (2022). *Invisible child: Poverty, survival, and hope in an American city.* Random House.

FindLaw. (2022). *Details on state right-to-work laws.* https://www.findlaw.com/state/employment-laws/details-on-state-right-to-work-laws.html

Goldblum, J. S., & Shaddox, C. (2021). *Broke in America: Seeing, understanding, and ending U.S. poverty.* BenBella Books.

Gorski, P. (2018). *Reaching and teaching students in poverty: Strategies for erasing the opportunity gap* (2nd ed.). Teachers College Press.

Gould IV, W. B. (2022). *For labor to build upon: Wars, depression and pandemic.* Cambridge University Press.

Haberman, M., Gillette, M. D., & Hill, D. A. (2018). *Star teachers of children in poverty* (2nd ed.). Routledge & Kappa Delta Pi.

Hallett, R. E., & Skrla, L. (2017). *Serving students who are homeless: A resource guide for schools, districts, and educational leaders.* Teachers College Press.

Henry, M., de Sousa, T., Roddey, C., Gayen, S., Bednar, T. J., & Abt Associates. (2021, January). *The 2020 annual homeless assessment report (AHAR) to Congress. Part 1: Point-in-time estimates of homelessness.* U.S. Department of Housing and Urban Development, Office of Community Planning and Development. https://www.huduser.gov/portal/datasets/ahar/2020-ahar-part-1-pit-estimates-of-homelessness-in-the-us.html

Henry, M., de Sousa, T., Tano, N. D., Hull, R., Shea, M., Morris, T., . . . Abt Associates. (2022, February). *The 2021 annual homeless assessment report (AHAR) to Congress. Part 1: Point-in-time estimates of sheltered homelessness.* U.S. Department of Housing and Urban Development, Office of Community Planning and Development. https://www.huduser.gov/portal/datasets/ahar.html

Hernandez, D. J. (2011, April). *Double jeopardy: How third-grade reading skills and poverty influence high school graduation.* Annie E. Casey Foundation. https://www.aecf.org/resources/double-jeopardy/

Hiefield, M., & Carter, H. (2021, September 26). *There is more to digital equity than devices and bandwidth.* https://www.iste.org/explore/education-leadership/there-more-digital-equity-devices-and-bandwidth

Ingram, E. S., Bridgeland, J. M., Reed, B., & Atwell, M. (2016). *Hidden in plain sight: Homeless students in America's public schools.* Civic Enterprises and Hart Research Associates. https://docs.wixstatic.com/ugd/03cac8_a5b464aa5411457e92d4192019874b05.pdf

Isenberg, N. (2017). *White trash: The 400-year untold history of class in America.* Penguin.

Jan, T. (2022, March 27). Home values soared during the pandemic, except for these Black families. *Washington Post.* https://www.washingtonpost.com/business/2022/03/23/home-appraisal-racial-bias/

Joint Center for Housing Studies of Harvard University. (2022). *The state of the nation's housing: 2022.* https://www.jchs.harvard.edu/state-nations-housing-2022

Jones, J. M. (2022, May 19). *Middle-class identification steady in U.S.* https://news.gallup.com/poll/392708/middle-class-identification-steady.aspx

King, M. L., Jr. (2010/1958). *Stride toward freedom: The Montgomery story.* Beacon.

Koball, H., Moore, A., & Hernandez, J. (2021, April). Basic facts about low-income children: Children under 18 years, 2019. National Center for Children in Poverty. https://www.nccp.org/publication/basic-facts-about-low-income-children-children-under-18-years-2019/

Kochhar, R., & Sechopoulos, S. (2022a, May 10). *Black and Hispanic Americans, those with less education are more likely to fall out of the middle class each year.* Pew Research Center. https://www.pewresearch.org/fact-tank/2022/05/10/black-and-hispanic-americans-those-with-less-education-are-more-likely-to-fall-out-of-the-middle-class-each-year/

Kochhar, R., & Sechopoulos, S. (2022b, April 20). *How the American middle class has changed in the past five decades.* Pew Research Center. https://www.pewresearch.org/fact-tank/2022/04/20/how-the-american-middle-class-has-changed-in-the-past-five-decades/

Krause, E., & Sawhill, I. V. (2018, June 5). Seven reasons to worry about the American middle class. Brookings Institution. https://www.brookings.edu/blog/social-mobility-memos/2018/06/05/seven-reasons-to-worry-about-the-american-middle-class/

Krugman, P. (2021, April 12). America needs to empower workers again. *New York Times.* https://www.nytimes.com/2021/04/12/opinion/us-unions-amazon.html

McCarthy, J. (2022, August 30). *U.S. approval of labor unions at highest point since 1965.* Gallup. https://news.gallup.com/poll/398303/approval-labor-unions-highest-point-1965.aspx

McKernan, S., Ratcliffe, C., Steuerle, E., & Zhang, S. (2014, April). *Impact of the great recession and beyond: Disparities in wealth building by generation and race.* Urban Institute.

Morton, M. H., Dworsky, A., & Samuels, G. M. (2017). *Missed opportunities: Youth homelessness in America. National estimates.* Chapin Hall at the University of Chicago. https://voicesofyouthcount.org/brief/national-estimates-of-youth-homelessness/

Murolo, P., & Chitty, B. B. (2018). *From the folks who brought you the weekend: An illustrated history of labor in the United States.* The New Press.

National Alliance to End Homelessness. (2021). *State of homelessness: 2021 edition.* https://endhomelessness.org/homelessness-in-america/homelessness-statistics/state-of-homelessness-2021/

National Assessment of Educational Progress. (2022a). *NAEP Data Explorer: Reading, grade 4, all students.* https://www.nationsreportcard.gov/ndecore/xplore/NDE

National Assessment of Educational Progress. (2022b). *The nation's report card: NAEP long-term trend assessment results: Reading and mathematics.* https://www.nationsreportcard.gov/highlights/ltt/2022/

National Center for Education Statistics. (2021). *Digest of Education Statistics.* https://nces.ed.gov/programs/digest/current_tables.asp

National Association of Colleges and Employers. (2022). *Equity.* https://www.naceweb.org/about-us/equity-definition/

National Center for Education Statistics. (2022a). Public high school graduation rates. *Condition of Education.* U.S. Department of Education, Institute of Education Sciences. https://nces.ed.gov/programs/coe/indicator/coi

National Center for Education Statistics. (2022b). *Public school revenue sources. Condition of Education.* https://nces.ed.gov/programs/coe/indicator/cma/public-school-revenue

National Center for Homeless Education. (2022). *National overview.* https://profiles.nche.seiservices.com/ConsolidatedState Profile.aspx

National Homelessness Law Center. (2022). Our work. https://homelesslaw.org/issue-areas-2/

National Law Center on Homelessness and Poverty. (2017). *Communities count people experiencing homelessness.* Retrieved from https://homelesslaw.org/hello-world/

National Law Center on Homelessness and Poverty. (2019). *Housing not handcuffs 2019.* https://homelesslaw.org/housing-not-handcuffs-2019/

National Low Income Housing Coalition. (2022). *Out of reach: The high cost of housing.* https://nlihc.org/oor

OECD. (2019). *Society at a glance 2019: OECD social indicators.* https://doi.org/10.1787/soc_glance-2019-en

Oxfam International. (2022, May 23). *Profiting from pain.* https://www.oxfamamerica.org/explore/research-publications/briefs/

Paycor. (2022, July 21). *Minimum wage by state 2022 and 2023 increases.* https://www.paycor.com/resource-center/articles/minimum-wage-by-state/

Persico, C. (2019, November 20). *How exposure to pollution affects educational outcomes and inequality.* Brookings Institution. https://www.brookings.edu/blog/brown-center-chalkboard/2019/11/20/how-exposure-to-pollution-affects-educational-outcomes-and-inequality/

Peterson-Withorn, C. (2022, September 27). The 2022 *Forbes* 400 list of richest Americans: Facts and figures. *Forbes.* https://www.forbes.com/sites/chasewithorn/2022/09/27/the-2022-forbes-400-list-of-richest-americans-facts-and-figures/?sh=a45445918e42

Pew Research Center. (2021). *Mobile fact sheet.* https://www.pewresearch.org/internet/fact-sheet/mobile/#who-is-smartphone-dependent

Reeves, R. V. (2018). *Dream hoarders: How the American upper middle class is leaving everyone else in the dust, why that is a problem, and what to do about it.* Brookings Institution.

Reeves, R. V. (2019, April 29). *Capitalism is failing. People want a job with a decent wage—why is that so hard.* Brookings Institution. https://www.brookings.edu/opinions/capitalism-is-failing-people-want-a-job-with-a-decent-wage-why-is-that-so-hard/

Reeves, R. V., Guyot, K., & Krause, E. (2018, May 7). *Defining the middle class: Cash, credentials, or culture?* Brookings Institution. https://www.brookings.edu/research/defining-the-middle-class-cash-credentials-or-culture/

Reeves, R. V., & Joo, N. (2017, October 4). *White, still: The American upper middle class.* Brookings Institution. https://www.brookings.edu/blog/social-mobility-memos/2017/10/04/white-still-the-american-upper-middle-class/

Reeves, R. V., & Nzau, S. (2021, June 14). *Poverty hurts the boys the most: Inequality at the intersection of class and gender.* Brookings Institution. https://www.brookings.edu/research/poverty-hurts-the-boys-the-most-inequality-at-the-intersection-of-class-and-gender/

Rideout, V. J., & Robb, M. B. (2021). *The Common Sense Census presents: Research brief. Remote learning and digital equity during the pandemic.* https://www.commonsensemedia.org/press-releases/the-common-sense-census-presents-remote-learning-and-digital-equity-during-the-pandemic-2021

Royce, E. (2023). *Poverty & power: The problem of structural inequality* (4th ed.). Rowman & Littlefield.

RRF Foundation for Aging. (2021, January). *Working together to achieve economic security in later life* (Issue Brief #1). https://rrf.issuelab.org/resource/working-together-to-achieve-economic-security-in-later-life.html

Saez, E., & Zucman, G. (2019). *The triumph of injustice: how the rich dodge taxes and how to make them pay.* Norton.

Saez, E., & Zucman, G. (2016, May). Wealth inequality in the United States since 1913: Evidence from capitalized income tax data. *Quarterly Journal of Economics, 131*(2), 519–578.

*San Antonio Independent School District v. Rodriguez,* 411 U.S. 1 (1973).

Shiro, E. G., Pulliam, C., Sabelhaus, J., & Smith, E. (2022, June). *Stuck on the ladder: Intragenerational wealth mobility in the United States.* Brookings Institution.

Shrider, E. A., Kollar, M., Chen, F., & Semega, J. (2021). *Income and poverty in the United States: 2020* (U.S. Census Bureau, Current Population Reports, P60-273). https://www.census.gov/library/publications/2021/demo/p60-273.html

Sitaraman, G. (2017). *The crisis of the middle-class constitution: Why economic inequality threatens our republic.* Vintage Books.

Smith, D. (2020). *The state of the world atlas* (10th ed.). Penguin Books.

Stiglitz, J. E. (2019). *People, power, and profits: Progressive capitalism for an age of discontent.* Norton.

Topoleski, J. J., & Myers, E. A. (2021, November 23). *Worker participation in employer-sponsored pensions: Data in brief* (R43439). https://crsreports.congress.gov/search/#/?term sToSearch=R43439&orderBy=Relevance

United Nations Educational, Scientific and Cultural Organization. (2022). *The right to education: Every human being has the right to quality education and lifelong learning opportunities.* https://www.unesco.org/en/education/right-education

U.S. Bureau of Labor Statistics. (2021a, May). *Major occupational groups as a percentage of total employment, May 2021.* https://www.bls.gov/oes/2021/may/featured_data.htm#largest3

U.S. Bureau of Labor Statistics. (2021b, May). *May 2021 national occupational employment and wage estimates: United States.* https://www.bls.gov/oes/current/oes_nat.htm#00-0000

U.S. Bureau of Labor Statistics. (2022a). *Employed persons by occupation, race, Hispanic or Latino ethnicity, and sex.* https://www.bls.gov/cps/cpsaat10.htm

U.S. Bureau of Labor Statistics. (2022b, September 2). *The employment situation—August 2022.* https://www.bls.gov/news.release/empsit.nr0.htm#

U.S. Bureau of Labor Statistics. (2022c). Fastest growing occupations. *Occupational Outlook Handbook.* https://www.bls.gov/ooh/fastest-growing.htm

U.S. Census Bureau. (2021a). *Female-headed households as a percent of families by poverty status: 1959 to 2021 (Table 12).* https://www.census.gov/data/tables/time-series/demo/income-poverty/historical-poverty-people.html

U.S. Census Bureau. (2021b). *Poverty status of people by age, race, and Hispanic origin: 1959 to 2020 (Table 3).* https://www.census.gov/data/tables/time-series/demo/income-poverty/historical-poverty-people.html

U.S. Census Bureau. (2021c). *Race and Hispanic origin of householder—Families by median and mean income (Table F-5).*

https://www.census.gov/data/tables/time-series/demo/income-poverty/historical-income-families.html

U.S. Census Bureau. (2021d). *Selected characteristics of families by total money income in: 2020 (FINC-01)*. https://www.census.gov/data/tables/time-series/demo/income-poverty/cps-finc/finc-01.html

U.S. Census Bureau. (2021e). *Selected characteristics of people 15 years old and over by total money income, work experience, race, Hispanic origin, and sex (PINC-01)*. https://www.census.gov/data/tables/time-series/demo/income-poverty/cps-pinc/pinc-01.html

U.S. Census Bureau. (2021f). *Type of family—All families by median and mean income: 1947 to 2020 (Table F-7)*. https://www.census.gov/data/tables/time-series/demo/income-poverty/historical-income-families.html

U.S. Census Bureau. (2022a). *Full-time, year-round workers and median earnings in past 12 months (in dollars) by sex, educational attainment and detailed occupation: ACS 2019 (Table 2)*. https://www.census.gov/data/tables/2022/demo/acs-2019.html

U.S. Census Bureau. (2022b). *Income limits for each fifth and top 5 percent of all families: 1947 to 2020 (Table F-1)*. https://www.census.gov/data/tables/time-series/demo/income-poverty/historical-income-families.html

U.S. Department of Health and Human Services. (2022). *HHS poverty guidelines for 2022*. https://aspe.hhs.gov/topics/poverty-economic-mobility/poverty-guidelines

U.S. Government Accountability Office. (2022, June). *Pandemic learning: Less academic progress overall, student and teacher strain, and implications for the future (GAO-22-105816)*. https://www.gao.gov/products/gao-22-105816

Van Dam, A. (2019, March 3). Working parents are an endangered species. That's why Democrats are talking child care. *Washington Post*. https://www.washingtonpost.com/us-policy/2019/02/26/working-parents-are-an-endangered-species-thats-why-democrats-are-talking-child-care/?utm_term=.8f986cff0cc2

Vespa, J., Medina, L., & Armstrong, D. M. (2020, February). *Demographic turning points for the United States: Population projections for 2020 to 2060 (U.S. Census Bureau, Current Population Reports, P25-1144)*. https://www.census.gov/library/publications/2020/demo/p25-1144.html

Waguespack, D., & Ryan, B. (2020). *2020 State index on youth homelessness*. https://homelesslaw.org/2020-state-index-on-youth-homelessness/

Wenger, J. B., & Zaber, M. A. (2021, May 14). *Most Americans consider themselves middle-class. But are they?* Rand Corporation. https://www.rand.org/blog/2021/05/most-americans-consider-themselves-middle-class-but.html

Whitford, E. (2021, March 25). Low-income high schools shut out. *Inside Higher Education*. https://www.insidehighered.com/news/2021/03/25/fall-college-enrollment-declined-more-among-graduates-low-income-high-schools

Will, M. (2022, September 19). Why teachers are going on strike this fall—and what could come next. *Education Week*. https://www.edweek.org/teaching-learning/why-teachers-are-going-on-strike-this-fall-and-what-could-come-next/2022/09

The World Bank. (2022). Nowcast of extreme poverty: 2015–2020. https://www.worldbank.org/en/understanding-poverty

Yang, A. (2018). *The war on normal people: The truth about America's disappearing jobs and why universal basic income is our future*. Hachette Books.

# Chapter 4

Ainsworth, C. (2018, October 22). Sex redefined: The idea of 2 sexes is overly simplistic. *Scientific American*. https://www.scientificamerican.com/article/sex-redefined-the-idea-of-2-sexes-is-overly-simplistic1/

American Association of University Women. (n.d.). *Fast facts: Women working in academia*. https://www.aauw.org/resources/article/fast-facts-academia/

American Civil Liberties Union. (2023). *Mapping attacks on LGBTQ rights in U.S. state legislatures*. https://www.aclu.org/legislative-attacks-on-lgbtq-rights

American Library Association. (2022a, March 24). Large majorities of voters oppose book bans and have confidence in libraries. *ALAnews*. https://www.ala.org/news/press-releases/2022/03/large-majorities-voters-oppose-book-bans-and-have-confidence-libraries

American Psychological Association. (2018). *Guidelines for psychological practice with boys and men*. https://www.apa.org/about/policy/boys-men-practice-guidelines.pdf

American Psychological Association. (2019). *What does transgender mean?* https://www.apa.org/topics/lgbt/transgender

Aragão, C. (2023, March 1). *Gender pay gap in U.S. hasn't changed much in two decades*. Pew Research Center. https://www.pewresearch.org/short-reads/2023/03/01/gender-pay-gap-facts/

Ashwell, K. (2019). *The brain book: Development • function • disorder • health*. Firefly Books.

Austin, A., Craig, S. L., D'Souza, S., & McInroy, L. B. (2020). Suicidality among transgender youth: Elucidating the role of interpersonal risk factors. *Journal of Interpersonal Violence, 37*(5–6), NP2696–NP2718.

Baker, C. N. (2022, Winter). The ERA is ratified, now what? *Ms. Magazine, XXXII*(1), 30–33.

Baker, K. J. M. (2023, January 22). When students change gender identity, and parents don't know. *New York Times*. https://www.nytimes.com/2023/01/22/us/gender-identity-students-parents.html

Beck, K. (2021). *White feminism: From the suffragettes to influencers and who they leave behind*. Atria.

Brink, M. (2022, July 19). Federal judge blocks Title IX guidance on transgender students. *Inside Higher Education*. https://www.insidehighered.com/news/2022/07/19/federal-judge-blocks-ed-dept-title-ix-guidance-trans-students

Brown, A. (2022, June 7). *About 5% of young adults in the U.S. say their gender is different from their sex assigned at birth*. Pew Research Center. https://www.pewresearch.org/short-reads/2022/06/07/about-5-of-young-adults-in-the-u-s-say-their-gender-is-different-from-their-sex-assigned-at-birth/

Brown, A., Horowitz, J. M., Parker, K., & Minkin, R. (2022, June 7). *The experiences, challenges and hopes of transgender and nonbinary U.S. adults*. Pew Research Center. https://www.pewresearch.org/social-trends/2022/06/07/the-experiences-challenges-and-hopes-of-transgender-and-nonbinary-u-s-adults/

Buchholz, K. (2022, March 10). *How has the number of female CEOs in Fortune 500 companies changed over the last 20 years?* World Economic Forum. https://www.weforum.org/agenda/2022/03/ceos-fortune-500-companies-female/

Cantor, D., Fisher, B., Chibnall, S., Harps, S., Townsend, R., Thomas, G., . . . Madden, K. (2020, January 17). *Report on the AAU campus climate survey on sexual assault and misconduct*.

Association of American Universities and Westat. https://www.aau.edu/key-issues/campus-climate-and-safety/aau-campus-climate-survey-2019

Catalano, C. C. J., Blumenfeld, W. J., & Hackman, H. W. (2018). Sexism, heterosexism, and trans* oppression: Introduction. In M. Adams, W. J. Blumenfeld, D. C. J. Catalano, K. S. DeJong, H. W. Hackman, L. E. Hopkins, . . . X. Zúñiga (Eds.), *Readings for diversity and social justice* (4th ed., pp. 341–353). Routledge.

Center for American Women and Politics. (2023). *Current numbers.* https://cawp.rutgers.edu/facts/current-numbers

Centers for Disease Control and Prevention (CDC). (2021, November 15). *About teen pregnancy.* https://www.cdc.gov/teenpregnancy/about/index.htm

Centers for Disease Control and Prevention (CDC). (2022a). *Fast facts: Preventing sexual violence.* https://www.cdc.gov/violenceprevention/sexualviolence/fastfact.html

Centers for Disease Control and Prevention (CDC). (2022b, November 10). *Youth and tobacco use.* https://www.cdc.gov/tobacco/data_statistics/fact_sheets/youth_data/tobacco_use/index.htm

Centers for Disease Control and Prevention (CDC). (2023a, May 11). *Suicide data and statistics.* https://www.cdc.gov/suicide/suicide-data-statistics.html

Centers for Disease Control and Prevention (CDC). (2023b). *WISQARS fatal and nonfatal injury report.* https://wisqars.cdc.gov/reports/

Chappell, S. V., Ketchum, K. E., & Richardson, L. (2018). *Gender diversity and LGBTQ inclusion in K–12 schools: A guide to supporting students, changing lives.* Routledge.

Ciesemier, K., & Strangio, C. (2023, April 27). *Why and how trans hate is spreading.* https://www.aclu.org/podcast/why-and-how-trans-hate-is-spreading

Clayton, H. B., Kilmer, G., DeGue, S, Estefan, L. F., Le, V. D., Suarez, N. A., . . . Thornton, J. E. (2023). Dating violence, sexual violence, and bullying victimization among high school students. Youth Risk Behavior Survey, United States, 2021. *Morbidity and Mortality Weekly Report, 72*(1, Suppl.), 66–74.

De La Cretaz, F. (2022, March 23). The IOC has a new trans-inclusion framework, but it the damage already done? *Sports Illustrated.* https://www.si.com/olympics/2022/03/23/transgender-athletes-testosterone-policies-ioc-framework

Dicker, R. (2016). *A history of U.S. feminisms.* Seal Press.

Editors of Rethinking Schools. (2016). Queering our schools. In A. Butler-Wall, K. Cosier, R. L. S. Harper, J. Sapp, J. Sokolower, & M. B. Tempel (Eds.), *Rethinking sexism, gender, and sexuality* (pp. 22–26). Rethinking Schools.

Eliot, L. (2012). *Pink brain, blue brain: How small differences grow into troublesome gaps—and what we can do about it.* One World.

Evans, E. (2015). *The politics of third wave feminisms: Neoliberalism, intersectionality, and the state in Britain and the US.* Palgrave Macmillan.

*G. G. v. Gloucester County School Board,* 822 F.3d 709 (2016).

GLAAD Media Institute. (2023). *Where we are on TV: 2022–2023.* https://glaad.org/whereweareontv22

Goldberg, S. K., & Santos, T. (2021, March). *Fact sheet: The importance of sports participation for transgender youth.* Center for American Progress. https://www.americanprogress.org/article/fact-sheet-importance-sports-participation-transgender-youth/

*Griswold v. Connecticut,* 381 U.S. 479 (1965).

Harper, C. R., Li, J., Sheats, K., Hertz, M. F., Merrill-Francis, M., Friar, N. W., . . . Hoots, B. E. (2023). Witnessing community violence, gun carrying, and associations with substance use and suicide risk among high school students. *Morbidity and Mortality Weekly Report, 72*(1, Suppl.), 22–28. https://www.cdc.gov/mmwr/ind2023_su.html

Hasenbush, A., Flores, A. R., & Herman, J. L. (2019). Gender identity nondiscrimination laws in public accommodations: A review of evidence regarding safety and privacy in public restrooms, locker rooms, and changing rooms. *Sexuality Research and Social Policy, 15,* 70–83.

Herbst, E., Golinkoff, R. M., & Hirsh-Pasek, K. (2021, November 10). *Holiday shopping in gender-neutral toy aisles? Planning for the future.* Brookings Institution. https://www.brookings.edu/blog/education-plus-development/2021/11/10/holiday-shopping-in-gender-neutral-toy-aisles-playing-for-the-future/

Herman, J. L., Flores, A. R., & O'Neill, K. K. (2022, June). *How many adults and youth identify as transgender in the United States.* Williams Institute, UCLA School of Law.

Hofmann, S. (2016). Miles of aisles of sexism: Helping students investigate toy stores. In E. Marshall & Ö. Sensoy (Eds.), *Rethinking popular culture and media* (2nd ed., pp. 200–208). Rethinking Schools.

Igielnik, R. (2022, April 21). *Most Americans who are familiar with Title IX say it's had a positive impact on gender equality.* Pew Research Center. https://www.pewresearch.org/short-reads/2022/04/21/most-americans-who-are-familiar-with-title-ix-say-its-had-a-positive-impact-on-gender-equality/

International Labour Organization. (2022a, February). *The gender gap in employment: What's holding women back?* https://www.ilo.org/infostories/en-GB/Stories/Employment/barriers-women#intro

International Labour Organization. (2022b, September 16). *Pay transparency can address the gender pay gap.* https://www.ilo.org/global/about-the-ilo/newsroom/news/WCMS_856203/lang--en/index.htm

Johnson, A. G. (2017). *Privilege, power, and difference* (3rd ed.). McGraw Hill.

Kim, R. (2023, April). Boys, men, and Title IX. *Kappan, 104*(7), 62–63.

Kochhar, R. (2023, March 1). *The enduring grip of the gender pay gap.* Pew Research Center. https://www.pewresearch.org/social-trends/2023/03/01/the-enduring-grip-of-the-gender-pay-gap/=

Kolakowski, V. S. (2022, July 5). *The role of religious objections to transgender and nonbinary inclusion and equality and/or gender identity protection.* American Bar Association. https://www.americanbar.org/groups/crsj/publications/human_rights_magazine_home/intersection-of-lgbtq-rights-and-religious-freedom/the-role-of-religious-objections-to-transgender-and-nonbinary-inclusion-and-equality/

Kosciw, J. G., Clark, C. M., & Menard, L. (2022). *The 2021 National School Climate Survey: The experiences of LGBTQ+ youth in our nation's schools.* GLSEN. https://www.glsen.org/school-climate-survey

Kuriloff, P., Andrus, S., & Jacobs, C. (2017). *Teaching girls: How teachers and parents can reach their brains and hearts.* Rowman & Littlefield.

Leech, M. (2022, August 3). Report finds a continued lack of diversity on boards of Fortune 500 companies. *Bizwomen.*

https://www.bizjournals.com/bizwomen/news/latest-news/2022/08/mogul-women-boards.html?page=all

LGBTQ+ Victory Institute. (2013). *Out for America 2023: An overview of LGBTQ+ elected officials in the U.S.* https://victoryinstitute.org/out-for-america-2023/

Lindsey, L. L. (2021). *Gender: Sociological perspectives* (7th ed.). Routledge.

Lorde, A. (1979). *An open letter to Mary Daly.* http://www.historyisaweapon.com/defcon1/lordeopenlettertomarydaly.html

Mangin, M. M. (2022). Teachers' strategies for supporting transgender and/or gender-expansive elementary school students. *Educational Researcher, 51*(5), 324–335.

Mangin, M. M. (2020). *Transgender students in elementary school: Creating an affirming and inclusive school culture.* Harvard Education Press.

Mayo Clinic. (2022, December 21). *Male depression: Understanding the issues.* https://www.mayoclinic.org/diseases-conditions/depression/in-depth/male-depression/art-20046216

Meckler, L. (2022, June 4). How schools are learning to teach gender identity. *Washington Post.* https://www.washingtonpost.com/education/2022/06/03/schools-gender-identity-transgender-lessons/

Meehan, K., & Friedman, J. (2023, April 20). *Update on book bans in the 2022–2023 school year shows expanded censorship of themes centered on race, history, sexual orientation and gender.* Pen America. https://pen.org/report/banned-in-the-usa-state-laws-supercharge-book-suppression-in-schools/

Melidona, D., Cecil, B. G., Cassell, A., & Chessman, H. M. (2023). *The American College President: 2023 edition.* American Council on Education.

Meyer, E. J. (2021, July 14). Trans youth in sports: What's the big idea? How to respond to common myths and misconceptions. *Psychology Today.* https://www.psychologytoday.com/us/blog/gender-and-schooling/202107/trans-youth-in-sports-whats-the-big-deal

Movement Advancement Project. (2023, June 28). *Equality maps: Identity document laws and policies.* https://www.lgbtmap.org/equality-maps/identity_document_laws

Myers, A. (2021). *Supporting transgender students: Understanding gender identity and reshaping school culture.* University of New Orleans Press.

National Academies of Sciences, Engineering, and Medicine. (2020). *Understanding the well-being of LGBTQI+ populations.* Author.

National Center for Education Statistics (NCES). (2022a, September). *Average total income, base salary, and other sources of school and nonschool income for full-time teachers in public and private elementary and secondary schools, by selected characteristics: School year 2020–21 (Table 211.10).* https://nces.ed.gov/programs/digest/d22/tables/dt22_211.10.asp

National Center for Education Statistics (NCES). (2022b, July). *Bachelor's, master's, and doctor's degrees conferred by postsecondary institutions, by sex of student and field of study: 2019–20 (Table 318.30).* https://nces.ed.gov/programs/digest/d21/tables/dt21_318.30.asp

National Center for Education Statistics (NCES). (2022c, September). *Highest degree, average years of experience, and salaries of principals in public and private elementary and secondary schools, by selected characteristics: Selected school years, 2007–08 through 2020–21 (Table 212.10).* https://nces.ed.gov/programs/digest/d22/tables/dt22_212.10.asp

National Center for Education Statistics (NCES). (2022d). *Principals' age and sex: Average and median age of K–12 school principals and percentage distribution of principals, by age category, sex, school type, and selected school characteristics: 2020–21.* https://nces.ed.gov/surveys/ntps/estable/table/ntps/ntps2021_fl02_a12n

National Center for Education Statistics (NCES). (2022e). *Teachers' age and sex: Average and median age of K–12 school teachers and percentage distribution of teachers by age category and by sex, by school type and selected school characteristics: 2020–21.* https://nces.ed.gov/surveys/ntps/estable/table/ntps/ntps2021_fl02_t12n

National Coalition Against Domestic Violence (NCADV). (2016.). *Domestic violence against American Indian and Alaska Native women.* https://www.speakcdn.com/assets/2497/american_indian_and_alaskan_native_women__dv.pdf

National Coalition Against Domestic Violence (NCADV). (n.d.). *National statistics.* https://ncadv.org/STATISTICS

The National Federation of State High School Associations. (2022). *High school athletics participation survey.* https://www.nfhs.org/media/5989280/2021-22_participation_survey.pdf

Parker, K., & Funk, C. (2017, December 14). *Gender discrimination comes in many forms for today's working women.* Pew Research Center. https://www.pewresearch.org/short-reads/2017/12/14/gender-discrimination-comes-in-many-forms-for-todays-working-women/

Parker, K., Horowitz, J. M., & Brown, A. (2022, June 28). *Americans' complex views on gender identity and transgender issues.* Pew Research Center. https://www.pewresearch.org/social-trends/2022/06/28/americans-complex-views-on-gender-identity-and-transgender-issues/

Patrick, K., & Chaudhry, N. (2017). *Let her learn: Stopping school pushout for girls who have suffered harassment and sexual violence.* National Women's Law Center. https://nwlc-ciw49tixgw5lbab.stackpathdns.com/wp-content/uploads/2017/04/final_nwlc_Gates_HarassmentViolence.pdf

Pendharkar, E. (2023, June 14). Pronouns for trans, nonbinary students: The states with laws that restrict them in schools. *Education Week.* https://www.edweek.org/leadership/pronouns-for-trans-nonbinary-students-the-states-with-laws-that-restrict-them-in-schools/2023/06

Reeves, R. V. (2022). *Of boys and men: Why the modern male is struggling, why it matters, and what to do about it.* Brookings Institution.

Sawchuk, S. (2022, June 1). Are teachers obliged to tell parents their child might be trans? Courts may soon decide. *Education Week.* https://www.edweek.org/policy-politics/are-teachers-obliged-to-tell-parents-their-child-might-be-trans-courts-may-soon-decide/2022/04

Schiappa, E. (2022). *The transgender exigency: Defining sex and gender in the 21st century.* Routledge.

Schutz, E. (2022). *Inequality, class, and economics.* Monthly Review Press.

Sensoy, Ö., & DiAngelo, R. (2017). *Is everyone really equal: An introduction to key concepts in social justice education* (2nd ed.). Teachers College Press.

Serano, J. (2018). Trans woman manifesto. In M. Adams, W. J. Blumenfeld, D. C. J. Catalano, K. S. DeJong, H. W. Hackman, L. E. Hopkins, . . . X. Zúñiga (Eds.), *Readings for diversity and social justice* (4th ed., pp. 447–455). Routledge.

Sokolower, J. (2016). As a mom and a teacher . . . In A. Butler-Wall, K. Cosier, R. L. S. Harper, J. Sapp, J. Sokoloer, & M. B. Tempel, *Rethinking sexism, gender, and sexuality* (pp. 100–102). Rethinking Schools.

Spillar, K. (2018, Spring). Marching to the polls. *Ms. Magazine, 28*(2), 20–21.

Steele, C. M. (2011) *Whistling Vivaldi: How stereotypes affect us and what we can do* (reprint ed.). Norton.

Stein, J. (2018, September 15). Census shows gender pay gap is narrowing. *Washington Post.* http://thewashingtonpost.newspaperdirect.com/epaper/viewer.aspx

UN Women. (2018). *Turning promises into action: Gender equality in the 2030 agenda for sustainable development.* http://www.onumulheres.org.br/wp-content/uploads/2018/02/SDG-report-Gender-equality-in-the-2030-Agenda-for-Sustainable-Development-2018-en.pdf

U.S. Bureau of Labor Statistics, U.S. Department of Labor. (2023a, March 7). Labor force participation rate for women highest in the District of Columbia in 2022. *The Economics Daily.* https://www.bls.gov/opub/ted/2023/labor-force-participation-rate-for-women-highest-in-the-district-of-columbia-in-2022.htm

U.S. Bureau of Labor Statistics, U.S. Department of Labor. (2023b, May 10). Preschool teachers. *Occupational Outlook Handbook.* https://www.bls.gov/ooh/Education-Training-and-Library/Preschool-teachers.htm

U.S. Census Bureau. (2021, October). *Degrees conferred by postsecondary institutions, by level of degree and sex of student: Selected years, 1869–70 through 2030–31 (Table 318.10).* https://nces.ed.gov/programs/digest/d21/tables/dt21_318.10.asp?current=yes

U.S. Census Bureau. (2022a). *Educational attainment of the population 18 years and over, by age, sex, race, and Hispanic origin: 2021 (Table 1).* https://www.census.gov/data/tables/2021/demo/educational-attainment/cps-detailed-tables.html

U.S. Census Bureau. (2022b). *Families and people in poverty by type of family: 2020 and 2021 (Table A-2).* https://www.census.gov/library/publications/2022/demo/p60-277.html

U.S. Census Bureau. (2023, March 9). *Full-time, year-round workers and median earnings in the past 12 months by sex and detailed occupation: 2021 (Table 1).* https://www.census.gov/data/tables/time-series/demo/industry-occupation/median-earnings.html

U.S. Department of Labor, Women's Bureau. (2023). *Gender earnings ratio and wage gap by race and Hispanic ethnicity (annual).* https://www.dol.gov/agencies/wb/data/earnings/earnings-ratio-wage-gap-race-ethnicity

U.S. Government Accountability Office. (2021, November). *K–12 education: Students' experiences with bullying, hate speech, hate crimes, and victimization in schools.* https://www.gao.gov/products/gao-22-104341

Wade, L. (2016). The new science of sex difference. In M. B. Zinn, P. Hondagneu-Sotelo, M. A. Messner, & A. M. Denissen (Eds.), *Gender through the prism of difference* (pp. 22–34). Oxford University Press.

Wade, L., & Ferree, M. M. (2023). *Gender: Ideas, interactions, institutions* (3rd ed.). Norton.

Wagner, S. R. (2019). *The women's suffrage movement.* Penguin.

Walsh, M. (2018, June 6). Courts take expansive view in transgender-rights cases. *Education Week, 37*(34), 26.

Weisman, J. (2022, March 23). A demand to define 'woman' injects gender politics into Jackson's confirmation hearing. *New York Times.* https://www.nytimes.com/2022/03/23/us/politics/ketanji-brown-jackson-woman-definition.html

*Whitaker v. Kenosha Unified School District.* No. 16-3522 (7th Cir. 2017).

Williams, J. (2017). *Women vs feminism: Why we all need liberating from the gender wars.* Emerald.

Wilson, A. (2022). *Title IX 50th anniversary: The status of women in college sports.* National Collegiate Athletic Association. https://www.ncaa.org/news/2022/6/23/media-center-title-ix-report-shows-gains-in-female-participation-though-rates-lag-increases-by-men.aspx

Wilson, G. D. M., Bouton, L. J. A., Badgett, M. V. L., & Mackin, M. L. (2023, February). *LGBT poverty in the United States: Trends at the onset of COVID-19.* Williams Institute at UCLA School of Law. https://williamsinstitute.law.ucla.edu/publications/lgbt-poverty-us/

The World Bank. (2016). *Primary school age children out-of school (%).* Gender Data Portal. https://genderdata.worldbank.org/indicators/se-lpv-prim-oos?gender=male and https://genderdata.worldbank.org/indicators/se-lpv-prim-oos

The World Bank. (2019). *Rate of out-of-school youth of upper secondary school age (%).* Gender Data Portal. https://genderdata.worldbank.org/indicators/uis-rofst-3-cp

The World Bank. (2022, March 1). *Nearly 2.4 billion women globally don't have same economic rights as men.* https://www.worldbank.org/en/news/press-release/2022/03/01/nearly-2-4-billion-women-globally-don-t-have-same-economic-rights-as-men

World Health Organization. (2021, March 9). *Devastatingly pervasive: 1 in 3 women globally experience violence.* https://www.who.int/news/item/09-03-2021-devastatingly-pervasive-1-in-3-women-globally-experience-violence

Zacharek, S., Dockterman, E., & Edwards, H. S. (2017, December 18). The silence breakers: The voices that launched a movement. *Time, 190*(25). http://time.com/time-person-of-the-year-2017-silence-breakers/

## Chapter 5

*303 Creative LLC et al. v. Elenis et al.,* 600 US 21–476. (2023)

Allen, E. (2023, July 12). Former York special education teacher sues district for discrimination. *Portland Press Herald.* https://www.pressherald.com/2023/07/11/former-york-special-education-teacher-sues-district-for-discrimination/

American Academy of Child and Adolescent Psychiatry. (2018). *Conversion therapy.* https://www.aacap.org/aacap/Policy_Statements/2018/Conversion_Therapy.aspx

American Civil Liberties Union (ACLU). (2023a). *An update on the status of sodomy laws.* https://www.aclu.org/other/update-status-sodomy-laws

American Civil Liberties Union (ACLU). (2023b). *Mapping attacks on LGBTQ rights in U.S. state legislatures.* www.aclu.org/legislative-attacks-on-lgbtq-rights

American Psychiatric Association. (2018). *APA reiterates strong opposition to conversion therapy.* https://www.psychiatry.org/newsroom/news-releases/apa-reiterates-strong-opposition-to-conversion-therapy

American Psychological Association. (2019). *Sexual orientation and homosexuality.* https://www.apa.org/topics/lgbt/orientation

Associated Press. (2021). *Court backs a teacher who refused to use transgender students' pronouns.* National Public Radio. https://www.npr.org/2021/08/31/1032929550/virginia-teacher-transgender-pronoun-supreme-court

Associated Press. (2023, July 1). *Designer in Supreme Court ruling cited client who denies making wedding site request.* National Public Radio. https://www.npr.org/2023/07/01/1185632827/web-designer-supreme-court-gay-couples

Bowman, M. (2023, June 6). *Hundreds of Floridians attend contentious school board meeting in Hernando County.*

National Public Radio. https://www.npr.org/2023/06/06/1180361024/hundreds-of-floridians-attend-contentious-school-board-meeting-in-hernando-count

Bronski, M., Pellegrini, A., & Amico, M. (2013). *"You can tell just by looking" and 20 other myths about LGBT life and people*. Beacon Press.

Bryant, A. (1977). *The Anita Bryant story: The survival of our nation's families and the threat of militant homosexuality*. Revell.

Burga, S. (2023, July 16). The implications of Supreme Court's 303 Creative decision are already being felt. *Time*. https://time.com/6295024/303-creative-supreme-court-future-implications/

California Department of Education. (2011). *Frequently asked questions: Senate Bill 48*. https://www.cde.ca.gov/ci/cr/cf/senatebill48faq.asp

California Department of Education. (2017). *History social science framework for California Public Schools*. https://www.cde.ca.gov/ci/hs/cf/documents/hssframeworkwhole.pdf

Catalano, D. C. J., Blumenfeld, W. J., & Hackman, H. W. (2018). Sexism, heterosexism, and trans* oppression. In M. Adams, W. J. Blumenfeld, D. C. J. Catalano, K. S. DeJong, H. W. Hackman, L. E. Hopkins, . . . X. Zúñiga (Eds.), *Readings for diversity and social justice* (4th ed., pp. 367–373). Routledge.

CBS Miami. (2018, February 9). *Catholic school teacher fired for marrying a woman*. https://miami.cbslocal.com/2018/02/09/teacher-married-woman-fired-catholic-lgbtq/

Center for Countering Digital Hate & Human Rights Campaign. (2022). *Digital hate: Social media's role in amplifying dangerous lies about LGBTQ+ people*. https://hrc-prod-requests.s3-us-west-2.amazonaws.com/CCDH-HRC-Digital-Hate-Report-2022-single-pages.pdf

Chappell, S. V., Ketchum, K. E., & Richardson, L. (2018). *Gender diversity and LGBTQ inclusion in K–12 schools: A guide to supporting students, changing lives*. Routledge.

College Board. (2023, August 3). *Statement on AP Psychology and Florida*. https://newsroom.collegeboard.org/statement-ap-psychology-and-florida

Desantis, R. (2022, March 28). *Governor Ron DeSantis signs historic bill to protect parental rights in education*. https://www.flgov.com/2022/03/28/governor-ron-desantis-signs-historic-bill-to-protect-parental-rights-in-education/

Dobbs v. Jackson Women's Health Organization, No. 19-1392, 597 U.S. 215 (2022).

Eagan, P. J., & Sherrill, K. (2009, January). *California's Proposition 8: What happened and what does the future hold?* National Gay and Lesbian Task Force.

Eaklor, V. L. (2008). *Queer America: A people's GLBT history of the United States*. The New Press.

Faderman, L. (2015). *The gay revolution: The story of the struggle*. Simon & Schuster.

Foody, K. (2023). *Court backs teacher firing over transgender students' names*. Associated Press. https://apnews.com/article/indiana-teacher-lawsuit-transgender-student-names-883b50e19088614d71df25f0f835ed08

Gallup. (2023). LGBTQ+ rights. https://news.gallup.com/poll/1651/gay-lesbian-rights.aspx

Ganna, A., Verweij, K. J. H., Nivard, M. G., Maier, R., Wedow, R., Busch, A. S., et al. (2019). Large-scale GWAS reveals insights into the genetic architecture of same-sex sexual behavior. *Science, 365*(6456), eaat7693.

Gates, G. J., & Newport, F. (2015, April 24). *An estimated 780,000 Americans in same-sex marriages*. Gallup. http://www.gallup.com/poll/182837/estimated-780-000-americans-sex-marriages.aspx?utm_source=SAME_SEX_RELATIONS&utm_medium=topic&utm_campaign=tiles

Gjelten, T. (2021, March 10). *Some faith leaders call Equality Act devastating; for others, it's God's will*. National Public Radio. https://www.npr.org/2021/03/10/974672313/some-faith-leaders-call-equality-act-devastating-for-others-its-gods-will

GLSEN. (2024). *Inclusive curricular standards policies*. https://maps.glsen.org/inclusive-curricular-standards-policies/

Hernandez, J. (2023a). *Florida is investigating a teacher who showed a Disney movie with a gay character*. National Public Radio. https://www.npr.org/2023/05/16/1176334055/florida-investigating-teacher-disney-movie-gay-character-desantis

Hernandez, J. (2023b). *Target removes some Pride Month products after threats against employees*. National Public Radio. https://www.npr.org/2023/05/24/1177963864/target-pride-month-lgbtq-products-threats

Human Rights Campaign. (2018). *2018 LGBTQ youth report*. https://assets2.hrc.org/files/assets/resources/2018-Youth-Report-NoVid.pdf?_ga=2.134619825.1102244158.1526302453-846000759.1523970534

Human Rights Campaign. (2019). *Explore: Coming out*. https://www.hrc.org/explore/topic/coming-out

Human Rights Campaign. (2023a). *The Equality Act*. https://www.hrc.org/resources/equality

Human Rights Campaign. (2023b). *LGBTQ+ Americans under attack: A report and reflection on the 2023 state legislative session*. https://hrc-prod-requests.s3-us-west-2.amazonaws.com/Anti-LGBTQ-Legislation-Impact-Report.pdf

Human Rights Campaign. (2023c). *Welcoming schools: Back-to-school toolkit*. https://hrc-prod-requests.s3-us-west-2.amazonaws.com/welcoming-schools/documents/Welcoming-Schools-Back-to-School-2023-Toolkit.pdf

Izaguirre, A. (2023, March 22). *DeSantis to expand 'don't say gay' law to all grades*. Associated Press. https://apnews.com/article/dont-say-gay-desantis-florida-gender-d3a9c91f4b5383a5bf6df6f7d8ff65b6

Izaguirre, A., & Farrington, B. (2023, April 19). *Florida expands "don't say gay"; house OKs anti-LGBTQ bills*. Associated Press. https://apnews.com/article/desantis-florida-dont-say-gay-ban-684ed25a303f83208a89c556543183cb

Johns, M. M., Lowry, R., Andrzejewski, J., Barrios, L. C., Zewditu, D., McManus, T., et al. (2019). Transgender identity and experiences of violence victimization, substance use, suicide risk, and sexual risk behaviors among high school student–19 states and large urban school districts, 2017. *Morbidity and Mortality Weekly Report, 68*(3), 65–71.

Johns, M. M., Lowry, R., Haderxhanaj, L. T., Rasberry, C. N., Robin, L., Scales, L., et al. (2020). Trends in violence victimization and suicide risk by sexual identity among high school students — Youth Risk Behavior Survey, United States, 2015–2019. *Morbidity and Mortality Weekly Report, 69*(Suppl. 1), 19–27.

Jones, J. M. (2022, February 17). *LGBT identification in U.S. tick up to 7.1%*. Gallup. https://news.gallup.com/poll/389792/lgbt-identification-ticks-up.aspx

Kosciw, J. G., Clark, C. M., & Menard, L. (2022). *The 2021 national school climate survey: The experiences of LGBTQ+ youth in our nation's schools*. GLSEN. https://www.glsen.org/sites/default/files/2022-10/NSCS-2021-Full-Report.pdf

Lavietes, M. (2022, April 1). *'I cannot teach in Florida': LGBTQ educators fear fallout from new school law*. NBC News. https://www.nbcnews.com/nbc-out/out-politics-and-policy/-cannot-teach-florida-lgbtq-educators-fear-fallout-new-school-law-rcna22106

*Lawrence v. Texas*, 539 U.S. 558 (2003).

Lindsey, R. (1985, October 22). Dan White, killer of San Francisco mayor, a suicide. *New York Times*. https://www.nytimes.com/1985/10/22/us/dan-white-killer-of-san-francisco-mayor-a-suicide.html

López Restrepo, M. (2023, March 6). *The anti-drag bills sweeping the U.S. are straight from history's playbook*. National Public Radio. https://www.npr.org/2023/03/06/1161452175/anti-drag-show-bill-tennessee-trans-rights-minor-care-anti-lgbtq-laws

*Lovell v. Comsewogue School District*, 214 F.Supp. 2d 319 (E.D.N.Y. 2002).

*L. W. v. Toms River Regional Schools Board of Education* (OAL Dkt. No.: CRT 8535-01), 2007.

Lugg, C. A., & Adelman, M. (2015). Sociolegal contexts of LGBTQ issues in education. In G. L. Wimberly (Ed.), *LGBTQ issues in education: Advancing a research agenda* (pp. 43–73). American Educational Research Association.

Maher, B., & Toledo, W. (2022). From pre-service to professional teaching: A longitudinal study of two LGBTQ+-identifying first-year elementary teachers' experiences. *Journal of Homosexuality, 69*(12), 2126–2147.

Mark, J. J. (2021, June 25). LGBTQ+ in the ancient world. *World History Encyclopedia*. https://www.worldhistory.org/article/1790/lgbtq-in-the-ancient-world/

McCarthy, M. M., Eckes, S. E., & Decker, J. R. (2019). *Legal rights of school leaders, teachers, and students* (8th ed.). Pearson.

Mora, H. L. (2015). Henry Gerber's bridge to the world. In A. Brooks (Ed.), *The right side of history: 100 years of LGBTQI activism* (pp. 10–15). Cleis Press.

*Morrison v. Board of Education*, 461 P.2d 375 (Cal. 1969).

Movement Advancement Project. (2023a). *Equality maps: Child welfare nondiscrimination laws*. https://www.lgbtmap.org/equality-maps/foster_and_adoption_laws

Movement Advancement Project. (2023b). *Equality maps: LGBTQ curricular laws*. https://www.lgbtmap.org/equality_maps/curricular_laws.

Movement Advancement Project (2023c). *Equality maps: Safe Schools Laws*. https://www.lgbtmap.org/equality-maps/safe_school_laws

Movement Advancement Project. (2023d). *Equality maps: Transgender healthcare "shield" laws*. https://www.lgbtmap.org/equality-maps/healthcare/trans_shield_laws

*Nabozny v. Mary Podlesny, William Davis, Thomas Blauert, et al*. 92 F.3d 446 (1996).

Nathanson, H. (2023, May 23). Objection to sexual, LGBTQ content propels spike in book challenges. *Washington Post*. https://www.washingtonpost.com/education/2023/05/23/lgbtq-book-ban-challengers/

National Center for Education Statistics. (2023). *Fast facts: Back to school statistics*. https://nces.ed.gov/fastfacts/display.asp?id=372

National Education Association. (2023). *Bostock and educator rights*. www.nea.org/sites/default/files/2023-04/27379-bostock-and-educator-rights-doc_final.pdf

National Education Association & Human Rights Campaign Foundation. (2023). *Welcoming Schools: What do you say to 'that's so gay' & other anti-LGBTQ* comments?* https://hrc-prod-requests.s3-us-west-2.amazonaws.com/welcoming-schools/documents/Welcoming-Schools-Back-to-School-2023-Toolkit.pdf

The NPD Group. (2022, June 15). *LGBTQ fiction sales are surging the U.S., NPD says*. https://www.npd.com/news/press-releases/2022/lgbtq-fiction-sales-are-surging-in-the-u-s-npd-says/

*Obergefell v. Hodges*, No. 14-556 (U.S. June 26, 2015).

*One, Inc. v. Olesen*, 355 U.S. 371. (1958).

Price-Feeney, M., Green, A. E., & Dorison, S. (2020). Understanding the mental health of transgender and nonbinary youth. *Journal of Adolescent Health, 66*(6), 684–690.

Rosales, I., & Garcia, J. (2023, May 23). *Florida school system has closed investigation into teacher who showed Disney movie with gay character*. CNN. https://www.cnn.com/2023/05/23/us/florida-teacher-lgbtq-disney-movie-investigation/index.html

Ryan, H. (2019, June 28). *How dressing in drag was labeled a crime in the 20th century*. History.com. https://www.history.com/news/stonewall-riots-lgbtq-drag-three-article-rule.

Sadowski, M. (2016). *Safe is not enough: Better schools for LGBTQ students*. Harvard Education Press.

*Schroeder v. Hamilton School District*, 282 F.3d 946 (7th Cir. 2002).

Sears, B., Mallory, C., Flores, A. R., & Conron, K. J. (2021). *LGBT people's experiences of workplace discrimination and harassment*. UCLA School of Law, Williams Institute. https://williamsinstitute.law.ucla.edu/wp-content/uploads/Workplace-Discrimination-Sep-2021.pdf

Southern Poverty Law Center. (2022). *Hate crimes laws, explained*. https://www.splcenter.org/news/2022/09/07/hate-crime-laws-timeline

Toledo, W., & Maher, B. (2021). On becoming an LGBTQ+-identifying teacher: A year-long study of two gay and lesbian preservice elementary teachers. *Journal of Homosexuality, 68*(10), 1609–1638.

The Trevor Project. (2022). *2022 national survey on LGBTQ youth mental health*. https://www.thetrevorproject.org/survey-2022/assets/static/trevor01_2022survey_final.pdf

Trans Legislation Tracker. (2023). *2023 anti-trans bill tracker*. https://translegislation.com/

Trotta, D. (2019, June 6). *New York police commissioner apologizes for Stonewall raid in 1969*. Reuters. https://www.reuters.com/article/us-usa-lgbt-stonewall-nypd/new-york-police-commissioner-apologizes-for-stonewall-raid-in-1969-idUSKCN1T72IR

U.S. Department of Health and Human Services. (2022). *HIV.gov data & trends*. https://www.hiv.gov/hiv-basics/overview/data-and-trends/statistics/

Verner Chappell, S., Ketchum, K. E., & Richardson, L. (2018). *Gender diversity and LGBTQ inclusion in K–12 schools: A guide to supporting students, changing lives*. Routledge.

*Walsh v. Tehachapi Unified School District*, 997 F.Supp.2d 1071 (2014).

Williams, P. (2022, October 31). The right-wing mother fueling the school-board wars. *The New Yorker*. https://www.newyorker.com/magazine/2022/11/07/the-right-wing-mothers-fuelling-the-school-board-wars

World Health Organization. (2022). *Summary of the global HIV epidemic, 2022*. https://www.who.int/data/gho/data/themes/hiv-aids

# Chapter 6

American School for the Deaf. (n.d.). *The American School for the Deaf—Today in history: April 15*. https://connecticuthistory.org/the-american-school-for-the-deaf-today-in-history/

Anti-Defamation League. (2017, March 5). *A brief history of the disability rights movement*. https://www.adl.org/resources/backgrounder/brief-history-disability-rights-movement

The Arc. (n.d.). *Civil rights: Overview*. https://thearc.org/policy-advocacy/civil-rights/

*Board of Education of the Hendrick Hudson School District v. Rowley*, 458 U.S. 176 (1982).

Bodenhamer, S., & Taylor, K. (2023). Special educator shortage: Examining teacher burnout and mental health. *Inside IES Research*. https://ies.ed.gov/blogs/research/post/special-educator-shortage-examining-teacher-burnout-and-mental-health

Bogart, K. R., & Dunn, D.S. (2019). Ableism special issue introduction. *Journal of Social Issues, 75*(3), 650–664.

Bogart, K. R., Lund, E. M., & Rottenstein, A. (2018). Disability pride protects self-esteem through the rejection-identification model. *Rehabilitation Psychology, 63*(1), 155–159. https://pubmed.ncbi.nlm.nih.gov/28758773/

Boskovich, L. A., Cannon, M., Hernández-Saca, Kahn, L. G., & Nusbaum, E. A. (2019). Self-study of intersectional and emotional narratives: Narrative inquiry, disability studies in education, and praxis in social science research. In *New narratives of disability: Constructions, clashes, and controversies (Research in social science and disability), 11*, 215–230. Emerald Publishing. https://doi.org/10.1108/S1479-354720190000011026

Brown, I. (2018). Spectacle, science, services and civil rights. In R. Hanes, I. Brown, & N. E. Hansen (Eds.), *The Routledge history of disability*. Routledge.

Brown, P. D. (2022, March). White educators working with Black parents: Resistance and trust. *Kappan, 103*(6), 46–51.

*Brown v. Board of Education of Topeka*, 347 U.S. 483 (1954).

*Buck v. Bell*, 274 U.S. 200 (1927).

Carmel, J. (2020a, July 22). Before the A.D.A., there was Section 504. *New York Times*. https://www.nytimes.com/2020/07/22/us/504-sit-in-disability-rights.html

Carmel, J. (2020b, July 29). "Nothing about us without us": 16 moments in the fight for disability rights. *New York Times*. https://www.nytimes.com/2020/07/22/us/ada-disabilities-act-history.html

Centers for Disease Control and Prevention (CDC). (2020a, September 16). *Disability and health healthy living*. https://www.cdc.gov/ncbddd/disabilityandhealth/healthyliving.html

Centers for Disease Control and Prevention (CDC). (2020b, September 16). *Disability and health overview*. https://www.cdc.gov/ncbddd/disabilityandhealth/disability.html

Centers for Disease Control and Prevention (CDC). (2023a, June 6). *Disability and health data now*. https://www.cdc.gov/ncbddd/disabilityandhealth/features/disability-health-data.html

Centers for Disease Control and Prevention (CDC). (2023b, May 15). *Disability impacts all of us*. https://www.cdc.gov/ncbddd/disabilityandhealth/infographic-disability-impacts-all.html

*Chandra Smith v. L.A. Unified Sch. Dist.*, 830 F.3d 843 (1996).

Dunn, L. (1968). Special education for the mildly retarded: Is much of it justifiable? *Exceptional Children, 7*, 5–24.

Dunn, D. A., & Burcaw, S. (2013). Disability identity: Exploring narrative accounts of disability. *Rehabilitation Psychology, 51*(4), 148–157.

*Endrew F. v. Douglas County School District* RE–1, 580 U.S. (2017).

*Felix v. Lingle* 1:93-cv-00367 (D. Haw.) (1993).

Fenning, P., & Johnson, M. (2022). Introductory comments: An interdisciplinary lens in addressing discipline disparities of students with disabilities. In P. Fenning & M. Johnson (Eds.), *Discipline disparities among students with disabilities: Creating equitable environments* (pp. 3–13). Teachers College Press.

Forber-Pratt, A. J., & Minotti, B. J. (2023). Disabled lives: Worthiness and identity in an ageist society. In F. R. Waitoller & K. A. K. Thorius (Eds.), *Sustaining disabled youth: Centering disability in asset pedagogies* (pp. 3–16). Teachers College Press.

Grim, A. (2015, July 8). Sitting-in for disability rights: The Section 504 protests of the 1970s. In National Museum of American History, *O say can you see?: Stories from the museum*. https://americanhistory.si.edu/blog/sitting-disability-rights-section-504-protests-1970s

Grissom, J., & Redding, C. (2016). Discretionary and disproportionality: Explaining the underrepresentation of high-achieving students of color in gifted programs. *AERA Open, 2*(1), 1–25.

Hacker, C., Zalani, A., Sanchez, J., & Stock, S. (2022, December 9). Handcuffs in hallways: hundreds of elementary students arrested at U.S. schools. *CBS News*. https://www.cbsnews.com/news/hundreds-of-elementary-students-arrested-at-us-schools/

Hallahan, D., Kauffman, J., & Pullen, P. (2019). *Exceptional learners: An introduction to special education* (14th ed.). Pearson.

Harry, B., & Klingner, J. (2022). *Why are so many students of color in speciation education: Understanding race and disability in schools*. Teachers College Press.

History.com Editors. (2019, January 18). *Helen Keller*. https://www.history.com/topics/womens-history/helen-keller

Human Rights Watch. (2015, May 12). *Callous and cruel: Use of force against inmates with mental disabilities in US jaoils and prisons*. https://www.hrw.org/report/2015/05/12/callous-and-cruel/use-force-against-inmates-mental-disabilities-us-jails-and

*Irving Independent School District v. Tatro*, 468 U.S. 883 (1984).

Jaffee, L. J. (2023). Disability matters: A materialist history of disability under U.S. settler-capitalism. In M. Cole, *Equality, education, and human rights in the United States: Issues of gender, race, sexuality, disability, and social class* (pp. 166–217). Routledge.

Jarrett, S. (2020). *Those they called idiots: The idea of the disabled mind from 1700 to the present day*. Reaktion Books.

Kart, A., & Kart, M. (2021). Academic and social effects of inclusion on students without disabilities: A review of the literature. *Education Sciences, 11*(1), Article No. 16. https://www.mdpi.com/2227-7102/11/1/16

Kauffman, J. M., & Badar, J. (2020). Definitions and other issues. In J. M. Kauffman (Ed.), *On educational inclusion: Meanings, history, issues and international perspectives* (pp. 1–24). Routledge.

Lane, K. L., Buckman, M. M., Oakes, W. P., & Menzies, H. (2020). Tiered systems and inclusion: Potential benefits, clarifications, and considerations. In J. M. Kauffman (Ed.), *On educational inclusion: Meanings, history, issues and international perspectives* (pp. 85–106). Routledge.

*Larry P. v. Riles*, 495 F.Supp. 926 (N.D. Cal. 1979).

Learning Disabilities Association of America. (2023, January 9). *Right to an evaluation of a child for special education services.* https://ldaamerica.org/advocacy/lda-position-papers/right-to-an-evaluation-of-a-child-for-special-education-services/

Library of Congress. (n.d.). Louis Braille (1809–1852). *National Library Service for the Blind and Print Disabled.* https://www.loc.gov/nls/braille-audio-reading-materials/lists-nls-produced-books-topic-genre/listings-on-narrow-topics-mini bibliographies/louis-braille-1809-1852/

Lieberman, M. (2023, April 27). How special education funding actually works. *Education Week.* https://www.edweek.org/teaching-learning/how-special-education-funding-actually-works/2023/04

Maslow, A. (1954). *Motivation and personality.* Harper.

Mastropieri, M. A., & Scruggs, T. E. (2018). *The inclusive classroom: Strategies for effective instruction* (6th ed.). Pearson.

Mayes, K. A. (2022). *The unteachables: Disability rights and the invention of Black special education.* University of Minnesota Press.

Mercer, J. (1973). *Labeling the mentally retarded.* University of California Press.

*Mills v. Board of Education of the District of Columbia*, 348 F.Supp. 866 (D.D.C. 1972).

Moll, L., & González, N. (2004). Engaging life: A funds-of-knowledge approach to multicultural education. In J. A. Banks & C. A. M. Banks (Eds.), *Handbook of research on multicultural education* (2nd ed., pp. 699–715). Jossey-Bass.

Morgan, P., Farkas, G., Cook, M., Strassfeld, N., Hillemeier, M., Pun, W., . . . Schussler, D. (2018). Are Hispanic, Asian, Native American, or language-minority children overrepresented in special education? *Exceptional Children, 84*(3), 261–279.

Murdick, N., Gartin, B., & Crabtree, T. (2014). *Special education law* (3rd ed.). Pearson.

National Archives. (1982). *Code of Federal Regulations: Part 15v— Nondiscrimination on the basis of handicap in programs or activities receiving federal financial assistance.* https://www.ecfr.gov/current/title-7/subtitle-A/part-15b

National Association for the Education of Young Children. (2022). *Developmentally appropriate practice in early childhood programs* (4th ed.). Author.

National Association for Gifted Children. (2019, July 11). *A definition of giftedness that guides best practice* [Position Statement]. https://nagc.org/page/position-statements

National Association for Gifted Education. (2023). *Jacob Javits Gifted and Talented Students Education Act.* https://nagc.org/page/jacob-javits-gifted-and-talented-students-education-act

National Center for Education Statistics (NCES). (2022a, February). *Children 3 to 21 years old served under Individuals with Disabilities Education Act (IDEA), Part B, by type of disability: Selected years, 1976–77 through 2021–22 (Table 204.30).* U.S. Department of Education. https://nces.ed.gov/programs/digest/d22/tables/dt22_204.30.asp

National Center for Education Statistics (NCES). (2022b, October). Percentage distribution of enrollment in public elementary and secondary schools, by race/ethnicity and state or jurisdiction: Fall 2010, fall 2020, and fall 2021 (Table 203.70). *Digest of Education Statistics.* U.S. Department of Education. https://nces.ed.gov/programs/digest/d22/tables/dt22_203.70.asp

National Center for Education Statistics (NCES). (2022c, March). *Percentage of public school students enrolled in gifted and talented programs, by sex, race/ethnicity, and state: Selected years, 2004 through 2017–18 (Table 204.90).* U.S. Department of Education. https://nces.ed.gov/programs/digest/d21/tables/dt21_204.90.asp?current=yes

National Center for Education Statistics (NCES). (2022d, June). *Public high school 4-year adjusted cohort graduation rate (ACGR), by selected student characteristics and locate: 2019–20 (Table 219.47).* U.S. Department of Education. https://nces.ed.gov/programs/digest/d21/tables/dt21_219.47.asp

National Center for Education Statistics (NCES). (2022e, July 25). *Special education—Grants to states: Funding status appropriations.* U.S. Department of Education. https://www2.ed.gov/programs/osepgts/funding.html

National Center for Education Statistics (NCES). (2023a, February). Children 3 to 21 years old served under Individuals with Disabilities Education Act (IDEA), Part B, by age group and sex, race/ethnicity, and type of disability: School year 2021–22 (Table 204.50). *Digest of Education Statistics.* U.S. Department of Education. https://nces.ed.gov/programs/digest/d22/tables/dt22_204.50.asp

National Center for Education Statistics (NCES). (2023b, February). Percentage distribution of school-age students served under Individuals with Disabilities Education Act (IDEA), Part B, by educational environment and type of disability: Selected years, fall 1989 through fall 2021 (Table 204.60). *Digest of Education Statistics.* U.S. Department of Education. https://nces.ed.gov/programs/digest/d22/tables/dt22_204.60.asp

National Center for Education Statistics (NCES). (2023c, May). Students with disabilities. *Condition of Education.* U.S. Department of Education. https://nces.ed.gov/programs/coe/indicator/cgg#suggested-citation

Nirje, B. (1985). The basis and logic of the normalization principle. *Australia and New Zealand Journal of Developmental Disabilities, 11*, 65–68.

Ocasio-Stoutenburg, L., & Harry, B. (2021). *Case studies in builind equity through family advocacy in special education.* Teachers College Press.

Osborne, A. G. Jr., & Russo, C. J. (2021). *Special education and the law: A guide for practitioners.* Corwin Press.

Pappas, S. (2020). Despite the ADA, equity is still out of reach: Psychologists are intensifying efforts to improve health care, justice, employment and more for people with disabilities. *Monitor on Psychology, 51*(8). https://www.apa.org/monitor/2020/11/feature-ada

*Parents in Action on Special Ed.(Pase) v. Hannon*, 506 F.Supp. 831 (N.D. Ill. 1980).

*Pennsylvania Association for Retarded Citizens (PARC) v. Commonwealth of Pennsylvania*, 334 F.Supp. 1257 (E.D. Pa. 1971).

Perry, D. M., & Carter-Long, L. (2016, March). *The Ruderman white paper on media coverage of law enforcement use of force and disability.* Ruderman Family Foundation.

Petek, G. (2019, November 6). *Overview of special education in California.* California Legislative Analyst's Office. https://lao.ca.gov/Publications/Detail/4110

Renzuli, J. S., & Brandon, L. E. (2017, August). Common sense about the under-representation issue: A school-wide approach to increase participation of diverse students in programs that develop talents and gifted behaviors in young people. *International Journal for Talent Development and Creativity.* http://morgridge.du.edu/wp-content/uploads/2019/01/Common-Sense-About-the-Under-Representation-Issue-2017.pdf

Rinn, A. N., Mun, R. U., & Hodges, J. (2022). *State of the states in gifted education.* National Association for Gifted Children and the Council of State Directors of Programs for the Gifted.

Rufo, J. M., & Causton, J. (2022). *Reimagining special education: Using inclusion as a framework to build equity and support all students.* Brookes.

Skiba, R. J. Chung, C., Trachok, M., Baker, T. L., Sheya, A., & Hughes, R. L. (2014). Parsing disciplinary disproportionality: Contributions of infraction, student, and school characteristics to out-of-school suspension and expulsion. *Research Journal, 51*(4), 640–670.

Skiba, R. J., Horner, R. H., Chung, C.-G., Rausch, M. K., May, S. L., & Tobin, T. (2011). Race is not neutral: A national investigation of African American and Latino disproportionality in school discipline. *School Psychology Review, 40*(2), 85–107.

Smith, D., Tyler, N., & Skow, K. G. (2018). *Introduction to contemporary special education: New horizons* (2nd ed.). Pearson.

Statistical Atlas. (n.d.) *School enrollment in the United States.* https://statisticalatlas.com/United-States/School-Enrollment

Steinweg, A. (2023, July 12). *Non-Hispanic Black adults have higher rates of disability due to arthritis, diabetes, hypertension than non-Hispanic white adults.* U.S. Census Bureau. https://www.census.gov/library/stories/2023/07/disparities-in-disabilities.html

Temple University. (n.d.). *Disability rights timeline.* College of Education and Human Development, Institute on Disabilities. https://disabilities.temple.edu/resources/disability-rights-timeline

Thorius, K. A. K., & Waitoller, F. R. (2023). Disability and asset pedagogies: An introduction to the book. In F. R. Waitoller & K. A. K. Thorius (Eds.), *Sustaining disabled youth: Centering disability in asset pedagogies* (pp. xv–xxxi). Teachers College Press.

Tomlinson, C. A. (2022). *Everybody's classroom: Differentiating for the shared and unique needs of diverse students.* Teachers College Press.

U.S. Bureau of Labor Statistics. (2023, February 23). *Persons with a disability: Labor force characteristics—2022.* U.S. Department of Labor. https://www.bls.gov/news.release/disabl.nr0.htm

U.S. Census Bureau. (2023, July 5). *Anniversary of Americans with Disabilities Act: July 26, 2023.* https://www.census.gov/newsroom/facts-for-features/2023/disabilities-act.html

U.S. Congress. (2004). *20 USC Ch. 33: Education of Individuals with Disabilities.* http://uscode.house.gov/view.xhtml?path=/prelim@title20/chapter33&edition=prelim

U.S. Department of Education, Office of Civil Rights. (2020, October). *The use of restraint and seclusion on children with disabilities in K–12 schools.* https://www2.ed.gov/about/offices/list/ocr/docs/restraint-and-seclusion.pdf

U.S. Department of Education, Office of Civil Rights. (2021, June). *An overview of exclusionary discipline practices in public schools for the 2017–2018 school year.* Civil Rights Data Collection. https://ocrdata.ed.gov/assets/downloads/crdc-exclusionary-school-discipline.pdf

Waitoller, F. R., & Thorius, K. A. K. (2016). Cross-pollinating culturally sustaining pedagogy and universal design for learning: Toward an inclusive pedagogy that accounts for dis/ability. *Harvard Educational Review, 86*(3), 366–389.

Wang, L. (2022, June). *Chronic punishment: The unmet health needs of people in state prisons.* Prison Policy Initiative. https://www.prisonpolicy.org/reports/chronicpunishment.html#disability

Wehmeyer, M. L., & Kurth, J. A. (2021). *Inclusive education in a strengths-based Era: Mapping the future of the field.* Norton.

Widra, E., & Jones, A. (2023, April 3). *Mortality, health, and poverty, The unmet needs of people on probation and parole.* https://www.prisonpolicy.org/blog/2023/04/03/nsduh_probation_parole/

Yell, M. (2018). *The law and special education* (5th ed.). Pearson.

## Chapter 7

Adger, C. T., Wolfram, W., & Christian, D. (2007). *Dialects in schools and communities* (2nd ed.). Erlbaum.

Allyn, B. (2019, September 26). *The "OK" hand gesture is now listed as a symbol of hate.* National Public Radio. https://www.npr.org/2019/09/26/764728163/the-ok-hand-gesture-is-now-listed-as-a-symbol-of-hate

American Councils for International Education. (2021, October 5). *2021 canvass of dual language and immersion (DLI) programs in U.S. public schools.* https://www.americancouncils.org/sites/default/files/documents/pages/2021-10/Canvass%20DLI%20-%20October%202021-2_ac.pdf

American Speech-Language-Hearing Association. (2019). *How does your child hear and talk?* http://www.asha.org/public/speech/development/chart/

Baker-Bell, A., Williams-Farrier, B. J., Jackson, D., Johnson, L., Kynard, C., & McMurtry, T. (2020, July). *This ain't another statement! This is a DEMAND for Black linguistic justice.* National Council of Teachers of English Conference on College Composition and Communication. https://cccc.ncte.org/cccc/demand-for-black-linguistic-justice

Breiseth, L. (2015). *What you need to know about ELLs: Fast facts.* http://www.colorincolorado.org/article/what-you-need-know-about-ells-fast-facts

Burgoon, J. K., Guerrero, L. K., & Floyd, K. (2010). *Nonverbal communication.* Allyn & Bacon.

California Alliance of Researchers for Equity in Education. (2020, September). *The shift to online education during and beyond the COVID-19 pandemic: Concerns and recommendations for California* [Research brief]. https://www.care-ed.org/_files/ugd/1e0c79_df201119763449f18419425ace9d509e.pdf

California Department of Education. (2022). *Facts about English learners in California.* https://www.cde.ca.gov/ds/ad/cefelfacts.asp.

Collier, V. P., & Thomas, W. P. (2004). The astounding effectiveness of dual language education for all. *NABE Journal of Research and Practice, 2*(1), 1–20.

Conference on College Composition & Communication. (2021). *CCCC Statement on Ebonics*. National Council of Teachers of English. https://cccc.ncte.org/cccc/resources/positions/ebonics

Council of Europe. (2023. *Plurilingual and intercultural education: Definition and founding principles*. https://www.coe.int/en/web/platform-plurilingual-intercultural-language-education/the-founding-principles-of-plurilingual-and-intercultural-education

Crawford, J., & Krashen, S. (2007). *English learners in American classrooms: 101 questions 101 answers*. Scholastic.

Eberhard, D. M., Simons, G. F., & Fenning, C. D. (Eds.). (2023). *Ethnologue: Languages of the world* (26th ed.). SIL International. http://www.ethnologue.com

Ethnologue. (2023) How many languages are there in the world? https://www.ethnologue.com/insights/how-many-languages/

Fuchs, C. (2018, April 25). *Research shows strong bilingual pre-K programs work. But how many states have them?* NBC News. https://www.nbcnews.com/news/latino/research-shows-strong-bilingual-pre-k-programs-work-how-many-n868696

Gans, J. (2023, March 30). *JD Vance bill sets English as official language*. The Hill. https://thehill.com/homenews/senate/3926341-jd-vance-bill-sets-english-as-official-language/

Gooskins, C., van Heuven, V. J., Golubović, J., Schüppert, A., Swarte, F., & Voigt, S. (2018). Mutual intelligibility between closely related languages in Europe. *International Journal of Multilingualism, 15*(2), 169–193.

Hall, E. T., & Hall, M. R. (1990). *Understanding cultural differences: Germans, French and Americans*. Intercultural Press.

Hankerson, S. (2023). "The world has to stop discriminating against African American Language" (AAL): Exploring the language ideologies of AAL-speaking students in college writing. *Written Communication, 40*(2), 587–619.

Heward, W. L., Alber-Morgan, S. R., & Konrad, M. (2017). *Exceptional Children* (11th ed.). Pearson Education.

Janse, A. M. (2023, March 11). *Lost in translation: 4 perfect words that have no English equivalent*. National Public Radio. https://www.npr.org/2023/03/11/1162340949/words-language-english-dictionary-translation

Katz, J., & Andrews, W. (2013, December 21). How y'all, youse and you guys talk. *New York Times*. https://www.nytimes.com/interactive/2014/upshot/dialect-quiz-map.html?_r=0

Kuhl, P. K. (2010). Brain mechanisms in early language acquisition. *Neuron, 67*(5), 713–727.

*Lau v. Nichols*, 414 U.S. 563–572 (Jan. 21, 1974).

Liu, C. (2020, February 12). *Black English matters*. JSTOR Daily. https://daily.jstor.org/black-english-matters/

McCluney, C. L., Robotham, K., Lee, S., Smith, R., & Durkee, M. (2019, November 15). The costs of code-switching. *Harvard Business Review*. https://hbr.org/2019/11/the-costs-of-codeswitching

Merriam-Webster [@MerriamWebster]. (2023, February 28). *Non-native English Speakers, what's a word from your language that you think is perfect that doesn't have an English equivalent?* [Tweet]. Twitter. https://twitter.com/MerriamWebster/status/1630580710208688129

Mitchell, C. (2019, May 23). Itinerant English learners pose challenges for school systems. *Education Week*. http://blogs.edweek.org/edweek/learning-the-language/2019/05/itinerant_english-learners_pos.html?cmp=eml-enl-tu-news3&M=58845387&U=1128256&UUID=7604ea5201dfb025772c4a7a44eea641

National Assessment of Educational Progress (NAEP). (2022). *The nation's report card: 2022*. https://www.nationsreportcard.gov/

National Center for Education Statistics (NCES). (2019). *English language learner students enrolled in public elementary and secondary schools, by state*. https://nces.ed.gov/programs/digest/d21/tables/dt21_204.20.asp

National Center for Education Statistics (NCES). (2023). English learners in public schools. *Condition of Education*. U.S. Department of Education, Institute of Education Sciences. https://nces.ed.gov/programs/coe/indicator/cgf/english-learners

National Clearinghouse for English Language Acquisition. (2020, September). *High school graduation rates for English Learners* [Fact sheet]. https://ncela.ed.gov/sites/default/files/2022-11/20200916-ELGraduationRatesFactSheet-508.pdf

National Clearinghouse for English Language Acquisition. (2021, June). *Teacher projections for English learners* [Fact sheet]. https://ncela.ed.gov/sites/default/files/legacy/files/fast_facts/Del4-4ELTeacher%20Projections_6.11.2021_508.pdf

National Clearinghouse for English Language Acquisition. (2023, February). *The top languages spoken by English learners in the United States* [Fact sheet]. https://ncela.ed.gov/sites/default/files/2023-02/OELATopLanguagesFS-508.pdf

National Education Association. (2020). *English language learners toolkit*. https://www.nea.org/resource-library/english-language-learners

National Governors Association Center for Best Practices & Council of Chief State School Officers. (2010). *Common Core State Standards for English language arts and literacy in history/social studies, science, and technical subjects*. Authors.

Owens, R. E., Jr. (2012). *Language development* (8th ed.). Pearson Education.

Raeburn, A. (2018, September 12). *10 Places where eye-contact is not recommended (10 places where the locals are friendly)*. TheTravel.com. https://www.thetravel.com/10-places-where-eye-contact-is-not-recommended-10-places-where-the-locals-are-friendly/

Reaser, J., Adger, C. T., Wolfram, W., & Christian, D. (2017). *Dialects at school*. Routledge.

Rolstad, K., Mahoney, K., & Glass, G. (2005). The big picture: A meta-analysis of program effectiveness research on English language learners. *Educational Policy, 19*(4), 572–594.

Samovar, L. A., Porter, R. E., McDaniel, E. R., & Roy, C. S. (2017). *Communication between cultures* (9th ed.). Cengage Learning.

Sanchez, C. (2017, February 23). *English language learners: How is your state doing*. National Public Radio. https://www.npr.org/sections/ed/2017/02/23/512451228/5-million-english-language-learners-a-vast-pool-of-talent-at-risk.

Sengupta, S. (2018, March 26). *The meaning of common hand gestures widely used across the world*. SocialMettle. https://socialmettle.com/hand-gestures-their-meanings

Smith, D., Tyler, N., & Skow, K. (2018). *Introduction to contemporary special education: New horizons* (2nd ed.). Pearson Education.

U.S. Census Bureau. (2022, August). *Language use in the United States: 2019*. https://www.census.gov/content/dam/Census/library/publications/2022/acs/acs-50.pdf

U.S. Department of Education. (2018). Academic performance and outcomes for English learners: Performance on national assessments and on-time graduation rates. https://www2.ed.gov/datastory/el-outcomes/index.html#introText

U.S. English. (2016). *About U.S. English*. https://www.usenglish.org/about-us/

U.S. Office of English Language Acquisition. (2023). *National Clearinghouse for English Language Acquisition fact sheet: The top languages spoken by English learners in the United States*. https://ncela.ed.gov/sites/default/files/2023-02/OELATopLanguagesFS-508.pdf

Vygotsky, L. S. (1962). *Thought and language*. MIT Press.

Worldatlas. (2020, December 18). *Major languages spoken in Asia*. https://www.worldatlas.com/articles/major-languages-spoken-in-asia.html

# Chapter 8

*Abington School District v. Schempp*, 374 U.S. 203 (1963).

Ahuvia, M. (2016). *Judaism, Jewish history, and anti-Jewish prejudice: An overview*. Stroum Center for Jewish Studies, University of Washington. https://jewishstudies.washington.edu/who-are-jews-jewish-history-origins-antisemitism/

Al Islam. (2023). *Are women allowed in mosques?* https://www.alislam.org/question/are-women-allowed-in-mosques/

Alper, B. (2018, August 18). *Why America's "nones" don't identify with a religion*. Pew Research Center. http://www.pewresearch.org/fact-tank/2018/08/08/why-americas-nones-dont-identify-with-a-religion/

American Academy of Child and Adolescent Psychiatry. (2018, February). *Conversion therapy*. https://www.aacap.org/AACAP/Policy_Statements/2018/Conversion_Therapy.aspx

American Library Association, Office for Intellectual Freedom. (2023). *Mapping challenges to the freedom to read*. https://www.ala.org/advocacy/bbooks/by-the-numbers

Anti-Defamation League. (2023). *Audit of antisemitic incidents 2022*. https://www.adl.org/resources/report/audit-antisemitic-incidents-2022

Asadu, C., & Crary, D. (2022, December 7). *Friction over LGBTQ issues worsens in global Anglican church*. Associated Press. https://apnews.com/article/anglican-church-lgbtq-issues-4f635708fdb24df166ac8237f9473f00

Bagby, I. (2020, June 2). The American mosque 2020: Growing and evolving (Report 1 of the US Mosque Survey 2020: Basic characteristics of the American mosque. Institute for Aoscial Policy and Understanding. https://www.ispu.org/report-1-mosque-survey-2020/

Bandera, G. (2023, May 27). *Which countries impose the death penalty on gay people?* Fair Planet. https://www.fairplanet.org/story/death-penalty-homosexualty-illegal/

Bowie, F. (2018). Ritual and performance. In C. Partridge & T. Dowley (Eds.), *A short introduction to world religions* (pp. 19–21). Fortress Press.

Brannon, V. C. (2022, June 30). *Kennedy v. Bremerton School District: School prayer and the Establishment Clause*. Congressional Research Service.

Brooks, D. (2022, February 4). The dissenters trying to save Evangelicalism from itself. *New York Times*. https://www.nytimes.com/2022/02/04/opinion/evangelicalism-division-renewal.html

Burge, R. P. (2022, January 21). What's new in Evangelical views on abortion?: The age gap. *Christianity Today*. https://www.christianitytoday.com/news/2022/january/evangelical-abortion-views-age-gap-younger-pro-life.html

Burge, R. (2023a, January 10). *Is Catholic teaching on birth control driving people from the pews?* Religious News Service. https://religionnews.com/2023/01/10/is-catholic-teaching-on-birth-control-driving-people-from-the-pews/

Burge, R. (2023b, January 17). *The concerns of young evangelicals offer political insights for 2024*. Religion & Politics. https://religionandpolitics.org/2023/01/17/the-concerns-of-young-evangelicals-offer-political-insights-for-2024/

Burke, K. J., Juzwik, M., & Prins, E. (2023, June/July). White Christian nationalism: What is it, and why does it matter for educational research? *Educational Researcher, 52*(5), 286–295.

Butler, A. (2021). *White evangelical racism: The politics of morality in America*. University of North Carolina Press.

Campbell-Reed, E. (2018, October). *State of clergywomen in the U.S.: A statistical update*. https://eileencampbellreed.org/state-of-clergy/

Carpenter, K. A. (2021, April). Living the sacred: Indigenous peoples and religious freedom. *Harvard Law Review, 134*(6), 2103–2156.

Chen, S. (2023, March 22). *An increasing number of U.S. school districts now observe Ramadan*. Axios. https://www.axios.com/2023/03/23/schools-ramadan-muslim-education

Chen, G. (2020, February 10). *The ongoing debate over school choice*. Public School Review. https://www.publicschoolreview.com/blog/the-ongoing-debate-over-school-choice

Chen, C., & Ho, T. C. (2023, March 22). *Asian American religions: Everywhere, all at once*. Social Science Research Council. https://tif.ssrc.org/2023/03/22/asian-american-religions-everywhere-all-at-once/

The Church of Jesus Christ of Latter-Day Saints. (2023a). *The Book of Mormon and the Bible are God's word*. https://www.churchofjesuschrist.org/welcome/bible-book-of-mormon-word-of-god?lang=eng

The Church of Jesus Christ of Latter-day Saints. (2023b). *Facts and statistics: United States*. https://newsroom.churchofjesuschrist.org/facts-and-statistics/country/united-states

Corichi, M., & Evans, J. (2019, December 20). *Many Catholics in Latin America-including a majority in Brazil-support allowing priests to marry*. Pew Research Center. https://www.pewresearch.org/short-reads/2019/12/20/many-catholics-in-latin-america-including-a-majority-in-brazil-support-allowing-priests-to-marry/

Davis, J., & Graham, M. (2023). *The great dechurching: Who's leaving, why are they going, and what will it take to bring them back?* Zondervan Reflective.

DeRose, J. (2023a, July 25). *Congregations leave United Methodist Church over defiance of LGBTQ bans*. National Public Radio. https://www.npr.org/2023/07/25/1189315875/congregations-leave-united-methodist-church-over-defiance-of-lgbtq-bans

DeRose, J. (2023b, June 14). *Southern Baptists say no to women pastors, uphold expulsion of Saddleback megachurch*. National Public Radio. https://www.npr.org/2023/06/14/1182141691/southern-baptist-convention-sbc-women-pastors-saddleback-megachurch

Diamant, J. (2017, November 8). *Key takeaways about Orthodox Christians*. Pew Research Center. https://www.pewresearch.org/short-reads/2017/11/08/key-takeaways-about-orthodox-christians/

Diamant, J. (2023, January 3). *Faith on the hill: The religious composition of the 118th Congress*. Pew Research Center. https://www.pewresearch.org/religion/2023/01/03/faith-on-the-hill-2023/

Du Mez, K. K. (2021). *Jesus and John Wayne: How White Evangelicals corrupted a faith and fractured a nation*. Liveright.

EdChoice. (2023, April 17). *Fast facts on school choice*. https://www.edchoice.org/school-choice/fast-facts/

*Edwards v. Aquillard*, 107 S. Ct. 2573 (1987).

Ekstrom, K. (2012, December 20). *From nuns to "nones," 10 ways religion shaped the news in 2012*. Religion News Service. http://www.religionnews.com/2012/12/20/from-nuns-to-nones-10-ways-religion-shaped-the-news-in-2012/

Elsheikh, E., & Sisemore, B. (2021, September). *Islamophobia through the eyes of Muslims: Assessing perceptions, experiences, and impacts*. Othering & Belonging Institute, University of California Berkeley.

Emerick, Y. (2023, September 25). *Muslim schools in America: A view from the inside*. Sound Vision Foundation. https://www.soundvision.com/article/muslim-schools-in-america-a-view-from-the-inside

*Engel v. Vitale*, 82 S. Ct. 1261 (1962).

*Epperson v. Arkansas*, 89 S. Ct. 266 (1968).

Equal Justice Initiative. (2016). *Racial segregation in the church*. https://eji.org/news/history-racial-injustice-racial-segregation-in-church/

Evangelical Council for Financial Accountability. (2023). *Life.Church*. https://www.ecfa.org/MemberProfile.aspx?ID=22274

Evans, J. (2022, October 26). *7 facts about Hindus around the world*. Pew Research Center. https://www.pewresearch.org/short-reads/2022/10/26/7-facts-about-hindus-around-the-world/

Fahmy, D. (2020, October 20). *8 key findings about Catholics and abortion*. Pew Research Center. https://www.pewresearch.org/short-reads/2020/10/20/8-key-findings-about-catholics-and-abortion/

Fairchild, M. (2019, April 27). *Eastern Orthodox denomination*. Learn Religions. https://www.learnreligions.com/eastern-orthodox-church-denomination-700624

Federal Bureau of Investigation. (2023). *FBI releases supplement to the 2021 hate crime statistics*. https://www.justice.gov/crs/highlights/2021-hate-crime-statistics

Fisher, M. P., & Rinehart, R. (2017). *Living religions* (10th ed.). Pearson.

Foundation for Apologetic Information and Research (FAIR). (n.d.). *Latter-day Saints and California Proposition 8. The Church of Jesus Christ of Latter-day Saints*. https://www.fairlatterdaysaints.org/answers/Mormonism_and_politics/California_Proposition_8

France, R. (2018). Jesus. In C. Partridge & T. Dowley (Eds.), *A short introduction to world religions* (pp. 236–244). Fortress Press.

Funk, C. (2019, February 6). *How highly religious Americans view evolution depends on how they're asked about it*. Pew Research Center. https://www.pewresearch.org/short-reads/2019/02/06/how-highly-religious-americans-view-evolution-depends-on-how-theyre-asked-about-it/

Gallup. (2023). *Religion*. https://news.gallup.com/poll/1690/Religion.aspx

Garretson, J., & Suhay, E. (2015, December 24). Scientific communication about biological influences on homosexuality and the politics of gay rights. *Political Research Quarterly*, 69(1), 17–29.

Gates, H. L., Jr. (2021). *The Black church: This is our story, this is our song*. Penguin Press.

Gjelten, T. (2017, April 20). *This Islamic school helps students build their American and Muslim identity*. National Public Radio. https://www.npr.org/sections/ed/2017/04/20/524510378/this-islamic-school-teaches-how-to-be-muslim-and-american

Good Feather, D. (2021). *Think indigenous: Native American spirituality for a modern world*. Hay House.

Gorski, P. S., & Perry, S. L. (2022). *The flag + the cross: White Christian nationalism and the threat to American democracy*. Oxford University Press.

Graham, R. (2021, October 19). Christian schools boom in a revolt against curriculum and pandemic rules. *New York Times*. https://www.jewishagency.org/jewish-population-rises-to-15-3-million-worldwide-with-over-7-million-residing-in-israel/

Graham, R. (2023, June 2). What the latest investigations into Catholic church sex abuse mean. *New York Times*. https://www.nytimes.com/2023/06/02/us/catholic-church-sex-abuse-investigations.html

Grant, S. (2017, June 9). *Are Muslims speaking out against terrorism? You bet they are*. ABC News. https://www.abc.net.au/news/2017-06-09/muslims-speak-out-against-terrorism/8606296

Green, E. (2017, March 10). White evangelicals believe they face more discrimination than Muslims. *The Atlantic*. https://www.theatlantic.com/politics/archive/2017/03/perceptions-discrimination-muslims-christians/519135/

Haberman, C. (2018, October 28). Religion and right-wing politics: How evangelicals reshaped elections. *New York Times*. https://www.nytimes.com/2018/10/28/us/religion-politics-evangelicals.html

Harris, E. J. (2018). Beliefs. In C. Partridge & T. Dowley (Eds.), *A short introduction to world religions* (pp. 117–123). Fortress Press.

Hayden, M. E. (2017, June 20). *Muslims "absolutely" the group most victimized by global terrorism, researchers say*. ABC News. https://abcnews.go.com/Politics/muslims-absolutely-group-victimized-global-terrorism-researchers/story?id=48131273

Helfand, D. (2008, September 11). Bishops in state oppose Prop. 8. *Los Angeles Times*. http://articles.latimes.com/2008/sep/11/local/me-gaymarriage11

History.com Editors. (2022, January 11). *Selma to Montgomery march*. https://www.history.com/topics/black-history/selma-montgomery-march#bloody-sunday

*Hollingsworth v. Perry*, 133 S. Ct. 2652 (2013).

Hopfe, L. M., Woodward, M. R., & Hendrickson, B. (2016). *Religions of the world* (13th ed.). Pearson.

Howard University School of Law. (2023, January 6). *A brief history of civil rights in the United States: Proposition 8*. https://library.law.howard.edu/civilrightshistory/lgbtq/prop8

Human Rights Campaign. (2022). *Marriage equality around the world*. https://www.hrc.org/resources/marriage-equality-around-the-world

Human Rights Campaign Foundation. (n.d.-a). *Stances of faiths on LGBTQ issues: Buddhism*. https://www.hrc.org/resources/stances-of-faiths-on-lgbt-issues-buddhism

Human Rights Campaign Foundation. (n.d.-b). *Stances of faiths on LGBTQ issues: Hinduism*. https://www.hrc.org/resources/stances-of-faiths-on-lgbt-issues-hinduism

Islam Faith Team. (2023). *What do Muslims believe about God?* https://www.islamfaith.com/muslims-believe-god/

Islam Icau. (2022, October 13). *Islamic education in the USA*. https://www.islamicau.org/islamic-education-in-the-usa/

Jaber, S. (2020). Stories from the front lines: Experiences of Arab and Muslim students in American classrooms—Introduction. In L. Ferlazzo, *Supporting Arab & Muslim students in the classroom*. Education Week. https://www.edweek.org/teaching-learning/opinion-supporting-arab-muslim-students-in-the-classroom/2020/09

Jaber. S. (2022, September 1). *The miseducation of Americans on Arab and Muslim identities*. National Council of Teachers of English. https://19thnews.org/2021/11/muslim-students-schools-hijab/

Jackson, K. (2019, February 26). *United Methodist Church strengthens ban on same-sex marriage, LGBT clergy*. Reuters. https://www.reuters.com/article/us-religion-lgbt-united-methodist-iduskcn1qg022

Jehovah's Witnesses. (2023). *Flag salute, voting, and civilian service*. https://www.jw.org/en/library/books/gods-love/flag-salute-voting-civilian-service/

The Jewish Agency for Israel. (2022, September 25). *Jewish population rises to 15.3 million worldwide, with over 7 million residing in Israel* [Press release]. https://www.jewishagency.org/jewish-population-rises-to-15-3-million-worldwide-with-over-7-million-residing-in-israel/

Johnson, A. (2023, May 24). Parents demand Germantown schools address antisemitic incidents. *Milwaukee Journal Sentinel*. https://www.jsonline.com/story/communities/north/2023/05/24/parents-want-germantown-school-district-to-address-swastika-incidents/70245343007/

Jones, J. M. (2023, September 22). *In U.S., 47% identify as religious, 33% as spiritual*. Gallup. https://news.gallup.com/poll/511133/identify-religious-spiritual.aspx

Jones, K. J. (2022, December 6). *U.S. Catholic population shows growth, trends southward*. Catholic News Agency. https://www.catholicnewsagency.com/news/252998/us-catholic-population-shows-growth-trends-southward

Jones, R. P. (2017). *The end of White Christian America*. Simon & Schuster.

Jones, R. P. (2020). *White too long: The legacy of White supremacy in American Christianity*. Simon & Schuster.

*Kennedy v. Bremerton Sch. Dist.*, 4 F.4th 910 (9th Cir. 2021).

Kerr, D. (2018). Worship and festivals. In C. Partridge & T. Dowley (Eds.), *A short introduction to world religions* (pp. 287–292). Fortress Press.

Kharroub, T. (2015, October 4). *Five things you need to know about women in Islam: Implications for advancing women's rights in the Middle East*. Arab Center Washington DC. https://arabcenterdc.org/resource/five-things-you-need-to-know-about-women-in-islam-implications-for-advancing-womens-rights-in-the-middle-east/

Kilgore, E. (2022, March 6). Refusal to accept LGBTQ equality is still causing divisions in churches. *Intelligencer*. https://nymag.com/intelligencer/2022/03/anti-lgbtq-equality-is-still-causing-divisions-in-churches.html

Krogstad, J. M., Alvarado, J., & Mohamed, B. (2023, April 13). *Among U.S. Latinos, Catholicism continues to decline but is still the largest faith*. Pew Research Center. https://www.pewresearch.org/religion/2023/04/13/among-u-s-latinos-catholicism-continues-to-decline-but-is-still-the-largest-faith/

Lapin, A. (2023, October 24). *Antisemitism reportedly spikes and US Jews face violent threats amid climate of fear over Israel-Hamas war*. Jewish Telegraphic Agency. https://www.jta.org/2023/10/24/united-states/antisemitism-reportedly-spikes-and-us-jews-face-violent-threats-amid-climate-of-fear-over-israel-hamas-war

*Lee v. Weisman*, 112 S. Ct. 2649 (1992).

*Lemon v. Kurtzman*, 91 S. Ct. 2105 (1971).

Lord, D. (2018, August 10). What happened at Charlottesville: Looking back on the rally that ended in death. *Atlanta Journal-Constitution*. https://www.ajc.com/news/national/what-happened-charlottesville-looking-back-the-anniversary-the-deadly-rally/fPpnLrbAtbxSwNI9BEy93K/

Lupu, I. C., Elwood, F., Davis, E., Masci, D., Tuttle, R. W., Berz, D. R., & Berz, K. B. (2019, October 3*). Religion in the public schools*. Pew Research Center. https://www.pewresearch.org/religion/2019/10/03/religion-in-the-public-schools-2019-update/

Masci, D., & Smith, G. A. (2016, April 8). *Pope's proclamation, like views of U.S. Catholics, indicates openness to nontraditional families*. Pew Research Center. https://www.pewresearch.org/short-reads/2016/04/08/popes-proclamation-like-views-of-u-s-catholics-indicates-openness-to-nontraditional-families/

Masci, D., & Smith, G. A. (2018, March 1). *5 facts about U.S. evangelical Protestants*. https://www.pewresearch.org/short-reads/2018/03/01/5-facts-about-u-s-evangelical-protestants/

McCutheon, R. T. (2018). What is religion? In C. Partridge & T. Dowley (Eds.), *A short introduction to world religions* (pp. 2–4). Fortress Press.

*McGirt v. Oklahoma*, 140 S. Ct. 2452, 2459 (2020).

McNally, M. (2020). *Defend the sacred: Native American religious freedom beyond the First Amendment*. Princeton University Press.

Media Portrayals of Minorities Project. (2021). *Report on Media Portrayals: 2020 Newspaper Coverage of African Americans, Asian Americans, Native Americans, Latinos, Jews, and Muslims*. Middlebury College. https://www.mediaandminorities.org/reports/

Meehan, K., Friedman, J., Baêta, S., & Magnusson, T. (2023). *Banned in the USA: The mounting pressure to censor*. PEN America. https://pen.org/report/book-bans-pressure-to-censor/

Millard, E. (2021, June 8). *For many LGBTQ Episcopalians, the struggle for full inclusion is not over – it's expanded*. Episcopal News Service. https://www.episcopalnewsservice.org/2021/06/08/for-many-lgbtq-episcopalians-the-struggle-for-full-inclusion-is-not-over-its-expanded/

Mohamed, B., Cox, K., Diamant, J., & Gecewicz, C. (2021, February 16). *A brief overview of Black religious history. in the U.S*. Pew Research Center. https://www.pewresearch.org/religion/2021/02/16/a-brief-overview-of-black-religious-history-in-the-u-s/#fnref-34217-30

Mohamed, B., & Diamant, J. (2019, January 17). *Black Muslims account for a fifth of all U.S. Muslims, and about half are converts to Islam*. Pew Research Center. https://www.pewresearch.org/short-reads/2019/01/17/black-muslims-account-for-a-fifth-of-all-u-s-muslims-and-about-half-are-converts-to-islam/

Moore, Russell. (2023, July 25). The American Evangelical church is in crisis. There's only one way out. *The Atlantic*. https://www.theatlantic.com/ideas/archive/2023/07/christian-evangelical-church-division-politics/674810/

Movement Advancement Project. (2023, October 3). *Conversion "therapy" laws*. https://www.lgbtmap.org/equality-maps/conversion_therapy

*Murray v. Curlett*, 374 U.S. 203 (1963).

My Jewish Learning. (2023). *The Torah*. https://www.myjewishlearning.com/article/the-torah/

National Catholic Educational Association. (2023). *Data brief: 2022–2023 Catholic school enrollment*. https://www.ncea.org/NCEA/How_We_Serve/News/Press_Releases/NCEA_Releases_2022-2023_Data_Brief_on_State_of_Catholic_Schools.aspx

National Education Association. (2021, December 2). *Vouchers*. https://www.publicschoolreview.com/blog/the-ongoing-debate-over-school-choice

National Public Radio. (2018, October 13). *Pope Francis defrocks 2 Chilean priests in deepening sex abuse scandal*. https://www.npr.org/2018/10/13/657125556/pope-francis-defrocks-2-chilean-priests-in-deepening-sex-abuse-scandal

Newbery, J. W. E. (2018). Native North Americans. In C. Partridge & T. Dowley (Eds.), *A short introduction to world religions* (pp. 62–64). Fortress Press.

Newport, F. (2009, April 10). *This Easter, smaller percentage of Americans are Christian*. Gallup. https://news.gallup.com/poll/117409/easter-smaller-percentage-americans-christian.aspx

Newport, F. (2017, December 22). *2017 update on Americans and religion*. Gallup. https://news.gallup.com/poll/224642/2017-update-americans-religion.aspx

Nittle, N. (2021, November 18). *Muslim students often feel unsafe or unwelcome in schools, report shows*. The 19th. https://19thnews.org/2021/11/muslim-students-schools-hijab/

Norman, J. (2018, April 6). *The religious regions of the U.S.* Gallup. https://news.gallup.com/poll/232223/religious-regions.aspx

Nortey, J. (2021, August 30). *Most White Americans who regularly attend worship services voted for Trump in 2020*. Pew Research Center. https://www.pewresearch.org/short-reads/2021/08/30/most-white-americans-who-regularly-attend-worship-services-voted-for-trump-in-2020/

*Obergefell v. Hodges* , 576 U.S. 644 (2015).

Oestreich, J. R. (2017, April 14). Bach's 'St. John Passion' has more humanity than anti-semitism. *New York Times*. https://www.nytimes.com/2017/04/14/arts/music/bachs-st-john-passion-has-more-humanity-than-anti-semitism.html

O'Grady, S. (2018, August 31). Despite scandals Australia's Catholic Church stands firm against reporting child abuse revealed in confession. *Washington Post*. https://www.washingtonpost.com/world/2018/08/31/despite-scandals-australias-catholic-church-stands-firm-against-reporting-child-abuse-revealed-confession/?utm_term=.67f55fb1fce5

Orthodox Church in America. (2023). *Ordination of women*. https://www.oca.org/questions/priesthoodmonasticism/ordination-of-women

Pandith, F. (2021, September 1). *The U.S., Muslims, and a turbulent post-9/11 world*. Council on Foreign Relations. https://www.cfr.org/article/us-muslims-and-turbulent-post-911-world

Paulsen, D. (2023, April 24). *In US visit, Anglican Communion secretary general defends structure, while conservatives call for changes*. Episcopal News Service. https://www.episcopalnewsservice.org/2023/04/24/anglican-communion-secretary-general-defends-structure-during-us-visit-while-conservatives-call-for-changes/

Pew Research Center. (2015, April 2). *The future of world religions: Population growth projections, 2010–2050*. http://www.pewforum.org/2015/04/02/religious-projections-2010-2050/

Pew Research Center. (2017, July 26). *U.S. Muslims concerned about their place in society, but continue to believe in the American Dream*. http://www.pewforum.org/2017/07/26/findings-from-pew-research-centers-2017-survey-of-us-muslims/

Pew Research Center. (2018, July 2). *5 facts about Episcopalians*. https://www.pewresearch.org/short-reads/2018/07/02/5-facts-about-episcopalians/

Pew Research Center. (2019a). *Americans see Catholic clergy sex abuse as an ongoing problem*. https://www.pewresearch.org/religion/2019/06/11/americans-see-catholic-clergy-sex-abuse-as-an-ongoing-problem/

Pew Research Center. (2019b). *Attitudes on same-sex marriage*. https://www.pewresearch.org/religion/fact-sheet/changing-attitudes-on-gay-marriage/

Pew Research Center. (2019c). *In U.S., decline of Christianity continues at rapid pace*. https://www.pewresearch.org/religion/2019/10/17/in-u-s-decline-of-christianity-continues-at-rapid-pace/

Pew Research Center. (2021, May 11). *Jewish Americans in 2020*. https://www.pewresearch.org/religion/2021/05/11/the-size-of-the-u-s-jewish-population/

Pew Research Center. (2022, September). *Modeling the future of religion in America*. https://www.pewresearch.org/religion/2022/09/13/modeling-the-future-of-religion-in-america/

Playlister. (2023). *Largest churches in America 2023: Pioneering the future of worship*. https://www.playlister.app/blog/largest-churches-in-america-2023-pioneering-the-future-of-worship

PRRI. (2021, July 8). *The 2020 census of American religion*. https://www.prri.org/research/2020-census-of-american-religion/

PRRI. (2023, February 24). *2022 census of American religion: Religious affiliation updates and trends*. https://www.prri.org/spotlight/prri-2022-american-values-atlas-religious-affiliation-updates-and-trends/

Ramsey, L. (2018). Judaism in the modern world. In C. Partridge & T. Dowley (Eds.), *A short introduction to world religions* (pp. 222–225). Fortress Press.

Reuters. (2018, August 20). *Factbox reports into abuse in the Irish Catholic Church*. https://www.reuters.com/article/us-pope-ireland-abuse-factbox/factbox-reports-into-abuse-in-the-irish-catholic-church-idUSKCN1L51J0

Riess, J. (2019, October 2). *Why it's important that Mormon women can now be official witnesses to a baptism*. Religion News Service. https://religionnews.com/2019/10/02/why-its-important-that-mormon-women-can-now-be-official-witnesses-to-a-baptism/

Saad, L., & Hrynowski, Z. (2022, June 24). *How many Americans believe in God?* Gallup. https://news.gallup.com/poll/268205/americans-believe-god.aspx

Sadgrove, M. (2018). Branches of the church. In C. Partridge & T. Dowley (Eds.), *A short introduction to world religions* (pp. 240–243). Fortress Press.

Sahgal, N. (2017, October 27). *500 years after the Reformation, 5 facts about Protestants around the world*. Pew Research Center. http://www.pewresearch.org/fact-tank/2017/10/27/500-years-after-the-reformation-5-facts-about-protestants-around-the-world/

Salter, E. (2018). Beliefs. In C. Partridge & T. Dowley (Eds.), *A short introduction to world religions* (pp. 170–174). Fortress Press.

Sandstrom, A. (2016, September 30). *6 facts about U.S. Mormons*. Pew Research Center. http://www.pewresearch.org/fact-tank/2016/09/30/6-facts-about-u-s-mormons/

Sawe, E. (2018, May 23). *Shia (Shi'a) Muslim countries*. World Atlas. https://www.worldatlas.com/articles/shia-shi-a-muslim-countries.html

Sergie, M. A. (2023, April 27). *The Sunni-Shia divide*. Council on Foreign Relations. https://www.cfr.org/article/sunni-shia-divide

Shaw, S. M. (2021, June 1). *How women in the Southern Baptist Convention have fought for decades to be ordained*. The Conversation. https://theconversation.com/how-women-in-the-southern-baptist-convention-have-fought-for-decades-to-be-ordained-161061

Siddiqui, S. (2023, September 25). *Muslim schools vs. public schools*. Sound Vision Foundation. https://www.soundvision.com/article/muslim-schools-vs-public-schools-0

Smith, C. (2022, December). Monuments to the unthinkable. *The Atlantic, 330*(5), 22–41.

Smith, G. A. (2021, December 14). *About three-in-ten U.S. adults are now religiously unaffiliated*. Pew Research Center. https://www.pewresearch.org/religion/2021/12/14/about-three-in-ten-u-s-adults-are-now-religiously-unaffiliated/

Stewart, K. (2019). *The power worshippers: Inside the dangerous rise of religious nationalism*. Bloomsbury.

*Stone v. Graham*, 449 U.S. 39 (1980).

Taketa, K. (2023, October 12). Antisemitic graffiti painted on the Torrey Pines High school campus—again. *San Diego Union-Tribune*. https://www.sandiegouniontribune.com/news/education/story/2023-10-12/antisemitic-graffiti-swastika-torrey-pines-high-school-campus-again

Thompson, A. Duffy, C., Gardella, R., & Dawson, C. (2018). *Thirteen states now investigating alleged sexual abuse linked to Catholic Church*. NBC News. https://www.nbcnews.com/news/religion/thirteen-states-now-investigating-alleged-sexual-abuse-linked-catholic-church-n916646

Union for Reform Judaism. (2023). *Hanukkah*. https://reformjudaism.org/jewish-holidays/hanukkah

United Nations. (2021, March 4). *UN expert says anti-Muslim hatred rises to epidemic proportions, urges states to act*. https://www.ohchr.org/en/press-releases/2021/03/un-expert-says-anti-muslim-hatred-rises-epidemic-proportions-urges-states

U.S. Conference of Catholic Bishops. (2023, August 1). *Bishops and dioceses*. http://www.usccb.org/about/bishops-and-dioceses/index.cfm

U.S. Department of Education. (2023, May 15). *Guidance on constitutionally protected prayer and religious expression in public elementary and secondary schools*. https://www2.ed.gov/policy/gen/guid/religionandschools/prayer_guidance.html

Vevea, B. (2023, June 12). *What is a school voucher?* https://www.greatschools.org/gk/articles/school-vouchers/

*Wallace v. Jaffree*, 105 S. Ct. 2479 (1985).

Warrier, M. (2018). A historical overview. In C. Partridge & T. Dowley (Eds.), *A short introduction to world religions* (pp. 72–77). Fortress Press.

Watt, M. (2018). A historical overview. In C. Partridge & T. Dowley (Eds.), *A short introduction to world religions* (pp. 266–273). Fortress Press.

Wehner, P. (2021, October 24). The Evangelical Church is breaking apart: Christians must reclaim Jesus from his church. *The Atlantic*. https://eppc.org/publication/the-evangelical-church-is-breaking-apart/

Whitehead, A. L., & Perry, S. L. (2020). *Taking America back for God: Christian nationalism in the United States*. Oxford University Press.

Williams, P. (2018). Sacred writings. In C. Partridge & T. Dowley (Eds.), *A short introduction to world religions* (pp. 112–116). Fortress Press.

Winter, M. (2021, July 26). The fastest-growing group of American evangelicals. *The Atlantic*. https://www.theatlantic.com/culture/archive/2021/07/latinos-will-determine-future-american-evangelicalism/619551/

World Population Review. (2023a). *Buddhist countries 2023*. https://worldpopulationreview.com/country-rankings/buddhist-countries

World Population Review. (2023b). *Hindu countries 2023*. https://worldpopulationreview.com/country-rankings/hindu-countries

World Population Review. (2023c). *Most Christian countries 2023*. https://worldpopulationreview.com/country-rankings/most-christian-countries

World Population Review. (2023d). *Muslim population by country 2023*. https://worldpopulationreview.com/country-rankings/muslim-population-by-country

World Population Review. (2023e). *Protestant Countries 2023*. https://worldpopulationreview.com/country-rankings/protestant-countries

## Chapter 9

Adams, R., & Farnsworth, M. (2020). Culturally responsive teacher education for rural and Native communitieis. *Multicultural Perspectives, 22*(2), 84–90.

Adamson, J., Evans, M. M., & Stein, R. (2002). *The environmental justice reader: Politics, poetics, and pedagogy*. University of Arizona Press.

Alter, C., Haynes, S., & Worland, J. (2019). Greta Thunberg: *Time* 2029 person of the year. *Time*. https://time.com/person-of-the-year-2019-greta-thunberg/

America Counts Staff. (2017, August 9). *One in five Americans live in rural areas*. U.S. Census Bureau. https://www.census.gov/library/stories/2017/08/rural-america.html

Anstreicher, G., Fletcher, J., & Thompson, O. (2022, April). *The long run impacts of court-ordered desegregation*. National Bureau of Economic Research. https://www.nber.org/papers/w29926

The Associated Press. (2021, January 19). *Vermont suit alleges school voucher bias*. https://www.nwaonline.com/news/2021/jan/19/vermont-suit-alleges-school-voucher-bias/

Asson, S., Frankenberg, E., Fowler, C. S., & Buck, R. K. (2023, February). Attendance zones in the suburbs. *Phi Delta Kappan, 104*(5), 11–17.

*Atlas Magazine*. (2023). Major natural disasters in January and February 2023. https://www.atlas-mag.net/en/category/menu-tags/divers/major-natural-disasters-in-january-and-february-2023

*Brown v. Board of Education*, 349 U.S. 294, at 300 (1955).

Bucholtz, S. (2020, August 3). *Urban. Suburban. Rural. How do households describe where they live?* U.S. Department of Housing and Urban Development. https://www.huduser.gov/portal/pdredge/pdr-edge-frm-asst-sec-080320.html

California Department of Education. (2019, January 14). *Magnets*. https://www.cde.ca.gov/sp/eo/mt/

Center for Place-Based Education. (2023). *Learning within the local community*. https://www.antioch.edu/centers-institutes/center-place-based-education/

Centers for Disease Control and Prevention. (2022, November 21). *Particle pollution*. https://www.cdc.gov/air/particulate_matter.html

City-as-School Toronto (CAST). (2021, May 26) *Place-based education: Principles, benefits, and examples*. https://www

.castschool.org/post/place-based-education-principles-benefits-and-examples

Davis, J. C., Rupasingha, A., Cromartie, J., & Sanders, A. (2022). *Rural America at a glance* (2022 ed.). U.S. Department of Agriculture, Economic Research Service. https://www.ers.usda.gov/publications/pub-details/?pubid=105154

Diamond, J. B., Posey-Maddox, L., & Valázquez. (2021, May). Reframing suburbs: Race, place, and opportunity in suburban educational spaces. *Educational Researcher, 50*(4), 249–255.

Dryden-Peterson, S. M. (2019). Inclusion and membership through refugee education?: Tensions between policy and practice. In M. M. Suárez-Orozco (Ed.), *Humanitarianism and mass migration: Confronting the world crisis* (pp. 218–231). University of California Press.

Farrigan, T. (2021, August 9). *Rural poverty has distinct regional and racial patterns.* U.S. Department of Agriculture, Economic Research Service. https://www.ers.usda.gov/amber-waves/2021/august/rural-poverty-has-distinct-regional-and-racial-patterns/

Fears, D. (2022, April 16). In redlined areas, higher levels of drilling and pollution. *Washington Post*, p. A3.

Fedinick, K. P. (2021, May 13). *Millions served by water systems detecting lead.* Natural Resources Defense Council. https://www.nrdc.org/resources/millions-served-water-systems-detecting-lead

Fleischman, L., & Franklin, M. (2017, November). *Fumes across the fence-line: The health impacts of air pollution from oil & gas facilities on African American communities.* NAACP and Clean Air Task Force. https://www.catf.us/resource/fumes-across-the-fence-line/

Frey, W. H. (2021a, April 26). *Census 2020: First results show near historically low population growth and a first-ever congressional seat loss for California.* Brookings Institution. https://www.brookings.edu/articles/census-2020-data-release/#1

Frey, W. H. (2021b, April 6). *Neighborhood segregation persists for Black, Latino or Hispanic, and Asian Americans.* Brookings Institution. https://www.brookings.edu/articles/neighborhood-segregation-persists-for-black-latino-or-hispanic-and-asian-americans/

Frey, W. H. (2022a, April 21). *A 2020 census portrait of America's largest metro areas: Population growth, diversity, segregation, and youth.* Brookings Mountain West. https://digitalscholarship.unlv.edu/brookings_policybriefs_reports/11/

Frey, W. H. (2022b, April 14). *New census data show a huge spike in movement out of big metro areas during the pandemic.* Brookings Institution. https://www.brookings.edu/articles/new-census-data-shows-a-huge-spike-in-movement-out-of-big-metro-areas-during-the-pandemic/

Frey, W. H. (2022c, June 25). *Today's suburbs are symbolic of America's rising diversity: A 2020 census portrait.* Brookings Institution. https://www.brookings.edu/articles/todays-suburbs-are-symbolic-of-americas-rising-diversity-a-2020-census-portrait/

Frey, W. H. (2023, January 4). *New census estimates show a tepid rise in U.S. population growth, buoyed by immigration.* Brookings Institution. https://www.brookings.edu/articles/new-census-estimates-show-a-tepid-rise-in-u-s-population-growth-buoyed-by-immigration/

Fry, R. (2020, July 29). *Prior to COVID-19, urban core counties in the U.S. were gaining vitality on key measures.* Pew Research Center. https://www.pewresearch.org/social-trends/2020/07/29/prior-to-covid-19-urban-core-counties-in-the-u-s-were-gaining-vitality-on-key-measures/

Gallup. (2019, February 9). *The religiously distinct states of America.* https://news.gallup.com/poll/226844/religiously-segregated-states-america.aspx?g_source=link_NEWSV9&g_medium=related_tile1&g_campaign=item_232223&g_content=The%2520Religiously%2520Distinct%2520States%2520of%2520America

Getting Smart. (n.d.). *What is place-based education and why does it matter?* Getting Smart, eduInnovation, & Teton Science Schools.

Global Footprint Network. (2023a). *FAQs: General.* https://www.footprintnetwork.org/faq/#nfba-source

Global Footprint Network. (2023b, July 27). *The power of food.* https://www.footprintnetwork.org/2023/07/27/the-power-of-food/

Gonzalez, D. J. X., Nardone, A., Nguyen, A. V., Morello-Frosch, R., & Casey, J. A. (2022, April). Historic redlining and the siting of oil and gas wells in the United States. *Journal of Exposure Science & Environmental Epidemiology, 33*, 76–83.

*Green v. County School Board of New Kent County*, 391 U.S. 430 (1968).

Green, E. L. (2019, November 6). Flint's children suffer in class after years of drinking the lead-poisoned water. *New York Times.* https://www.nytimes.com/2019/11/06/us/politics/flint-michigan-schools.html

Heissel, J., Persico, C., & Simon, D. (2019, January). *Does pollution drive achievement?: The effect of traffic pollution on academic performance.* National Bureau of Economic Research. https://www.nber.org/papers/w25489

Hill, P. T. (2019, December 16). *Desegregating schools: More than just getting the numbers right.* Brookings Institution. https://www.brookings.edu/articles/desegregating-schools-more-than-just-getting-the-numbers-right/

Hirsh, S. (2023, March 1). *Cancer alley might be our country's most toxic symbol of environmental racism.* Greenmatters. https://www.greenmatters.com/news/cancer-alley-louisiana

Hopkins, J. P. (2020). *Indian education for all: Decolonizing indigenous education in public schools.* Teachers College Press.

Jan, T. (2018, March 28). Redlining was banned 50 years ago. It's still hurting minorities today. *Washington Post.* https://www.washingtonpost.com/news/wonk/wp/2018/03/28/redlining-was-banned-50-years-ago-its-still-hurting-minorities-today/?utm_term=.3254cf3c1a3c

Janke, T., Cumpston, Z., Hill, R., Woodward, E., Harkness, P, von Gavel, S., & Morrison, J. (2021). *Australia state of the environment 2021: Indigenous* (Independent report to the Australian Government Minister for the Environment). Commonwealth of Australia. https://soe.dcceew.gov.au/

Johnson, R. C. (2019). *Children of the dream: Why school integration works.* Basic Books.

Jordan, R. (2021, February 22). Air pollution puts children at higher risk of disease in adulthood, according to Stanford researchers and others. *Stanford News.* https://news.stanford.edu/2021/02/22/air-pollution-impacts-childrens-health/

Lane, H. M., Morello-Frosch, R., Marshall, J. D., & Apte, J. S. (2022). Historical redlining is associated with present-day air pollution disparities in U. S. cities. *Environmental Science & Technology Letters, 9*(4), 345–350.

Mader, J. (2018, March 6). Can online learning level the AP playing field for rural students? *The Hechinger Report.* https://www.kqed.org/mindshift/50701/can-online-learning-level-the-ap-playing-field-for-rural-students

McCarthy, J. (2019, September 17). *Most Americans say segregation in schools a serious problem.* Gallup. https://news.gallup.com/

poll/266756/americans-say-segregation-schools-serious-problem.aspx

*Méndez v. Westminster, School District of Orange County, et al.*, 64 F.Supp. 544 (S.D. Cal. 1946).

*Meredith v. Jefferson County (Ky.) Board of Education*, 551 U.S. 701 (2007).

Natarajan, A., Moslimani, M., & Lopez, M. H. (2022, December 16). *Key facts about recent trends in global migration.* Pew Research Center. https://www.pew research.org/short-reads/2022/12/16/key-facts-about-recent-trends-in-global-migration/

National Academies of Sciences, Engineering, and Medicine. (2022). *Building resilience into the nation's medical product supply chains.* Author.

National Center for Education Statistics (NCES). (2021a, March). Percentage of persons 18 to 24 years old and age 25 and over, by educational attainment and state: 2000 and 2019 (Table 104.80). *Digest of Education Statistics.* https://nces.ed.gov/programs/digest/d21/tables/dt21_104.80.asp

National Center for Education Statistics (NCES). (2021b, May). Percentage of related children ages 5 to 17 living in poverty, by locale, region, and state: 2019 (Table 102.45). *Digest of Education Statistics.* https://nces.ed.gov/programs/digest/d21/tables/dt21_102.45.asp

National Center for Education Statistics. (2021c, November). Public elementary and secondary school enrollment, by locale and state: Fall 2019 (Table 203.72). *Digest of Education Statistics.* https://nces.ed.gov/programs/digest/d21/tables/dt21_203.72.asp

National Center for Education Statistics (NCES). (2022a, October). Enrollment and percentage distribution of enrollment in public elementary and secondary schools, by race/ethnicity and region: Selected years, fall 1995 through fall 2031 (Table 203.50). *Digest of Education Statistics.* https://nces.ed.gov/programs/digest/d22/tables/dt22_203.50.asp

National Center for Education Statistics (NCES). (2022b, April). Enrollment, poverty, and federal funds for the 120 largest school districts, by enrollment size in 2019: 2018–19 and fiscal year 2021 (Table 215.30). *Digest of Education Statistics.* https://nces.ed.gov/programs/digest/d21/tables/dt21_215.30.asp

National Center for Education Statistics (NCES). (2022c, October). Number and percentage distribution of public school students, by percentage of students in school who are eligible for free or reduced-price lunch, school level, locale, and student race/ethnicity: Fall 2021 (Table 216.60). *Digest of Education Statistics.* https://nces.ed.gov/programs/digest/d22/tables/dt22_216.60.asp

National Center for Education Statistics. (2022d, November). Public elementary and secondary school enrollment, number of schools, and other selected characteristics, by locale: Fall 2015 through fall 2021 (Table 214.40). https://nces.ed.gov/programs/digest/d22/tables/dt22_214.40.asp

National Center for Education Statistics (NCES). (2023, May). Concentration of public school students eligible for free or reduced-price lunch. *Condition of Education.* https://nces.ed.gov/programs/coe/indicator/clb

National Education Association. (2023, April 24). *Teacher salaries not keeping up with inflation, NEA report finds.* https://www.nea.org/advocating-for-change/new-from-nea/teacher-salaries-not-keeping-inflation-nea-report-finds

National Public Radio, the Robert Wood Johnson Foundation, and Harvard T.H. Chan School of Public Health. (2018,

October). *Life in rural America.* https://www.rwjf.org/en/insights/our-research/2018/10/life-in-rural-america.html

Natural Resources Defense Council. (2018, November 8). *Flint water crisis: Everything you need to know.* https://www.nrdc.org/stories/flint-water-crisis-everything-you-need-know#summary

Norman, J. (2018, April 6). *The religious regions of the U.S.* Gallup. https://news.gallup.com/poll/232223/religious-regions.aspx

Omi, M., & Winant, H. (2015). *Racial formation in the United States* (3rd ed.). Routledge.

Orum, P., Moore, R., Roberts, M., & Sánchez, J. (2014, May). *Who's in danger?: Race, poverty, and chemical disasters: A demographic analysis of chemical disaster vulnerability zones.* Environmental Justice and Health Alliance for Chemical Policy Reform.

*Parents Involved in Community Schools v. Seattle School District #1*, 551 U.S. 701 (2007).

Persico, C. (2019, November 20). *How exposure to pollution affects educational outcomes and inequality.* Brookings Institution. https://www.brookings.edu/blog/brown-center-chalkboard/2019/11/20/how-exposure-to-pollution-affects-educational-outcomes-and-inequality/

Persico, C., Figlio, D., & Roth, J. (2020, October). The developmental consequences of superfund sites. *Journal of Labor Economics, 38*(4), 1055–1097.

Persico, C. L., & Venator, J. (2023, July). The effects of local industrial pollution on students and schools. *Journal of Human Resources, 58*(4), 406–445.

*Plessy v. Ferguson*, 163 U.S. 537 (1896).

Potter, H., & Burris, M. (2020, December 2). *Here is what school integration in America looks like today.* The Century Foundation. https://tcf.org/content/report/school-integration-america-looks-like-today/

Potter, H. Lallinger, S., Burris, M., Kahlenberg, R. D., & Edwards, A. (2021, June 3). *School integration is popular. We can make it more so.* The Century Foundation. https://tcf.org/content/commentary/school-integration-is-popular-we-can-make-it-more-so/

Ramos, P. (2020). *Finding Latinx: In search of the voices redefining Latino identity.* Vintage Books.

Rathke, L. (2018, January 21). *With just 3 students, small-town high school closing down.* https://www.boston.com/news/education/2018/01/21/with-just-3-students-a-small-town-vermont-high-school-is-closing-down

Reardon, S. F., & Owens, A. (2014). 60 Years after Brown: Trends and Consequences of School Segregation. *Annual Review of Sociology, 40*:199–218.

Reardon, S. F., Weathers, E., Fahle, E., Jang, H., & Kalogrides, D. (2022). *Is separate still unequal?: New evidence on school segregation and racial academic achievement gaps* (CEPA Working Paper No.19-06). Stanford Center for Education Policy Analysis. https://cepa.stanford.edu/content/separate-still-unequal-new-evidence-school-segregation-and-racial-academic-achievement-gaps

Rose, M. (2022). Reflections on the public school and the social fabric. In D. C. Berliner & C. Hermanns (Eds.), *Public education: Defending a cornerstone of American democracy* (pp. 52–60). Teachers College Press.

Rowlands, DW, & Love, H. (2021, September 28). *Mapping rural America's diversity and demographic change.* Brookings Institution. https://www.brookings.edu/articles/mapping-rural-americas-diversity-and-demographic-change/

Saenz-Armstrong, P. (2023, May 11). *Teacher salaries, cost of rent, and home prices: Can teachers afford to live where they teach.* National Council on Teacher Quality. https://www.nctq .org/blog/Teacher-salaries,-cost-of-rent,-and-home-prices:- Can-teachers-afford-to-live-where-they-teach

Sageman, J. (2022, March). School closures and rural population decline. *Rural Sociology, 87*(3), 960–992.

Seventh Generation Fund for Indigenous Peoples. (n.d.). *Celebrating Indigenous peoples' self-determination.* https:// 7genfund.org/who-we-are/

Shrider, E. A., Kollar, M., Chen, F., & Semega, J. (2021, September). *Income and poverty in the United States: 2020* (P60-273). U.S. Census Bureau. https://www.census.gov/ library/publications/2021/demo/p60-273.html

Sipple, J. W., Francis, J. D., & Fiduccia, P. C. (2019). Exploring the gradient: The economic benefits of 'nearby' schools on rural communities. *Journal of Rural Studies, 68*, 251–263.

Slack, T., & Jensen, L. (2020, September). The changing demography of rural and small-town America. *Population Research and Policy Review, 39*, 775–783.

Smith, A. S., & Trevelyan, E. (2019, October 22). *In some states, more than half of older residents live in rural areas.* U.S. Census Bureau. https://www.census.gov/library/stories/2019/10/older- population-in-rural-america.html

Southern Poverty Law Center. (2023, June 28). *Mississippi city's water problems stem from generations of neglect.* https://www .splcenter.org/news/2023/06/28/timeline-jackson- mississippi-water-problems

Statista. (2023, August 3). *Percentage of the population aged 25 and over who have completed an advanced degree in the U.S. in 2021, by state.* https://www.statista.com/statistics/725335/ us-population-that-held-advanced-degree-by-state/

Suárez-Orozco, M. M. (2020). Global migration, education, and the nation-state. *Intercultural Education, 31*(5), 506–518.

Trounstine, J. (2018). *Segregation by design: Local politics and inequality in American cities.* Cambridge University Press.

United National Convention on the Rights of the Child. (1989). *Convention on the Rights of the Child: For every child, every right.* UNICEF. http://www.ohchr.org/en/professionalinterest/ pages/crc.aspx

United Nations. (2017). *World population projected to reach 9.8 billion in 2050, and 11.2 billion in 2100.* https://www .un.org/en/desa/world-population-projected-reach-98- billion-2050-and-112-billion-2100

United Nations Development Programme. (2021, July 29). *10 things to know about indigenous peoples.* https://stories .undp.org/10-things-we-all-should-know-about- indigenous-people

United Nations High Commissioner for Refugees. (2023). *Global trends report 2022.* https://www.unhcr.org/ global-trends

U.S. Census Bureau. (2021a, April 26). *2020 census: Apportionment of the U.S. House of Representatives.* https://www.census.gov/ library/visualizations/2021/dec/2020-apportionment-map .html

U.S. Census Bureau. (2021b, April 26). *Historical population change data (1910–2020).* https://www.census.gov/data/ tables/time-series/dec/popchange-data-text.html

U.S. Census Bureau. (2021c, May). *Percentage of related children ages 5 to 17 living in poverty, by locale, region, and state: 2019 (Table 102.45).* https://nces.ed.gov/programs/digest/d21/ tables/dt21_102.45.asp

U.S. Census Bureau. (2021d, August 12). *Race and ethnicity in the United States: 2010 census and 2020 census.* https://www .census.gov/library/visualizations/interactive/race-and- ethnicity-in-the-united-state-2010-and-2020-census.html

U.S. Census Bureau. (2022a). *Annual resident population estimates for metropolitan and micropolitan statistical areas and their geographic components for the United States: April 1, 2020 to July 1, 2022.* https://www.census.gov/data/tables/ time-series/demo/popest/2020s-total-metro-and-micro- statistical-areas.html

U.S. Census Bureau. (2022b). *Income summary measures by selected characteristics: 2020 and 2021 (Table A-1).* https:// www.census.gov/data/tables/2022/demo/income- poverty/p60-276.html

U.S. Census Bureau. (2022d) *People in poverty by selected characteristics: 2019 and 2020 (Table B-1).* https://www .census.gov/data/tables/2021/demo/income-poverty/ p60-273.html

U.S. Census Bureau. (2022e, October). *Population by sex, metropolitan status, nativity, and U.S. citizenship status: 2020 (Table 1.16).* https://www.census.gov/data/tables/2021/ demo/foreign-born/cps-2021.html

U.S. Census Bureau. (2023a, June 2023). *2020 census urban areas facts.* https://www.census.gov/programs-surveys/ geography/guidance/geo-areas/urban-rural/2020-ua- facts.html

U.S. Census Bureau. (2023b, May 18). *Public school spending per pupil experiences largest year-to-year increase in more than a decade.* https://www.census.gov/newsroom/press- releases/2023/public-school-spending.html

U.S. Census Bureau. (2023c, July). *State-level 2020 and 2010 census urban and rural information for the U.S., Puerto Rico, and island areas sorted by state FIPS code.* https://www .census.gov/programs-surveys/geography/guidance/ geo-areas/urban-rural.html

U.S. Department of Agriculture, Economic Research Service. (2022, November 29). *Rural poverty & well-being.* https:// www.ers.usda.gov/topics/rural-economy-population/ rural-poverty-well-being/

U.S. Department of Agriculture, Economic Research Service. (2023, March 14). *Farming and farm income.* https://www .ers.usda.gov/data-products/ag-and-food-statistics-charting- the-essentials/farming-and-farm-income/

U.S. Department of Energy, Office of Legacy Management. (n.d.). *What is environmental justice?* https://www.energy .gov/lm/what-environmental-justice

U.S. Government Accountability Office. (2022, June). *K–12 education: Student population has significantly diversified, but many schools remain divided along racial, ethnic, and economic lines.* https://www.gao.gov/products/gao-22-104737

Vander Ark, T., Liebtag, E., & McClennen, N. (2020). *The power of place: Authentic learning through place-based education.* Association of Supervision and Curriculum Development.

Vogels, E. A. (2021, August 19). *Some digital divides persist between rural, urban and suburban America.* Pew Research Center. https://www.pewresearch.org/short- reads/2021/08/19/some-digital-divides-persist-between- rural-urban-and-suburban-america/

Warikoo, N. (2022). *Race at the top: Asian Americans and whites in pursuit of the American dream in suburban schools.* University of Chicago Press.

Wang, S. (2019, March 22). *A new American dream: The rise of immigrants in rural America.* Civil Eats. https://civileats .com/2019/03/22/a-new-american-dream-the-rise-of- immigrants-in-rural-america/

Water Defense. (2023). *Flint water explained: Summary, facts & resolution.* https://waterdefense.org/flint-water-crisis/

Wells, A. S., Fox, L., & Cordova-Cobo, D. (2016). *How racially diverse school and classrooms can benefit all students.* The Century Foundation. https://tcf.org/content/report/how-racially-diverse-schools-and-classrooms-can-benefit-all-students/?agreed=1

Williams. J. (2021). *Climate change\* \*is racist: Race, privilege and the Struggle for climate justice.* Icon Books.

WorldAtlas. (2023a). *The 4 hemispheres of the world.* https://www.worldatlas.com/geography/the-4-hemispheres-of-the-world.html

WorldAtlas. (2023b). *The 10 largest cities in the world.* https://www.worldatlas.com/articles/the-10-largest-cities-in-the-world.html

World Bank. (2022). *Poverty and shared prosperity 2022: Correcting course.* https://www.worldbank.org/en/publication/poverty-and-shared-prosperity

World Bank. (2023). *World Development Indicators.* https://databank.worldbank.org/reports.aspx?dsid=2&series=SP.RUR.TOTL

World Health Organization. (2018, October 29). *More than 90% of the world's children breathe toxic air every day.* https://www.who.int/news/item/29-10-2018-more-than-90-of-the-worlds-children-breathe-toxic-air-every-day

World Population Review. (2023a). *Asia Population 2023.* https://worldpopulationreview.com/continents/asia-population

World Population Review. (2023b). *Carbon footprint by country 2023.* https://worldpopulationreview.com/country-rankings/carbon-footprint-by-country

World Population Review. (2023c). *Politics.* https://worldpopulationreview.com/state-rankings/topic/politics

World Population Review. (2023d). *Total population by country 2023.* http://worldpopulationreview.com/countries/

## Chapter 10

Abrams, Z. (2023, January/February). *2023 trends report: Kids' mental health is in crisis. Here's what psychologists are doing to help.* American Psychological Association. https://www.apa.org/monitor/2023/01/trends-improving-youth-mental-health

American Academy of Pediatrics, the American Academy of Child and Adolescent Psychiatry, & the Children's Hospital Association. (2022). *A declaration from the American Academy of Pediatrics, American Academy of Child and Adolescent Psychiatry and Children's Hospital Association.* https://www.aap.org/en/advocacy/child-and-adolescent-healthy-mental-development/aap-aacap-cha-declaration-of-a-national-emergency-in-child-and-adolescent-mental-health/

American Lung Association. (2023). *E-cigarettes & vaping: What parents should know.* https://www.lung.org/quit-smoking/e-cigarettes-vaping/e-cigarettes-parents

American School Counselor Association. (2023, January 4). *ASCA releases updated student-to-school-counselor ratio data.* https://www.schoolcounselor.org/getmedia/a0565224-7cc7-4119-883a-2aa900e296b6/student-to-sc-ratios.pdf

Anderson, M., Vogels, E. A., Perrin, A., & Rainie, L. (2022, November 16). *Connection, creativity and drama: Teen life on social media in 2022.* Pew Research Center. https://www.pewresearch.org/internet/2022/11/16/connection-creativity-and-drama-teen-life-on-social-media-in-2022/

Au, W. (2016). "And ya don't stop:" Using hip-hop in the language arts classroom. In E. Marshall & Ö. Sensoy, *Rethinking popular culture and media* (2nd ed., pp. 279–287). Rethinking Schools.

Austin, A., Craig, S. L., D'Souza, S., & McInroy, L.B. (2022, March). Suicidality among transgender youth: Elucidating the role of interpersonal risk factors. *Journal of Interpersonal Violence, 37*(5–6), 2696–2718.

Banks, J. A. (2023). Series Foreword. In T. S. Jenkins, *The hip-hop mindset: Success strategies for educators and other professionals* (pp. xi–xvi). Teachers College Press.

Barclay, R. (2018). *Alienation.* Healthline. https://www.healthline.com/health/alienation

Blake, J. J., & Epstein, R. (2017). *Listening to Black women and girls: Lived experiences of adultification bias.* Center on Poverty and Inequality, Georgetown Law.

Buchanan, C. M., & Hughes, J. L. (2009). Construction of social reality during early adolescence: Can expecting storm and stress increase real or perceived storm and stress? *Journal of Research on Adolescence, 19*, 261–285.

Buchanan, C. M., Romer, D., Wray-Lake, L., & Butler-Barnes, S. T. (2023). Editorial: Adolescent storm and stress: A 21st century evaluation. *Frontiers in Psychology, 14*, 1–7.

Burns, S. (2020, January 3). *Transforming how the media portrays young people.* American Friends Service Committee. https://afsc.org/news/transforming-how-media-portrays-young-people

Campaign for Tobacco-Free Kids. (2023). *States & localities that have restricted the sale of flavored tobacco products.* https://assets.tobaccofreekids.org/factsheets/0398.pdf

Cavanagh, T. (2018). Restorative justice: An alternative approach to school discipline. In G. E. Hall, L. F. Quinn, & D. M. Gollnick (Eds.), *The Wiley handbook of teaching and learning* (pp. 529–548). Wiley-Blackwell.

Center for Behavioral Health Statistics and Quality. (2022). *Results from the 2021 National Survey on Drug Use and Health: Detailed tables.* Substance Abuse and Mental Health Services Administration. https://www.samhsa.gov/data/report/2021-nsduh-detailed-tables

Centers for Disease Control and Prevention (CDC). (2020, April 28). *Tobacco-related mortality.* https://www.cdc.gov/tobacco/data_statistics/fact_sheets/health_effects/tobacco_related_mortality/index.htm

Centers for Disease Control and Prevention (CDC). (2021, April 8). *Adolescents and young adults.* https://www.cdc.gov/std/life-stages-populations/adolescents-youngadults.htm

Centers for Disease Control and Prevention (CDC). (2022a). *High-risk substance use among youth.* https://www.cdc.gov/healthyyouth/substance-use/index.htm

Centers for Disease Control and Prevention (CDC). (2022b). *Underage drinking.* https://www.cdc.gov/alcohol/fact-sheets/underage-drinking.htm

Centers for Disease Control and Prevention (CDC). (2022c). *Youth and tobacco use.* https://www.cdc.gov/tobacco/data_statistics/fact_sheets/youth_data/tobacco_use/index.htm

Centers for Disease Control and Prevention (CDC). (2022d). *Youth risk behavior survey: Data summary & trends report 2011–2021.* National Center for HIV, Viral Hepatitis, STD, and TB Prevention. https://www.cdc.gov/healthyyouth/mental-health/index.htm

Centers for Disease Control and Prevention (CDC). (2023a, July 25). *Adolescent health.* National Center for Health Statistics. https://www.cdc.gov/nchs/fastats/adolescent-health.htm

Centers for Disease Control and Prevention (CDC). (2023b, May 4). *Cigarette smoking in the U.S.* https://www.cdc.gov/tobacco/data_statistics/fact_sheets/fast_facts/cigarette-smoking-in-the-us.html

Centers for Disease Control and Prevention (CDC). (2023c, September 6). *Fentanyl facts.* https://www.cdc.gov/stopoverdose/fentanyl/index.html

Centers for Disease Control and Prevention (CDC). (2023d, June 1). *Mental health: Poor mental health impacts adolescent well-being.* Division of Adolescent and School Health. https://www.cdc.gov/healthyyouth/mental-health/index.htm

Centers for Disease Control and Prevention (CDC). (2023e, August 2). *School connectedness.* Division of Population Health. https://www.cdc.gov/healthyschools/school_connectedness.htm

Centers for Disease Control and Prevention (CDC). (2023f, August 10). *Suicide data and statistics.* https://www.cdc.gov/suicide/suicide-data-statistics.html

Center for Information & Research on Civic Learning and Engagement (CIRCLE). (2021, July 20). *What the research says: Youth, media, and democracy.* Tufts University, Tisch College. https://circle.tufts.edu/latest-research/what-research-says-youth-media-and-democracy

Children's Defense Fund. (2023). *Gun violence prevention.* https://www.childrensdefense.org/policy/policy-priorities/gun-violence-prevention/

Cooper, A., Swartz, S., & Mahali, A. (2019). Disentangled, decentered and democratised: Youth studies for the global south. *Journal of Youth Studies, 22*(1), 29–45.

Cornell, D., & Crowley, B. (2021). Preventing school violence and advancing school safety. In P. J. Lazarus, S. M. Suldo, & B. Doll (Eds.), *Fostering the emotional well-being of our youth: A school-based approach* (pp. 137–162). Oxford University Press.

Cross, W. E. (1991). *Shades of Black: Diversity in African-American identity.* Temple University Press.

Damour, L. (2023). *The emotional lives of teenagers: Raising connected, capable and compassionate adolescents.* Allen Unwin.

De Witte, M. (2022, January 3). Gen Z are not "coddled." They are highly collaborative, self-reliant and pragmatic, according to new Stanford-affiliated research. *Stanford News.* https://news.stanford.edu/2022/01/03/know-gen-z/

Dimock, M. (2023, May 22). *5 things to keep in mind when you hear about Gen Z, millennials, boomers and other generations.* Pew Research Center. https://www.pewresearch.org/short-reads/2023/05/22/5-things-to-keep-in-mind-when-you-hear-about-gen-z-millennials-boomers-and-other-generations/

Ehnie, K. (2022, August 24). *6 ways to use student smartphones for learning.* International Society for Technology in Education. https://www.iste.org/explore/toolbox/6-ways-use-student-smartphones-learning

Emdin, C. (2016). *For white folks who teach in the hood . . . and the rest of y'all too: Reality pedagogy and urban education.* Beacon Press.

Gershenson, S., Hart, C., Lindsay, C., & Papageorge, N.W. (2017). *The long-run impacts of same-race teachers* (IZA DP No. 10630). IZA Institute of Labor Economics. https://www.iza.org/publications/dp/10630

Gramlich, J. (2023, April 6). *Gun deaths among U.S. children and teens rose 50% in two years.* Pew Research Center. https://www.pewresearch.org/short-reads/2023/04/06/gun-deaths-among-us-kids-rose-50-percent-in-two-years/

Griffiths, A. J., Diamond, E., Maupin, Z., Alsip, J., Keller, M. J., Moffa, K., & Furlong, M. J. (2021). Promoting school safety, school climate, and student mental health: Interdependent constructs built upon comprehensive multidisciplinary planning. In P. J. Lazarus, S. M. Suldo, & B. Doll (Eds.), *Fostering the emotional well-being of our youth: A school-based approach* (pp. 117–136). Oxford University Press.

Guttmacher Institute. (2023, August 1). *Sex and HIV education.* https://www.guttmacher.org/state-policy/explore/sex-and-hiv-education

Harper, C. R., Li, J. Sheats, K., Mertz, M. F., Merrill-Francis, M., Friar, N. W., et al. (2023). Witnessing community violence, gun carrying, and associations with substance use and suicide risk among high school students—Youth risk behavior survey, United States, 2021. *Morbidity and Mortality Weekly Report, 72*(1), 22–28.

Helms, J. E. (1990). *Black and White racial identity: Theory, research, and practice.* Greenwood Press.

Hoots, B. E., Li, J., Hertz, M. F., Esser, M. B., Rico, A., Zavala, E. Y., & Jones, C. M. (2023). Alcohol and other substance use before and during the COVID-19 pandemic among high school students—Youth risk behavior survey, United States, 2021. *Morbidity and Mortality Weekly Report, 72*(Suppl. 1), 84–92.

Jean, J. Y. (2022, November 9). Why school nurses are leaving the career. *NurseJournal.* https://nursejournal.org/articles/why-school-nurses-are-leaving/

Jenkins, T. S. (2023). *The hip-hop mindset: Success strategies for educators and other professionals.* Teachers College Press.

Jones, S. E., Ethier, K. A., Hertz, M., DeGue, S., Le, V. D., Thornton, J., et al. (2022). Mental health, suicidality, and connectedness among high school students during the COVID-19 pandemic—Adolescent behaviors and experiences survey, United States, January–June 2021. *Morbidity and Mortality Weekly Report, 71*(3), 16–21.

Katz, R., Ogilvie, S., Shaw, J., & Woodhead, L. (2021). *Gen Z, Explained: The art of living in a digital age.* University of Chicago Press.

Lansford, J. E., French, D. C., & Gauvain, M. (2021). *Child and adolescent development in cultural context.* American Psychological Association.

Lazarus, P. J., Suldo, S. M., & Doll, B. (2021). Introduction: Are our youth all right? In P. J. Lazarus, S. M. Suldo, & B. Doll (Eds.), *Fostering the emotional well-being of our youth: A school-based approach* (pp. 1–19). Oxford University Press.

Lightfoot, C. (1997). *The culture of adolescent risk-taking.* Guilford Press.

Loudermilk, B. (2017, April 25). Countries with the lowest teen pregnancy rates. *WorldAtlas.* https://www.worldatlas.com/articles/countries-with-the-lowest-teen-pregnancy-rates.html

Mailman School of Public Health. (2021, September 27). *Just how harmful is social media? Our experts weigh-in.* Columbia University. https://www.publichealth.columbia.edu/news/just-how-harmful-social-media-our-experts-weigh

Marberry, J. (2019, May 9). *Here's what teens say they need.* Association for Supervision and Curriculum Development. http://www.ascd.org/ascd-express/vol14/num26/heres-what-teens-say-they-need.aspx?utm_source=ascdexpress&utm_medium=email&utm_campaign=Express%2014-26

McGough, M., Amin, K., Panchal, N., & Cox, C. (2023, July 18). *Child and teen firearm mortality in the U.S. and peer countries.* KFF. https://www.kff.org/mental-health/issue-brief/child-and-teen-firearm-mortality-in-the-u-s-and-peer-countries/

Merlo, C. L., Jones, S. E., Michael, S. L., Chen, T. J., Siliwa, S. A., Lee, S. H., et al. (2020). Dietary and physical activity behaviors among high school students—Youth Risk Behavior Survey, United States, 2019. *Morbidity and Mortality Weekly Report, 69*(1), 64–76.

Michael, S. L., Jones, S. E., Merlo, C. L., Siliwa, S. A., Lee, S. M., Cornett, K., et al. (2023). Dietary and physical activity behaviors in 2021 and changes from 2019 to 2021 among high school students—Youth Risk Behavior Survey, United States, 2021. *Morbidity and Mortality Weekly Report, 72*(1), 75–83.

Miech, R. A., Johnston, L. D., Patrick, M. E., O'Malley, P. M., Bachman, J. G., & Schulenberg, J. E., (2023). *Monitoring the Future national survey results on drug use, 1975–2022: Secondary school students.* Monitoring the Future Monograph Series. Institute for Social Research, University of Michigan. https://monitoringthefuture.org/results/publications/monographs/

Moore, L. F. Jr, & Jones, K. (2023). Krip-hop nation puts back the fourth element of hip-hop: Knowledge with a political limp. In F. R. Waitoller & K. A. K. Thorius (Eds.), *Sustaining disabled youth: Centering disability in asset pedagogies* (pp. 86–94). Teachers College Press.

Murthy, V. H. (2022). The mental health of minority and marginalized young people: An opportunity for action. *Harvard Education Public Health Reports, 137*(4), 613–616.

Nakkula, M. J., & Toshalis, E. (2021). *Understanding youth: Adolescent development for educators.* Harvard Education Press.

National Academies of Sciences, Engineering, and Medicine. (2017). *Communities in action: Pathways to health equity.* National Academies Press.

National Academies of Sciences, Engineering, and Medicine. (2019). *The promise of adolescence: Realizing opportunity for all youth.* Author.

National Association of School Psychologists. (2023). *State shortages data dashboard.* https://www.nasponline.org/about-school-psychology/state-shortages-data-dashboard

National Association of Social Workers. (2018, March 27). *NASW highlights the growing need for school social workers to prevent school violence.* https://www.socialworkers.org/news/news-releases/id/1633/nasw-highlights-the-growing-need-for-school-social-workers-to-prevent-school-violence

National Center for Education Statistics. (2021, November). High school graduates, by sex and control of school; public high school averaged freshman graduation rate (AFGR); and total graduates as a ratio of 17-year-old population: Selected years, 1869–70 through 2030–31 (Table 219.10). *Digest of Education Statistics.* https://nces.ed.gov/programs/digest/d21/tables/dt21_219.10.asp

National Center for Education Statistics. (2022, May 31). *Roughly half of public schools report that they can effectively provide mental health services to all students in need.* U.S. Department of Education. https://nces.ed.gov/whatsnew/press_releases/05_31_2022_2.asp

National Institute on Alcohol Abuse and Alcoholism. (2023, April 26). *Alcohol-related emergencies and deaths in the United States.* https://www.niaaa.nih.gov/alcohols-effects-health/alcohol-topics/alcohol-facts-and-statistics/alcohol-related-emergencies-and-deaths-united-states.

National Institute on Drug Abuse. (2023, June 30). *Drug overdose death rates.* https://nida.nih.gov/research-topics/trends-statistics/overdose-death-rates

National Institute of Mental Health (NIMH). (2023a, March). *Child and adolescent mental health.* https://www.nimh.nih.gov/health/topics/child-and-adolescent-mental-health

National Institute of Mental Health (NIMH). (2023b, March). *Mental illness.* https://www.nimh.nih.gov/health/statistics/mental-illness#part_2632

Okonofua, J. A., & Eberhardt, J. L. (2015). Two strikes: Race and disciplining of young students. *Psychological Science, 26*(5), 617–624.

Oliver, B. E., Jones, S. E., Hops, E. D., Ashley, C. L. Miech, R., & Mpofu, J. J. (2023). Electronic vapor product use among high school students—Youth risk behavior survey, United States, 2021. *Morbidity and Mortality Weekly Report, 72*(1), 93–99.

Omary, A. (2022, September 30). How stereotypes about teens cause harm: Negative preconceptions about teens create a self-fulfilling prophecy. *Psychology Today.* https://www.psychologytoday.com/us/blog/natured-nurture/202209/how-stereotypes-about-teens-cause-harm

Orben, A., & Przybylski, A. K. (2019). The association between adolescent well-being and digital technology. *Nature Human Behaviour. 3*(2019), 173–182.

Osgerby, B. (2021). *Youth culture and the media: Global perspectives* (2nd ed.). Routledge.

Parker, K., Graf, N., & Igielnik, R. (2019, January 17). *Generation Z looks a lot like millennials on key social and political issues.* Pew Research Center. Retrieved from http://www.pewsocialtrends.org/2019/01/17/generation-z-looks-a-lot-like-millennials-on-key-social-and-political-issues/

Parker, K., & Igielnik, R. (2020, May 14). *On the cusp of adulthood and facing an uncertain future: What we know about Gen Z so far.* Pew Research Center. https://www.pewresearch.org/social-trends/2020/05/14/on-the-cusp-of-adulthood-and-facing-an-uncertain-future-what-we-know-about-gen-z-so-far-2/

Pate, A. (2023, February 23). Setting the financial stage for Gen Alpha by engaging millennial parents. *Forbes.* https://www.forbes.com/sites/columbiabusinessschool/2023/02/23/setting-the-financial-stage-for-gen-alpha-by-engaging-millennial-parents/?sh=46ca7f84700d

Pinzone, C., & Reschly, A. L. (2021). Cultivating student engagement and connectedness. In P. J. Lazarus, S. M. Suldo, & B. Doll (Eds.), *Fostering the emotional well-being of our youth: A school-based approach* (pp. 163–182). Oxford University Press.

Protzko, J., & Schooler, J. W. (2022, May 30). Who denigrates today's youth?: The role of age, implicit theories, and sharing the same negative trait. *Frontiers in Psychology, 13*(2022), 1–10.

Puzzanchera, C., Hockenberry, S., & Sickmund, M. (2022, December). *Youth and the juvenile justice system: 2022 national report.* National Center for Juvenile Justice. https://ojjdp.ojp.gov/library/publications/youth-and-juvenile-justice-system-2022-national-report

Qu, Y., Galvan, A., Fuligni, A. J., Lieberman, M. D., & Telzer, E. H. (2015). Longitudinal changes in prefrontal cortex activation underlie declines in adolescent risk taking. *Journal of Neuroscience, 35*(32), 11308–11314.

Qu, Y., Pomerantz, E. M., McCormick, E. & Telzer, E. H. (2018). Youth's conceptions of adolescence predict longitudinal changes in prefrontal cortex activation and risk taking during adolescence. *Child Development, 89*(3), 773–783. https://doi.org/10.1111/cdev.13017

Reinert, M., Fritze, D., & Nguyen, T. (2021, October). *The state of mental health in America 2022.* Mental Health America. https://mhanational.org/research-reports/2022-state-mental-health-america-report

Rideout, V., Peebles, A., Mann, S., & Robb, M. B. (2022, March 9). *The Common Sense census: Media use by tweens and teens, 2021.* Common Sense. https://www.common sensemedia.org/research/the-common-sense-census-media-use-by-tweens-and-teens-2021

School shootings this year: How many and where. (2023, August 29). *Education Week.* https://www.edweek.org/leadership/school-shootings-this-year-how-many-and-where/2023/01

Skiba, R. J., Horner, R. H., Chung, C.-G., Rausch, M. K., May, S. L., & Tobin, T. (2011). Race is not neutral: A national investigation of African American and Latino disproportionality in school discipline. *School Psychology Review, 40*(2), 85–107.

Society of Health and Physical Educators. (2019). *Aligning SHAPE American national standards and grade-level outcomes for K–12 physical education with CASEL social and emotional learning core competencies.* https://www.shapeamerica.org/standards/guidelines/sel-crosswalk.aspx

Solmi, M., Radua, J., Olivola, M., Croce, E., Soardo, L., de Pablo, G. S., et al. (2022). Age at onset of mental disorders worldwide: Large=scale meta-analysis of 192 epidemiological studies. *Molecular Psychiatry, 27*(1), 281–295.

St. George, D. (2023, August 31). In a crisis, schools are 100,000 mental health staff short. *Washington Post.* https://www.washingtonpost.com/education/2023/08/31/mental-health-crisis-students-have-third-therapists-they-need/

Superville, D. R. (2017, November 20). Absences, trauma, and orphaned children: How the opioid crisis is ravaging schools. *Education Week.* https://www.edweek.org/ew/articles/2017/11/20/absences-trauma-and-orphaned-children-how-the.html

Szabo, R. (2023). Let's talk about mental health. *Educational Leadership, 81*(1), 56–61.

Twenge, J. M. (2023). *The real differences between Gen A, Millennials, Gen X, Boomers, and Silents—and what they mean for America's future.* Atria Books.

U.S. Census Bureau. (2023, June). *Annual estimates of the resident population by single year of age and sex for the United States: April 1, 2020 to July 1, 2022 (NC-EST2022-SYASEXN).* https://www.census.gov/data/tables/time-series/demo/popest/2020s-national-detail.html

U.S. Department of Health and Human Services, Office of Population Affairs. (n.d.-a). *About teen pregnancy and childbearing.* https://www.opa.hhs.gov/adolescent-health/reproductive-health-and-teen-pregnancy/about-teen-pregnancy-and-childbearing

U.S. Department of Health and Human Services, Office of Population Affairs. (n.d.-b). *Trends in teen pregnancy and childbearing.* https://opa.hhs.gov/adolescent-health/reproductive-health-and-teen-pregnancy/trends-teen-pregnancy-and-childbearing

U.S. Department of Health and Human Services. (2023, May 23). *Surgeon General issues new advisory about effects social media use has on youth mental health.* https://www.hhs.gov/about/news/2023/05/23/surgeon-general-issues-new-advisory-about-effects-social-media-use-has-youth-mental-health.html

U.S. Department of Justice, Office of Juvenile Justice and Delinquency Prevention. (2020, September 11). *Supporting youth and families impacted by opioid use.* https://ojjdp.ojp.gov/programs/supporting-youth-and-families-impacted-by-opioid-use

Vogels, E. A., & Gelles-Watnick, R. (2023, April 24). *Teens and social media: Key findings from Pew Research Center surveys.* Pew Research Center. https://www.pewresearch.org/short-reads/2023/04/24/teens-and-social-media-key-findings-from-pew-research-center-surveys/

Ware, M. A., & Rath, J. (2019, May 9). *4 must-haves for positive teacher teen relationships.* Association for Supervision and Curriculum Development. http://www.ascd.org/ascd-express/vol14/num26/4-must-haves-for-positive-teacher-teen-relationships.aspx?utm_source=ascdexpress&utm_medium=email&utm_campaign=Express%2014–26

Waterford.org. (2020, January 23). *Technology and digital media in the classroom: A guide for educators.* https://www.waterford.org/education/technology-in-the-classroom/

Weinstein, E., & James, C. (2022). *Behind their screens: What teens are facing (and adults are missing).* MIT Press.

Wilkens. N. J., Krause, K. H., Verlenden, J. V., Szucs, L. E., Ussery, E. N., Allen, C. T., et al. (2023). School connectedness and risk behaviors and experiences among high school students—Youth risk behavior survey, United States, 2021. *Morbidity and Mortality Weekly Report, 72*(1), 13–21.

World Health Organization. (2022, June 17). *Mental health.* https://www.who.int/news-room/fact-sheets/detail/mental-health-strengthening-our-response

youth,gov. (n.d.). *School based mental health.* https://youth.gov/youth-topics/youth-mental-health/school-based

## Chapter 11

Alim, H. S., & Paris, D. (2017). What is culturally sustaining pedagogy and why does it matter? In H. S. Alim & D. Paris (Eds.), *Culturally sustaining pedagogies: Teaching and learning for justice in a changing world* (pp. 1–21). Teachers College Press.

Applebaum, Y. (2018, October). Americans aren't practicing democracy anymore. *The Atlantic, 322*(3). https://www.theatlantic.com/magazine/archive/2018/10/losing-the-democratic-habit/568336/

Ayers, R., & Ayers, W. (2014). *Teaching the taboo: Courage and imagination in the classroom.* Teachers College Press.

Baines, A. M., Medina, D., & Healy, C. (2023). *Amplify student voices: Equitable practices to build confidence in the classroom.* Association for Supervision and Curriculum Development.

Banks, J. A. (2019). *An introduction to multicultural education* (6th ed.). Pearson.

Benson, T. A., & Fiarman, S. E. (2019). *Unconscious bias in schools: A developmental approach to exploring race and racism.* Harvard University Press.

Bucholtz, M., Casillas, D. I., & Lee, J. S. (2017). Language and culture as sustenance. In H. S. Alim & D. Paris (Eds.), *Culturally sustaining pedagogies: Teaching and learning for justice in a changing world.* Teachers College Press.

Children's Defense Fund. (2023). *State of America's children*. https://www.childrensdefense.org/the-state-of-americas-children/soac-2023-gun-violence/

Christensen, L. (2017). *Reading, writing, and rising up: Teaching about social justice and the power of the written word*. Rethinking Schools.

CNN Money. (2021). *Education vs prison costs*. https://money.cnn.com/infographic/economy/education-vs-prison-costs/

Collaborative for Academic, Social, and Emotional Learning. (2023). *SEL in the school*. https://casel.org/systemic-implementation/sel-in-the-school/

Darling-Hammond, K., & Darling-Hammond, L. (2022). *The civil rights road to deeper learning*. Teachers College Press.

Dorris, M. (2016). Why I'm not thankful for Thanksgiving. In E. Marshall & Ö. Sensoy (Eds.), *Rethinking popular culture and media* (2nd ed., pp. 101–106). Rethinking Schools.

Duncan-Andrade, J. M. R. (2022). *Equality or equity: Toward a model of community-responsive education*. Harvard Education Press.

Emdin, C. (2016). *For White folks who teach in the hood . . . and the rest of y'all too: Reality pedagogy and urban education*. Beacon Press.

Epstein, V. (2019, June 12). *What happens in the democratic classroom?* https://www.kars4kids.org/blog/education/what-happens-in-the-democratic-classroom/

Frey, N., Fisher, D., & Smith, D. (2019). *All learning is social and emotional: Helping students develop essential skills for the classroom and beyond*. Association for Supervision and Curriculum Development.

Gay, G. (2018). *Culturally responsive teaching: Theory, research, and practice* (3rd ed.). Teachers College Press.

Gay, G. (2023). *Educating for equity and excellence: Enacting culturally responsive teaching*. Teachers College Press.

German, L. E. (2021). *Textured teaching: A framework for culturally sustaining practices*. Heinemann.

Gershenson, S., Hart, C. M. D., Hyman, J., Lindsay, C., & Papageorge, N. W. (2017, March). The long-run impacts of same-race teachers (IZA DP No. 10630). http://ftp.iza.org/dp10630.pdf

Gershenson, S., Hansen, M., & Lindsay, C. A. (2021). *Teacher diversity and student success: Why racial representation matters in the classroom*. Harvard Education Press.

Gorski, P., & Swalwell, K. (2023). *Fix injustice not kids: and other Principles for transformative equity leadership*. Association for Supervision and Curriculum Development.

Harry, B., & Klingner, J. (2022). *Why are so many students of color in special education: Understanding race and disability in schools*. Teachers College Press.

Hattie, J., & Zierer, K. (2019). *Visible learning insights*. Routledge.

Howard, T. C. (2019). *Why race and culture matter in schools: Closing the achievement gap in America's classrooms* (2nd ed.). Teachers College Press.

Johnson, J. (2018, Summer). Howling at the ocean: Surviving my first year teaching. *Rethinking Schools, 32*(4), 30–34.

Jones, J., & Miranda, A. H. (2021). Building culturally responsive school: A model based on the Association for Supervision and Curriculum development's whole child approach. In P. J. Lazarus, S. M. Suldo, & B. Doll, *Fostering the emotional well-being of our youth: A school-based approach* (pp. 61–78). Oxford University Press.

Jones, S., Bailey, R., Brush, K., & Kahn, J. (2018). *Preparing for effective SEL implementation*. Harvard Graduate School of Education.

Ladson-Billings, G. (2001). *Crossing over to Canaan*. Jossey-Bass.

Ladson-Billings, G. (2021). *Culturally relevant pedagogy: Asking a different question*. Teachers College Press.

Ladson-Billings, G. (2022). *The dream-keepers: Successful teachers of African American children*. Jossey-Bass.

Lazarus, P. J., Suldo, S. M., & Doll, B. (2021). Introduction: Are our youth all right? In P. J. Lazarus, S. M. Suldo, & B. Doll, *Fostering the emotional well-being of our youth: A school-based approach* (pp. 1–19). Oxford University Press.

Leonardo, Z., & Grubb, W. N. (2019). *Education and racism: A primer on issues and dilemmas* (2nd ed.). Routledge.

Liu, J., Penner, E. K., & Gao, W. (2023). Troublemakers?: The role of frequent teacher referrers in expanding racial disciplinary disproportionalities. *Educational Researcher, 52*(9), 469–481.

Love, B. L. (2019). *We want to do more than survive: Abolitionist teaching and the pursuit of educational freedom*. Beacon Press.

Milner IV, H. R. (2020). *Start where you are, but don't stay there: Understanding diversity, opportunity gaps, and teaching in today's classrooms* (2nd ed.). Harvard Education Press.

National Assessment of Educational Progress. (2023). *The Nation's Report Card*. U.S. Department of Education. https://www.nationsreportcard.gov/

National Science Board. (2018). *2018 science & engineering indicators*. https://www.nsf.gov/statistics/2018/nsb20181/assets/nsb20181.pdf

Nguyen, U. S., Smith, S., & Granja, M. R. (2020, October). *Young children in deep poverty: Racial/ethnic disparities and child well-being compared to other income groups*. National Center for Children in Poverty, Bank Street Graduate School of Education. https://www.nccp.org/publication/young-children-in-deep-poverty-racial-ethnic-disparities-and-child-well-being-compared-to-other-income-groups/

Nieto, S. (2018). *Language, culture, and teaching: Critical perspectives* (3rd ed.). Routledge.

Noguera, P., & Syeed, E. (2021). The role of schools is reducing racial inequality. In J. A. Banks (Ed.), *Transforming multi cultural education policy and practice: Expanding educational opportunity*. Teachers College Press.

Perry, B. D., & Szalavitz, M. (2017). *The boy who was raised as a dog*. Basic Books.

Samuels, D. R. (2014). *The culturally inclusive educator*. Teachers College Press.

Sanders, W. I., & Rivers, J. C. (1996). *Cumulative and residual effects of teachers on future student academic achievement*. University of Tennessee, Value-Added Research and Assessment Center.

Sapon-Shevin, M. (2010). *Because we can change the world: A practical guide to building cooperative, inclusive classroom communities* (2nd ed.). Corwin Press.

Schwartz, S. (2019, June 11). Teachers push for books with more diversity, fewer stereotypes. *Education Week, 38*(35), 6.

Seider, S., & Graves, D. (2020). *Schooling for critical consciousness: Engaging Black and Latinx youth in analyzing, navigating, and challenging racial injustice*. Harvard University Press.

Southern Poverty Law Center. (2019). *Hate at school.* https://www.splcenter.org/sites/default/files/tt_2019_hate_at_school_report_final_0.pdf

Spencer, J. A., & Ullucci, K. (2022). *Anti-Blackness at school: Creating affirming educational spaces for African American students.* Teachers College Press.

Sprenger, M. (2020). *Social emotional learning and the brain: Strategies to help your students thrive.* Association for Supervision and Curriculum Development.

Startz, D. (2019, January 15). *Equal opportunity in American education.* https://www.brookings.edu/blog/brown-center-chalkboard/2019/01/15/equal-opportunity-in-american-education/

Stenhouse, V. L. (2009, Fall). Rethinking Thanksgiving: Myths and misgivings. *Rethinking Schools, 24*(1). https://rethinkingschools.org/articles/rethinking-thanksgiving-myths-and-misgivings/

Stone, M. (2023, October 25). Why America has a youth mental health crisis, and how schools can help. *Education Week, 43*(9), 3–7.

Tatum, B. D. (2017). *Why are all the black kids sitting together in the cafeteria? And other conversations about race* (Revised and updated). Basic Books.

Toldson, I. A. (2019). *No BS (bad stats): Black people need people who believe in Black people enough not to believe every bad thing they hear about Black people.* Brill Sense.

United Nations. (2015). *Universal Declaration of Human Rights.* https://www.un.org/en/udhrbook/pdf/udhr_booklet_en_web.pdf

U.S. Census Bureau. (2023). *Poverty status of people by age, race, and Hispanic origin: 1959 to 2022 (Table A-3).* https://www.census.gov/library/publications/2023/demo/p60-280.html

U.S. Department of Education, Office of Civil Rights. (2021, June). *An overview of exclusionary discipline practices in public schools for the 2017–2018 school year.* Civil Rights Data Collection. https://ocrdata.ed.gov/assets/downloads/crdc-exclusionary-school-discipline.pdf

Wright, T. (2023). Reframing trauma-informed practices. *Kappan, 105*(3), 9–13.

# Author Index

# Subject Index